Taxing Wages 2014

SPECIAL FEATURE:
CHANGES IN STRUCTURAL LABOUR INCOME TAX PROGRESSIVITY OVER THE 2000-12 PERIOD IN OECD MEMBER COUNTRIES

OECD
BETTER POLICIES FOR BETTER LIVES

This work is published on the responsibility of the Secretary-General of the OECD. The opinions expressed and arguments employed herein do not necessarily reflect the official views of the OECD or of the governments of its member countries.

This document and any map included herein are without prejudice to the status of or sovereignty over any territory, to the delimitation of international frontiers and boundaries and to the name of any territory, city or area.

Please cite this publication as:
OECD (2014), *Taxing Wages 2014*, OECD Publishing.
http://dx.doi.org/10.1787/tax_wages-2014-en

ISBN 978-92-64-20916-9 (print)
ISBN 978-92-64-20917-6 (PDF)

Annual:
ISSN 1995-3844 (print)
ISSN 2072-5124 (online)

The statistical data for Israel are supplied by and under the responsibility of the relevant Israeli authorities. The use of such data by the OECD is without prejudice to the status of the Golan Heights, East Jerusalem and Israeli settlements in the West Bank under the terms of international law.

Corrigenda to OECD publications may be found on line at: *www.oecd.org/about/publishing/corrigenda.htm*.

Foreword

This annual publication provides details of taxes paid on wages in all thirty-four member countries of the OECD. The information contained in the Report covers the personal income tax and social security contributions paid by employees, the social security contributions and payroll taxes paid by their employers and cash benefits received by families. The objective of the Report is to illustrate how personal income taxes, social security contributions and payroll taxes are calculated and to examine how these levies and cash family benefits impact on net household incomes. The results also allow quantitative cross-country comparisons of labour cost levels and of the overall tax and benefit position of single persons and families.*

The Report shows the amounts of taxes, social security contributions, payroll taxes and cash benefits for eight family-types, which differ by income level and household composition. It also presents the resulting average and marginal tax rates. Average tax rates show that part of gross wage earnings or total labour costs which are taken in personal income taxes (before and after cash benefits), social security contributions and payroll taxes. Marginal tax rates show the part of an increase of gross earnings or total labour costs that is paid in these levies.

The focus of the Report is the presentation of accurate estimates of the tax/benefit position of employees in 2013. In addition, the Report shows definitive data on the tax/benefit position of employees for the year 2012. It is important to note that, the average worker is designated as a full-time employee (including manual and non-manual) in either industry Sectors C-K inclusive with reference to the International Standard Industrial Classification of All Economic Activities, Revision 3 (ISIC Rev. 3) or industry Sectors B-N inclusive with reference to the International Standard Industrial Classification of All Economic Activities, Revision 4 (ISIC Rev. 4).

The Report is structured as follows:

- *The Overview at the start of the Report reviews the main results for 2013.*
- *Part I (International Comparisons) reviews the main results for 2013 and 2012 and is divided into three sections. The first section reviews the main results for 2013, which are summarised in comparative tables and figures included at the end of that section. The second section presents a graphical exposition of the estimated tax burden on labour income in 2013 for gross wage earnings between 50 per cent and 250 per cent of the average wage. The third section reviews the main results for 2012, which are summarized in the comparative tables at the end of that section and compares them with the 2013 figures.*
- *Part II focuses on the historical trends in the tax burden for the period 2000-13.*
- *Part III contains individual country tables specifying the wage levels considered and the associated tax burdens for eight separate family types, together with descriptions of each tax/benefit system.*

* *Previous editions were published under the title* The Tax/Benefit Position of Employees *(1996-98 editions) and* The Tax/Benefit Position of Production Workers *(editions published before 1996).*

- *The Annex describes the methodology and its limitations.*

The Report has been prepared under the auspices of the Working Party on Tax Policy Analysis and Tax Statistics of the Committee on Fiscal Affairs. This document has been produced with the financial assistance of the European Union. The views expressed herein can in no way be taken to reflect the official opinion of the European Union.

Table of contents

PART I

INTERNATIONAL COMPARISONS

PART II

TAX BURDEN TRENDS 2000-13

PART III

COUNTRY DETAILS, 2013

Taxing Wages 2014
Changes in structural labour income tax progressivity
over 2000-12 period in OECD member countries

Executive summary

The tax burden on wages continued to rise in OECD countries in 2013 by 0.2 percentage points to an average 35.9%. The rate of increase was higher than in 2012 but slower than in 2011. The tax burden or tax wedge is measured by taking the total taxes and social security contributions paid by employees and employers, minus family benefits received as a proportion of the total labour costs for employers. This makes it possible to examine how these levies and cash benefits affect net household income.

The main contributors to the 2013 increase were changes to personal income taxes, with increases in the statutory income tax rates in eight OECD countries. Increases in employee social security contributions also played a role in some countries. Reductions in employer social security contributions and personal income tax were key factors in those countries where the tax level fell in 2013.

Over the past three years, the tax burden has increased in 21 OECD countries and fallen in 9. At the same time, personal income tax burdens have risen in 25 out of 34 countries, largely because a higher proportion of earnings was subject to tax as the value of tax free allowances and tax credits fell relative to earnings. In 2013, only 6 countries had higher statutory income tax rates for workers on average earnings than in 2010, and in 5 countries they were lower.

This report looks at how these changes affect various types of household, such as single earners, families with or without children, or single parents. In most OECD countries, for example, the tax wedge for families with children is lower than that for single earners without children.

It also looks at how the levels of progressivity of the tax systems in OECD countries – that is how far income tax systems operate to achieve a more equal distribution of income after tax than before it – have changed since the year 2000. On average across the OECD, there have been strong increases in tax progression for low income families with children. Otherwise, there has been little change for the single workers without children and at higher income levels generally, although there are considerable differences between countries.

Key findings

Tax burdens continued to rise in 2013

- Across OECD countries the average tax and social security burden on employment incomes increased by 0.2 of a percentage point to 35.9% in 2013. This followed rises of 0.1 and 0.5 percentage points in 2012 and 2011 respectively, reversing the decline from 36.1% to 35.1% between 2007 and 2010.

- In 2013, the tax wedge increased in 21 of 34 countries, fell in 12 and remained unchanged in 1.
- Changes to the personal income taxes (PIT) were the main contributor to the increase in the average OECD total tax wedge in 2013, with increases in 20 of the OECD countries. The largest increase was in Portugal (+3.5percentage points) due to higher statutory income tax rates.
- Changes to PIT and employer social security contributions were the primary factors in countries where the tax burden fell. The largest decreases in the tax burden were in the Netherlands (-1.8 percentage points), Greece (-1.4 percentage points) and in France (-1.2 percentage points). In France, a tax credit for competitiveness and employment was introduced, which reduced the burden of employer social security contributions by 1.9 percentage points.
- The highest average tax burdens for childless single workers earning the average national wage were in Belgium (55.8%), Germany (49.3%), Austria (49.1%) and Hungary (49.0%). The lowest were in Chile (7%), New Zealand (16.9%), Mexico (19.2%) and Israel (20.7%).

Tax burdens in families with children

- The highest tax wedges for one-earner/two children families at the average wage were in Greece (44.5%), France (41.6%), Belgium (41.0%) and Austria (38.4%). New Zealand had the smallest tax wedge for these families (2.4%), followed by Ireland (6.8%), Chile (7%), and Switzerland (9.5%). The average for OECD countries was 26.4%.
- The largest increases in the tax burden for one earner families with children were in New Zealand and Portugal (both +1.9 percentage points) and the Slovak Republic (+1.8 percentage points) and the largest fall was in France and the Netherlands (-1.5 percentage points). In New Zealand, the tax burden increase for one earner families with children was higher than for the average single worker without children (+0.5 percentage point) because the basic amounts in the Family Tax Credit and the In Work Tax Credit for families with dependent children were frozen.
- In all OECD countries except Mexico and Chile, the tax wedge for families with children is lower than that for single individuals without children. The differences are particularly large in the Czech Republic, Luxembourg, Germany, Ireland and Slovenia.

Tax progressivity between 2000 and 2012

- On average across the OECD, personal income tax systems (as measured by the average PIT rate progression) have become slightly more progressive at lower income levels since the year 2000. The opposite is the case at higher income levels, although the changes at especially higher income levels are very small. There has been little change since 2007, except for the considerable increase in PIT progression for low-income families with 2 children.
- Over the period, increases in average PIT rate progression for single workers without children were highest in Ireland, Sweden and Slovenia. For single parents with 2 children, it increased the most in the Czech Republic, France, Sweden and the United Kingdom. The largest decreases for single taxpayers without children were in Germany, Hungary and Israel, and for single parents with 2 children in Germany, Hungary and Luxembourg.

- The progression of average tax wedges for low-income taxpayers with 2 children increased strongly between 2000 and 2012 as a result of an increased targeting of tax and benefit systems to low income workers (e.g. through in-work tax provisions) and especially lower-income families with children (through child benefits). The corresponding increase for low-income taxpayers without children was less pronounced although it increased considerably before 2007. On average, tax wedge progression for higher-income intervals hardly changed over the 2000-12 period.
- Average tax wedge progression for single workers without children increased the most in Turkey and decreased the most in Hungary, Germany and Mexico. For single parents with 2 children, the largest increases were in Australia, Canada, Hungary, Ireland, New Zealand, Portugal, Spain, Turkey and the United Kingdom. The largest decreases for this family-type were in Estonia, Germany, Iceland, Luxembourg, Norway, Mexico and Poland.

Overview

This Report provides unique information for each of the thirty four OECD countries on the income taxes paid by workers, their social security contributions, the family benefits they receive in the form of cash transfers as well as the social security contributions and payroll taxes paid by their employers. Results reported include the marginal and average tax burden for one- and two-earner households, and the implied total labour costs for employers. These data are widely used in academic research and in the formulation and evaluation of social and economic policies. The taxpayer specific detail in this Report enables it to complement the information provided annually in the Revenue Statistics, a publication providing internationally comparative data on tax levels and tax structures in OECD countries. The methodology followed in this Report is described briefly in the introduction section below and in more detail in the Annex.

The tables and charts present estimates of tax burdens and of the tax "wedge" between labour costs and net take-home pay for eight illustrative family types on comparable levels of income. The key results for 2013 are summarised in Section 2 below. Part I of the Report presents more detailed results for 2013, together with definitive results for 2012 and discusses the changes between the two years. Part II of the Report reviews historical changes in tax burdens between 2000 and 2013.

The statistical data for Israel are supplied by and under the responsibility of the relevant Israeli authorities. The use of such data by the OECD is without prejudice to the status of the Golan Heights, East Jerusalem and Israeli settlements in the West Bank under the terms of international law.

1. Introduction

This section briefly introduces the methodology employed for this Report, which focuses on full-time employees. It is assumed that their annual income from employment is equal to a given ratio of the average full-time adult gross wage earnings for each OECD economy, also referred to as the average wage (AW). This covers both manual and non-manual workers for either industry Sectors C-K inclusive with reference to the International Standard Industrial Classification of All Economic Activities, Revision 3 (ISIC Rev. 3) or industry Sectors B-N inclusive with reference to the International Standard Industrial Classification of All Economic Activities, Revision 4 (ISIC Rev. 4).[1] Further details are provided in Table 0.6 as well as in the Annex of this Report. Additional assumptions are made about the personal circumstances of these wage earners in order to determine their tax/benefit position. The taxes included in the present Report are confined to personal income tax, social security contributions and payroll taxes (which are aggregated with employer social contributions in the calculation of tax rates) payable on gross wage earnings. Consequently, any income tax that might be due on non-wage income and other kinds of taxes – e.g. corporate income tax, net wealth tax and consumption taxes – is not taken into account. The benefits included are those paid by general government as cash transfers, usually in respect of dependent children.

For most OECD countries, the tax year is equivalent to the calendar year, the exceptions being Australia, New Zealand and the United Kingdom. In the case of New Zealand and the United Kingdom, where the tax year starts in April, the calculations apply a "forward looking" approach. This implies that, for example, the tax rates reported for 2013 are those for the fiscal year 2013-14. However, in Australia, where the tax year starts in July, it has been decided to take a "backward looking" approach in order to present more reliable results. So, for example, the year 2013 in respect of Australia has been defined to mean its fiscal year 2012-13.

The Report presents several measures of taxation on labour. Most emphasis is given to the tax wedge – a measure of the difference between labour costs to the employer and the corresponding net take-home pay of the employee – which is calculated by expressing the sum of personal income tax, employee plus employer social security contributions together with any payroll tax, minus benefits as a percentage of labour costs. Employer social security contributions and – in some countries – payroll taxes are added to gross wage earnings of employees in order to determine a measure of total labour costs. However, it should be recognised that this measure may be less than the true labour costs faced by employers because, for example, employers may also have to make non-tax compulsory payments. The average tax wedge measures identify that part of total labour costs which is taken in tax and social security contributions net of cash benefits. In contrast, the marginal tax wedge measures identify the part of an increase of total labour costs that is paid in these levies.

The calculations also focus on the net personal average tax rate. This is the term used when the personal income tax and employee social security contributions net of cash benefits are expressed as a percentage of gross wage earnings. The net personal marginal tax rate shows the part of an increase of gross wage earnings that is paid in personal income tax and employee social security contributions net of cash benefits.

2. Review of results for 2013

2.1. Tax wedge

Table 0.1 shows that the tax wedge between total labour costs to the employer and the corresponding net take-home pay for single workers without children, at average earnings levels, varied widely across OECD countries in 2013 (see column 1). While in Austria, Belgium, France, Germany and Hungary, the tax wedge is around 50 per cent or higher, it is under 20 per cent in Chile, Mexico and New Zealand. The highest tax wedge is observed in Belgium (55.8 per cent) and the lowest in Chile (7.0 per cent).

The changes in tax wedge between 2012 and 2013 for the average worker without children are described in column 2 of Table 0.1. The tax wedges increased in twenty one countries and fell in twelve. The largest increases were in Portugal (3.54 percentage points), the Slovak Republic and the United States (1.51 percentage points). The Netherlands (-1.78 percentage points), Greece (-1.35 percentage points) and France (-1.20 percentage points) were the countries with a decrease of more than one percentage point. There was no change in the tax wedge for Chile.

In general, the rises in tax wedge rates are driven by higher income taxes (see column 3). This was the major factor in fourteen of the countries showing an overall increase. The largest increases in income taxes as a percentage of labour costs were in Portugal (3.54 percentage points) and in Luxembourg (1.09 percentage points). By contrast, higher employee and employer social security contributions account for virtually all of the increased tax wedge in Canada, Ireland, Israel and Japan. In the Slovak Republic and the United States, the increases in the tax wedge were mainly due to employee or employers' social security contributions that rose by more than one percentage point of labour costs.

Table 0.2 and Figure 0.1 show the constituent components of the tax wedge in 2013, i.e. income tax, employee and employer social security contributions (including payroll taxes where applicable), as a percentage of labour costs for the average worker without children. The labour costs in Table 0.2 are expressed in terms of dollars with equivalent purchasing power. Figure 0.1 shows that the average tax wedge in OECD countries was 35.9 per cent in 2013.

The percentage of labour costs paid in income tax varies considerably within OECD countries. The lowest figures are in Chile (zero) and Korea (4.6 per cent). The highest values are in Denmark (35.8 per cent), with Australia, Belgium and Iceland all over 20 per cent. The percentage of labour costs paid in employee social security contributions also varies widely ranging from zero in Australia and New Zealand to 17.1 per cent in Germany and 19.0 per cent in Slovenia. Employers in France pay 28.7 per cent of total labour costs in social security contributions, the highest amongst OECD countries. The corresponding figures are also more than 20 per cent in ten other countries – Austria, Belgium, the Czech Republic, Estonia, Greece, Hungary, Italy, the Slovak Republic, Spain and Sweden.

As a percentage of labour costs, the total of employee and employer social security contributions exceeds 20 per cent in more than half of the OECD countries. It also exceeds

Table 0.1. Comparison of total tax wedge

As % of labour costs[1]

Country[2]	Total tax wedge 2013	Annual change 2013/12 (in percentage points)[3]			
		Tax wedge	Income tax	Employee SSC	Employer SSC[4]
	(1)	(2)	(3)	(4)	(5)
Belgium	55.8	-0.19	-0.06	0.02	-0.16
Germany	49.3	-0.30	0.12	-0.21	-0.21
Austria	49.1	0.28	0.28	0.00	0.00
Hungary	49.0	-0.49	-0.49	0.00	0.00
France	48.9	-1.20	0.39	0.32	-1.92
Italy	47.8	0.08	0.08	0.00	0.00
Finland	43.1	0.56	0.57	-0.01	0.00
Sweden	42.9	0.07	0.09	-0.02	0.00
Czech Republic	42.4	-0.09	-0.09	0.00	0.00
Slovenia	42.3	-0.16	-0.16	0.00	0.00
Greece	41.6	-1.35	-0.79	0.11	-0.67
Portugal	41.1	3.54	3.54	0.00	0.00
Slovak Republic	41.1	1.51	-0.21	-0.27	1.98
Spain	40.7	0.05	0.05	0.00	0.00
Estonia	39.9	-0.51	0.30	-0.59	-0.22
Turkey	38.6	0.26	0.26	0.00	0.00
Denmark	38.2	-0.31	-0.33	0.01	0.00
Norway	37.3	-0.08	-0.01	0.01	-0.08
Luxembourg	37.0	1.09	1.09	0.00	0.00
Netherlands	36.9	-1.78	-0.91	0.48	-1.35
Poland	35.6	0.05	0.05	0.00	0.00
Iceland	33.4	0.05	0.14	-0.01	-0.09
Japan	31.6	0.37	0.00	0.18	0.18
United Kingdom	31.5	-0.61	-0.60	0.00	-0.02
United States	31.3	1.51	-0.29	1.82	-0.02
Canada	31.1	0.24	0.03	0.07	0.14
Australia	27.4	0.20	0.20	0.00	0.00
Ireland	26.6	0.69	-0.05	0.73	0.00
Switzerland	22.0	0.04	0.04	0.00	0.00
Korea	21.4	0.37	0.17	0.13	0.06
Israel	20.7	0.27	0.03	-0.04	0.28
Mexico	19.2	0.22	0.21	0.00	0.02
New Zealand	16.9	0.50	0.50	0.00	0.00
Chile	7.0	0.00	0.00	0.00	0.00

1. Single individual without children at the income level of the average worker.
2. Countries ranked by decreasing total tax wedge.
3. Due to rounding, the changes in tax wedge in column (2) may differ by one tenth of percentage point from the sum of columns (3)-(5). For Denmark, the Green Check (cash benefit) contributes to the difference as it is not included in columns (3)-(5).
4. Includes payroll taxes where applicable.

Sources: Country submissions, *OECD Economic Outlook Volume 2013* (No. 94).

StatLink http://dx.doi.org/10.1787/888933003839

one-third of total labour costs in eight OECD countries: Austria, Belgium, the Czech Republic, France, Germany, Greece, Hungary and the Slovak Republic.

2.2. Personal average tax rates

The personal average tax rate is defined as income tax plus employee social security contributions as a percentage of gross wage earnings.[2] Table 0.3 and Figure 0.2 show the

Table 0.2. **Income tax plus employee and employer social security contributions**

As % of labour costs, 2013[1]

Country[2]	Total tax wedge[3]	Income tax	Social security contributions		Labour costs[5]
			Employee	Employer[4]	
	(1)	(2)	(3)	(4)	(5)
Belgium	55.8	22.0	10.8	23.0	72 974
Germany	49.3	16.0	17.1	16.2	68 962
Switzerland	22.0	10.2	5.9	5.9	68 317
Norway	37.3	18.9	6.9	11.5	67 289
Austria	49.1	12.6	14.0	22.6	64 980
Luxembourg	37.0	15.1	11.0	11.0	64 680
Netherlands	36.9	14.3	14.2	8.4	63 585
France	48.9	10.4	9.8	28.7	61 648
Sweden	42.9	13.7	5.3	23.9	59 649
Finland	43.1	18.4	6.2	18.6	57 406
United Kingdom	31.5	13.3	8.5	9.8	56 797
Australia	27.4	21.8	0.0	5.6	55 766
Japan	31.6	6.7	12.2	12.8	54 790
United States	31.3	15.4	7.0	8.9	53 223
Italy	47.8	16.3	7.2	24.3	52 080
Korea	21.4	4.6	7.5	9.3	51 895
Denmark	38.2	35.8	2.7	0.0	51 772
Spain	40.7	12.8	4.9	23.0	49 723
Iceland	33.4	25.9	0.4	7.1	48 334
Ireland	26.6	13.3	3.6	9.7	44 494
Canada	31.1	13.7	6.6	10.8	43 643
Greece	41.6	7.1	12.9	21.5	40 650
New Zealand	16.9	16.9	0.0	0.0	36 381
Portugal	41.1	13.1	8.9	19.2	35 511
Turkey	38.6	11.6	12.9	14.2	34 293
Slovenia	42.3	9.4	19.0	13.9	34 282
Israel	20.7	8.4	7.5	4.8	34 046
Czech Republic	42.4	8.8	8.2	25.4	30 096
Hungary	49.0	12.5	14.4	22.2	29 465
Estonia	39.9	13.0	1.5	25.4	28 430
Poland	35.6	5.9	15.3	14.4	26 822
Slovak Republic	41.1	7.1	10.2	23.8	25 867
Chile	7.0	0.0	7.0	0.0	18 989
Mexico	19.2	7.5	1.2	10.5	13 964

1. Single individual without children at the income level of the average worker.
2. Countries ranked by decreasing labour costs.
3. Due to rounding, the total in column(1) may differ by one or more percentage points from the sum of columns (2)-(4). For Denmark, the Green Check (cash benefit) contributes to the difference as it is not included in columns (2)-(4).
4. Includes payroll taxes where applicable.
5. Dollars with equal purchasing power.

Sources: Country submissions, *OECD Economic Outlook Volume 2013* (No. 94).

StatLink http://dx.doi.org/10.1787/888933003858

personal average tax rates in 2013 for a single worker without children at the average earnings level. The gross wage earnings figures in Table 0.3 are expressed in terms of dollars with equivalent purchasing power. Figure 0.2 provides a graphical representation of the personal average tax rate decomposed between income tax and employee social security contributions.

Figure 0.1. Income tax plus employees' and employers' social security contributions, 2013

As a % of labour costs[1, 2]

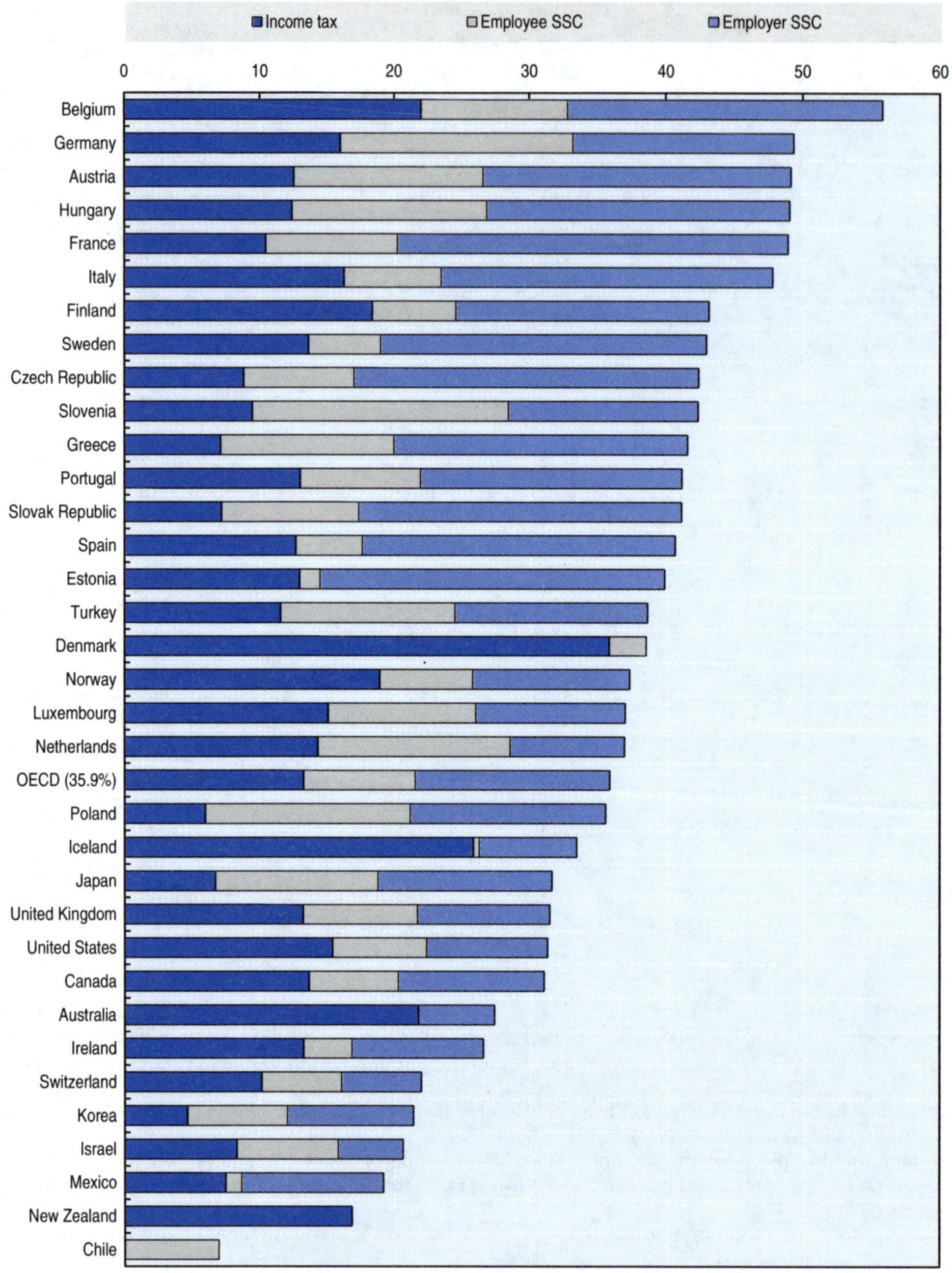

1. Single individual without children at the income level of the average worker.
2. Includes payroll taxes where applicable.

StatLink http://dx.doi.org/10.1787/888933003782

Figure 0.2 shows that on average, the personal average tax rate in OECD countries is 25.4 per cent. Belgium at 42.6 per cent of gross earnings has the highest rate with Denmark and Germany being the only other countries with rates of more than 35 per cent. Chile and Mexico have the lowest personal average tax rates with 7.0 and 9.8 per cent of gross average earnings respectively. Korea is the only other country with a rate of less than 15 per cent.

Table 0.3. **Income tax plus employee social security contributions, 2013**[1]

As % of gross wage earnings

Country[2]	Total payment[3]	Income tax	Empoyee social security contributions	Gross wage earnings[4]
	(1)	(2)	(3)	(4)
Switzerland	17.1	10.9	6.3	64 298
Norway	29.2	21.4	7.8	59 548
Netherlands	31.2	15.7	15.5	58 252
Germany	39.6	19.1	20.4	57 818
Luxembourg	29.3	17.0	12.3	57 591
Belgium	42.6	28.6	14.0	56 171
Australia	23.1	23.1	0.0	52 639
Denmark	38.6	35.8	2.7	51 772
United Kingdom	24.1	14.7	9.4	51 255
Austria	34.3	16.2	18.1	50 322
United States	24.6	16.9	7.7	48 463
Japan	21.6	7.7	13.9	47 771
Korea	13.4	5.1	8.3	47 075
Finland	30.2	22.5	7.6	46 748
Sweden	25.0	18.0	7.0	45 388
Iceland	28.3	27.9	0.5	44 883
France	28.4	14.6	13.8	43 984
Ireland	18.7	14.7	4.0	40 175
Italy	31.0	21.5	9.5	39 430
Canada	22.7	15.3	7.4	38 948
Spain	22.9	16.6	6.4	38 278
New Zealand	16.9	16.9	0.0	36 381
Israel	16.7	8.8	7.9	32 419
Greece	25.5	9.0	16.5	31 892
Slovenia	33.1	11.0	22.1	29 528
Turkey	28.5	13.5	15.0	29 436
Portugal	27.2	16.2	11.0	28 696
Poland	24.7	6.9	17.8	22 968
Hungary	34.5	16.0	18.5	22 930
Czech Republic	22.8	11.8	11.0	22 460
Estonia	19.5	17.5	2.0	21 217
Slovak Republic	22.8	9.4	13.4	19 716
Chile	7.0	0.0	7.0	18 989
Mexico	9.8	8.4	1.4	12 501

1. Single individual without children at the income level of the average worker.
2. Countries ranked by decreasing gross wage earnings.
3. Due to rounding total may differ one percentage point from aggregate of columns for income tax and social security contributions.
4. Dollars with equal purchasing power.

Sources: Country submissions, *OECD Economic Outlook Volume 2013* (No. 94).

StatLink http://dx.doi.org/10.1787/888933003877

The impact of taxes and benefits on worker's take-home pay varies greatly among OECD countries. Such wide variations in the size and make-up of tax wedges reflect in part differences in:

- the overall ratio of aggregate tax revenues to Gross Domestic Product; and,
- the share of personal income tax and social security contributions in national tax mixes.

The mix of taxes paid out of gross wage earnings also varies greatly between countries as illustrated in Figure 0.2.

Figure 0.2. **Percentage of gross wage earnings paid in income tax and employee social security contributions, 2013**[1, 2]

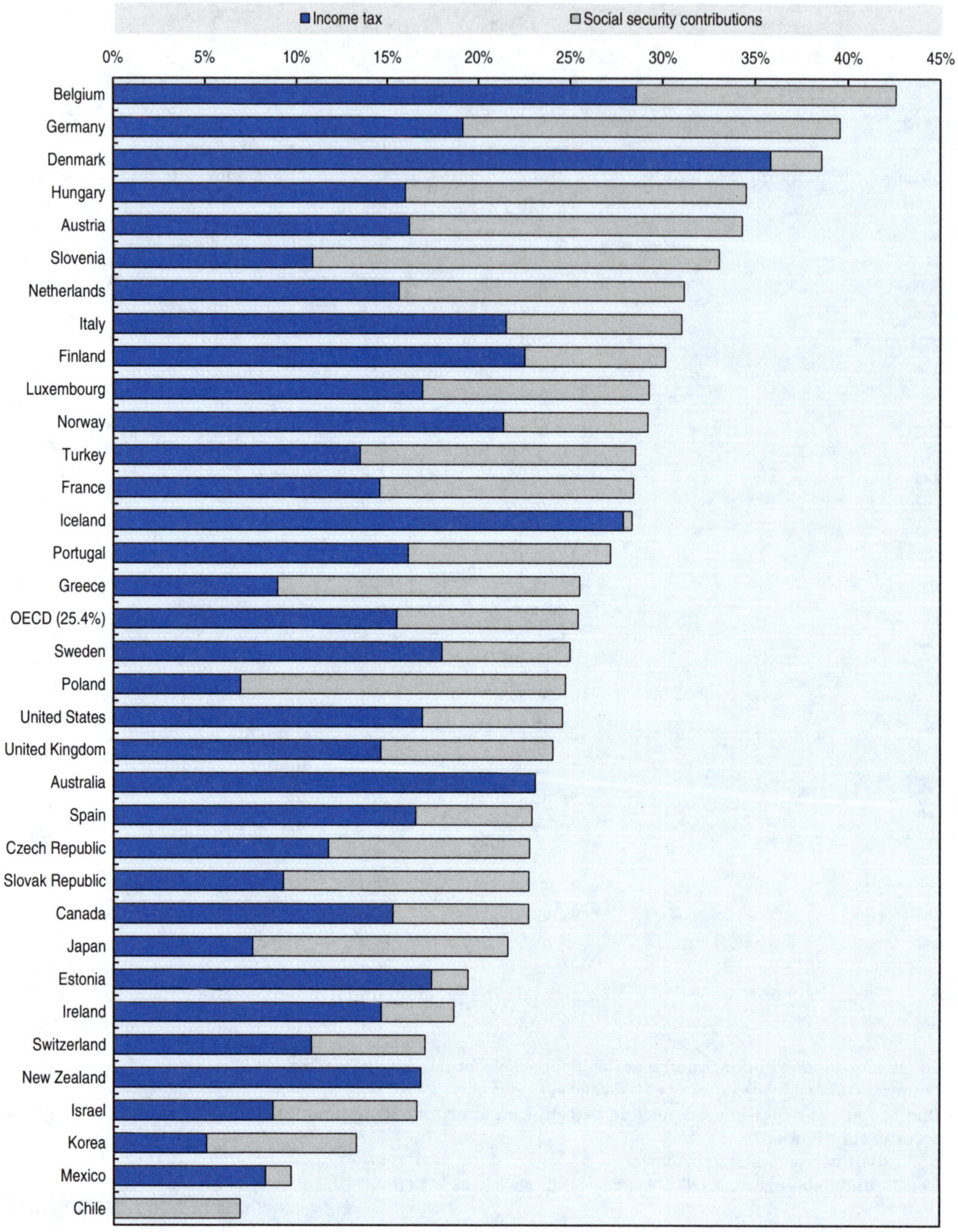

1. Countries ranked by decreasing tax burden.
2. Single workers at the income level of the average worker.

StatLink http://dx.doi.org/10.1787/888933003801

In 2013, the share of income tax within the personal average tax rate is more important than the share of the employee social security contributions for 23 of 34 OECD member countries. No employee social security contributions are levied in Australia and New Zealand and the rates are comparatively small in Denmark, Estonia, Iceland, Ireland and Mexico. In contrast, the single worker at the average wage level paid substantially more employee social security contributions than personal income tax in seven countries – Greece, Japan, Korea, Poland, the Slovak Republic and Slovenia plus Chile, where the average worker did not pay personal income tax in 2013. In eight countries – Austria, the Czech Republic, France, Germany, Hungary, Israel, the Netherlands, and Turkey – the income tax and employee social security contributions as percentages of gross earnings are almost equivalent (differences of less than 3 percentage points).

2.3. Family tax rates

Table 0.4 compares the tax wedges for a one-earner married couple with two children and a single individual without children, at average earnings levels. These tax wedges varied widely across OECD countries in 2013 (see columns 1 and 2). The size of the tax wedge for the family is generally lower than the one observed for the individual without children, since many OECD countries provide a fiscal benefit to families with children through advantageous tax treatment and/or cash transfers.

The savings realised by a one-earner married couple compared to a single worker are greater than 20 per cent of labour costs in the Czech Republic and Luxembourg, and greater than 15 per cent of labour costs in three other countries – Germany, Ireland and Slovenia. The tax burdens are the same in Chile and Mexico and different by less than three percentage points in Greece, Korea and Turkey (see columns 1 and 2).

In 28 of 34 OECD countries, the change in the tax wedge of an average one-earner married couple with two children between 2012 and 2013 does not exceed plus or minus one percentage point (see column 3). There are increases of greater than 1 percentage point in four countries: Portugal and New Zealand (1.9), the Slovak Republic (1.8) and the United States (1.6). The tax wedge fell by 1.5 percentage points in France and the Netherlands. In 2013, the tax wedge of families also decreased by less than one percentage point in ten other countries: Belgium, the Czech Republic, Denmark, Estonia, Germany, Hungary, Italy, Slovenia, Switzerland and the United Kingdom. By comparison, the change in the tax wedge of a single taxpayer without children at the average wage level was greater than one percentage point or more in seven OECD countries. Detailed explanations on the latter are given in the above Section 2.1.

A comparison of the changes in tax wedges between 2012 and 2013 between one-earner married couples with two children and single persons without children, at the average wage level, is shown in column 5 of Table 0.4. The fiscal preference for families increased in seven OECD member countries: Belgium, the Czech Republic, France, Italy, Luxembourg, Portugal and Switzerland. Additionally, the effects of changes in the tax system on the tax wedge were independent of the family type in Chile, Denmark, Ireland, Japan, Mexico and Turkey.

Figure 0.3 compares the net personal average tax rate for the average worker between single individuals and a one-earner married couple with two children. These results show the same pattern as those for the tax wedge results. This is because employer social security contributions which are not taken into account in the former but included in the latter are independent of family type. The savings realised by a one-earner married couple are equal to or greater than 20 per cent of earnings in four countries – the Czech Republic (29.3 per cent), Luxembourg (25.5 per cent), Slovenia (22.4 per cent) and Ireland (21.9 per cent). In contrast, the savings as percentage of gross earnings are less than 10 per cent of earnings in eleven countries – Spain (7.6 per cent), Norway (7.0 per cent), Sweden (6.9 per

Table 0.4. Comparison of total tax wedge by family type

As % of labour costs

Country[1]	Family[2] total tax wedge 2013	Single[3] total tax wedge 2013	Annual change 2013/12 (in percentage points) Family tax wedge	Single Tax wedge	Difference between single and family (4)-(3)[4]
	(1)	(2)	(3)	(4)	(5)
Greece	44.5	41.6	0.6	-1.4	-2.0
France	41.6	48.9	-1.5	-1.2	0.3
Belgium	41.0	55.8	-0.3	-0.2	0.1
Austria	38.4	49.1	0.5	0.3	-0.3
Italy	38.2	47.8	-0.5	0.1	0.6
Finland	38.1	43.1	0.7	0.6	-0.1
Sweden	37.7	42.9	0.1	0.1	-0.1
Turkey	37.4	38.6	0.2	0.3	0.0
Spain	34.8	40.7	0.1	0.0	0.0
Hungary	34.1	49.0	-0.1	-0.5	-0.4
Germany	33.8	49.3	-0.2	-0.3	-0.1
Estonia	32.3	39.9	-0.1	-0.5	-0.4
Norway	31.2	37.3	0.1	-0.1	-0.1
Netherlands	30.8	36.9	-1.5	-1.8	-0.3
Poland	29.8	35.6	0.2	0.1	-0.1
Portugal	29.8	41.1	1.9	3.5	1.7
Slovak Republic	27.6	41.1	1.8	1.5	-0.3
Denmark	27.6	38.2	-0.3	-0.3	0.0
United Kingdom	27.0	31.5	-0.5	-0.6	-0.1
Japan	26.1	31.6	0.4	0.4	0.0
Slovenia	23.1	42.3	-0.1	-0.2	-0.1
Czech Republic	20.5	42.4	-0.5	-0.1	0.4
United States	20.3	31.3	1.6	1.5	-0.1
Mexico	19.2	19.2	0.2	0.2	0.0
Iceland	19.1	33.4	0.9	0.0	-0.8
Korea	19.0	21.4	0.4	0.4	-0.1
Canada	18.7	31.1	0.4	0.2	-0.1
Israel	17.4	20.7	0.9	0.3	-0.6
Australia	16.9	27.4	0.4	0.2	-0.2
Luxembourg	14.3	37.0	0.8	1.1	0.3
Switzerland	9.5	22.0	-0.4	0.0	0.4
Chile	7.0	7.0	0.0	0.0	0.0
Ireland	6.8	26.6	0.7	0.7	0.0
New Zealand	2.4	16.9	1.9	0.5	-1.4

1. Countries ranked by decreasing tax wedge of the family.
2. One earner married couple with two children and earnings at the average wage level.
3. Single individual without children and earnings at the average wage level.
4. Due to rounding total may differ one percentage point from the subtraction results of columns 4 and 3.

Sources: Country submissions, *OECD Economic Outlook Volume 2013* (No. 94).

StatLink http://dx.doi.org/10.1787/888933003896

cent), the Netherlands and Poland (6.7 per cent), Japan (6.4 per cent), Finland (6.2 per cent), the United Kingdom (4.9 per cent), Israel (3.4 per cent), Korea (2.7 per cent) and Turkey (1.4 per cent). The burden is the same in Chile and in Mexico. It is also interesting to note that when cash benefits are taken into account, the tax burden measure for the average one-earner married couples with two children becomes negative in the Czech Republic and Ireland because cash benefits exceed the income tax and social security payments.

Figure 0.3. **Income tax plus employee contributions less cash benefits, 2013**

As % of gross wage earnings, by family-type[1, 2]

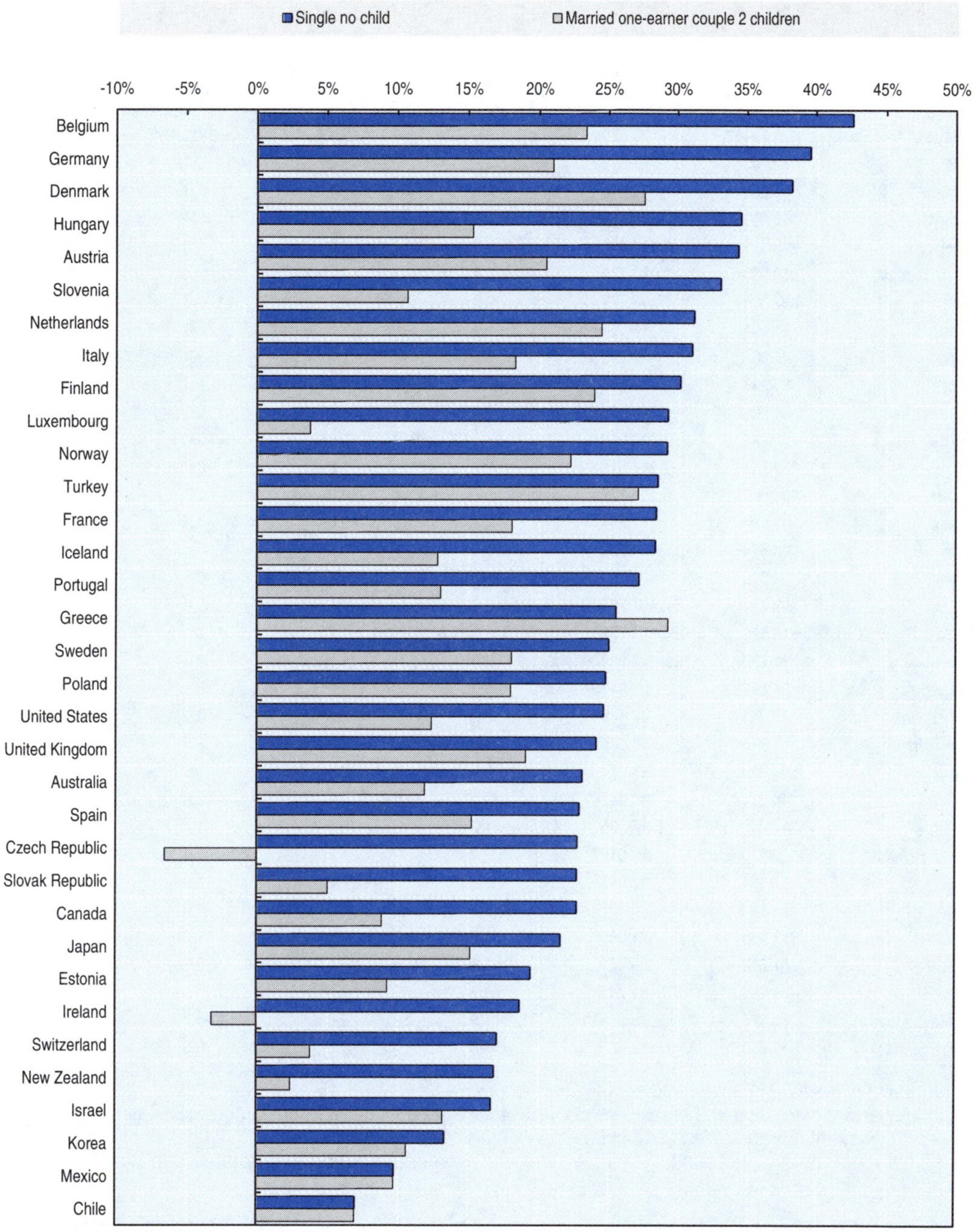

1. Countries ranked by decreasing rates for single taxpayer without children.
2. Family types: a single individual without children and earnings at the average wage level and a one earner married couple with two children and earnings at the average wage level.

StatLink http://dx.doi.org/10.1787/888933003820

2.4. Wages

Table 0.5 shows the gross wage earnings in national currency of the average worker in each OECD member country for 2012 and 2013. The figures for 2013 are estimated by the OECD Secretariat by applying the change in the compensation per employee in the total

Table 0.5. **Comparison of wage levels**

Country	Gross wage in national currency		Annual change 2013/12 (in percentage)			
	2012	2013	Gross wage	Inflation[1]	Real wage before tax	Change in personal average tax rate[2]
	(1)	(2)	(3)	(4)	(5)	(6)
Australia	73 494	77 530	5.5	2.1	3.3	0.2
Austria	40 708	41 693	2.4	2.0	0.4	0.4
Belgium	45 886	46 810	2.0	1.1	0.9	-0.1
Canada	46 940	48 078	2.4	1.0	1.4	0.1
Chile	6 218 613	6 607 476	6.3	2.0	4.2	0.0
Czech Republic	302 993	298 770	-1.4	1.4	-2.7	-0.1
Denmark	392 000	395 722	0.9	0.7	0.2	-0.3
Estonia	11 004	11 664	6.0	3.6	2.3	-0.4
Finland	41 662	42 493	2.0	2.3	-0.3	0.7
France	36 248	36 980	2.0	1.0	1.0	0.2
Germany	44 300	45 170	2.0	1.7	0.3	-0.2
Greece	22 240	20 604	-7.4	-0.7	-6.7	-1.1
Hungary	2 838 864	2 914 514	2.7	1.9	0.8	-0.6
Iceland	5 856 000	6 191 179	5.7	4.0	1.7	0.1
Ireland	32 514	32 381	-0.4	0.6	-1.0	0.8
Israel	128 549	131 033	1.9	1.5	0.4	0.0
Italy	29 315	29 704	1.3	1.4	-0.1	0.1
Japan	4 893 341	4 901 704	0.2	0.2	0.0	0.3
Korea	38 811 570	39 829 650	2.6	1.2	1.4	0.3
Luxembourg	51 752	52 902	2.2	1.7	0.5	1.2
Mexico	94 875	97 941	3.2	3.8	-0.5	0.2
Netherlands	47 075	48 109	2.2	2.8	-0.6	-0.9
New Zealand	51 278	53 234	3.8	0.9	2.9	0.5
Norway	504 929	524 177	3.8	2.2	1.6	0.0
Poland	40 205	41 442	3.1	1.1	2.0	0.1
Portugal	17 040	17 335	1.7	0.5	1.2	4.4
Slovak Republic	9 810	10 015	2.1	1.6	0.4	0.0
Slovenia	17 538	17 611	0.4	2.2	-1.8	-0.2
Spain	25 894	26 027	0.5	1.6	-1.0	0.1
Sweden	387 960	391 990	1.0	0.1	1.0	0.1
Switzerland	87 662	88 161	0.6	-0.4	0.9	0.0
Turkey	29 209	31 744	8.7	7.5	1.1	0.3
United Kingdom	34 877	35 548	1.9	2.6	-0.7	-0.7
United States	47 960	48 463	1.0	1.5	-0.5	-0.3

1. Estimated percentage change in the total consumer price index.
2. Difference in the personal average tax rate of the average worker (single without children) between 2013 and 2012.

Sources: Country submissions, *OECD Economic Outlook Volume* 2013 (No. 94).

StatLink http://dx.doi.org/10.1787/888933003915

economy as presented in the OECD Economic Outlook (No 94) Database to the final average wage values provided by OECD member countries. More information on the values of the average wage and the estimation methodology is included in Section 5 of the Annex of this Report.

The annual change in 2013 – shown in column 3 – varied between a decrease of -7.4 per cent in Greece and an increase of 8.7 per cent in Turkey. To a large extent, the changes reflect the different inflation levels of individual OECD countries – see column 4 of Table 0.5. The annual change in real wage levels (before personal income tax and employee social security contributions) is found to be in the -2 to +2 per cent range for most

Table 0.6. Average Wage Industry Classification

	Years for which ISIC Rev. 3.1 or any variant (Sectors C-K) has been used to calculate the AW	Years for which ISIC Rev. 4 or any variant (Sectors B-N) has been used to calculate the AW
Australia[1]		2000-13
Austria[2]	2004-07	2008-13
Belgium	2000-07	2008-13
Canada		2000-13
Chile[3]	2000-13	
Czech Republic		2000-13
Denmark	2000-07	2008-13
Estonia		2000-13
Finland		2000-13
France	2000-07	2008-13
Germany	2000-05	2006-13
Greece[4]	2000-07	2008-13
Hungary		2000-13
Iceland[5]		2000-13
Ireland[6]	2000-07	2008-13
Israel	2000-13	
Italy		2000-13
Japan		2000-13
Korea[7]	2000-07	2008-13
Luxembourg	2000-04	2005-13
Mexico[8]		
Netherlands	2000-07	2008-13
New Zealand[9]	2000-03	2004-13
Norway	2000-08	2009-13
Poland	2000-07	2008-13
Portugal	2000-05	2006-13
Slovak Republic[10]		2000-13
Slovenia		2000-13
Spain		2000-13
Sweden		2000-13
Switzerland		2000-13
Turkey[11]		
United Kingdom	2000-06	2007-13
United States	2000-06	2007-13

1. Australia: Based on ANZSIC06 such that the categories substantially overlap with ISIC 4, Sectors B-N.
2. Austria: 2000-03 average wage values are not based on the NACE (ISIC) classification.
3. Chile: The AW values are based on sectors C to O from years 2006 to 2012. From 2010 onwards Sectors L (7522) and L (7523) are excluded.
4. Greece: The average annual earnings refer to full time employees for the Sectors B to N of NACE Rev. 2, including Division 95 and excluding Divisions 37, 39 and 75 for 2008 onwards.
5. Iceland: Using national classification system that corresponds with the NACE Rev. 2 classification system.
6. Ireland: Values from 2000 to 2007 are based on Sectors C-E (NACE). From 2008 onwards, they are based on Sectors B-E (NACE Rev. 2).
7. Korea: Average wage values are based on 6th Korean Standard Industrial Classification (KSIC) C-K for 2000-01, 8th KISC C-M for 2002 to 2007 and 9th KISC B-N except E for 2008 onwards.
8. Mexico: 2000-13 AW values are based on the Mexican Classification of Economic Activities (Clasificación Mexicana de Actividades Económicas [CMAE]) which is based on one of the first versions of ISIC.
9. New Zealand: See the note for Australia which applies from 2004.
10. Slovak Republic: Average wage values based on ISIC Rev. 4 classification (B to N) and still include the self-employment data.
11. Turkey: The average wage is based on the average production worker wage ISIC Rev. 3.1, Sector D.

StatLink http://dx.doi.org/10.1787/888933003934

countries; see column 5 of Table 0.5 Greece (-6.7 per cent), the Czech Republic (-2.7 per cent), Estonia (2.3 per cent), New Zealand (2.9 per cent), Australia (3.3 per cent) and Chile (4.2 per cent) show changes that are outside this range.

When comparing wage levels, it is important to note that the definition of average wage earnings can vary between countries due to data limitations. For instance, some countries do not include the wages earned by supervisory and managerial workers and not all countries exclude the wage earnings from part-time workers.

Table 0.6 provides more information on whether the average wages for the years 2000 to 2013 are based on industry Sectors C-K inclusive with reference to the International Standard Industrial Classification of All Economic Activities, Revision 3 (ISIC Rev. 3) or industry Sectors B-N inclusive with reference to the International Standard Industrial Classification of All Economic Activities, Revision 4 (ISIC Rev. 4).

Most OECD countries have calculated average wage earnings on the basis of Sectors B-N in the ISIC Rev. 4 Industry Classification at least since 2008. Some countries have revised the average wage values using the ISIC Rev. 4 Classification or any variant for prior years as well. This is the case, for example, in Australia, Canada, the Czech Republic, Estonia, Finland, Hungary, Iceland, Italy, Japan, the Slovak Republic, Slovenia, Spain, Sweden and Switzerland. Australia (for all years) and New Zealand (years 2004 to 2013) have provided values based on the 2006 ANZSIC industry classification, divisions B to N, which substantially overlaps the ISIC Rev. 4, Sectors B to N. For New Zealand, the years prior 2004 continue to be based on Sectors C-K in ANZSIC. In general, the change in the industry classification has had only a small impact on the level of the average wage earnings but the results reported in this Report for the years before 2013 may slightly deviate from the values reported in last year's edition on this account.

Notes

1. Not all national statistical agencies use ISIC Rev. 3 or Rev. 4 to classify industries. However, the Statistical Classification of Economic Activities in the European Community (NACE Rev. 1 or Rev. 2), the North American Industry Classification System (US NAICS 2002) and the Australian and New Zealand Standard Industrial Classification (ANZSIC 2006) include a classification which broadly conforms either with industries C-K in ISIC Rev. 3 or industries B-N in ISIC Rev. 4.
2. In the Netherlands, the division made between personal income taxes and employee social security contributions is slightly different to the methodology generally applied in this Report.

Taxing Wages 2014
Changes in structural labour income tax progressivity
over 2000-12 period in OECD member countries

Special Feature: Changes in structural labour income tax progressivity over the 2000-12 period in OECD member countries*

This Special Feature analyses the changes in the progressivity of taxes on wage earnings in OECD countries over the 2000-12 period. This chapter also studies changes in progressivity over the 2000-07 and the 2007-12 periods, and whether changes in personal income taxes, benefits or social security contributions have been the drivers of these changes.

The statistical data for Israel are supplied by and under the responsibility of the relevant Israeli authorities. The use of such data by the OECD is without prejudice to the status of the Golan Heights, East Jerusalem and Israeli settlements in the West Bank under the terms of international law.

1. Introduction

This Special Feature analyses the changes in the progressivity of taxes on wage earnings in OECD countries over the 2000-12 period. This chapter also studies changes in progressivity over the 2000-07 and the 2007-12 periods, and whether changes in personal income taxes, benefits or social security contributions have been the drivers of these changes.

The progressivity of the taxes on wage earnings depends on the design and interaction of the personal income tax (PIT) system, social security contributions (SSCs) and the benefit system. First, the progressivity of the PIT depends on the progressivity of the statutory PIT rate schedule, which depends on the number and width of the tax brackets and on the difference between the tax rates and especially between the top and bottom tax rates.

Second, the progressivity also depends on the specific design of "standard" and "non-standard" PIT provisions that reduce the taxpayer's tax liability. Provisions can take the form of allowances, deductions, exemptions and credits and may depend on the level of income (e.g. in-work tax credits and other make-work-pay provisions) and/or specific family characteristics (e.g. the number of children, a dependent spouse, etc.). As is the case in *Taxing Wages*, non-standard PIT reliefs are not taken into account in the analysis of PIT progressivity in this Special Feature.

Third, in addition to PIT, wage earnings are also subject to employee and employer SSCs and possibly payroll taxes. As these are often levied at flat rates, they tend to reduce the progressivity of the tax system. SSC ceilings may result in regressive taxes on wage earnings. SSC ceilings will typically have an impact on the social security benefits that can be received, but a discussion of this impact goes beyond the scope of this Special Feature. On the other hand, provisions in social security contributions, which are typically targeted at low-income earners, may (locally) increase the tax system's progressivity.

Also, taxpayers may receive direct benefits, which are typically targeted at lower income households and especially at families with children. These benefits make the tax system more progressive as lump-sum benefits reduce the average tax burden more for low income households. Benefits that are decreasing in income, as often is the case, also result in higher marginal tax rates (and therefore increased progressivity) over the tapering interval.

In order to capture the impact and interaction of all features of the tax and benefit system, this paper calculates average-rate progression indicators, which measure the change in the average tax rates over a particular income interval and for different family types. As average PIT rates and average tax wedges are (amongst) the key indicators included in the OECD's *Taxing Wages* report, the tax progressivity indicators that are presented in this Special Feature have been calculated using the *Taxing Wages* country calculation models.

The Special Feature builds on and extends last year's Special Feature (Paturot, Mellbye and Brys, 2012), which has calculated statutory progressivity indicators for OECD member countries in 2011. As last year's Special Feature included a detailed discussion of the advantages and disadvantages of different types of structural progressivity indicators, including the structural average tax rate progression indicator, this discussion is not repeated here.

This Special Feature is organized as follows. Section 2 briefly reviews the structural labour income tax progressivity indicators that are presented and discussed in this Special Feature. Section 3 presents results for the average PIT rate and average tax wedge progression on average across the OECD. The overall average PIT rate and average tax wedge progression and the deviation across income intervals is presented in Section 4. Section 5 analyses the level of country-specific progression rates and aims at identifying the tax systems that are the most and the least progressive in the OECD. Section 6 identifies the countries that have increased the progressivity of their tax system the most over time.

An analysis of the drivers of the changes in progressivity over time (e.g. changes in PITs, SSCs and payroll taxes and/ or benefits) is left for future work.

A selection of the charts that have been prepared for this analysis has been included in the main part of the text. The remaining charts can be found in the Annexes to this Special Feature.

2. Structural labour income tax progressivity indicators

This Special Feature presents results on average PIT rate and average tax wedge progression for 7 income intervals: 50%-67%, 67%-100%, 100%-133%, 133%-167%, 167%-200%, 200%-300% and 300%-500% of the AW in OECD countries in 2000, 2007 and 2012 as well as changes in these progression rates over time.

The average PIT rate and tax wedge progression is calculated for 6 different household types: singles without children, single parents with 2 children, one-earner married couples without and with 2 children and two-earner married couples without and with 2 children. In case of two-earner couples, it is assumed that one partner earns 67% of the AW while the other partner's earnings vary between 50% and 500% of the AW.

For each family type, also the overall progression rate for the 50%-500% of the AW income interval is presented, as well as the standard deviation in progression across the 7 income intervals.

Please note that the standard deviations in progression across income intervals should be interpreted with care, as similar standard deviations can hide large differences in actual tax progressivity across countries (as the standard deviation is calculated using the mean progression over the intervals and this mean progression deviates across countries and over time). Alternatively, coefficients of variation, which divide the standard deviation by the mean as a way to show normalized dispersion, could be calculated using the progression results. Also, the standard deviations would change if the number of intervals would increase or decrease (keeping the 50%-500% of the AW income interval fixed).

The "structural" tax progression indicator is defined as:

$$(\text{AETR } X_2\% \text{ AW} - \text{AETR } X_1\% \text{ AW}) / (X_2\% \text{ AW} - X_1\% \text{ AW})$$

Where AETR X_1%AW and AETR X_2%AW are the average effective tax rates or tax wedges corresponding to two different income levels X_1 and X_2, respectively. The income levels are expressed as multiples of the average wage (AW). *The indicator measures how the average PIT rate or the average tax wedge increases per percentage point increase in income, measured as a multiple of the AW, over the X_2%AW – X_1%AW income range.*

The value of this indicator is zero, and hence the slope of the average effective tax rate curve is flat, in case of a proportional tax (in the absence of a basic allowance). A progressive tax is reflected by a positive value of the indicator, and a regressive tax by a negative value. The higher is the value of this indicator, the higher is the increase in the average tax rate with income and therefore the more progressive is the tax system. (Average tax rates that increase with income or marginal tax rates that are higher than average tax rates at any income level are similar definitions of tax progressivity).

The average PIT rate progression captures the progressivity of the PIT system in isolation. The average tax wedge progression takes also into account the effect of employee and employer social security contributions, payroll taxes and cash benefits on progressivity.

The following example shows how to interpret the progression rates. An average personal income tax rate progression of 0.4 over the 50%-67% of the AW income interval means that the personal average tax rate increases with 0.4 percentage points per percentage point increase in the AW over the 50%-67% income level. The increase in the average PIT rate at 67% of the AW compared to the rate at 50% of the AW then equals 0.4 multiplied by 17, i.e. 6.8 percentage points.

This example shows that values of progression rates are dependent on the level of the average tax burden. Information on progression rates, as well as standard deviations in progression rates across income intervals, should therefore be complemented with levels of average effective tax rates. This information is included in the main *Taxing Wages* report.

Compared to the Special Feature prepared for the 2013 edition of *Taxing Wages*, this Special Feature extends the analysis by adding two additional income intervals (200%-300% and 300%-500% of the AW) in order to capture the effect of top PIT rates which are levied in some countries at very high incomes, and two additional family types (two-earner married couples without and with 2 children).

Because the extension of the range of the analysis to 500% of the AW has an impact on the overall PIT rate and tax wedge progression and the standard deviation in progression across income intervals, the analysis not only focuses on changes in progressivity over time, but also presents results for the individual years (i.e. 2000, 2007 and 2012).

Note that small changes in progressivity may not necessarily reflect the impact of tax reforms, but may reflect the effect on tax burdens of, for instance, fiscal drag. Throughout this paper, small changes in progression rates should therefore be interpreted with care.

3. The average PIT rate and tax wedge progression on average across the OECD

Figure S.1 shows average PIT rate and tax wedge progression on average across the OECD in 2012 for the six family types and the seven income intervals that are considered in the analysis. The graph indicates that when only PIT is considered, the OECD average progression rate is the highest at the bottom income interval and that it decreases with income regardless of the family situation. These results are strongly driven by the impact of basic and other types of tax allowances or credits which, as they are not increasing in

Figure S.1. **Average PIT rate and tax wedge progression on average across the OECD in 2012**

For 6 household types, by income intervals

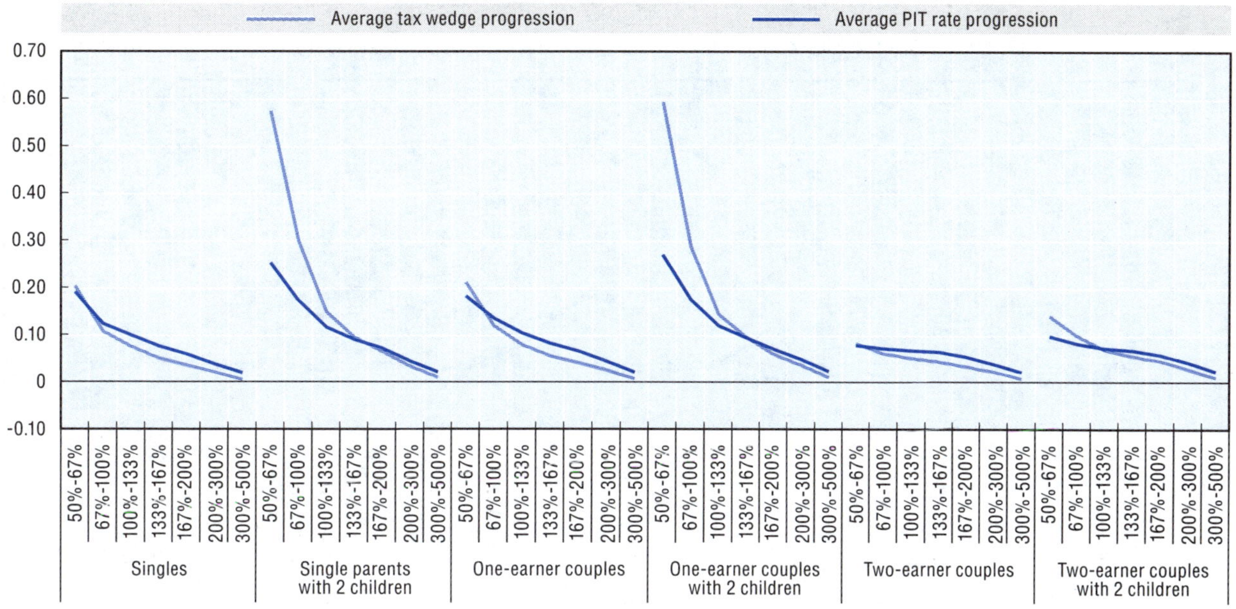

StatLink http://dx.doi.org/10.1787/888933005416

income, reduce average tax rates more at lower income levels.* The average tax wedge progression, which takes also social security contributions and cash transfers into account, shows a similar pattern.

However, some differences between average PIT rate and tax wedge progression indicators can be observed. First, the average tax wedge progression is lower than the average PIT rate progression for households without children except at the bottom income interval. As families without children usually do not receive benefits, this result shows that SSCs tend to reduce tax progressivity because they are typically levied at flat rates (and in some cases because ceilings apply). The higher tax wedge progression at the bottom income interval is the result of SSC provisions targeted at lower income levels. Second, the average tax wedge progression is higher than the average PIT rate progression for households with children, except at higher income intervals. Thus, for households with children, the effect of cash benefits, which reduce the tax wedge, and the fact that these benefits are i) lump-sum amounts and ii) typically phased out when income increases, result in an increase in tax progressivity. This effect tends to be stronger than the flattening effect from social security contributions at the lower and middle-income intervals.

Average PIT rate and tax wedge progression on average across the OECD has followed a similar pattern in 2007 and 2000 (see Annex S.A), although progression has slightly changed when progression rates in 2012 are compared with the rates in 2000. To show this more clearly, Figure S.2 presents the change in the average PIT rate and tax wedge progression on average across the OECD over the 2000-12 time interval.

Compared to the year 2000, personal income tax systems (as measured by the average PIT rate progression) have become slightly more progressive in 2012 at lower income levels

* This is in line with the analysis in OECD (2006) which demonstrated that a significant amount of progressivity can be achieved in a flat tax system through a basic allowance.

Figure S.2. **Change in the average PIT rate and tax wedge progression on average across the OECD over the 2000-12 time interval**

For 6 household types, by income intervals

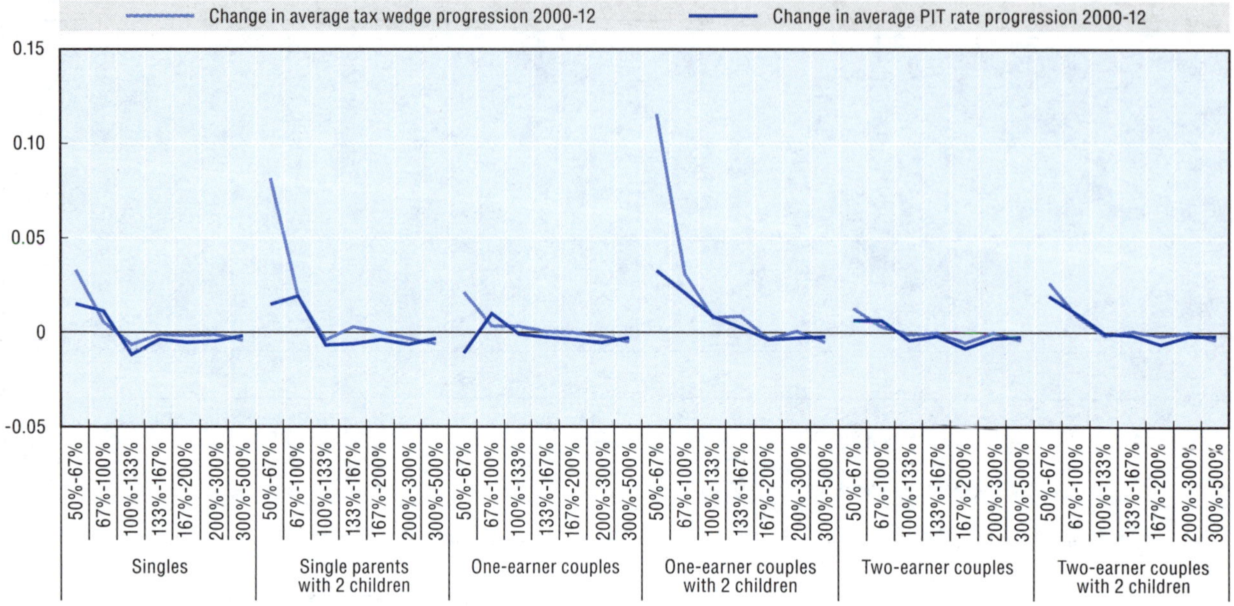

StatLink http://dx.doi.org/10.1787/888933005435

while they have turned slightly less progressive at higher income levels, on average across the OECD, although the differences at especially higher income levels are very small.

In addition to the fact that small changes do not necessarily reflect tax reforms but rather fiscal drag, these results should be interpreted with care because higher progressivity can arise as a result of a drop in the tax burden on the income at the "start" of a particular income interval or an increase in the tax burden on the income at the "end" of that interval. In fact, higher progressivity because of an increase in the tax burden on income at the end of the interval may result in a drop in progressivity in the following interval if the tax burden on income at the end of the following income interval has not changed. Hence, progression points are (possibly) interlinked.

Also, when comparing tax wedges in 2012 with 2000, we notice highly increased progressivity for families with children at bottom income intervals (as measured by the change in the average tax wedge progression). This may be the result of more generous child benefits and/ or that child benefits in 2012 are more targeted at children living in lower-income families compared to 2000 (e.g. that benefits are tapered out more rapidly with income).

Figure S.3 presents the change in the average PIT rate, on average across the OECD, over the 2000-12 time interval as well as its decomposition in changes that occurred during the sub-periods 2000-07 and 2007-12. The analysis shows that the decrease in progressivity over the 2000-12 interval for higher incomes is a result of personal income tax changes which have been implemented before 2007, and that the increase in progressivity for low-income single parents and one-earner married couples with 2 children is a result of changes that have occurred after 2007. In fact, since 2007, the progressivity of the personal income tax for all intervals except the bottom income interval, on average across the OECD, has hardly changed.

Figure S.3. **Change in the average PIT rate progression on average across the OECD over time**

For 6 household types, by income intervals

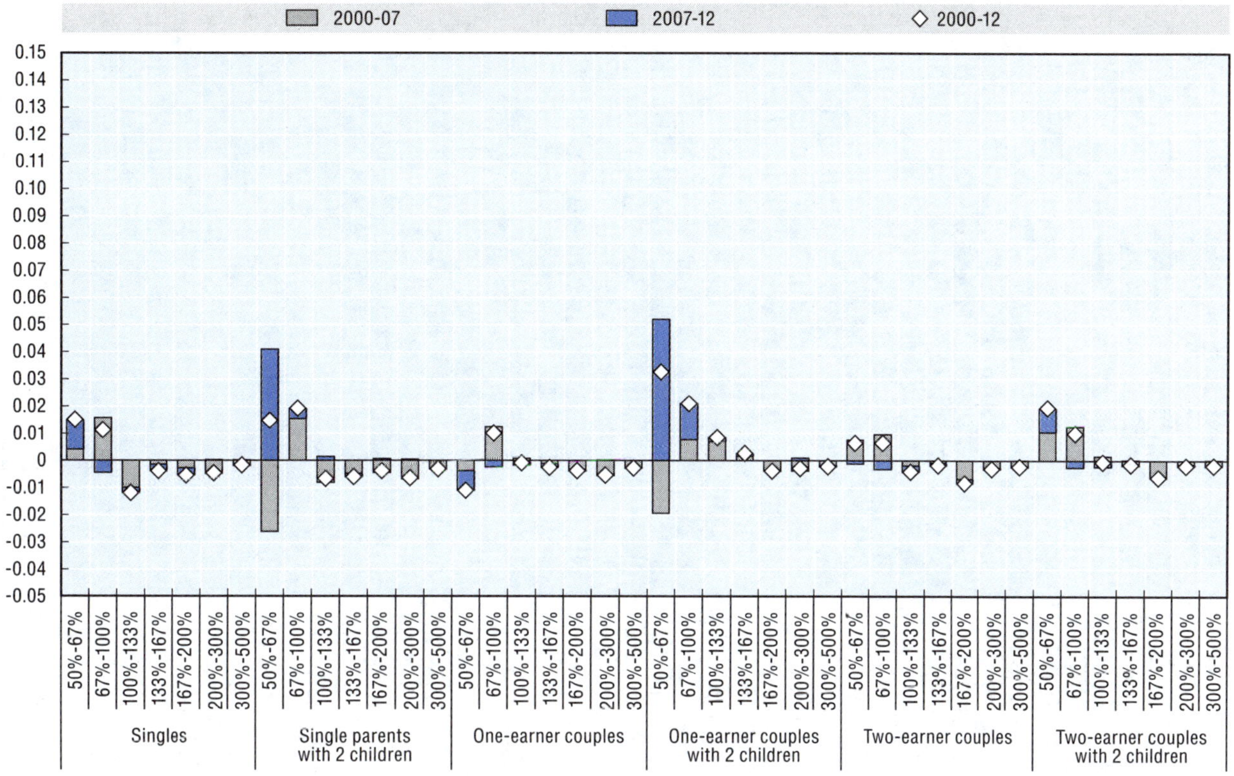

StatLink http://dx.doi.org/10.1787/888933005454

Figure S.4 presents the change in the average tax wedge, on average across the OECD, over the 2000-12 time interval as well as its decomposition over the sub-periods 2000-07 and 2007-12. The increased progressivity for families with children at bottom income intervals, and to a much lower extent also for other low-income families, is the results of increased progressivity implemented before 2007. Only progressivity for one-earner married couples with 2 children, and to a smaller extent, single parents with 2 children at the bottom income interval increased considerably after 2007. The progressivity of the tax burden on bottom-income one-earner couples without children has decreased since 2007. Although the changes are very minor, there seem to be a slight trend of a decrease in tax wedge progressivity since 2007 for all families and income levels, except bottom-income families with 2 children. This decrease has offset the slight increase in progressivity that occurred before 2007. Although this result is relatively small, it likely is the result of the increased SSCs in some countries as part of their fiscal consolidation efforts.

Table S.1 summarizes the changes in progressivity over time for the lower income intervals (i.e. the lowest 3 to 4 intervals) and the higher income intervals (i.e. the top 3 to 4 intervals). The direction and number of arrows indicates approximately whether progressivity has increased (↗) or decreased (↘).

Figure S.4. **Change in the average tax wedge progression on average across the OECD over time**

For 6 household types, by income intervals

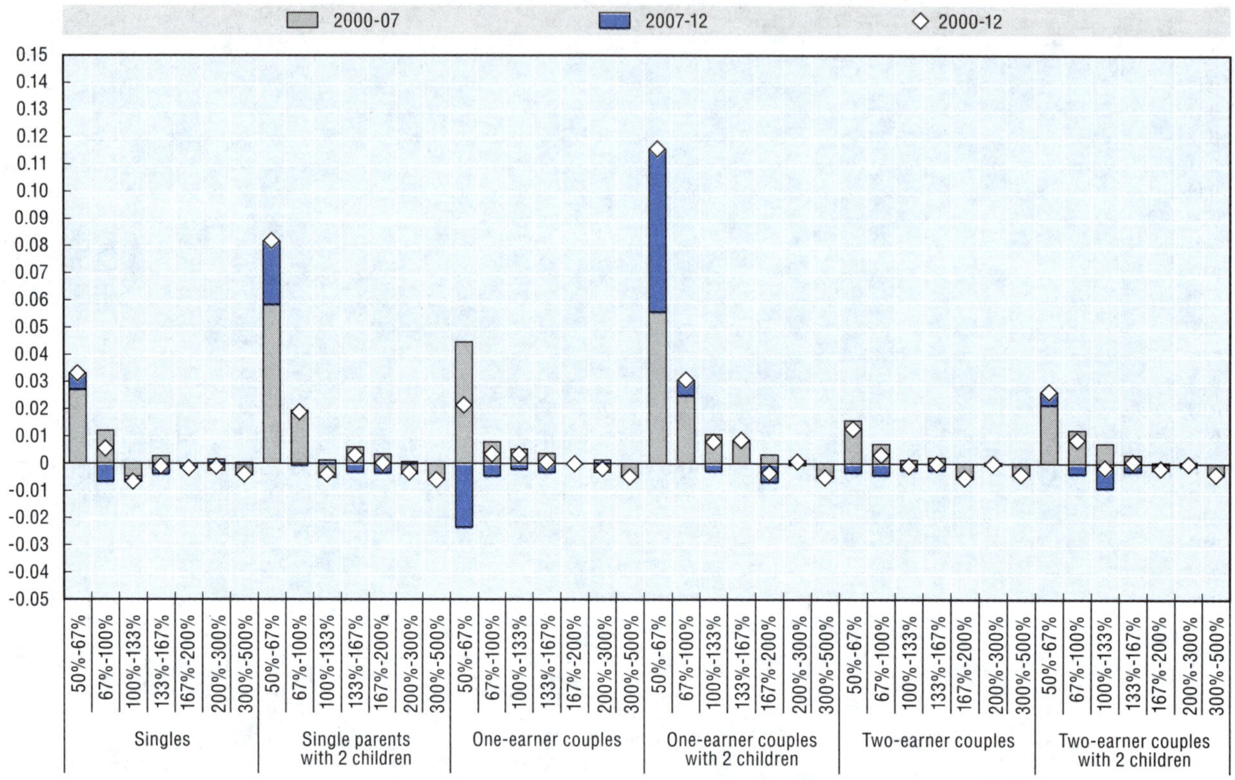

StatLink http://dx.doi.org/10.1787/888933005473

Table S.1. **Changes over time in average PIT rate and tax wedge progression on average across the OECD: Summary table**

			2000-12	2000 – 2007	2007 – 2012
PIT progression	Lower-income intervals	0 children	↗	↗	–
		2 children	↗	↘	↗↗
	Higher-income intervals	0 children	↘	↘	–
		2 children	↘	↘	–
Tax wedge progression	Lower-income intervals	0 children	↗	↗↗	↘
		2 children	↗↗↗↗	↗↗	↗↗
	Higher-income intervals	0 children	–	–	–
		2 children	–	–	–

4. Overall average PIT rate and tax wedge progression and deviation across income intervals

Figure S.5 shows the overall PIT rate progression level over the 50% to 500% of the AW income interval for single taxpayers in 2012. The highest overall PIT progression can be observed in the Netherlands (0.087), Ireland (0.086) and Sweden (0.078), while the lowest overall PIT rate progression is observed in Poland (0.013), Estonia (0.010), Chile (0.008) and Hungary (0.008).

The standard deviations in Figure S.5 show the degree of variation in PIT rate progression across the seven income intervals for each country. Countries with similar overall PIT rate progression (over the 50% to 500% of the AW income range) may differ considerably in their rate progression across the seven income intervals. France and the United Kingdom, for instance, face almost the same overall PIT rate progression for earnings ranging from 50% to 500% of the AW (around 0.06), but the PIT rate progression is relatively more constant across income intervals in the United Kingdom than it is in France (see also Figure S.E.1).

Figure S.5. **Overall average PIT rate and average tax wedge progression and standard deviation for single tax payers without children**[1, 2]

Across income intervals ranging from 50% to 500% of the AW, in 2012

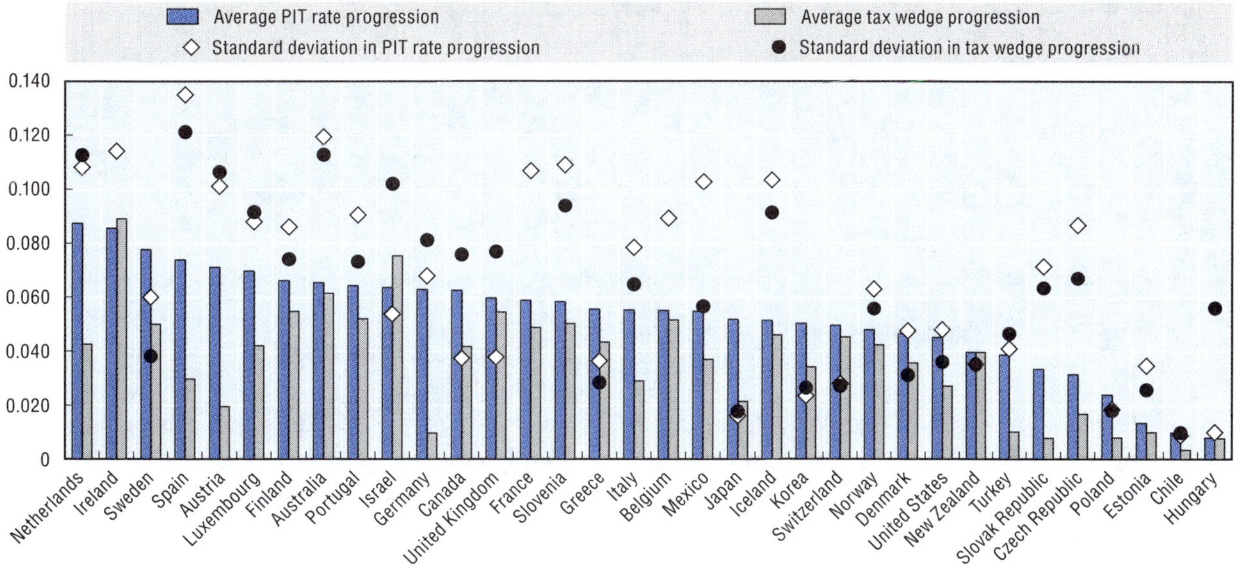

1. The standard deviation indicates the level of variation in the average PIT rate progression across the 7 income intervals for each country.
2. STD in tax wedge progression in France is 0.243, in Ireland it is 0.186 and in Belgium 0.158.

StatLink http://dx.doi.org/10.1787/888933005492

Figure S.5 also presents the overall tax wedge progression for the 50% to 500% of the AW income interval. It shows that the overall progression decreases for most OECD member countries, except in Ireland and Israel, when the flattening effect of social security contributions – although the inclusion of benefits might go in the opposite direction – are taken into account. This also explains why, for most countries, the standard deviation in tax wedge progression across income levels is substantially lower (or very similar) than the standard deviation in PIT progression. However, cuts in SSCs targeted at lower incomes and/ or child benefits result in a higher standard deviation of the tax wedge progression in Canada, the United Kingdom, Hungary, Israel, Belgium, Ireland and especially France.

Figure S.6 shows the change in the overall PIT rate and tax wedge progression, as well as the change in the standard deviations of the progression rates across income intervals, over the 50% to 500% of the AW income interval over the 2000-12 time period for single taxpayers (measured as the difference in the corresponding values in 2012 and 2000). The strongest increase in overall PIT rate progression, over the 2000-12 period, has taken place in the United Kingdom, Slovenia, Ireland and especially Sweden, while the strongest

Figure S.6. **Change in the overall average PIT rate and average tax wedge progression and standard deviation for single taxpayers without children**[1, 2]

Over the 2000-12 time interval, income ranging from 50% to 500% of the AW

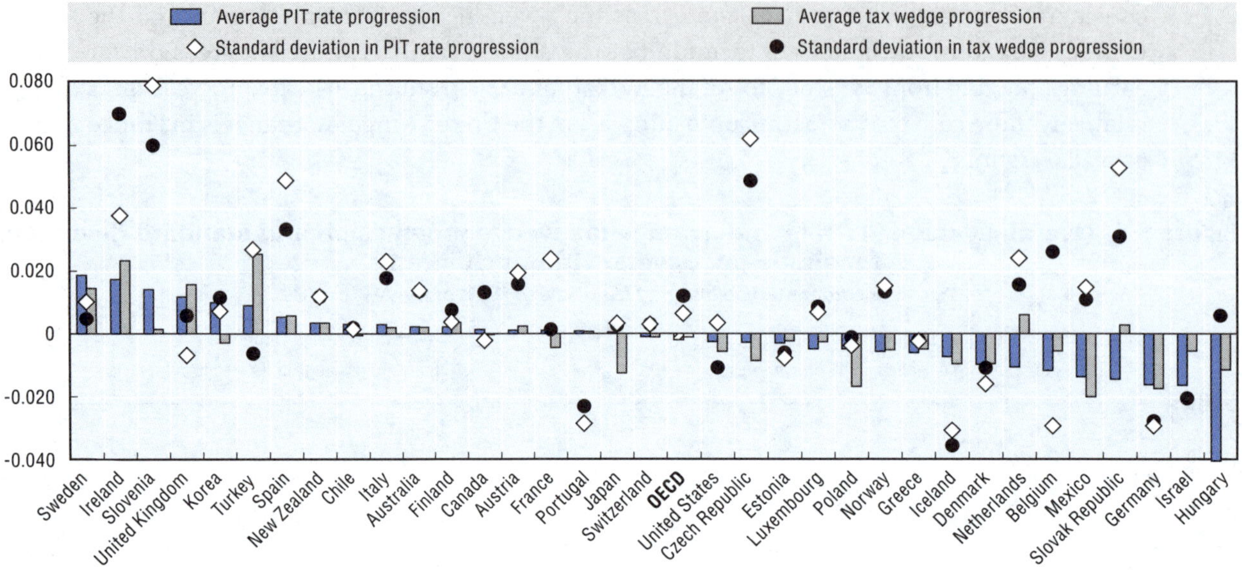

1. The standard deviation indicates the level of variation in the average PIT rate progression across the 7 income intervals for each country.
2. Change in STD in PIT rate progression in Israel is -0.058 and in Hungary -0.07.

StatLink http://dx.doi.org/10.1787/888933005511

decrease occurred in Germany, Israel and especially Hungary. Progressivity of personal income tax systems, measured in this way, has hardly changed on average across OECD countries (i.e. increased PIT progressivity in some countries offset decreased progressivity in other countries).

Figure S.6 also shows that the largest increase in the variation of PIT rate progression over the 2000-12 period, as measured by the increase in the standard deviation in the PIT rate progression over the 7 income intervals (note that this is not necessarily a measure of increased "global" but rather of "local" PIT progressivity) has occurred in Ireland, Spain, the Slovak Republic, the Czech Republic and especially Slovenia. The largest decrease in the standard deviation, reflecting the flattening of personal income taxes over time, is observed in Iceland, Israel and especially Hungary.

For single taxpayers, Figure S.6 also shows that the strongest increase in overall tax wedge progression (i.e. over the 50% to 500% of the AW income range), over the 2000-12 period, has taken place in the United Kingdom, Ireland and especially Turkey, while the strongest decrease occurred in Poland, Germany and especially Mexico. On average across the OECD, average tax wedge progression, measured in this way, has hardly changed.

Figure S.7 shows the same data as Figure S.5 but focuses on single parents with 2 children instead. Progression is considerably higher, as are the differences across income intervals, in the presence of children. This result holds for other family types as well.

Figure S.8 is similar to Figure S.6 but focuses on single parents with 2 children instead of single taxpayers. The analysis shows that overall PIT rate and tax wedge progression has changed more significantly for this family type. The strongest increase in PIT rate progression has occurred in the United Kingdom while the strongest decrease occurred in

Figure S.7. **Overall average PIT rate and average tax wedge progression and standard deviation for single parents with 2 children**[1, 2]

Across income intervals ranging from 50% to 500% of the AW, in 2012

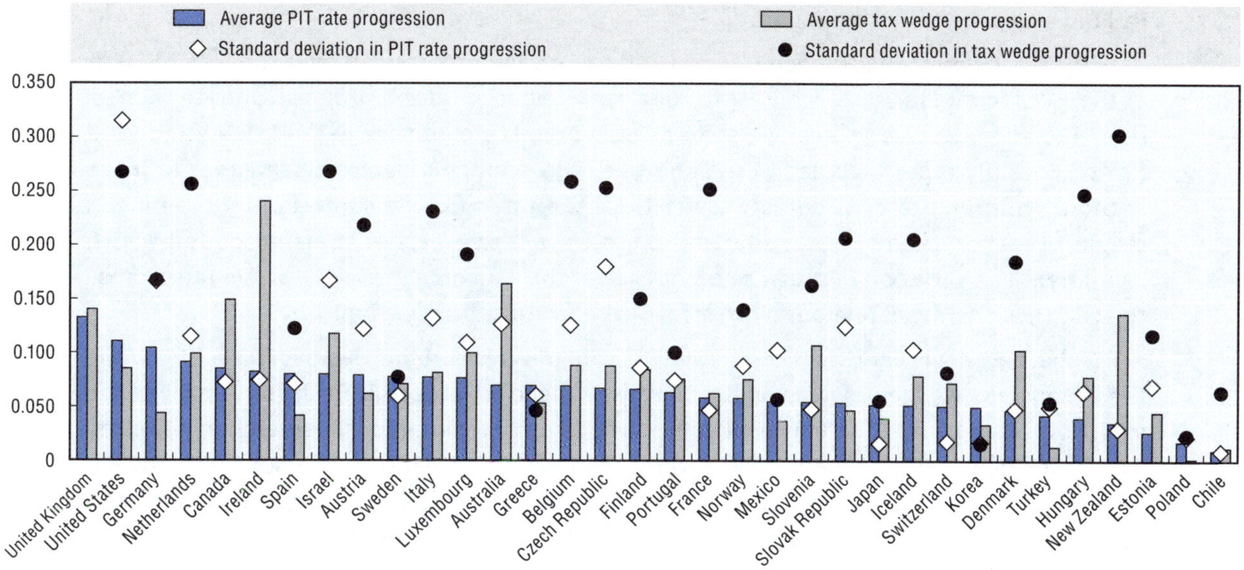

1. The standard deviation indicates the level of variation in the average PIT rate progression across the 7 income intervals for each country.
2. STD in tax wedge progression not included in chart: Australia (0.557), Canada (0.457), Ireland (0.751) and the United Kingdom (0.513). The STD in PIT rate progression in the United Kingdom is 0.439.

StatLink http://dx.doi.org/10.1787/888933005530

Figure S.8. **Change in the overall average PIT rate and average tax wedge progression and standard deviation For single parents with 2 children**[1, 2]

Over the 2000-12 time interval, income ranging from 50% to 500% of the AW

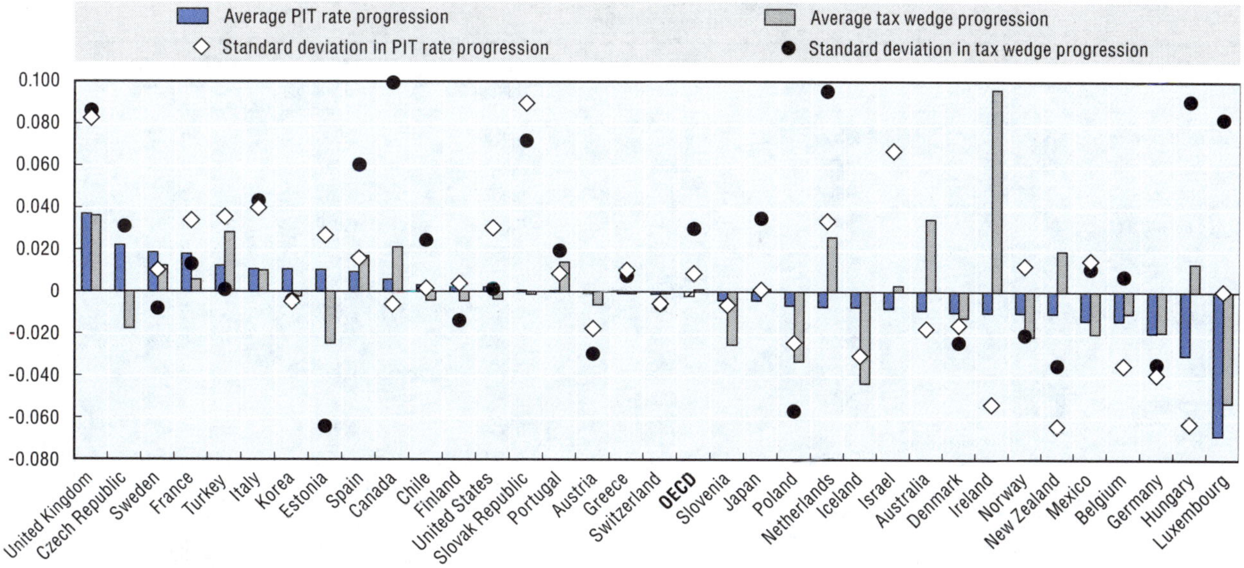

1. The standard deviation indicates the level of variation in the average PIT rate progression across the 7 income intervals for each country.
2. Change in STD in PIT rate progression in the Czech Republic is +0.14. Change in the STD of the tax wedge progression in Israel is +0.147, in Australia +0.153 and in Ireland +0.292; while the decrease was -0.08 in Iceland and -0.105 in Slovenia.

StatLink http://dx.doi.org/10.1787/888933005549

Luxembourg. Note also the strong increase in tax wedge progression in Canada, the Netherlands, Turkey, Australia, the United Kingdom and especially Ireland, while the overall tax wedge progression decreased strongly Norway, Estonia, Slovenia, Poland, Iceland and especially Luxembourg.

Table S.2 shows the average PIT rate and tax wedge progression over the 50% to 500% of the AW income range as well as the standard deviation in the progression rates across the 7 income intervals on average across OECD member countries in 2000, 2007 and 2012 for the 6 family types included in the analysis. The average progression rates for families without children are considerably lower than the rates for the same family type (i.e. a single taxpayer, a one-earner married couple, or a two-earner married couple) with 2 children. The variation in progression rates over the 7 income intervals, on average across the OECD, is positively related to the level of the average progression.

Table S.2 shows also that the average PIT rate progression has decreased slightly while the average tax wedge progression has hardly changed for most family types. However, the variation in average PIT rate as well as tax wedge progression has considerably increased over time, in line with previous observations of increased targeting by personal income tax and benefit systems to lower income workers (through in-work tax provisions) and especially lower-income families with children (through child benefits).

The changes in the overall PIT rate and tax wedge progression over the 2000-12 period for each country can be decomposed in changes that occurred during the sub-periods 2000-07 and 2007-12. The corresponding charts with the changes in the sub-periods for all family types are available upon request.

Table S.2. **Average PIT rate and tax wedge progression over the 50% to 500% of the AW income range and standard deviation in progression rates across the 7 income intervals on average across the OECD in 2000, 2007 and 2012 for 6 family types**

Summary table

		Average PIT rate progr.	STD in av. PIT rate progr.	Average tax wedge progr.	STD in av. tax wedge progr.
Single, 0 children	2012	0.053	0.058	0.036	0.068
	2007	0.053	0.055	0.037	0.066
	2000	0.055	0.052	0.037	0.056
Lone parent, 2 children	2012	0.064	0.080	0.080	0.201
	2007	0.062	0.068	0.080	0.193
	2000	0.066	0.071	0.079	0.171
One-earner couples, 0 ch.	2012	0.057	0.055	0.041	0.070
	2007	0.057	0.057	0.042	0.078
	2000	0.059	0.055	0.042	0.062
One-earner couples, 2 ch.	2012	0.067	0.085	0.080	0.206
	2007	0.064	0.068	0.079	0.185
	2000	0.066	0.071	0.075	0.164
Two-earner couples, 0 ch.	2012	0.042	0.020	0.027	0.025
	2007	0.043	0.021	0.028	0.026
	2000	0.044	0.018	0.029	0.020
Two-earner couples, 2 ch.	2012	0.046	0.025	0.038	0.044
	2007	0.046	0.024	0.039	0.043
	2000	0.046	0.019	0.038	0.035

Figures S.9 and S.10 show that changes in the overall PIT rate progression and tax wedge progression in 2000-07 for single parents with 2 children are hardly correlated with the changes that occurred in 2007-12. These results hold for other family types as well. On the basis of this overall progressivity measure (i.e. for the 50% to 500% of the AW income range), there is no evidence that countries which have increased progressivity over the 2000-07 period have continued doing so afterwards or have reversed their policies.

Figure S.9. **Correlation in the changes in the overall average PIT rate progression for single parents with 2 children over time**

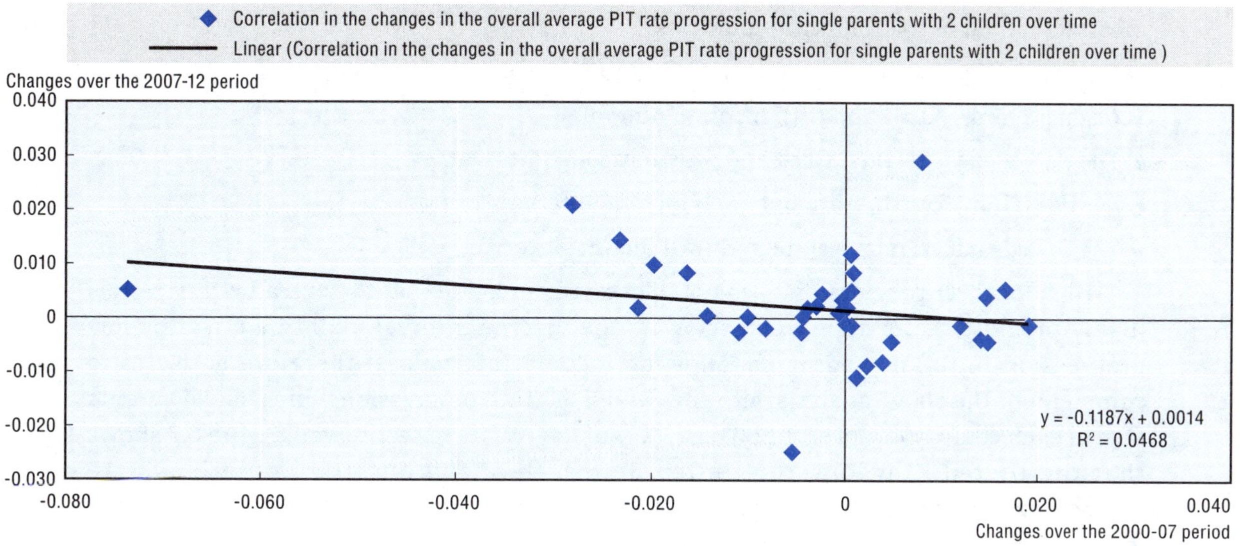

StatLink http://dx.doi.org/10.1787/888933005568

Figure S.10. **Correlation in the changes in the overall average tax wedge progression for single parents with 2 children over time**

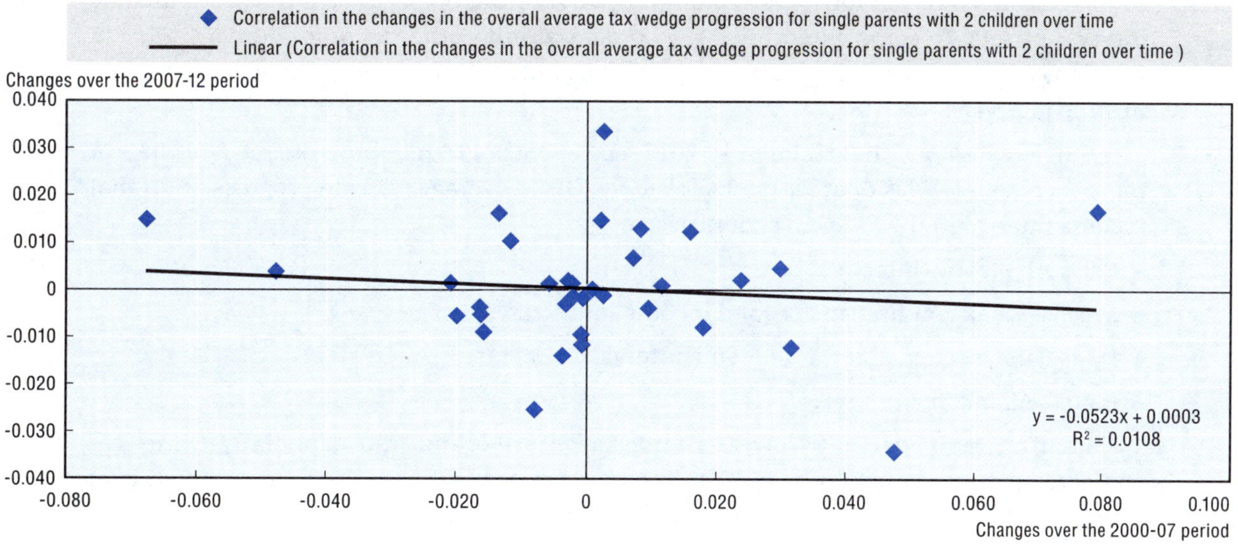

StatLink http://dx.doi.org/10.1787/888933005587

5. Average tax rate progression varies widely across OECD countries

Average rate progression in 2012 varies considerably across countries and family types, as can be observed from the data charts included in Annex S.E. As an example, Figure S.11 shows the average rate progression for single parents with 2 children in 9 OECD countries in 2012.

PIT rate progression for single parents with 2 children

Single parents with 2 children in 2012 face average PIT rate progression rates in 3 or more income intervals of at least 50% *above* the OECD average PIT rate progression in that income interval in the following countries:

- *Germany*: All income intervals except the top interval.
- *Ireland*: Third, fourth and fifth income interval.
- *The Netherlands*: Second, third and fourth income interval.
- *Sweden*: Third, fourth, fifth and sixth income interval.
- *The United States*: First, second and fifth income interval.

High local PIT progression does not necessarily indicate that the overall PIT system is highly progressive, as high progression in one income interval might be offset by low progression in the preceding or following income intervals. It therefore is useful to complement the above analysis with the overall PIT rate progression which single parents face in each country (i.e. over the 50% to 500% of the AW income interval). Figure S.7 shows that the United Kingdom, the United States, Germany and the Netherlands are characterized by the highest overall PIT rate progression with an overall rate which is at least 40% above the OECD average.

The United Kingdom has the highest overall PIT rate progression because of its highly progressive personal income tax system at the second but especially at the bottom income interval. In the other income intervals, the progression is also considerably above the OECD average. In Ireland, the low progression (only 25% of the average) at the bottom income interval offsets, to some extent, the high progression in other income intervals. Also in Sweden, the very low progression at the bottom offsets the high progression at other income intervals.

Single parents with 2 children in 2012 face average PIT rate progression rates in 3 or more income intervals of at least 50% *below* the OECD average PIT rate progression in that income interval in the following countries:

- *Chile:* All income intervals.
- *Estonia*: All except first and second income interval.
- *Japan*: First, second and third income interval.
- *Poland*: All income intervals.

Figure S.7 shows that New Zealand, Estonia, Poland and especially Chile are characterized by the lowest overall PIT rate progression with an overall rate which is at least 40% below the OECD average, closely followed by Hungary. Japan's PIT system is considerably less progressive at lower income levels but the low bottom-income progression rates are somewhat compensated for by average progression rates on middle incomes and a progression rate which is at least 50% above the average in the top income interval. Single parents in New Zealand face progression rates which are below average but especially low progression rates in the 2 bottom income intervals.

In summary, the least progressive PIT systems for single parents with 2 children are found in Hungary, New Zealand, Estonia, Poland and especially Chile, while they face the most progressive tax system in the Netherlands, Germany, the United States and the United Kingdom and also in Ireland and Sweden although not at the bottom income interval(s) in these last 2 countries.

PIT rate progression for single taxpayers without children

Single taxpayers without children in 2012 face average PIT rate progression rates in 3 or more income intervals of at least 50% *above* the OECD average PIT rate progression in that income interval in the following countries:

- *Ireland:* First, third, fourth and fifth income interval.
- *The Netherlands:* Second, third, fourth and fifth income interval.
- *Sweden:* Second, third, fourth and fifth income interval.

In addition to these three countries, also Spain has an overall average PIT rate progression (over the 50% to 500% of the AW income range) which is at least 40% above the OECD average (see Figure S.5). Spain has very high progression in the first and second income interval as well as in the top three income intervals, but below average progression on income ranging between 100%-133%-167% of the AW (third and fourth income interval).

In contrast to single parents with 2 children, the PIT system in Germany and the United Kingdom is not amongst the most progressive tax systems for single taxpayers without children. This is especially the case in the United States.

Single taxpayers without children in 2012 face average PIT rate progression rates in 3 or more income intervals of at least 50% *below* the OECD average PIT rate progression in that income interval in the following countries:

- *Chile:* All income intervals.
- *The Czech Republic*: Fourth, fifth, sixth and seventh income interval.
- *Estonia*: All except the first income interval.
- *Hungary*: All income intervals.
- *Japan*: First, second and third income interval.
- *Poland*: All except sixth and seventh income interval.
- *The Slovak Republic*: Fourth, fifth and seventh income interval.

Figure S.5 shows that the Slovak Republic, the Czech Republic, Poland, Estonia, Chile and especially Hungary are characterized by the lowest overall PIT rate progression with an overall rate which is about 40% or more below the OECD average. Single taxpayers in Japan face very low progression at lower income intervals but above average progression at middle and high income intervals.

Single taxpayers without children in the Slovak Republic and the Czech Republic face especially low progression rates (see Figure S.5). In both of these countries, the tax system is more progressive for single parents with 2 children (see Figure S.7).

In summary, the least progressive PIT systems for single taxpayers without children are found in the Slovak Republic, the Czech Republic, Poland, Estonia, Chile and Hungary, while they face the most progressive tax system in Spain (but not "middle" income earners), Sweden, Ireland and the Netherlands.

Tax wedge progression for single parents with 2 children

Single parents with 2 children in 2012 face average tax wedge progression rates in 3 or more income intervals of at least 50% above the OECD average tax wedge progression in that income interval in the following countries:

- *Australia*: All income intervals except 3th and 5th income interval.
- *Canada*: First, second and last income interval.
- *Denmark*: All income intervals except first and second income interval.
- *Ireland*: All income intervals.
- *Israel*: All except first two income intervals.
- *Luxembourg*: All except the first and last 2 income intervals.
- *New Zealand*: Second, third and fourth income interval.
- *Slovenia*: Third and last 2 income intervals.
- *The United Kingdom*: First, second and last income interval.

Note also that Finland, Sweden and Switzerland face high (i.e. 50% above the average) average tax wedge progression in the last two income intervals. A similar observation holds for Portugal where single parents face high progression in the 5th and 7th income interval, while the progression in the 6th income interval is at about the OECD average.

Local average tax wedge progression does not necessarily indicate that the overall tax system is progressive, as high progression in one income interval can be offset by low progression in the preceding or following income intervals. It therefore is useful to complement the above analysis with the overall average tax wedge progression rate single parents face in each country (i.e. over the 50% to 500% of the AW income interval). In Australia, Canada, Ireland, Israel, New Zealand and the United Kingdom, the overall progression is at least 40% above the OECD average progression rate (see Table S.2 and Figure S.7). Denmark, Luxembourg and Slovenia face an overall tax wedge progression of at least 25% above the OECD average.

In summary: single taxpayers with 2 children face a relatively highly progressive tax (including the effect of SSCs and benefits) system in Luxembourg, Denmark and Slovenia, and even more so in Israel, New Zealand, the United Kingdom, Canada and Australia. The most progressive tax system can be found in Ireland.

The highly progressive tax systems in New Zealand, the United Kingdom, Canada, Australia and Ireland are, to a large extent, the result of the withdrawal of the generous benefits (e.g. in relation to children and/ or in-work benefits). While strengthening equity, these benefits have to be designed with care in order to prevent too large work disincentives.

Single parents with 2 children in 2012 face average tax wedge progression rates in 3 or more income intervals of at least 50% below the OECD average tax wedge progression in that income interval. This is the case in:

- *Austria*: All except first three income intervals.
- *Chile*: All income intervals.

- *France*: Second, third and fourth income interval.
- *Germany*: All except first and second income interval.
- *Japan*: All except fourth and last two income intervals.
- *Korea*: All except last two income intervals.
- *Mexico*: All except second and last two income intervals.
- *Poland*: All income intervals.
- *Spain*: Fourth, fifth and sixth income interval.
- *Turkey*: All income intervals.

Figure S.7 shows that the overall average tax wedge progression for single parents in Germany, Spain, Japan, Mexico, Korea, Turkey, Chile and especially in Poland is less than 55% of the OECD average progression rate.

The low overall progressivity of the tax system in Spain and Germany is a result of the SSC ceiling, which turns the tax system regressive at higher income levels. France has a considerably higher tax wedge progression at the first income interval, partly offsetting the effect of the low progression rates in the second to fourth interval. In Austria the progression in the first two income intervals is equal to the OECD average; it is even higher than the average in the third income interval. Again, these progression results offset the lower than average progression for higher incomes (as a result of the SSC ceiling).

In summary, single taxpayers with 2 children face a relatively low progressive tax (including the effect of SSCs and benefits) system in Japan, Mexico, Korea, Turkey and Chile. The least progressive tax system can be found in Poland.

Figure S.11. **Average rate progression in 2012 for single taxpayers with 2 children for 9 OECD countries**

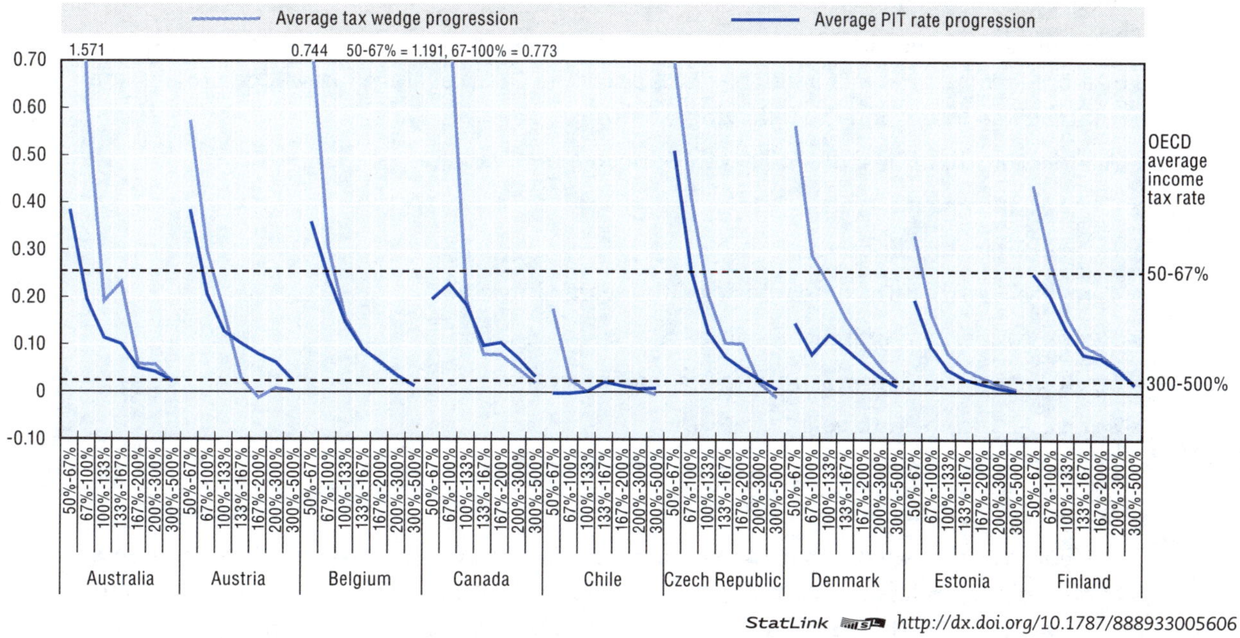

StatLink http://dx.doi.org/10.1787/888933005606

Tax wedge progression for single taxpayers without children

Single taxpayers without children in 2012 face average tax wedge progression rates in 3 or more income intervals of at least 50% *above* the OECD average tax wedge progression in that income interval in the following countries:

- *Australia*: First, second, sixth and seventh income interval.
- *Belgium*: First and second income interval (third income interval is considerably above the average as well).
- *Finland*: Second, fifth, sixth and seventh income interval.
- *Greece*: Fifth, sixth and seventh income interval.
- *Ireland*: All income intervals.
- *Israel*: All income intervals.
- *Luxembourg*: Second, third and fourth income interval.
- *Portugal*: Fourth, fifth and seventh income interval.
- *Slovenia*: Fourth, fifth, sixth and seventh income interval.
- *Sweden*: All except first and second income interval.
- *The United Kingdom*: Fourth, sixth and seventh income interval.

Figure S.5 shows that the overall progression over the 50% to 500% of the AW income interval in Ireland, Israel, Australia, Finland, the United Kingdom, Portugal, Belgium, Slovenia and Sweden is at least 40% above the OECD average progression over that income interval. In Greece, the relatively high progression at top income intervals (in comparison to other countries) is to some extent offset by the very low progression in the bottom income interval. A similar conclusion can be drawn for Denmark. In Luxembourg, the high progression at the bottom income intervals is partly offset by the regressivity in the sixth and seventh income interval.

Single taxpayers without children in 2012 face average tax wedge progression rates in 3 or more income intervals of at least 50% *below* the OECD average tax wedge progression in that income interval in the following countries:

- *Austria:* Fourth, fifth, sixth and seventh income interval.
- *Chile*: All income intervals.
- *Estonia*: All income intervals.
- *Germany*: Fourth, fifth, sixth and seventh income interval.
- *Hungary*: All except first income interval.
- *Japan*: First, second, third and fifth income interval.
- *Poland*: All income intervals.
- *Slovak Republic*: Fourth, fifth, sixth and seventh income interval.
- *Spain*: Fourth, fifth and sixth income interval.

Figure S.5 also shows that the overall progression over the 50% to 500% of the AW income interval in Japan, Austria, the Czech Republic, Turkey, Estonia, Germany, Poland, the Slovak Republic, Hungary and Chile is at least 40% below the OECD average progression over that income interval. In Spain, the low progression at top income intervals is partly offset by the high progression at the bottom interval. The tax system is also weakly progressive and even regressive at the top 2 income intervals in Turkey.

Single taxpayers without children face a regressive tax system (when personal income taxes, SSCs and benefits are taken into account) in:

- *Austria*: Fourth to the seventh income interval.
- *Chile*: Seventh income interval.
- *Czech Republic*: Seventh income interval.
- *Germany*: Fifth to the seventh income interval.
- *Hungary*: Seventh income interval.
- *Italy*: Seventh income interval.
- *Luxembourg*: Sixth and seventh income interval.
- *Slovak Republic*: Seventh income interval.
- *Spain*: Fifth income interval.
- *Turkey*: Sixth and seventh income interval.

In summary, single taxpayers without children face the least progressive tax system (when also SSCs and benefits are taken into account) in Spain, Japan, Austria, the Czech Republic, Turkey, Estonia, Germany, Poland, the Slovak Republic, Hungary and especially in Chile; they face the most progressive tax system (across all income levels) in Ireland, Israel, Australia, Finland, the United Kingdom, Portugal, Belgium, Slovenia and Sweden.

6. Changes in average tax rate progression over time vary widely across OECD countries

The changes in the average rate progression over time are presented in Figure S.12 for the 2000-12 time period for a random selection of countries. Information on changes for the 2000-12 period for all countries is included in Annex S.F; graphical representation of the changes in the 2 other periods has not been included but is available upon request.

For single taxpayers without children, the personal income tax has become considerably more progressive over the 2000-12 period (increase of at least 0.05 in at least two income intervals) in the Czech Republic, Ireland, the Netherlands, and the Slovak Republic; and has become considerably less progressive (decrease of at least 0.05 in at least two income intervals) in Hungary, Israel and the Netherlands.

Note that this type of analysis does not indicate whether the tax system has become globally more progressive, but focuses rather on local progression (i.e. at one or more income intervals). This explains why progressivity has both increased and decreased considerably in the Netherlands.

More specially, Figure S.6 shows that the largest increases in the overall PIT rate progression have occurred in Sweden, Ireland and Slovenia, while the overall PIT rate progression has decreased the most in Germany, Israel and especially Hungary. In the Czech Republic, the strong increases in PIT progression at the bottom income intervals is offset by very modest increases in progression at middle income intervals and decreases in progression at the top income intervals. In the Slovak Republic and the Netherlands, the strong increases in PIT progression at the first two income intervals is offset by decreases in progression in all other income intervals. The strong overall increase in progression in Sweden is the result of increases in progression in the middle income intervals. The PIT system has become less progressive in Germany at most but especially at the lower income intervals (Figure S.F.1).

When also SSCs and benefits are taken into account, single taxpayers without children face in 2012 a considerably more progressive tax system (increase of at least 0.05 in at least two income intervals) in the Czech Republic, the Netherlands and Turkey. Similarly to the results for the PIT, however, the overall tax wedge progression did not strongly increase in the Czech Republic and the Netherlands because the strong increases at the bottom income intervals are offset by decreases in progression as from the fourth or third income interval, respectively. When also SSCs and benefits are taken into account, single taxpayers without children face a considerably less progressive tax system (decrease of at least 0.05 in at least two income intervals) in Hungary (but not single taxpayers with income at the bottom income interval). Strong decreases in progression are also noted for Germany and Mexico.

For single parents with 2 children, the personal income tax has become considerably more progressive over the 2000-12 period (increase of at least 0.05 in at least two income intervals) in the Czech Republic, the Slovak Republic, Spain and the United Kingdom, while the PIT has become considerably less progressive (decrease of at least 0.05 in at least two income intervals) in Australia, Germany, Hungary, Luxembourg, the Netherlands and Poland.

Figure S.8 shows that the largest increases in the overall PIT rate progression have occurred in the United Kingdom, the Czech Republic, Sweden and France, while the overall PIT rate progression has decreased the most in Germany, Hungary and especially Luxembourg. In Spain and the Slovak Republic, the strong increase in progression at lower income intervals is partly offset by low increases or decreases in progression at other income intervals. In France, the PIT has become especially more progressive at the bottom income interval while in Sweden the progressivity of the PIT system focused on middle-income intervals. In the Netherlands, the decrease in progression at middle and top income intervals is largely offset by an increase in progression at the bottom income intervals. The reverse happened in Poland, where the strong decrease in progression at the bottom income intervals is offset by increased progression at especially the middle income intervals.

When also SSCs and benefits are taken into account, single parents with 2 children face in 2012 a considerably more progressive tax system (increase of at least 0.05 in at least two income intervals) in Australia, Canada, the Czech Republic, Hungary, Ireland, Japan, Luxembourg, New Zealand, Portugal, Spain, Turkey and the United Kingdom, while they face a considerably less progressive tax system (decrease of at least 0.05 in at least two income intervals) in Estonia, Germany, Iceland, Luxembourg, Poland and the Slovak Republic. In the list of countries which are characterized by considerable increased "local" progression, only Japan, the Czech Republic and especially Luxembourg do not face an increase in "global" progression as measured by an increase in the overall progression rate (i.e. measured over the 50% to 500% of the AW income range). Figure S.F.2 shows that, to some extent, progression also decreased considerably in Norway and Mexico while it decreased considerably at lower income intervals only in Slovenia. In the Slovak Republic, the decreased progression at middle income intervals is offset by increased progression at the bottom (and also 6th) income interval.

Figure S.12. **Change in the average rate progression over the 2000-12 time interval for singe taxpayers with 2 children in 9 OECD countries**

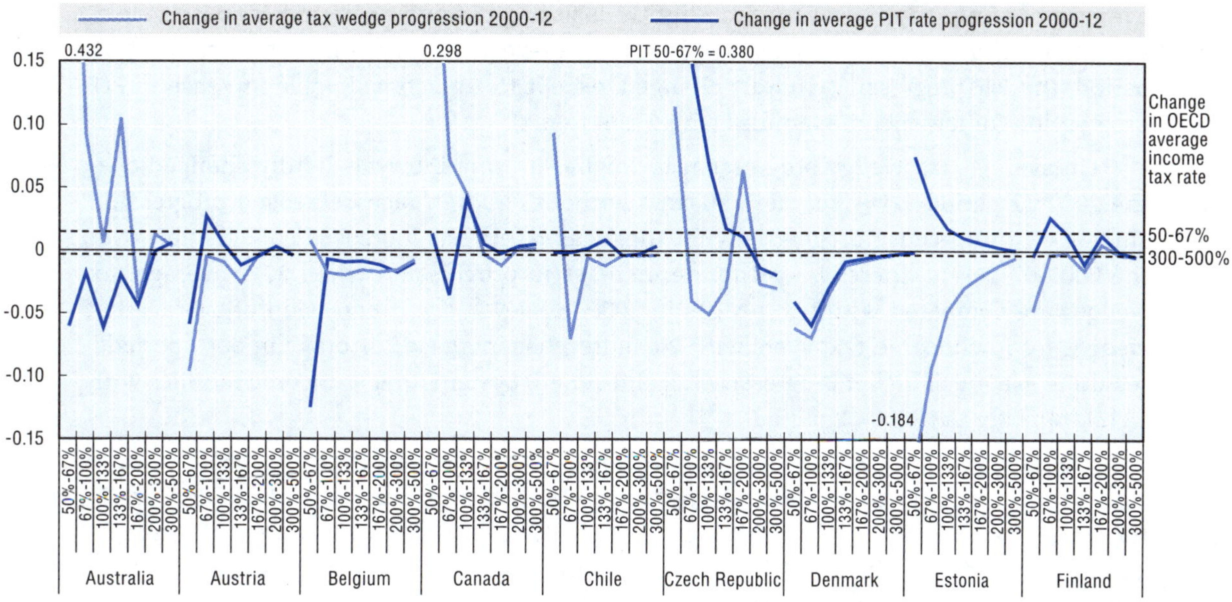

StatLink http://dx.doi.org/10.1787/888933005625

7. Conclusion

This paper has analysed average PIT rate and average tax wedge progression for 7 income intervals (50%-67%, 67%-100%, 100%-133%, 133%-167%, 167%-200%, 200%-300% and 300%-500% of the AW) in OECD countries in 2000, 2007, 2012 and the corresponding changes that have occurred over time. The average PIT rate progression captures the progressivity of the PIT system in isolation. The average tax wedge progression takes also the effect of employee and employer social security contributions, payroll taxes and cash benefits on progressivity into account. Average rate progression has been calculated for 6 different household types: singles without children and single parents with 2 children, one-earner married couples without and with 2 children, and two-earner married couples without and with 2 children (it is assumed that one partner earns a fixed gross wage of 67% of the AW, while the other partner's gross wage earnings vary between 50% and 500% of the AW). The overall progression rate for the 50%-500% of the AW income interval has also been presented, as well as the standard deviation in progression across the 7 income intervals.

Similarly to the analysis in the Special Feature of the 2013 edition of *Taxing Wages*, the results show a clear pattern of progression rates across the 7 income intervals. On average across the OECD, the highest tax progression can be observed at the bottom income interval, while progression decreases for each higher income interval. This pattern emerges for the 6 household types considered and for the average PIT rate as well as the average tax wedge progression. These results indicate that this pattern is observed in many OECD countries, although considerable differences among countries exist. In most countries, however, the top average rate progression can be found at the bottom income interval and the lowest average rate progression is reached at the top income interval, as the country charts in Annex S.E clearly show.

On average across the OECD, personal income tax systems (as measured by the average PIT rate progression) have become slightly more progressive at lower income levels over time, while they have turned slightly less progressive at higher income levels, although the changes at especially higher income levels are very small. Over the 2007-12 period, the PIT progressivity hardly changed, except for the considerable increase in PIT progression for low-income families with 2 children.

On average, tax wedge progression for higher-income intervals hardly changed over the 2000-12 period. Low-income taxpayers without children face decreased progression since 2007, but because progressivity for these taxpayers has increased considerably over the 2000-07 period, there is a moderate increase in progression when 2012 average tax wedges are compared with tax wedges in 2000. However, the progression of average tax wedges for low-income taxpayers with 2 children has increased strongly in both periods, resulting in a much higher progressive tax and benefit system for low-income families with 2 children over the 2000-12 period.

The highest average PIT rate progression for single taxpayers over the 50% to 500% of the AW income range in 2012 is observed in the Netherlands, Ireland and Sweden, while the lowest progression can be found in Poland, Estonia, Chile and Hungary. For single parents with 2 children in 2012, the highest PIT rate progression over the 50% to 500% of the AW income range is observed in the United Kingdom, the United States and Germany while the lowest progression is found in Estonia, Poland and Chile.

The average PIT rate progression over the 50% to 500% of the AW income range has decreased slightly while the corresponding average tax wedge progression has hardly changed over time for most family types. However, the variation in average PIT rate as well as tax wedge progression has considerably increased over time as a result of an increased targeting of the tax and benefit system to lower-income workers (e.g. through in-work tax provisions) and especially lower-income families with children (through child benefits).

The analysis has also shown that changes in PIT rate and tax wedge progression in the 2000-07 and the 2007-12 period are not significantly related. On average, countries that changed tax progression in 2000-07 have not made changes along the same lines in the 2007-12 period, nor have they reversed in 2007-12 the previously implemented reforms.

Although tax progression tends to be relatively similar for both one-earner married couples and single taxpayers without children, some countries do have a more progressive PIT system for married couples as a result of a dependent spouse allowance. However, progressivity might also decrease if some taxable income can be transferred from the principal earner to the spouse.

SSCs and cash benefits have a strong impact on tax progressivity, as reflected by the considerable differences between average PIT rate and average tax wedge progression on average across the OECD. The direction of the difference in these rates strongly depends on whether the taxpayer has children or not.

First, the average tax wedge progression is lower than the average PIT rate progression for households without children except at the bottom income interval. As families without children typically do not receive cash benefits, this result shows that SSCs tend to reduce tax progressivity because they are typically levied at flat rates. A SSC ceiling might even lead to overall regressivity at the top income intervals. The higher tax wedge progression at the bottom income interval is the result of SSC provisions targeted at lower income levels in some countries. This result is driven by the low-income SSC provisions in Canada, the United Kingdom, Israel, the Netherlands, and especially in Ireland, Belgium and France.

Second, the average tax wedge progression is higher than the average PIT rate progression for households with children, except at the top income intervals. Thus, for households with children, the effect of cash benefits, which reduce the tax wedge, and the fact that these benefits are typically phased out when income increases, results in an increase in (local) tax progressivity in a large majority of OECD countries. This effect tends to be stronger than the flattening effect from social security contributions, except at the top income intervals.

The variation in progression over the 7 income intervals, on average across the OECD, is positively related to the level of the average progression. For instance, the higher OECD average PIT rate progression for families with children compared to families without children results also in a higher deviation across the 7 income levels, basically indicating that PIT provisions for children reduce the average effective tax rate more for lower-income than for higher-income earners.

Across the OECD, single taxpayers without children face the least progressive PIT system in the Slovak Republic, the Czech Republic, Poland, Estonia, Chile and Hungary, while single taxpayers with 2 children face the least progressive PIT system in Hungary, New Zealand, Estonia, Poland and especially Chile. The most progressive PIT system for single taxpayers without children is found in Spain (but not for Spanish middle income families), Sweden, Ireland and the Netherlands and for single parents with 2 children in the Netherlands, Germany, the United States and the United Kingdom and also in Ireland and Sweden although not at the bottom income interval(s) in these last 2 countries.

Over the 2000-12 period, average PIT rate progression increased the most in Ireland, Sweden and Slovenia for single taxpayers without children; for single parents with 2 children, it increased the most in the Czech Republic, France, Sweden and the United Kingdom. For single taxpayers without children, average PIT rate progression decreased the most in Germany, Hungary and Israel, while for single parents with 2 children it decreased the most in Germany, Hungary and Luxembourg.

Single taxpayers without children face the least progressive tax system, when also SSCs and benefits are taken into account, in Spain, Japan, Austria, the Czech Republic, Turkey, Estonia, Germany, Poland, the Slovak Republic, Hungary and especially in Chile. Single parents with 2 children face the lowest average tax wedge progression in Japan, Mexico, Korea, Turkey and Chile. The least progressive tax system can be found in Poland. Single taxpayers without children face the most progressive tax system (across all income levels) in Ireland, Israel, Australia, Finland, the United Kingdom, Portugal, Belgium, Slovenia and Sweden. Single parents with 2 children face a relatively highly progressive average tax wedge in Luxembourg, Denmark and Slovenia, and even more so in Israel, New Zealand, the United Kingdom, Canada and Australia. The most progressive tax system can be found in Ireland.

Over the 2000-12 period, average tax wedge progression increased the most in Turkey for single taxpayers without children; for single parents with 2 children, it increased the most in Australia, Canada, Hungary, Ireland, New Zealand, Portugal, Spain, Turkey and the United Kingdom. For single taxpayers without children, average tax wedge progression decreased the most in Hungary, Germany and Mexico, while for single parents with 2 children it decreased the most in Estonia, Germany, Iceland, Luxembourg, Norway, Mexico and Poland.

Bibliography

Musgrave, R.A. and P.B. Musgrave (1989), *Public finance in theory and practice*, 5th edition, McGraw-Hill Book Company.

Musgrave, R.A. and T. Thin (1948), "Income tax progression, 1929-1948", *Journal of Political Economy*, Vol. 56, No. 6, pp. 498-514.

OECD (2006), "Fundamental reform of personal income tax", *OECD Tax Policy Studies*, No. 13, OECD Publishing.

Paturot, D., K. Mellbye and B. Brys (2013), "Average personal income tax rate and tax wedge progression in OECD countries", *OECD Taxation Working Papers*, No. 15, OECD Publishing.

Torres, C., K. Mellbye and B. Brys (2012), "Trends in personal income tax and employee social security contribution schedules", *OECD Taxation Working Papers*, No. 12, OECD Publishing.

ANNEX S.A

Average personal income tax rate and tax wedge progression on average across the OECD in 2007 and 2000, for 6 household types, by income intervals

Figures available online only:

Figure S.A.1. **Average PIT rate and tax wedge progression on average across the OECD in 2000**

StatLink http://dx.doi.org/10.1787/888933005644

Figure S.A.2. **Average PIT rate and tax wedge progression on average across the OECD in 2007**

StatLink http://dx.doi.org/10.1787/888933005663

ANNEX S.B

Changes over time in the average personal income tax rate and tax wedge progression on average across the OECD

Figures available online only:

Figure S.B.1. **Change in the average PIT rate and tax wedge progression on average across the OECD over the 2007-12 time interval**

StatLink http://dx.doi.org/10.1787/888933005682

Figure S.B.2. **Change in the average PIT rate and tax wedge progression on average across the OECD over the 2000-07 time interval**

StatLink http://dx.doi.org/10.1787/888933005701

ANNEX S.C

Overall average pit tax rate and tax wedge progression and standard deviation across 7 income intervals in 2012 for 6 family types

Figures available online only:

Figure S.C.1. **Overall average rate progression and standard deviation for single taxpayers without children**

StatLink http://dx.doi.org/10.1787/888933005720

Figure S.C.2. **Overall average rate progression and standard deviation for single parents with 2 children**

StatLink http://dx.doi.org/10.1787/888933005739

Figure S.C.3. **Overall average rate progression and standard deviation for one-earner married couples without children**

StatLink http://dx.doi.org/10.1787/888933005758

Figure S.C.4. **Overall average rate progression and standard deviation for one-earner married couples with 2 children**

StatLink http://dx.doi.org/10.1787/888933005777

Figure S.C.5. **Overall average rate progression and standard deviation for two-earner married couples without children**

StatLink http://dx.doi.org/10.1787/888933005796

Figure S.C.6. **Overall average rate progression and standard deviation for two-earner married couples with 2 children**

StatLink http://dx.doi.org/10.1787/888933005815

ANNEX S.D

Changes in the overall average tax rate progression and changes in the standard deviation across 7 income intervals over the 2000-12 time interval for 6 family types

Figures available online only:

Figure S.D.1. **Changes in overall average rate progression and standard deviation for single taxpayers without children**

StatLink http://dx.doi.org/10.1787/888933005834

Figure S.D.2. **Changes in overall average rate progression and standard deviation for single parents with 2 children**

StatLink http://dx.doi.org/10.1787/888933005853

Figure S.D.3. **Changes in overall average rate progression and standard deviation for one-earner married couples without children**

StatLink http://dx.doi.org/10.1787/888933005872

Figure S.D.4. **Changes in overall average rate progression and standard deviation for one-earner married couples with 2 children**

StatLink http://dx.doi.org/10.1787/888933005891

Figure S.D.5. **Changes in overall average rate progression and standard deviation for two-earner married couples without children**

StatLink http://dx.doi.org/10.1787/888933005910

Figure S.D.6. **Changes in overall average rate progression and standard deviation for two-earner married couples with 2 children**

StatLink http://dx.doi.org/10.1787/888933005929

ANNEX S.E

Average tax rate progression in 2012: Country charts

Figures available online only:

Figure S.E.1. **Average rate progression in 2012 for single taxpayers without children**

StatLink http://dx.doi.org/10.1787/888933005948

Figure S.E.2. **Average rate progression in 2012 for single parents with 2 children**

StatLink http://dx.doi.org/10.1787/888933005967

Figure S.E.3. **Average rate progression in 2012 for one-earner married couples without children**

StatLink http://dx.doi.org/10.1787/888933005986

Figure S.E.4. **Average rate progression in 2012 for one-earner married couples with 2 children**

StatLink http://dx.doi.org/10.1787/888933006005

Figure S.E.5. **Average rate progression in 2012 for two-earner married couples without children**

StatLink http://dx.doi.org/10.1787/888933006024

Figure S.E.6. **Average rate progression in 2012 for two-earner married couples with 2 children**

StatLink http://dx.doi.org/10.1787/888933006043

ANNEX S.F

Change in average tax rate progression over the 2000-12 time interval: Country charts

Figures available online only:

Figure S.F.1. **Change in average rate progression over the 2000-12 time interval for single taxpayers without children**

StatLink http://dx.doi.org/10.1787/888933006062

Figure S.F.2. **Change in average rate progression over the 2000-12 time interval for single parents with 2 children**

StatLink http://dx.doi.org/10.1787/888933006081

Figure S.F.3. **Change in average rate progression over the 2000-12 time interval for one-earner married couples without children**

StatLink http://dx.doi.org/10.1787/888933006100

Figure S.F.4. **Change in average rate progression over the 2000-12 time interval for one-earner married couples with 2 children**

StatLink http://dx.doi.org/10.1787/888933006119

Figure S.F.5. **Change in average rate progression over the 2000-12 time interval for two-earner married couples without children**

StatLink http://dx.doi.org/10.1787/888933006138

Figure S.F.6. **Change in average rate progression over the 2000-12 time interval for two-earner married couples with 2 children**

StatLink http://dx.doi.org/10.1787/888933006157

PART I

International comparisons

This section provides unique information for each of the OECD countries on the income taxes paid by workers, their social security contributions, the family benefits they receive in the form of cash transfers as well as the social security contributions and payroll taxes paid by their employers. It provides detailed results for 2013; definitive results for 2012 and discusses the changes between the two years. Results reported include the marginal and average tax burden for eight different family types.

Taxing Wages 2014
Changes in structural labour income tax progressivity
over 2000-12 period in OECD member countries

Tax burdens, 2013 estimates

This section comments on Tables I.1-I.11 and Figures I.1-I.6. These summary tables show results for eight family-types, characterised by different family status (single/married, 0-2 children), economic status (one-/two-earner household) and wage level (33 per cent, 67 per cent, 100 per cent and 167 per cent of annual gross wage earnings of an average worker).

Table I.1 and Figure I.1 in Part I show the average tax wedge (combined burden of income tax, employee and employer social security contributions) taking into account the amount of cash benefits each specific family-type is entitled to. Total levies due minus transfers received are expressed as a percentage of total labour costs, defined as gross wage plus employers' social security contributions (including payroll taxes). In the case of a single person at the average wage level the wedge ranges from 7.0 per cent (Chile) and 16.9 per cent (New Zealand) to 49.3 per cent (Germany) and 55.8 per cent (Belgium). For a one-earner married couple with two children at the same wage level the wedge is lowest in New Zealand (2.4 per cent) and Ireland (6.8 per cent) and highest in Greece (44.5 per cent) and France (41.6 per cent). As stated in Section 2.3 of the Overview, the wedge tends to be lower for a married couple with two-children at this wage level than for a single individual without children due to receipt of cash benefits and/or more advantageous tax treatment. It is also interesting to note that the wedge for a single parent with two children earning 67 per cent of the average wage level is negative in Australia (-2.9 per cent), Canada (-6.3 per cent), New Zealand (-17.1 per cent) and Ireland (-24.9 per cent). This result is because the value of the cash benefits received by these families plus any applicable non-wastable tax credits exceeds the sum of the total tax and social security contributions that are due.

Table I.2 and Figure I.2 present the combined burden of the personal income tax and employee social security contributions, expressed as a percentage of gross wage earnings (the corresponding measures for income tax and employee contributions separately are shown in Tables I.4 and I.5). A single person at the average wage level without children is liable to an average tax plus contributions burden of over 40 per cent in Belgium (42.6 per cent). The lowest average rates (below 20 per cent) were in Estonia (19.5 per cent), Ireland (18.7 per cent), Switzerland (17.1 per cent), New Zealand (16.9 per cent), Israel (16.7 per cent), Korea (13.4 per cent), Mexico (9.8 per cent) and Chile (7.0 per cent).

Table I.3 shows the combined burden of income tax and employee social security contributions with the levies due being reduced by the entitlement to cash benefits for each family-type. Figure I.3 illustrates this burden for single individuals without children and one-earner married couples with two children at average earnings, respectively. Comparing Tables I.2 and I.3, the average tax rates for families with children (columns 4-7) are lower in Table I.3 because many OECD countries support families with children through cash benefits. A lower burden is observed for a single individual without children at 67 per cent of the average wage in the case of Canada because of a cash transfer paid to mitigate the burden imposed by the federal consumption tax (further details can be found in the country chapter contained in Part III of this Report) and in Denmark for single taxpayers at 67 and 100 per cent of the average wage and two-earner married couples without children, one partner at average earnings and the other partner at 33 per cent of the average wage, receiving a green check to compensate for increased environmental taxes.

Cash benefits are provided in a majority of OECD countries. For single parents with two children earning 67 per cent of the average wage level, 26 countries provide benefits that range from 46.1 per cent of income (Ireland) to 0.9 per cent (Chile). The benefits are at least 25 per cent of income in 4 other countries: Denmark (25.9 per cent), Australia (26.2 per cent), Canada (27.3 per cent) and New Zealand (31.8 per cent). 25 countries provide benefits for a one-earner married couple with two children earning 100 per cent of the average wage level, although these are less generous relative to income, ranging from 14.5 per cent (New Zealand) to 3.4 per cent (Israel). The lower level of importance of cash benefits for the married couple can be attributed to three reasons: single parents may be eligible for more generous treatment; the benefits themselves may be fixed in absolute amount; and/or the benefits may be subject to income testing.

Table I.4 shows personal income tax due as a percentage of gross wage earnings. For single persons without children at the average wage (column 2) – the income tax burden varies between 0 per cent (Chile) and 35.8 per cent (Denmark). In most OECD member countries, at the average wage level, the income tax burden for one-earner married couples with two children is substantially lower than that faced by single persons (compare columns 2 and 5). This difference is clearly illustrated in Figure I.4. In twelve OECD countries, the income tax burden faced by a one-earner married couple with two children is less than half that faced by a single individual (the Czech Republic, Germany, Hungary, Ireland, Korea, Luxembourg, Poland, Portugal, the Slovak Republic, Slovenia, Switzerland and the United States). In contrast, there is no difference in eight countries – Australia, Chile, Finland, Israel, Mexico, New Zealand, Sweden and the United Kingdom.

There are only two OECD member countries where a married average worker with 2 children faces a personal income tax burden less than zero. This result is due to non-wastable tax credits, whereby credit amounts in excess of the taxes otherwise due are paid to the family, resulting in tax burdens of -5.5 per cent in the Czech Republic and -2.8 per cent in the Slovak Republic. Similarly, in five countries – the Czech Republic, Germany, the Slovak Republic, the United Kingdom and the United States – single parents with two children earning 67 per cent of the average wage show a negative tax burden. In seven other countries – Chile, Israel, Korea, Mexico, Poland and Slovenia – this family-type pays no or almost no income tax.

A comparison of columns 5 and 6 in Table I.4 demonstrates that if the previously non-employed spouse finds a job which pays 33 per cent of the average wage level, the income tax burden of the family (now expressed as a percentage of 4/3 times the average wage level) is (slightly) higher in nineteen countries, the largest increases being in the Czech Republic (7.6 percentage points) and Germany and the Slovak Republic (both 5.7 percentage points). At the same time, the income tax burden is lower in fourteen countries, the largest falls being in Mexico (-4.5 percentage points), Australia (-4.4 percentage points) and Finland (-4.3 percentage points). There is no impact on the tax burden in Chile.

An important consideration in the design of an income tax is progressivity – the rate at which the income tax burden increases with income. A comparison of columns 1 to 3 in Table I.4 provides an insight into the levels of progressivity in the income tax systems of OECD countries. Comparing the income tax burden of single individuals at the average wage level with their counterparts at 167 per cent of the average (columns 2 and 3), the lower paid worker faces a lower tax burden in most OECD countries. In Hungary, where a flat tax rate is applied on labour income, the households without children pay the same percentage of income tax. Similarly, single individuals at 67 per cent of the average wage level pay a lower percentage of their income in income tax (columns 1 and 2) than the average except in Hungary as explained above and also in Chile where these workers do not pay income tax. Finally the burden faced by single individuals at 67 per cent of the average wage level is less than one-quarter of the burden faced by their counterparts at 167 per cent in five OECD countries: the Netherlands (20 per cent), Korea (18 per cent), Greece (11 per cent), Mexico (5 per cent) and Chile (0 per cent).

The addition of social security contributions to the average tax rate reduces this progressivity as well as the proportional fiscal savings enjoyed by families (compare Table I.2 and Table I.4). The OECD personal average tax burden of single individuals at 67 per cent of the average wage level is only 32 per cent lower than their counterparts at 167 per cent compared to the OECD average savings of 50 per cent for personal income taxes alone. The average fiscal savings observed for one-earner married couples with two children at 100 per cent of the average wage level relative to single individuals falls from 37 per cent to 21 per cent. These lower figures are consistent with the observation that there is little variation between social security contribution rates across family types, as shown in Table I.5.

Table I.5 shows employee social security contributions as a percentage of gross wage earnings. For a single worker without children at the average wage level (column 2) the rate of contributions varies between zero per cent (Australia and New Zealand) and 22.1 per cent (Slovenia). Australia and New Zealand levy no social security contributions at all on employees and there are four other countries with very low rates – Iceland (0.5 per cent), Mexico (1.4 per cent), Estonia (2.0 per cent), and Denmark (2.7 per cent). Social security contributions are usually levied at a flat rate on all earnings, i.e. without any exempt threshold. In a number of OECD member countries a ceiling applies. However, this 'capping' provision usually applies to wage levels higher than 167 per cent of the average wage. These rate structures are reflected in a roughly constant average burden of employee social security contributions for most countries between 33 and 167 per cent of average wage earnings. Some typical examples of the proportional burden of employee social security contributions for all family-types at all wage levels considered here, are (in decreasing order) Slovenia (22.1 per cent), Hungary (18.5 per cent), Poland (17.8 per cent), Greece (16.5 per cent), Turkey (15.0 per cent), the Slovak Republic (13.4 per cent), the Czech Republic and Portugal (11 per cent), Norway (7.8 per cent), the United States (7.7 per cent), Chile (7.0 per cent) and Estonia (2.0 per cent).

Also, at the 100 per cent average wage level all OECD member countries, except Germany and the Netherlands, impose the same burden of social security contributions on employees; regardless of their family status (see Figure I.5).

Marginal rates

Assuming a marginal increase in labour costs, Table I.6 and Figure I.6 show the percentage of the rise in labour costs that is deducted through the personal income tax and both employee and employer (including payroll taxes) social security contributions. Therefore, they trace the marginal wedge. In most cases, the marginal tax wedge absorbs 25-55 per cent of a rise in labour costs for single individuals without children at 100 per cent of the average wage level. However, in six OECD countries these individuals face higher marginal wedges – Belgium (69.7 per cent), Canada (63.7 per cent), Austria (60.6 per cent), Germany (60.0 per cent), France (59.7 per cent) and Finland (57.6 per cent). Mexico (23.4 per cent) and Chile (7.0 per cent) have the lowest marginal tax rates.

In twenty OECD member countries, the marginal tax wedge for one-earner married couples at average earnings with 2 children is either the same or within 5 percentage points as that for single persons at average wage earnings with no children. The marginal wedge is more than 5 percentage points lower for the one-earner married couples in seven countries: Luxembourg (16.1 percentage points), Portugal (14.1 percentage points), France (11.3 percentage points), the United States (9.3 percentage points), Switzerland (8.0 percentage points), Germany (7.8 percentage points), and Slovenia (7.4 percentage points). In contrast, in the Czech Republic (5.5 percentage points), Netherlands (6.6 percentage points), Iceland (7.1 percentage points), Australia (16.5 percentage points), New Zealand (21.3 percentage points), Canada (27.2 percentage points) and Ireland (37.4 percentage points), the marginal rate for one-earner married couples with two children is more than 5 percentage points higher than it is for single workers with no children.

Table I.7 and Figure I.7 show the incremental change to personal income tax and employee social security contributions less cash benefits when gross wage earnings rise marginally. As in the case of the tax wedge, in most cases personal income tax and employee social security contributions absorb 25-55 per cent of a worker's pay rise for single individuals without children at 100 per cent of the average wage level. The marginal tax rate is lower than 25 per cent only in Chile (7.0 per cent), Mexico (17.6 per cent), Korea (21.8 per cent) and Estonia (22.6 per cent) and it exceeds 55 per cent in Belgium (59.4 per cent) and in Canada (60.1 per cent).

As in the case of the tax wedge, in twenty OECD member countries, the net marginal personal tax rate for one-earner married couples with two children at the average wage level is either the same or within five percentage points as that for single persons with no children. The marginal rate is more than 5 percentage points lower for the one-earner married couples in seven countries: Luxembourg (18.1 percentage points), Portugal (17.5 percentage points), France (15.9 percentage points), the United States (10.0 percentage points), Germany (9.2 percentage points), Switzerland (8.6 percentage points) and Slovenia (8.5 percentage points). By contrast, in the Netherlands (7.2 percentage points), the Czech Republic (7.3 percentage points), Iceland (7.7 percentage points), Australia (17.5 percentage points, New Zealand (21.3 percentage points), Canada (29.9 percentage points) and Ireland (41.4 percentage points), the marginal rate for one-earner married couples with two children is more than 5 percentage points higher than it is for single persons with no children. These higher marginal rates are due to the phase out of income-tested tax reliefs and/or cash transfers. When an income-tested measure is being phased out, the reduction in the relief or benefit compounds the increase in the tax otherwise payable. These programmes are set out in greater detail in the relevant country chapters, in Part III of the Report.

Table I.8 shows the percentage increase in net income when gross wage earnings increase by 1 currency unit, i.e. the elasticity of after-tax income.[1] Under a proportional tax system, net income would increase by the same percentage as the increase in gross earnings, in which case the elasticity is equal to 1. The elasticity is measured as 0.8 when an increase of gross wage by 1 currency unit leads to a corresponding rise of net take-home pay of only 0.8 of a unit. The more progressive the system is – at the income level considered – the lower this elasticity will be. In the case, for example, of the one-earner married households with two children at the average wage level, column 5 of Table I.8 shows that of all OECD member countries Canada (0.11), Ireland (0.27), New Zealand (0.50), Australia (0.55), the Czech Republic (0.58) and Belgium (0.59) have, on this measure, the most progressive systems of income tax plus employee social security contributions taking into account tax provisions and cash transfers for children at this income level. In contrast, Chile (1.00) and, Mexico (0.91) either implement or are close to a proportional system of income tax plus employee social security contributions – at least for this family type.

It is interesting to note that the elasticity exceeds one for a single individual at 167 per cent of the average earnings in Austria (1.02), indicating that the income tax system at this point in the income scale is regressive. In other words, a percentage increase in gross pay leads to an increase in net income in excess of the percentage increase in gross wage earnings.

Table I.9 provides a different elasticity measure: the percentage increase in net income when labour costs (i.e. gross wage earnings plus employer social security contributions and payroll taxes) rise by 1 currency unit.[2] In this case taxes and social security contributions paid by employers are also part of the analysis. In most OECD member countries the value of this elasticity lies between 0.5 and 0.97 for the eight selected family-types. This elasticity is below 0.5 for single parents earning 67 per cent of the average wage level in Australia (0.41), Canada (0.37), Ireland (0.26) and the United Kingdom (0.25), and for one-earner married households at the average wage level with two children in Ireland (0.27) and Canada (0.11). In contrast, the elasticity is greater than or equal to 0.97 for some family types in Austria, Chile, Estonia, Germany, Hungary, Japan, Korea, Poland and Spain. It is interesting to mention that under this elasticity measure the income tax system is regressive for a single individual at 167 per cent of average earnings in Spain (1.08), Germany (1.14) and Austria (1.20).

Table I.10 sets out figures for gross wage earnings and net income for the eight family-types after all amounts have been converted into US. dollars with the same purchasing power. Single workers with the average wage take home (see Table I.10, column 4) over USD 37 000 in six countries: Switzerland (USD 53 296), Norway (USD 42 166), Korea (USD 40 782), Luxembourg (USD 40 743), Australia (USD 40 481), the Netherlands (USD 40 096), the United Kingdom (USD 38 918) and Japan (USD 37 452). The corresponding lowest levels were in Mexico (USD 11 281), in Hungary (USD 15 019) and in the Slovak Republic (USD 15 227). In the case of a one-earner married couple with two children at the average earnings level, families take home over USD 50 000 in Luxembourg and Switzerland; with the lowest level again being in Mexico. It is interesting to observe that with the exceptions of Chile and Mexico, the one-earner married couple takes home more than the single individual at the average wage due to the favourable tax treatment of this family and/or the cash transfers to which they are entitled.

Table I.11 shows the corresponding figures to Table I.10 for labour costs and net income. So the "net" columns in Tables I.10 and I.11 are identical. Usually, labour costs are found to be much higher, because any employer social security contributions (including payroll taxes) are now taken into account. If measured in US dollars with equal purchasing power, labour costs for single workers earning the average wage level are the highest in Belgium (USD 72 974) and Germany (USD 68 962), and the lowest in Mexico (USD 13 964) and Chile (USD 18 989). It is interesting to note that the annual labour costs are equal to the annual gross wage in Chile, Denmark and New Zealand. In those countries neither employer social security contributions nor payroll taxes are levied on wages. However, employers in Chile and Denmark are subject to non-tax compulsory payments related notably to pension schemes.

Notes

1. The reported elasticities in Table I.8 are calculated as (100 – METR)/(100 – AETR), where METR is the marginal rate of income tax plus employee social security contributions less cash benefits reported in Table I.7 and AETR is the average rate plus employee social security contributions less cash benefits reported in Table I.3.
2. The reported elasticities in Table I.9 are calculated as (100 – METR)/(100 – AETR), where METR is the marginal rate of income tax plus employee and employer social security contributions less cash benefits reported in Table I.6 and AETR is the average rate plus employee and employer social security contributions less cash benefits reported in Table I.1.

Table I.1. **Income tax plus employee and employer contributions less cash benefits, 2013**

As % of labour costs, by family-type and wage level

	Single no ch 67 (% AW)	Single no ch 100 (% AW)	Single no ch 167 (% AW)	Single 2 ch 67 (% AW)	Married 2 ch 100-0 (% AW)	Married 2 ch 100-33 (% AW)[2]	Married 2 ch 100-67 (% AW)[2]	Married no ch 100-33 (% AW)[2]
Australia	21.9	27.4	33.1	-2.9	16.9	19.9	25.2	23.2
Austria	44.5	49.1	51.9	28.5	38.4	38.2	41.6	45.2
Belgium	50.1	55.8	60.9	36.4	41.0	42.3	48.7	48.5
Canada	26.3	31.1	33.1	-6.3	18.7	24.1	27.3	27.9
Chile	7.0	7.0	7.8	6.1	7.0	4.8	6.6	7.0
Czech Republic	39.3	42.4	44.9	14.3	20.5	29.7	33.9	40.2
Denmark	36.6	38.2	44.3	11.2	27.6	32.1	33.8	36.9
Estonia	38.7	39.9	40.8	26.4	32.3	34.8	36.3	38.7
Finland	37.6	43.1	48.9	26.6	38.1	35.6	37.9	39.4
France	45.6	48.9	54.1	37.2	41.6	39.5	44.2	44.9
Germany	45.1	49.3	51.2	31.0	33.8	38.6	42.1	45.1
Greece	36.9	41.6	49.2	38.7	44.5	42.0	42.5	40.6
Hungary	49.0	49.0	49.0	25.2	34.1	36.2	40.1	47.7
Iceland	28.7	33.4	37.8	16.5	19.1	26.5	30.5	29.0
Ireland	21.0	26.6	38.5	-24.9	6.8	13.5	19.2	20.1
Israel	13.9	20.7	29.5	1.4	17.4	14.0	14.3	17.2
Italy	44.7	47.8	53.2	28.4	38.2	40.2	42.9	44.7
Japan	30.3	31.6	34.5	23.9	26.1	27.6	28.5	30.8
Korea	18.3	21.4	22.9	17.4	19.0	18.9	19.0	20.3
Luxembourg	29.9	37.0	44.3	4.4	14.3	18.8	24.3	28.3
Mexico	13.9	19.2	22.2	13.9	19.2	16.9	17.1	16.9
Netherlands	32.1	36.9	41.9	11.0	30.8	28.7	30.5	33.5
New Zealand	13.3	16.9	22.8	-17.1	2.4	10.1	15.8	15.7
Norway	34.1	37.3	43.0	21.9	31.2	31.7	33.7	34.6
Poland	34.7	35.6	36.2	29.6	29.8	31.3	32.5	34.7
Portugal	34.7	41.1	47.4	24.9	29.8	30.9	36.7	34.7
Slovak Republic	38.4	41.1	43.3	26.3	27.6	33.0	35.2	39.1
Slovenia	38.5	42.3	46.1	13.0	23.1	30.5	34.3	40.0
Spain	37.2	40.7	44.3	30.3	34.8	36.4	37.6	37.5
Sweden	40.8	42.9	50.6	33.0	37.7	37.2	38.9	41.2
Switzerland	19.2	22.0	26.5	4.3	9.5	12.6	15.7	19.8
Turkey[1]	36.5	38.6	42.1	35.5	37.4	38.1	38.8	38.6
United Kingdom	26.9	31.5	37.7	6.3	27.0	23.5	27.0	26.9
United States	29.3	31.3	36.2	11.1	20.3	24.9	26.7	29.8
Unweighted average								
OECD-Average	**32.2**	**35.9**	**40.3**	**17.2**	**26.4**	**28.3**	**31.2**	**32.9**
OECD-EU 21	**38.2**	**42.0**	**46.6**	**21.8**	**31.0**	**33.0**	**36.2**	**38.5**

Note: ch = children

1. Wage figures are based on the old definition of average worker (ISIC D, Rev. 3).
2. Two-earner family.

StatLink http://dx.doi.org/10.1787/888933006176

Figure I.1. **Income tax plus employee and employer contributions less cash benefits, 2013**

As a % of labour costs, by family-type[1]

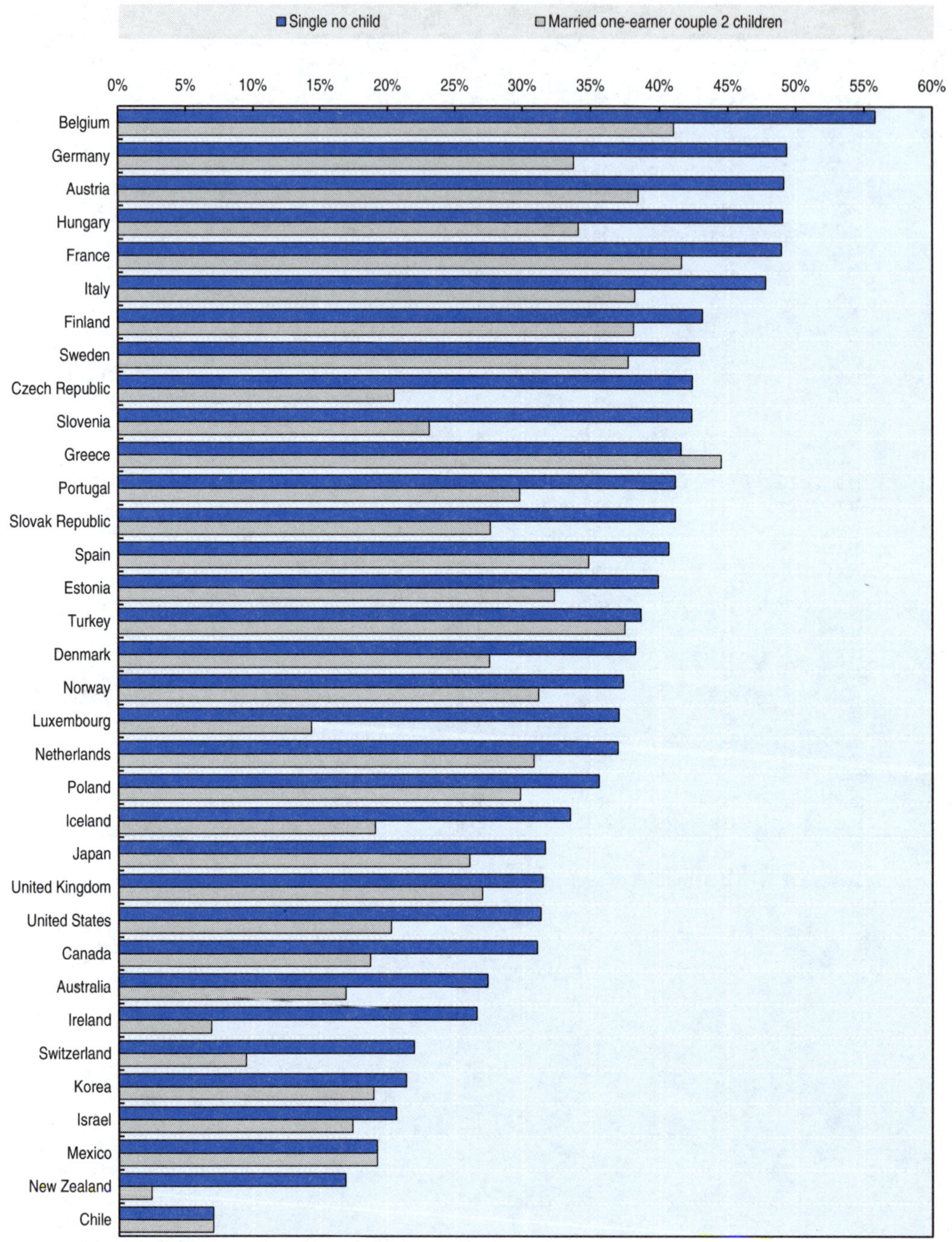

1. Corresponds to Table I.1, columns 2 and 5.

Source: OECD calculations based on country submissions and *OECD Economic Outlook*, Volume 2013 (No. 94).

StatLink http://dx.doi.org/10.1787/888933003953

Table I.2. **Income tax plus employee contributions, 2013**

As % of gross wage earnings, by family-type and wage level

	Single no ch 67 (% AW)	Single no ch 100 (% AW)	Single no ch 167 (% AW)	Single 2 ch 67 (% AW)	Married 2 ch 100-0 (% AW)	Married 2 ch 100-33 (% AW)[2]	Married 2 ch 100-67 (% AW)[2]	Married no ch 100-33 (% AW)[2]
Australia	17.2	23.1	29.2	-9.0	12.0	15.2	20.7	18.7
Austria	28.3	34.3	39.0	7.7	20.5	20.1	24.5	29.3
Belgium	36.1	42.6	49.4	18.6	23.4	27.1	33.7	35.0
Canada	17.5	22.8	26.8	-19.0	8.9	15.1	18.5	19.4
Chile	7.0	7.0	7.8	6.1	7.0	4.8	6.6	7.0
Czech Republic	18.6	22.8	26.1	-14.8	-6.5	5.8	11.5	19.8
Denmark	36.6	38.2	44.3	11.2	27.6	32.1	33.8	36.9
Estonia	17.9	19.5	20.7	1.4	9.3	12.6	14.6	17.9
Finland	23.3	30.2	37.3	9.9	24.0	21.0	23.7	25.6
France	26.4	28.4	34.0	15.1	18.1	19.1	22.8	26.4
Germany	34.6	39.6	43.7	17.7	21.0	26.7	31.0	34.6
Greece	19.6	25.5	35.3	21.8	29.3	26.1	26.7	24.3
Hungary	34.5	34.5	34.5	3.9	15.3	20.1	23.0	34.5
Iceland	23.2	28.3	33.0	10.1	12.9	20.9	25.2	23.5
Ireland	12.6	18.7	31.9	-38.3	-3.2	4.7	10.5	11.9
Israel	10.2	16.7	25.5	-2.8	13.3	10.0	10.3	13.4
Italy	27.0	31.0	38.2	5.5	18.3	21.0	24.6	27.0
Japan	20.0	21.6	25.4	12.7	15.2	17.0	18.0	20.6
Korea	9.9	13.4	16.0	9.0	10.7	10.6	10.7	12.2
Luxembourg	21.2	29.3	37.4	-7.4	3.8	8.8	15.0	19.5
Mexico	1.9	9.8	14.3	1.9	9.8	5.2	6.6	5.2
Netherlands	26.1	31.2	38.4	3.1	24.5	22.3	24.2	27.5
New Zealand	13.3	16.9	22.8	-17.1	2.4	10.1	15.8	15.7
Norway	25.5	29.2	35.6	11.7	22.2	22.8	25.1	26.2
Poland	23.8	24.7	25.5	17.8	18.0	19.8	21.1	23.8
Portugal	19.3	27.2	34.9	7.0	13.1	14.4	21.7	19.3
Slovak Republic	19.2	22.8	25.6	3.3	5.1	12.1	15.0	20.1
Slovenia	28.5	33.1	37.4	-1.0	10.7	19.3	23.8	30.3
Spain	18.4	22.9	28.5	9.5	15.3	17.4	18.9	18.8
Sweden	22.2	25.0	35.0	11.9	18.1	17.5	19.8	22.7
Switzerland	14.2	17.1	22.0	-1.7	3.8	7.1	10.4	14.8
Turkey[1]	26.1	28.5	32.6	24.8	27.1	27.9	28.7	28.5
United Kingdom	20.1	24.1	30.2	2.5	19.1	16.4	19.5	20.1
United States	21.5	24.6	30.5	1.4	12.4	16.7	19.2	22.1
Unweighted average								
OECD-Average	**21.2**	**25.4**	**30.8**	**3.8**	**14.2**	**16.7**	**19.9**	**22.1**
OECD-EU 21	**24.5**	**28.8**	**34.6**	**4.8**	**15.5**	**18.3**	**21.9**	**25.0**

Note: ch = children

1. Wage figures are based on the old definition of average worker (ISIC D, Rev. 3).
2. Two-earner family.

StatLink http://dx.doi.org/10.1787/888933006195

Figure I.2. **Income tax plus employee contributions, 2013**

As % of gross wage earnings, by family-type and wage level[1]

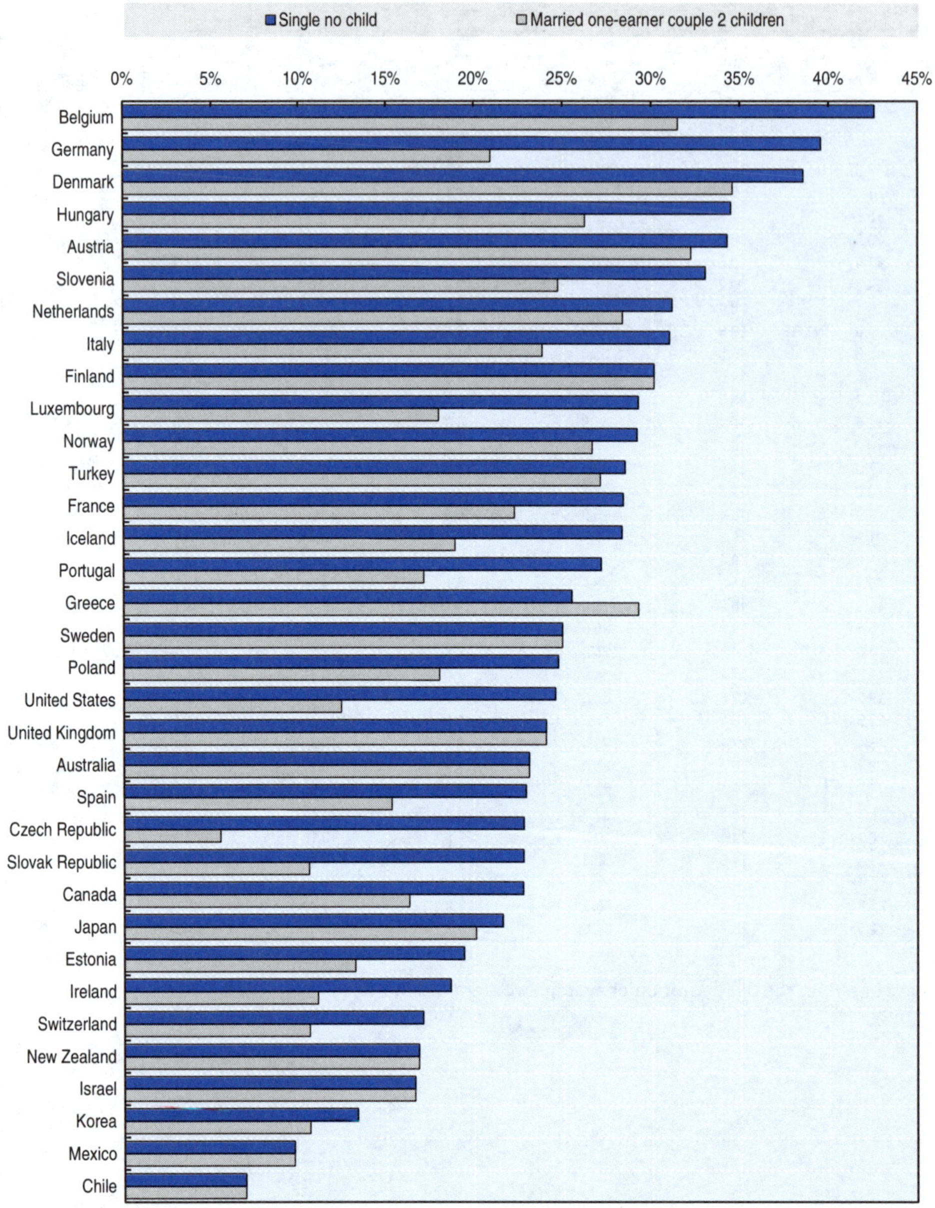

1. Corresponds to Table I.2, columns 2 and 5.

Sources: Country submissions, *OECD Economic Outlook*, Volume 2013 (No. 94).

StatLink http://dx.doi.org/10.1787/888933003972

Table I.3. **Income tax plus employee contributions less cash benefits, 2013**

As % of gross wage earnings, by family-type and wage level

	Single no ch 67 (% AW)	Single no ch 100 (% AW)	Single no ch 167 (% AW)	Single 2 ch 67 (% AW)	Married 2 ch 100-0 (% AW)	Married 2 ch 100-33 (% AW)[2]	Married 2 ch 100-67 (% AW)[2]	Married no ch 100-33 (% AW)[2]
Australia	17.2	23.1	29.2	-9.0	12.0	15.2	20.7	18.7
Austria	28.3	34.3	39.0	7.7	20.5	20.1	24.5	29.3
Belgium	36.1	42.6	49.4	18.6	23.4	27.1	33.7	35.0
Canada	17.5	22.8	26.8	-19.0	8.9	15.1	18.5	19.4
Chile	7.0	7.0	7.8	6.1	7.0	4.8	6.6	7.0
Czech Republic	18.6	22.8	26.1	-14.8	-6.5	5.8	11.5	19.8
Denmark	36.6	38.2	44.3	11.2	27.6	32.1	33.8	36.9
Estonia	17.9	19.5	20.7	1.4	9.3	12.6	14.6	17.9
Finland	23.3	30.2	37.3	9.9	24.0	21.0	23.7	25.6
France	26.4	28.4	34.0	15.1	18.1	19.1	22.8	26.4
Germany	34.6	39.6	43.7	17.7	21.0	26.7	31.0	34.6
Greece	19.6	25.5	35.3	21.8	29.3	26.1	26.7	24.3
Hungary	34.5	34.5	34.5	3.9	15.3	20.1	23.0	34.5
Iceland	23.2	28.3	33.0	10.1	12.9	20.9	25.2	23.5
Ireland	12.6	18.7	31.9	-38.3	-3.2	4.7	10.5	11.9
Israel	10.2	16.7	25.5	-2.8	13.3	10.0	10.3	13.4
Italy	27.0	31.0	38.2	5.5	18.3	21.0	24.6	27.0
Japan	20.0	21.6	25.4	12.7	15.2	17.0	18.0	20.6
Korea	9.9	13.4	16.0	9.0	10.7	10.6	10.7	12.2
Luxembourg	21.2	29.3	37.4	-7.4	3.8	8.8	15.0	19.5
Mexico	1.9	9.8	14.3	1.9	9.8	5.2	6.6	5.2
Netherlands	26.1	31.2	38.4	3.1	24.5	22.3	24.2	27.5
New Zealand	13.3	16.9	22.8	-17.1	2.4	10.1	15.8	15.7
Norway	25.5	29.2	35.6	11.7	22.2	22.8	25.1	26.2
Poland	23.8	24.7	25.5	17.8	18.0	19.8	21.1	23.8
Portugal	19.3	27.2	34.9	7.0	13.1	14.4	21.7	19.3
Slovak Republic	19.2	22.8	25.6	3.3	5.1	12.1	15.0	20.1
Slovenia	28.5	33.1	37.4	-1.0	10.7	19.3	23.8	30.3
Spain	18.4	22.9	28.5	9.5	15.3	17.4	18.9	18.8
Sweden	22.2	25.0	35.0	11.9	18.1	17.5	19.8	22.7
Switzerland	14.2	17.1	22.0	-1.7	3.8	7.1	10.4	14.8
Turkey[1]	26.1	28.5	32.6	24.8	27.1	27.9	28.7	28.5
United Kingdom	20.1	24.1	30.2	-2.5	19.1	16.4	19.5	20.1
United States	21.5	24.6	30.5	1.4	12.4	16.7	19.2	22.1
Unweighted average								
OECD-Average	**21.2**	**25.4**	**30.8**	**3.8**	**14.2**	**16.7**	**19.9**	**22.1**
OECD-EU 21	**24.5**	**28.8**	**34.6**	**4.8**	**15.5**	**18.3**	**21.9**	**25.0**

Note: ch = children

1. Wage figures are based on the old definition of average worker (ISIC D, Rev. 3).
2. Two-earner family.

StatLink http://dx.doi.org/10.1787/888933006214

Figure I.3. **Income tax plus employee contributions less cash benefits, 2013**

As % of gross wage earnings, by family-type and wage level[1]

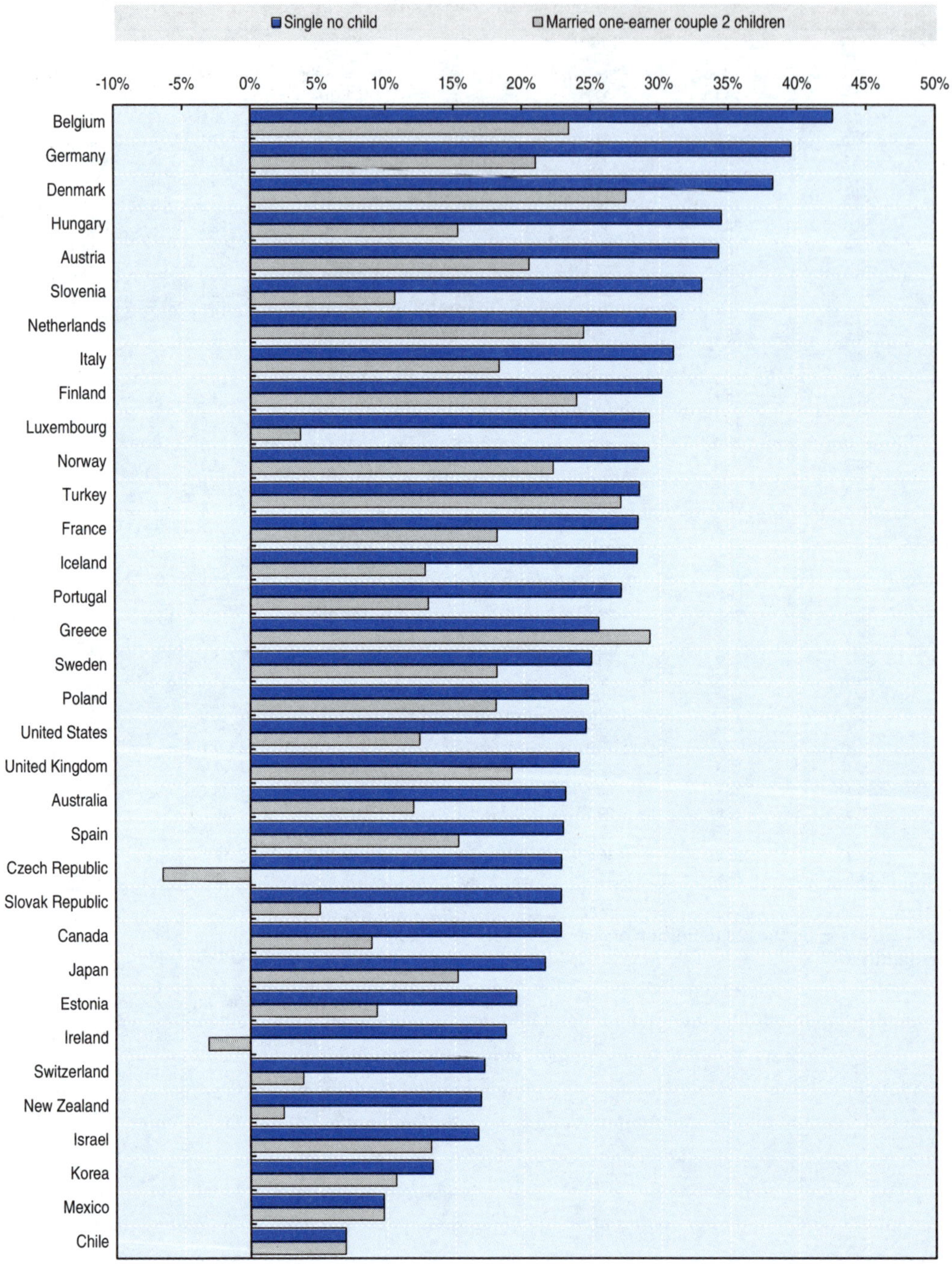

1. Corresponds to Table I.3, columns 2 and 5.

Source: OECD calculations based on country submissions and *OECD Economic Outlook*, Volume 2013 (No. 94).

StatLink http://dx.doi.org/10.1787/888933003991

Table I.4. **Income tax, by family-type and wage level, 2013**

As % of gross wage earnings

	Single no ch 67 (% AW)	Single no ch 100 (% AW)	Single no ch 167 (% AW)	Single 2 ch 67 (% AW)	Married 2 ch 100-0 (% AW)	Married 2 ch 100-33 (% AW)[2]	Married 2 ch 100-67 (% AW)[2]	Married no ch 100-33 (% AW)[2]
Australia	17.2	23.1	29.2	17.2	23.1	18.7	20.7	18.7
Austria	10.2	16.2	22.9	7.2	14.2	11.6	13.5	12.0
Belgium	22.2	28.6	35.3	16.8	17.5	22.4	24.6	24.3
Canada	11.6	15.3	21.8	1.1	8.9	11.3	13.0	12.4
Chile	0.0	0.0	0.8	0.0	0.0	0.0	0.0	0.0
Czech Republic	7.6	11.8	15.1	-5.8	-5.5	2.1	4.7	8.8
Denmark	33.0	35.8	42.7	33.0	31.8	33.3	34.7	33.3
Estonia	15.9	17.5	18.7	11.2	11.2	13.6	15.0	15.9
Finland	15.8	22.5	29.6	15.8	22.5	18.2	19.8	18.2
France	12.6	14.6	20.9	7.6	8.5	8.4	11.5	12.6
Germany	14.1	19.1	27.7	-2.4	0.8	6.5	10.8	14.1
Greece	3.1	9.0	18.8	5.3	12.8	9.6	10.2	7.8
Hungary	16.0	16.0	16.0	3.6	7.8	9.8	11.1	16.0
Iceland	22.5	27.9	32.8	22.5	18.5	22.8	25.7	22.8
Ireland	8.6	14.7	27.9	3.8	7.1	8.9	12.2	8.9
Israel	4.4	8.8	16.0	0.0	8.8	5.8	5.3	6.6
Italy	17.5	21.5	28.6	9.5	14.4	13.9	16.9	17.5
Japan	6.1	7.7	12.2	6.1	6.2	6.7	7.0	6.7
Korea	1.6	5.1	9.0	0.7	2.4	2.3	2.4	3.9
Luxembourg	9.0	17.0	25.0	1.7	5.7	7.2	11.2	7.2
Mexico	0.7	8.4	12.9	0.7	8.4	3.9	5.3	3.9
Netherlands	5.6	15.7	28.1	3.2	15.2	12.0	11.2	12.4
New Zealand	13.3	16.9	22.8	14.7	16.9	15.7	16.0	15.7
Norway	17.7	21.4	27.8	13.9	18.9	18.4	19.9	18.4
Poland	6.0	6.9	7.7	0.0	0.2	1.9	3.3	6.0
Portugal	8.3	16.2	23.9	3.3	6.1	6.2	10.7	8.3
Slovak Republic	5.8	9.4	12.2	-1.8	-2.8	2.9	4.9	6.7
Slovenia	6.4	11.0	15.3	0.0	2.6	3.6	5.5	8.2
Spain	12.0	16.6	22.5	3.1	9.0	11.0	12.5	12.4
Sweden	15.2	18.0	30.1	15.2	18.0	15.7	16.9	15.7
Switzerland	7.9	10.9	15.8	2.2	4.4	6.0	8.2	8.6
Turkey[1]	11.1	13.5	17.6	9.8	12.1	12.9	13.7	13.5
United Kingdom	12.0	14.7	22.8	-3.1	14.7	12.0	13.6	12.0
United States	13.9	16.9	22.8	-6.2	4.8	9.0	11.5	14.5
Unweighted average								
OECD-Average	**11.3**	**15.5**	**21.6**	**6.2**	**10.2**	**10.7**	**12.5**	**12.5**
OECD-EU 21	**12.2**	**16.8**	**23.4**	**6.1**	**10.1**	**11.0**	**13.1**	**13.3**

Note: ch = children

1. Wage figures are based on the old definition of average worker (ISIC D, Rev. 3).
2. Two-earner family.

StatLink http://dx.doi.org/10.1787/888933006233

Figure I.4. **Income tax, by family-type, 2013**

As % of gross wage earnings[1]

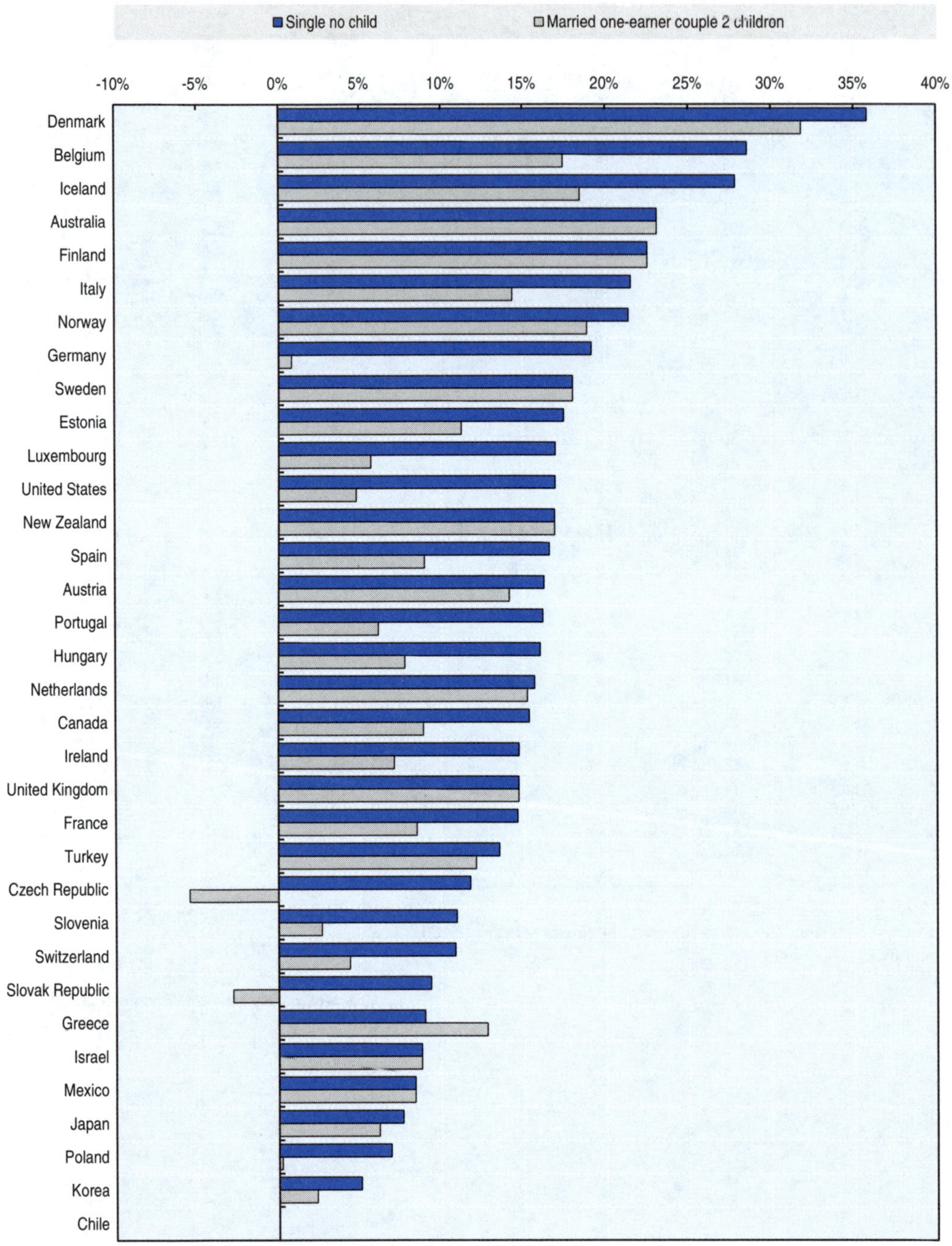

1. Corresponds to Table I.4, columns 2 and 5.

Source: OECD calculations based on country submissions and *OECD Economic Outlook*, Volume 2013 (No. 94)

StatLink http://dx.doi.org/10.1787/888933004010

Table I.5. **Employee contributions, 2013**

As % of gross wage earnings, by family-type and wage level

	Single no ch 67 (% AW)	Single no ch 100 (% AW)	Single no ch 167 (% AW)	Single 2 ch 67 (% AW)	Married 2 ch 100-0 (% AW)	Married 2 ch 100-33 (% AW)[2]	Married 2 ch 100-67 (% AW)[2]	Married no ch 100-33 (% AW)[2]
Australia	0.0	0.0	0.0	0.0	0.0	0.0	0.0	0.0
Austria	18.1	18.1	16.2	18.1	18.1	17.3	18.1	17.3
Belgium	13.9	14.0	14.0	13.9	14.0	10.8	14.0	10.8
Canada	7.2	7.4	5.0	7.2	7.4	7.0	7.3	7.0
Chile	7.0	7.0	7.0	7.0	7.0	7.0	7.0	7.0
Czech Republic	11.0	11.0	11.0	11.0	11.0	11.0	11.0	11.0
Denmark	4.1	2.7	1.6	4.1	2.7	4.1	3.3	4.1
Estonia	2.0	2.0	2.0	2.0	2.0	2.0	2.0	2.0
Finland	7.5	7.6	7.7	7.5	7.6	7.4	7.6	7.4
France	13.8	13.8	13.1	13.8	13.8	13.8	13.8	13.8
Germany	20.4	20.4	16.1	20.2	20.2	20.2	20.2	20.4
Greece	16.5	16.5	16.5	16.5	16.5	16.5	16.5	16.5
Hungary	18.5	18.5	18.5	18.5	18.5	18.5	18.5	18.5
Iceland	0.7	0.5	0.3	0.7	0.5	0.7	0.6	0.7
Ireland	4.0	4.0	4.0	4.0	4.0	3.0	4.0	3.0
Israel	5.8	7.9	9.5	5.8	7.9	6.8	7.1	6.8
Italy	9.5	9.5	9.6	9.5	9.5	9.5	9.5	9.5
Japan	13.9	13.9	13.2	13.9	13.9	13.9	13.9	13.9
Korea	8.3	8.3	7.0	8.3	8.3	8.3	8.3	8.3
Luxembourg	12.2	12.3	12.4	12.2	12.3	12.2	12.3	12.2
Mexico	1.3	1.4	1.5	1.3	1.4	1.3	1.3	1.3
Netherlands	20.5	15.5	10.3	9.3	13.2	13.2	15.3	15.1
New Zealand	0.0	0.0	0.0	0.0	0.0	0.0	0.0	0.0
Norway	7.8	7.8	7.8	7.8	7.8	7.8	7.8	7.8
Poland	17.8	17.8	17.8	17.8	17.8	17.8	17.8	17.8
Portugal	11.0	11.0	11.0	11.0	11.0	11.0	11.0	11.0
Slovak Republic	13.4	13.4	13.4	13.4	13.4	13.4	13.4	13.4
Slovenia	22.1	22.1	22.1	22.1	22.1	22.1	22.1	22.1
Spain	6.4	6.4	6.0	6.4	6.4	6.4	6.4	6.4
Sweden	7.0	7.0	4.9	7.0	7.0	7.0	7.0	7.0
Switzerland	6.3	6.3	6.2	6.3	6.3	6.3	6.3	6.3
Turkey[1]	15.0	15.0	15.0	15.0	15.0	15.0	15.0	15.0
United Kingdom	8.1	9.4	7.4	8.1	9.4	8.1	8.9	8.1
United States	7.7	7.7	7.7	7.7	7.7	7.7	7.7	7.7
Unweighted average								
OECD-Average	**10.0**	**9.9**	**9.3**	**9.6**	**9.8**	**9.6**	**9.8**	**9.7**
OECD-EU 21	**12.3**	**12.0**	**11.2**	**11.7**	**11.9**	**11.7**	**12.0**	**11.8**

Note: ch = children

1. Wage figures are based on the old definition of average worker (ISIC D, Rev. 3).
2. Two-earner family.

StatLink http://dx.doi.org/10.1787/888933006252

Figure I.5. **Employee contributions, 2013**

As % of gross wage earnings, by family-type[1]

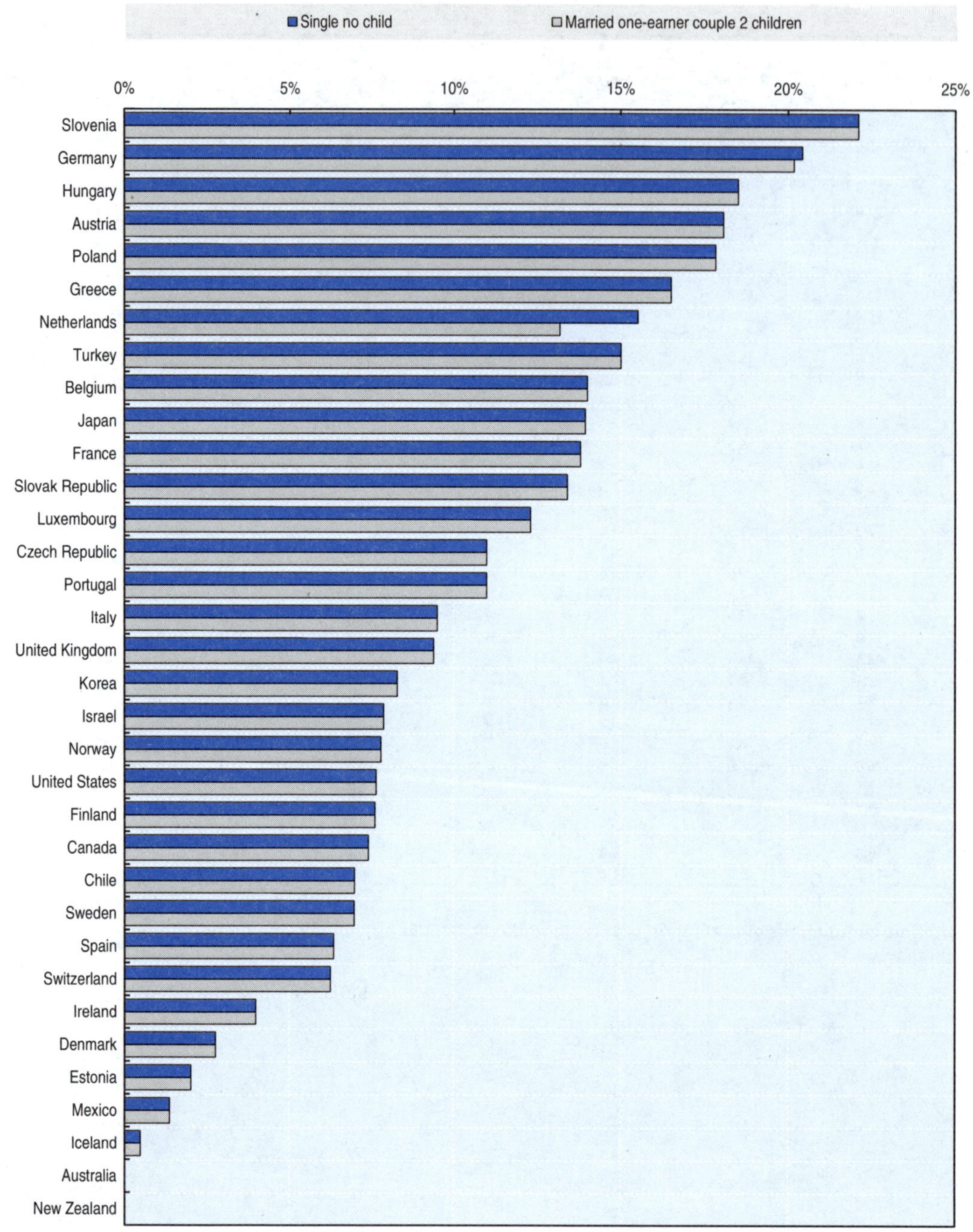

1. Corresponds to Table I.5, columns 2 and 5.

Source: OECD calculations based on country submissions and *OECD Economic Outlook*, Volume 2013 (No. 94)

StatLink http://dx.doi.org/10.1787/888933004029

Table I.6. **Marginal rate of income tax plus employee and employer contributions less cash benefits, 2013[1]**

As % of labour costs, by family-type and wage level

	Single no ch 67 (% AW)	Single no ch 100 (% AW)	Single no ch 167 (% AW)	Single 2 ch 67 (% AW)	Married 2 ch 100-0 (% AW)	Married 2 ch 100-33 (% AW)[3]	Married 2 ch 100-67 (% AW)[3]	Married no ch 100-33 (% AW)[3]
Australia	39.1	37.7	41.9	58.0	54.2	66.0	37.7	37.7
Austria	56.9	60.6	42.2	56.9	60.6	60.6	60.6	60.6
Belgium	66.3	69.7	68.5	66.3	66.3	69.7	68.8	69.7
Canada	33.8	63.7	38.4	60.7	90.9	67.3	67.3	63.7
Chile	7.0	7.0	10.2	7.0	7.0	7.0	7.0	7.0
Czech Republic	48.6	48.6	48.6	55.7	54.1	54.1	54.1	48.6
Denmark	40.3	49.4	56.2	40.3	49.4	49.4	49.4	49.4
Estonia	42.2	42.2	42.2	42.2	42.2	42.2	42.2	42.2
Finland	53.7	57.6	57.6	53.7	57.6	57.6	57.6	57.6
France	62.9	59.7	59.8	57.3	48.4	55.1	51.4	51.4
Germany	55.5	60.0	44.3	53.7	52.2	55.2	57.5	55.5
Greece	48.9	49.6	56.8	49.6	50.2	50.2	50.2	49.6
Hungary	49.0	49.0	49.0	49.0	49.0	49.0	49.0	49.0
Iceland	43.0	43.0	48.3	50.1	50.1	50.1	47.5	43.0
Ireland	37.7	37.7	56.7	67.9	75.1	37.7	37.7	37.7
Israel	30.5	37.1	46.5	17.4	37.1	69.5	37.1	37.1
Italy	54.1	54.1	62.0	55.3	55.3	55.3	54.7	54.1
Japan	32.3	36.6	35.3	32.3	36.5	36.6	36.6	36.6
Korea	24.8	29.0	31.8	18.9	29.0	29.0	29.0	29.0
Luxembourg	45.8	55.1	55.1	47.5	39.0	42.4	49.2	42.4
Mexico	17.4	23.4	28.4	17.4	23.4	23.4	23.4	23.4
Netherlands	45.1	48.5	49.3	51.7	55.1	48.5	48.5	48.5
New Zealand	17.5	30.0	33.0	17.5	51.3	51.3	51.3	30.0
Norway	43.2	51.2	53.8	43.2	51.2	51.2	51.2	51.2
Poland	37.2	37.2	37.2	29.6	37.2	37.2	37.2	37.2
Portugal	53.9	53.9	60.8	51.1	39.8	51.1	51.1	53.9
Slovak Republic	46.5	46.5	46.5	46.5	46.5	46.5	46.5	46.5
Slovenia	43.6	51.0	60.4	32.9	43.6	43.6	43.6	51.0
Spain	45.7	49.5	40.0	53.0	49.5	49.5	49.5	49.5
Sweden	45.8	48.1	67.1	45.8	48.1	48.1	48.1	48.1
Switzerland	26.3	30.1	35.9	18.9	22.1	26.1	29.4	26.9
Turkey[2]	42.3	47.4	47.4	42.3	47.4	47.4	47.4	47.4
United Kingdom	40.2	40.2	49.0	76.3	40.2	40.2	40.2	40.2
United States	34.3	43.6	43.6	50.4	34.3	34.3	34.3	34.3
Unweighted average								
OECD-Average	**41.5**	**45.5**	**47.2**	**44.6**	**46.9**	**47.1**	**45.5**	**44.4**
OECD-EU 21	**48.6**	**50.9**	**52.8**	**51.5**	**50.5**	**49.7**	**49.9**	**49.7**

Note: ch = children

1. Assumes a rise in gross earnings of the principal earner in the household. The outcome may differ if the wage of the spouse goes up, especially if partners are taxed individually.
2. Wage figures are based on the old definition of average worker (ISIC D, Rev. 3).
3. Two-earner family.

StatLink http://dx.doi.org/10.1787/888933006271

Figure I.6. **Marginal rate of income tax plus employee and employer contributions less cash benefits, 2013**

As % of labour costs, by family-type[1]

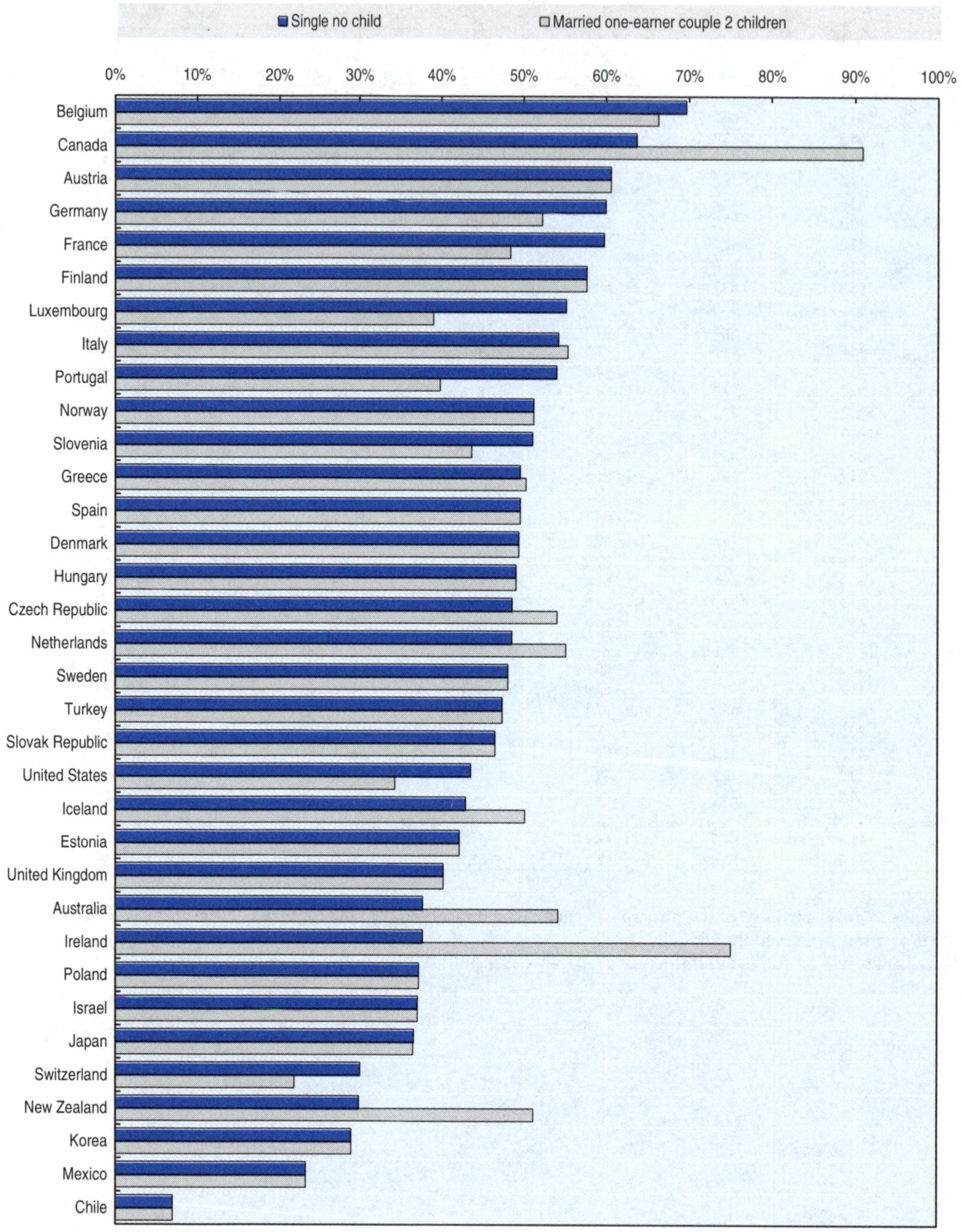

1. Corresponds to Table I.6, columns 2 and 5.

Source: OECD calculations based on country submissions and *OECD Economic Outlook*, Volume 2013 (No. 94)

StatLink *http://dx.doi.org/10.1787/888933004048*

Table I.7. **Marginal rate of income tax plus employee contributions less cash benefits, 2013**[1]

As % of gross wage earnings, by family-type and wage level

	Single no ch 67 (% AW)	Single no ch 100 (% AW)	Single no ch 167 (% AW)	Single 2 ch 67 (% AW)	Married 2 ch 100-0 (% AW)	Married 2 ch 100-33 (% AW)[3]	Married 2 ch 100-67 (% AW)[3]	Married no ch 100-33 (% AW)[3]
Australia	35.5	34.0	38.5	55.5	51.5	64.0	34.0	34.0
Austria	44.4	49.1	37.9	44.4	49.1	49.1	49.1	49.1
Belgium	54.9	59.4	59.8	54.9	54.9	59.4	58.4	59.4
Canada	25.5	60.1	35.4	55.8	90.0	64.1	64.1	60.1
Chile	7.0	7.0	10.2	7.0	7.0	7.0	7.0	7.0
Czech Republic	31.1	31.1	31.1	40.7	38.4	38.4	38.4	31.1
Denmark	40.3	49.4	56.2	40.3	49.4	49.4	49.4	49.4
Estonia	22.6	22.6	22.6	22.6	22.6	22.6	22.6	22.6
Finland	43.1	48.0	48.0	43.1	48.0	48.0	48.0	48.0
France	31.9	43.6	42.4	21.7	27.7	37.0	31.9	31.9
Germany	46.9	52.2	44.3	44.8	43.0	46.6	49.3	46.9
Greece	34.9	35.7	44.9	35.7	36.5	36.5	36.5	35.7
Hungary	34.5	34.5	34.5	34.5	34.5	34.5	34.5	34.5
Iceland	38.6	38.6	44.4	46.3	46.3	46.3	43.4	38.6
Ireland	31.0	31.0	52.0	64.4	72.4	31.0	31.0	31.0
Israel	26.0	33.0	43.0	12.0	33.0	67.5	33.0	33.0
Italy	39.3	39.4	49.9	40.9	41.0	41.0	40.2	39.4
Japan	22.4	27.3	31.2	22.4	27.2	27.3	27.3	27.3
Korea	17.1	21.8	27.9	10.6	21.8	21.8	21.8	21.8
Luxembourg	39.1	49.6	49.6	41.0	31.5	35.3	42.9	35.3
Mexico	12.1	17.6	22.9	12.1	17.6	17.6	17.6	17.6
Netherlands	39.8	43.6	49.3	47.0	50.8	43.6	43.6	43.6
New Zealand	17.5	30.0	33.0	17.5	51.3	51.3	51.3	30.0
Norway	35.8	44.8	47.8	35.8	44.8	44.8	44.8	44.8
Poland	26.7	26.7	26.7	17.8	26.7	26.7	26.7	26.7
Portugal	43.0	43.0	51.5	39.5	25.5	39.5	39.5	43.0
Slovak Republic	29.9	29.9	29.9	29.9	29.9	29.9	29.9	29.9
Slovenia	34.6	43.1	54.0	22.1	34.6	34.6	34.6	43.1
Spain	29.5	34.4	40.0	38.9	34.4	34.4	34.4	34.4
Sweden	28.7	31.7	56.7	28.7	31.7	31.7	31.7	31.7
Switzerland	21.7	25.8	32.2	13.8	17.2	21.5	25.0	22.3
Turkey[2]	32.8	38.7	38.7	32.8	38.7	38.7	38.7	38.7
United Kingdom	32.0	32.0	42.0	73.0	32.0	32.0	32.0	32.0
United States	29.3	39.3	39.3	46.6	29.3	29.3	29.3	29.3
Unweighted average								
OECD-Average	**31.7**	**36.7**	**40.2**	**35.1**	**37.9**	**38.3**	**36.5**	**35.4**
OECD-EU 21	**36.1**	**39.5**	**44.0**	**39.3**	**38.8**	**38.1**	**38.3**	**38.0**

Note: ch = children

1. Assumes a rise in gross earnings of the principal earner in the household. The outcome may differ if the wage of the spouse goes up, especially if partners are taxed individually.
2. Wage figures are based on the old definition of average worker (ISIC D, Rev. 3).
3. Two-earner family.

StatLink http://dx.doi.org/10.1787/888933006290

Figure I.7. **Marginal rate of income tax plus employee contributions less cash benefits, 2013**

As % of gross wage earnings, by family-type[1]

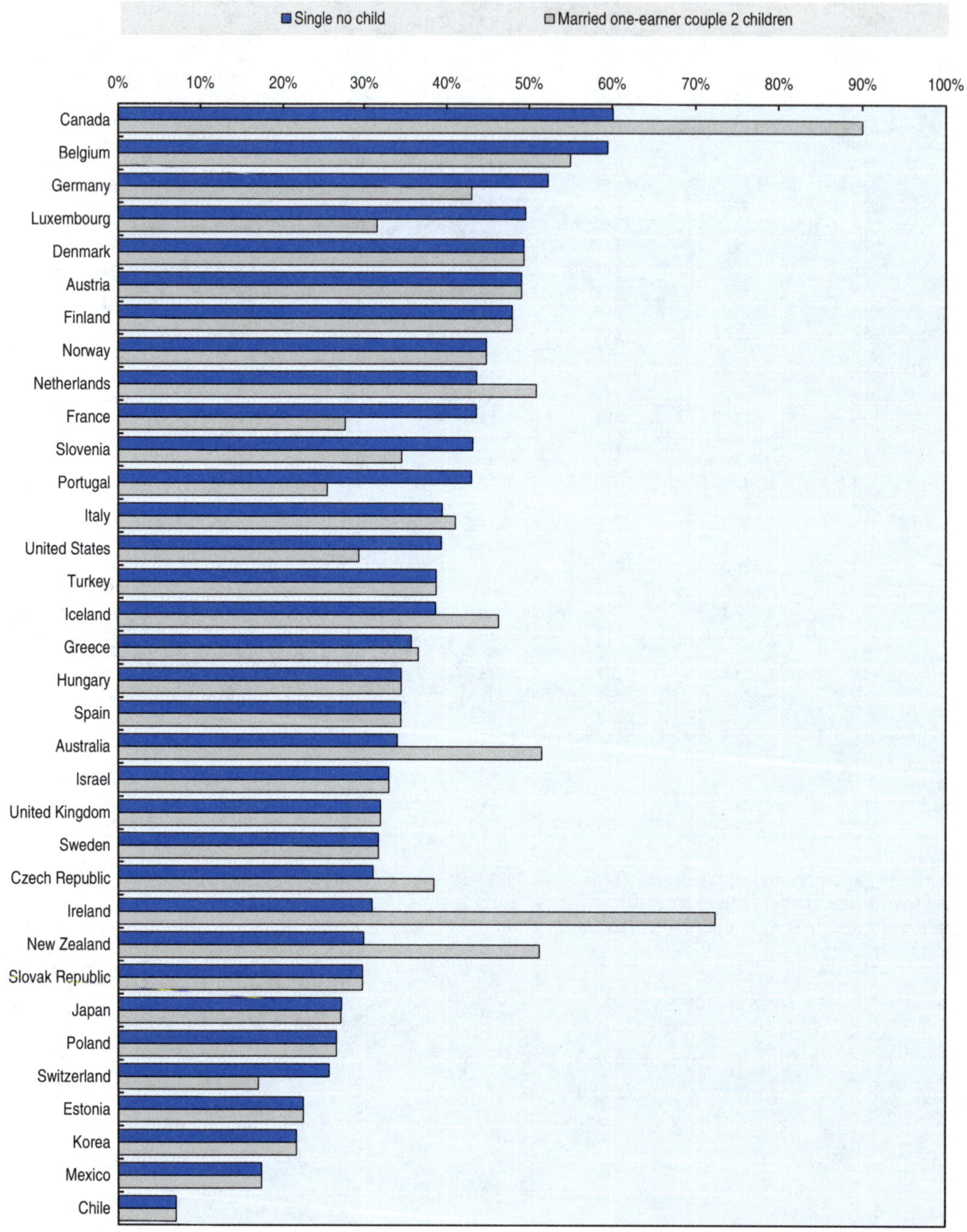

1. Corresponds to Table I.7, columns 2 and 5.

Source: OECD calculations based on country submissions and *OECD Economic Outlook*, Volume 2013 (No. 94)

StatLink http://dx.doi.org/10.1787/888933004067

Table I.8. **Increase in net income after an increase of 1 currency unit in gross wages, 2013**[1]

By family-type and wage level (%)

	Single no ch 67 (% AW)	Single no ch 100 (% AW)	Single no ch 167 (% AW)	Single 2 ch 67 (% AW)	Married 2 ch 100-0 (% AW)	Married 2 ch 100-33 (% AW)[3]	Married 2 ch 100-67 (% AW)[3]	Married no ch 100-33 (% AW)[3]
Australia	0.78	0.86	0.87	0.41	0.55	0.42	0.83	0.81
Austria	0.78	0.78	1.02	0.60	0.64	0.64	0.68	0.72
Belgium	0.71	0.71	0.80	0.55	0.59	0.56	0.63	0.62
Canada	0.90	0.52	0.88	0.37	0.11	0.42	0.44	0.50
Chile	1.00	1.00	0.97	0.99	1.00	0.98	1.00	1.00
Czech Republic	0.85	0.89	0.93	0.52	0.58	0.65	0.70	0.86
Denmark	0.94	0.82	0.79	0.67	0.70	0.75	0.77	0.80
Estonia	0.94	0.96	0.90	0.79	0.85	0.89	0.91	0.94
Finland	0.74	0.75	0.83	0.63	0.68	0.66	0.68	0.70
France	0.93	0.79	0.87	0.92	0.88	0.78	0.88	0.93
Germany	0.81	0.79	0.99	0.67	0.72	0.73	0.74	0.81
Greece	0.81	0.86	0.85	0.82	0.90	0.86	0.87	0.85
Hungary	1.00	1.00	1.00	0.68	0.77	0.82	0.85	1.00
Iceland	0.80	0.86	0.83	0.60	0.62	0.68	0.76	0.80
Ireland	0.79	0.85	0.70	0.26	0.27	0.72	0.77	0.78
Israel	0.82	0.80	0.77	0.86	0.77	0.36	0.75	0.77
Italy	0.83	0.88	0.81	0.63	0.72	0.75	0.79	0.83
Japan	0.97	0.93	0.92	0.89	0.86	0.88	0.89	0.92
Korea	0.92	0.90	0.86	0.98	0.88	0.88	0.88	0.89
Luxembourg	0.77	0.71	0.81	0.55	0.71	0.71	0.67	0.80
Mexico	0.90	0.91	0.90	0.90	0.91	0.87	0.88	0.87
Netherlands	0.81	0.82	0.82	0.55	0.65	0.73	0.74	0.78
New Zealand	0.95	0.84	0.87	0.71	0.50	0.54	0.58	0.83
Norway	0.86	0.78	0.81	0.73	0.71	0.72	0.74	0.75
Poland	0.96	0.97	0.99	1.00	0.90	0.91	0.93	0.96
Portugal	0.71	0.78	0.75	0.65	0.86	0.71	0.77	0.71
Slovak Republic	0.87	0.91	0.94	0.73	0.74	0.80	0.83	0.88
Slovenia	0.92	0.85	0.73	0.77	0.73	0.81	0.86	0.82
Spain	0.86	0.85	0.84	0.68	0.77	0.79	0.81	0.81
Sweden	0.92	0.91	0.67	0.81	0.83	0.83	0.85	0.88
Switzerland	0.91	0.90	0.87	0.85	0.86	0.85	0.84	0.91
Turkey[2]	0.91	0.86	0.91	0.89	0.84	0.85	0.86	0.86
United Kingdom	0.85	0.90	0.83	0.26	0.84	0.81	0.85	0.85
United States	0.90	0.81	0.87	0.54	0.81	0.85	0.88	0.91
Unweighted average								
OECD-Average	**0.87**	**0.85**	**0.86**	**0.69**	**0.73**	**0.74**	**0.79**	**0.83**
OECD-EU 21	**0.85**	**0.85**	**0.85**	**0.65**	**0.73**	**0.76**	**0.79**	**0.83**

Note: ch = children

1. Net income is calculated as gross earnings minus personal income tax and employees' social security contributions plus family benefits. The increase reported in the Table represents a form of elasticity. In a proportional tax system the plus elasticity would equal 1. The more progressive the system at these income levels, the lower is the elasticity.
2. Wage figures are based on the old definition of average worker (ISIC D, Rev. 3).
3. Two-earner family. Assumes a rise in the labour costs associated with the principal earner in the household.

StatLink http://dx.doi.org/10.1787/888933006309

Table I.9. Increase in net income after an increase of 1 currency unit in gross labour cost, 2013[1]

By family-type and wage level (%)

	Single no ch 67 (% AW)	Single no ch 100 (% AW)	Single no ch 167 (% AW)	Single 2 ch 67 (% AW)	Married 2 ch 100-0 (% AW)	Married 2 ch 100-33 (% AW)[3]	Married 2 ch 100-67 (% AW)[3]	Married no ch 100-33 (% AW)[3]
Australia	0.78	0.86	0.87	0.41	0.55	0.42	0.83	0.81
Austria	0.78	0.78	1.20	0.60	0.64	0.64	0.68	0.72
Belgium	0.68	0.69	0.81	0.53	0.57	0.53	0.61	0.59
Canada	0.90	0.53	0.92	0.37	0.11	0.43	0.45	0.50
Chile	1.00	1.00	0.97	0.99	1.00	0.98	1.00	1.00
Czech Republic	0.85	0.89	0.93	0.52	0.58	0.65	0.70	0.86
Denmark	0.94	0.82	0.79	0.67	0.70	0.75	0.77	0.80
Estonia	0.94	0.96	0.98	0.79	0.85	0.89	0.91	0.94
Finland	0.74	0.75	0.83	0.63	0.68	0.66	0.68	0.70
France	0.68	0.79	0.88	0.68	0.88	0.74	0.87	0.88
Germany	0.81	0.79	1.14	0.67	0.72	0.73	0.74	0.81
Greece	0.81	0.86	0.85	0.82	0.90	0.86	0.87	0.85
Hungary	1.00	1.00	1.00	0.68	0.77	0.80	0.85	0.97
Iceland	0.80	0.86	0.83	0.60	0.62	0.68	0.76	0.80
Ireland	0.79	0.85	0.70	0.26	0.27	0.72	0.77	0.78
Israel	0.81	0.79	0.76	0.84	0.76	0.36	0.73	0.76
Italy	0.83	0.88	0.81	0.63	0.72	0.75	0.79	0.83
Japan	0.97	0.93	0.99	0.89	0.86	0.88	0.89	0.92
Korea	0.92	0.90	0.89	0.98	0.88	0.88	0.88	0.89
Luxembourg	0.77	0.71	0.81	0.55	0.71	0.71	0.67	0.80
Mexico	0.96	0.95	0.92	0.96	0.95	0.92	0.92	0.92
Netherlands	0.81	0.82	0.87	0.54	0.65	0.72	0.74	0.77
New Zealand	0.95	0.84	0.87	0.71	0.50	0.54	0.58	0.83
Norway	0.86	0.78	0.81	0.73	0.71	0.72	0.74	0.75
Poland	0.96	0.97	0.99	1.00	0.90	0.91	0.93	0.96
Portugal	0.71	0.78	0.75	0.65	0.86	0.71	0.77	0.71
Slovak Republic	0.87	0.91	0.94	0.73	0.74	0.80	0.83	0.88
Slovenia	0.92	0.85	0.73	0.77	0.73	0.81	0.86	0.82
Spain	0.86	0.85	1.08	0.68	0.77	0.79	0.81	0.81
Sweden	0.92	0.91	0.67	0.81	0.83	0.83	0.85	0.88
Switzerland	0.91	0.90	0.87	0.85	0.86	0.85	0.84	0.91
Turkey[2]	0.91	0.86	0.91	0.89	0.84	0.85	0.86	0.86
United Kingdom	0.82	0.87	0.82	0.25	0.82	0.78	0.82	0.82
United States	0.93	0.82	0.88	0.56	0.82	0.87	0.90	0.94
Unweighted average								
OECD-Average	**0.86**	**0.85**	**0.88**	**0.68**	**0.73**	**0.74**	**0.79**	**0.83**
OECD-EU 21	**0.83**	**0.84**	**0.88**	**0.64**	**0.73**	**0.75**	**0.79**	**0.82**

Note: ch = children

1. Net income is calculated as gross earnings minus personal income tax and employees' social security contributions plus family benefits. The increase reported in the Table represents a form of elasticity. In a proportional tax system the plus elasticity would equal 1. The more progressive the system at these income levels, the lower is the elasticity.
2. Wage figures are based on the old definition of average worker (ISIC D, Rev. 3).
3. Two-earner family. Assumes a rise in the labour costs associated with the principal earner in the household.

StatLink http://dx.doi.org/10.1787/888933006328

Table I.10a. **Annual gross wage and net income, single person, 2013**

In US dollars using PPP, by family-type and wage level

	Single no ch 67 (% AW)		Single no ch 100 (% AW)		Single no ch 167 (% AW)		Single 2 ch 67 (% AW)	
	Total gross earnings before taxes	Net income after taxes	Total gross earnings before taxes	Net income after taxes	Total gross earnings before taxes	Net income after taxes	Total gross earnings before taxes	Net income after taxes
Australia	35 093	29 053	52 639	40 481	87 732	62 139	35 093	38 253
Austria	33 548	24 058	50 322	33 064	83 870	51 139	33 548	30 970
Belgium	37 447	23 911	56 171	32 252	93 618	47 414	37 447	30 478
Canada	25 965	21 411	38 948	30 088	64 914	47 503	25 965	30 901
Chile	12 659	11 773	18 989	17 660	31 648	29 168	12 659	11 888
Czech Republic	14 973	12 184	22 460	17 342	37 433	27 659	14 973	17 187
Denmark	34 515	21 885	51 772	31 976	86 286	48 051	34 515	30 660
Estonia	14 145	11 611	21 217	17 086	35 361	28 037	14 145	13 946
Finland	31 165	23 896	46 748	32 651	77 913	48 868	31 165	28 073
France	29 323	21 577	43 984	31 489	73 307	48 385	29 323	24 887
Germany	38 545	25 224	57 818	34 945	96 363	54 226	38 545	31 711
Greece	21 261	17 098	31 892	23 756	53 154	34 401	23 388	18 288
Hungary	15 287	10 013	22 930	15 019	38 217	25 032	15 287	14 696
Iceland	29 922	22 983	44 883	32 168	74 804	50 087	29 922	26 901
Ireland	26 783	23 420	40 175	32 660	66 958	45 625	26 783	37 047
Israel	21 613	19 413	32 419	27 013	54 031	40 247	21 613	22 217
Italy	26 287	19 185	39 430	27 196	65 717	40 622	26 287	24 842
Japan	31 848	25 472	47 771	37 452	79 619	59 389	31 848	27 811
Korea	31 384	28 273	47 075	40 782	78 459	65 905	31 384	28 568
Luxembourg	38 394	30 246	57 591	40 743	95 985	60 092	38 394	41 232
Mexico	8 334	8 174	12 501	11 281	20 835	17 845	8 334	8 174
Netherlands	38 835	28 702	58 252	40 096	97 086	59 835	38 835	37 636
New Zealand	24 254	21 035	36 381	30 237	60 636	46 831	24 254	28 397
Norway	39 698	29 572	59 548	42 166	99 246	63 925	39 698	35 039
Poland	15 312	11 669	22 968	17 284	38 280	28 512	15 312	12 582
Portugal	19 131	15 448	28 696	20 900	47 827	31 131	19 131	17 782
Slovak Republic	13 144	10 617	19 716	15 227	32 859	24 447	13 144	12 711
Slovenia	19 686	14 067	29 528	19 767	49 214	30 820	19 686	19 889
Spain	25 518	20 823	38 278	29 505	63 796	45 631	25 518	23 098
Sweden	30 259	23 537	45 388	34 044	75 647	49 161	30 259	26 663
Switzerland	42 865	36 782	64 298	53 296	107 164	83 594	42 865	43 604
Turkey[1]	19 624	14 508	29 436	21 042	49 060	33 069	19 624	14 753
United Kingdom	34 170	27 300	51 255	38 918	85 426	59 587	34 170	35 018
United States	32 309	25 349	48 463	36 549	80 772	56 160	32 309	31 843
Unweighted average								
OECD-Average	**26 862**	**20 890**	**40 292**	**29 592**	**67 154**	**45 428**	**26 924**	**25 816**
OECD-EU 21	**26 558**	**19 832**	**39 838**	**27 901**	**66 396**	**42 318**	**26 660**	**25 209**

Note: ch = children

1. Wage figures are based on the old definition of average worker (ISIC D, Rev. 3).

StatLink http://dx.doi.org/10.1787/888933006347

Table I.10b. Insert Annual gross wage and net income, married couple, 2013

In US dollars using PPP, by family-type and wage level

	Married 2 ch 100-0 (% AW)		Married 2 ch 100-33 (% AW)[2]		Married 2 ch 100-67 (% AW)[2]		Married no ch 100-33 (% AW)[2]	
	Total gross earnings before taxes	Net income after taxes	Total gross earnings before taxes	Net income after taxes	Total gross earnings before taxes	Net income after taxes	Total gross earnings before taxes	Net income after taxes
Australia	52 639	46 334	70 186	59 525	87 732	69 534	70 186	57 081
Austria	50 322	40 011	67 096	53 585	83 870	63 287	67 096	47 445
Belgium	56 171	43 034	74 894	54 585	93 618	62 054	74 894	48 658
Canada	38 948	35 471	51 931	44 109	64 914	52 886	51 931	41 871
Chile	18 989	17 660	25 318	24 111	31 648	29 547	25 318	23 546
Czech Republic	22 460	23 926	29 946	28 212	37 433	33 145	29 946	24 005
Denmark	51 772	37 502	69 029	46 850	86 286	57 122	69 029	43 589
Estonia	21 217	19 244	28 289	24 719	35 361	30 194	28 289	23 222
Finland	46 748	35 546	62 330	49 267	77 913	59 442	62 330	46 372
France	43 984	36 009	58 645	47 461	73 307	56 575	58 645	43 155
Germany	57 818	45 687	77 091	56 503	96 363	66 539	77 091	50 444
Greece	38 271	27 073	51 027	37 725	63 784	46 727	46 775	35 416
Hungary	22 930	19 419	30 574	24 425	38 217	29 432	30 574	20 026
Iceland	44 883	39 108	59 843	47 347	74 804	55 961	59 843	45 774
Ireland	40 175	41 459	53 566	51 052	66 958	59 951	53 566	47 181
Israel	32 419	28 118	43 225	38 912	54 031	48 474	43 225	37 441
Italy	39 430	32 200	52 574	41 537	65 717	49 532	52 574	38 394
Japan	47 771	40 491	63 695	52 883	79 619	65 263	63 695	50 544
Korea	47 075	42 050	62 767	56 095	78 459	70 068	62 767	55 120
Luxembourg	57 591	55 421	76 788	70 028	95 985	81 598	76 788	61 840
Mexico	12 501	11 281	16 668	15 798	20 835	19 454	16 668	15 798
Netherlands	58 252	43 987	77 669	60 341	97 086	73 566	77 669	56 310
New Zealand	36 381	35 503	48 508	43 601	60 636	51 029	48 508	40 912
Norway	59 548	46 311	79 397	61 277	99 246	74 383	79 397	58 632
Poland	22 968	18 824	30 624	24 572	38 280	30 186	30 624	23 339
Portugal	28 696	24 939	38 261	32 735	47 827	37 467	38 261	30 896
Slovak Republic	19 716	18 718	26 287	23 097	32 859	27 938	26 287	21 003
Slovenia	29 528	26 367	39 371	31 771	49 214	37 525	39 371	27 434
Spain	38 278	32 416	51 037	42 160	63 796	51 739	51 037	41 454
Sweden	45 388	37 170	60 518	49 924	75 647	60 707	60 518	46 797
Switzerland	64 298	61 835	85 731	79 635	107 164	96 014	85 731	73 031
Turkey[1]	29 436	21 450	39 248	28 302	49 060	34 978	39 248	28 056
United Kingdom	51 255	41 451	68 340	57 133	85 426	68 751	68 340	54 600
United States	48 463	42 433	64 618	53 854	80 772	65 276	64 618	50 320
Unweighted average								
OECD-Average	**40 480**	**34 366**	**53 973**	**44 504**	**67 467**	**53 422**	**53 848**	**41 462**
OECD-EU 21	**40 141**	**33 353**	**53 522**	**43 223**	**66 902**	**51 594**	**53 319**	**39 599**

Note: ch = children

1. Wage figures are based on the old definition of average worker (ISIC D, Rev. 3).
2. Two-earner family.

StatLink http://dx.doi.org/10.1787/888933006366

Table I.11a. **Insert Annual labour costs and net income, single person, 2013**

In US dollars using PPP, by family-type and wage level

	Single no ch 67 (% AW)		Single no ch 100 (% AW)		Single no ch 167 (% AW)		Single 2 ch 67 (% AW)	
	Total gross labour costs before taxes	Net income after taxes	Total gross labour costs before taxes	Net income after taxes	Total gross labour costs before taxes	Net income after taxes	Total gross labour costs before taxes	Net income after taxes
Australia	37 178	29 053	55 766	40 481	92 944	62 139	37 178	38 253
Austria	43 320	24 058	64 980	33 064	106 387	51 139	43 320	30 970
Belgium	47 946	23 911	72 974	32 252	121 251	47 414	47 946	30 478
Canada	29 058	21 411	43 643	30 088	70 994	47 503	29 058	30 901
Chile	12 659	11 773	18 989	17 660	31 648	29 168	12 659	11 888
Czech Republic	20 064	12 184	30 096	17 342	50 160	27 659	20 064	17 187
Denmark	34 515	21 805	51 772	31 976	86 286	48 051	34 515	30 660
Estonia	18 954	11 611	28 430	17 086	47 384	28 037	18 954	13 946
Finland	38 271	23 896	57 406	32 651	95 677	48 868	38 271	28 073
France	39 652	21 577	61 648	31 489	105 445	48 385	39 652	24 887
Germany	45 975	25 224	68 962	34 945	111 153	54 226	45 975	31 711
Greece	27 100	17 098	40 650	23 756	67 750	34 401	29 810	18 288
Hungary	19 644	10 013	29 465	15 019	49 109	25 032	19 644	14 696
Iceland	32 223	22 983	48 334	32 168	80 557	50 087	32 223	26 901
Ireland	29 662	23 420	44 494	32 660	74 156	45 625	29 662	37 047
Israel	22 538	19 413	34 046	27 013	57 064	40 247	22 538	22 217
Italy	34 720	19 185	52 080	27 196	86 799	40 622	34 720	24 842
Japan	36 527	25 472	54 790	37 452	90 716	59 389	36 527	27 811
Korea	34 597	28 273	51 895	40 782	85 501	65 905	34 597	28 568
Luxembourg	43 120	30 246	64 680	40 743	107 801	60 092	43 120	41 232
Mexico	9 489	8 174	13 964	11 281	22 930	17 845	9 489	8 174
Netherlands	42 300	28 702	63 585	40 096	102 976	59 835	42 300	37 636
New Zealand	24 254	21 035	36 381	30 237	60 636	46 831	24 254	28 397
Norway	44 859	29 572	67 289	42 166	112 148	63 925	44 859	35 039
Poland	17 881	11 669	26 822	17 284	44 703	28 512	17 881	12 582
Portugal	23 674	15 448	35 511	20 900	59 185	31 131	23 674	17 782
Slovak Republic	17 245	10 617	25 867	15 227	43 111	24 447	17 245	12 711
Slovenia	22 855	14 067	34 282	19 767	57 137	30 820	22 855	19 889
Spain	33 148	20 823	49 723	29 505	81 873	45 631	33 148	23 098
Sweden	39 766	23 537	59 649	34 044	99 416	49 161	39 766	26 663
Switzerland	45 545	36 782	68 317	53 296	113 770	83 594	45 545	43 604
Turkey[1]	22 862	14 508	34 293	21 042	57 154	33 069	22 862	14 753
United Kingdom	37 354	27 300	56 797	38 918	95 683	59 587	37 354	35 018
United States	35 832	25 349	53 223	36 549	88 003	56 160	35 832	31 843
Unweighted average								
OECD-Average	**31 317**	**20 890**	**47 082**	**29 592**	**78 162**	**45 428**	**31 397**	**25 816**
OECD-EU 21	**32 246**	**19 832**	**48 565**	**27 901**	**80 640**	**42 318**	**32 375**	**25 209**

Note: ch = children

1. Wage figures are based on the old definition of average worker (ISIC D, Rev. 3).

StatLink http://dx.doi.org/10.1787/888933006385

Table I.11b. **Insert Annual labour costs and net income, married couple, 2013**

In US dollars using PPP, by family-type and wage level

	Married 2 ch 100-0 (% AW)		Married 2 ch 100-33 (% AW)[2]		Married 2 ch 100-67 (% AW)[2]		Married no ch 100-33 (% AW)[2]	
	Total gross labour costs before taxes	Net income after taxes	Total gross labour costs before taxes	Net income after taxes	Total gross labour costs before taxes	Net income after taxes	Total gross labour costs before taxes	Net income after taxes
Australia	55 766	46 334	74 355	59 525	92 944	69 534	74 355	57 081
Austria	64 980	40 011	86 640	53 585	108 300	63 287	86 640	47 445
Belgium	72 974	43 034	94 528	54 585	120 921	62 054	94 528	48 658
Canada	43 643	35 471	58 102	44 109	72 701	52 886	58 102	41 871
Chile	18 989	17 660	25 318	24 111	31 648	29 547	25 318	23 546
Czech Republic	30 096	23 926	40 128	28 212	50 160	33 145	40 128	24 005
Denmark	51 772	37 502	69 029	46 850	86 286	57 122	69 029	43 589
Estonia	28 430	19 244	37 907	24 719	47 384	30 194	37 907	23 222
Finland	57 406	35 546	76 542	49 267	95 677	59 442	76 542	46 372
France	61 648	36 009	78 386	47 461	101 300	56 575	78 386	43 155
Germany	68 962	45 687	91 950	56 503	114 937	66 539	91 950	50 444
Greece	48 780	27 073	65 040	37 725	81 299	46 727	59 620	35 416
Hungary	29 465	19 419	38 267	24 425	49 109	29 432	38 267	20 026
Iceland	48 334	39 108	64 445	47 347	80 557	55 961	64 445	45 774
Ireland	44 494	41 459	59 023	51 052	74 156	59 951	59 023	47 181
Israel	34 046	28 118	45 225	38 912	56 584	48 474	45 225	37 441
Italy	52 080	32 200	69 439	41 537	86 799	49 532	69 439	38 394
Japan	54 790	40 491	73 053	52 883	91 317	65 263	73 053	50 544
Korea	51 895	42 050	69 193	56 095	86 491	70 068	69 193	55 120
Luxembourg	64 680	55 421	86 241	70 028	107 801	81 598	86 241	61 840
Mexico	13 964	11 281	19 017	15 798	23 454	19 454	19 017	15 798
Netherlands	63 585	43 987	84 632	60 341	105 885	73 566	84 632	56 310
New Zealand	36 381	35 503	48 508	43 601	60 636	51 029	48 508	40 912
Norway	67 289	46 311	89 718	61 277	112 148	74 383	89 718	58 632
Poland	26 822	18 824	35 762	24 572	44 703	30 186	35 762	23 339
Portugal	35 511	24 939	47 348	32 735	59 185	37 467	47 348	30 896
Slovak Republic	25 867	18 718	34 489	23 097	43 111	27 938	34 489	21 003
Slovenia	34 282	26 367	45 710	31 771	57 137	37 525	45 710	27 434
Spain	49 723	32 416	66 297	42 160	82 871	51 739	66 297	41 454
Sweden	59 649	37 170	79 532	49 924	99 416	60 707	79 532	46 797
Switzerland	68 317	61 835	91 089	79 635	113 861	96 014	91 089	73 031
Turkey[1]	34 293	21 450	45 723	28 302	57 154	34 978	45 723	28 056
United Kingdom	56 797	41 451	74 709	57 133	94 152	68 751	74 709	54 600
United States	53 223	42 433	71 665	53 854	89 055	65 276	71 665	50 320
Unweighted average								
OECD-Average	**47 322**	**34 366**	**62 853**	**44 504**	**78 798**	**53 422**	**62 694**	**41 462**
OECD-EU 21	**48 953**	**33 353**	**64 838**	**43 223**	**81 457**	**51 594**	**64 580**	**39 599**

Note: ch = children

1. Wage figures are based on the old definition of average worker (ISIC D, Rev. 3.).
2. Two-earner family.

StatLink http://dx.doi.org/10.1787/888933006404

Graphical exposition of the 2013 estimated tax burden

The graphs in this section show the estimated tax burden on labour income in 2013 for gross wage earnings between 50 per cent and 250 per cent of the average wage (AW). For each OECD member country, there are separate graphs for four family types: single taxpayers without children, single parents with two children, one-earner married couples without children and one-earner married couples with two children. The net personal average and marginal tax rates ((the change in) personal income taxes and employee social security contributions net of cash benefits as a percentage of (the change in) gross wage earnings) are included in the graphs that show respectively the average and the marginal tax wedge.*

The different components of the tax wedges are also presented; central income taxes, local income taxes, employee social security contributions, employer social security contributions (including payroll taxes where applicable) and family benefits as a percentage of total labour costs (TLC). It should be noted that a decreasing share in total labour costs does not necessarily imply that the corresponding taxes or cash benefits are decreasing in cash terms income. A decreasing share in the tax wedge only implies that the corresponding taxes and benefits are not increasing as rapidly as total labour costs.

Low-income families with children are treated favourably by the tax-benefit system in many OECD countries. When cash benefits are also taken into account, single parents and one-earner married couples with 2 children do not pay income taxes and employee social security contributions up to income levels between 50 and 85 per cent of the AW in 13 OECD member countries. The net personal average tax rate for single parents with two children becomes positive at 87 per cent of the AW (Average Wage) in Canada, 91 per cent of the AW in the Czech Republic, 96 per cent of the AW in New Zealand and 104 per cent of the AW in Ireland. The net personal average tax rate for one-earner married couples with 2 children becomes positive at 88 per cent of the AW in Canada and Luxembourg, 96 per

* The marginal tax wedges in the graphs are calculated in a slightly different manner than the marginal tax rates that are included in the rest of the *Taxing Wages* publication. In *Taxing Wages*, marginal rates are usually calculated by increasing gross earnings by one currency unit (except for the spouse in the one-earner married couple whose earnings increase by 1/3 of the average wage). However, the "+1 currency unit" approach requires the calculation of marginal rates for every single currency unit within the income range included in the graphs. It otherwise would not be correct to draw a line through the different data points because the data for the income levels in between the different points would be missing. In order to reduce the required number of calculations, the marginal rates that are shown in the graphs are calculated by increasing gross earnings by 1 percentage point – each line in the graph therefore consists of 200 data points – instead of 1 currency unit.

cent of the AW in New Zealand, 106 per cent of the AW in Ireland and 117 per cent of the AW in the Czech Republic.

Negative central government income taxes are observed in the Czech Republic, Germany, the Slovak Republic and the United Kingdom because of the non-wastable child tax credits, in Canada because of the non-wastable working income tax benefit, in Mexico because of the non-wastable employment subsidy credit, in Israel because of the non-wastable earned income tax credit for families with children, in Sweden because of the non-wastable earned income tax credit and in the United States because of the non-wastable earned income credit and the child tax credit.

There are large differences in cash benefits across OECD countries. They represent 25 per cent or more of total labour costs for low-income single parents and/or one-earner married couples with two children in Australia, Canada, Denmark, Ireland, Luxembourg, New Zealand and Slovenia.

The marginal tax wedge is relatively flat across the earnings distribution in some countries because of the flat social security contribution and personal income tax rates. Single taxpayers without children face a flat marginal tax wedge of 42.2 per cent in Estonia (over the 50-250% income range) and 48.6 per cent in the Czech Republic. The tax wedge is also relatively flat in Chile, Hungary, Iceland, Poland, the Slovak Republic and the United Kingdom. In Chile, it is 7.0 per cent on earnings below 123 per cent of the AW and 10.2 per cent on earnings between 124 and 250 per cent of the AW. In Hungary, it is 55.9 per cent on earnings below 55 per cent of the AW and 49.0 per cent between 56 and 250 per cent of the AW. In Iceland, it is 43.0 per cent on earnings below 149 per cent of the AW and 48.3 per cent on earnings between 150 and 250 per cent of the AW. In Poland, it is 37.2 per cent on earnings below 242 per cent of the AW and 47.6 per cent on earnings between 243 and 250 per cent of the AW. In the Slovak Republic, it is 46.5 per cent on earnings below 224 per cent of the AW and 49.7 per cent on earnings between 225 and 250 per cent of the AW. In the United Kingdom, it is 40.3 per cent on earnings below 116 per cent of the AW and then 49.0 per cent on earnings between 117 and 250 per cent of the AW.

In Turkey, single taxpayers without children face a constant marginal tax wedge of 42.3 per cent from 50 per cent to 96 per cent of the AW, and of 47.4 per cent on earnings ranging from 97 per cent to 245 per cent of the AW. It drops to 27.8 per cent on earnings between 246 and 250 per cent of the AW. In Denmark, the marginal tax wedge is 56.2 per cent on earnings exceeding 115 per cent of the AW. In France and in Ireland, the marginal tax wedges are constant on earnings exceeding the AW with respectively 59.8 per cent and 56.7 per cent. In Belgium, the reduction in social security contribution rates offsets the impact of the progressivity of the personal income tax system for single taxpayers without children. The marginal tax wedge is about 68 per cent for single taxpayers with above average earnings in 2013.

Social security contributions are levied at flat rates in many OECD countries. Some countries have an earnings ceiling above which no additional social security contributions have to be paid. The marginal employer social security rates fall to zero as a result of income ceilings in Germany, Luxembourg, the Netherlands, Spain and Turkey and to a large extent in the United States (the rate drops from 7.65 per cent to 1.45 per cent on earnings above USD 113 700). Employee social security ceilings are implemented in Austria, Canada, Germany, the Netherlands, Spain, Sweden and Turkey and to a large extent in Luxembourg (employee social security contributions drop to 1.4 per cent on earnings above

EUR 112 451.28), the United Kingdom (employee national insurance contributions drop to 2 per cent of earnings above GBP 41 450) and the United States (the rate drops from 6.2 per cent to 1.45 per cent on earnings above USD 113 700).

Taxpayers in some OECD countries face marginal social security contribution rates as percentage of total labour costs that decrease as income increases (for gross earnings between 50 per cent and 250 per cent of the AW). For single taxpayers without children, this can be observed in Austria, Belgium, Canada, France, Germany, Hungary, Japan, Korea, the Netherlands and Switzerland.

Taxpayers face marginal tax rates and wedges of about 80 per cent or more in several of OECD countries. This is the case for low-income taxpayers without children in France, Greece, Ireland, Mexico, Portugal and Slovenia. They also apply to families with children only (at particular income levels) in Australia, Belgium, Canada, Chile, the Czech Republic, Greece, Ireland, Italy, Japan, Mexico, Portugal, the Slovak Republic, Slovenia and Spain. In many countries, these high marginal tax rates for low-income taxpayers are partly the result of a reduction in benefits, allowances or tax credits that are targeted at low-income taxpayers and that are decreasing in income.

The zigzag movement in the marginal tax burdens arises when the taxes, social security contributions, and/or cash benefits, and/or the changes in these amounts vary over (small changes in) the income range in a non-continuous way. This is the case in Germany and Sweden because of the rounding rules; because of the discrete characteristics of the income tax credit in Greece and of the PAYE (Pay As You Earn) tax credit, the spouse tax credit and the child transfers in Italy; in Luxembourg and Switzerland because of the rounding of taxable income; and in the United States because of the truncation of gross earnings in the calculation of the child tax credit.

Australia 2013: Average tax wedge decomposition

By level of gross earnings expressed as a % of the average wage

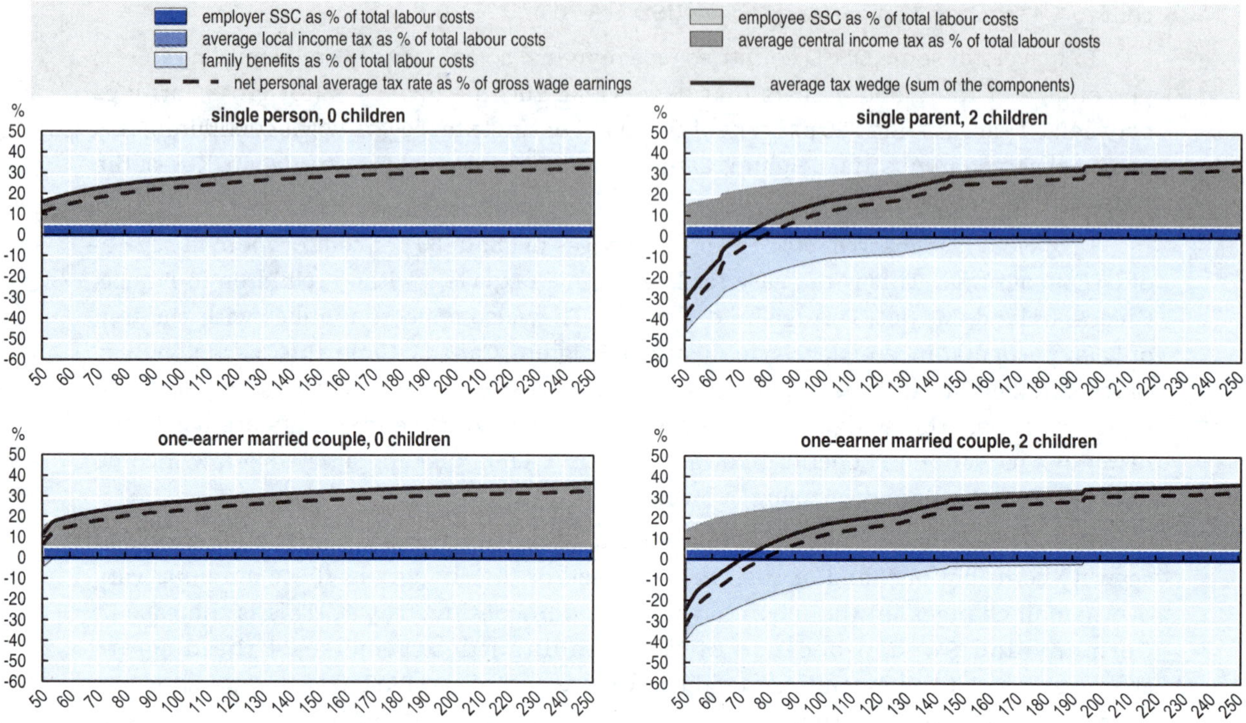

StatLink http://dx.doi.org/10.1787/888933004124

Australia 2013: Marginal tax wedge decomposition

By level of gross earnings expressed as a % of the average wage

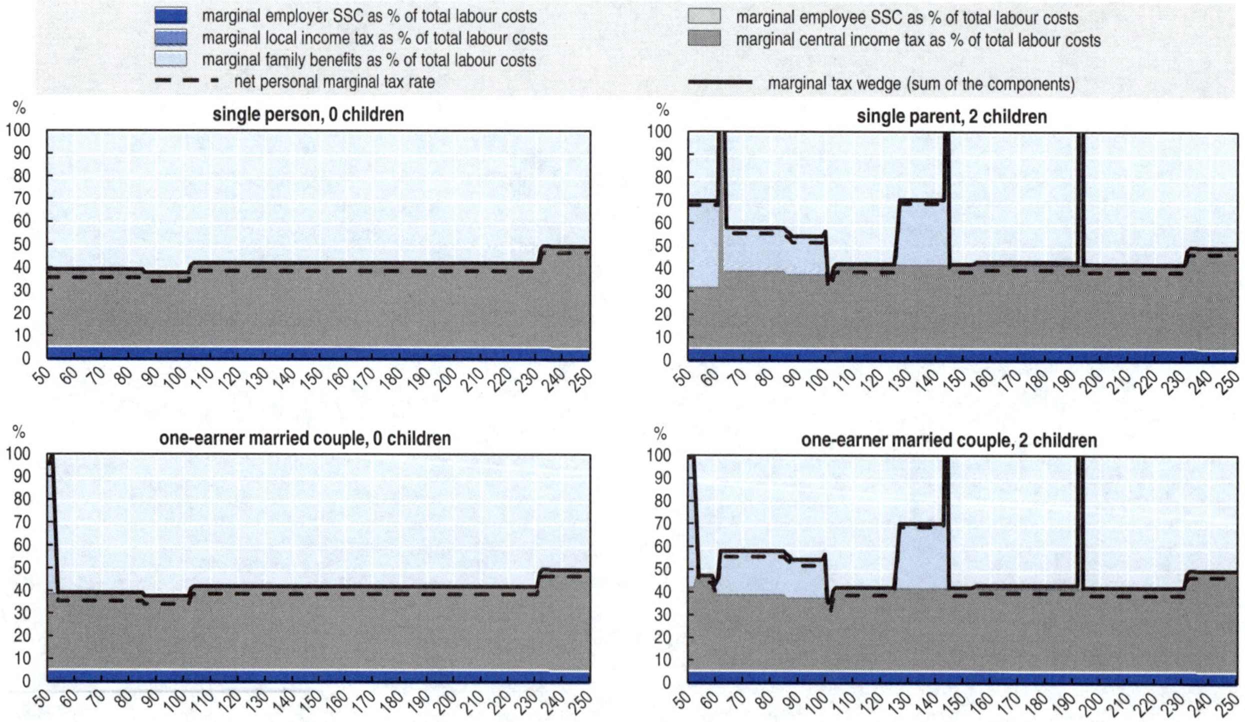

StatLink http://dx.doi.org/10.1787/888933004770

Austria 2013: Average tax wedge decomposition

By level of gross earnings expressed as a % of the average wage

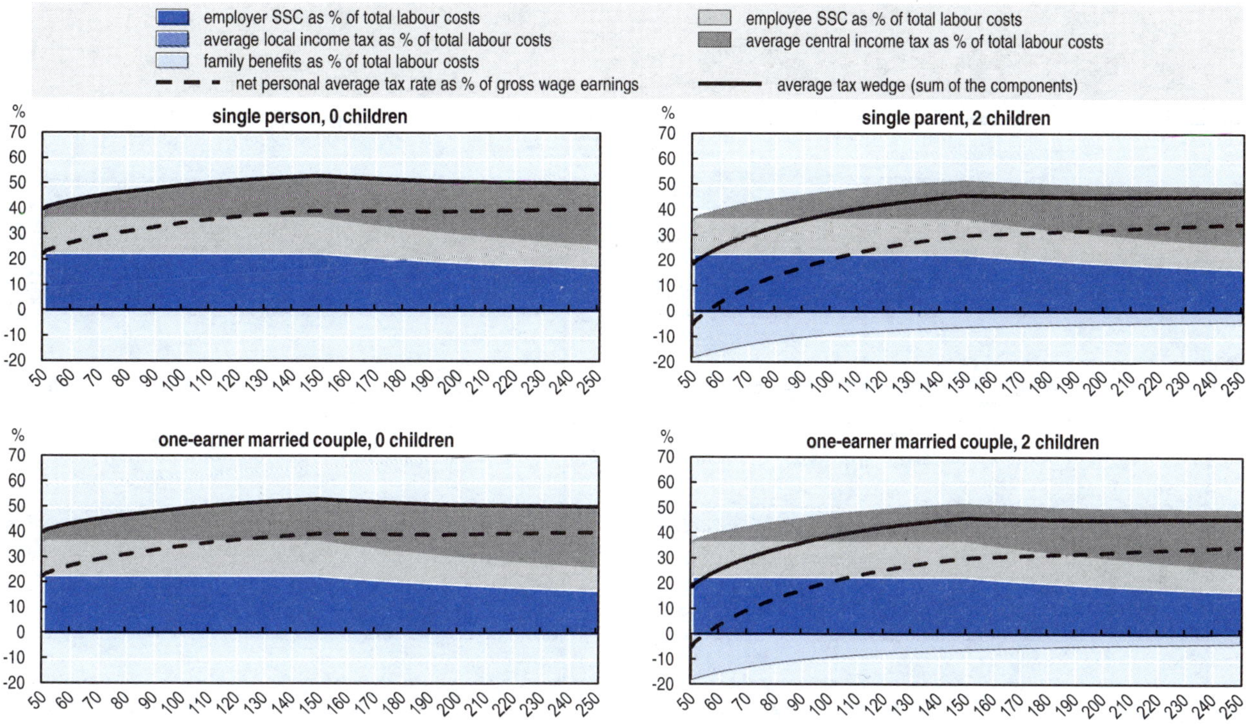

StatLink http://dx.doi.org/10.1787/888933004143

Austria 2013: Marginal tax wedge decomposition

By level of gross earnings expressed as a % of the average wage

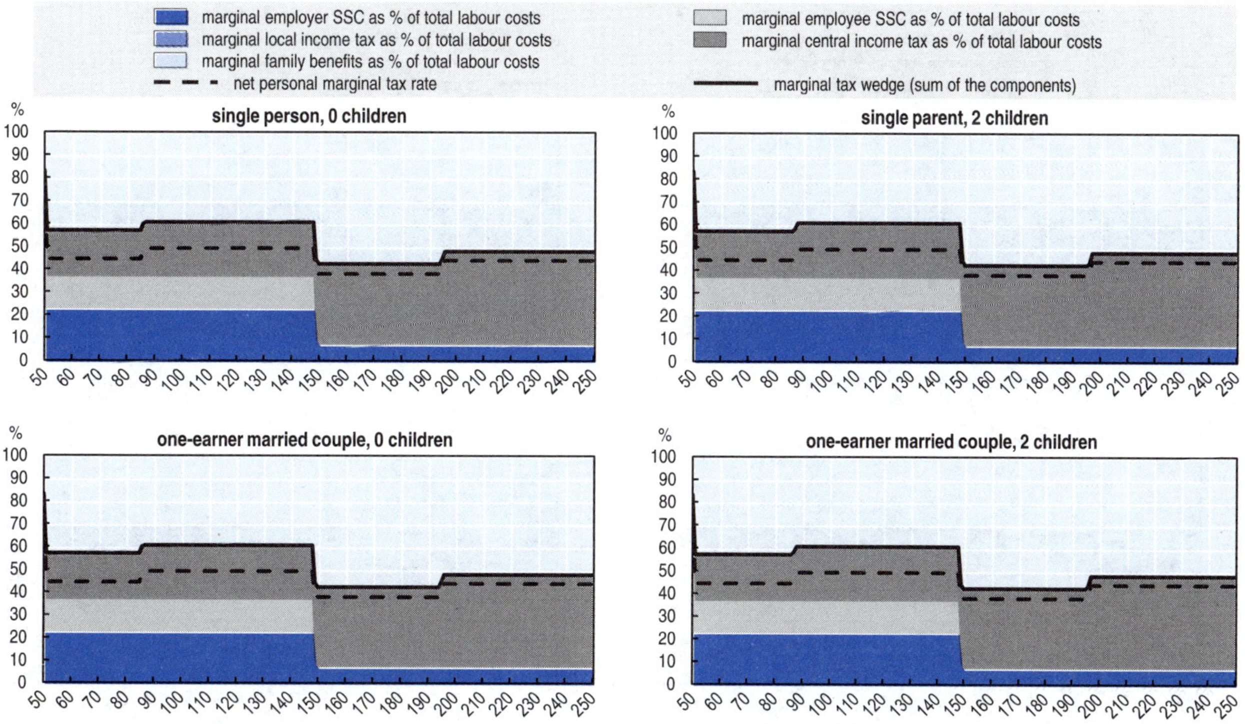

StatLink http://dx.doi.org/10.1787/888933004789

Belgium 2013: Average tax wedge decomposition

By level of gross earnings expressed as a % of the average wage

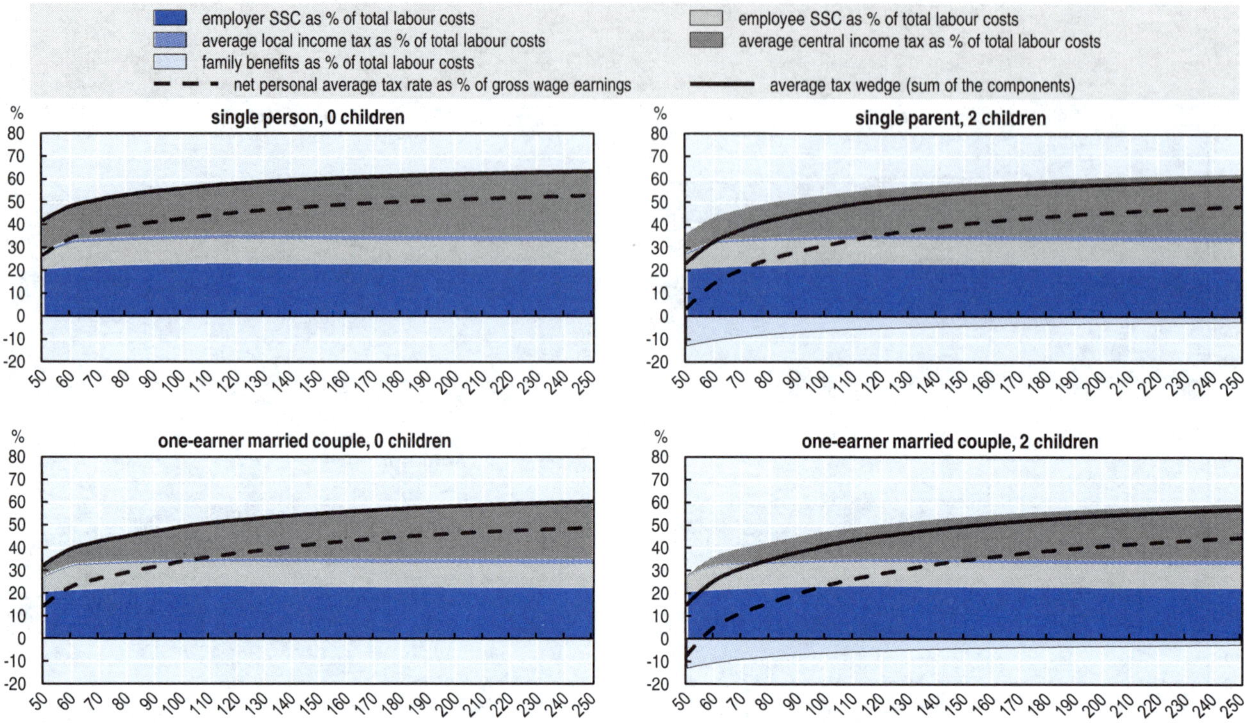

StatLink http://dx.doi.org/10.1787/888933004162

Belgium 2013: Marginal tax wedge decomposition

By level of gross earnings expressed as a % of the average wage

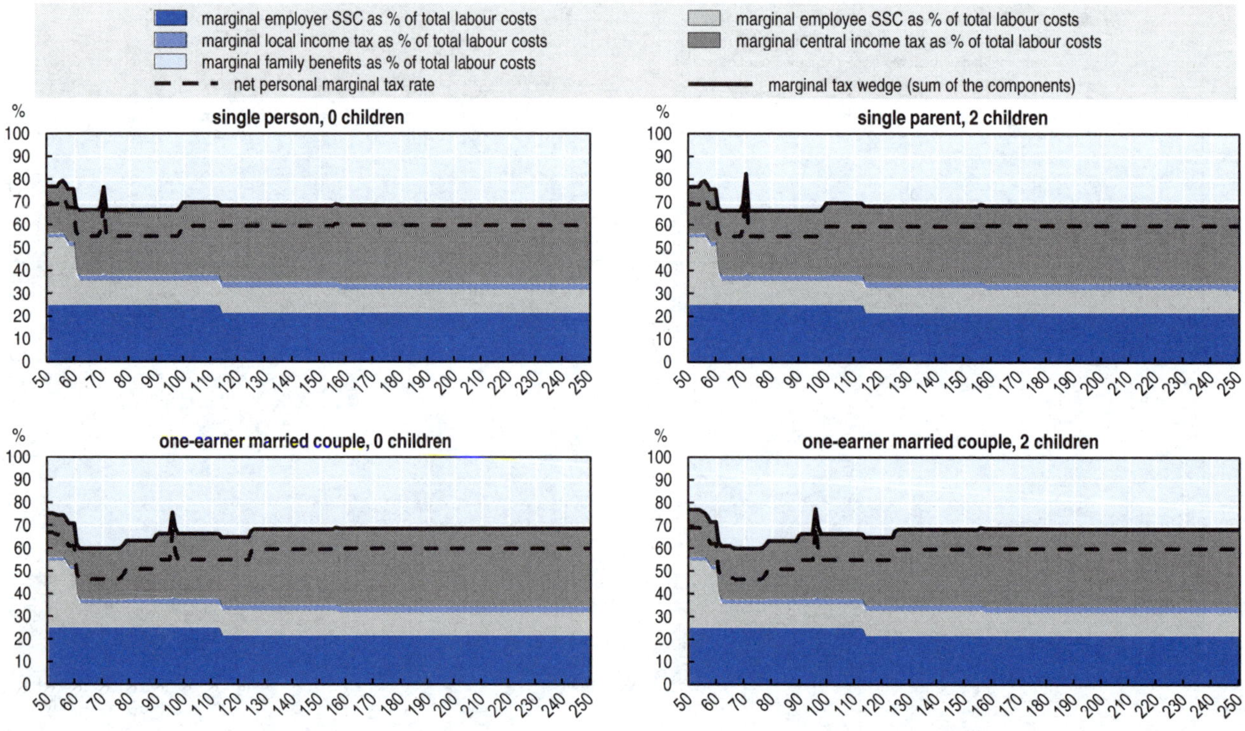

StatLink http://dx.doi.org/10.1787/888933004808

Canada 2013: Average tax wedge decomposition

By level of gross earnings expressed as a % of the average wage

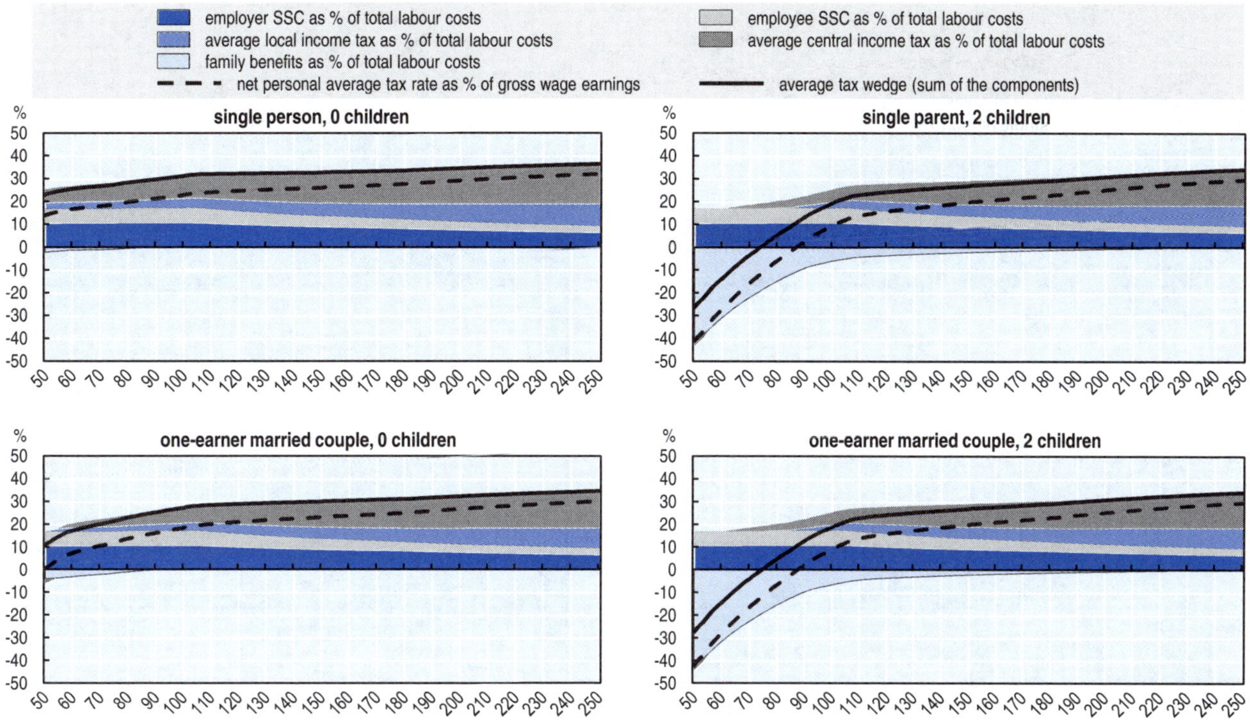

StatLink http://dx.doi.org/10.1787/888933004181

Canada 2013: Marginal tax wedge decomposition

By level of gross earnings expressed as a % of the average wage

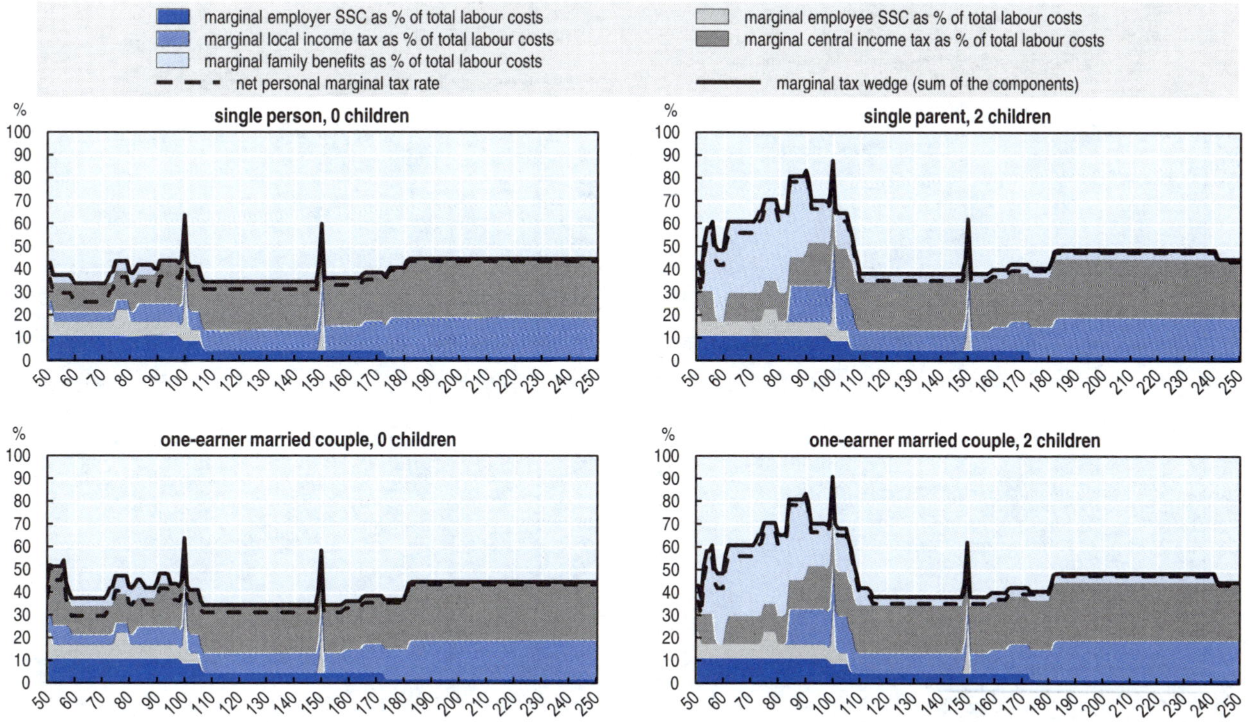

StatLink http://dx.doi.org/10.1787/888933004827

Chile 2013: Average tax wedge decomposition

By level of gross earnings expressed as a % of the average wage

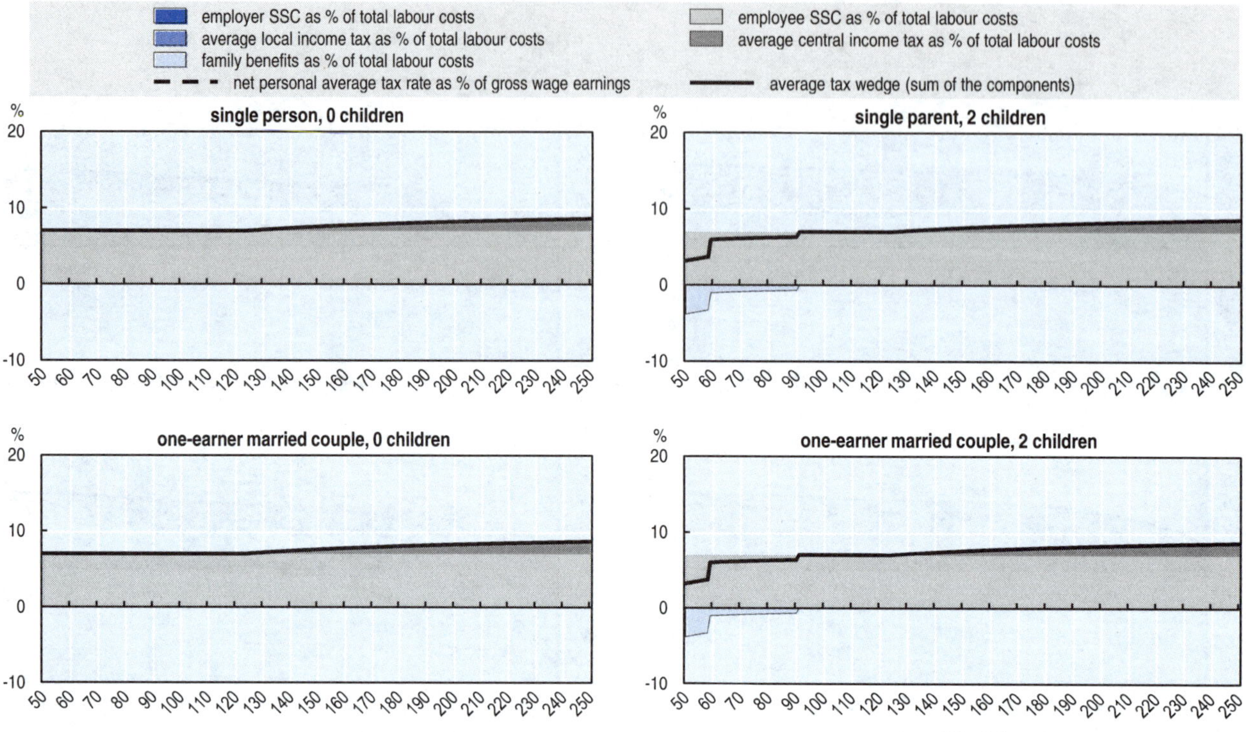

StatLink http://dx.doi.org/10.1787/888933004219

Chile 2013: Marginal tax wedge decomposition

By level of gross earnings expressed as a % of the average wage

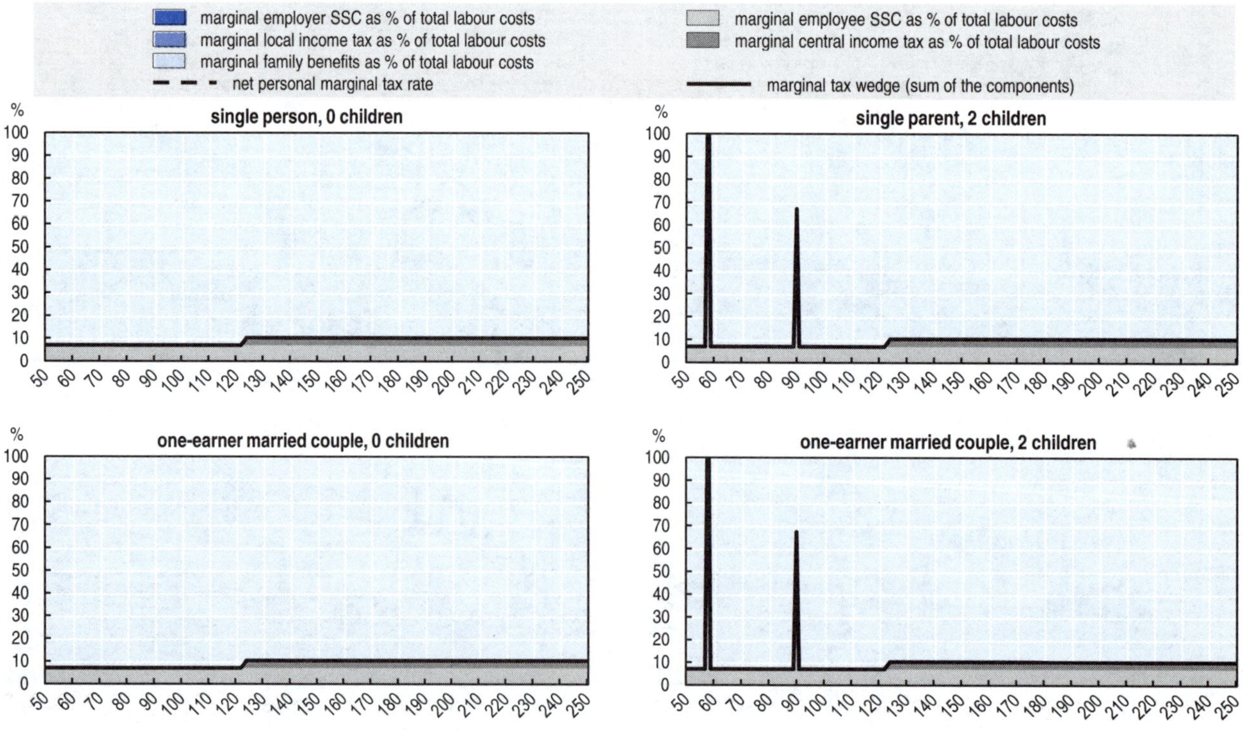

StatLink http://dx.doi.org/10.1787/888933004865

Czech Republic 2013: Average tax wedge decomposition

By level of gross earnings expressed as a % of the average wage

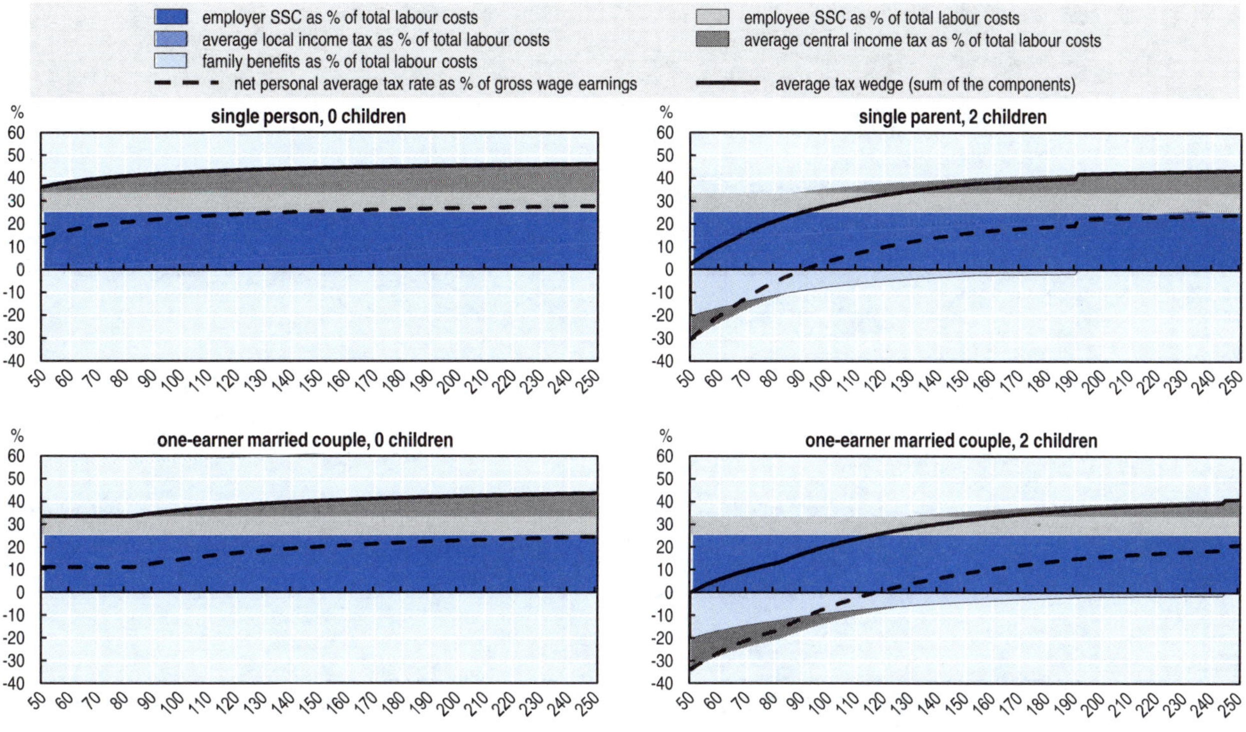

StatLink http://dx.doi.org/10.1787/888933004238

Czech Republic 2013: Marginal tax wedge decomposition

By level of gross earnings expressed as a % of the average wage

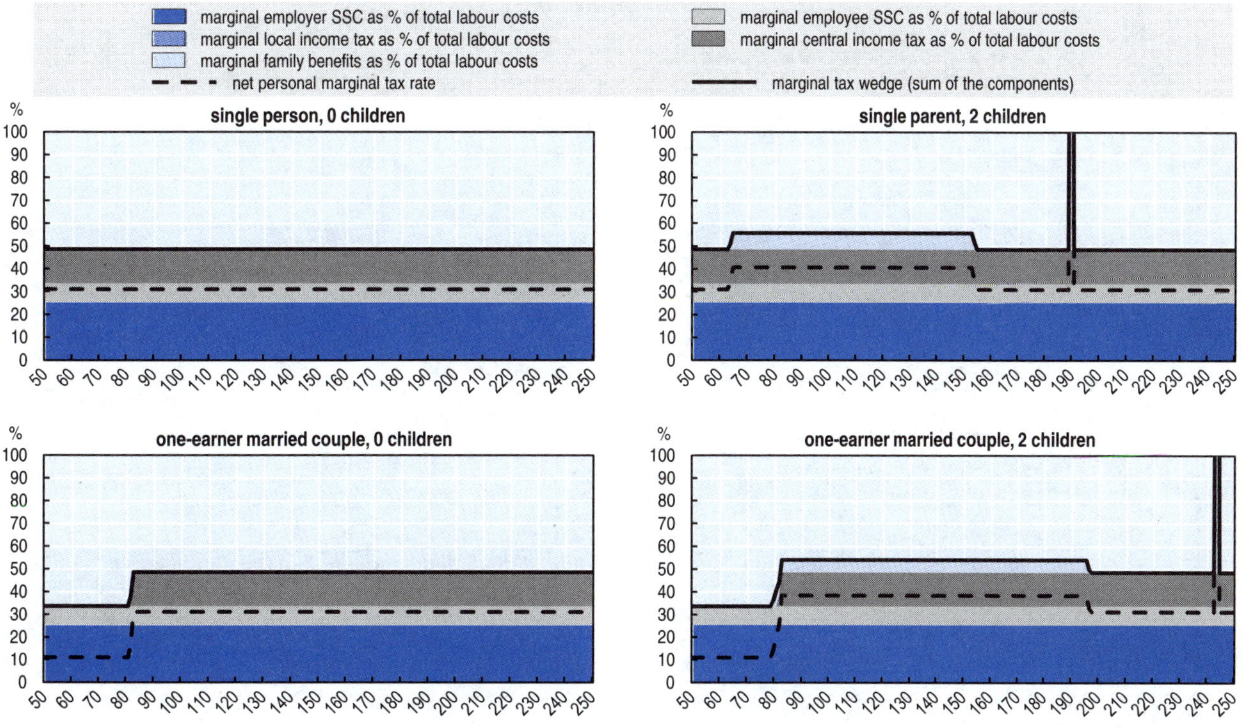

StatLink http://dx.doi.org/10.1787/888933004884

Denmark 2013: Average tax wedge decomposition

By level of gross earnings expressed as a % of the average wage

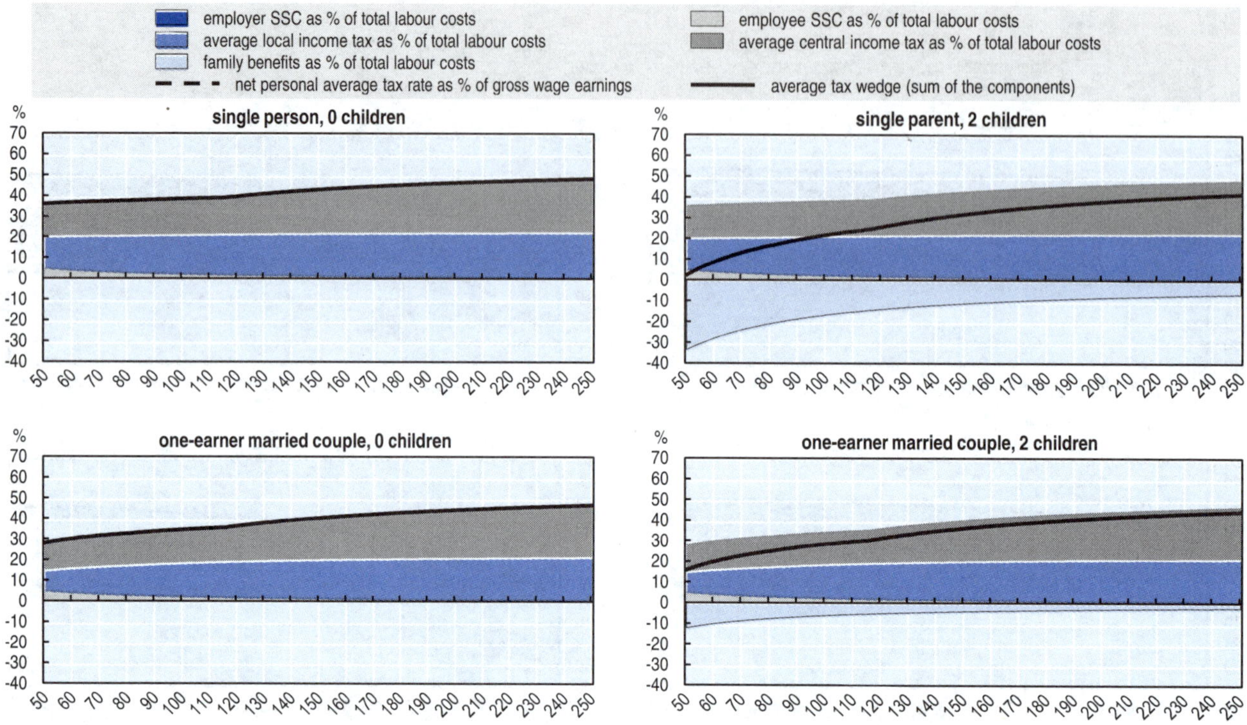

StatLink http://dx.doi.org/10.1787/888933004276

Denmark 2013: Marginal tax wedge decomposition

By level of gross earnings expressed as a % of the average wage

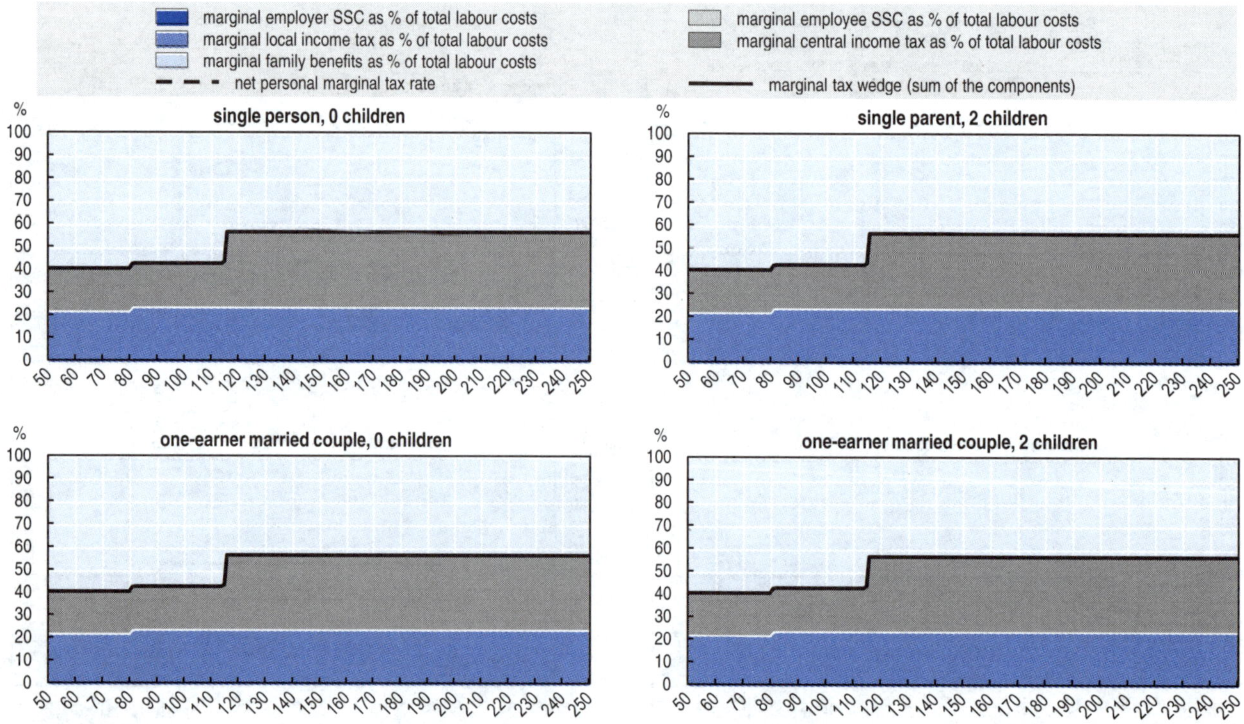

StatLink http://dx.doi.org/10.1787/888933004922

Estonia 2013: Average tax wedge decomposition

By level of gross earnings expressed as a % of the average wage

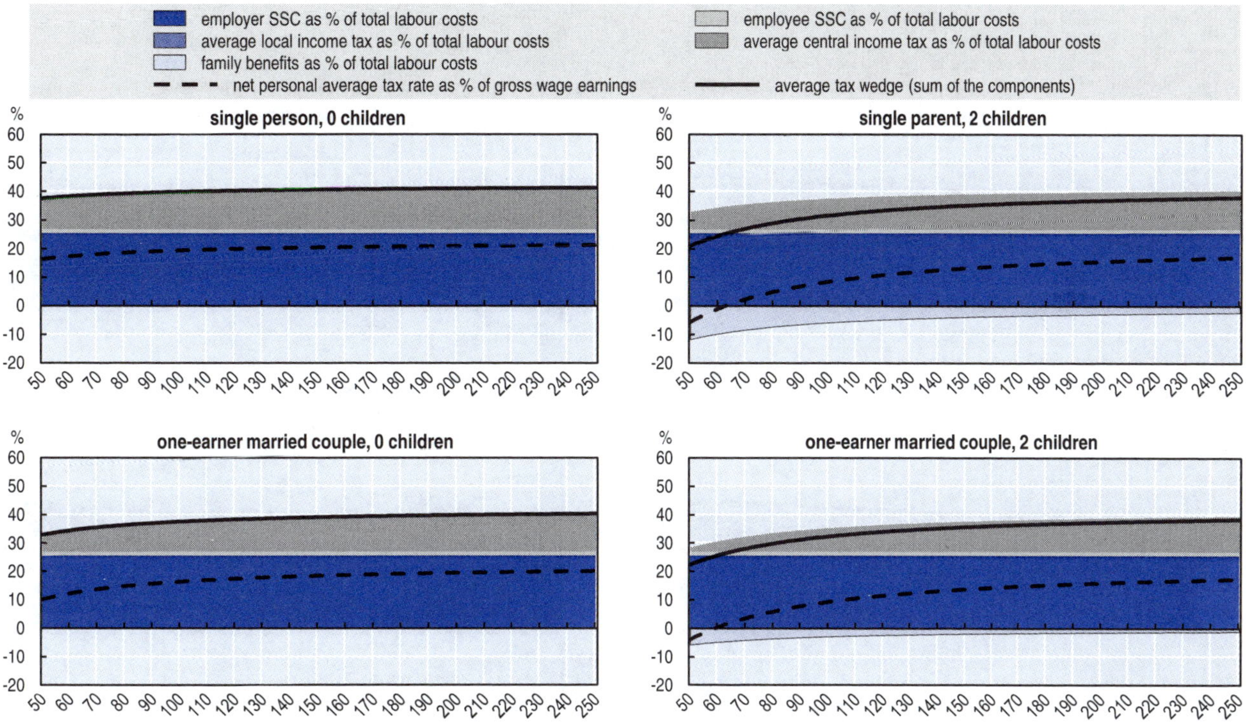

StatLink http://dx.doi.org/10.1787/888933004314

Estonia 2013: Marginal tax wedge decomposition

By level of gross earnings expressed as a % of the average wage

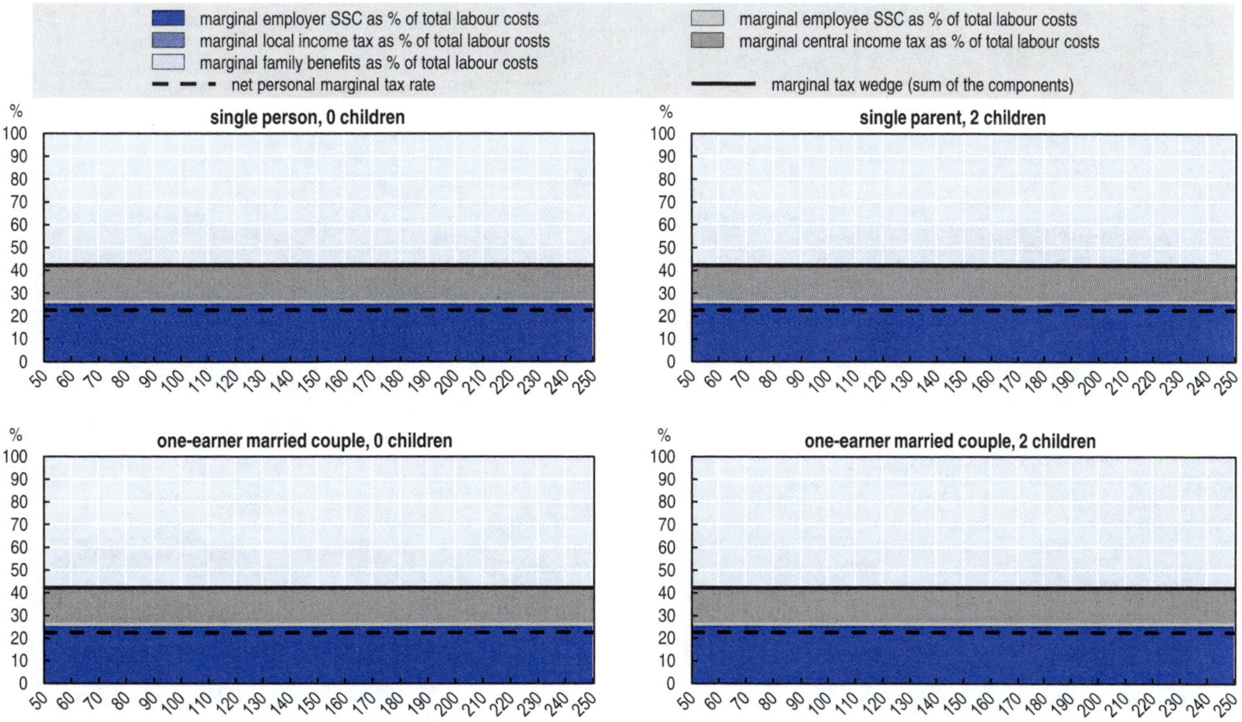

StatLink http://dx.doi.org/10.1787/888933004960

Finland 2013: Average tax wedge decomposition

By level of gross earnings expressed as a % of the average wage

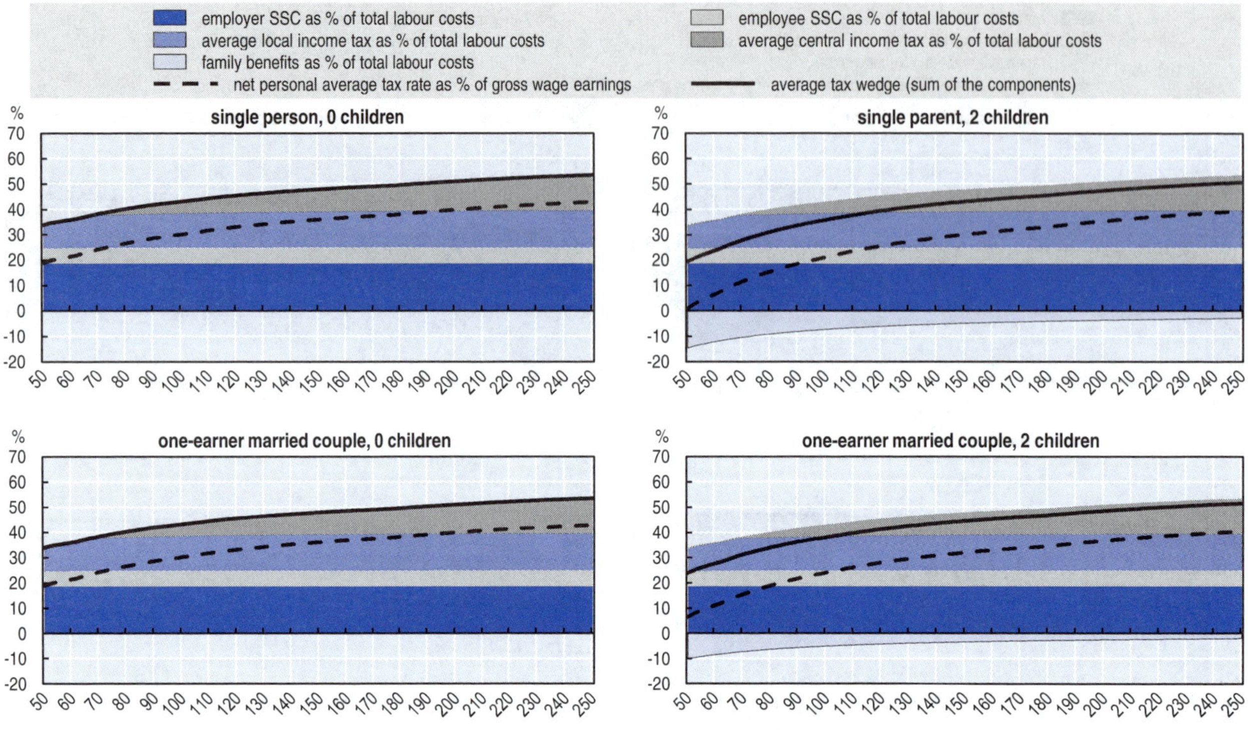

StatLink http://dx.doi.org/10.1787/888933004333

Finland 2013: Marginal tax wedge decomposition

By level of gross earnings expressed as a % of the average wage

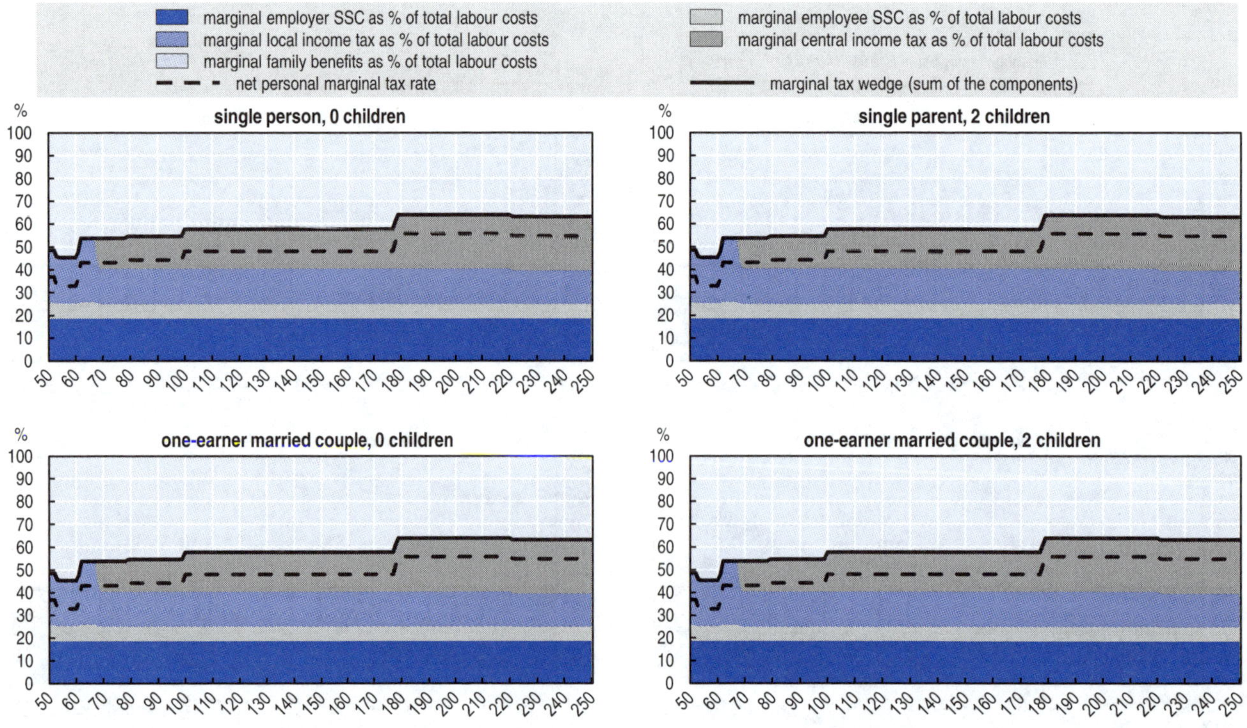

StatLink http://dx.doi.org/10.1787/888933004979

France 2013: Average tax wedge decomposition

By level of gross earnings expressed as a % of the average wage

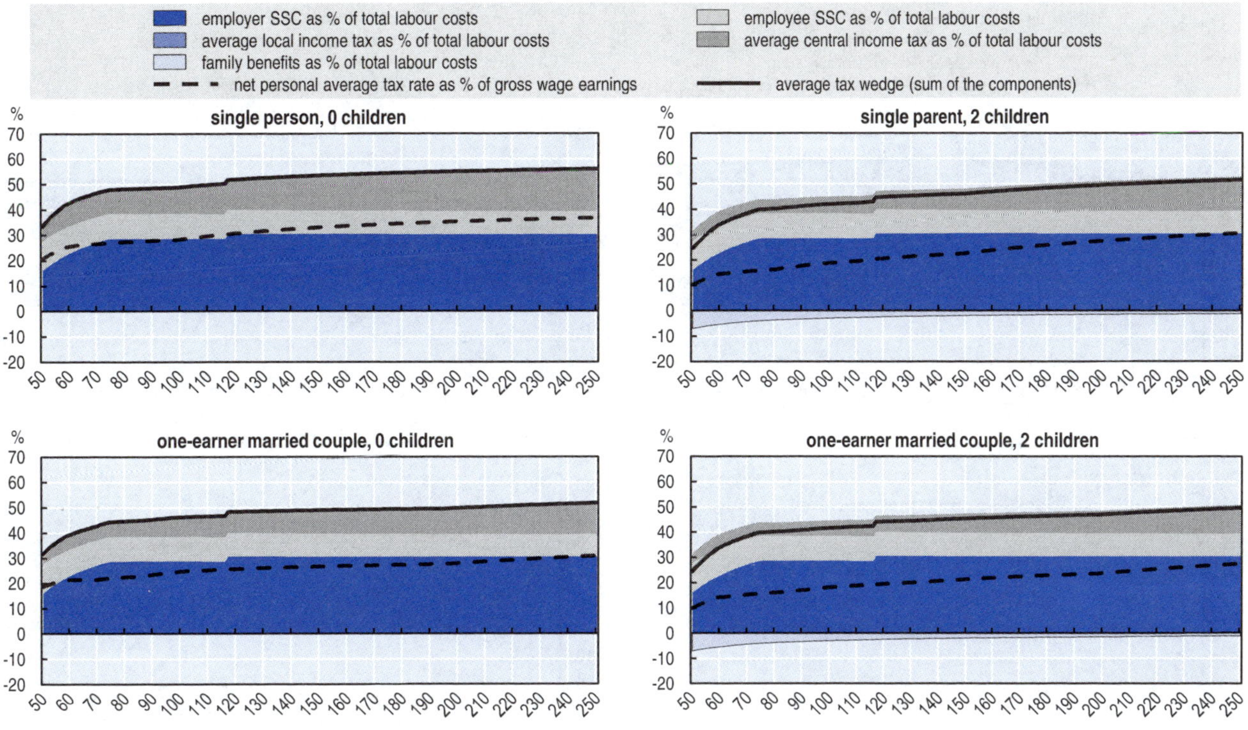

StatLink http://dx.doi.org/10.1787/888933004352

France 2013: Marginal tax wedge decomposition

By level of gross earnings expressed as a % of the average wage

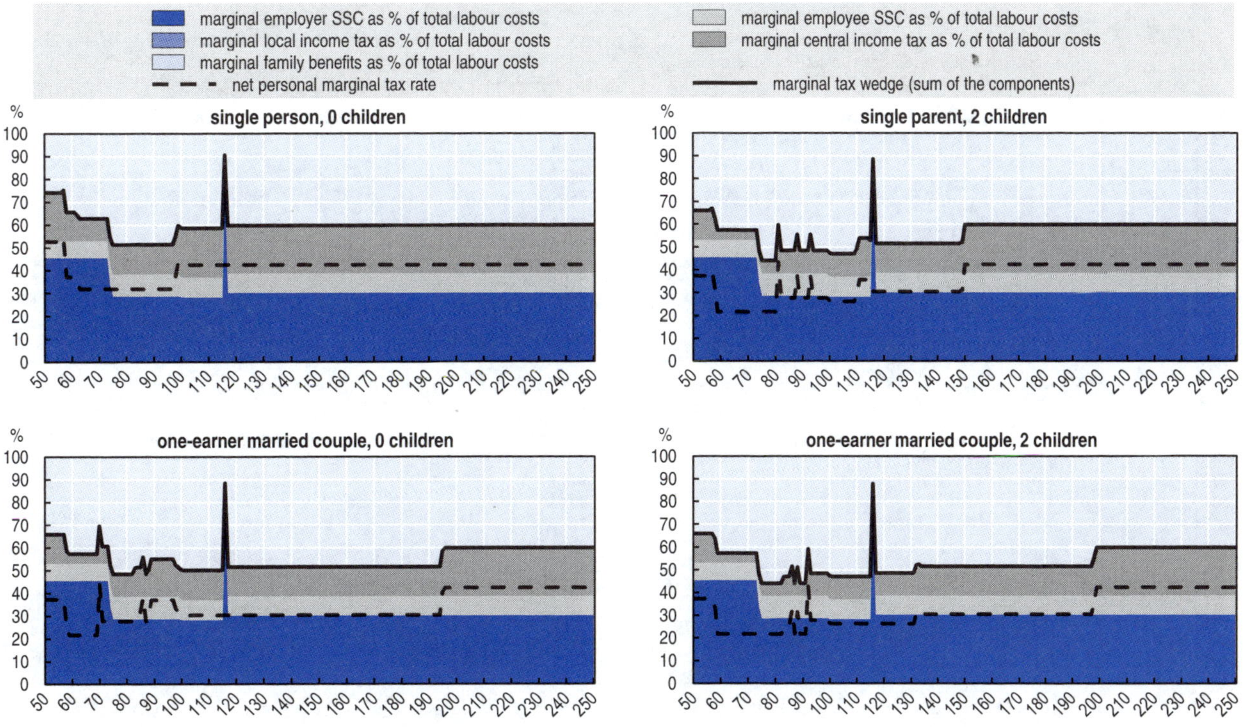

StatLink http://dx.doi.org/10.1787/888933004998

Germany 2013: Average tax wedge decomposition

By level of gross earnings expressed as a % of the average wage

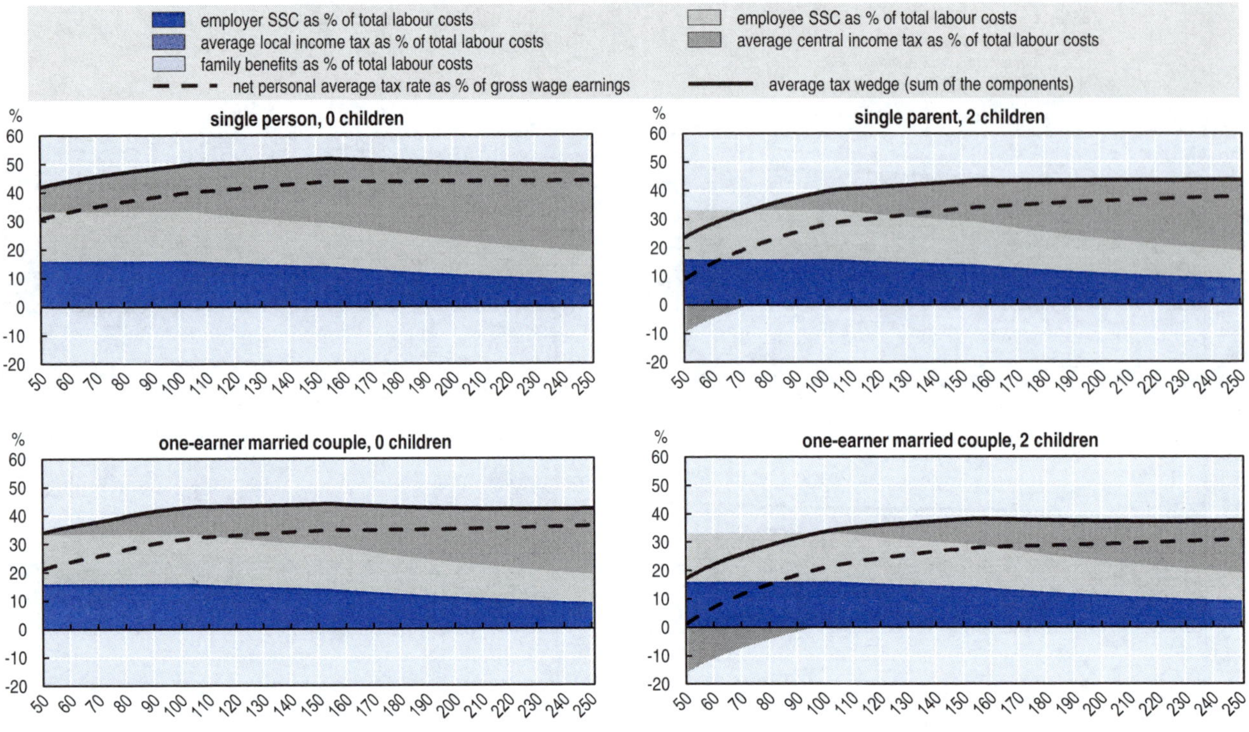

StatLink http://dx.doi.org/10.1787/888933004257

Germany 2013: Marginal tax wedge decomposition

By level of gross earnings expressed as a % of the average wage

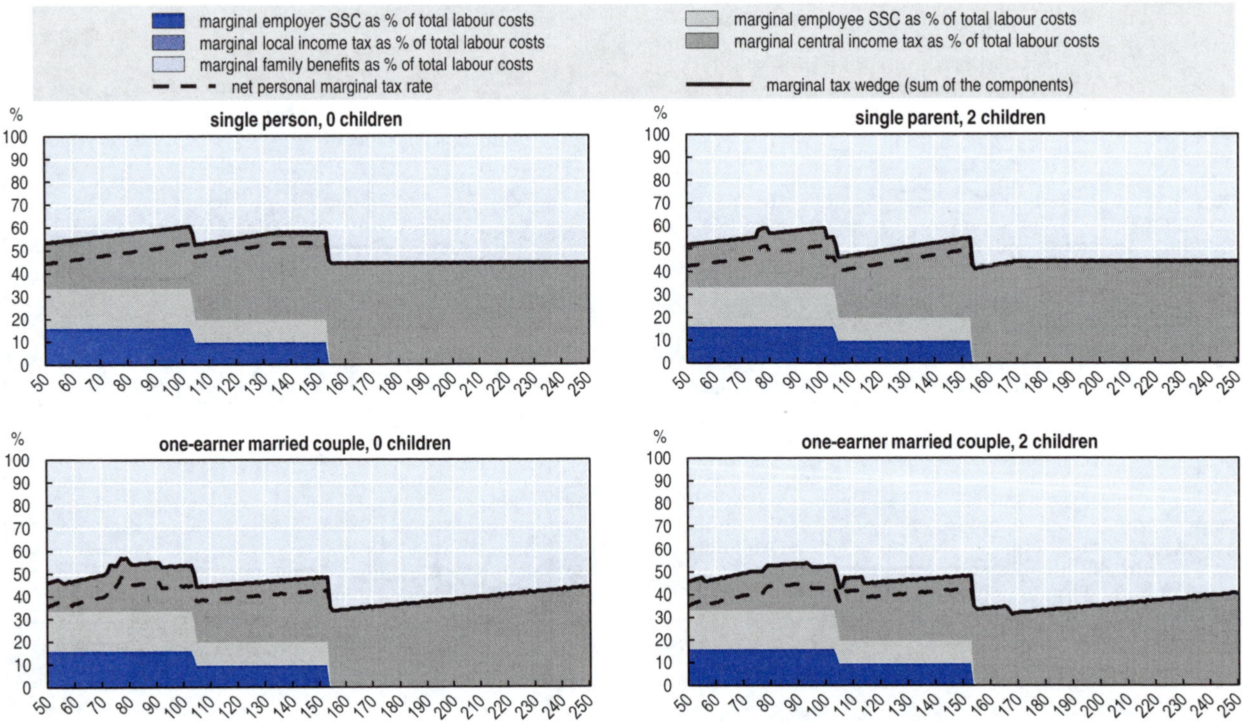

StatLink http://dx.doi.org/10.1787/888933004903

Greece 2013: Average tax wedge decomposition

By level of gross earnings expressed as a % of the average wage

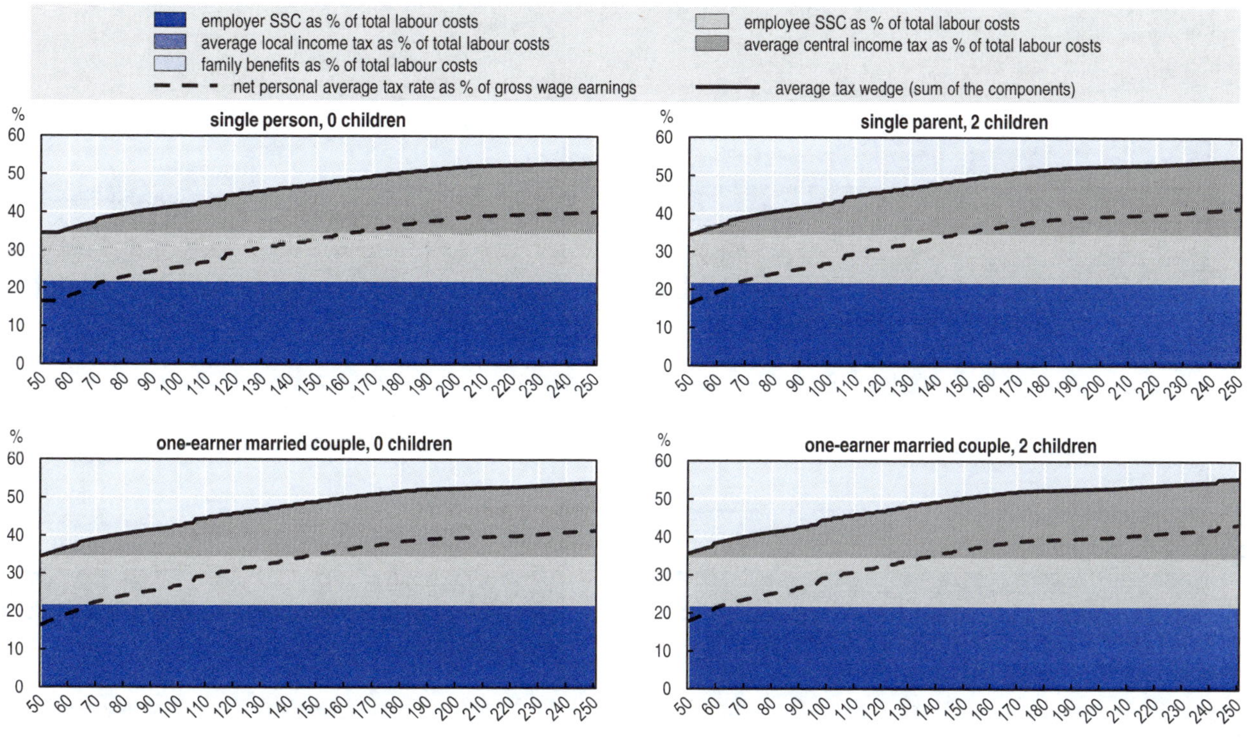

StatLink http://dx.doi.org/10.1787/888933004390

Greece 2013: Marginal tax wedge decomposition

By level of gross earnings expressed as a % of the average wage

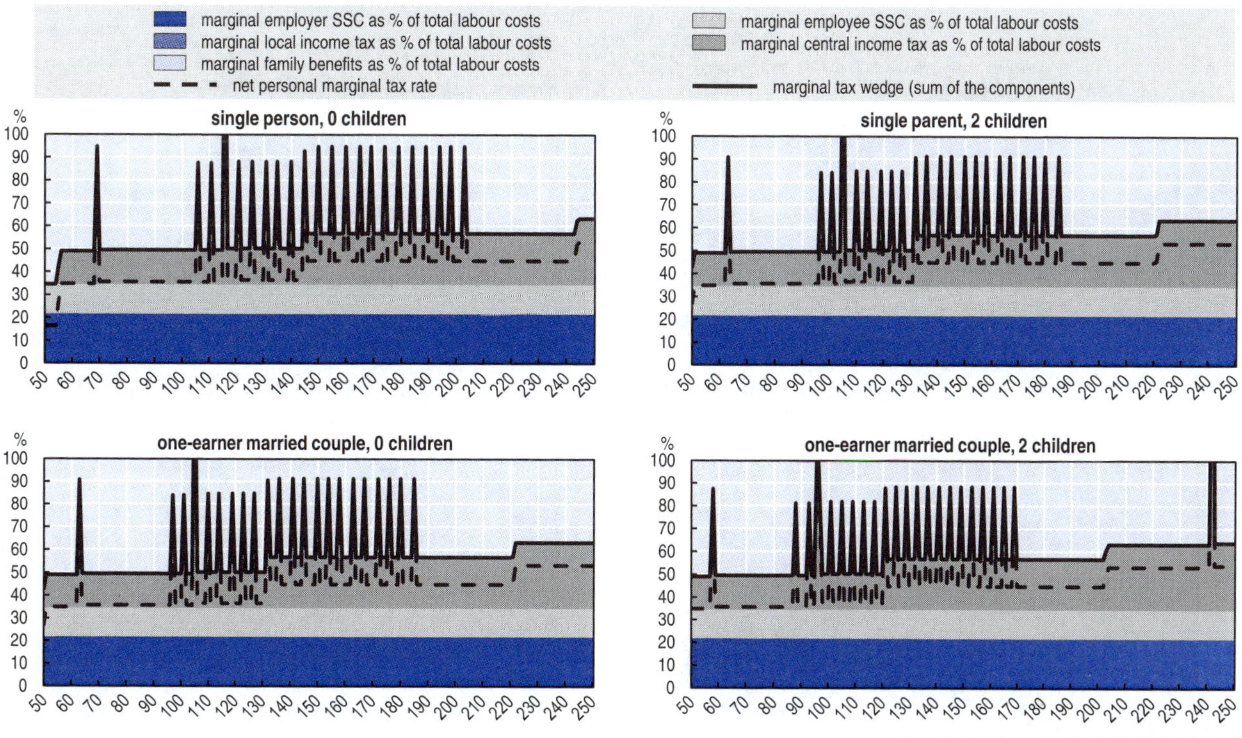

StatLink http://dx.doi.org/10.1787/888933005036

Hungary 2013: Average tax wedge decomposition

By level of gross earnings expressed as a % of the average wage

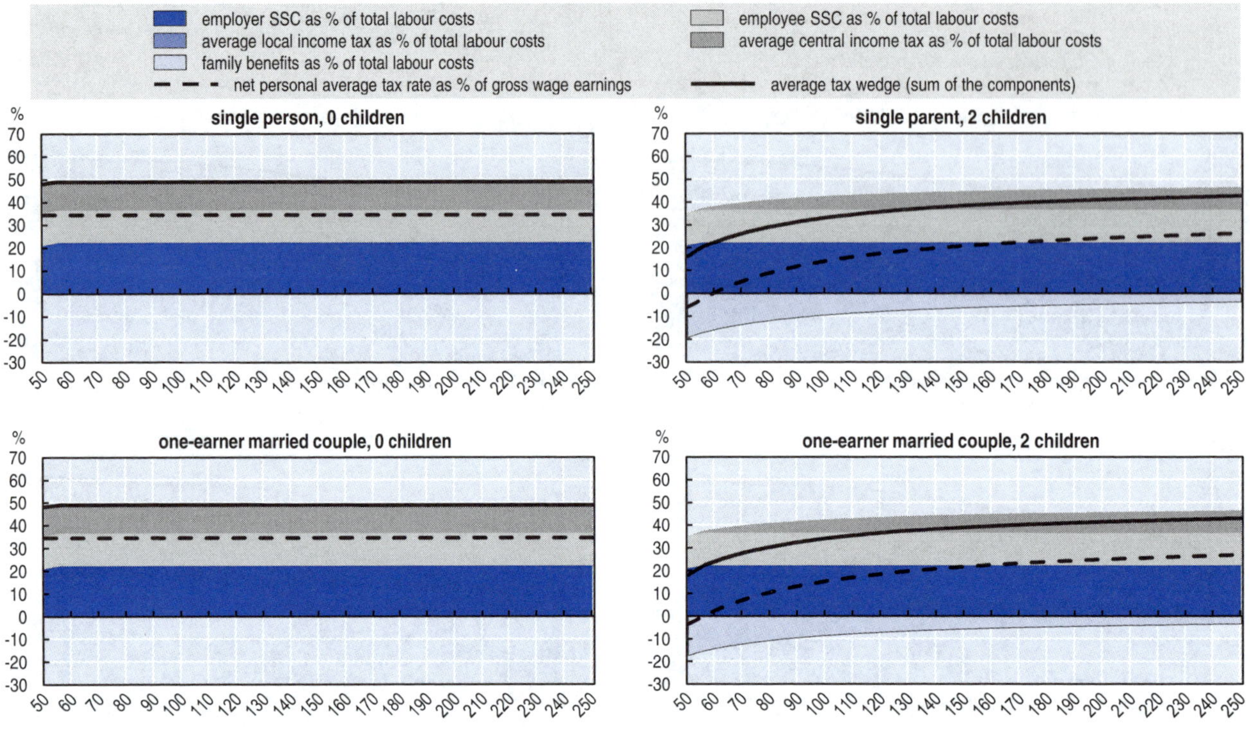

StatLink http://dx.doi.org/10.1787/888933004409

Hungary 2013: Marginal tax wedge decomposition

By level of gross earnings expressed as a % of the average wage

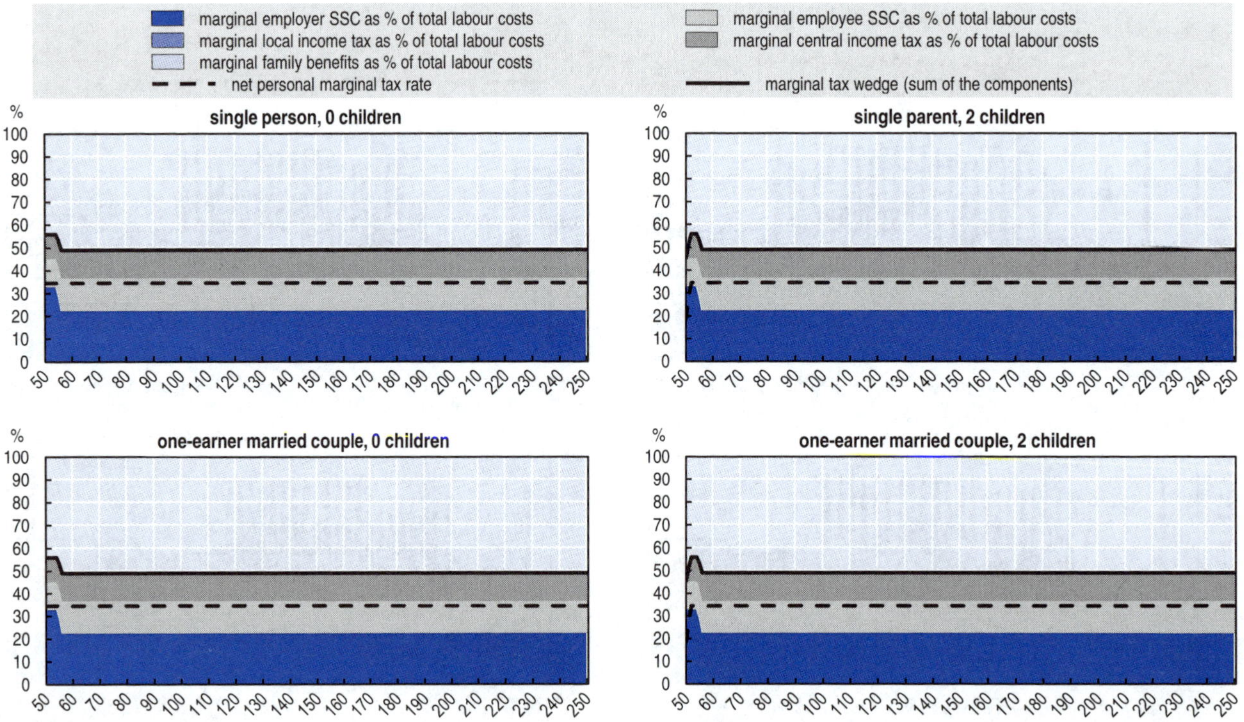

StatLink http://dx.doi.org/10.1787/888933005055

Iceland 2013: Average tax wedge decomposition

By level of gross earnings expressed as a % of the average wage

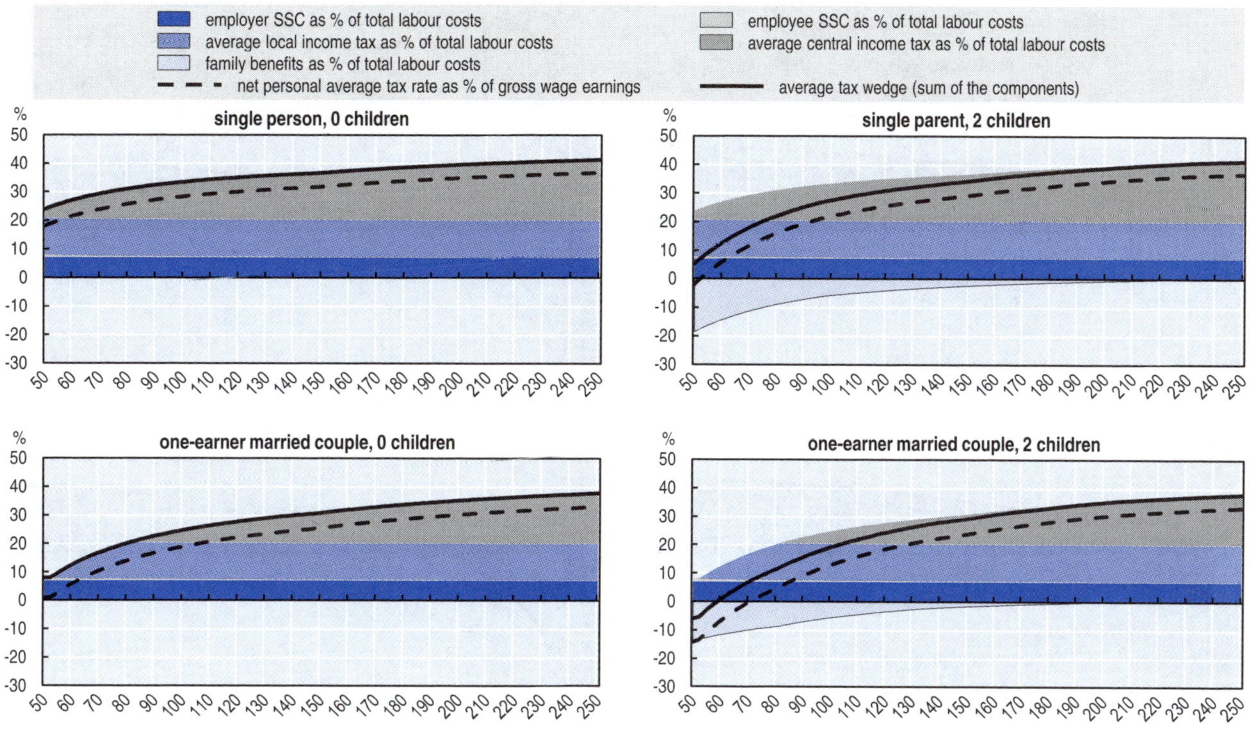

StatLink http://dx.doi.org/10.1787/888933004447

Iceland 2013: Marginal tax wedge decomposition

By level of gross earnings expressed as a % of the average wage

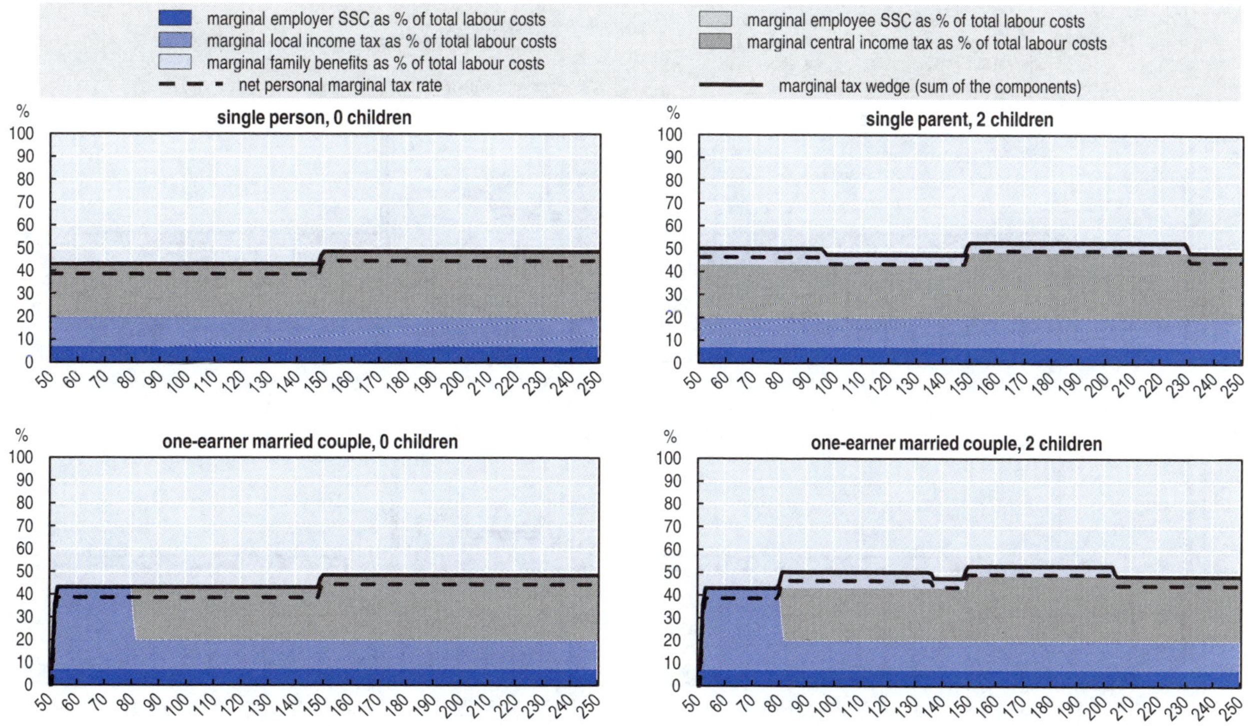

StatLink http://dx.doi.org/10.1787/888933005093

Ireland 2013: Average tax wedge decomposition

By level of gross earnings expressed as a % of the average wage

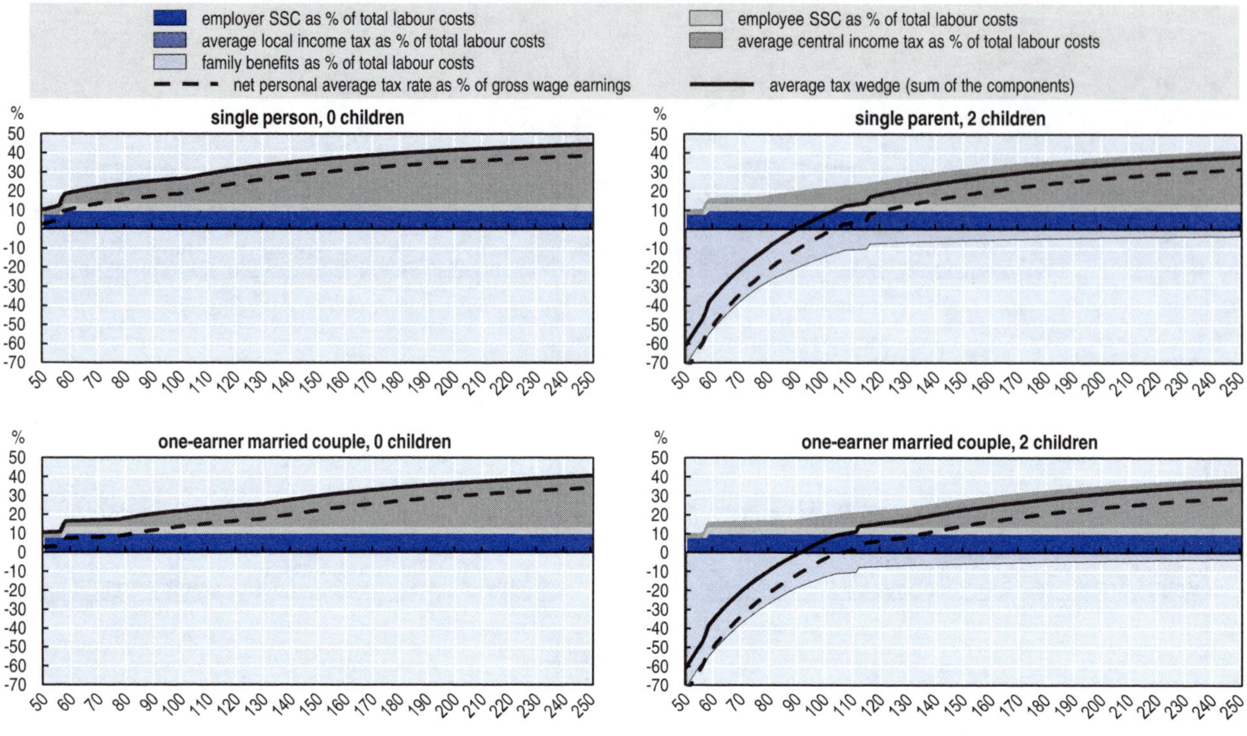

StatLink http://dx.doi.org/10.1787/888933004428

Ireland 2013: Marginal tax wedge decomposition

By level of gross earnings expressed as a % of the average wage

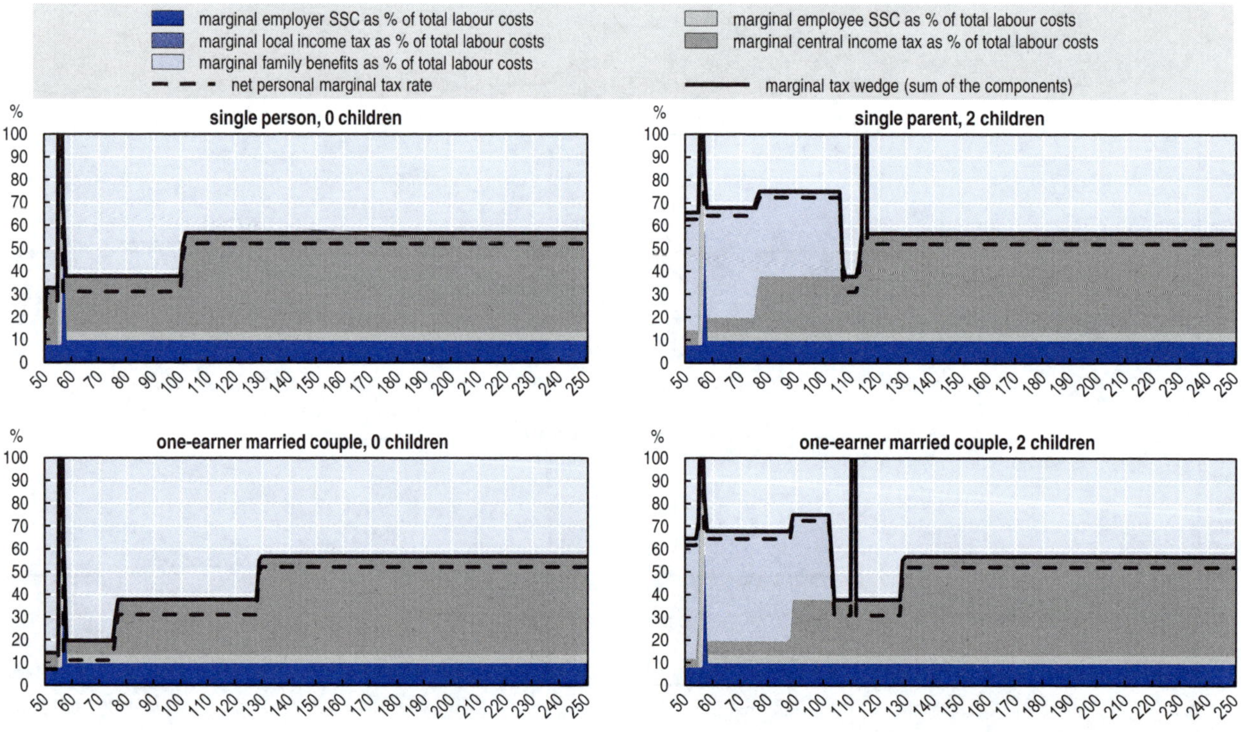

StatLink http://dx.doi.org/10.1787/888933005074

Israel 2013: Average tax wedge decomposition

By level of gross earnings expressed as a % of the average wage

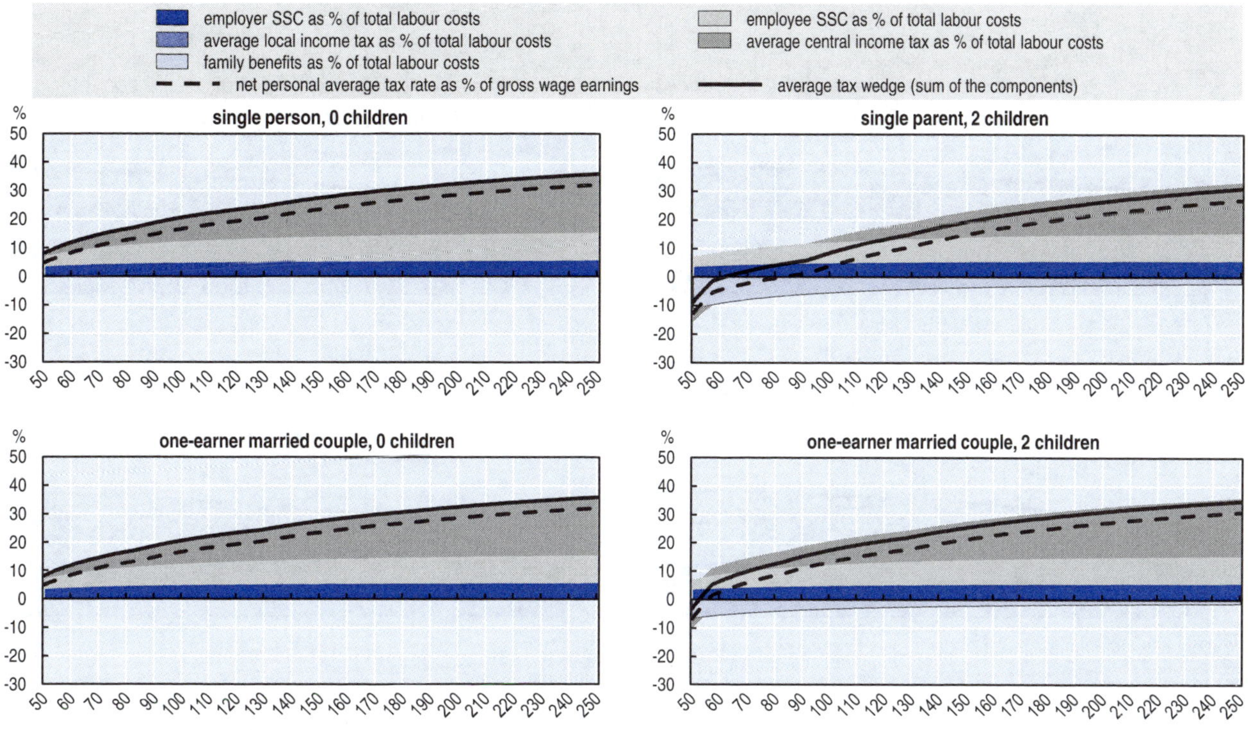

StatLink http://dx.doi.org/10.1787/888933004466

Israel 2013: Marginal tax wedge decomposition

By level of gross earnings expressed as a % of the average wage

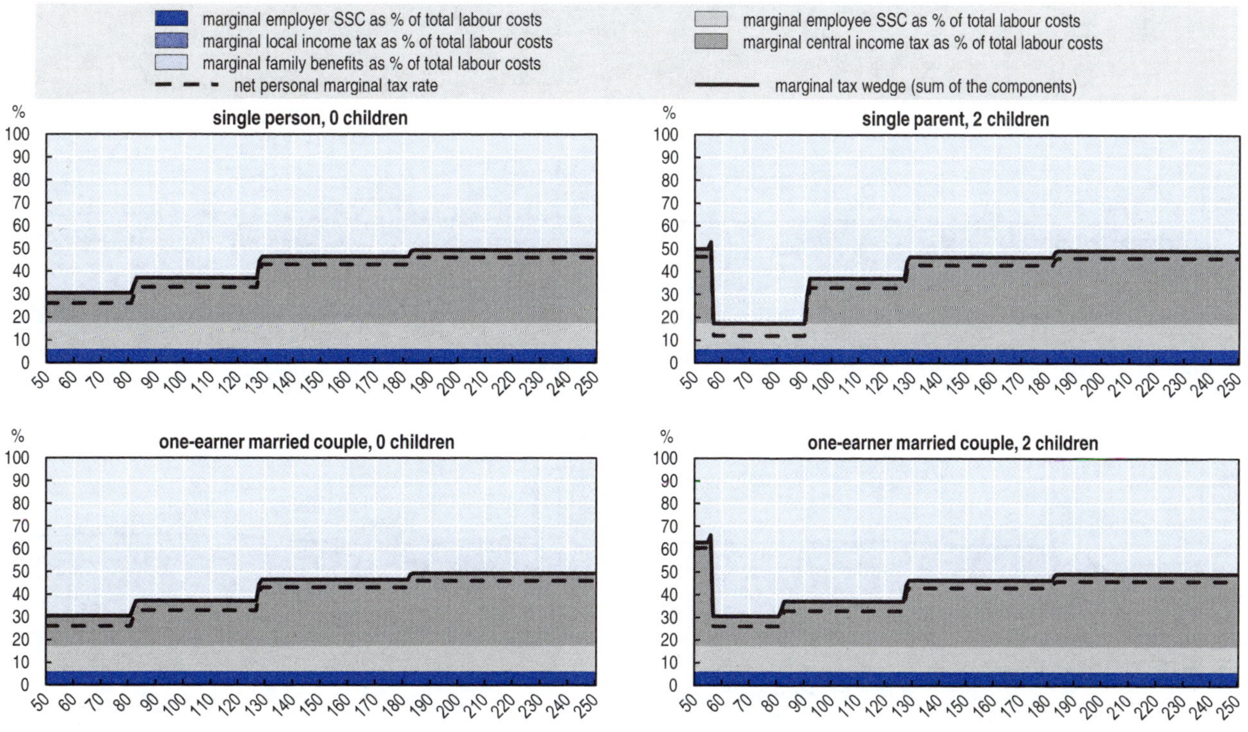

StatLink http://dx.doi.org/10.1787/888933005112

Italy 2013: Average tax wedge decomposition

By level of gross earnings expressed as a % of the average wage

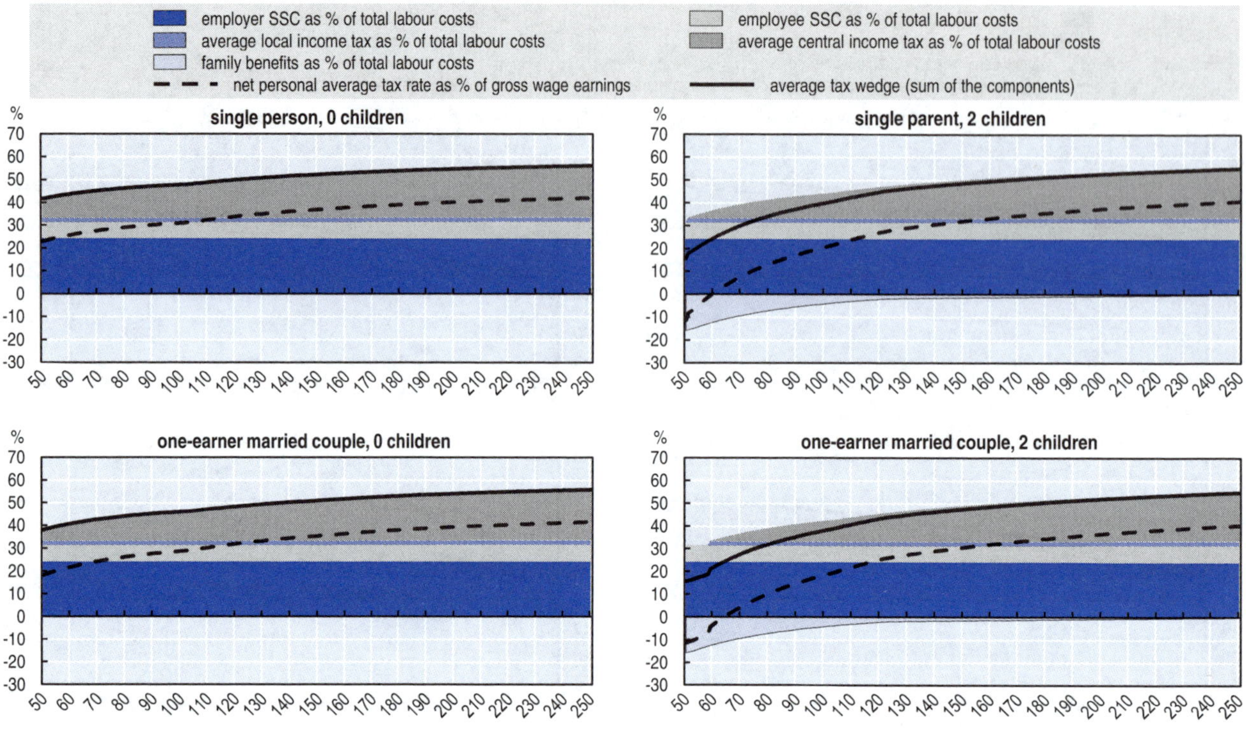

StatLink http://dx.doi.org/10.1787/888933004485

Italy 2013: Marginal tax wedge decomposition

By level of gross earnings expressed as a % of the average wage

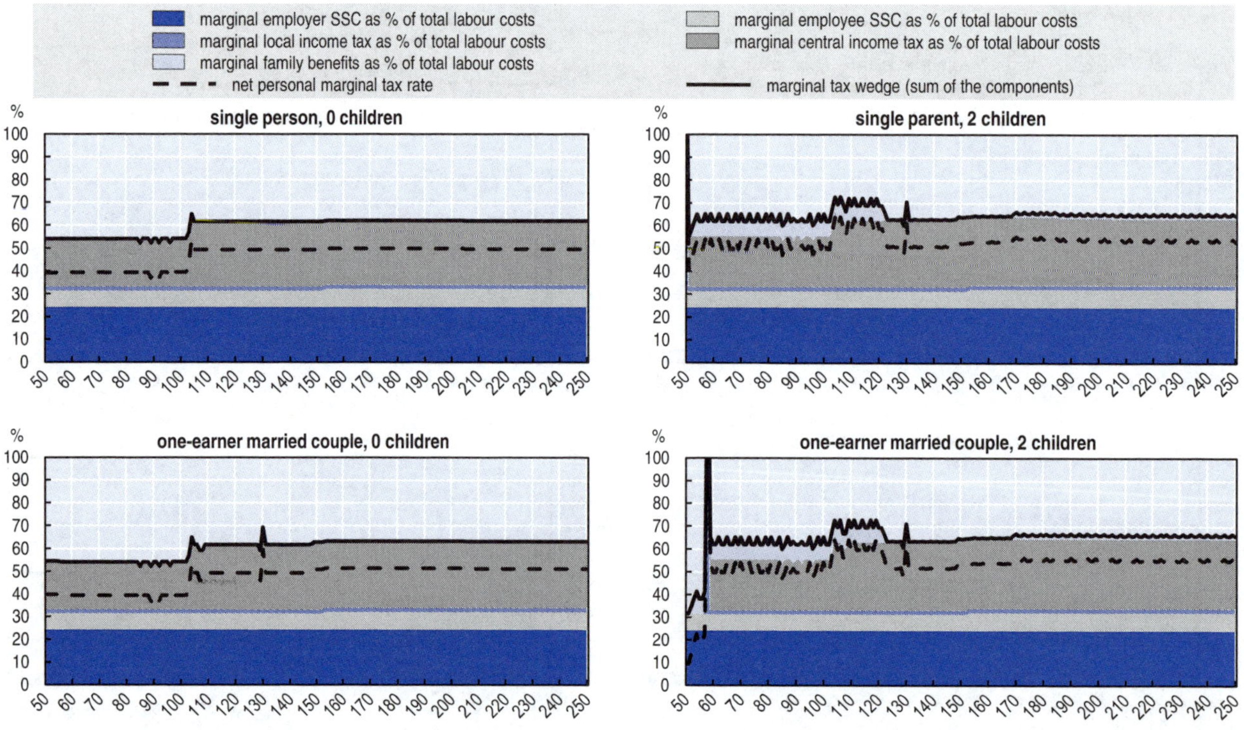

StatLink http://dx.doi.org/10.1787/888933005131

Japan 2013: Average tax wedge decomposition

By level of gross earnings expressed as a % of the average wage

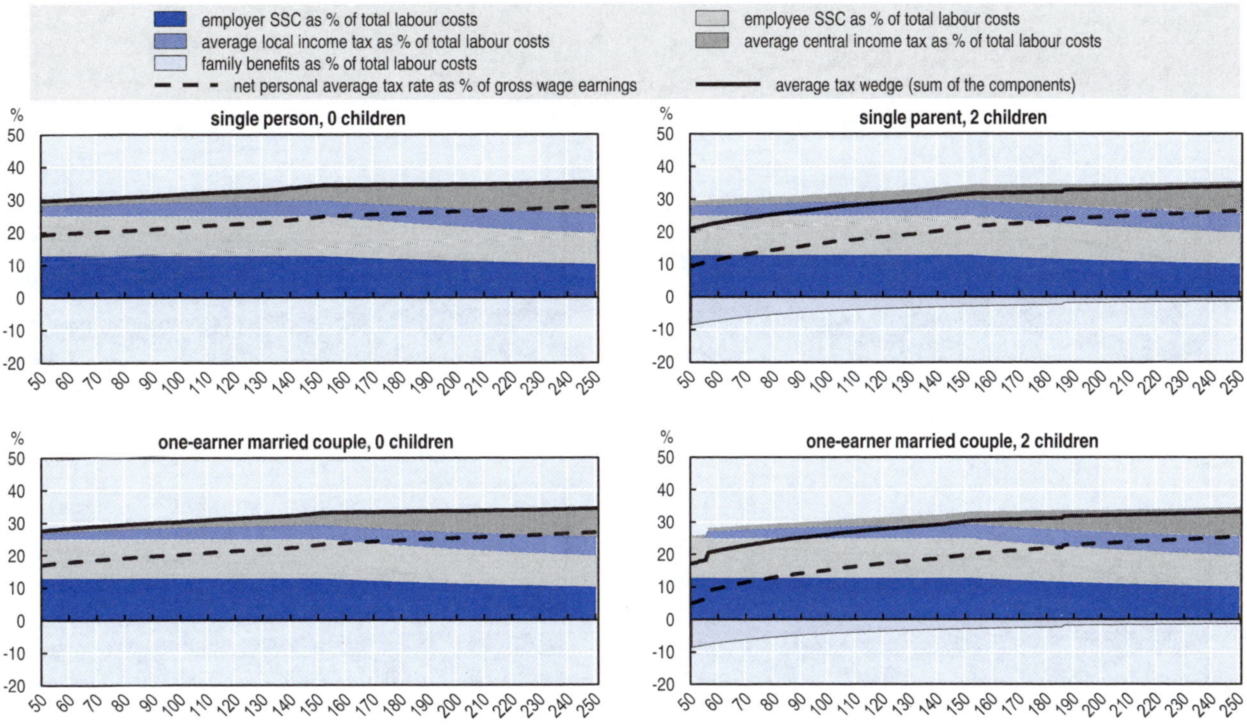

StatLink http://dx.doi.org/10.1787/888933004504

Japan 2013: Marginal tax wedge decomposition

By level of gross earnings expressed as a % of the average wage

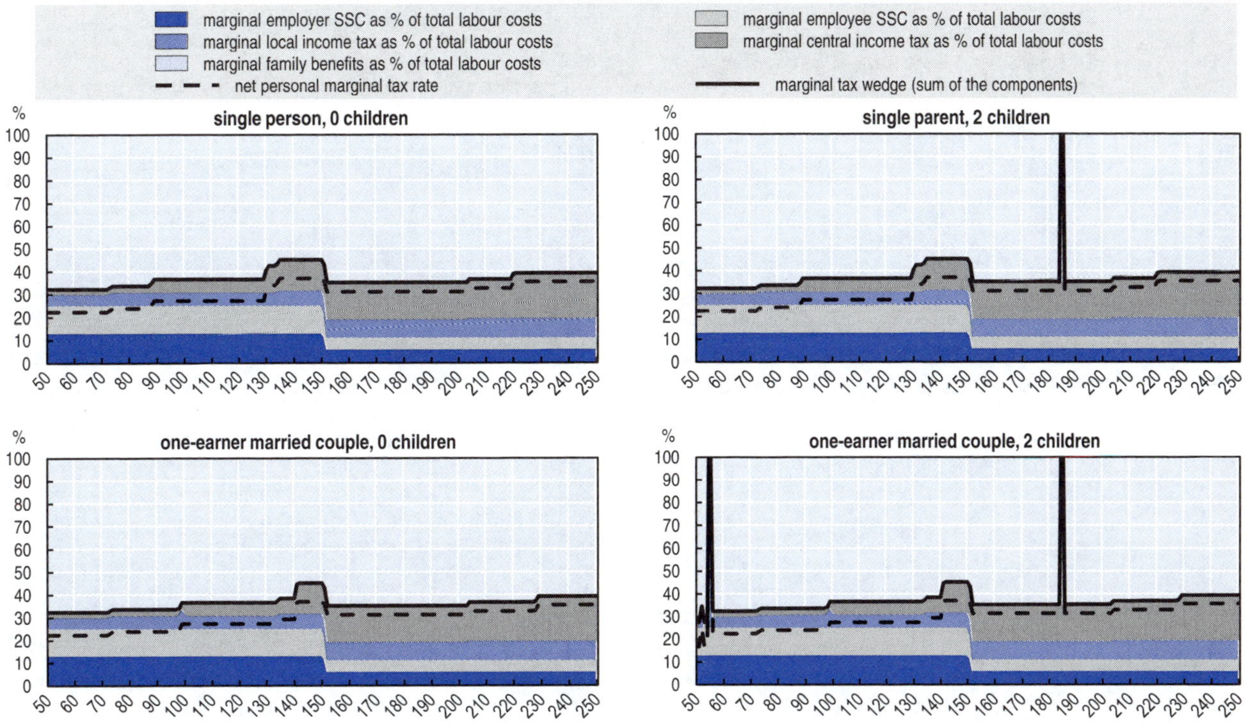

StatLink http://dx.doi.org/10.1787/888933005150

Korea 2013: Average tax wedge decomposition

By level of gross earnings expressed as a % of the average wage

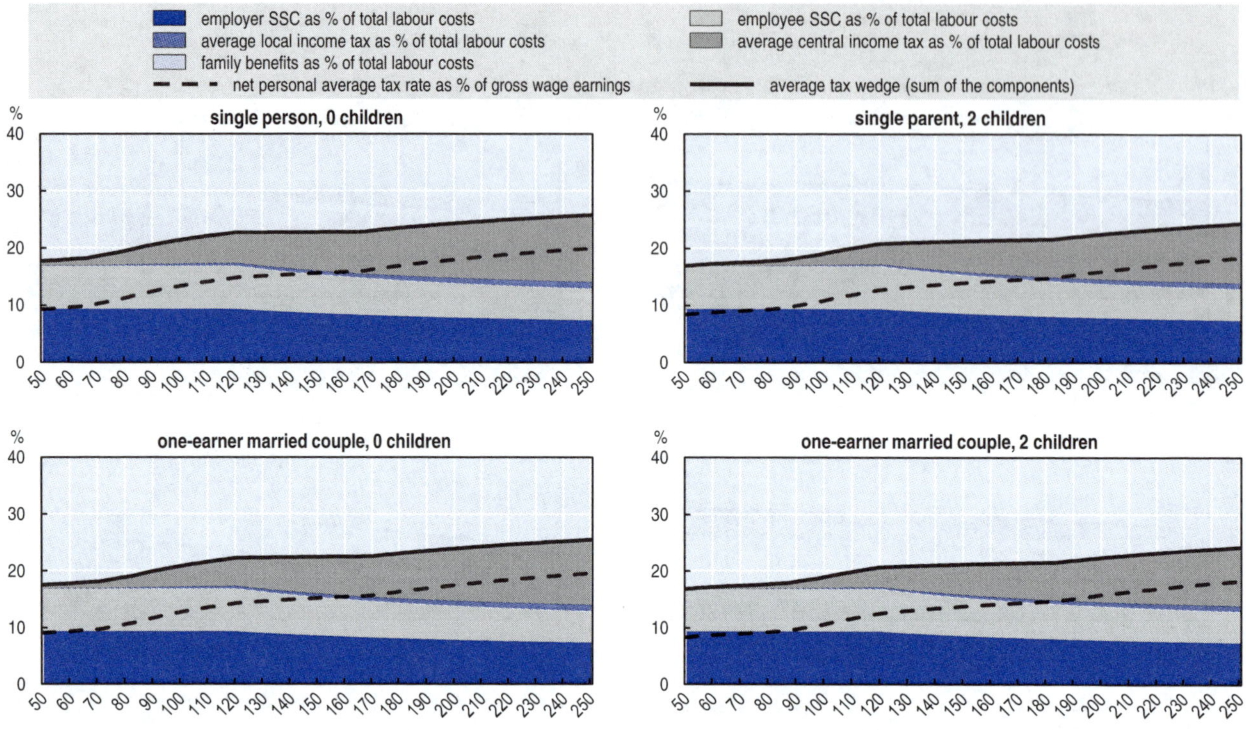

StatLink http://dx.doi.org/10.1787/888933004523

Korea 2013: Marginal tax wedge decomposition

By level of gross earnings expressed as a % of the average wage

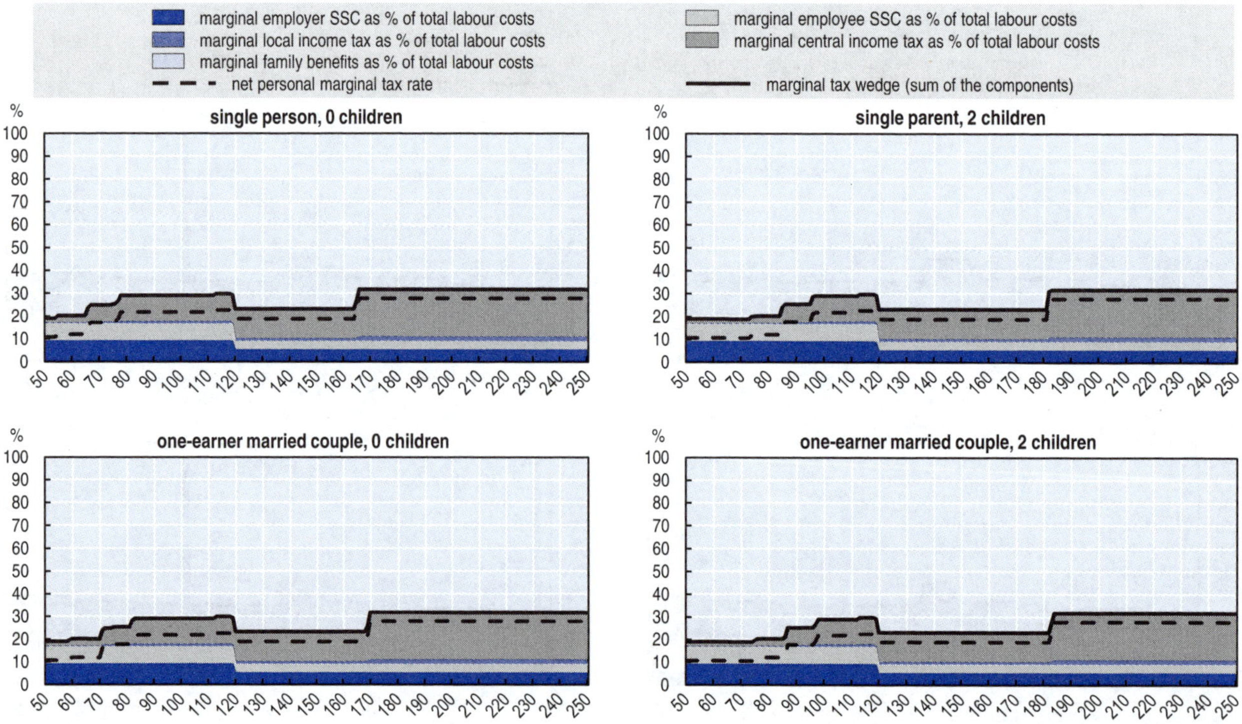

StatLink http://dx.doi.org/10.1787/888933005169

Luxembourg 2013: Average tax wedge decomposition

By level of gross earnings expressed as a % of the average wage

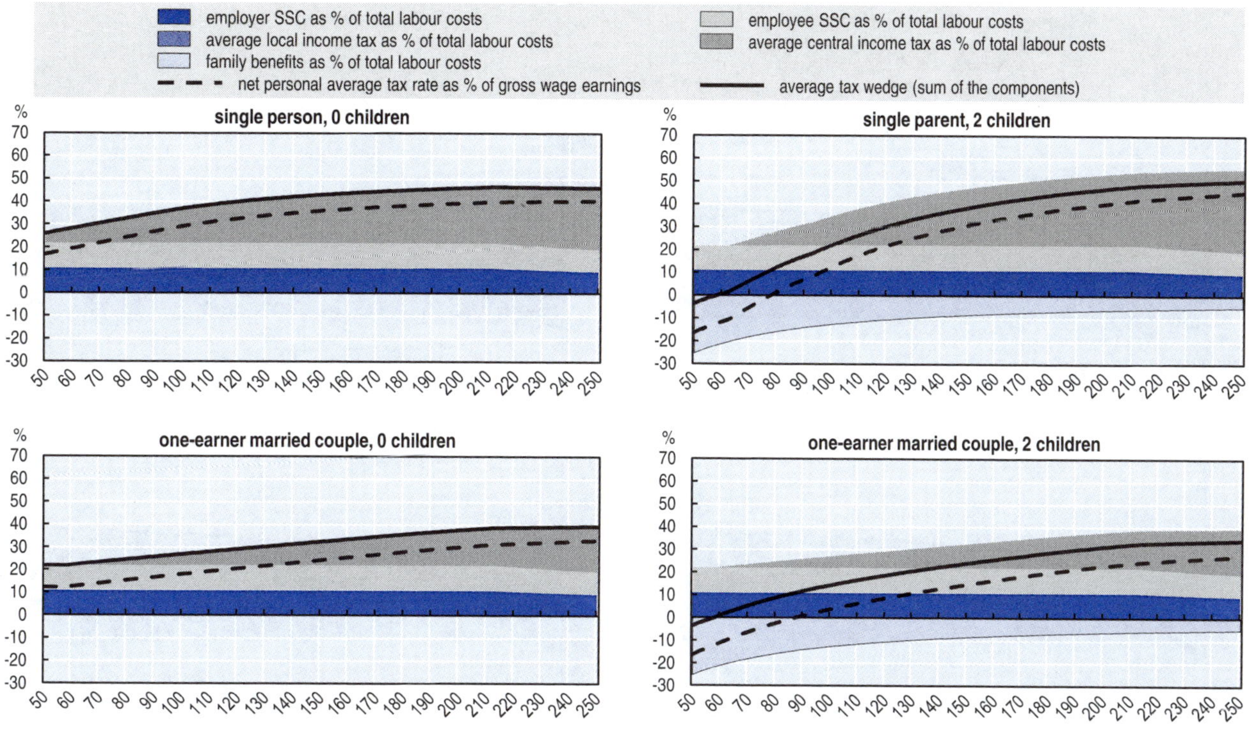

StatLink http://dx.doi.org/10.1787/888933004542

Luxembourg 2013: Marginal tax wedge decomposition

By level of gross earnings expressed as a % of the average wage

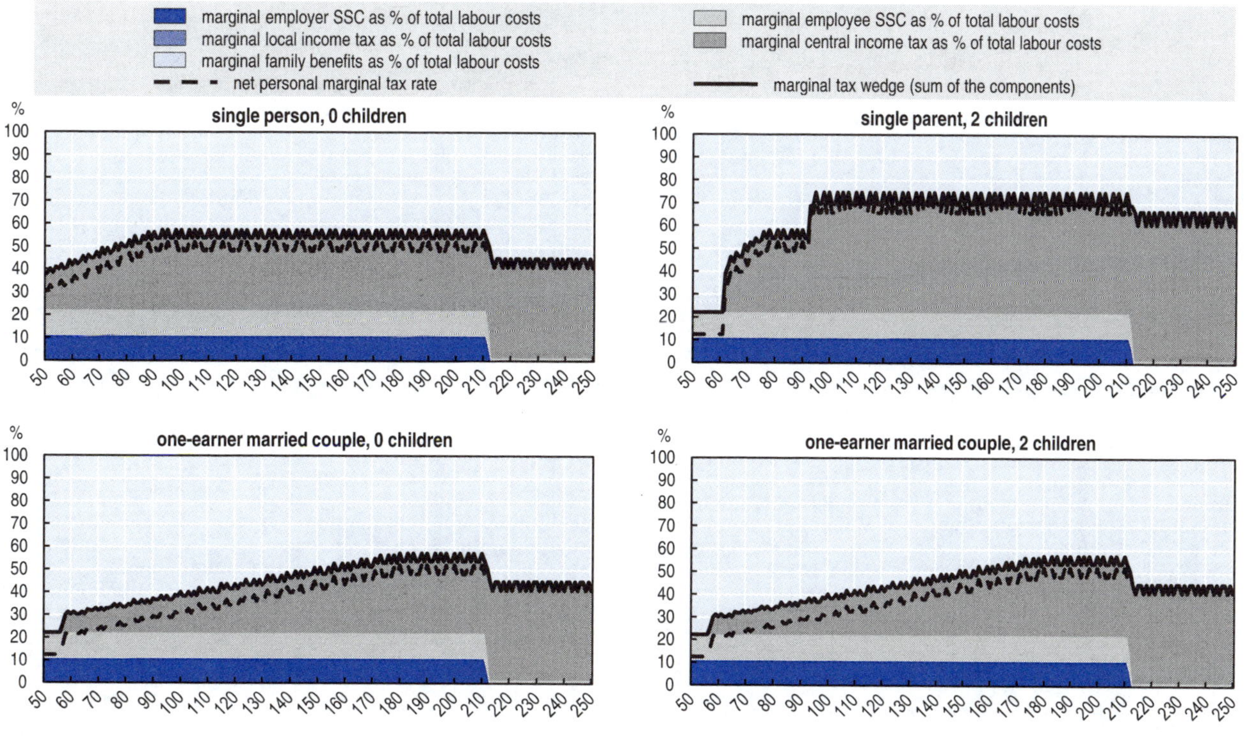

StatLink http://dx.doi.org/10.1787/888933005188

Mexico 2013: Average tax wedge decomposition

By level of gross earnings expressed as a % of the average wage

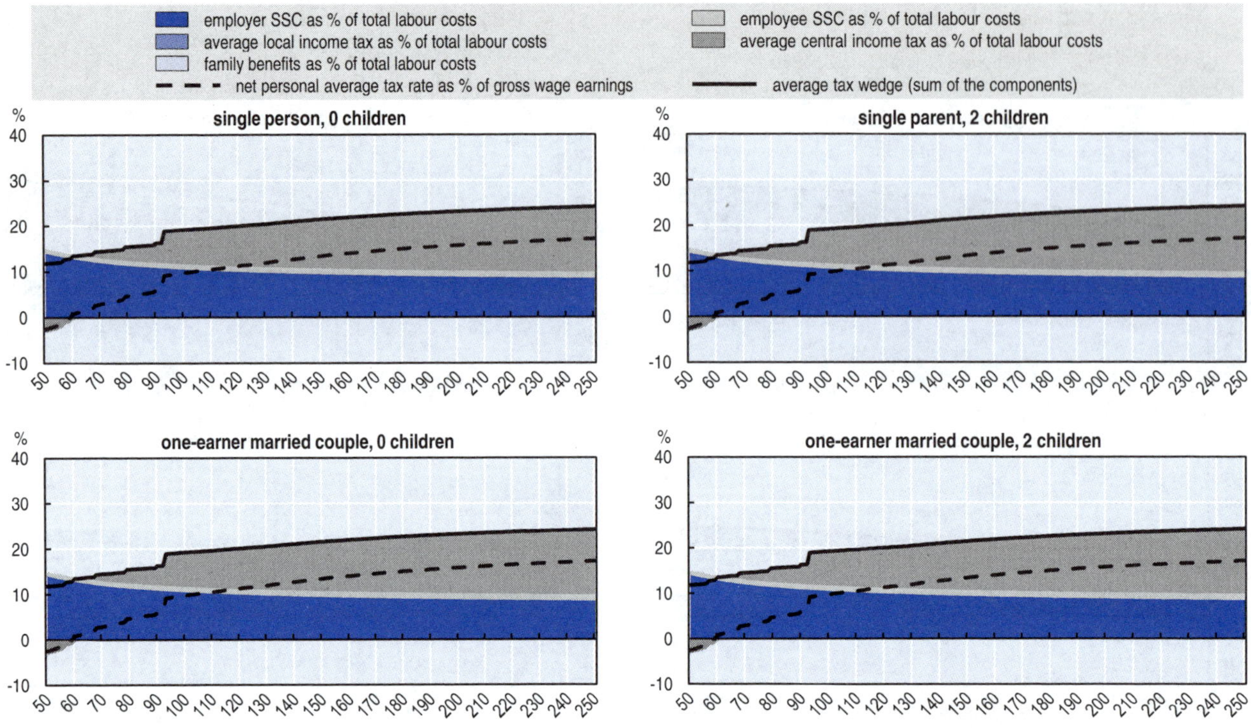

StatLink http://dx.doi.org/10.1787/888933004561

Mexico 2013: Marginal tax wedge decomposition

By level of gross earnings expressed as a % of the average wage

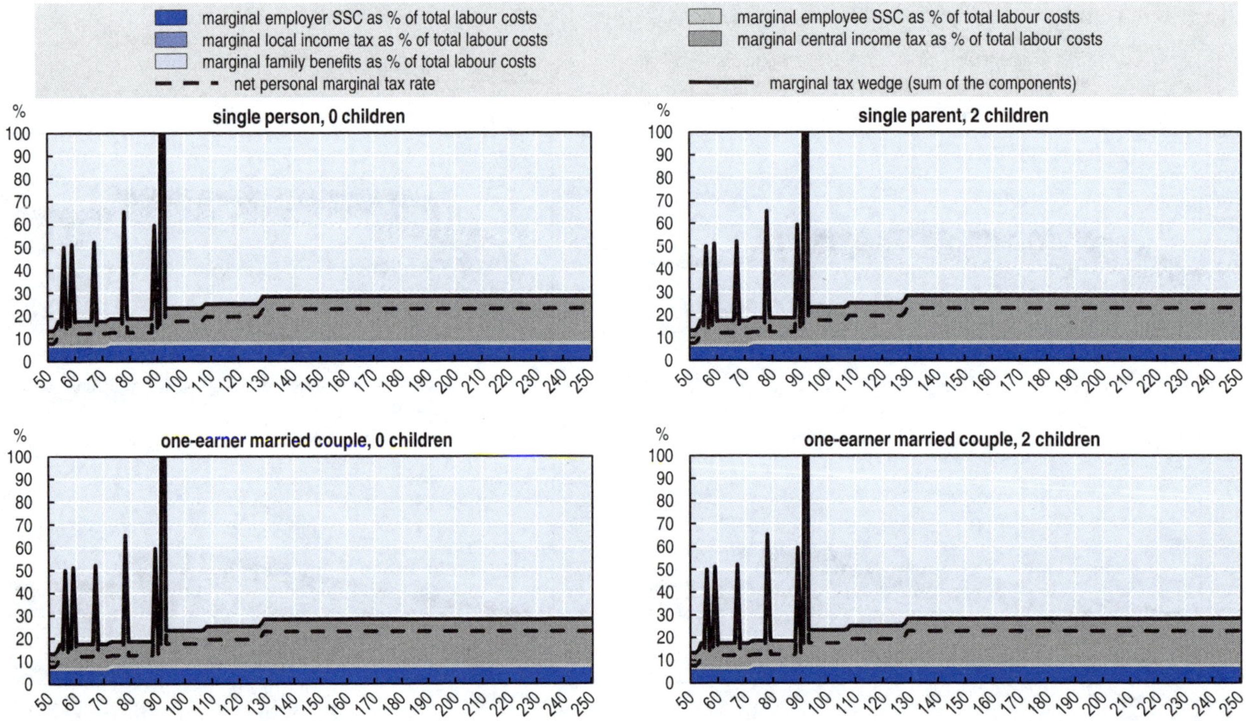

StatLink http://dx.doi.org/10.1787/888933005207

Netherlands 2013: Average tax wedge decomposition

By level of gross earnings expressed as a % of the average wage

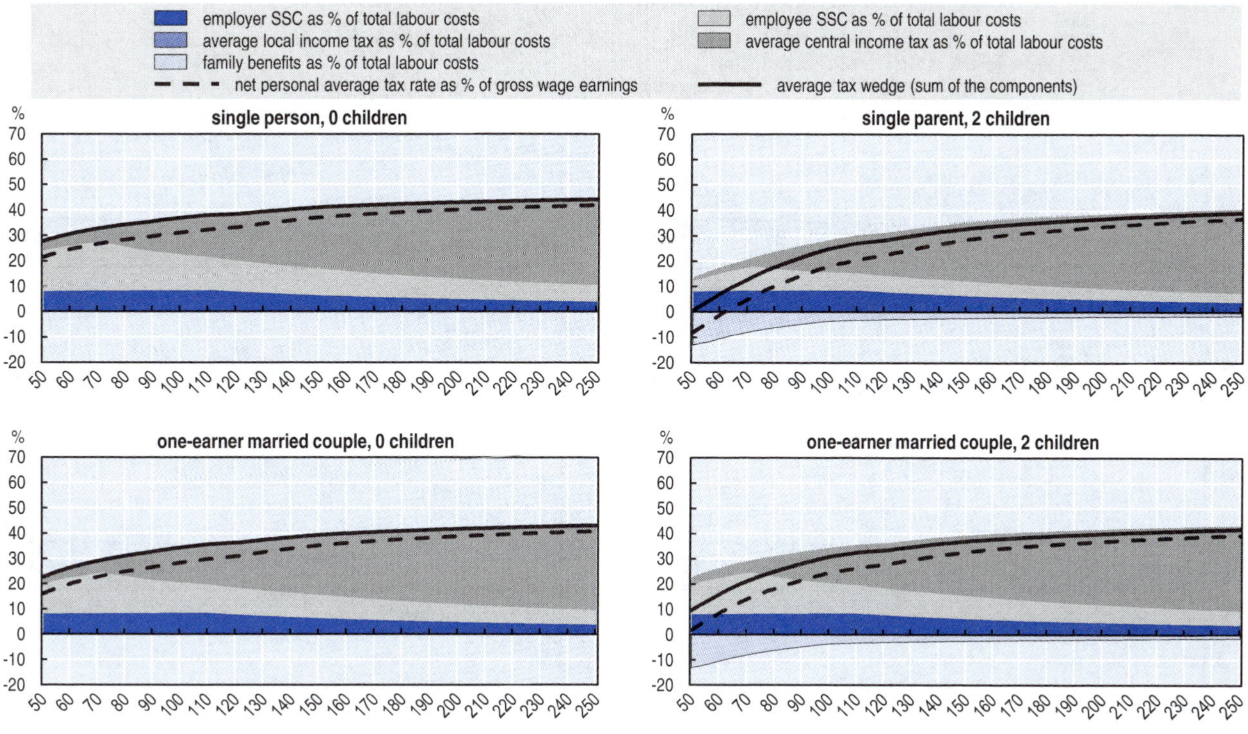

StatLink http://dx.doi.org/10.1787/888933004580

Netherlands 2013: Marginal tax wedge decomposition

By level of gross earnings expressed as a % of the average wage

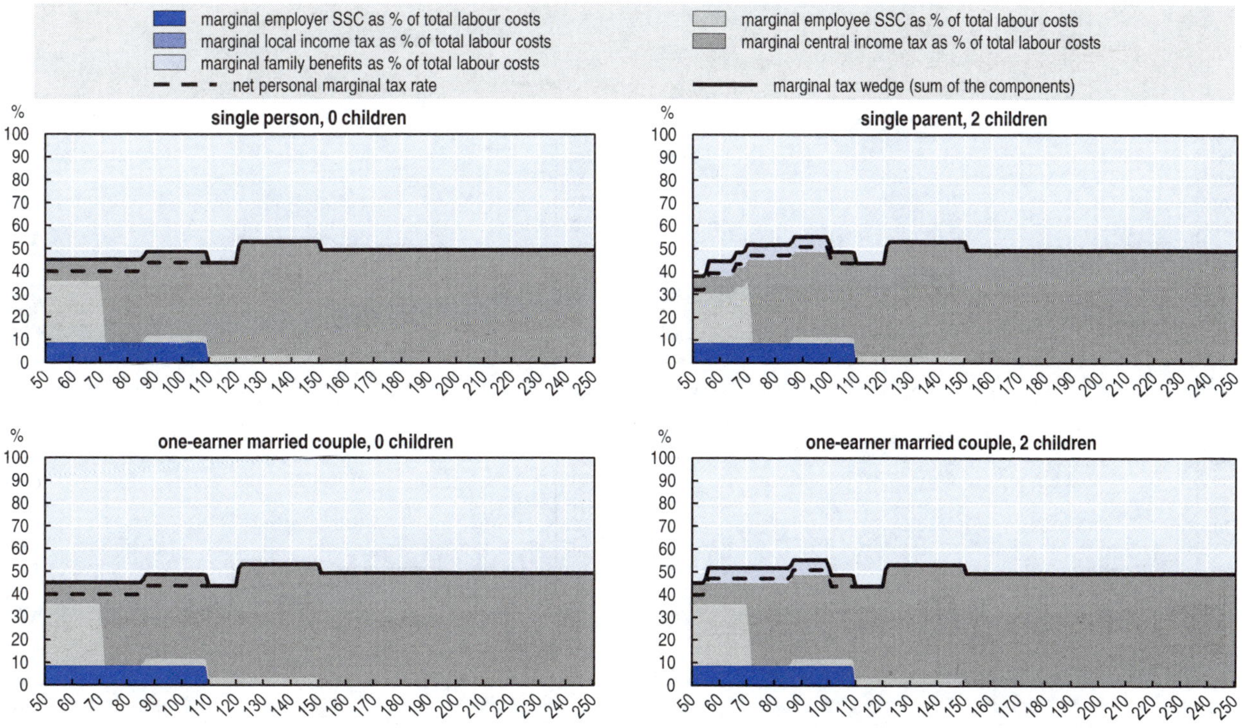

StatLink http://dx.doi.org/10.1787/888933005226

New Zealand 2013: Average tax wedge decomposition

By level of gross earnings expressed as a % of the average wage

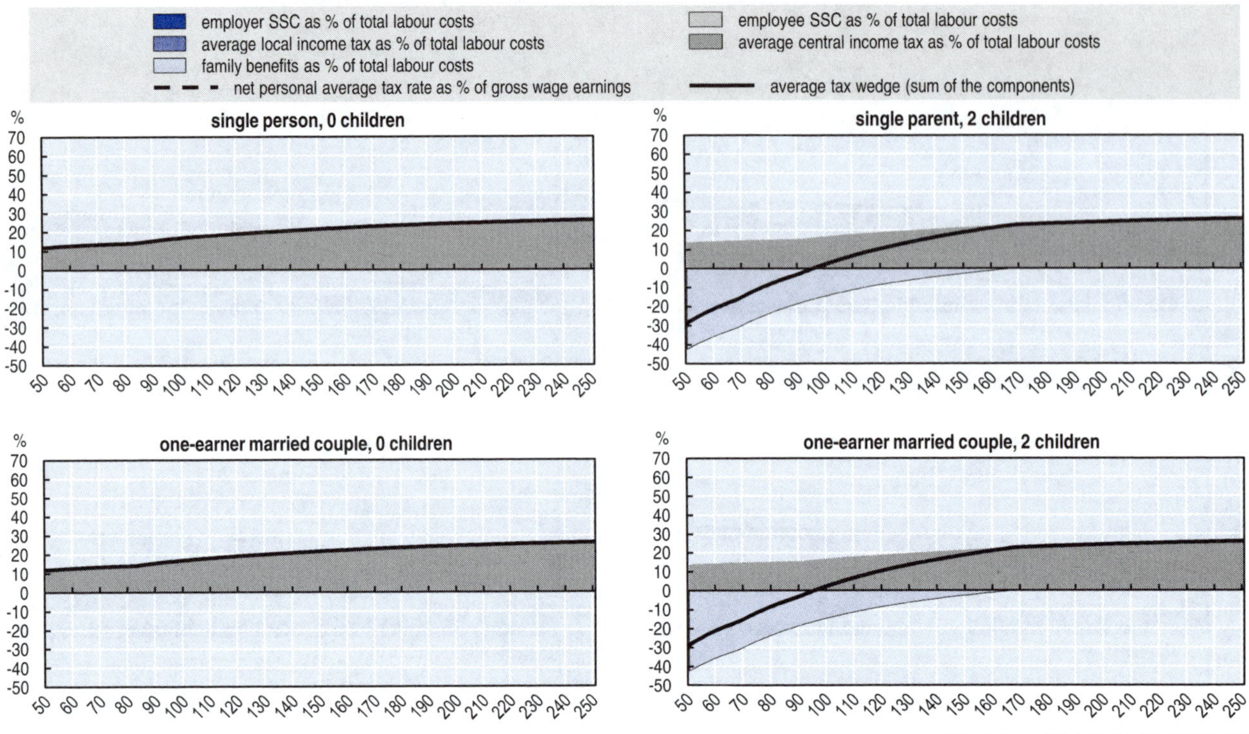

StatLink http://dx.doi.org/10.1787/888933004618

New Zealand 2013: Marginal tax wedge decomposition

By level of gross earnings expressed as a % of the average wage

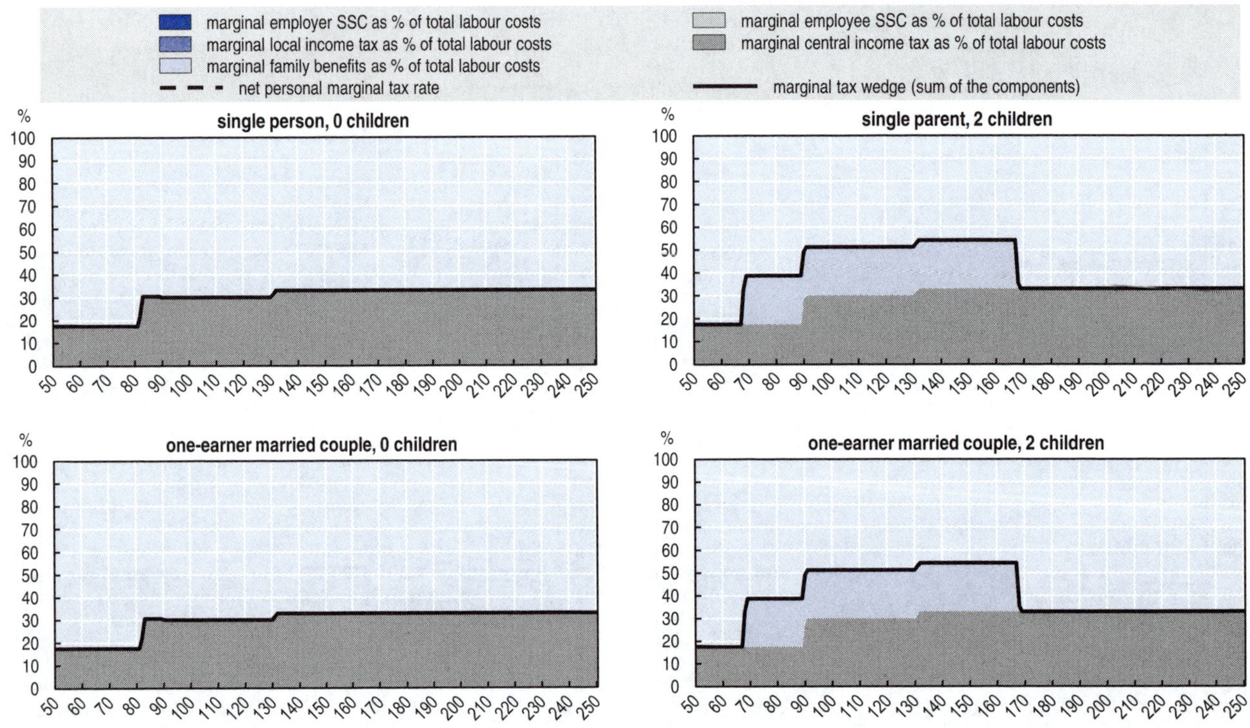

StatLink http://dx.doi.org/10.1787/888933005264

Norway 2013: Average tax wedge decomposition

By level of gross earnings expressed as a % of the average wage

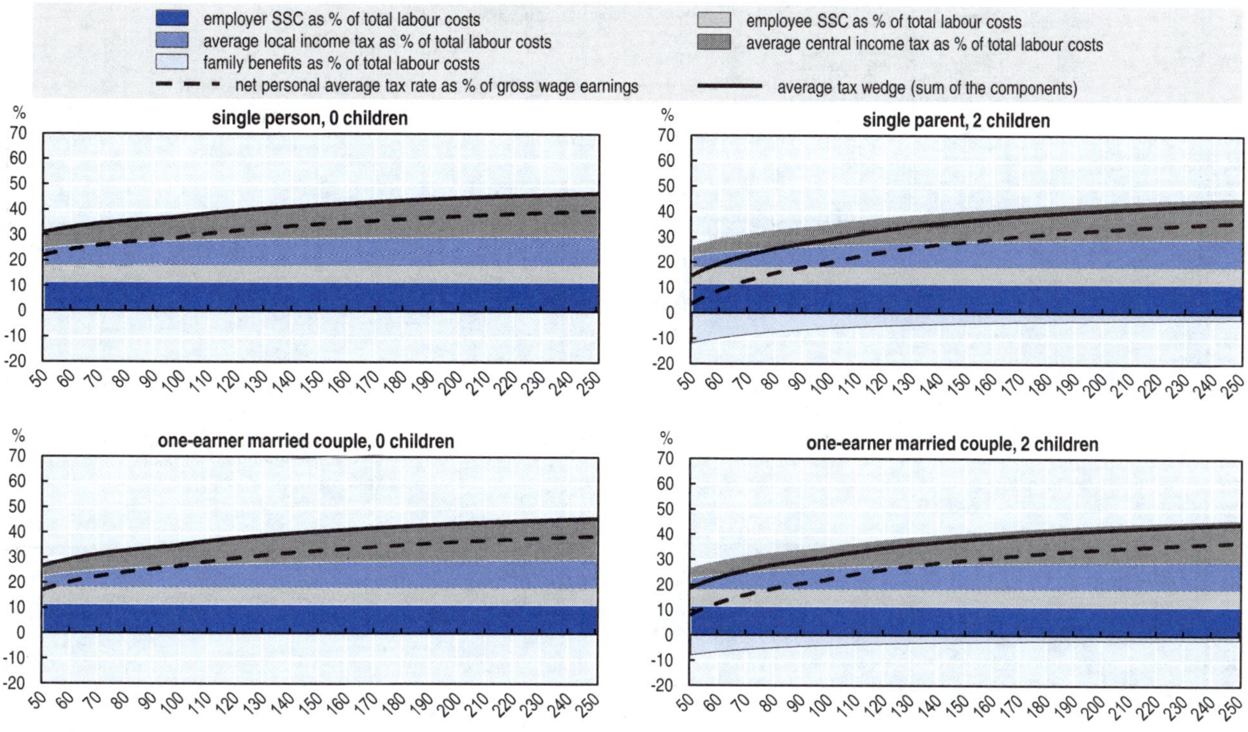

StatLink http://dx.doi.org/10.1787/888933004599

Norway 2013: Marginal tax wedge decomposition

By level of gross earnings expressed as a % of the average wage

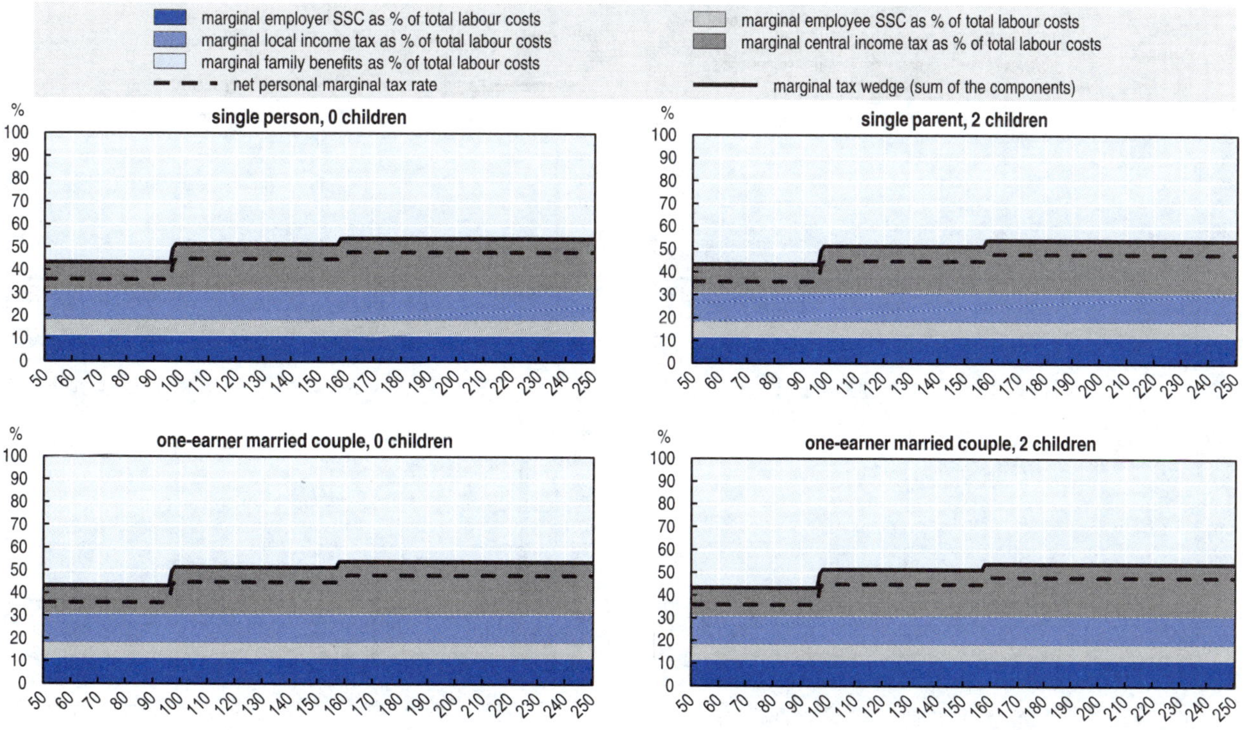

StatLink http://dx.doi.org/10.1787/888933005245

Poland 2013: Average tax wedge decomposition

By level of gross earnings expressed as a % of the average wage

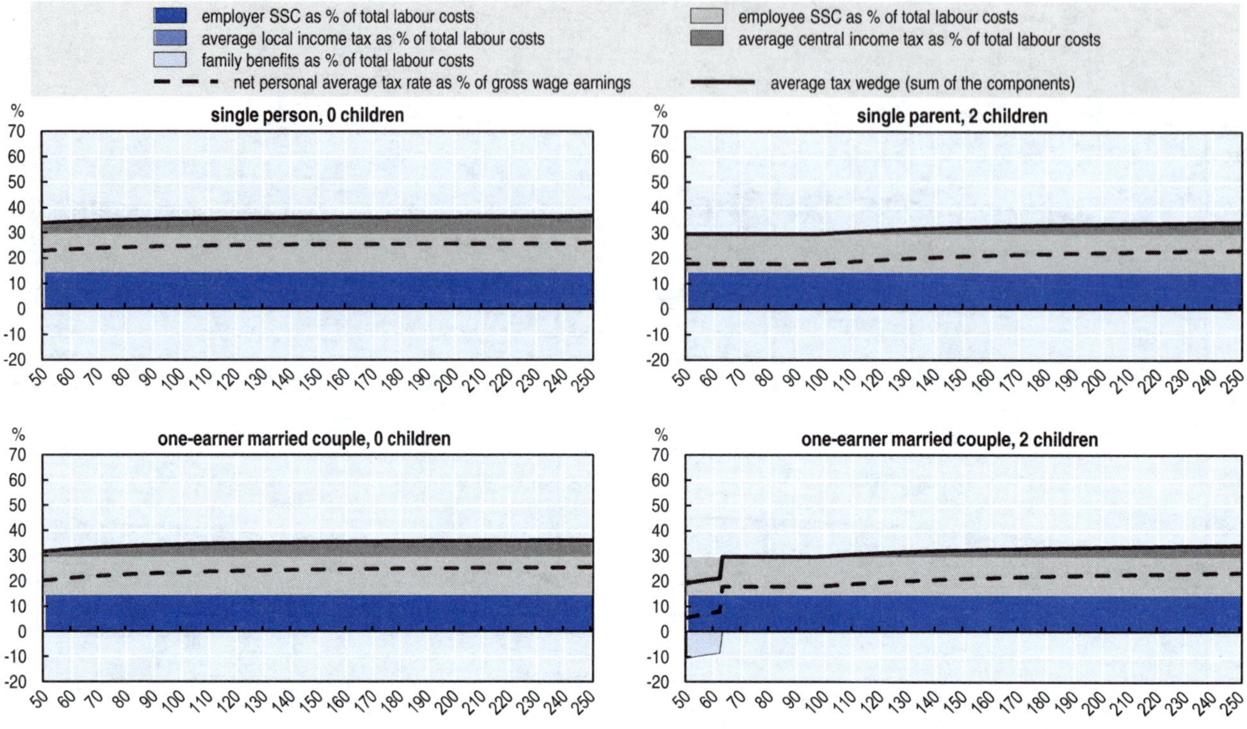

StatLink http://dx.doi.org/10.1787/888933004637

Poland 2013: Marginal tax wedge decomposition

By level of gross earnings expressed as a % of the average wage

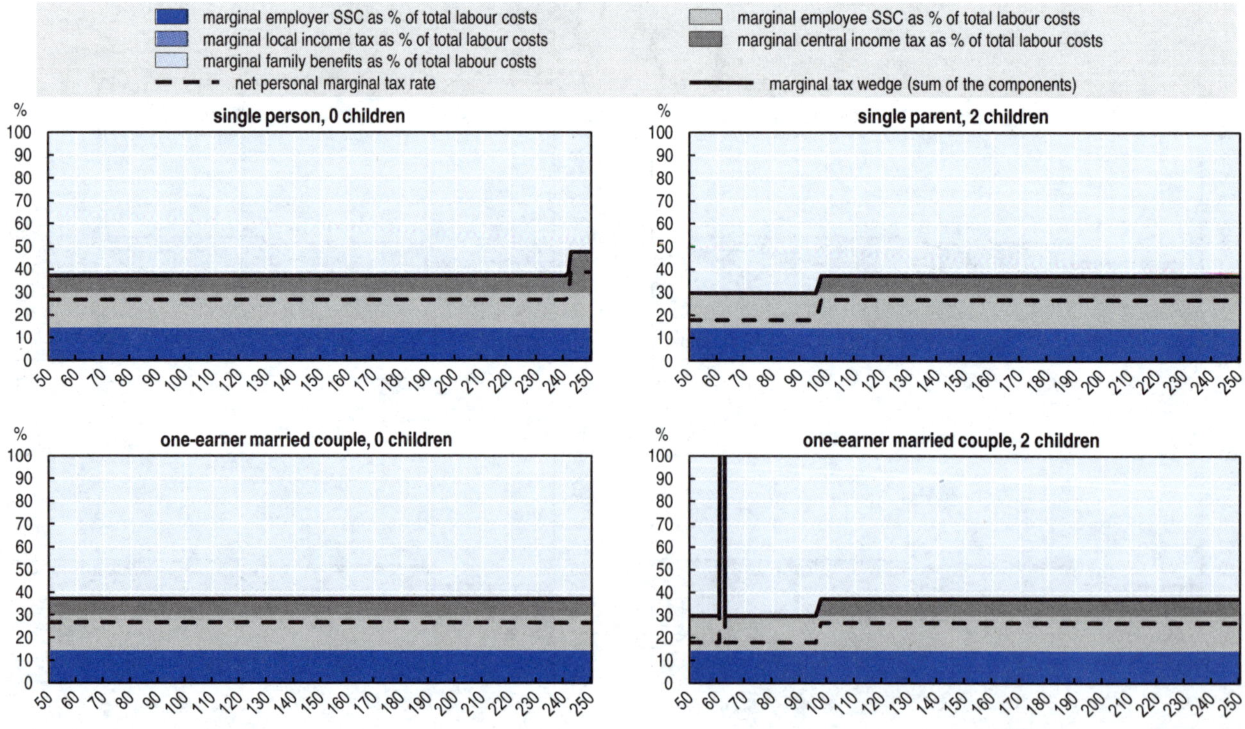

StatLink http://dx.doi.org/10.1787/888933005283

Portugal 2013: Average tax wedge decomposition

By level of gross earnings expressed as a % of the average wage

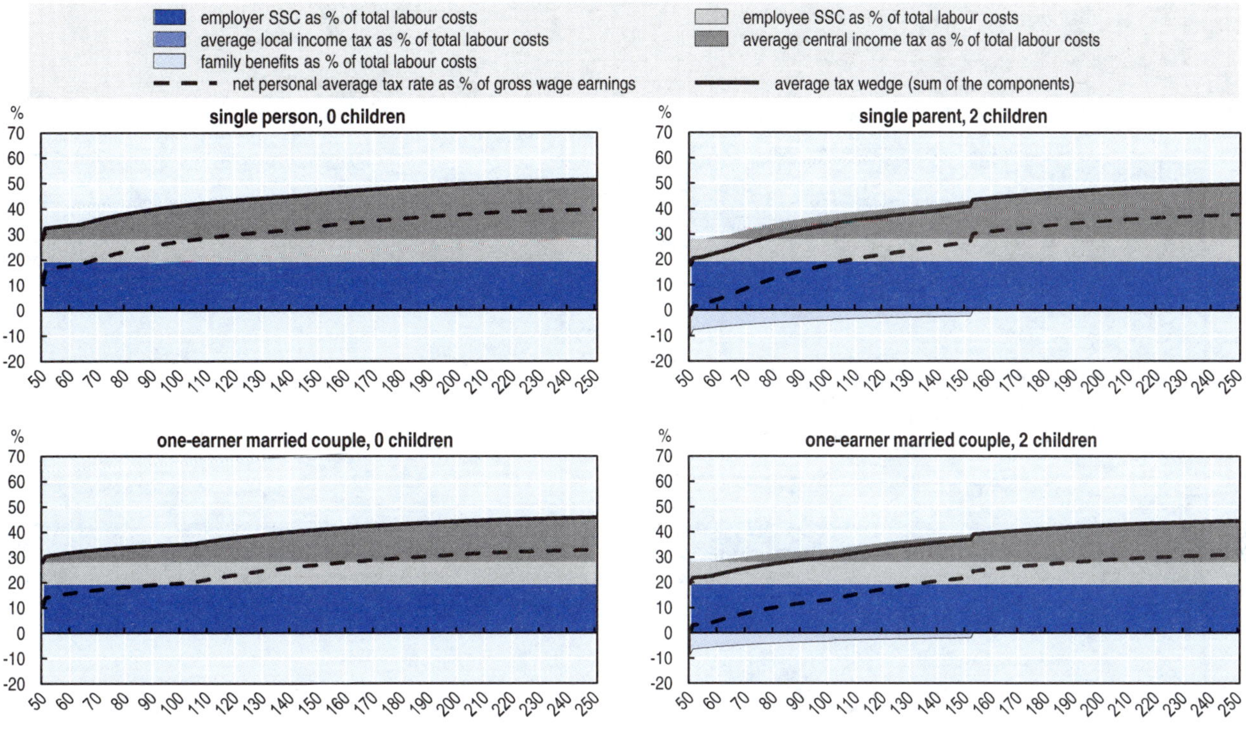

StatLink http://dx.doi.org/10.1787/888933004656

Portugal 2013: Marginal tax wedge decomposition

By level of gross earnings expressed as a % of the average wage

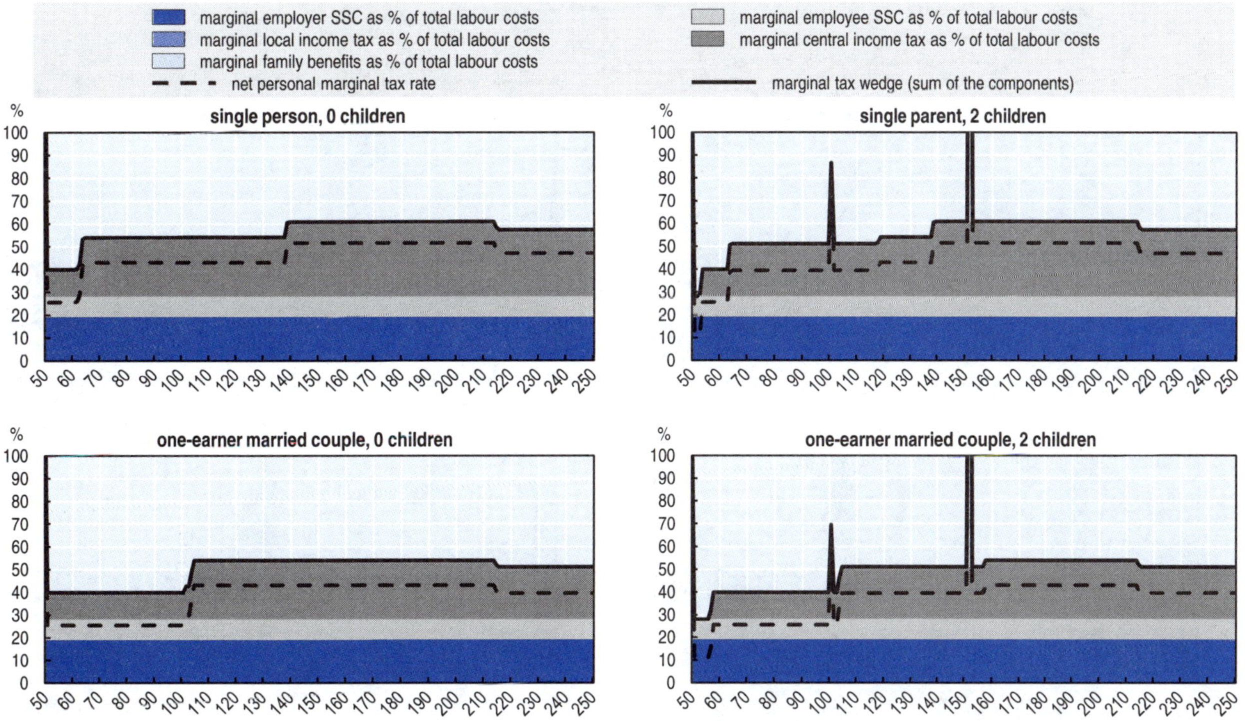

StatLink http://dx.doi.org/10.1787/888933005302

Slovak Republic 2013: Average tax wedge decomposition

By level of gross earnings expressed as a % of the average wage

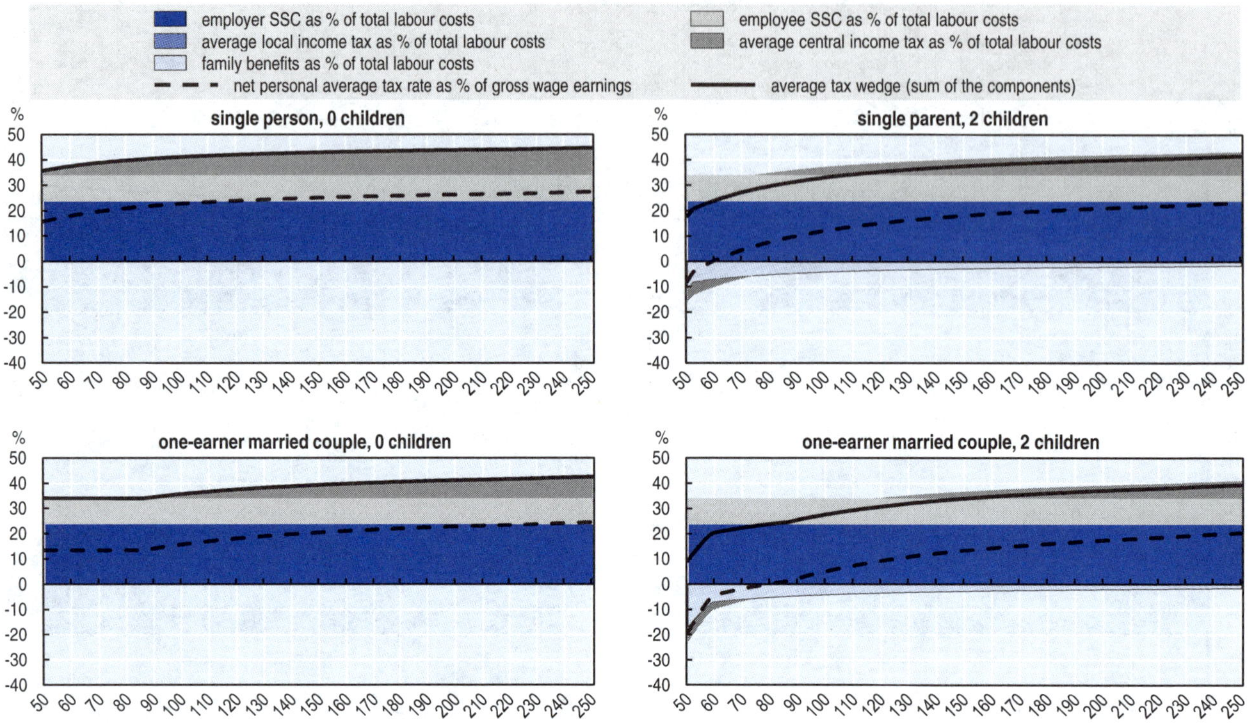

StatLink http://dx.doi.org/10.1787/888933004675

Slovak Republic 2013: Marginal tax wedge decomposition

By level of gross earnings expressed as a % of the average wage

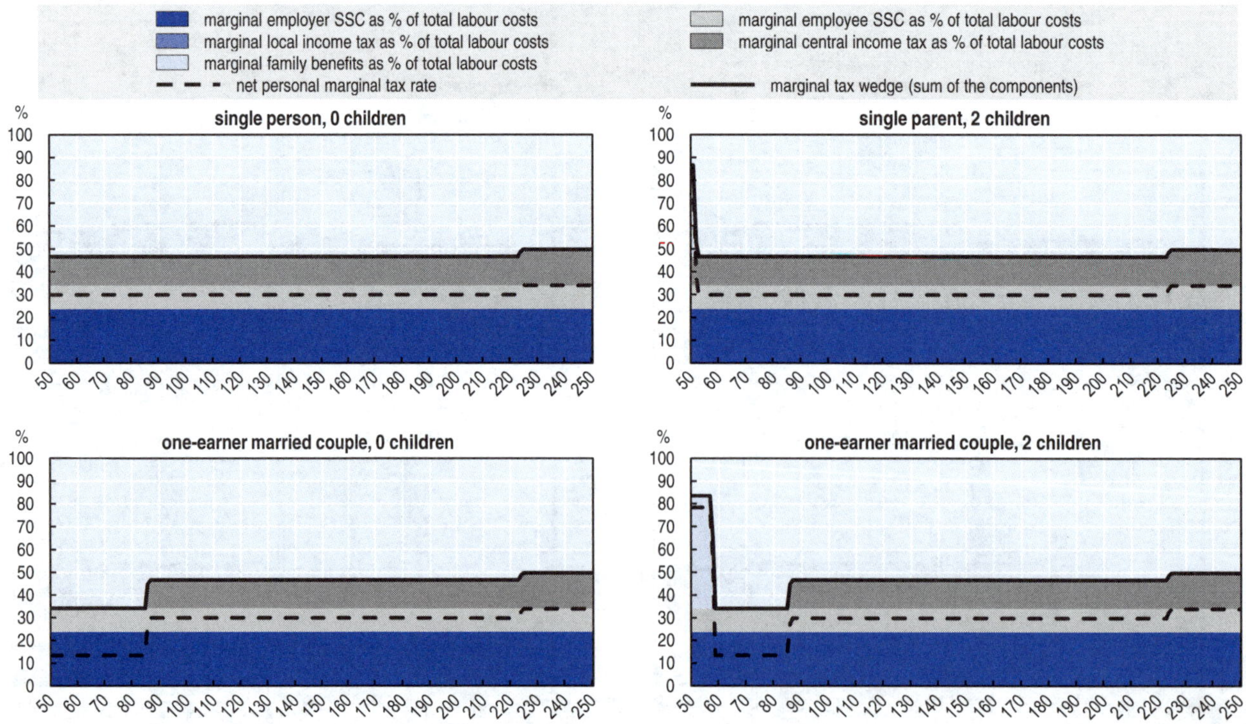

StatLink http://dx.doi.org/10.1787/888933005321

Slovenia 2013: Average tax wedge decomposition

By level of gross earnings expressed as a % of the average wage

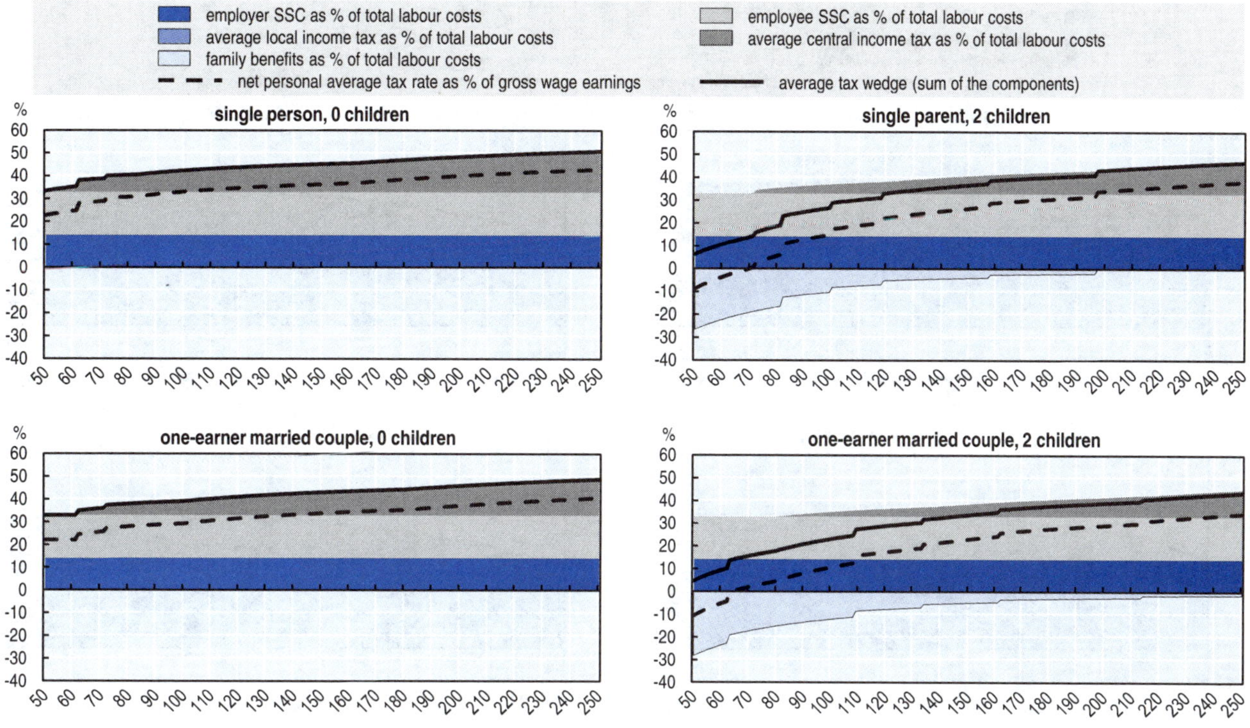

StatLink http://dx.doi.org/10.1787/888933004694

Slovenia 2013: Marginal tax wedge decomposition

By level of gross earnings expressed as a % of the average wage

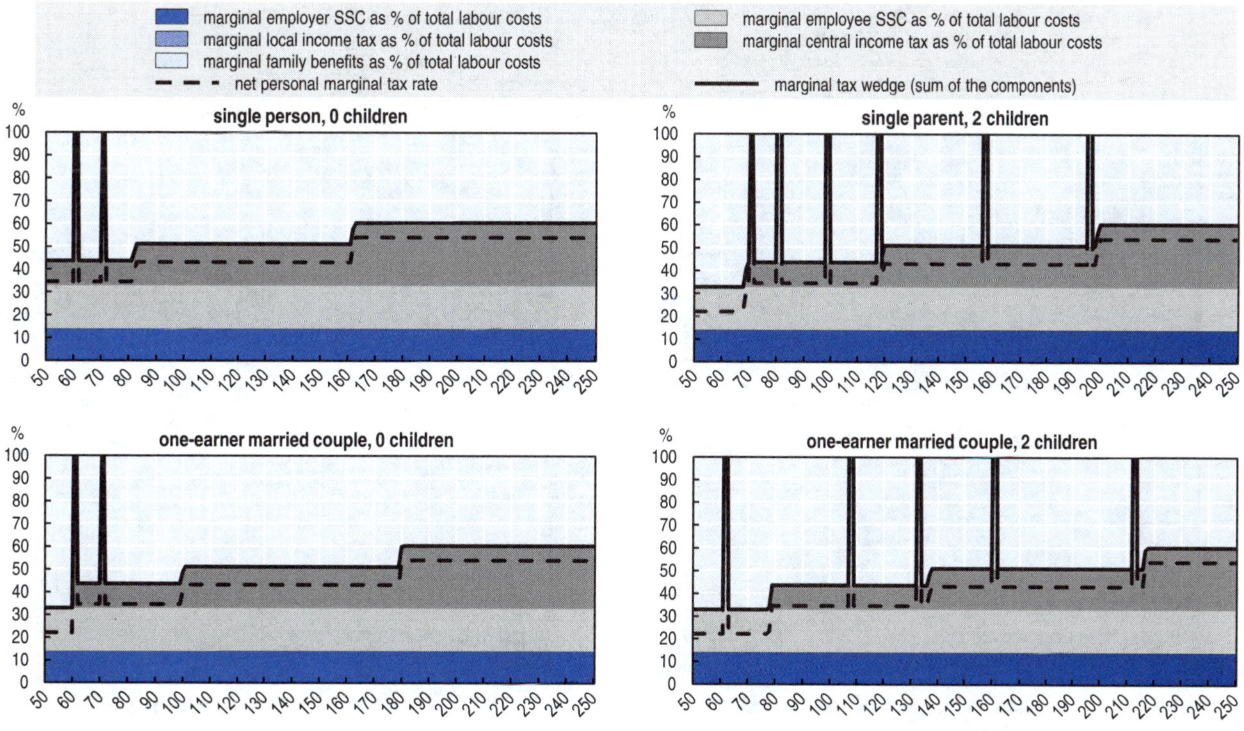

StatLink http://dx.doi.org/10.1787/888933005340

Spain 2013: Average tax wedge decomposition

By level of gross earnings expressed as a % of the average wage

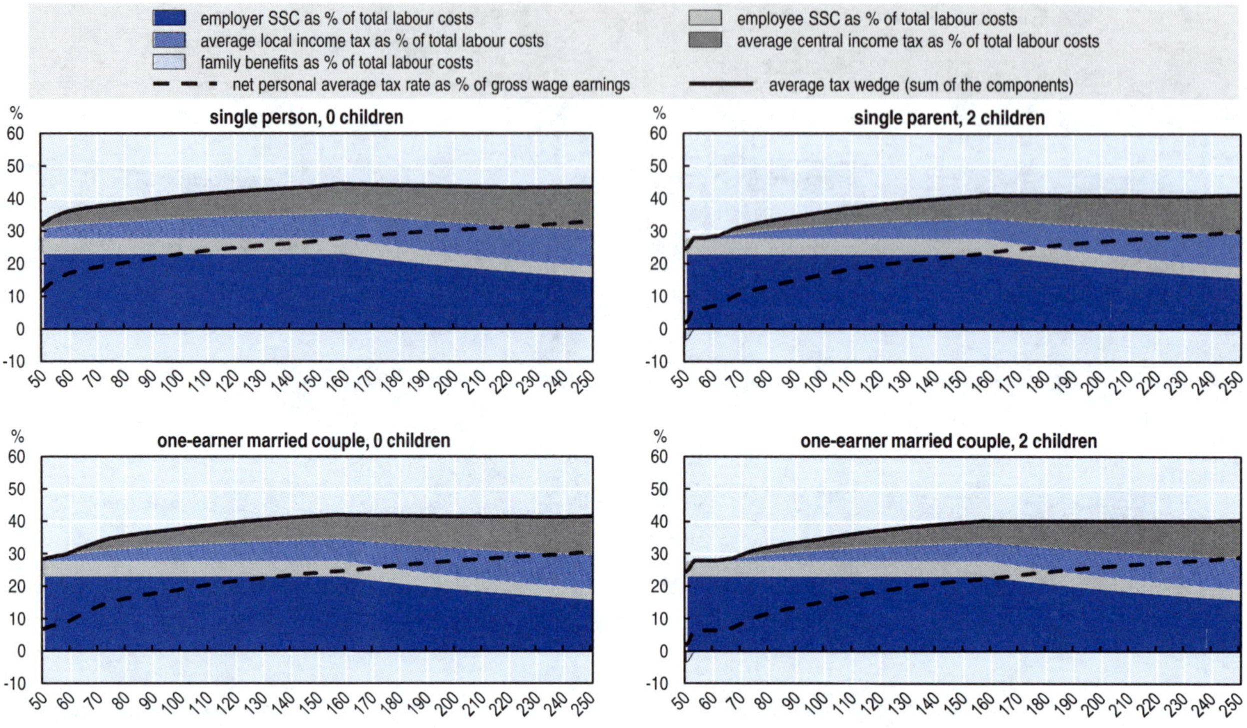

StatLink http://dx.doi.org/10.1787/888933004295

Spain 2013: Marginal tax wedge decomposition

By level of gross earnings expressed as a % of the average wage

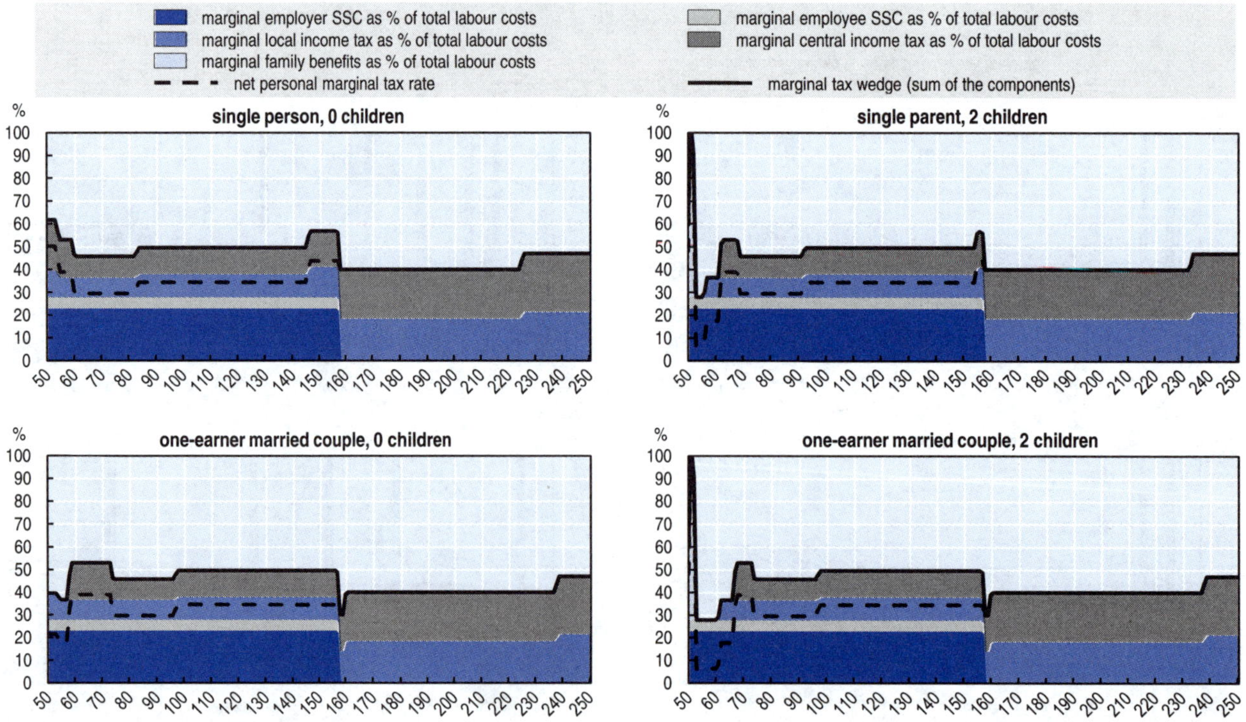

StatLink http://dx.doi.org/10.1787/888933004941

Sweden 2013: Average tax wedge decomposition

By level of gross earnings expressed as a % of the average wage

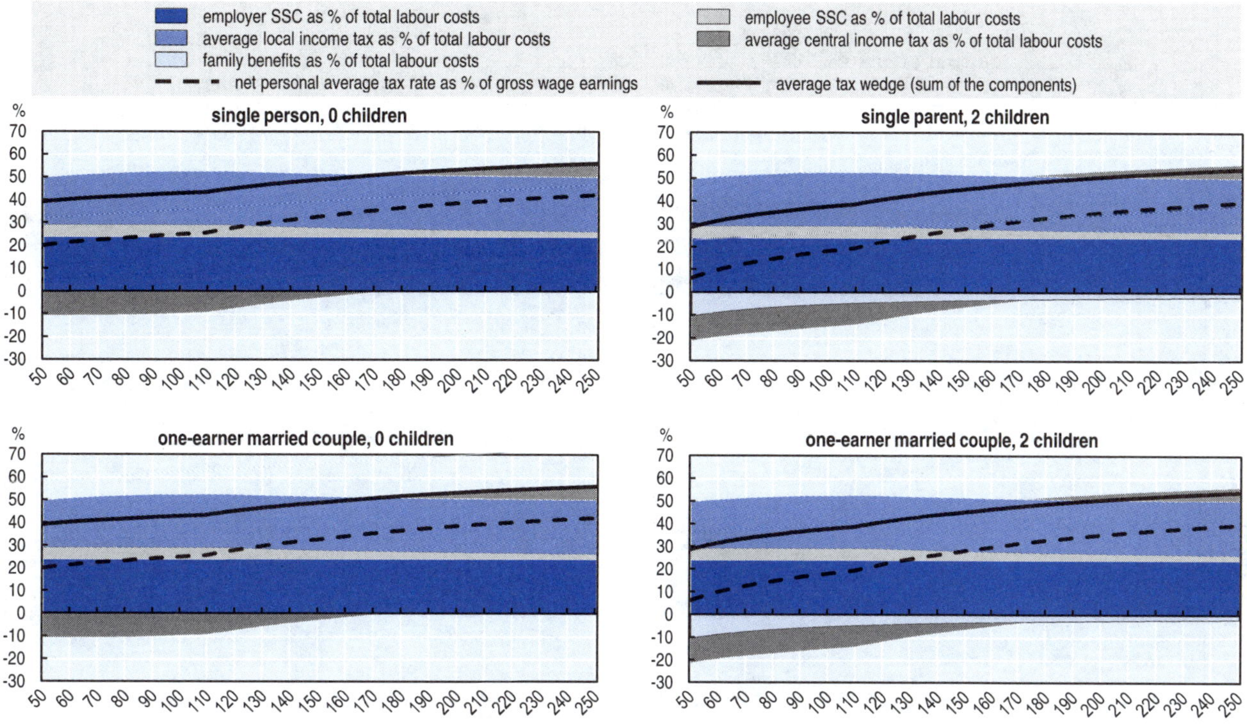

StatLink http://dx.doi.org/10.1787/888933004713

Sweden 2013: Marginal tax wedge decomposition

By level of gross earnings expressed as a % of the average wage

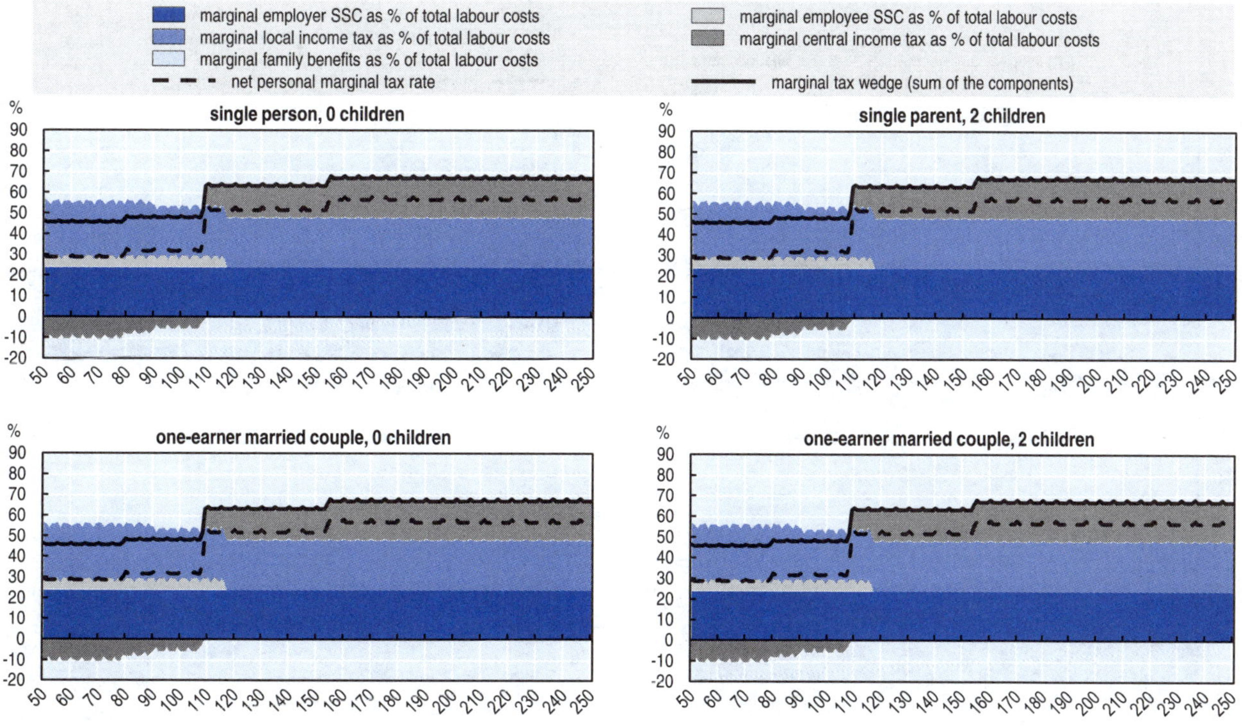

StatLink http://dx.doi.org/10.1787/888933005359

Switzerland 2013: Average tax wedge decomposition

By level of gross earnings expressed as a % of the average wage

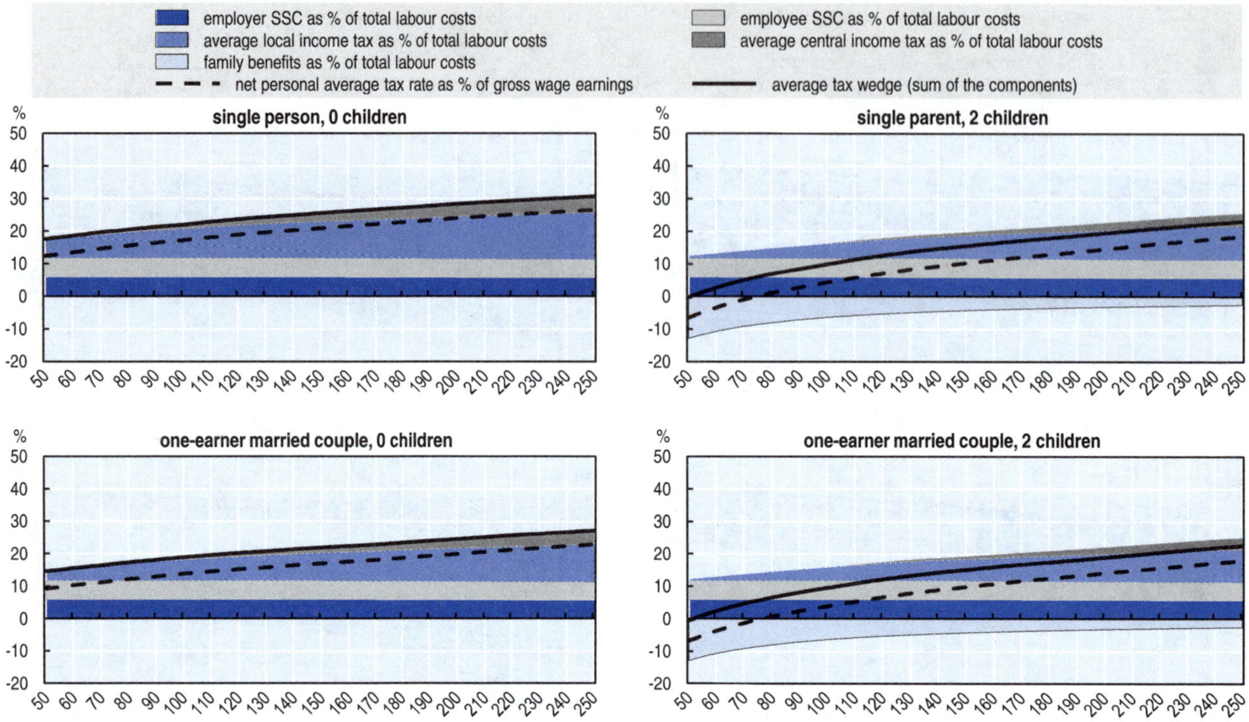

StatLink http://dx.doi.org/10.1787/888933004200

Switzerland 2013: Marginal tax wedge decomposition

By level of gross earnings expressed as a % of the average wage

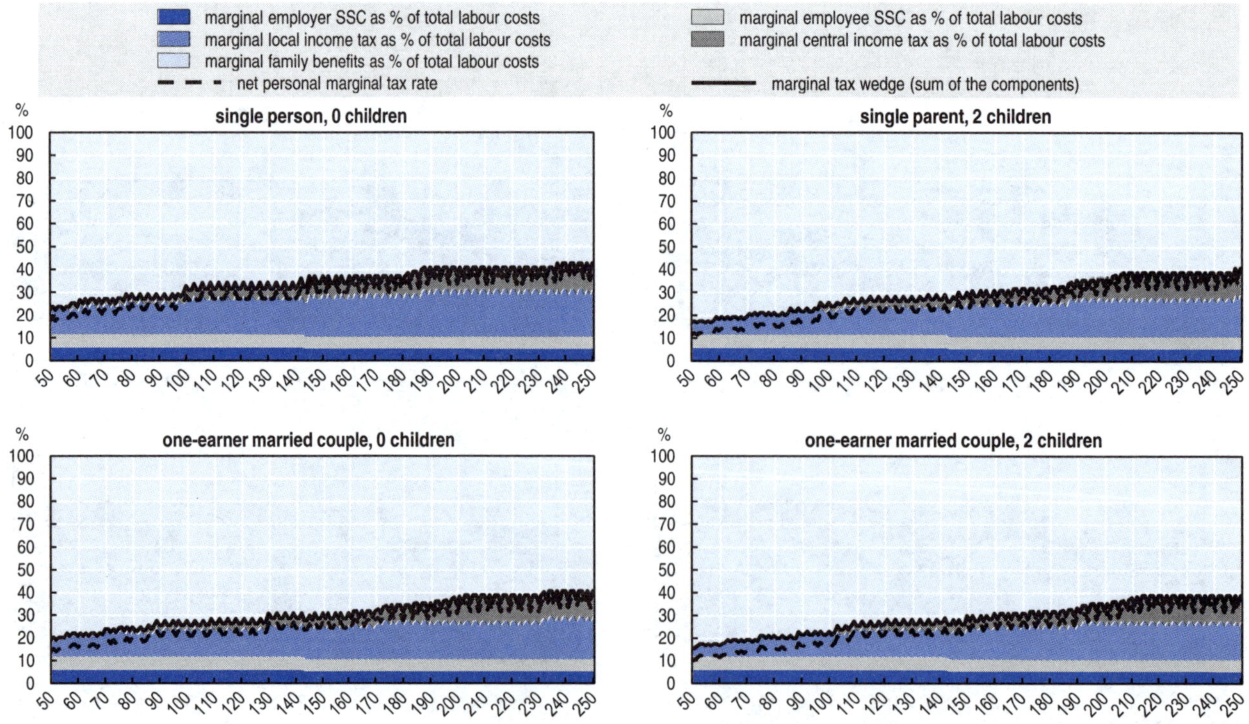

StatLink http://dx.doi.org/10.1787/888933004846

Turkey 2013: Average tax wedge decomposition

By level of gross earnings expressed as a % of the average wage

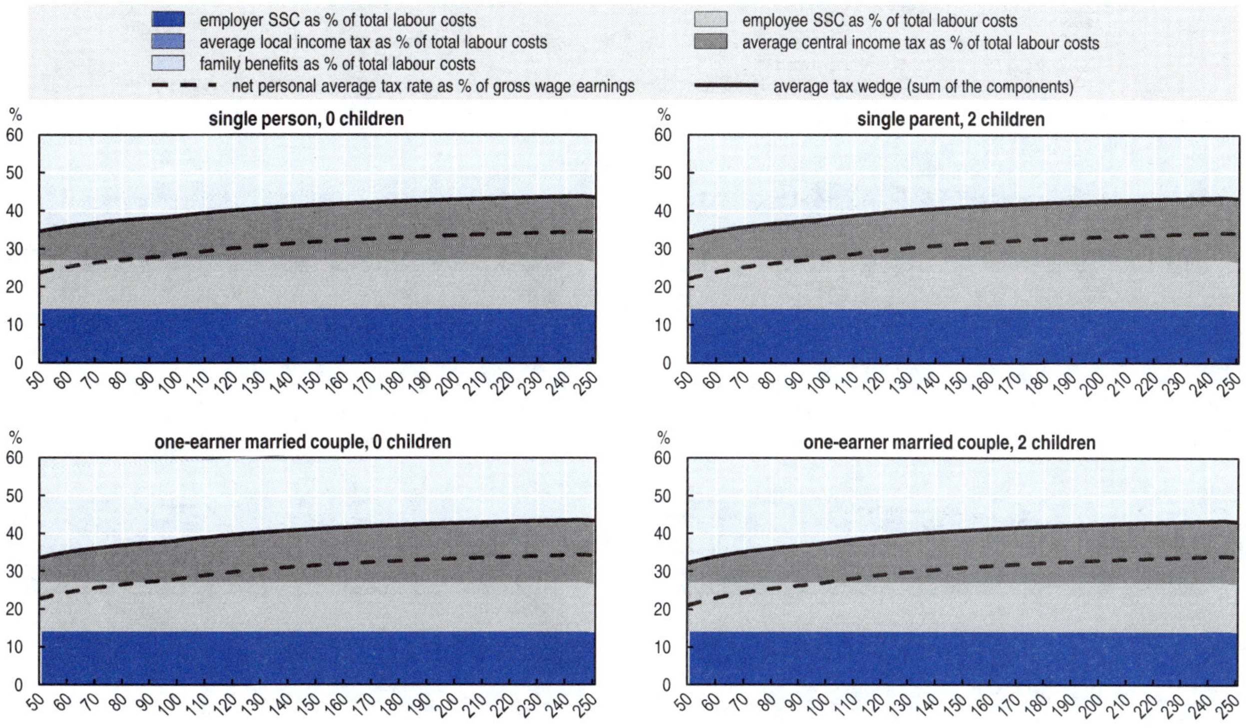

StatLink http://dx.doi.org/10.1787/888933004732

Turkey 2013: Marginal tax wedge decomposition

By level of gross earnings expressed as a % of the average wage

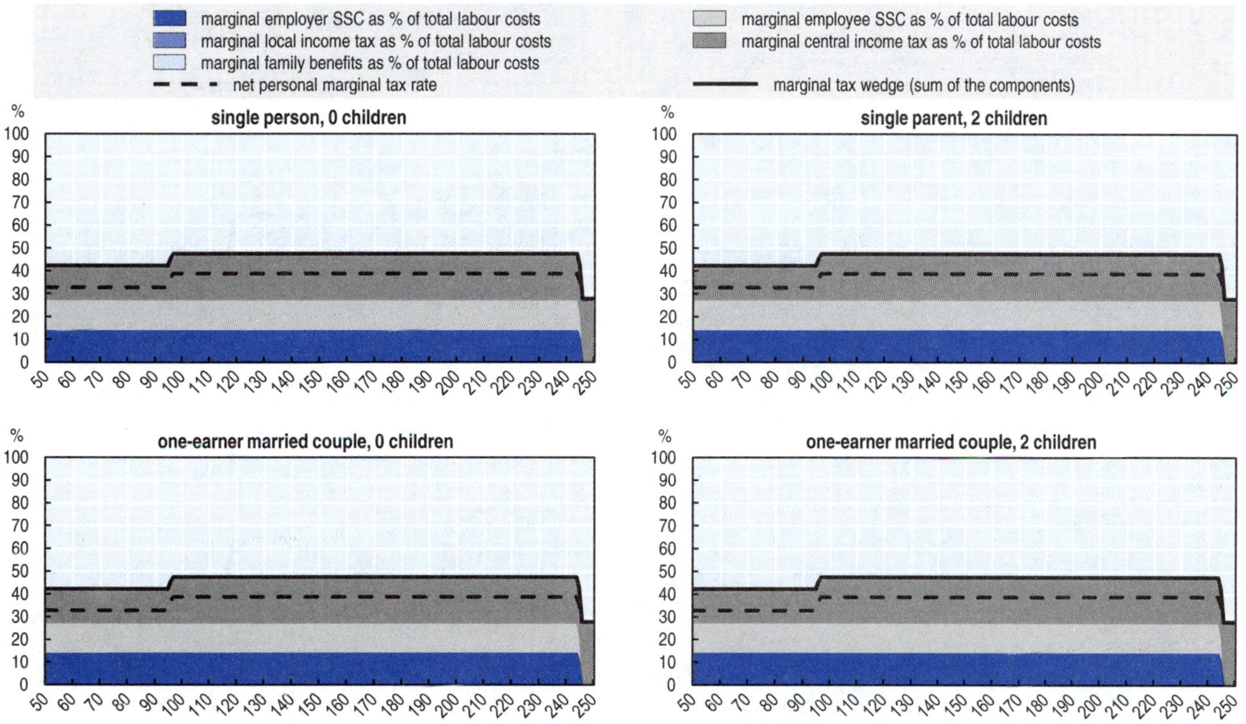

StatLink http://dx.doi.org/10.1787/888933005378

United Kingdom 2013: Average tax wedge decomposition

By level of gross earnings expressed as a % of the average wage

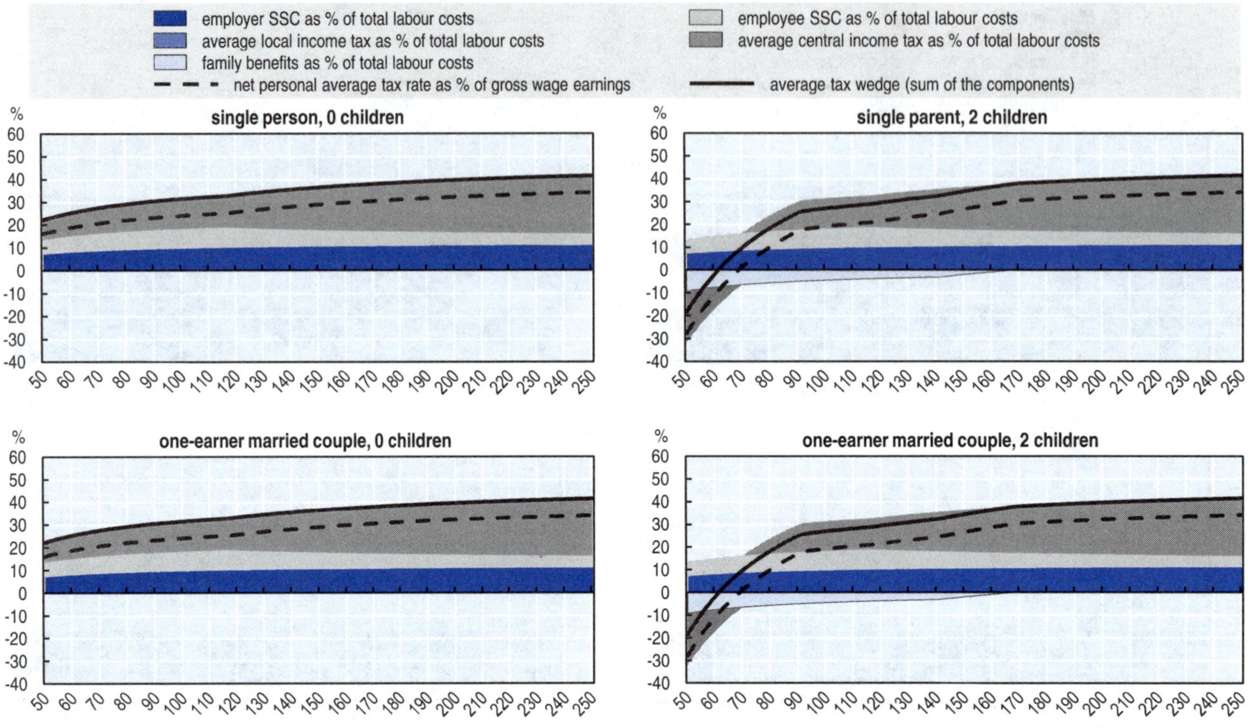

StatLink http://dx.doi.org/10.1787/888933004371

United Kingdom 2013: Marginal tax wedge decomposition

By level of gross earnings expressed as a % of the average wage

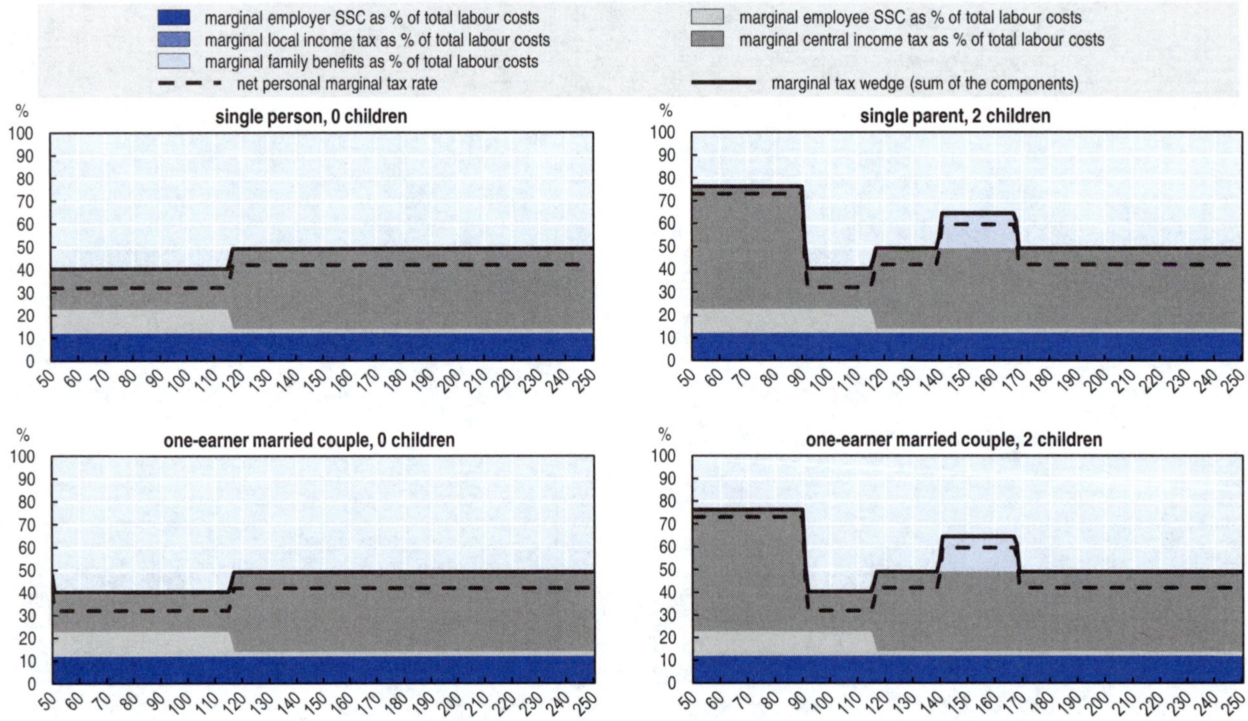

StatLink http://dx.doi.org/10.1787/888933005017

United States 2013: Average tax wedge decomposition

By level of gross earnings expressed as a % of the average wage

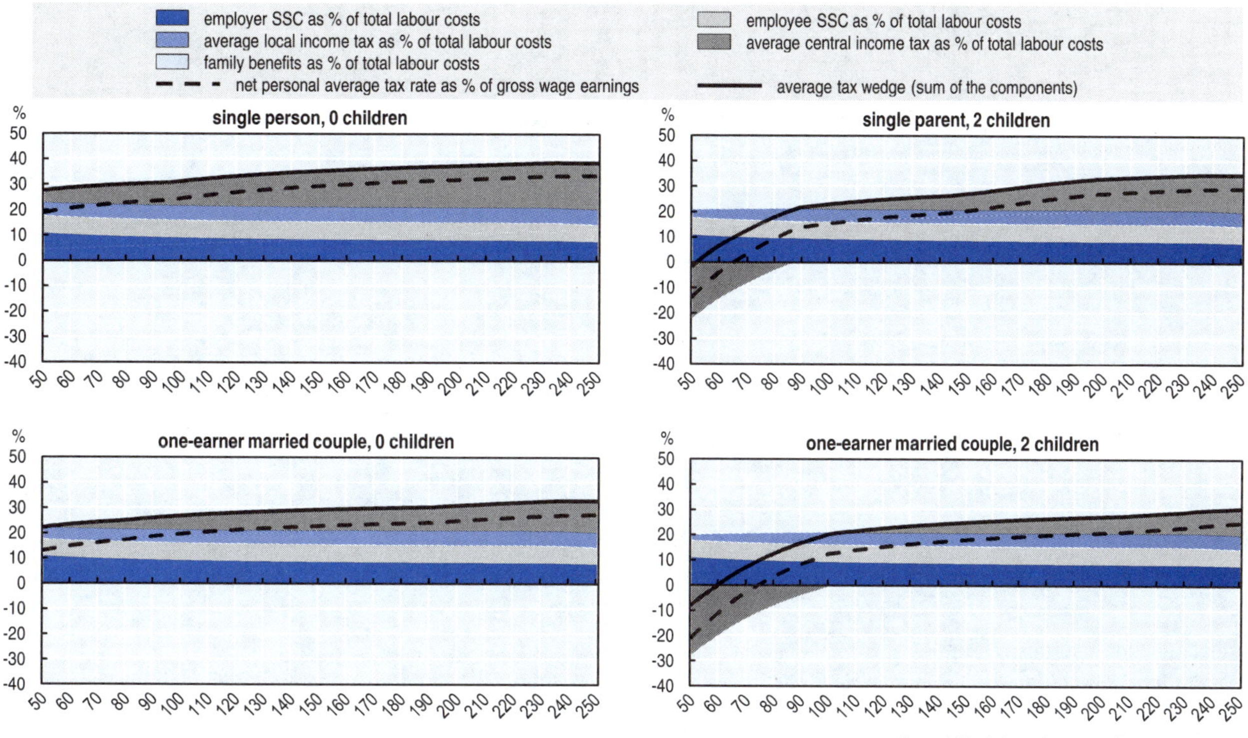

StatLink http://dx.doi.org/10.1787/888933004751

United States 2013: Marginal tax wedge decomposition

By level of gross earnings expressed as a % of the average wage

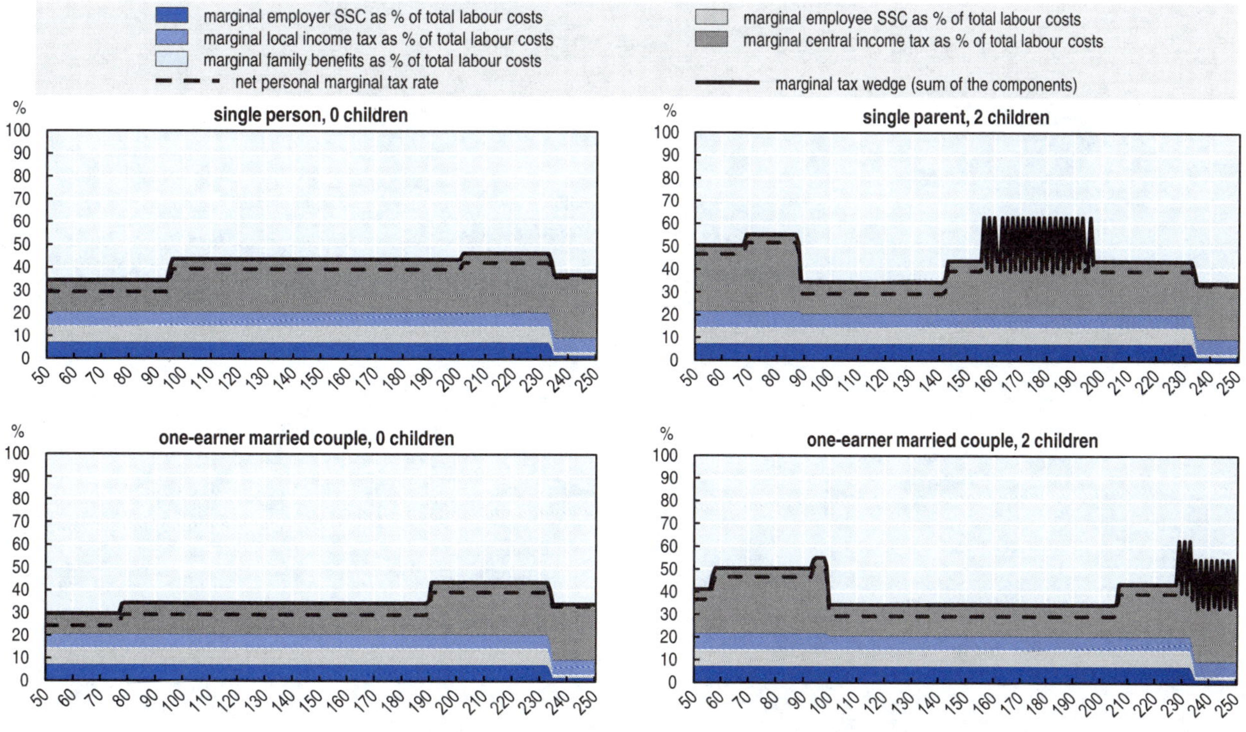

StatLink http://dx.doi.org/10.1787/888933005397

Taxing Wages 2014
Changes in structural labour income tax progressivity
over 2000-12 period in OECD member countries

Tax burdens, 2012 definitive results (and changes to 2013)

This section briefly reviews the definitive results for 2012 reported in Tables I.12-I.22 and what they show about changes between 2012 and 2013. The comparable 2013 data is shown in Tables I.1-I.11 and the formats of the two sets of tables are identical meaning that the changes for each family-type between the two years can be traced by comparing the corresponding columns in the two sets of Tables.

The following commentary focuses on changes in tax burdens and marginal tax rates for two of the eight family-types – single employees without children at the average wage level (column 2 of the tables) and one-earner married families with two children at the average wage level (column 5 of the tables). Comparing the columns 1, 3-4 and 6-8 of the tables gives corresponding results for the six other family-types. Generally, only those changes exceeding 1 percentage point for average effective rates and 5 percentage points for marginal effective rates are flagged.

Table I.12 presents the total tax wedge, income tax plus employee and employer's social security contributions less cash benefits by family-type as a percentage of total labour costs [gross wage plus employers' social security contributions (including payroll taxes)]. In the majority of countries, changes in the gap between total labour costs and the corresponding net take-home pay in 2013 as compared to 2012 were within plus or minus one percentage point. Comparing column 2 in Tables I.1 and I.12, the OECD average tax wedge increased by 0.1 percentage point for a single average worker between 2012 and 2013. It increased by more than one percentage point in Portugal (3.5 percentage points), the Slovak republic and the United States (both 1.5 percentage points) and Luxembourg (1.1 percentage points) and it fell by more than one percentage point in the Netherlands (-1.8 percentage points), Greece (-1.4 percentage points) and France (-1.2 percentage points).

For one-earner married couples (comparing column 5 of Tables I.1 and I.12), the OECD average tax wedge increased this time by 0.3 percentage points. The wedge increased by more than one percentage point in four countries: Portugal (1.9 percentage points), New Zealand and the Slovak republic (1.8 percentage points) and the United States (1.6 percentage points) and decreased by more than one percentage point in France and the Netherlands (both -1.5 percentage points).

Table I.13 shows the combined burden of income tax and employee social security contributions in the form of personal average tax rates as a percentage of gross wage earnings. For single persons on average earnings, this changed by more than one percentage point between 2012 and 2013 in Portugal (+4.4 percentage points), the United States (+1.7 percentage points), Luxembourg (+1.2 percentage points) and Greece

(-1.1 percentage points). For one-earner married couples with 2 children it increased by more than 1 percentage point in Portugal (2.3 percentage points), the United States (1.7 percentage points), Greece (1.4 percentage points) and Australia (1.3 percentage points).

Table I.14 provides the combined burden of income tax and employee social security contributions less the amount of cash family benefits (net personal average tax rate). Comparing column 2 of Tables I.3 and I.14, for single persons at average earnings, there was an increase of more than one percentage point between 2012 and 2013 in Portugal (4.4 percentage points), the United States (1.7 percentage points) and Luxembourg (1.3 percentage points) and a reduction in Greece (-1.1 percentage points). Comparing column 5 of Tables I.3 and I.14, increases in the net personal average tax rate of one-earner married couples exceeding one percentage point are noted for Portugal (2.3 percentage points), New Zealand (1.8 percentage points), the United States (1.7 percentage points), Greece (1.4 percentage points) and Iceland (1.1 percentage point).

Table I.15 presents information on income tax due as a percentage of gross wage earnings. In most OECD member countries, the income tax for single persons at average earnings has changed only slightly between 2012 and 2013. The OECD average income tax has increased by 0.1 percentage point for the single average worker. Comparing column 2 of Tables I.4 and I.15, the income tax rate increased by more than one percentage point only in Portugal (4.4 percentage points) and in Luxembourg (1.3 percentage points); there were decrease of more than one percentage point in the Netherlands (-1.2 percentage points) and Greece (-1.1 percentage points) only.

The OECD average income tax rate for the one-earner married couple with two children also increased by 0.1 percentage point during this period. Increases by greater than one percentage point were observed in two countries: Portugal (2.2 percentage points), Greece (1.4 percentage points) and Australia (1.3 percentage points). As for the single average worker, there was a decrease of more than one percentage point in the Netherlands (-1.5 percentage points) only.

Table I.16 shows information on employee social security contributions as a percentage of gross wage earnings. Comparing columns 2 and 5 of Tables I.5 and I.16, there were changes of more than one percentage point in the United States only. In the latter, the average employee social security contributions increased by 2.0 percentage points for both the average single person and the average one-earner married couple with two children during this period. The OECD average has increased by 0.1 percentage point for the two family-types.

Table I.17 shows the marginal tax wedge (rate of income tax plus employee and employer social security contributions and payroll taxes where applicable minus benefits) in 2012. Comparing columns 2 and 5 respectively in Tables I.6 and I.17, changes between 2012 and 2013 in the marginal wedge were generally within the range of plus or minus five percentage points. There were changes of more than five percentage points in five OECD countries for the two family-types. The marginal tax wedge increased for both family-types by 22.8 percentage points in Canada, by 7.1 percentage points in Denmark and by 5.2 percentage points in Turkey. It increased in Portugal (6.1 percentage points) for the single average worker and in Poland (7.6 percentage points) and the Netherlands (5.1 percentage points) for the one-earner married couples with two children at the average wage.

Table I.18 presents the marginal rate of income tax plus employee social security contributions minus benefits by family-type and wage level. Comparing columns 2 and 5 respectively in Tables I.7 and I.18, the pattern of changes between 2012 and 2013 in the marginal rate were similar to that for the tax wedge discussed above. For the two family-types being focused on, the examples of changes outside the range of plus or minus five percentage points were in Canada (+25.0 percentage points for both family-types), Denmark (+7.1 percentage points for both family-types), the Netherlands (+6.8 percentage points for the one-earner married couple), Poland (+8.9 percentage points for the one-earner married couple), Portugal (+7.5 percentage points for the single worker) and Turkey (+6.0 percentage points for both family-types). Table I.19 shows the increase in net income (in per cent) after an increase of one currency unit in gross wage earnings for 2012.[1] Table I.20 provides the percentage increase in net income given an increase in one currency unit of gross labour costs for the same year.[2] The results shown in these two tables are directly dependent upon the marginal and average tax rates that have been discussed in the paragraphs above. Tables I.21 and I.22 report background information on levels of labour costs plus gross and net wages in 2012.

Notes

1. The reported elasticities in Table I.19 are calculated as (100 – METR)/(100 – AETR), where METR is the marginal rate of income tax plus employee social security contributions less cash benefits reported in Table I.18 and AETR is the average rate plus employee social security contributions less cash benefits reported in Table I.14.
2. The reported elasticities in Table I.20 are calculated as (100 – METR)/(100 – AETR), where METR is the marginal rate of income tax plus employee and employer social security contributions less cash benefits reported in Table I.17 and AETR is the average rate plus employee and employer social security contributions less cash benefits reported in Table I.12.

Table I.12. **Income tax plus employee and employer contributions less cash benefits, 2012**

As % of labour costs, by family-type and wage level

	Single no ch 67 (% AW)	Single no ch 100 (% AW)	Single no ch 167 (% AW)	Single 2 ch 67 (% AW)	Married 2 ch 100-0 (% AW)	Married 2 ch 100-33 (% AW)[2]	Married 2 ch 100-67 (% AW)[2]	Married no ch 100-33 (% AW)[2]
Australia	21.5	27.2	33.0	-4.0	16.5	18.6	24.9	23.4
Austria	44.2	48.8	51.4	27.8	37.9	37.8	41.1	45.0
Belgium	50.4	56.0	60.9	36.8	41.3	42.5	48.9	48.8
Canada	26.1	30.8	33.0	-6.9	18.4	23.7	27.0	27.7
Chile	7.0	7.0	7.9	6.1	7.0	4.8	6.6	7.0
Czech Republic	39.4	42.5	44.9	14.9	21.0	30.0	34.2	40.2
Denmark	37.0	38.5	45.1	11.6	27.8	32.5	34.1	37.2
Estonia	39.2	40.4	41.4	26.2	32.4	35.0	36.6	39.2
Finland	36.8	42.6	48.5	25.7	37.4	35.0	37.2	38.9
France	46.9	50.1	54.0	38.7	43.1	41.0	45.5	46.4
Germany	45.5	49.6	51.3	31.1	34.0	38.8	42.3	45.5
Greece	39.7	42.9	48.2	38.5	43.9	42.2	42.7	42.5
Hungary	47.9	49.5	50.7	22.8	34.2	35.4	39.6	47.4
Iceland	28.6	33.4	37.8	15.3	18.2	25.9	30.2	28.9
Ireland	20.0	25.9	38.1	-26.0	6.1	12.5	18.0	19.6
Israel	13.7	20.4	28.6	0.4	16.6	12.7	13.8	17.0
Italy	44.6	47.7	53.1	29.1	38.7	40.4	43.2	44.6
Japan	29.9	31.3	34.2	23.5	25.7	27.2	28.2	30.4
Korea	18.0	21.0	22.6	17.3	18.5	18.6	18.6	20.0
Luxembourg	29.0	35.9	43.2	3.1	13.5	17.8	23.2	27.5
Mexico	13.6	19.0	21.9	13.6	19.0	16.6	16.8	16.6
Netherlands	33.4	38.7	42.4	11.8	32.3	29.8	32.0	34.6
New Zealand	13.1	16.4	22.4	-18.4	0.6	8.7	14.7	15.2
Norway	34.2	37.4	43.1	21.6	31.1	31.8	33.7	34.9
Poland	34.7	35.5	36.2	29.6	29.6	31.1	32.3	34.7
Portugal	32.6	37.6	43.6	23.1	27.9	29.0	34.5	32.6
Slovak Republic	36.9	39.6	41.6	24.4	25.8	30.4	33.5	36.6
Slovenia	38.5	42.5	47.5	12.9	23.2	30.6	34.3	40.1
Spain	37.1	40.6	43.6	30.2	34.7	36.4	37.5	37.4
Sweden	40.7	42.9	50.7	32.8	37.6	37.1	38.8	41.1
Switzerland	19.2	21.9	26.5	4.6	9.9	12.9	16.0	19.8
Turkey[1]	36.5	38.4	41.9	35.4	37.2	37.9	38.6	38.4
United Kingdom	27.9	32.1	37.8	6.4	27.5	24.4	27.7	27.9
United States	27.7	29.8	34.6	9.9	18.7	23.3	25.1	28.2
Unweighted average								
OECD-Average	**32.1**	**35.7**	**40.0**	**16.8**	**26.1**	**28.0**	**30.9**	**32.8**
OECD-EU 21	**38.2**	**41.9**	**46.4**	**21.5**	**30.9**	**32.8**	**36.1**	**38.5**

Note: ch = children

1. Wage figures are based on the old definition of average worker (ISIC D, Rev. 3).
2. Two-earner family.

StatLink http://dx.doi.org/10.1787/888933006423

Table I.13. **Income tax plus employee contributions, 2012**

As % of gross wage earnings, by family-type and wage level

	Single no ch 67 (% AW)	Single no ch 100 (% AW)	Single no ch 167 (% AW)	Single 2 ch 67 (% AW)	Married 2 ch 100-0 (% AW)	Married 2 ch 100-33 (% AW)[2]	Married 2 ch 100-67 (% AW)[2]	Married no ch 100-33 (% AW)[2]
Australia	16.8	22.9	29.1	15.2	21.8	18.0	20.5	18.8
Austria	27.9	33.9	38.6	24.8	31.8	28.7	31.2	29.0
Belgium	36.3	42.7	49.5	31.0	31.7	33.5	38.7	35.3
Canada	18.8	22.6	26.8	8.3	16.1	18.2	20.2	19.2
Chile	7.0	7.0	7.9	7.0	7.0	7.0	7.0	7.0
Czech Republic	18.8	22.9	26.2	5.5	5.9	13.3	16.0	19.9
Denmark	37.5	38.9	45.1	37.5	34.8	37.7	38.3	37.7
Estonia	18.3	19.9	21.2	13.3	13.3	15.8	17.3	18.3
Finland	22.4	29.5	36.8	22.4	29.5	24.9	26.6	24.9
France	26.3	28.2	33.9	21.3	22.2	22.0	25.2	26.3
Germany	34.8	39.8	43.8	17.7	21.0	26.8	31.0	34.8
Greece	22.5	26.6	33.4	21.0	27.9	25.7	26.4	26.1
Hungary	34.5	35.1	36.6	21.8	26.7	28.6	29.8	35.0
Iceland	23.0	28.2	32.9	23.0	18.7	23.3	26.1	23.3
Ireland	11.4	17.9	31.5	6.6	10.4	11.4	15.3	11.4
Israel	10.2	16.6	24.9	5.8	16.6	11.9	12.3	13.4
Italy	26.9	30.9	38.0	19.9	24.4	23.7	26.7	26.8
Japan	19.8	21.3	25.1	19.8	19.9	20.4	20.7	20.4
Korea	9.7	13.0	15.7	8.9	10.3	10.3	10.4	11.9
Luxembourg	20.3	28.0	36.2	12.9	17.4	18.6	22.5	18.6
Mexico	1.6	9.5	14.1	1.6	9.5	4.9	6.4	4.9
Netherlands	26.7	32.1	38.3	12.7	28.9	25.6	27.2	27.9
New Zealand	13.1	16.4	22.4	14.6	16.4	15.2	15.7	15.2
Norway	25.5	29.2	35.6	21.8	26.7	26.3	27.7	26.3
Poland	23.7	24.7	25.5	17.8	17.8	19.6	21.0	23.7
Portugal	16.6	22.8	30.2	12.2	14.9	14.9	18.9	16.6
Slovak Republic	19.3	22.8	25.4	11.6	10.7	15.1	18.3	18.9
Slovenia	28.7	33.2	39.0	22.1	24.9	25.8	27.7	30.5
Spain	18.3	22.9	28.2	9.3	15.2	17.3	18.8	18.7
Sweden	22.1	24.9	35.2	22.1	24.9	22.6	23.8	22.6
Switzerland	14.1	17.1	21.9	8.9	11.1	12.6	14.8	14.8
Turkey[1]	26.0	28.2	32.3	24.8	26.9	27.7	28.5	28.3
United Kingdom	21.1	24.7	30.3	5.2	24.7	21.1	23.3	21.1
United States	19.8	22.9	28.7	0.1	10.7	14.9	17.4	20.3
Unweighted average								
OECD-Average	**21.2**	**25.2**	**30.6**	**15.5**	**19.7**	**20.1**	**22.1**	**22.0**
OECD-EU 21	**24.5**	**28.7**	**34.4**	**17.6**	**21.9**	**22.5**	**25.0**	**25.0**

Note: ch = children

1. Wage figures are based on the old definition of average worker (ISIC D, Rev. 3).
2. Two-earner family.

StatLink http://dx.doi.org/10.1787/888933006442

Table I.14. **Income tax plus employee contributions less cash benefits, 2012**

As % of gross wage earnings, by family-type and wage level

	Single no ch 67 (% AW)	Single no ch 100 (% AW)	Single no ch 167 (% AW)	Single 2 ch 67 (% AW)	Married 2 ch 100-0 (% AW)	Married 2 ch 100-33 (% AW)[2]	Married 2 ch 100-67 (% AW)[2]	Married no ch 100-33 (% AW)[2]
Australia	16.8	22.9	29.1	-10.2	11.6	13.7	20.5	18.8
Austria	27.9	33.9	38.6	6.8	19.8	19.6	24.0	29.0
Belgium	36.3	42.7	49.5	18.8	23.6	27.4	33.9	35.3
Canada	17.5	22.6	26.8	-19.4	8.7	14.8	18.3	19.2
Chile	7.0	7.0	7.9	6.1	7.0	4.8	6.6	7.0
Czech Republic	18.8	22.9	26.2	-14.0	-5.9	6.2	11.8	19.9
Denmark	37.0	38.5	45.1	11.6	27.8	32.5	34.1	37.2
Estonia	18.3	19.9	21.2	0.8	9.1	12.7	14.8	18.3
Finland	22.4	29.5	36.8	8.7	23.1	20.2	22.8	24.9
France	26.3	28.2	33.9	15.0	18.0	18.9	22.6	26.3
Germany	34.8	39.8	43.8	17.7	21.0	26.8	31.0	34.8
Greece	22.5	26.6	33.4	21.0	27.9	25.7	26.4	26.1
Hungary	34.5	35.1	36.6	3.1	15.4	20.2	23.1	35.0
Iceland	23.0	28.2	32.9	8.7	11.8	20.1	24.7	23.3
Ireland	11.4	17.9	31.5	-39.5	-3.9	3.6	9.1	11.4
Israel	10.2	16.6	24.9	-3.7	12.6	8.9	9.9	13.4
Italy	26.9	30.9	38.0	6.4	19.0	21.3	24.9	26.8
Japan	19.8	21.3	25.1	12.4	15.0	16.7	17.8	20.4
Korea	9.7	13.0	15.7	8.9	10.3	10.3	10.4	11.9
Luxembourg	20.3	28.0	36.2	-8.9	2.9	7.7	13.7	18.6
Mexico	1.6	9.5	14.1	1.6	9.5	4.9	6.4	4.9
Netherlands	26.7	32.1	38.3	3.0	25.0	22.6	24.9	27.9
New Zealand	13.1	16.4	22.4	-18.4	0.6	8.7	14.7	15.2
Norway	25.5	29.2	35.6	11.4	22.1	22.9	25.0	26.3
Poland	23.7	24.7	25.5	17.8	17.8	19.6	21.0	23.7
Portugal	16.6	22.8	30.2	4.8	10.8	12.1	18.9	16.6
Slovak Republic	19.3	22.8	25.4	3.4	5.1	11.0	15.0	18.9
Slovenia	28.7	33.2	39.0	-1.1	10.8	19.4	23.7	30.5
Spain	18.3	22.9	28.2	9.3	15.2	17.3	18.8	18.7
Sweden	22.1	24.9	35.2	11.7	17.9	17.4	19.6	22.6
Switzerland	14.1	17.1	21.9	-1.3	4.2	7.4	10.7	14.8
Turkey[1]	26.0	28.2	32.3	24.8	26.9	27.7	28.5	28.3
United Kingdom	21.1	24.7	30.3	-2.3	19.7	17.3	20.3	21.1
United States	19.8	22.9	28.7	0.1	10.7	14.9	17.4	20.3
Unweighted average								
OECD-Average	**21.1**	**25.2**	**30.6**	**3.4**	**13.9**	**16.3**	**19.6**	**22.0**
OECD-EU 21	**24.5**	**28.7**	**34.4**	**4.5**	**15.3**	**18.1**	**21.6**	**24.9**

Note: ch = children

1. Wage figures are based on the old definition of average worker (ISIC D, Rev. 3).
2. Two-earner family.

StatLink http://dx.doi.org/10.1787/888933006461

Table I.15. **Income tax, 2012**

As % of gross wage earnings, by family-type and wage level

	Single no ch 67 (% AW)	Single no ch 100 (% AW)	Single no ch 167 (% AW)	Single 2 ch 67 (% AW)	Married 2 ch 100-0 (% AW)	Married 2 ch 100-33 (% AW)[2]	Married 2 ch 100-67 (% AW)[2]	Married no ch 100-33 (% AW)[2]
Australia	16.8	22.9	29.1	15.2	21.8	18.0	20.5	18.8
Austria	9.8	15.9	22.8	6.8	13.8	11.4	13.2	11.7
Belgium	22.4	28.7	35.4	17.0	17.7	22.7	24.7	24.5
Canada	11.6	15.3	21.8	1.1	8.8	11.3	13.0	12.3
Chile	0.0	0.0	0.9	0.0	0.0	0.0	0.0	0.0
Czech Republic	7.8	11.9	15.2	-5.5	-5.1	2.3	5.0	8.9
Denmark	33.4	36.2	43.4	33.4	32.1	33.6	35.1	33.6
Estonia	15.5	17.1	18.4	10.5	10.5	13.0	14.5	15.5
Finland	14.9	21.8	29.1	14.9	21.8	17.5	19.1	17.5
France	12.6	14.4	20.8	7.6	8.5	8.3	11.5	12.6
Germany	14.1	19.0	27.6	-2.8	0.6	6.3	10.6	14.1
Greece	6.0	10.1	16.9	4.5	11.4	9.2	9.9	9.6
Hungary	16.0	16.6	18.1	3.3	8.2	10.1	11.3	16.5
Iceland	22.3	27.7	32.7	22.3	18.2	22.6	25.5	22.6
Ireland	8.6	14.8	27.9	3.9	7.2	9.0	12.3	9.0
Israel	4.3	8.7	15.4	0.0	8.7	5.1	5.2	6.6
Italy	17.4	21.4	28.5	10.4	14.9	14.2	17.2	17.3
Japan	6.1	7.6	12.1	6.1	6.2	6.7	7.0	6.7
Korea	1.5	4.9	8.8	0.8	2.1	2.1	2.2	3.7
Luxembourg	8.1	15.7	23.9	0.7	5.1	6.4	10.2	6.4
Mexico	0.4	8.2	12.6	0.4	8.2	3.6	5.0	3.6
Netherlands	5.2	16.9	29.1	3.3	16.7	12.8	12.1	12.9
New Zealand	13.1	16.4	22.4	14.6	16.4	15.2	15.7	15.2
Norway	17.7	21.4	27.8	14.0	18.9	18.5	19.9	18.5
Poland	5.9	6.9	7.7	0.0	0.0	1.7	3.1	5.9
Portugal	5.6	11.8	19.2	1.2	3.9	3.9	7.9	5.6
Slovak Republic	5.9	9.4	12.3	-1.8	-2.7	1.7	4.9	5.5
Slovenia	6.6	11.1	16.9	0.0	2.8	3.7	5.6	8.4
Spain	12.0	16.5	22.5	3.0	8.9	11.0	12.5	12.4
Sweden	15.1	17.9	30.5	15.1	17.9	15.6	16.8	15.6
Switzerland	7.9	10.8	15.8	2.7	4.8	6.3	8.6	8.5
Turkey[1]	11.0	13.2	17.3	9.8	11.9	12.7	13.5	13.3
United Kingdom	13.0	15.4	22.6	-2.9	15.4	13.0	14.4	13.0
United States	14.1	17.3	23.1	-5.6	5.1	9.2	11.7	14.7
Unweighted average								
OECD-Average	**11.2**	**15.4**	**21.4**	**6.0**	**10.0**	**10.6**	**12.3**	**12.4**
OECD-EU 21	**12.2**	**16.6**	**23.3**	**5.8**	**10.0**	**10.8**	**12.9**	**13.2**

Note: ch = children

1. Wage figures are based on the old definition of average worker (ISIC D, Rev. 3).
2. Two-earner family.

StatLink http://dx.doi.org/10.1787/888933006480

Table I.16. **Employee contributions, 2012**

As % of gross wage earnings, by family type and wage level

	Single no ch 67 (% AW)	Single no ch 100 (% AW)	Single no ch 167 (% AW)	Single 2 ch 67 (% AW)	Married 2 ch 100-0 (% AW)	Married 2 ch 100-33 (% AW)[2]	Married 2 ch 100-67 (% AW)[2]	Married no ch 100-33 (% AW)[2]
Australia	0.0	0.0	0.0	0.0	0.0	0.0	0.0	0.0
Austria	18.1	18.1	15.8	18.1	18.1	17.3	18.1	17.3
Belgium	13.9	14.0	14.0	13.9	14.0	10.8	14.0	10.8
Canada	7.2	7.3	5.0	7.2	7.3	6.9	7.3	6.9
Chile	7.0	7.0	7.0	7.0	7.0	7.0	7.0	7.0
Czech Republic	11.0	11.0	11.0	11.0	11.0	11.0	11.0	11.0
Denmark	4.1	2.7	1.6	4.1	2.7	4.1	3.3	4.1
Estonia	2.8	2.8	2.8	2.8	2.8	2.8	2.8	2.8
Finland	7.5	7.6	7.7	7.5	7.6	7.4	7.6	7.4
France	13.7	13.7	13.1	13.7	13.7	13.7	13.7	13.7
Germany	20.7	20.7	16.1	20.5	20.5	20.5	20.5	20.7
Greece	16.5	16.5	16.5	16.5	16.5	16.5	16.5	16.5
Hungary	18.5	18.5	18.5	18.5	18.5	18.5	18.5	18.5
Iceland	0.7	0.5	0.3	0.7	0.5	0.7	0.6	0.7
Ireland	2.8	3.2	3.5	2.8	3.2	2.4	3.0	2.4
Israel	5.8	7.9	9.5	5.8	7.9	6.8	7.1	6.8
Italy	9.5	9.5	9.6	9.5	9.5	9.5	9.5	9.5
Japan	13.7	13.7	13.0	13.7	13.7	13.7	13.7	13.7
Korea	8.1	8.1	6.9	8.1	8.1	8.1	8.1	8.1
Luxembourg	12.2	12.3	12.4	12.2	12.3	12.2	12.3	12.2
Mexico	1.3	1.4	1.5	1.3	1.4	1.3	1.3	1.3
Netherlands	21.5	15.2	9.2	9.4	12.2	12.8	15.2	15.0
New Zealand	0.0	0.0	0.0	0.0	0.0	0.0	0.0	0.0
Norway	7.8	7.8	7.8	7.8	7.8	7.8	7.8	7.8
Poland	17.8	17.8	17.8	17.8	17.8	17.8	17.8	17.8
Portugal	11.0	11.0	11.0	11.0	11.0	11.0	11.0	11.0
Slovak Republic	13.4	13.4	13.2	13.4	13.4	13.4	13.4	13.4
Slovenia	22.1	22.1	22.1	22.1	22.1	22.1	22.1	22.1
Spain	6.4	6.4	5.8	6.4	6.4	6.4	6.4	6.4
Sweden	7.0	7.0	4.8	7.0	7.0	7.0	7.0	7.0
Switzerland	6.3	6.3	6.2	6.3	6.3	6.3	6.3	6.3
Turkey[1]	15.0	15.0	15.0	15.0	15.0	15.0	15.0	15.0
United Kingdom	8.1	9.4	7.7	8.1	9.4	8.1	8.9	8.1
United States	5.7	5.7	5.7	5.7	5.7	5.7	5.7	5.7
Unweighted average								
OECD-Average	**9.9**	**9.8**	**9.2**	**9.6**	**9.7**	**9.5**	**9.8**	**9.6**
OECD-EU 21	**12.3**	**12.0**	**11.2**	**11.7**	**11.9**	**11.7**	**12.0**	**11.8**

Note: ch = children

1. Wage figures are based on the old definition of average worker (ISIC D, Rev. 3).
2. Two-earner family.

StatLink http://dx.doi.org/10.1787/888933006499

Table I.17. **Marginal rate of income tax plus employee and employer contributions less cash benefits, 2012**[1]

As % of labour costs, by family-type and wage level

	Single no ch 67 (% AW)	Single no ch 100 (% AW)	Single no ch 167 (% AW)	Single 2 ch 67 (% AW)	Married 2 ch 100-0 (% AW)	Married 2 ch 100-33 (% AW)[3]	Married 2 ch 100-67 (% AW)[3]	Married no ch 100-33 (% AW)[3]
Australia	39.1	35.8	42.9	58.0	54.7	35.8	35.8	35.8
Austria	56.9	60.6	42.2	56.9	60.6	60.6	60.6	60.6
Belgium	66.3	69.7	68.5	66.3	66.3	69.7	68.8	69.7
Canada	33.6	40.9	38.3	60.6	68.1	44.5	44.5	40.9
Chile	7.0	7.0	11.0	7.0	7.0	7.0	7.0	7.0
Czech Republic	48.6	48.6	48.6	55.7	54.1	54.1	54.1	48.6
Denmark	40.9	42.3	56.1	40.9	42.3	42.3	42.3	42.3
Estonia	42.9	42.9	42.9	42.9	42.9	42.9	42.9	42.9
Finland	53.6	54.5	57.5	53.6	54.5	54.5	54.5	54.5
France	63.6	60.8	59.8	58.1	49.7	48.3	52.7	52.7
Germany	55.7	60.2	44.3	54.0	52.5	55.5	57.7	55.7
Greece	47.4	51.9	59.1	47.4	52.6	52.6	52.6	52.6
Hungary	54.0	52.4	52.4	54.0	52.4	52.4	52.4	52.4
Iceland	43.1	43.1	48.4	50.2	50.2	50.2	47.5	43.1
Ireland	37.7	37.7	56.7	67.9	75.1	37.7	37.7	37.7
Israel	30.1	36.7	45.2	16.9	36.7	69.3	36.7	36.7
Italy	54.1	54.1	62.0	54.6	55.1	55.1	290.9	54.1
Japan	32.0	36.2	34.8	32.0	36.2	36.2	36.2	36.2
Korea	20.0	28.9	23.1	18.8	25.2	28.9	28.9	28.9
Luxembourg	43.5	54.2	54.2	44.3	36.9	41.8	48.4	41.8
Mexico	17.4	23.4	28.4	17.4	23.4	23.4	23.4	23.4
Netherlands	48.9	50.1	49.3	55.8	50.1	50.1	50.1	50.1
New Zealand	17.5	30.0	33.0	17.5	51.3	51.3	51.3	30.0
Norway	43.2	51.2	53.8	43.2	51.2	51.2	51.2	51.2
Poland	37.2	37.2	37.2	29.6	29.6	37.2	37.2	37.2
Portugal	39.4	47.9	56.8	39.4	39.4	39.4	47.9	39.4
Slovak Republic	45.1	45.1	43.5	45.1	45.1	45.1	45.1	45.1
Slovenia	43.6	51.0	60.4	32.9	43.6	43.6	43.6	51.0
Spain	45.7	49.5	40.0	53.0	49.5	49.5	49.5	49.5
Sweden	45.7	48.0	67.0	45.7	48.0	48.0	48.0	48.0
Switzerland	26.3	30.2	35.9	18.9	22.1	26.1	29.4	26.9
Turkey[2]	42.2	42.2	47.3	42.2	42.2	42.2	42.2	42.2
United Kingdom	40.2	40.2	49.0	76.3	40.2	40.2	40.2	40.2
United States	32.6	41.9	41.9	48.7	32.6	32.6	32.6	32.6
Unweighted average								
OECD-Average	**41.0**	**44.3**	**46.8**	**44.3**	**45.3**	**44.7**	**51.3**	**43.0**
OECD-EU 21	**48.1**	**50.4**	**52.7**	**51.2**	**49.5**	**48.6**	**60.8**	**48.9**

Note: ch = children

1. Assumes a rise in gross earnings of the principal earner in the household. The outcome may differ if the wage of the spouse goes up, especially if partners are taxed individually.
2. Wage figures are based on the old definition of average worker (ISIC D, Rev. 3).
3. Two-earner family.

StatLink http://dx.doi.org/10.1787/888933006518

Table I.18. Marginal rate of income tax plus employee contributions less cash benefits, 2012[1]

As % of gross wage earnings, by family type and wage level

	Single no ch 67 (% AW)	Single no ch 100 (% AW)	Single no ch 167 (% AW)	Single 2 ch 67 (% AW)	Married 2 ch 100-0 (% AW)	Married 2 ch 100-33 (% AW)[3]	Married 2 ch 100-67 (% AW)[3]	Married no ch 100-33 (% AW)[3]
Australia	35.5	32.0	39.5	55.5	52.0	32.0	32.0	32.0
Austria	44.4	49.1	37.9	44.4	49.1	49.1	49.1	49.1
Belgium	54.9	59.4	59.8	54.9	54.9	59.4	58.4	59.4
Canada	25.5	35.1	35.4	55.8	65.0	39.1	39.1	35.1
Chile	7.0	7.0	11.0	7.0	7.0	7.0	7.0	7.0
Czech Republic	31.1	31.1	31.1	40.7	38.4	38.4	38.4	31.1
Denmark	40.9	42.3	56.1	40.9	42.3	42.3	42.3	42.3
Estonia	23.2	23.2	23.2	23.2	23.2	23.2	23.2	23.2
Finland	43.0	44.1	47.8	43.0	44.1	44.1	44.1	44.1
France	31.8	43.5	42.4	21.6	27.6	25.6	31.8	31.8
Germany	47.1	52.4	44.3	45.0	43.2	46.8	49.4	47.1
Greece	32.4	38.2	47.4	32.4	39.0	39.0	39.0	39.0
Hungary	34.5	38.8	38.8	34.5	38.8	38.8	38.8	38.8
Iceland	38.6	38.6	44.4	46.3	46.3	46.3	43.4	38.6
Ireland	31.0	31.0	52.0	64.4	72.4	31.0	31.0	31.0
Israel	26.0	33.0	42.0	12.0	33.0	67.5	33.0	33.0
Italy	39.3	39.4	49.9	40.0	40.7	40.7	352.1	39.4
Japan	22.1	27.0	30.8	22.1	27.0	27.0	27.0	27.0
Korea	11.9	21.6	18.7	10.5	17.6	21.6	21.6	21.6
Luxembourg	36.5	48.5	48.5	37.4	29.1	34.7	42.1	34.7
Mexico	12.1	17.6	22.9	12.1	17.6	17.6	17.6	17.6
Netherlands	42.6	44.0	49.3	50.4	44.0	44.0	44.0	44.0
New Zealand	17.5	30.0	33.0	17.5	51.3	51.3	51.3	30.0
Norway	35.8	44.8	47.8	35.8	44.8	44.8	44.8	44.8
Poland	26.7	26.7	26.7	17.8	17.8	26.7	26.7	26.7
Portugal	25.0	35.5	46.5	25.0	25.0	25.0	35.5	25.0
Slovak Republic	29.9	29.9	28.7	29.9	29.9	29.9	29.9	29.9
Slovenia	34.6	43.1	54.0	22.1	34.6	34.6	34.6	43.1
Spain	29.5	34.4	40.0	38.9	34.4	34.4	34.4	34.4
Sweden	28.6	31.6	56.6	28.6	31.6	31.6	31.6	31.6
Switzerland	21.7	25.8	32.3	13.8	17.2	21.5	25.0	22.3
Turkey[2]	32.7	32.7	38.6	32.7	32.7	32.7	32.7	32.7
United Kingdom	32.0	32.0	42.0	73.0	32.0	32.0	32.0	32.0
United States	27.4	37.4	37.4	44.8	27.4	27.4	27.4	27.4
Unweighted average								
OECD-Average	**31.0**	**35.3**	**39.9**	**34.5**	**36.2**	**35.5**	**44.4**	**33.7**
OECD-EU 21	**35.2**	**39.0**	**44.0**	**38.5**	**37.7**	**36.7**	**52.8**	**37.0**

Note: ch = children

1. Assumes a rise in gross earnings of the principal earner in the household. The outcome may differ if the wage of the spouse goes up, especially if partners are taxed individually.
2. Wage figures are based on the old definition of average worker (ISIC D, Rev. 3).
3. Two-earner family.

StatLink http://dx.doi.org/10.1787/888933006537

Table I.19. **Increase in net income after an increase of 1 currency unit in gross wages, 2012**[1]

By family-type and wage level (%)

	Single no ch 67 (% AW)	Single no ch 100 (% AW)	Single no ch 167 (% AW)	Single 2 ch 67 (% AW)	Married 2 ch 100-0 (% AW)	Married 2 ch 100-33 (% AW)[3]	Married 2 ch 100-67 (% AW)[3]	Married no ch 100-33 (% AW)[3]
Australia	0.78	0.88	0.85	0.40	0.54	0.79	0.86	0.84
Austria	0.77	0.77	1.01	0.60	0.64	0.63	0.67	0.72
Belgium	0.71	0.71	0.80	0.56	0.59	0.56	0.63	0.63
Canada	0.90	0.84	0.88	0.37	0.38	0.72	0.75	0.80
Chile	1.00	1.00	0.97	0.99	1.00	0.98	1.00	1.00
Czech Republic	0.85	0.89	0.93	0.52	0.58	0.66	0.70	0.86
Denmark	0.94	0.94	0.80	0.67	0.80	0.85	0.88	0.92
Estonia	0.94	0.96	0.98	0.77	0.85	0.88	0.90	0.94
Finland	0.74	0.79	0.83	0.63	0.73	0.70	0.73	0.75
France	0.93	0.79	0.87	0.92	0.88	0.92	0.88	0.93
Germany	0.81	0.79	0.99	0.67	0.72	0.73	0.73	0.81
Greece	0.87	0.84	0.79	0.86	0.85	0.82	0.83	0.82
Hungary	1.00	0.94	0.97	0.68	0.72	0.77	0.80	0.94
Iceland	0.80	0.86	0.83	0.59	0.61	0.67	0.75	0.80
Ireland	0.78	0.84	0.70	0.26	0.27	0.72	0.76	0.78
Israel	0.82	0.80	0.77	0.85	0.77	0.36	0.74	0.77
Italy	0.83	0.88	0.81	0.64	0.73	0.75	-3.36	0.83
Japan	0.97	0.93	0.92	0.89	0.86	0.88	0.89	0.92
Korea	0.98	0.90	0.96	0.98	0.92	0.87	0.87	0.89
Luxembourg	0.80	0.72	0.81	0.58	0.73	0.71	0.67	0.80
Mexico	0.89	0.91	0.90	0.89	0.91	0.87	0.88	0.87
Netherlands	0.78	0.83	0.82	0.51	0.75	0.72	0.75	0.78
New Zealand	0.95	0.84	0.86	0.70	0.49	0.53	0.57	0.83
Norway	0.86	0.78	0.81	0.72	0.71	0.72	0.74	0.75
Poland	0.96	0.97	0.98	1.00	1.00	0.91	0.93	0.96
Portugal	0.90	0.84	0.77	0.79	0.84	0.85	0.80	0.90
Slovak Republic	0.87	0.91	0.96	0.73	0.74	0.79	0.83	0.87
Slovenia	0.92	0.85	0.75	0.77	0.73	0.81	0.86	0.82
Spain	0.86	0.85	0.84	0.67	0.77	0.79	0.81	0.81
Sweden	0.92	0.91	0.67	0.81	0.83	0.83	0.85	0.88
Switzerland	0.91	0.90	0.87	0.85	0.87	0.85	0.84	0.91
Turkey[2]	0.91	0.94	0.91	0.90	0.92	0.93	0.94	0.94
United Kingdom	0.86	0.90	0.83	0.26	0.85	0.82	0.85	0.86
United States	0.90	0.81	0.88	0.55	0.81	0.85	0.88	0.91
Unweighted average								
OECD-Average	**0.87**	**0.86**	**0.86**	**0.69**	**0.75**	**0.77**	**0.68**	**0.85**
OECD-EU 21	**0.86**	**0.85**	**0.85**	**0.66**	**0.74**	**0.77**	**0.59**	**0.84**

Note: ch = children

1. Net income is calculated as gross earnings minus personal income tax and employees' social security contributions plus family benefits. The increase reported in the Table represents a form of elasticity. In a proportional tax system the plus elasticity would equal 1. The more progressive the system at these income levels, the lower is the elasticity.
2. Wage figures are based on the old definition of average worker (ISIC D, Rev. 3).
3. Two-earner family. Assumes a rise in the labour costs associated with the principal earner in the household.

StatLink http://dx.doi.org/10.1787/888933006556

Table I.20. Increase in net income after an increase of 1 currency unit in gross labour cost, 2012[1]

By family-type and wage level (%)

	Single no ch 67 (% AW)	Single no ch 100 (% AW)	Single no ch 167 (% AW)	Single 2 ch 67 (% AW)	Married 2 ch 100-0 (% AW)	Married 2 ch 100-33 (% AW)[3]	Married 2 ch 100-67 (% AW)[3]	Married no ch 100-33 (% AW)[3]
Australia	0.78	0.88	0.85	0.40	0.54	0.79	0.86	0.84
Austria	0.77	0.77	1.19	0.60	0.64	0.63	0.67	0.72
Belgium	0.68	0.69	0.81	0.53	0.57	0.53	0.61	0.59
Canada	0.90	0.86	0.92	0.37	0.39	0.73	0.76	0.82
Chile	1.00	1.00	0.97	0.99	1.00	0.98	1.00	1.00
Czech Republic	0.85	0.89	0.93	0.52	0.58	0.66	0.70	0.86
Denmark	0.94	0.94	0.80	0.67	0.80	0.85	0.88	0.92
Estonia	0.94	0.96	0.98	0.77	0.85	0.88	0.90	0.94
Finland	0.74	0.79	0.83	0.63	0.73	0.70	0.73	0.75
France	0.69	0.79	0.87	0.68	0.88	0.88	0.87	0.88
Germany	0.81	0.79	1.14	0.67	0.72	0.73	0.73	0.81
Greece	0.87	0.84	0.79	0.86	0.85	0.82	0.83	0.82
Hungary	0.88	0.94	0.97	0.60	0.72	0.74	0.79	0.91
Iceland	0.80	0.86	0.83	0.59	0.61	0.67	0.75	0.80
Ireland	0.78	0.84	0.70	0.26	0.27	0.71	0.76	0.78
Israel	0.81	0.80	0.77	0.83	0.76	0.35	0.73	0.76
Italy	0.83	0.88	0.81	0.64	0.73	0.75	-3.36	0.83
Japan	0.97	0.93	0.99	0.89	0.86	0.88	0.89	0.92
Korea	0.98	0.90	0.99	0.98	0.92	0.87	0.87	0.89
Luxembourg	0.80	0.72	0.81	0.58	0.73	0.71	0.67	0.80
Mexico	0.96	0.95	0.92	0.96	0.95	0.92	0.92	0.92
Netherlands	0.77	0.82	0.88	0.50	0.74	0.71	0.73	0.76
New Zealand	0.95	0.84	0.86	0.70	0.49	0.53	0.57	0.83
Norway	0.86	0.78	0.81	0.72	0.71	0.72	0.74	0.75
Poland	0.96	0.97	0.98	1.00	1.00	0.91	0.93	0.96
Portugal	0.90	0.84	0.77	0.79	0.84	0.85	0.80	0.90
Slovak Republic	0.87	0.91	0.97	0.73	0.74	0.79	0.83	0.87
Slovenia	0.92	0.85	0.75	0.77	0.73	0.81	0.86	0.82
Spain	0.86	0.85	1.06	0.67	0.77	0.79	0.81	0.81
Sweden	0.92	0.91	0.67	0.81	0.83	0.83	0.85	0.88
Switzerland	0.91	0.90	0.87	0.85	0.87	0.85	0.84	0.91
Turkey[2]	0.91	0.94	0.91	0.90	0.92	0.93	0.94	0.94
United Kingdom	0.83	0.88	0.82	0.25	0.83	0.79	0.83	0.83
United States	0.93	0.83	0.89	0.57	0.83	0.88	0.90	0.94
Unweighted average								
OECD-Average	**0.86**	**0.86**	**0.89**	**0.68**	**0.75**	**0.77**	**0.68**	**0.85**
OECD-EU 21	**0.84**	**0.85**	**0.88**	**0.64**	**0.74**	**0.77**	**0.59**	**0.83**

Note: ch = children

1. Net income is calculated as gross earnings minus personal income tax and employees' social security contributions plus family benefits. The increase reported in the Table represents a form of elasticity. In a proportional tax system the plus elasticity would equal 1. The more progressive the system at these income levels, the lower is the elasticity.
2. Wage figures are based on the old definition of average worker (ISIC D, Rev. 3).
3. Two-earner family. Assumes a rise in the labour costs associated with the principal earner in the household.

StatLink http://dx.doi.org/10.1787/888933006575

Table I.21a. **Annual gross wage and net income, single person, 2012**

In US dollars using PPP, by family-type and wage level

	Single no ch 67 (% AW)		Single no ch 100 (% AW)		Single no ch 167 (% AW)		Single 2 ch 67 (% AW)	
	Total gross earnings before taxes	Net income after taxes	Total gross earnings before taxes	Net income after taxes	Total gross earnings before taxes	Net income after taxes	Total gross earnings before taxes	Net income after taxes
Australia	33 081	27 515	49 622	38 266	82 703	58 678	33 081	36 445
Austria	32 880	23 707	49 320	32 582	82 200	50 496	32 880	30 645
Belgium	36 739	23 406	55 108	31 571	91 847	46 417	36 739	29 831
Canada	25 258	20 847	37 887	29 323	63 146	46 252	25 258	30 166
Chile	11 909	11 075	17 863	16 612	29 771	27 419	11 909	11 187
Czech Republic	15 194	12 337	22 791	17 571	37 985	28 040	15 194	17 323
Denmark	34 239	21 575	51 358	31 562	85 597	47 032	34 239	30 251
Estonia	13 691	11 190	20 536	16 447	34 227	26 960	13 691	13 586
Finland	30 613	23 757	45 920	32 390	76 533	48 404	30 613	27 942
France	28 735	21 184	43 103	30 962	71 838	47 519	28 735	24 432
Germany	38 037	24 805	57 056	34 365	95 094	53 489	38 037	31 322
Greece	22 105	17 128	33 158	24 335	55 263	36 794	24 316	19 219
Hungary	15 152	9 924	22 728	14 743	37 879	24 013	15 152	14 689
Iceland	28 821	22 191	43 231	31 034	72 052	48 315	28 821	26 307
Ireland	26 585	23 550	39 877	32 722	66 462	45 556	26 585	37 084
Israel	21 391	19 218	32 087	26 749	53 478	40 158	21 391	22 182
Italy	25 935	18 971	38 902	26 875	64 837	40 168	25 935	24 270
Japan	31 162	25 001	46 744	36 768	77 906	58 344	31 162	27 294
Korea	30 515	27 562	45 772	39 811	76 287	64 326	30 515	27 800
Luxembourg	38 205	30 457	57 308	41 242	95 513	60 902	38 205	41 594
Mexico	8 097	7 967	12 146	10 988	20 243	17 392	8 097	7 967
Netherlands	38 024	27 876	57 035	38 722	95 059	58 688	38 024	36 890
New Zealand	23 606	20 511	35 409	29 606	59 015	45 810	23 606	27 950
Norway	38 411	28 606	57 617	40 782	96 028	61 831	38 411	34 039
Poland	14 751	11 255	22 127	16 664	36 878	27 480	14 751	12 122
Portugal	18 780	15 669	28 170	21 752	46 950	32 789	18 780	17 883
Slovak Republic	12 855	10 378	19 282	14 887	32 136	23 959	12 855	12 421
Slovenia	19 393	13 836	29 089	19 418	48 481	29 550	19 393	19 612
Spain	25 209	20 585	37 813	29 169	63 022	45 223	25 209	22 856
Sweden	29 732	23 153	44 598	33 493	74 330	48 138	29 732	26 256
Switzerland	42 002	36 060	63 002	52 250	105 004	81 966	42 002	42 562
Turkey[1]	18 867	13 962	28 300	20 315	47 167	31 909	18 867	14 194
United Kingdom	33 714	26 600	50 572	38 062	84 286	58 718	33 714	34 505
United States	31 973	25 656	47 960	36 972	79 933	56 977	31 973	31 950
Unweighted average								
OECD-Average	**26 343**	**20 515**	**39 514**	**29 089**	**65 857**	**44 697**	**26 408**	**25 435**
OECD-EU 21	**26 217**	**19 588**	**39 326**	**27 597**	**65 544**	**41 921**	**26 323**	**24 987**

Note: ch = children

1. Wage figures are based on the old definition of average worker (ISIC D, Rev. 3).

StatLink http://dx.doi.org/10.1787/888933006594

Table I.21b. Annual gross wage and net income, married couple, 2012

In US dollars using PPP, by family-type and wage level

	Married 2 ch 100-0 (% AW)		Married 2 ch 100-33 (% AW)[2]		Married 2 ch 100-67 (% AW)[2]		Married no ch 100-33 (% AW)[2]	
	Total gross earnings before taxes	Net income after taxes	Total gross earnings before taxes	Net income after taxes	Total gross earnings before taxes	Net income after taxes	Total gross earnings before taxes	Net income after taxes
Australia	49 622	43 888	66 162	57 085	82 703	65 782	66 162	53 698
Austria	49 320	39 556	65 760	52 843	82 200	62 477	65 760	46 680
Belgium	55 108	42 123	73 477	53 354	91 847	60 729	73 477	47 548
Canada	37 887	34 606	50 516	43 035	63 146	51 568	50 516	40 805
Chile	17 863	16 612	23 817	22 664	29 771	27 799	23 817	22 150
Czech Republic	22 791	24 136	30 388	28 508	37 985	33 491	30 388	24 333
Denmark	51 358	37 069	68 478	46 255	85 597	56 377	68 478	43 014
Estonia	20 536	18 660	27 382	23 917	34 227	29 173	27 382	22 380
Finland	45 920	35 290	61 227	48 876	76 533	59 048	61 227	45 975
France	43 103	35 339	57 470	46 633	71 838	55 569	57 470	42 368
Germany	57 056	45 057	76 075	55 702	95 094	65 570	76 075	49 609
Greece	39 790	28 697	53 053	39 410	66 316	48 815	48 632	35 961
Hungary	22 728	19 220	30 303	24 182	37 879	29 144	30 303	19 705
Iceland	43 231	38 119	57 641	46 047	72 052	54 248	57 641	44 192
Ireland	39 877	41 452	53 170	51 238	66 462	60 393	53 170	47 118
Israel	32 087	28 037	42 783	38 975	53 478	48 178	42 783	37 070
Italy	38 902	31 515	51 870	40 807	64 837	48 674	51 870	37 965
Japan	46 744	39 738	62 325	51 907	77 906	64 061	62 325	49 614
Korea	45 772	41 075	61 029	54 751	76 287	68 373	61 029	53 778
Luxembourg	57 308	55 661	76 410	70 524	95 513	82 384	76 410	62 195
Mexico	12 146	10 988	16 195	15 398	20 243	18 955	16 195	15 398
Netherlands	57 035	42 767	76 047	58 855	95 059	71 421	76 047	54 799
New Zealand	35 409	35 214	47 212	43 120	59 015	50 350	47 212	40 021
Norway	57 617	44 888	76 822	59 261	96 028	72 045	76 822	56 605
Poland	22 127	18 182	29 502	23 734	36 878	29 143	29 502	22 510
Portugal	28 170	25 132	37 560	33 019	46 950	38 076	37 560	31 338
Slovak Republic	19 282	18 291	25 709	22 890	32 136	27 308	25 709	20 847
Slovenia	29 089	25 938	38 785	31 268	48 481	36 998	38 785	26 972
Spain	37 813	32 060	50 418	41 674	63 022	51 155	50 418	40 973
Sweden	44 598	36 597	59 464	49 134	74 330	59 749	59 464	46 030
Switzerland	63 002	60 333	84 003	77 750	105 004	93 764	84 003	71 599
Turkey[1]	28 300	20 701	37 734	27 300	47 167	33 736	37 734	27 068
United Kingdom	50 572	40 610	67 429	55 747	84 286	67 210	67 429	53 199
United States	47 960	42 828	63 947	54 430	79 933	66 031	63 947	50 934
Unweighted average								
OECD-Average	**39 709**	**33 835**	**52 946**	**43 832**	**66 182**	**52 582**	**52 816**	**40 719**
OECD-EU 21	**39 642**	**33 017**	**52 856**	**42 789**	**66 070**	**51 091**	**52 645**	**39 120**

Note: ch = children

1. Wage figures are based on the old definition of average worker (ISIC D, Rev. 3).
2. Two-earner family.

StatLink http://dx.doi.org/10.1787/888933006613

Table I.22a. **Annual labour costs and net income, single person, 2012**

In US dollars using PPP, by family-type and wage level

	Single no ch 67 (% AW)		Single no ch 100 (% AW)		Single no ch 167 (% AW)		Single 2 ch 67 (% AW)	
	Total gross labour costs before taxes	Net income after taxes	Total gross labour costs before taxes	Net income after taxes	Total gross labour costs before taxes	Net income after taxes	Total gross labour costs before taxes	Net income after taxes
Australia	35 046	27 515	52 569	38 266	87 616	58 678	35 046	36 445
Austria	42 457	23 707	63 686	32 582	103 883	50 496	42 457	30 645
Belgium	47 187	23 406	71 741	31 571	118 850	46 417	47 187	29 831
Canada	28 227	20 847	42 388	29 323	68 984	46 252	28 227	30 166
Chile	11 909	11 075	17 863	16 612	29 771	27 419	11 909	11 187
Czech Republic	20 360	12 337	30 540	17 571	50 900	28 040	20 360	17 323
Denmark	34 239	21 575	51 358	31 562	85 597	47 032	34 239	30 251
Estonia	18 400	11 190	27 601	16 447	46 001	26 960	18 400	13 586
Finland	37 593	23 757	56 390	32 390	93 983	48 404	37 593	27 942
France	39 869	21 184	62 081	30 962	103 262	47 519	39 869	24 432
Germany	45 483	24 805	68 225	34 365	109 766	53 489	45 483	31 322
Greece	28 419	17 128	42 628	24 335	71 047	36 794	31 261	19 219
Hungary	19 033	9 924	29 205	14 743	48 675	24 013	19 033	14 689
Iceland	31 066	22 191	46 599	31 034	77 665	48 315	31 066	26 307
Ireland	29 443	23 550	44 164	32 722	73 607	45 556	29 443	37 084
Israel	22 274	19 218	33 601	26 749	56 254	40 158	22 274	22 182
Italy	34 255	18 971	51 382	26 875	85 637	40 168	34 255	24 270
Japan	35 666	25 001	53 499	36 768	88 600	58 344	35 666	27 294
Korea	33 615	27 562	50 422	39 811	83 082	64 326	33 615	27 800
Luxembourg	42 908	30 457	64 362	41 242	107 270	60 902	42 908	41 594
Mexico	9 216	7 967	13 565	10 988	22 276	17 392	9 216	7 967
Netherlands	41 846	27 876	63 188	38 722	101 946	58 688	41 846	36 890
New Zealand	23 606	20 511	35 409	29 606	59 015	45 810	23 606	27 950
Norway	43 443	28 606	65 164	40 782	108 607	61 831	43 443	34 039
Poland	17 226	11 255	25 839	16 664	43 066	27 480	17 226	12 122
Portugal	23 240	15 669	34 860	21 752	58 100	32 789	23 240	17 883
Slovak Republic	16 437	10 378	24 656	14 887	41 011	23 959	16 437	12 421
Slovenia	22 515	13 836	33 772	19 418	56 287	29 550	22 515	19 612
Spain	32 746	20 585	49 119	29 169	80 116	45 223	32 746	22 856
Sweden	39 074	23 153	58 610	33 493	97 684	48 138	39 074	26 256
Switzerland	44 627	36 060	66 940	52 250	111 480	81 966	44 627	42 562
Turkey[1]	21 980	13 962	32 970	20 315	54 949	31 909	21 980	14 194
United Kingdom	36 869	26 600	56 052	38 062	94 419	58 718	36 869	34 505
United States	35 471	25 656	52 681	36 972	87 100	56 977	35 471	31 950
Unweighted average								
OECD-Average	**30 757**	**20 515**	**46 269**	**29 089**	**76 662**	**44 697**	**30 841**	**25 435**
OECD-EU 21	**31 886**	**19 588**	**48 070**	**27 597**	**79 576**	**41 921**	**32 021**	**24 987**

Note: ch = children

1. Wage figures are based on the old definition of average worker (ISIC D, Rev. 3).

StatLink http://dx.doi.org/10.1787/888933006632

Table I.22b. Annual labour costs and net income, married couple, 2012

In US dollars using PPP, by family-type and wage level

	Married 2 ch 100-0 (% AW)		Married 2 ch 100-33 (% AW)[2]		Married 2 ch 100-67 (% AW)[2]		Married no ch 100-33 (% AW)[2]	
	Total gross labour costs before taxes	Net income after taxes	Total gross labour costs before taxes	Net income after taxes	Total gross labour costs before taxes	Net income after taxes	Total gross labour costs before taxes	Net income after taxes
Australia	52 569	43 888	70 093	57 085	87 616	65 782	70 093	53 698
Austria	63 686	39 556	84 915	52 843	106 144	62 477	84 915	46 680
Belgium	71 741	42 123	92 781	53 354	118 928	60 729	92 781	47 548
Canada	42 388	34 606	56 432	43 035	70 615	51 568	56 432	40 805
Chile	17 863	16 612	23 817	22 664	29 771	27 799	23 817	22 150
Czech Republic	30 540	24 136	40 720	28 508	50 900	33 491	40 720	24 333
Denmark	51 358	37 069	68 478	46 255	85 597	56 377	68 478	43 014
Estonia	27 601	18 660	36 801	23 917	46 001	29 173	36 801	22 380
Finland	56 390	35 290	75 186	48 876	93 983	59 048	75 186	45 975
France	62 081	35 339	79 039	46 633	101 950	55 569	79 039	42 368
Germany	68 225	45 057	90 967	55 702	113 708	65 570	90 967	49 609
Greece	51 154	28 697	68 205	39 410	85 256	48 815	62 521	35 961
Hungary	29 205	19 220	37 443	24 182	48 238	29 144	37 443	19 705
Iceland	46 599	38 119	62 132	46 047	77 665	54 248	62 132	44 192
Ireland	44 164	41 452	58 586	51 238	73 607	60 393	58 586	47 118
Israel	33 601	28 037	44 665	38 975	55 874	48 178	44 665	37 070
Italy	51 382	31 515	68 509	40 807	85 637	48 674	68 509	37 965
Japan	53 499	39 738	71 332	51 907	89 165	64 061	71 332	49 614
Korea	50 422	41 075	67 230	54 751	84 037	68 373	67 230	53 778
Luxembourg	64 362	55 661	85 816	70 524	107 270	82 384	85 816	62 195
Mexico	13 565	10 988	18 470	15 398	22 781	18 955	18 470	15 398
Netherlands	63 188	42 767	83 781	58 855	105 034	71 421	83 781	54 799
New Zealand	35 409	35 214	47 212	43 120	59 015	50 350	47 212	40 021
Norway	65 164	44 888	86 886	59 261	108 607	72 045	86 886	56 605
Poland	25 839	18 182	34 453	23 734	43 066	29 143	34 453	22 510
Portugal	34 860	25 132	46 480	33 019	58 100	38 076	46 480	31 338
Slovak Republic	24 656	18 291	32 874	22 890	41 093	27 308	32 874	20 847
Slovenia	33 772	25 938	45 030	31 268	56 287	36 998	45 030	26 972
Spain	49 119	32 060	65 492	41 674	81 865	51 155	65 492	40 973
Sweden	58 610	36 597	78 147	49 134	97 684	59 749	78 147	46 030
Switzerland	66 940	60 333	89 253	77 750	111 567	93 764	89 253	71 599
Turkey[1]	32 970	20 701	43 960	27 300	54 949	33 736	43 960	27 068
United Kingdom	56 052	40 610	73 737	55 747	92 921	67 210	73 737	53 199
United States	52 681	42 828	70 942	54 430	88 152	66 031	70 942	50 934
Unweighted average								
OECD-Average	**46 519**	**33 835**	**61 761**	**43 832**	**77 444**	**52 582**	**61 594**	**40 719**
OECD-EU 21	**48 476**	**33 017**	**64 164**	**42 789**	**80 632**	**51 091**	**63 893**	**39 120**

Note: ch = children

1. Wage figures are based on the old definition of average worker (ISIC D, Rev. 3).
2. Two-earner family.

StatLink http://dx.doi.org/10.1787/888933006651

PART II

Tax burden trends 2000-13

This section presents detailed results of the evolution of the tax burden between 2000 and 2013. It provides information for each of the OECD countries on the income taxes paid by workers, their social security contributions, the family benefits they receive in the form of cash transfers as well as the social security contributions and payroll taxes paid by their employers over this period.

Taxing Wages 2014
Changes in sructural labour income tax progressivity
over 2000-12 period in OECD member countries

Evolution of the tax burden (2000-13)

1. Historical trends

The evolution of the tax burden for the eight family types over the period 2000 to 2013 is presented in Tables II.1 to II.8 in the second section of Part II titled "Income taxes, social security contributions and cash benefits". Each of the Tables 1 to 8 corresponds to a particular family type and each is divided into three parts.

The discussion focuses on the main observable trends over the period and highlights selected important year-to-year changes.

2. Important trends

The OECD average tax wedge, the income tax burden and the net tax burden (personal income tax plus social security contributions less cash benefits) have all declined between 2000 and 2013 for each of the selected family types.

The reductions over the period in the OECD average tax wedge ranged from 0.8 percentage points (for single workers earning the average wage) to 1.5 percentage points (for single parents at 67 per cent of the average wage level).

The decrease in the OECD net personal average tax burden ranges from 0.6 percentage points (for single workers earning the average wage) to 1.1 percentage points (for the two-earner married couples with children where the spouse is earning 33 per cent of the average wage level).

The OECD average income tax burden has also declined for all family types in the period considered. The reduction ranges from 0.5 percentage points (for single workers at the average wage level) to 1.3 percentage points (for single parents at 67 per cent of the average wage level).

3. Tax wedge

Focusing on the overall (average) tax wedge (a.-tables), there are thirteen OECD member countries with a reduction of more than five percentage points between 2000 and 2013 for at least one of the family types – Australia, Canada, Denmark, Finland, Germany, Hungary, Ireland, Israel, the Netherlands, New Zealand, Poland, Sweden and the United Kingdom.

The largest decline is observed in Ireland where single parents have benefited from a reduction in the wedge of 24.0 percentage points. Married couples with two children on average earnings and 133 per cent of the average in Ireland also enjoyed reductions of 8.7 and 6.8 percentage points respectively. In New Zealand married couples with two children earning the average wage level and single parents at 67 per cent of the average wage level enjoyed a reduction of more than 10 percentage points in the wedge.

A reduction of seven percentage points or more in the tax wedge for at least one family-type was observed in five other countries – Denmark, Hungary, Israel, the Netherlands and Sweden. In Denmark, the largest decrease was for the single person earning 167 per cent of the average wage level (-7.1 percentage points). In Hungary, there were reductions of between 2.4 and 10.1 percentage points over the range of family types. The largest decreases were for single workers earning 167 per cent of the average wage level (-10.1 percentage points) and the one-earner married couples with 2 children at average earnings (-9.8 percentage points). In Israel, the tax wedge decreased by more than 7 percentage points for all the household types except for the single parents earning 67 per cent of the average wage level (-1.6 percentage points). In the Netherlands, single parents earning 67 per cent of the average wage level (-15.3 percentage points) and single workers earning 67 per cent of the average wage (-10.1 percentage points) benefited most from the reduction in the tax wedge. In Sweden, all but one of the families enjoyed a reduction in the tax wedge of 6 to 8 percentage points, the exception being the single workers earning 167 per cent of the average wage level (-5.1 percentage points). It is interesting to note that in Iceland the single worker earning 167 per cent of the average wage level enjoyed a reduction in the tax wedge (-1.7 percentage points), while the tax burden increased by more than 4 percentage points for all the other family types and notably by 10.8 percentage points for the single parents earning 67 per cent of the average wage.

The tax wedge has decreased for all family types in twelve of the OECD member countries (Australia, Canada, Denmark, Finland, Germany, Hungary, Israel, New Zealand, Poland, Slovenia, Sweden and Switzerland) while it has increased across all family types in six countries (Austria, Greece, Japan, Korea, Mexico and Spain).

4. Average income tax rate

Between 2000 and 2013, the average income tax burden (b.-tables) has decreased for all family types in twelve of the OECD member countries: Canada, Estonia, Finland, Hungary, Israel, New Zealand, Slovenia, Sweden, Switzerland, Turkey, the United Kingdom and the United States. The most significant reductions affecting all of the family types are noted in Sweden where all the family types enjoyed decreases of around 8-10 percentage points except the single taxpayer earning 167 per cent of the average wage level where the decrease was -6.2 percentage points. In Estonia, the average income tax burden has decreased by at least four percentage points for all family types with single parents at 67 per cent of the average wage enjoying an income tax reduction of 8.7 percentage points. In Finland, there was a reduction of 4-6 percentage points for all family types. In Hungary, there were significant decreases of more than 10 percentage points for the single persons earning 167 per cent of the average wage level and the one-earner married couples with children earning the average wage. In Israel, the average income tax rate decreased by 7 to 10 percentage points in all family types except for single parents at 67 per cent of the average wage who had a reduction of 1 percentage point. Other decreases of more than 5 percentage points were observed in Canada (from -5.5 to -6.1 percentage points for families with children where the earnings are at 67 and 100 per cent of the average wage), New Zealand (-5.3 percentage points for the single workers earning 67 per cent of the average wage without children) and the United Kingdom where there was a reduction of 11.5 percentage points for the single parents at 67 per cent of the average wage. Reductions of less than 5 percentage points in average income tax rates are observed for all family types in Slovenia, Switzerland, Turkey and the United States.

There are thirteen other OECD member countries with reductions in the personal income tax in some family types: Australia, Belgium, the Czech Republic, France, Germany, Iceland, Ireland, Italy, Luxembourg, Norway, Poland, Portugal and the Slovak Republic. In three of those countries the reductions in average income tax rates exceeded six percentage points including both the Czech Republic (-9.5 percentage points for the one-earner married couples with children at the average wage level and -8.0 percentage points for the single parents earning 67 per cent of the average) and the Slovak Republic (-7.6 percentage points for the one-earner married couples at the average wage level with children).

At the other extreme, the personal income tax burden has increased across all family types in eight OECD member countries: Austria, Denmark, Greece, Japan, Korea, Mexico, the Netherlands and Spain. In Mexico the increases were in the range 5 to 8 percentage points for each family type. In the Netherlands, there were increases of 10.4 percentage points for the one-earner married couple with two children and 6.1 percentage points for the single person on average earnings. In contrast, in Chile the average income tax burden slightly increased only for the single worker earning 167 per cent of the average wage level (+0.4 percentage points). The average income tax rates stayed constant for the other family types since they do not pay income taxes.

5. Net personal average tax rate

The *net* tax burden takes into account personal income taxes and employee social security contributions as well as cash benefits (c.-tables). It decreased between 2000 and 2013 for all family types in nine OECD countries: Australia, Canada, Denmark, Israel, New Zealand, Poland, Sweden, Switzerland and the United States. Of these, the most significant reductions were observed in Sweden, ranging from -9.6 percentage points (the two-earning married couples without children where the spouse is earning 33 per cent of the average wage) to -6.1 percentage points (single taxpayer earning 167 per cent of the average wage level). In Australia, the net personal average tax burden has significantly decreased for most family types, notably by with 6.4 percentage points for single parents earning 67 per cent of the average wage and 6.5 percentage points for one-earner married couples at average earnings with children. Significant reductions were also observed in Israel for all but one family type (reductions ranging between 7.4 and 9.5 percentage points), the exception being single parents earning 67 per cent of the average wage where the reduction was only 1.1 percentage point. The net personal average tax rate also decreased strongly in Ireland for most families with children and especially for single parents at 67 per cent of the average wage (-28.9 percentage points), in the Netherlands and the United Kingdom for the single parents earning 67 per cent of the average wage level (-11.3 percentage points and -9.9 respectively) and in New Zealand for families with children and especially if these families have low earnings (single parents at 67 per cent of the average wage enjoyed a reduction of 13.8 percentage points).

There are five other OECD member countries with reductions in the net personal average tax rate exceeding five percentage points in some family types: Canada, Denmark, Germany, Hungary and Poland. In Canada, there were reductions of 6.9 percentage points for the single parents at 67 per cent of the average wage and 5.2 percentage points for one earner married couples with two children. In Hungary, the reduction for the latter was 5.2 percentage points with a 8.3 percentage point reduction for the single worker on 167 per cent of the average wage. In Denmark, there were reductions for single workers at the average wage level and at 167 per cent of it of -5.9 and -7.2 percentage points respectively. In Poland, there was a reduction of 6.2 percentage points for the two-earner married couple with two children and the spouse earning 67 per cent of the average wage.

Between 2000 and 2013, an increase of five or more percentage points in the net tax burden for one or more family types is only observed in eight countries. In most of these, Austria, Estonia, Iceland, Mexico, Norway and the Slovak Republic, the single parents earning 67 per cent of the average wage saw increases of between 5 and 10 percentage points. There were increases of similar size for other family types in four countries. In Iceland, all the family types with married couples and children saw increase between 3 and 9 percentage points. In Mexico there were increases of between 4 and 8 percentage points for each of the other family types. In Portugal and Turkey, the net personal average tax rate increased by 5-6 percentage points for the single worker on 167 per cent of the average wage. In Greece, it increased by 5 percentage points for the married couple with children on average earnings.

6. Progressivity

The discussion of the results for 2013 in Part I of this publication gave some to consideration to their use in assessing the progressivity of personal income taxes and the results presented in Part II can also be used to look at the evolution of this measure.

The degree of progressivity of the personal income tax system can be assessed by comparing the burden faced by single persons earning 67 per cent of the average wage with that faced by their counterparts earning 167 per cent of the average wage. Hence Table II.1b is compared with Table II.3b. For all OECD countries and for all years the lower paid worker always pays a lower percentage of income in personal income tax than the higher paid worker.

On average, the progressivity of the personal income taxes has not changed drastically in OECD countries. On average (excluding Mexico), the single worker earning 67 per cent of the average wage level paid 52 per cent in 2000 and 51 per cent in 2013 of the tax burden of the worker earning 167 per cent of the average wage level.

Comparing the situation in each OECD country, personal income taxes have become more progressive in seventeen countries. The most significant reductions were in Israel, where the burden of the lower paid worker was about 46 per cent of the higher paid worker in 2000 and 27 per cent in 2013; in New Zealand where the corresponding reduction was from 77 per cent to 58 per cent; and in Sweden, where it was from about 68 per cent to about 51 per cent.

Personal income taxes have become slightly less progressive (using this measure) in eleven OECD countries: Austria, Denmark, Estonia, France, Hungary, Iceland, Italy, Korea, Norway, Poland and Spain. The most significant change occurred in Hungary where the burden of the lower paid worker was about 58 per cent the higher paid worker in 2000 and about 100 per cent in 2013.

7. Families

The results presented in Tables II.5 and II.2 can be used to compare the tax burdens faced by a one-earner married couple with two children at the average wage and the single worker without children at the same income level. Focusing on the net tax burden (personal income tax plus employee social security contributions less cash benefits which can be found in Part c of the Tables), one observes that the OECD average fiscal savings for the married couple compared with the single worker increased slightly between 2000 and 2013 (by about 0.4 of a percentage point).

The savings for the one-earner married couple have increased in fifteen countries and declined in eighteen others. There were three countries where the fiscal savings have increased by more than 5 percentage points; in New Zealand increasing by 8.7 percentage points from 5.8 to 14.5 per cent of income and in Ireland and Portugal where the increases were between 5 and 7 percentage points.

Income taxes, social security contributions and cash benefits

The evolution of the income taxes, social security contributions and cash benefits for the eight family types over the period 2000 to 2013 is presented in the Tables II.1 to II.8. Each of the Tables 1 to 8 corresponds to a particular family type and each is divided into three parts.

- Part a.-tables containing the (average) tax wedge comprising income taxes plus employee and employer social security contributions (including any applicable payroll taxes) less cash benefits,
- Part b.-tables providing the (average) burden of personal income taxes, and the
- Part c.-tables depicting the (average) burden of income taxes plus employee social security contributions less cash benefits (*net* personal average tax rates).

Tables II.9 and II.10 show the average gross and net earnings of a single individual over the 2000 to 2013 period in US dollar using purchasing power parities of national currencies and in national currencies.

Table II.1a. **Income tax plus employee and employer contributions less cash benefits, single persons, 67% of average earnings**

Tax burden as a % of labour costs, single persons without children

	2000	2005	2006	2007	2008	2009	2010	2011	2012	2013
Australia	25.8	25.1	24.7	23.7	21.9	20.7	20.9	20.6	21.5	21.9
Austria	43.2	43.3	43.7	44.2	44.5	43.2	43.4	43.8	44.2	44.5
Belgium	51.3	49.3	49.4	49.6	50.2	49.9	50.3	50.5	50.4	50.1
Canada	27.7	27.4	27.3	26.6	26.5	26.1	25.8	26.0	26.1	26.3
Chile	7.0	7.0	7.0	7.0	7.0	7.0	7.0	7.0	7.0	7.0
Czech Republic	41.3	42.0	40.0	40.5	40.1	38.7	38.9	39.6	39.4	39.3
Denmark	40.8	38.9	38.9	38.9	38.5	38.0	36.7	36.8	37.0	36.6
Estonia	39.8	38.1	37.3	37.6	37.0	37.7	38.7	39.0	39.2	38.7
Finland	42.7	39.3	38.8	38.6	38.6	37.1	36.7	36.7	36.8	37.6
France	43.8	46.4	46.0	46.3	46.5	46.5	46.7	46.9	46.9	45.6
Germany	47.5	47.3	47.4	46.9	46.5	45.9	44.9	45.5	45.5	45.1
Greece	36.0	35.4	36.4	36.4	36.2	36.5	35.7	39.9	39.7	36.9
Hungary	51.4	43.1	43.3	46.0	46.7	46.2	43.8	45.2	47.9	49.0
Iceland	23.8	28.2	28.2	27.0	27.6	26.1	28.3	29.4	28.6	28.7
Ireland	18.1	16.8	16.1	14.9	15.0	16.2	16.7	19.9	20.0	21.0
Israel	23.1	18.0	16.3	16.8	15.4	14.4	14.0	13.9	13.7	13.9
Italy	43.6	42.5	42.7	42.8	43.2	43.5	44.0	44.4	44.6	44.7
Japan	23.4	26.5	27.4	27.8	28.0	27.8	28.9	29.5	29.9	30.3
Korea	15.0	15.6	16.0	16.8	17.4	16.9	17.3	17.8	18.0	18.3
Luxembourg	31.1	28.7	29.1	29.9	28.2	27.4	27.7	29.4	29.0	29.9
Mexico	7.5	10.0	10.6	11.1	10.9	11.9	12.3	13.2	13.6	13.9
Netherlands	42.2	41.6	33.2	33.3	34.0	33.3	33.5	33.4	33.4	32.1
New Zealand	18.6	18.8	18.9	19.0	18.0	15.5	14.2	12.9	13.1	13.3
Norway	35.1	34.2	34.3	34.2	34.2	34.0	34.0	34.3	34.2	34.1
Poland	37.0	37.5	37.8	37.1	33.6	33.1	33.3	33.4	34.7	34.7
Portugal	33.2	32.1	32.8	32.5	32.1	31.8	32.2	32.2	32.6	34.7
Slovak Republic	40.6	34.8	35.2	35.5	36.0	34.4	34.7	36.0	36.9	38.4
Slovenia	42.6	41.8	41.3	40.9	40.3	39.7	38.6	38.6	38.5	38.5
Spain	34.8	35.7	35.9	35.7	34.0	34.3	36.5	36.7	37.1	37.2
Sweden	48.6	46.6	45.9	43.3	42.5	41.3	40.6	40.7	40.7	40.8
Switzerland	20.1	19.4	19.4	19.6	19.1	19.1	19.2	19.5	19.2	19.2
Turkey[1]	39.1	41.9	41.8	41.8	37.8	35.0	35.7	36.2	36.5	36.5
United Kingdom	29.1	30.5	30.6	30.8	29.7	29.1	29.4	28.4	27.9	26.9
United States	28.3	27.6	27.7	27.9	27.1	27.6	27.9	27.4	27.7	29.3
Unweighted average										
OECD-Average	**33.3**	**32.7**	**32.4**	**32.4**	**31.9**	**31.3**	**31.4**	**31.9**	**32.1**	**32.2**
OECD-EU 21	**39.9**	**38.6**	**38.2**	**38.2**	**37.8**	**37.3**	**37.3**	**38.0**	**38.2**	**38.2**

1. Wage figures are based on the old definition of average worker (ISIC D, Rev. 3).

StatLink http://dx.doi.org/10.1787/888933006670

Table II.1b. **Income tax, single persons, 67% of average earnings**

Tax burden as a % of gross wage earnings of single persons without children

	2000	2005	2006	2007	2008	2009	2010	2011	2012	2013
Australia	21.1	20.6	20.2	19.1	17.2	15.7	15.9	15.9	16.8	17.2
Austria	7.5	8.7	9.3	9.8	10.3	8.6	8.9	9.4	9.8	10.2
Belgium	22.7	21.7	21.6	21.8	22.1	21.8	22.4	22.5	22.4	22.2
Canada	15.0	12.9	12.9	12.2	12.4	11.9	11.5	11.6	11.6	11.6
Chile	0.0	0.0	0.0	0.0	0.0	0.0	0.0	0.0	0.0	0.0
Czech Republic	8.2	9.2	6.6	7.2	6.6	6.9	7.1	8.1	7.8	7.6
Denmark	27.6	26.6	26.7	26.8	26.5	25.9	25.1	33.3	33.4	33.0
Estonia	19.9	16.3	15.8	16.2	15.5	14.9	14.8	15.2	15.5	15.9
Finland	20.8	18.5	17.5	17.2	17.7	16.4	15.6	15.4	14.9	15.8
France	12.5	12.3	11.8	12.1	12.1	12.2	12.2	12.4	12.6	12.6
Germany	16.3	14.9	14.9	15.2	15.4	14.7	13.7	13.9	14.1	14.1
Greece	2.2	1.3	2.5	2.5	2.3	2.7	1.7	6.6	6.0	3.1
Hungary	17.5	8.7	8.9	10.1	11.0	11.7	10.8	12.1	16.0	16.0
Iceland	19.9	23.9	23.9	22.9	23.0	20.7	21.4	22.5	22.3	22.5
Ireland	11.1	5.2	4.4	3.1	3.1	4.4	5.0	8.5	8.6	8.6
Israel	12.0	6.5	6.4	7.1	5.6	4.9	4.3	4.3	4.3	4.4
Italy	15.2	14.3	15.2	15.0	15.6	15.8	16.5	17.1	17.4	17.5
Japan	5.5	5.2	5.7	6.4	6.3	6.3	6.1	6.1	6.1	6.1
Korea	0.8	1.0	1.1	1.5	1.7	1.3	1.4	1.4	1.5	1.6
Luxembourg	10.2	7.2	7.8	8.3	8.1	6.8	7.2	7.7	8.1	9.0
Mexico	-6.1	-3.3	-2.8	-2.3	-2.6	-1.5	-1.1	-0.1	0.4	0.7
Netherlands	5.3	4.2	4.4	4.8	5.2	5.4	5.3	5.3	5.2	5.6
New Zealand	18.6	18.8	18.9	19.0	18.0	15.5	14.2	12.9	13.1	13.3
Norway	18.9	17.8	17.8	17.9	18.0	17.8	17.8	17.9	17.7	17.7
Poland	5.3	5.0	5.2	5.5	6.0	5.4	5.6	5.8	5.9	6.0
Portugal	6.3	4.9	5.8	5.4	5.0	4.6	5.1	5.1	5.6	8.3
Slovak Republic	6.0	4.3	4.9	5.1	5.9	3.8	4.2	5.9	5.9	5.8
Slovenia	10.2	8.1	8.0	7.9	8.0	7.9	6.6	6.7	6.6	6.4
Spain	8.5	9.6	10.0	10.0	7.8	8.4	11.1	11.5	12.0	12.0
Sweden	24.7	22.2	21.5	17.9	16.9	15.8	15.0	15.1	15.1	15.2
Switzerland	8.4	8.5	8.5	8.7	8.1	8.2	8.3	8.3	7.9	7.9
Turkey[1]	13.2	14.5	14.2	14.3	10.2	9.3	10.1	10.6	11.0	11.1
United Kingdom	15.1	15.4	15.5	15.6	14.6	14.2	14.3	13.4	13.0	12.0
United States	14.9	14.3	14.4	14.6	13.7	12.3	12.6	14.0	14.1	13.9
Unweighted average										
OECD-Average	**12.2**	**11.2**	**11.2**	**11.1**	**10.8**	**10.3**	**10.3**	**11.1**	**11.2**	**11.3**
OECD-EU 21	**13.0**	**11.4**	**11.3**	**11.3**	**11.2**	**10.9**	**10.9**	**11.9**	**12.2**	**12.2**

1. Wage figures are based on the old definition of average worker (ISIC D, Rev. 3).

StatLink http://dx.doi.org/10.1787/888933006689

Table II.1c. Income tax plus employee contributions less cash benefits, single persons, 67% of average earnings

Tax burden as a % of gross wage earnings, single persons without children

	2000	2005	2006	2007	2008	2009	2010	2011	2012	2013
Australia	21.1	20.6	20.2	19.1	17.2	15.7	15.9	15.9	16.8	17.2
Austria	25.6	26.7	27.3	27.9	28.4	26.6	27.0	27.5	27.9	28.3
Belgium	35.8	35.0	35.1	35.3	36.0	35.7	36.3	36.4	36.3	36.1
Canada	19.4	19.0	18.9	18.1	18.2	17.6	17.3	17.4	17.5	17.5
Chile	7.0	7.0	7.0	7.0	7.0	7.0	7.0	7.0	7.0	7.0
Czech Republic	20.7	21.7	19.1	19.7	19.1	17.9	18.1	19.1	18.8	18.6
Denmark	40.9	38.9	38.9	38.9	38.5	38.0	36.7	36.8	37.0	36.6
Estonia	19.9	17.3	16.4	16.8	16.1	16.7	17.6	18.0	18.3	17.9
Finland	27.8	24.7	24.2	23.8	23.8	22.6	22.6	22.5	22.4	23.3
France	25.9	25.9	25.5	25.8	25.8	25.9	25.9	26.1	26.3	26.4
Germany	36.8	36.3	36.6	36.3	36.0	35.3	34.2	34.8	34.8	34.6
Greece	18.1	17.3	18.5	18.5	18.3	18.7	17.7	22.8	22.5	19.6
Hungary	30.0	22.2	23.3	27.1	28.0	28.7	27.8	29.6	34.5	34.5
Iceland	20.1	24.1	24.1	23.1	23.7	21.5	22.1	23.3	23.0	23.2
Ireland	11.1	7.9	7.0	5.8	5.9	7.2	7.8	11.3	11.4	12.6
Israel	19.3	13.3	12.0	13.0	11.7	10.8	10.3	10.3	10.2	10.2
Italy	24.4	23.5	24.3	24.5	25.0	25.3	26.0	26.6	26.9	27.0
Japan	15.5	17.1	17.9	18.4	18.5	18.4	19.1	19.5	19.8	20.0
Korea	7.5	8.1	8.3	8.9	9.3	8.9	9.2	9.5	9.7	9.9
Luxembourg	21.8	18.9	19.4	20.3	20.1	19.0	19.4	20.7	20.3	21.2
Mexico	-4.8	-2.1	-1.6	-1.1	-1.4	-0.2	0.1	1.2	1.6	1.9
Netherlands	32.9	31.9	27.1	27.1	27.6	27.0	27.0	27.1	26.7	26.1
New Zealand	18.6	18.8	18.9	19.0	18.0	15.5	14.2	12.9	13.1	13.3
Norway	26.7	25.6	25.6	25.7	25.8	25.6	25.6	25.7	25.5	25.5
Poland	26.5	27.0	27.4	26.5	23.8	23.2	23.4	23.6	23.7	23.8
Portugal	17.3	15.9	16.8	16.4	16.0	15.6	16.1	16.1	16.6	19.3
Slovak Republic	18.0	17.7	18.3	18.5	19.3	17.2	17.6	19.3	19.3	19.2
Slovenia	32.3	30.2	30.1	30.0	30.1	30.0	28.7	28.8	28.7	28.5
Spain	14.9	16.0	16.3	16.3	14.2	14.7	17.5	17.8	18.3	18.4
Sweden	31.7	29.2	28.5	24.9	23.9	22.8	22.0	22.1	22.1	22.2
Switzerland	14.9	14.6	14.5	14.8	14.2	14.2	14.3	14.5	14.1	14.2
Turkey[1]	27.2	29.5	29.2	29.3	25.2	24.3	25.1	25.6	26.0	26.1
United Kingdom	22.7	23.8	23.8	24.0	22.9	22.4	22.6	21.6	21.1	20.1
United States	22.6	21.9	22.0	22.3	19.3	20.0	20.2	19.6	19.8	21.5
Unweighted average										
OECD-Average	**22.1**	**21.3**	**21.2**	**21.2**	**20.8**	**20.3**	**20.4**	**20.9**	**21.1**	**21.2**
OECD-EU 21	**25.5**	**24.2**	**24.0**	**24.0**	**23.8**	**23.4**	**23.4**	**24.2**	**24.5**	**24.5**

1. Wage figures are based on the old definition of average worker (ISIC D, Rev. 3).

StatLink http://dx.doi.org/10.1787/888933006708

Table II.2a. **Income tax plus employee and employer contributions less cash benefits, single persons, 100% of average earnings**

Tax burden as a % of labour costs, single persons without children

	2000	2005	2006	2007	2008	2009	2010	2011	2012	2013
Australia	31.0	28.5	28.3	27.7	26.9	26.7	26.8	26.7	27.2	27.4
Austria	47.3	48.1	48.5	48.8	49.0	47.9	48.2	48.5	48.8	49.1
Belgium	57.1	55.5	55.5	55.6	55.9	55.7	55.9	56.1	56.0	55.8
Canada	32.9	31.9	31.8	31.3	31.3	30.5	30.4	30.7	30.8	31.1
Chile	7.0	7.0	7.0	7.0	7.0	7.0	7.0	7.0	7.0	7.0
Czech Republic	42.6	43.7	42.5	42.9	43.4	42.0	42.1	42.6	42.5	42.4
Denmark	44.1	40.9	41.0	41.1	40.9	39.5	38.3	38.4	38.5	38.2
Estonia	41.3	39.9	39.0	39.0	38.4	39.2	40.1	40.3	40.4	39.9
Finland	47.5	44.4	44.0	43.9	43.8	42.5	42.3	42.3	42.6	43.1
France	50.4	50.5	49.7	49.7	49.8	49.8	49.9	50.0	50.1	48.9
Germany	52.9	52.1	52.3	51.8	51.3	50.8	49.1	49.7	49.6	49.3
Greece	39.1	41.2	42.3	42.1	41.5	41.3	40.1	43.2	42.9	41.6
Hungary	54.7	51.1	51.9	54.5	54.1	53.1	46.6	49.5	49.5	49.0
Iceland	28.8	32.1	31.8	30.5	30.9	30.5	33.4	34.1	33.4	33.4
Ireland	28.9	23.5	23.0	22.2	22.3	24.7	25.8	25.8	25.9	26.6
Israel	29.6	25.5	24.3	24.9	22.9	21.3	20.7	20.8	20.4	20.7
Italy	47.1	45.9	46.1	46.4	46.6	46.8	47.2	47.6	47.7	47.8
Japan	24.7	27.7	28.8	29.3	29.5	29.2	30.2	30.8	31.3	31.6
Korea	16.4	17.3	18.2	19.7	20.0	19.5	20.1	20.5	21.0	21.4
Luxembourg	37.1	34.7	35.3	36.3	34.7	33.9	34.3	36.3	35.9	37.0
Mexico	12.4	14.7	15.0	15.9	15.1	15.3	15.5	18.7	19.0	19.2
Netherlands	40.0	38.9	38.4	38.7	39.2	38.0	38.1	38.0	38.7	36.9
New Zealand	19.4	20.0	20.4	21.1	20.5	18.1	17.0	15.9	16.4	16.9
Norway	38.6	37.2	37.4	37.5	37.6	37.3	37.3	37.6	37.4	37.3
Poland	38.2	38.7	39.0	38.2	34.7	34.1	34.2	34.3	35.5	35.6
Portugal	37.3	36.8	37.5	37.3	36.9	36.5	37.1	38.0	37.6	41.1
Slovak Republic	41.9	38.0	38.3	38.4	38.8	37.7	37.9	38.8	39.6	41.1
Slovenia	46.3	45.6	45.3	43.3	42.9	42.2	42.5	42.6	42.5	42.3
Spain	38.6	39.0	39.1	39.0	38.0	38.3	39.7	40.0	40.6	40.7
Sweden	50.1	48.1	47.8	45.3	44.8	43.2	42.8	42.8	42.9	42.9
Switzerland	22.9	22.2	22.1	22.4	21.9	22.0	22.1	22.3	21.9	22.0
Turkey[1]	40.4	42.8	42.7	42.7	39.9	37.4	37.9	38.2	38.4	38.6
United Kingdom	32.6	33.9	34.0	34.1	32.8	32.4	32.6	32.5	32.1	31.5
United States	30.4	29.8	29.9	30.3	29.8	30.1	30.5	29.7	29.8	31.3
Unweighted average										
OECD-Average	**36.7**	**36.1**	**36.1**	**36.1**	**35.7**	**35.1**	**35.1**	**35.6**	**35.7**	**35.9**
OECD-EU 21	**43.6**	**42.4**	**42.4**	**42.3**	**41.9**	**41.4**	**41.2**	**41.8**	**41.9**	**42.0**

1. Wage figures are based on the old definition of average worker (ISIC D, Rev. 3).

StatLink http://dx.doi.org/10.1787/888933006727

Table II.2b. **Income tax, single persons, 100% of the average earnings**

Tax burden as a % of gross wage earnings, single persons without children

	2000	2005	2006	2007	2008	2009	2010	2011	2012	2013
Australia	26.6	24.2	24.0	23.4	22.5	22.1	22.3	22.3	22.9	23.1
Austria	12.9	15.0	15.4	15.8	16.2	14.7	15.0	15.5	15.9	16.2
Belgium	29.0	28.0	27.9	28.1	28.5	28.3	28.7	28.8	28.7	28.6
Canada	19.2	16.3	16.3	16.0	16.1	15.2	15.1	15.3	15.3	15.3
Chile	0.0	0.0	0.0	0.0	0.0	0.0	0.0	0.0	0.0	0.0
Czech Republic	10.0	11.5	9.9	10.4	11.1	11.3	11.5	12.1	11.9	11.8
Denmark	32.3	30.1	30.2	30.4	30.2	28.8	27.9	36.1	36.2	35.8
Estonia	21.9	18.8	18.1	18.1	17.3	16.8	16.7	16.9	17.1	17.5
Finland	26.9	24.7	23.8	23.7	24.2	23.0	22.3	22.2	21.8	22.5
France	15.7	15.3	14.0	14.1	14.1	14.1	14.2	14.2	14.4	14.6
Germany	22.7	20.8	20.8	21.0	21.2	20.6	18.7	18.9	19.0	19.1
Greece	6.1	8.8	10.1	9.8	9.1	8.8	7.2	10.8	10.1	9.0
Hungary	23.2	20.1	20.9	21.8	21.3	20.8	14.4	17.6	16.6	16.0
Iceland	25.3	28.0	27.7	26.7	26.8	25.7	27.1	27.9	27.7	27.9
Ireland	15.2	10.2	9.6	8.7	8.8	10.2	10.7	14.7	14.8	14.7
Israel	18.0	13.3	12.6	13.3	11.2	9.7	9.0	9.1	8.7	8.8
Italy	19.9	18.8	19.6	19.7	20.0	20.2	20.7	21.3	21.4	21.5
Japan	7.0	6.7	7.2	8.1	8.0	7.9	7.6	7.6	7.6	7.7
Korea	2.3	2.8	3.4	4.7	4.6	4.1	4.5	4.4	4.9	5.1
Luxembourg	17.0	14.2	14.9	15.6	15.3	14.0	14.6	15.3	15.7	17.0
Mexico	0.7	3.1	3.5	4.6	3.8	4.1	4.2	7.9	8.2	8.4
Netherlands	9.6	11.2	13.2	14.6	15.5	16.6	16.2	16.4	16.9	15.7
New Zealand	19.4	20.0	20.4	21.1	20.5	18.1	17.0	15.9	16.4	16.9
Norway	22.9	21.2	21.3	21.7	21.8	21.5	21.5	21.6	21.4	21.4
Poland	6.6	6.4	6.5	6.8	7.2	6.6	6.7	6.8	6.9	6.9
Portugal	11.4	10.8	11.7	11.4	11.0	10.5	11.2	12.3	11.8	16.2
Slovak Republic	7.8	8.4	8.7	8.9	9.4	8.0	8.3	9.4	9.4	9.4
Slovenia	13.5	12.6	12.7	10.7	11.0	10.8	11.2	11.3	11.1	11.0
Spain	13.5	13.9	14.1	14.2	12.9	13.4	15.4	15.7	16.5	16.6
Sweden	26.7	24.2	23.9	20.6	19.9	18.4	17.8	17.9	17.9	18.0
Switzerland	11.3	11.5	11.3	11.7	11.1	11.2	11.3	11.2	10.8	10.9
Turkey[1]	14.7	15.5	15.4	15.4	12.7	12.1	12.6	13.0	13.2	13.5
United Kingdom	17.4	17.6	17.7	17.7	16.4	16.1	16.2	15.6	15.4	14.7
United States	17.3	16.6	16.8	17.2	16.8	15.7	16.1	17.2	17.3	16.9
Unweighted average										
OECD-Average	**16.0**	**15.3**	**15.4**	**15.5**	**15.2**	**14.7**	**14.5**	**15.4**	**15.4**	**15.5**
OECD-EU 21	**17.1**	**16.3**	**16.4**	**16.3**	**16.2**	**15.8**	**15.5**	**16.6**	**16.6**	**16.8**

1. Wage figures are based on the old definition of average worker (ISIC D, Rev. 3).

StatLink http://dx.doi.org/10.1787/888933006746

Table II.2c. **Income tax plus employee contributions less cash benefits, single persons, 100% of average earnings**

Tax burden as a % of gross wage earnings, single persons without children

	2000	2005	2006	2007	2008	2009	2010	2011	2012	2013
Australia	26.6	24.2	24.0	23.4	22.5	22.1	22.3	22.3	22.9	23.1
Austria	31.0	33.0	33.4	33.8	34.3	32.8	33.1	33.6	33.9	34.3
Belgium	43.0	42.0	41.9	42.1	42.5	42.3	42.7	42.8	42.7	42.6
Canada	25.1	23.9	23.8	23.3	23.4	22.5	22.4	22.5	22.6	22.8
Chile	7.0	7.0	7.0	7.0	7.0	7.0	7.0	7.0	7.0	7.0
Czech Republic	22.5	24.0	22.4	22.9	23.6	22.3	22.5	23.1	22.9	22.8
Denmark	44.2	40.9	41.0	41.1	40.9	39.5	38.3	38.4	38.5	38.2
Estonia	21.9	19.8	18.7	18.7	17.9	18.6	19.5	19.7	19.9	19.5
Finland	33.9	31.0	30.6	30.4	30.4	29.3	29.4	29.4	29.5	30.2
France	29.2	28.9	27.7	27.8	27.8	27.8	27.8	27.9	28.2	28.4
Germany	43.2	42.2	42.5	42.2	41.9	41.2	39.2	39.8	39.8	39.6
Greece	22.0	24.8	26.1	25.8	25.1	24.8	23.2	27.0	26.6	25.5
Hungary	35.7	33.6	35.2	38.8	38.3	37.8	31.4	35.1	35.1	34.5
Iceland	25.4	28.2	27.8	26.8	27.2	26.2	27.6	28.4	28.2	28.3
Ireland	20.3	15.2	14.7	13.9	13.9	16.7	17.9	17.8	17.9	18.7
Israel	26.1	21.3	20.3	21.2	19.3	17.7	17.0	17.0	16.6	16.7
Italy	29.0	28.0	28.7	29.2	29.5	29.7	30.2	30.7	30.9	31.0
Japan	17.0	18.5	19.4	20.2	20.2	20.0	20.6	21.0	21.3	21.6
Korea	9.0	9.9	10.6	12.1	12.1	11.7	12.3	12.5	13.0	13.4
Luxembourg	28.7	25.9	26.6	27.7	27.4	26.2	26.8	28.4	28.0	29.3
Mexico	2.2	4.6	5.0	6.0	5.1	5.4	5.6	9.2	9.5	9.8
Netherlands	33.6	32.5	32.5	32.5	32.8	31.8	31.7	31.7	32.1	31.2
New Zealand	19.4	20.0	20.4	21.1	20.5	18.1	17.0	15.9	16.4	16.9
Norway	30.7	29.0	29.1	29.5	29.6	29.3	29.3	29.4	29.2	29.2
Poland	27.8	28.4	28.7	27.8	25.0	24.4	24.5	24.6	24.7	24.7
Portugal	22.4	21.8	22.7	22.4	22.0	21.5	22.2	23.3	22.8	27.2
Slovak Republic	19.8	21.8	22.1	22.3	22.8	21.4	21.7	22.8	22.8	22.8
Slovenia	35.6	34.7	34.8	32.8	33.1	32.9	33.3	33.4	33.2	33.1
Spain	19.8	20.3	20.5	20.6	19.3	19.8	21.7	22.0	22.9	22.9
Sweden	33.7	31.2	30.9	27.6	26.9	25.4	24.8	24.8	24.9	25.0
Switzerland	17.8	17.5	17.4	17.7	17.1	17.3	17.4	17.5	17.1	17.1
Turkey[1]	28.7	30.5	30.4	30.4	27.7	27.1	27.6	28.0	28.2	28.5
United Kingdom	25.8	26.9	26.9	27.0	25.6	25.2	25.4	25.1	24.7	24.1
United States	24.9	24.3	24.4	24.8	23.1	23.3	23.8	22.8	22.9	24.6
Unweighted average										
OECD-Average	**26.0**	**25.5**	**25.5**	**25.6**	**25.2**	**24.7**	**24.6**	**25.1**	**25.2**	**25.4**
OECD-EU 21	**29.7**	**28.9**	**29.0**	**28.9**	**28.6**	**28.2**	**28.0**	**28.6**	**28.7**	**28.8**

1. Wage figures are based on the old definition of average worker (ISIC D, Rev. 3).

StatLink http://dx.doi.org/10.1787/888933006765

Table II.3a. **Income tax plus employee and employer contributions less cash benefits, single persons, 167% of average earnings**

Tax burden as a % of labour costs, single persons without children

	2000	2005	2006	2007	2008	2009	2010	2011	2012	2013
Australia	38.8	36.0	34.7	32.8	32.7	32.6	32.4	32.2	33.0	33.1
Austria	50.4	51.4	51.6	51.7	51.8	51.2	51.4	51.5	51.4	51.9
Belgium	62.6	60.9	60.8	60.9	61.1	60.8	61.0	61.1	60.9	60.9
Canada	35.2	33.2	33.2	32.9	32.9	32.6	32.7	32.8	33.0	33.1
Chile	7.4	7.0	7.0	7.0	7.0	7.0	7.6	7.7	7.9	7.8
Czech Republic	44.8	46.1	46.0	46.7	46.1	44.6	44.7	45.0	44.9	44.9
Denmark	51.4	49.2	49.4	49.6	49.6	48.5	44.5	44.9	45.1	44.3
Estonia	42.5	41.4	40.5	40.1	39.5	40.3	41.2	41.3	41.4	40.8
Finland	53.2	50.2	49.9	49.7	49.5	48.3	48.2	48.2	48.5	48.9
France	52.5	53.3	53.3	53.4	53.4	53.6	53.6	53.8	54.0	54.1
Germany	56.3	54.9	55.0	53.8	53.1	53.1	51.5	51.3	51.3	51.2
Greece	45.0	48.0	49.0	47.3	46.4	45.9	45.6	48.6	48.2	49.2
Hungary	59.1	56.7	56.7	58.6	59.1	58.3	53.1	51.6	50.7	49.0
Iceland	39.6	37.0	34.6	33.4	33.6	34.1	37.8	38.3	37.8	37.8
Ireland	39.4	34.9	34.0	33.0	33.0	35.1	36.4	38.0	38.1	38.5
Israel	38.0	34.6	33.7	34.2	32.2	29.9	29.4	29.2	28.6	29.5
Italy	51.1	50.6	50.9	51.4	51.8	52.0	52.5	52.9	53.1	53.2
Japan	28.5	30.3	31.6	32.4	32.5	32.3	33.3	33.8	34.2	34.5
Korea	20.4	21.4	21.8	22.5	22.6	21.8	21.7	22.2	22.6	22.9
Luxembourg	45.1	41.9	42.3	43.0	41.7	41.3	41.6	43.7	43.2	44.3
Mexico	19.2	21.8	21.9	22.0	20.6	20.9	21.3	21.6	21.9	22.2
Netherlands	44.9	42.4	41.3	42.0	42.5	41.8	41.8	41.8	42.4	41.9
New Zealand	24.2	25.8	26.2	26.8	26.3	24.6	23.3	22.0	22.4	22.8
Norway	45.2	43.8	43.0	43.1	43.2	43.0	43.0	43.2	43.1	43.0
Poland	39.1	39.6	40.1	39.0	36.0	34.9	35.0	35.0	36.2	36.2
Portugal	42.3	42.3	43.3	43.0	42.6	42.2	43.0	44.6	43.6	47.4
Slovak Republic	45.2	40.2	40.4	40.5	40.7	40.1	40.3	40.8	41.6	43.3
Slovenia	51.0	52.3	51.6	49.0	48.3	47.1	47.6	47.7	47.5	46.1
Spain	41.0	42.4	42.6	42.3	41.4	41.6	42.4	42.5	43.6	44.3
Sweden	55.7	54.7	54.5	53.0	52.7	51.1	50.9	50.9	50.7	50.6
Switzerland	27.4	26.6	26.4	26.7	26.4	26.5	26.5	26.8	26.5	26.5
Turkey[1]	35.0	44.6	44.3	44.5	42.8	40.2	41.1	41.6	41.9	42.1
United Kingdom	35.8	37.7	37.8	37.9	37.5	36.9	37.2	37.9	37.8	37.7
United States	36.8	35.1	35.2	35.5	35.3	35.4	35.7	34.5	34.6	36.2
Unweighted average										
OECD-Average	**41.3**	**40.8**	**40.7**	**40.6**	**40.2**	**39.7**	**39.7**	**40.0**	**40.0**	**40.3**
OECD-EU 21	**48.0**	**47.2**	**47.2**	**47.0**	**46.6**	**46.1**	**45.9**	**46.3**	**46.4**	**46.6**

1. Wage figures are based on the old definition of average worker (ISIC D, Rev. 3).

StatLink http://dx.doi.org/10.1787/888933006784

Table II.3b. **Income tax, single persons at 167% of average earnings**

Tax burden as a % of gross wage earnings, single persons without children

	2000	2005	2006	2007	2008	2009	2010	2011	2012	2013
Australia	34.9	32.2	30.7	28.7	28.7	28.3	28.2	28.2	29.1	29.2
Austria	20.3	22.1	22.4	22.8	23.1	22.0	22.1	22.5	22.8	22.9
Belgium	36.0	34.7	34.7	34.9	35.2	35.1	35.4	35.5	35.4	35.3
Canada	25.5	22.3	22.3	22.2	22.3	21.6	21.7	21.8	21.8	21.8
Chile	0.4	0.0	0.0	0.0	0.0	0.0	0.6	0.7	0.9	0.8
Czech Republic	13.0	14.8	14.7	15.6	14.8	14.8	14.9	15.3	15.2	15.1
Denmark	40.7	39.5	39.7	40.0	40.0	38.9	34.9	43.2	43.4	42.7
Estonia	23.6	20.8	20.0	19.6	18.7	18.3	18.2	18.3	18.4	18.7
Finland	34.0	31.9	31.0	30.9	31.2	30.0	29.4	29.4	29.1	29.6
France	21.2	20.0	19.9	20.1	20.1	20.3	20.3	20.5	20.8	20.9
Germany	31.6	28.8	28.8	29.0	29.2	28.6	27.1	27.5	27.6	27.7
Greece	13.8	17.4	18.7	16.5	15.4	14.8	14.3	17.7	16.9	18.8
Hungary	30.3	28.1	27.6	27.5	28.1	27.6	22.7	20.3	18.1	16.0
Iceland	36.6	33.3	30.7	29.7	29.8	29.7	32.1	32.7	32.7	32.8
Ireland	26.7	22.7	21.6	20.5	20.6	21.3	22.0	27.8	27.9	27.9
Israel	26.2	21.9	20.7	21.2	19.2	16.9	16.4	16.0	15.4	16.0
Italy	25.2	25.1	25.9	26.3	26.8	27.0	27.6	28.2	28.5	28.6
Japan	11.1	10.8	11.6	12.8	12.8	12.4	12.0	12.0	12.1	12.2
Korea	6.7	8.1	8.6	9.4	9.3	8.6	8.6	8.5	8.8	9.0
Luxembourg	26.2	22.4	22.8	23.3	23.1	22.3	22.6	23.6	23.9	25.0
Mexico	7.8	11.7	12.0	12.3	11.1	11.5	11.9	12.3	12.6	12.9
Netherlands	25.4	25.0	25.6	27.2	27.9	28.8	28.4	28.6	29.1	28.1
New Zealand	24.2	25.8	26.2	26.8	26.3	24.6	23.3	22.0	22.4	22.8
Norway	30.3	28.7	27.6	28.1	28.1	27.9	27.8	28.0	27.8	27.8
Poland	7.7	7.5	7.9	7.8	8.7	7.5	7.5	7.6	7.7	7.7
Portugal	17.6	17.6	18.8	18.4	18.0	17.4	18.5	20.4	19.2	23.9
Slovak Republic	12.4	11.7	11.9	12.0	12.3	11.4	11.6	12.3	12.3	12.2
Slovenia	19.1	18.8	18.7	16.3	16.7	16.5	17.0	17.2	16.9	15.3
Spain	18.5	18.8	19.1	19.1	18.5	19.1	20.5	21.0	22.5	22.5
Sweden	36.3	35.3	35.2	33.2	32.8	31.0	30.8	30.7	30.5	30.1
Switzerland	16.2	16.4	16.3	16.6	16.0	16.1	16.2	16.1	15.8	15.8
Turkey[1]	18.0	17.7	17.4	17.6	16.2	15.3	16.4	17.0	17.3	17.6
United Kingdom	23.0	24.1	24.2	24.5	23.2	21.9	22.4	22.4	22.6	22.8
United States	24.2	22.4	22.6	22.8	22.8	22.1	22.4	23.0	23.1	22.8
Unweighted average										
OECD-Average	**22.5**	**21.7**	**21.6**	**21.6**	**21.4**	**20.9**	**20.8**	**21.4**	**21.4**	**21.6**
OECD-EU 21	**23.9**	**23.2**	**23.3**	**23.1**	**23.1**	**22.6**	**22.3**	**23.3**	**23.3**	**23.4**

1. Wage figures are based on the old definition of average worker (ISIC D, Rev. 3).

StatLink http://dx.doi.org/10.1787/888933006803

Table II.3c. **Income tax plus employee contributions less cash benefits, single persons at 167% of average earnings**

Tax burden as a % of gross wage earnings, single persons without children

	2000	2005	2006	2007	2008	2009	2010	2011	2012	2013
Australia	34.9	32.2	30.7	28.7	28.7	28.3	28.2	28.2	29.1	29.2
Austria	36.3	38.3	38.6	38.8	39.0	38.1	38.3	38.5	38.6	39.0
Belgium	50.0	48.8	48.7	48.9	49.3	49.2	49.5	49.6	49.5	49.4
Canada	29.3	27.2	27.2	26.9	27.0	26.5	26.6	26.7	26.8	26.8
Chile	7.4	7.0	7.0	7.0	7.0	7.0	7.6	7.7	7.9	7.8
Czech Republic	25.5	27.3	27.2	28.1	27.3	25.8	25.9	26.3	26.2	26.1
Denmark	51.5	49.2	49.4	49.6	49.6	48.5	44.5	44.9	45.1	44.3
Estonia	23.6	21.8	20.6	20.2	19.3	20.1	21.0	21.1	21.2	20.7
Finland	41.1	38.3	37.8	37.6	37.4	36.4	36.6	36.6	36.8	37.3
France	33.1	33.0	33.0	33.1	33.2	33.3	33.3	33.6	33.9	34.0
Germany	48.8	46.9	47.1	46.2	45.7	45.5	43.8	43.8	43.8	43.7
Greece	29.7	33.4	34.7	32.5	31.4	30.8	30.3	33.9	33.4	35.3
Hungary	42.8	41.6	41.9	44.5	45.1	44.6	39.7	37.8	36.6	34.5
Iceland	36.7	33.4	30.8	29.8	30.1	30.0	32.4	33.0	32.9	33.0
Ireland	32.1	27.9	26.9	25.8	25.8	28.2	29.5	31.3	31.5	31.9
Israel	35.0	30.8	30.1	30.8	28.8	26.5	25.9	25.6	24.9	25.5
Italy	34.5	34.3	35.1	35.8	36.3	36.6	37.2	37.8	38.0	38.2
Japan	21.1	21.9	23.1	24.1	24.2	24.0	24.5	24.8	25.1	25.4
Korea	13.4	14.7	15.1	15.8	15.8	15.1	15.0	15.3	15.7	16.0
Luxembourg	37.9	34.1	34.6	35.4	35.2	34.6	34.9	36.8	36.2	37.4
Mexico	9.8	13.4	13.7	13.9	12.6	12.9	13.4	13.7	14.1	14.3
Netherlands	40.6	38.3	37.5	38.1	38.5	37.9	37.7	37.8	38.3	38.4
New Zealand	24.2	25.8	26.2	26.8	26.3	24.6	23.3	22.0	22.4	22.8
Norway	38.1	36.5	35.4	35.9	35.9	35.7	35.6	35.8	35.6	35.6
Poland	28.9	29.5	30.1	28.8	26.6	25.3	25.4	25.4	25.5	25.5
Portugal	28.6	28.6	29.8	29.4	29.0	28.4	29.5	31.4	30.2	34.9
Slovak Republic	24.4	24.8	25.0	25.1	25.4	24.6	24.8	25.4	25.4	25.6
Slovenia	41.2	40.9	40.8	38.4	38.8	38.6	39.1	39.3	39.0	37.4
Spain	24.4	25.1	25.3	25.3	24.6	25.1	26.4	26.8	28.2	28.5
Sweden	41.1	40.0	39.8	37.8	37.4	35.8	35.5	35.4	35.2	35.0
Switzerland	22.7	22.3	22.1	22.4	22.0	22.1	22.2	22.3	21.9	22.0
Turkey[1]	26.9	32.7	32.4	32.6	31.2	30.3	31.4	32.0	32.3	32.6
United Kingdom	28.8	30.5	30.6	30.8	30.3	29.7	30.0	30.4	30.3	30.2
United States	31.9	30.1	30.2	30.5	29.6	29.7	30.0	28.6	28.7	30.5
Unweighted average										
OECD-Average	**31.6**	**31.2**	**31.1**	**31.0**	**30.7**	**30.3**	**30.3**	**30.6**	**30.6**	**30.8**
OECD-EU 21	**35.5**	**34.9**	**35.0**	**34.8**	**34.5**	**34.1**	**34.0**	**34.5**	**34.4**	**34.6**

1. Wage figures are based on the old definition of average worker (ISIC D, Rev. 3).

StatLink http://dx.doi.org/10.1787/888933006822

Table II.4a. **Income tax plus employee and employer contributions less cash benefits, single parent at 67% of average earnings**

Tax burden as a % of labour costs, single parent with two children

	2000	2005	2006	2007	2008	2009	2010	2011	2012	2013
Australia	3.5	-3.5	-3.5	-4.6	-5.2	-7.4	-6.9	-6.0	-4.0	-2.9
Austria	25.1	25.6	26.6	27.5	28.3	25.4	25.9	27.1	27.8	28.5
Belgium	36.3	35.2	35.4	35.4	35.8	35.6	36.6	36.9	36.8	36.4
Canada	-0.6	-1.2	-0.5	-2.7	-6.4	-10.1	-7.7	-7.4	-6.9	-6.3
Chile	2.8	3.0	3.0	3.1	3.1	3.2	6.0	6.0	6.1	6.1
Czech Republic	12.5	17.6	19.0	16.4	14.9	15.4	15.6	17.0	14.9	14.3
Denmark	14.7	12.5	12.9	13.6	13.5	12.9	11.1	11.6	11.6	11.2
Estonia	18.3	21.7	18.0	21.8	18.6	22.6	24.0	25.1	26.2	26.4
Finland	28.2	26.4	26.6	27.0	26.8	25.5	25.4	25.6	25.7	26.6
France	34.4	37.9	37.8	38.2	38.5	38.4	38.6	38.8	38.7	37.2
Germany	31.7	33.3	33.7	33.4	33.1	31.1	29.7	30.9	31.1	31.0
Greece	35.3	35.1	36.6	35.3	35.2	35.7	34.4	38.8	38.5	38.7
Hungary	33.9	26.0	25.9	29.0	29.8	29.7	27.3	20.1	22.8	25.2
Iceland	5.7	14.6	15.4	15.2	14.8	12.1	16.5	18.8	15.3	16.5
Ireland	-0.9	-19.6	-31.0	-26.1	-25.5	-29.9	-28.2	-26.7	-26.0	-24.9
Israel	3.1	4.6	2.1	2.3	2.4	1.8	1.5	0.7	0.4	1.4
Italy	29.4	27.4	27.9	24.9	26.3	26.7	27.9	28.7	29.1	28.4
Japan	21.0	22.5	21.6	21.7	21.9	21.5	18.6	19.8	23.5	23.9
Korea	14.4	15.3	15.7	16.1	16.6	16.3	16.7	17.1	17.3	17.4
Luxembourg	6.2	4.9	5.1	6.0	2.0	0.2	0.7	2.9	3.1	4.4
Mexico	7.5	10.0	10.6	11.1	10.9	11.9	12.3	13.2	13.6	13.9
Netherlands	26.3	22.7	12.8	12.8	13.6	11.2	12.0	12.0	11.8	11.0
New Zealand	-3.3	-6.4	-15.3	-17.1	-17.5	-17.3	-17.9	-18.5	-18.4	-17.1
Norway	16.2	18.6	19.4	19.9	20.5	20.5	20.8	21.5	21.6	21.9
Poland	29.7	35.1	35.5	32.4	28.4	28.4	28.4	28.4	29.6	29.6
Portugal	26.5	23.5	24.8	24.1	22.7	19.4	20.5	22.2	23.1	24.9
Slovak Republic	25.2	20.9	21.5	22.7	24.1	21.5	21.8	23.5	24.4	26.3
Slovenia	13.3	14.8	15.0	15.4	13.5	12.4	12.3	12.7	12.9	13.0
Spain	28.5	30.0	30.2	28.2	28.3	28.4	29.1	29.8	30.2	30.3
Sweden	39.9	38.4	36.7	34.4	34.1	33.0	32.3	32.5	32.8	33.0
Switzerland	6.4	6.0	5.6	6.0	3.1	4.4	4.6	4.9	4.6	4.3
Turkey[1]	39.1	41.9	41.8	41.8	36.7	33.8	34.6	35.1	35.4	35.5
United Kingdom	15.0	13.4	14.1	15.6	11.3	8.2	9.0	6.7	6.4	6.3
United States	9.6	6.2	7.0	8.5	7.4	7.1	8.4	8.6	9.9	11.1
Unweighted average										
OECD-Average	**18.7**	**18.1**	**17.3**	**17.3**	**16.5**	**15.6**	**15.9**	**16.4**	**16.8**	**17.2**
OECD-EU 21	**24.3**	**23.0**	**22.1**	**22.3**	**21.6**	**20.5**	**20.7**	**21.2**	**21.5**	**21.8**

1. Wage figures are based on the old definition of average worker (ISIC D, Rev. 3).

StatLink http://dx.doi.org/10.1787/888933006841

Table II.4b. Income tax, single parent at 67% of average earnings

Tax burden as a % of gross wage earnings, single parent with two children

	2000	2005	2006	2007	2008	2009	2010	2011	2012	2013
Australia	15.3	20.5	20.2	18.8	17.1	13.9	14.2	14.2	15.2	17.2
Austria	5.7	5.7	6.4	7.1	7.6	5.3	5.7	6.3	6.8	7.2
Belgium	16.5	16.2	16.1	16.3	16.7	16.3	17.0	17.2	17.0	16.8
Canada	6.6	5.0	4.9	1.1	1.3	0.4	0.9	1.0	1.1	1.1
Chile	0.0	0.0	0.0	0.0	0.0	0.0	0.0	0.0	0.0	0.0
Czech Republic	2.2	1.0	-1.2	0.1	-5.2	-4.5	-5.0	-3.7	-5.5	-5.8
Denmark	27.6	26.6	26.7	26.8	26.5	25.9	25.1	33.3	33.4	33.0
Estonia	19.9	16.3	8.7	10.5	4.6	9.2	9.2	9.9	10.5	11.2
Finland	20.8	18.5	17.5	17.2	17.7	16.4	15.6	15.4	14.9	15.8
France	7.1	7.2	7.0	7.4	7.4	7.4	7.4	7.5	7.6	7.6
Germany	-2.8	-1.6	-1.4	-0.9	-0.3	-2.7	-4.1	-3.4	-2.8	-2.4
Greece	1.4	0.9	2.9	1.2	1.1	1.6	0.0	5.1	4.5	5.3
Hungary	10.2	0.8	8.9	10.1	11.0	11.7	10.8	0.0	3.3	3.6
Iceland	19.9	23.9	23.9	22.9	23.0	20.7	21.4	22.5	22.3	22.5
Ireland	2.2	0.0	0.0	0.0	0.0	1.7	2.0	3.8	3.9	3.8
Israel	1.0	0.0	0.0	0.0	0.0	0.0	0.0	0.0	0.0	0.0
Italy	9.9	6.3	7.3	7.0	7.9	8.3	9.2	10.0	10.4	9.5
Japan	2.8	2.6	2.7	3.1	3.1	2.9	2.7	4.1	6.1	6.1
Korea	0.1	0.6	0.7	0.8	0.8	0.6	0.7	0.7	0.8	0.7
Luxembourg	0.0	0.0	0.0	0.0	3.0	0.0	0.0	0.2	0.7	1.7
Mexico	-6.1	-3.3	-2.8	-2.3	-2.6	-1.5	-1.1	-0.1	0.4	0.7
Netherlands	3.0	2.5	2.2	2.4	3.5	3.5	3.5	3.5	3.3	3.2
New Zealand	18.6	18.8	18.9	19.0	18.0	17.2	15.9	14.5	14.6	14.7
Norway	13.2	14.0	14.1	14.3	14.3	14.0	14.0	14.1	14.0	13.9
Poland	2.5	2.2	2.5	0.0	0.0	0.0	0.0	0.0	0.0	0.0
Portugal	3.3	0.9	2.0	1.3	0.7	0.1	0.5	0.5	1.2	3.3
Slovak Republic	3.3	-2.8	-3.8	-2.9	-1.8	-4.1	-3.6	-1.7	-1.8	-1.8
Slovenia	3.3	0.5	0.6	0.8	1.0	0.9	0.0	0.0	0.0	0.0
Spain	0.3	2.2	2.5	0.2	0.4	0.7	1.6	2.5	3.0	3.1
Sweden	24.7	22.2	21.5	17.9	16.9	15.8	15.0	15.1	15.1	15.2
Switzerland	4.0	4.2	3.6	3.8	3.4	3.3	3.3	3.2	2.7	2.2
Turkey[1]	13.2	14.5	14.2	14.3	8.9	7.9	8.8	9.4	9.8	9.8
United Kingdom	8.4	4.3	4.7	6.0	1.7	-1.0	-0.3	-2.6	-2.9	-3.1
United States	-5.2	-8.9	-8.0	-6.4	-7.0	-10.4	-8.9	-6.9	-5.6	-6.2
Unweighted average										
OECD-Average	**7.4**	**6.5**	**6.6**	**6.4**	**5.9**	**5.3**	**5.3**	**5.8**	**6.0**	**6.2**
OECD-EU 21	**8.1**	**6.2**	**6.2**	**6.1**	**5.7**	**5.4**	**5.2**	**5.7**	**5.8**	**6.1**

1. Wage figures are based on the old definition of average worker (ISIC D, Rev. 3).

StatLink http://dx.doi.org/10.1787/888933006860

Table II.4c. **Income tax plus employee contributions less cash benefits, single parent at 67% of average earnings**

Tax burden as a % of gross wage earnings, single parent with two children

	2000	2005	2006	2007	2008	2009	2010	2011	2012	2013
Australia	-2.7	-9.7	-9.8	-10.9	-11.5	-14.3	-13.5	-12.3	-10.2	-9.0
Austria	1.8	3.9	5.2	6.4	7.5	3.6	4.4	5.8	6.8	7.7
Belgium	15.9	16.9	17.1	17.1	17.5	17.4	18.8	18.9	18.8	18.6
Canada	-12.1	-12.9	-12.1	-14.6	-18.6	-22.6	-20.0	-19.8	-19.4	-19.0
Chile	2.8	3.0	3.0	3.1	3.1	3.2	6.0	6.0	6.1	6.1
Czech Republic	-18.1	-11.3	-9.3	-12.9	-14.8	-13.3	-13.1	-11.2	-14.0	-14.8
Denmark	14.9	12.5	12.9	13.6	13.5	12.9	11.1	11.6	11.6	11.2
Estonia	-8.6	-4.6	-9.3	-4.3	-8.5	-3.6	-2.2	-0.6	0.8	1.4
Finland	9.5	8.8	8.9	9.5	9.2	8.4	8.8	8.8	8.7	9.9
France	13.5	14.1	14.2	14.5	14.8	14.6	14.7	14.8	15.0	15.1
Germany	17.7	19.5	20.0	20.0	20.1	17.7	16.1	17.3	17.7	17.7
Greece	17.3	16.9	18.9	17.2	17.1	17.6	16.0	21.3	21.0	21.8
Hungary	4.8	-1.2	-0.3	4.0	5.2	6.8	6.6	-2.6	3.1	3.9
Iceland	1.2	9.7	10.5	10.6	10.2	6.6	9.3	11.8	8.7	10.1
Ireland	-9.5	-32.5	-45.1	-39.6	-39.0	-43.9	-42.0	-40.3	-39.5	-38.3
Israel	-1.7	-0.9	-3.0	-2.1	-1.8	-2.3	-2.7	-3.4	-3.7	-2.8
Italy	5.3	3.3	4.7	0.8	2.6	3.2	4.8	5.9	6.4	5.5
Japan	12.8	12.6	11.4	11.6	11.6	11.3	7.4	8.4	12.4	12.7
Korea	6.8	7.7	7.9	8.1	8.4	8.2	8.5	8.7	8.9	9.0
Luxembourg	-6.5	-8.1	-7.9	-6.8	-9.0	-11.3	-10.7	-9.0	-8.9	-7.4
Mexico	-4.8	-2.1	-1.6	-1.1	-1.4	-0.2	0.1	1.2	1.6	1.9
Netherlands	14.4	9.8	5.0	4.6	5.2	2.9	3.4	3.6	3.0	3.1
New Zealand	-3.3	-6.4	-15.3	-17.1	-17.5	-17.3	-17.9	-18.5	-18.4	-17.1
Norway	5.5	8.0	8.7	9.6	10.3	10.3	10.7	11.3	11.4	11.7
Poland	18.0	24.2	24.7	21.0	17.8	17.8	17.8	17.8	17.8	17.8
Portugal	9.0	5.4	6.9	6.0	4.4	0.2	1.6	3.7	4.8	7.0
Slovak Republic	-3.2	0.2	0.9	2.4	4.3	0.9	1.3	3.4	3.4	3.3
Slovenia	-2.2	-2.2	-1.3	-0.1	-1.3	-1.8	-1.8	-1.4	-1.1	-1.0
Spain	6.7	8.5	8.9	6.6	6.7	7.0	7.9	8.8	9.3	9.5
Sweden	20.1	18.4	16.3	13.1	12.7	11.9	11.0	11.3	11.7	11.9
Switzerland	0.2	0.3	-0.1	0.3	-2.8	-1.4	-1.2	-1.0	-1.3	-1.7
Turkey[1]	27.2	29.5	29.2	29.3	23.9	22.9	23.8	24.4	24.8	24.8
United Kingdom	7.4	5.0	5.8	7.3	2.7	-0.6	0.3	-2.2	-2.3	-2.5
United States	2.4	-1.2	-0.3	1.3	-2.5	-2.7	-1.3	-1.2	0.1	1.4
Unweighted average										
OECD-Average	**4.8**	**4.3**	**3.7**	**3.8**	**2.9**	**2.1**	**2.5**	**3.0**	**3.4**	**3.8**
OECD-EU 21	**6.1**	**5.1**	**4.6**	**4.8**	**4.2**	**3.3**	**3.6**	**4.1**	**4.5**	**4.8**

1. Wage figures are based on the old definition of average worker (ISIC D, Rev. 3).

StatLink http://dx.doi.org/10.1787/888933006879

Table II.5a. **Income tax plus employee and employer contributions less cash benefits, married couple at 100% of average earnings**

Tax burden as a % of labour costs, one-earner married couple with two children

	2000	2005	2006	2007	2008	2009	2010	2011	2012	2013
Australia	23.4	17.0	17.1	14.9	14.9	14.2	14.6	15.2	16.5	16.9
Austria	35.2	36.3	37.0	37.7	38.2	36.0	36.4	37.3	37.9	38.4
Belgium	42.6	40.3	40.3	40.3	40.6	40.4	41.2	41.4	41.3	41.0
Canada	23.1	21.2	21.5	19.7	19.0	16.6	17.7	18.1	18.4	18.7
Chile	6.1	6.1	6.1	6.1	6.2	6.2	6.3	7.0	7.0	7.0
Czech Republic	22.0	27.0	26.0	21.3	20.8	20.9	21.1	22.2	21.0	20.5
Denmark	30.7	28.9	29.1	29.4	29.3	28.7	27.2	27.6	27.8	27.6
Estonia	32.8	30.7	27.3	29.5	26.8	29.8	31.0	31.8	32.4	32.3
Finland	40.3	38.0	37.9	38.2	38.4	37.2	37.1	37.2	37.4	38.1
France	41.3	42.2	42.4	42.5	42.5	42.7	42.9	43.0	43.1	41.6
Germany	35.3	35.4	35.8	35.5	35.1	33.5	32.6	33.8	34.0	33.8
Greece	40.7	42.5	43.7	42.4	41.8	41.6	40.4	44.2	43.9	44.5
Hungary	43.9	40.6	41.1	44.0	43.9	43.2	36.7	33.0	34.2	34.1
Iceland	13.1	19.6	19.8	19.1	18.4	15.0	19.2	21.3	18.2	19.1
Ireland	15.5	5.7	1.9	4.0	3.8	2.8	4.7	5.6	6.1	6.8
Israel	25.5	22.9	21.1	21.9	20.0	18.3	17.5	17.1	16.6	17.4
Italy	39.3	36.3	36.6	35.7	36.6	36.9	37.8	38.4	38.7	38.2
Japan	21.0	23.9	23.6	23.8	24.0	23.6	22.1	23.1	25.7	26.1
Korea	15.7	16.2	16.8	17.5	17.8	17.1	17.8	18.0	18.5	19.0
Luxembourg	13.5	10.8	11.4	12.7	11.2	11.1	11.6	13.7	13.5	14.3
Mexico	12.4	14.7	15.0	15.9	15.1	15.3	15.5	18.7	19.0	19.2
Netherlands	29.9	29.7	29.1	29.6	30.3	29.7	30.8	31.1	32.3	30.8
New Zealand	13.6	12.8	0.5	0.8	0.7	-0.3	-0.9	-1.1	0.6	2.4
Norway	28.4	29.6	30.0	30.5	30.8	30.6	30.7	31.2	31.1	31.2
Poland	33.3	37.1	37.4	32.4	28.4	28.4	28.4	28.4	29.6	29.8
Portugal	30.2	27.5	28.3	27.7	26.3	25.4	26.3	27.3	27.9	29.8
Slovak Republic	30.8	22.1	23.0	23.9	25.3	22.8	22.9	24.9	25.8	27.6
Slovenia	25.0	24.2	24.2	24.5	23.1	22.1	22.9	23.2	23.2	23.1
Spain	32.3	33.4	33.6	32.9	32.0	32.4	34.0	34.3	34.7	34.8
Sweden	44.3	42.6	41.6	39.4	39.2	37.7	37.2	37.4	37.6	37.7
Switzerland	11.7	11.4	11.0	11.4	9.2	10.1	10.3	10.3	9.9	9.5
Turkey[1]	40.4	42.8	42.7	42.7	38.7	36.0	36.6	37.0	37.2	37.4
United Kingdom	27.8	27.9	28.0	28.4	26.9	26.2	26.5	26.4	27.5	27.0
United States	20.6	17.4	17.8	18.5	17.0	17.2	18.2	18.3	18.7	20.3
Unweighted average										
OECD-Average	**27.7**	**26.9**	**26.4**	**26.3**	**25.7**	**25.0**	**25.2**	**25.8**	**26.1**	**26.4**
OECD-EU 21	**32.7**	**31.4**	**31.2**	**31.0**	**30.5**	**30.0**	**30.0**	**30.6**	**30.9**	**31.0**

1. Wage figures are based on the old definition of average worker (ISIC D, Rev. 3).

StatLink http://dx.doi.org/10.1787/888933006898

Table II.5b. **Income tax, married couple at 100% of average earnings**

Tax burden as a % of gross wage earnings, one-earner married couple with two children

	2000	2005	2006	2007	2008	2009	2010	2011	2012	2013
Australia	25.6	24.2	24.0	23.4	22.5	20.9	21.1	21.1	21.8	23.1
Austria	11.7	13.0	13.5	13.9	14.4	12.5	12.8	13.3	13.8	14.2
Belgium	18.9	16.5	16.5	16.7	17.3	17.0	17.7	17.8	17.7	17.5
Canada	15.0	11.7	11.6	9.5	9.8	8.2	8.5	8.7	8.8	8.9
Chile	0.0	0.0	0.0	0.0	0.0	0.0	0.0	0.0	0.0	0.0
Czech Republic	4.0	1.0	-2.6	-1.7	-5.8	-5.1	-5.3	-4.2	-5.1	-5.5
Denmark	25.6	24.9	25.0	25.2	24.9	24.3	23.7	31.9	32.1	31.8
Estonia	17.9	13.8	8.7	10.5	6.4	9.2	9.2	9.9	10.5	11.2
Finland	26.9	24.7	23.8	23.7	24.2	23.0	22.3	22.2	21.8	22.5
France	7.3	7.9	7.8	8.1	7.9	8.3	8.3	8.4	8.5	8.5
Germany	1.5	0.9	1.1	1.7	2.1	0.2	-0.6	0.1	0.6	0.8
Greece	8.2	10.4	11.9	10.2	9.5	9.2	7.7	12.0	11.4	12.8
Hungary	18.4	14.9	20.9	21.8	21.3	20.8	14.4	8.5	8.2	7.8
Iceland	16.1	19.8	20.1	19.1	19.3	15.8	17.0	18.5	18.2	18.5
Ireland	5.0	2.0	1.6	0.6	0.4	1.7	2.2	7.0	7.2	7.1
Israel	18.0	13.3	12.6	13.3	11.2	9.7	9.0	9.1	8.7	8.8
Italy	15.6	11.5	12.4	12.1	12.8	13.2	13.9	14.6	14.9	14.4
Japan	2.9	3.5	3.8	4.3	4.3	4.1	3.9	4.9	6.2	6.2
Korea	1.5	1.5	1.9	2.3	2.2	1.4	1.9	1.7	2.1	2.4
Luxembourg	2.3	0.2	0.8	1.4	5.3	4.2	4.5	4.9	5.1	5.7
Mexico	0.7	3.1	3.5	4.6	3.8	4.1	4.2	7.9	8.2	8.4
Netherlands	4.8	10.9	12.8	14.2	15.1	16.3	15.9	16.2	16.7	15.2
New Zealand	19.4	20.0	20.4	21.1	20.5	18.4	17.0	15.9	16.4	16.9
Norway	18.1	18.7	18.8	19.3	19.4	19.0	19.0	19.1	18.9	18.9
Poland	4.8	4.5	4.7	0.0	0.0	0.0	0.0	0.0	0.0	0.2
Portugal	6.2	3.7	4.3	3.7	3.2	2.8	3.3	3.4	3.9	6.1
Slovak Republic	4.8	-4.4	-4.8	-4.0	-2.8	-5.2	-5.1	-2.7	-2.7	-2.8
Slovenia	4.8	2.0	2.2	2.4	2.6	2.5	2.9	3.0	2.8	2.6
Spain	5.2	6.6	7.0	6.3	5.2	5.8	7.9	8.3	8.9	9.0
Sweden	26.7	24.2	23.9	20.6	19.9	18.4	17.8	17.9	17.9	18.0
Switzerland	6.2	6.6	6.0	6.3	5.8	5.8	5.9	5.4	4.8	4.4
Turkey[1]	14.7	15.5	15.4	15.4	11.2	10.5	11.1	11.6	11.9	12.1
United Kingdom	17.4	15.8	15.9	16.1	14.7	14.5	14.6	14.0	15.4	14.7
United States	6.8	3.3	3.7	4.5	4.1	1.6	2.7	4.8	5.1	4.8
Unweighted average										
OECD-Average	**11.3**	**10.2**	**10.3**	**10.2**	**9.8**	**9.2**	**9.1**	**9.9**	**10.0**	**10.2**
OECD-EU 21	**11.3**	**9.8**	**9.9**	**9.7**	**9.5**	**9.2**	**9.0**	**9.8**	**10.0**	**10.1**

1. Wage figures are based on the old definition of average worker (ISIC D, Rev. 3).

StatLink http://dx.doi.org/10.1787/888933006917

Table II.5c. Income tax plus employee contributions less cash benefits, married couple at 100% of average earnings

Tax burden as a % of gross wage earnings, one-earner married couple with two children

	2000	2005	2006	2007	2008	2009	2010	2011	2012	2013
Australia	18.4	12.0	12.1	9.8	9.8	8.7	9.3	10.1	11.6	12.0
Austria	15.1	17.8	18.7	19.5	20.3	17.4	17.9	19.0	19.8	20.5
Belgium	23.7	22.1	22.1	22.1	22.6	22.4	23.6	23.7	23.6	23.4
Canada	14.2	12.0	12.3	10.4	9.7	7.0	8.2	8.5	8.7	8.9
Chile	6.1	6.1	6.1	6.1	6.2	6.2	6.3	7.0	7.0	7.0
Czech Republic	-5.3	1.4	0.0	-6.2	-6.9	-6.0	-5.7	-4.2	-5.9	-6.5
Denmark	30.8	28.9	29.1	29.4	29.3	28.7	27.2	27.6	27.8	27.6
Estonia	10.6	7.5	3.1	6.0	2.5	6.1	7.3	8.3	9.1	9.3
Finland	24.8	23.2	23.1	23.3	23.6	22.7	23.0	23.1	23.1	24.0
France	16.1	16.9	17.1	17.3	17.4	17.6	17.7	17.8	18.0	18.1
Germany	22.0	22.0	22.6	22.6	22.5	20.6	19.6	20.8	21.0	21.0
Greece	24.1	26.4	27.9	26.2	25.5	25.2	23.7	28.2	27.9	29.3
Hungary	20.5	19.5	20.7	24.7	24.6	24.7	18.7	14.0	15.4	15.3
Iceland	8.9	15.0	15.2	14.8	14.0	9.7	12.2	14.5	11.8	12.9
Ireland	5.4	-4.4	-8.7	-6.4	-6.6	-7.6	-5.5	-4.5	-3.9	-3.2
Israel	21.8	18.5	16.9	18.1	16.2	14.5	13.6	13.2	12.6	13.3
Italy	18.6	15.2	16.2	15.1	16.3	16.7	17.8	18.7	19.0	18.3
Japan	12.9	14.2	13.6	13.9	14.0	13.8	11.3	12.2	15.0	15.2
Korea	8.2	8.7	9.1	9.6	9.8	9.0	9.7	9.8	10.3	10.7
Luxembourg	1.9	-1.2	-0.6	0.9	1.3	0.8	1.5	3.1	2.9	3.8
Mexico	2.2	4.6	5.0	6.0	5.1	5.4	5.6	9.2	9.5	9.8
Netherlands	22.4	22.3	22.3	22.4	23.0	22.6	23.6	24.0	25.0	24.5
New Zealand	13.6	12.8	0.5	0.8	0.7	-0.3	-0.9	-1.1	0.6	2.4
Norway	19.3	20.3	20.7	21.6	21.9	21.7	21.8	22.2	22.1	22.2
Poland	22.1	26.5	26.9	21.0	17.8	17.8	17.8	17.8	17.8	18.0
Portugal	13.6	10.3	11.2	10.5	8.8	7.7	8.8	10.1	10.8	13.1
Slovak Republic	4.4	1.7	2.8	4.0	5.8	2.5	2.6	5.2	5.1	5.1
Slovenia	10.1	9.1	9.8	10.6	9.9	9.6	10.4	10.8	10.8	10.7
Spain	11.5	13.0	13.3	12.6	11.5	12.2	14.2	14.7	15.2	15.3
Sweden	26.0	24.0	22.8	19.8	19.4	18.1	17.4	17.7	17.9	18.1
Switzerland	5.9	6.1	5.6	6.0	3.7	4.7	4.9	4.6	4.2	3.8
Turkey[1]	28.7	30.5	30.4	30.4	26.2	25.5	26.1	26.6	26.9	27.1
United Kingdom	20.6	20.2	20.3	20.6	19.0	18.4	18.7	18.3	19.7	19.1
United States	14.4	10.9	11.4	12.1	9.0	9.3	10.4	10.4	10.7	12.4
Unweighted average										
OECD-Average	**15.1**	**14.5**	**14.1**	**14.0**	**13.4**	**12.7**	**12.9**	**13.6**	**13.9**	**14.2**
OECD-EU 21	**16.1**	**15.3**	**15.3**	**15.1**	**14.6**	**14.2**	**14.3**	**15.0**	**15.3**	**15.5**

1. Wage figures are based on the old definition of average worker (ISIC D, Rev. 3).

StatLink http://dx.doi.org/10.1787/888933006936

Table II.6a. **Income tax plus employee and employer contributions less cash benefits, married couple with two children at 100% and 33% of average earnings**

Tax burden as a % of labour costs

	2000	2005	2006	2007	2008	2009	2010	2011	2012	2013
Australia	24.6	20.8	20.5	19.6	19.1	18.0	18.0	17.9	18.6	19.9
Austria	36.3	37.3	37.8	38.3	38.7	36.4	36.7	37.4	37.8	38.2
Belgium	44.3	41.4	41.3	41.2	41.7	41.6	42.3	42.4	42.5	42.3
Canada	26.9	25.2	25.5	24.1	24.0	23.0	23.2	23.5	23.7	24.1
Chile	4.8	5.0	4.9	4.5	4.5	4.5	4.8	4.8	4.8	4.8
Czech Republic	31.1	35.1	33.5	29.5	30.5	30.3	30.3	31.0	30.0	29.7
Denmark	35.7	33.8	34.0	34.1	33.9	33.4	31.9	32.2	32.5	32.1
Estonia	35.7	34.0	31.1	32.6	30.4	33.1	34.1	34.5	35.0	34.8
Finland	39.3	36.6	36.4	36.4	36.4	35.2	35.0	35.1	35.0	35.6
France	40.5	40.3	40.0	40.0	39.4	40.4	40.6	40.7	41.0	39.5
Germany	41.2	40.8	41.1	40.7	40.3	39.0	37.7	38.7	38.8	38.6
Greece	39.1	40.5	41.4	40.4	39.9	39.8	38.9	42.4	42.2	42.0
Hungary	44.8	40.0	40.2	42.8	42.8	42.1	36.4	34.5	35.4	36.2
Iceland	20.2	26.3	26.0	25.2	24.6	22.6	26.3	27.7	25.9	26.5
Ireland	20.3	9.6	8.6	7.3	7.4	8.8	10.6	12.4	12.5	13.5
Israel	21.7	19.6	17.9	18.3	16.8	15.4	14.9	13.5	12.7	14.0
Italy	41.2	38.2	39.2	37.8	38.6	39.0	39.6	40.2	40.4	40.2
Japan	22.4	24.7	24.8	25.1	25.2	24.9	24.0	25.1	27.2	27.6
Korea	15.3	16.0	16.6	17.3	17.6	17.1	17.8	18.0	18.6	18.9
Luxembourg	17.5	15.5	16.1	17.3	15.8	15.4	16.0	18.0	17.8	18.8
Mexico	9.5	12.2	12.7	13.7	13.1	13.5	13.8	16.3	16.6	16.9
Netherlands	34.4	32.2	29.6	29.6	30.2	29.2	29.5	29.4	29.8	28.7
New Zealand	18.6	19.2	9.6	9.8	9.3	8.1	7.5	7.1	8.7	10.1
Norway	30.8	31.3	31.3	31.4	31.6	31.5	31.6	32.0	31.8	31.7
Poland	34.6	37.5	37.8	32.5	29.1	29.0	29.3	29.7	31.1	31.3
Portugal	30.6	28.7	29.6	28.9	28.4	27.7	28.3	28.4	29.0	30.9
Slovak Republic	35.1	28.2	28.9	29.1	30.1	26.7	27.2	29.4	30.4	33.0
Slovenia	33.7	32.3	32.2	32.1	30.7	30.0	30.4	30.6	30.6	30.5
Spain	35.0	35.3	35.5	35.1	34.4	34.6	35.7	35.9	36.4	36.4
Sweden	44.7	42.5	41.6	39.1	38.8	37.3	36.8	37.0	37.1	37.2
Switzerland	14.5	14.1	13.7	14.1	12.5	13.1	13.3	13.3	12.9	12.6
Turkey[1]	39.7	42.4	42.3	42.3	39.5	37.1	37.5	37.7	37.9	38.1
United Kingdom	25.5	25.9	26.1	26.4	25.2	24.4	24.8	24.9	24.4	23.5
United States	24.2	21.6	21.9	22.4	21.4	22.9	23.3	22.9	23.3	24.9
Unweighted average										
OECD-Average	**29.8**	**29.0**	**28.5**	**28.2**	**27.7**	**27.2**	**27.3**	**27.8**	**28.0**	**28.3**
OECD-EU 21	**35.3**	**33.6**	**33.4**	**32.9**	**32.5**	**32.1**	**32.0**	**32.6**	**32.8**	**33.0**

1. Wage figures are based on the old definition of average worker (ISIC D, Rev. 3).

StatLink http://dx.doi.org/10.1787/888933006955

Table II.6b. **Income tax, married couple with two children at 100% and 33% of average earnings**

Tax burden as a % of gross wage earnings

	2000	2005	2006	2007	2008	2009	2010	2011	2012	2013
Australia	22.1	21.0	20.6	19.6	19.0	17.3	17.4	17.4	18.0	18.7
Austria	9.4	11.0	11.3	11.6	11.9	10.5	10.7	11.1	11.4	11.6
Belgium	24.0	21.9	22.0	22.1	22.6	22.3	22.9	22.8	22.7	22.4
Canada	16.3	13.5	13.5	11.9	12.1	11.0	11.1	11.2	11.3	11.3
Chile	0.0	0.0	0.0	0.0	0.0	0.0	0.0	0.0	0.0	0.0
Czech Republic	5.2	5.1	2.7	3.7	2.5	2.8	2.5	3.2	2.3	2.1
Denmark	27.6	26.7	26.8	26.9	26.7	26.1	25.3	33.5	33.6	33.3
Estonia	19.9	16.3	12.2	13.4	10.1	12.0	12.0	12.5	13.0	13.6
Finland	23.4	21.0	20.1	19.8	20.2	19.1	18.4	18.2	17.5	18.2
France	8.9	7.7	7.2	7.3	6.3	7.7	7.8	8.0	8.3	8.4
Germany	8.7	7.4	7.5	7.9	8.3	6.7	5.5	5.9	6.3	6.5
Greece	6.2	7.8	8.9	7.7	7.1	6.9	5.8	9.8	9.2	9.6
Hungary	15.8	11.1	15.7	16.4	16.1	15.9	10.8	7.4	10.1	9.8
Iceland	19.9	23.9	23.9	22.9	23.0	20.7	21.7	22.8	22.6	22.8
Ireland	11.1	5.2	4.4	3.1	3.1	4.0	4.5	8.9	9.0	8.9
Israel	13.5	9.9	9.4	10.0	8.4	7.3	6.8	5.8	5.1	5.8
Italy	14.4	10.7	11.8	11.1	12.1	12.4	13.2	13.9	14.2	13.9
Japan	4.4	4.2	4.5	5.1	5.0	4.9	4.7	5.7	6.7	6.7
Korea	1.1	1.4	1.8	2.0	2.0	1.5	1.9	1.7	2.1	2.3
Luxembourg	3.9	2.2	2.8	3.4	6.4	5.2	5.6	6.1	6.4	7.2
Mexico	-4.3	-1.5	-0.9	0.2	-0.4	0.0	0.3	3.2	3.6	3.9
Netherlands	7.8	8.5	10.1	11.1	11.7	12.5	12.3	12.4	12.8	12.0
New Zealand	18.6	19.2	19.5	20.1	19.2	17.2	15.9	14.8	15.2	15.7
Norway	19.2	19.1	18.7	18.9	19.0	18.7	18.7	18.8	18.5	18.4
Poland	5.3	5.0	5.2	0.2	0.7	0.6	1.0	1.5	1.7	1.9
Portugal	5.7	3.7	4.7	3.9	3.4	2.9	3.3	3.4	3.9	6.2
Slovak Republic	4.6	1.5	1.2	1.1	2.0	-1.6	-1.0	1.7	1.7	2.9
Slovenia	6.8	4.3	4.3	4.3	3.6	3.6	3.8	3.8	3.7	3.6
Spain	8.7	9.2	9.4	9.1	8.2	8.6	10.1	10.4	11.0	11.0
Sweden	25.3	22.3	21.8	18.2	17.5	16.1	15.4	15.5	15.6	15.7
Switzerland	7.5	7.8	7.3	7.6	7.2	7.2	7.3	6.8	6.3	6.0
Turkey[1]	14.0	15.0	14.9	14.9	12.2	11.7	12.2	12.4	12.7	12.9
United Kingdom	15.1	14.1	14.2	14.4	13.3	13.0	13.1	13.4	13.0	12.0
United States	10.5	7.8	8.1	8.7	8.5	7.1	7.5	9.0	9.2	9.0
Unweighted average										
OECD-Average	**11.8**	**10.7**	**10.8**	**10.5**	**10.3**	**9.8**	**9.7**	**10.4**	**10.6**	**10.7**
OECD-EU 21	**12.3**	**10.6**	**10.7**	**10.3**	**10.2**	**9.9**	**9.7**	**10.6**	**10.8**	**11.0**

1. Wage figures are based on the old definition of average worker (ISIC D, Rev. 3).

StatLink http://dx.doi.org/10.1787/888933006974

Table II.6c. **Income tax plus employee contributions less cash benefits, married couple with two children at 100% and 33% of average earnings**

Tax burden as a % of gross wage earnings

	2000	2005	2006	2007	2008	2009	2010	2011	2012	2013
Australia	19.8	16.1	15.7	14.8	14.3	12.7	12.9	13.0	13.7	15.2
Austria	16.5	19.1	19.7	20.3	20.9	17.9	18.3	19.1	19.6	20.1
Belgium	29.3	26.8	26.5	26.5	26.8	26.7	27.6	27.5	27.4	27.1
Canada	18.6	16.6	16.9	15.4	15.4	14.3	14.5	14.6	14.8	15.1
Chile	4.8	5.0	4.9	4.5	4.5	4.5	4.8	4.8	4.8	4.8
Czech Republic	7.0	12.4	10.2	4.8	6.2	6.5	6.6	7.6	6.2	5.8
Denmark	35.9	33.8	34.0	34.1	33.9	33.4	31.9	32.2	32.5	32.1
Estonia	14.4	11.8	8.2	10.1	7.2	10.2	11.3	12.0	12.7	12.6
Finland	23.5	21.3	21.1	21.1	21.2	20.3	20.5	20.4	20.2	21.0
France	18.8	17.9	17.6	17.7	16.8	18.1	18.3	18.5	18.9	19.1
Germany	29.2	28.6	29.0	28.8	28.7	27.1	25.7	26.6	26.8	26.7
Greece	22.1	23.8	24.9	23.7	23.1	22.9	21.8	26.0	25.7	26.1
Hungary	20.5	18.0	19.1	22.8	22.8	23.1	18.3	15.8	20.2	20.1
Iceland	16.4	22.1	21.8	21.2	20.6	17.8	19.9	21.5	20.1	20.9
Ireland	11.4	0.4	-0.7	-2.2	-2.1	-0.5	1.5	3.4	3.6	4.7
Israel	17.8	15.0	13.6	14.4	13.0	11.8	11.1	9.7	8.9	10.0
Italy	21.2	17.8	19.7	17.9	19.0	19.4	20.2	21.0	21.3	21.0
Japan	14.4	15.1	14.9	15.3	15.4	15.2	13.5	14.5	16.7	17.0
Korea	7.8	8.5	9.0	9.4	9.6	9.1	9.7	9.8	10.3	10.6
Luxembourg	6.4	4.0	4.7	6.0	6.4	5.7	6.3	8.0	7.7	8.8
Mexico	-2.9	-0.1	0.5	1.5	0.9	1.3	1.6	4.5	4.9	5.2
Netherlands	26.7	24.2	23.2	22.9	23.3	22.5	22.6	22.6	22.6	22.3
New Zealand	18.6	19.2	9.6	9.8	9.3	8.1	7.5	7.1	8.7	10.1
Norway	22.0	22.3	22.1	22.6	22.9	22.7	22.8	23.1	22.9	22.8
Poland	23.6	27.0	27.4	21.2	18.6	18.5	18.8	19.3	19.6	19.8
Portugal	14.1	11.7	12.8	12.0	11.4	10.6	11.2	11.4	12.1	14.4
Slovak Republic	10.5	9.4	10.2	10.5	11.8	7.5	8.2	11.0	11.0	12.1
Slovenia	21.2	19.5	19.8	20.0	18.9	18.8	19.2	19.4	19.4	19.3
Spain	15.1	15.5	15.7	15.5	14.6	15.0	16.5	16.8	17.3	17.4
Sweden	26.5	23.9	22.7	19.4	18.9	17.6	16.9	17.2	17.4	17.5
Switzerland	9.0	9.0	8.5	8.9	7.2	7.9	8.0	7.9	7.4	7.1
Turkey[1]	28.0	30.0	29.9	29.9	27.2	26.7	27.2	27.4	27.7	27.9
United Kingdom	18.8	18.8	18.9	19.2	18.0	17.2	17.5	17.7	17.3	16.4
United States	18.2	15.4	15.8	16.3	13.0	14.7	15.1	14.6	14.9	16.7
Unweighted average										
OECD-Average	**17.8**	**17.1**	**16.7**	**16.4**	**15.9**	**15.4**	**15.5**	**16.1**	**16.3**	**16.7**
OECD-EU 21	**19.6**	**18.4**	**18.3**	**17.7**	**17.5**	**17.1**	**17.1**	**17.8**	**18.1**	**18.3**

1. Wage figures are based on the old definition of average worker (ISIC D, Rev. 3).

StatLink http://dx.doi.org/10.1787/888933006993

Table II.7a. Income tax plus employee and employer contributions less cash benefits, married couple at 100% and 67% of average earnings

Tax burden as a % of labour costs, two-earner married couple with two children

	2000	2005	2006	2007	2008	2009	2010	2011	2012	2013
Australia	26.7	23.5	23.9	23.4	22.9	22.3	23.7	24.2	24.9	25.2
Austria	39.0	40.0	40.6	41.1	41.6	39.7	40.0	40.7	41.1	41.6
Belgium	50.9	48.2	48.2	48.2	48.5	48.3	48.8	49.0	48.9	48.7
Canada	29.7	28.4	28.6	27.4	27.3	26.5	26.5	26.8	27.0	27.3
Chile	5.3	5.4	5.4	5.4	5.5	5.5	6.6	6.6	6.6	6.6
Czech Republic	36.3	38.9	37.8	34.1	34.5	34.2	34.3	35.0	34.2	33.9
Denmark	38.7	35.6	35.7	35.9	35.6	35.1	33.7	34.0	34.1	33.8
Estonia	37.4	35.9	33.4	34.4	32.5	34.7	35.8	36.2	36.6	36.3
Finland	41.2	38.5	38.3	38.3	38.5	37.1	36.9	37.0	37.2	37.9
France	43.2	44.6	44.6	44.9	45.0	45.1	45.2	45.4	45.5	44.2
Germany	45.4	44.7	45.0	44.5	44.2	43.0	41.4	42.3	42.3	42.1
Greece	39.4	40.7	41.9	41.1	40.6	40.5	39.3	43.0	42.7	42.5
Hungary	46.9	41.6	42.0	44.8	45.0	44.4	39.5	37.9	39.6	40.1
Iceland	25.4	30.3	29.7	28.8	28.1	26.9	30.4	31.6	30.2	30.5
Ireland	21.8	14.6	13.8	12.7	12.8	14.5	16.2	17.8	18.0	19.2
Israel	21.5	18.5	16.8	17.2	16.0	14.8	14.4	14.1	13.8	14.3
Italy	44.2	41.7	41.9	41.1	41.6	41.9	42.4	43.0	43.2	42.9
Japan	22.9	25.4	25.7	26.0	26.2	25.9	25.4	26.4	28.2	28.5
Korea	15.5	16.1	16.7	17.4	17.8	17.2	17.9	18.2	18.6	19.0
Luxembourg	22.9	20.7	21.4	22.6	21.2	20.7	21.3	23.4	23.2	24.3
Mexico	10.4	12.8	13.2	14.0	13.4	13.9	14.2	16.5	16.8	17.1
Netherlands	38.0	36.5	32.7	32.9	33.5	31.6	31.8	31.8	32.0	30.5
New Zealand	19.0	19.6	15.9	16.1	15.6	14.7	13.8	13.2	14.7	15.8
Norway	33.0	32.8	33.1	33.2	33.4	33.3	33.4	33.7	33.7	33.7
Poland	37.7	38.2	38.5	34.1	30.6	30.4	30.6	31.0	32.3	32.5
Portugal	32.9	32.0	33.3	32.8	32.2	31.2	32.5	34.3	34.5	36.7
Slovak Republic	36.9	31.1	31.6	32.1	33.0	31.2	31.5	32.7	33.5	35.2
Slovenia	37.1	36.2	35.9	35.7	34.9	34.2	34.0	34.1	34.3	34.3
Spain	35.4	36.1	36.3	35.8	34.6	34.9	36.7	37.0	37.5	37.6
Sweden	46.0	44.2	43.3	41.0	40.5	39.1	38.6	38.7	38.8	38.9
Switzerland	17.6	17.2	16.8	17.2	15.6	16.2	16.4	16.4	16.0	15.7
Turkey[1]	39.9	42.5	42.3	42.4	40.0	37.6	38.1	38.4	38.6	38.8
United Kingdom	28.3	29.9	29.3	29.9	28.6	28.0	28.4	28.0	27.7	27.0
United States	26.3	24.1	24.3	24.7	24.0	25.2	25.4	24.8	25.1	26.7
Unweighted average										
OECD-Average	**32.1**	**31.4**	**31.1**	**30.9**	**30.5**	**30.0**	**30.2**	**30.7**	**30.9**	**31.2**
OECD-EU 21	**38.1**	**36.7**	**36.5**	**36.1**	**35.7**	**35.2**	**35.2**	**35.8**	**36.1**	**36.2**

1. Wage figures are based on the old definition of average worker (ISIC D, Rev. 3).

StatLink http://dx.doi.org/10.1787/888933007012

Table II.7b. **Income tax, married couple at 100% and 67% of average earnings**

Tax burden as a % of gross wage earnings, two-earner married couple with two children

	2000	2005	2006	2007	2008	2009	2010	2011	2012	2013
Australia	23.8	22.8	22.5	21.7	20.4	18.8	19.0	19.7	20.5	20.7
Austria	10.7	12.5	12.9	13.4	13.9	11.9	12.2	12.7	13.2	13.5
Belgium	26.4	24.0	23.9	24.0	24.5	24.2	24.7	24.9	24.7	24.6
Canada	17.5	14.9	14.9	13.6	13.8	13.0	12.8	12.9	13.0	13.0
Chile	0.0	0.0	0.0	0.0	0.0	0.0	0.0	0.0	0.0	0.0
Czech Republic	6.8	7.1	5.5	6.2	4.6	5.0	4.9	5.5	5.0	4.7
Denmark	30.4	28.3	28.4	28.5	28.2	27.7	26.8	35.0	35.1	34.7
Estonia	21.1	17.8	14.3	15.1	12.2	13.8	13.7	14.1	14.5	15.0
Finland	24.4	22.2	21.3	21.1	21.6	20.3	19.6	19.5	19.1	19.8
France	10.8	10.8	10.6	10.9	11.0	11.1	11.1	11.2	11.5	11.5
Germany	13.7	12.1	12.2	12.5	12.9	11.5	9.9	10.3	10.6	10.8
Greece	6.5	8.1	9.7	8.6	8.0	7.8	6.2	10.5	9.9	10.2
Hungary	18.0	12.4	16.1	17.1	17.2	17.1	12.9	10.0	11.3	11.1
Iceland	23.1	26.4	26.2	25.2	25.3	23.7	24.8	25.7	25.5	25.7
Ireland	13.3	8.2	7.5	6.5	6.5	7.9	8.4	12.2	12.3	12.2
Israel	12.4	8.0	7.5	8.0	6.7	5.8	5.4	5.5	5.2	5.3
Italy	16.8	14.0	14.8	14.8	15.3	15.6	16.3	16.9	17.2	16.9
Japan	4.9	4.7	5.2	5.8	5.7	5.6	5.5	6.2	7.0	7.0
Korea	1.3	1.5	1.8	2.2	2.2	1.6	2.0	1.9	2.2	2.4
Luxembourg	8.2	6.2	6.8	7.6	9.9	8.8	9.2	9.8	10.2	11.2
Mexico	-2.0	0.5	1.0	1.8	1.2	1.8	2.1	4.7	5.0	5.3
Netherlands	7.9	8.3	9.6	10.6	11.2	11.9	11.7	11.8	12.1	11.2
New Zealand	19.0	19.6	19.8	20.3	19.5	17.9	16.5	15.3	15.7	16.0
Norway	20.6	19.9	19.9	20.2	20.3	20.0	20.0	20.1	19.9	19.9
Poland	6.1	5.9	6.0	2.0	2.5	2.3	2.6	2.9	3.1	3.3
Portugal	8.1	7.3	8.4	7.8	7.2	6.5	7.2	7.6	7.9	10.7
Slovak Republic	5.8	4.0	3.7	4.2	4.9	3.2	3.5	5.0	4.9	4.9
Slovenia	8.1	5.9	6.0	6.0	6.1	6.0	5.6	5.7	5.6	5.5
Spain	9.3	10.2	10.5	10.0	8.5	9.1	11.4	11.8	12.5	12.5
Sweden	25.9	23.4	22.9	19.5	18.7	17.4	16.7	16.7	16.8	16.9
Switzerland	9.8	10.1	9.6	9.9	9.4	9.4	9.5	9.1	8.6	8.2
Turkey[1]	14.1	15.1	14.9	15.0	12.9	12.3	12.9	13.2	13.5	13.7
United Kingdom	16.5	16.7	16.0	16.5	15.4	15.0	15.3	14.7	14.4	13.6
United States	12.8	10.5	10.7	11.2	11.1	10.0	10.3	11.5	11.7	11.5
Unweighted average										
OECD-Average	**13.3**	**12.3**	**12.4**	**12.3**	**12.0**	**11.6**	**11.5**	**12.2**	**12.3**	**12.5**
OECD-EU 21	**14.0**	**12.6**	**12.7**	**12.5**	**12.4**	**12.1**	**11.9**	**12.8**	**12.9**	**13.1**

1. Wage figures are based on the old definition of average worker (ISIC D, Rev. 3).

StatLink http://dx.doi.org/10.1787/888933007031

Table II.7c. Income tax plus employee contributions less cash benefits, married couple at 100% and 67% of average earnings

Tax burden as a % of gross wage earnings, two-earner married couple with two children

	2000	2005	2006	2007	2008	2009	2010	2011	2012	2013
Australia	22.0	18.9	19.3	18.8	18.3	17.3	18.9	19.7	20.5	20.7
Austria	20.0	22.6	23.3	24.0	24.6	22.1	22.6	23.4	24.0	24.5
Belgium	34.9	32.9	32.9	32.9	33.3	33.1	33.9	34.0	33.9	33.7
Canada	21.6	20.0	20.3	19.0	18.9	18.1	18.1	18.2	18.3	18.5
Chile	5.3	5.4	5.4	5.4	5.5	5.5	6.6	6.6	6.6	6.6
Czech Republic	14.0	17.5	16.0	11.0	11.6	11.8	11.9	12.8	11.8	11.5
Denmark	38.8	35.6	35.7	35.9	35.6	35.1	33.7	34.0	34.1	33.8
Estonia	16.7	14.4	11.2	12.6	10.1	12.6	13.7	14.2	14.8	14.6
Finland	26.0	23.8	23.5	23.5	23.7	22.7	22.9	22.8	22.8	23.7
France	21.4	21.6	21.6	22.0	22.1	22.1	22.2	22.4	22.6	22.8
Germany	34.2	33.3	33.7	33.4	33.3	31.9	30.1	30.9	31.0	31.0
Greece	22.4	24.1	25.7	24.6	24.0	23.8	22.2	26.7	26.4	26.7
Hungary	24.3	20.6	21.8	25.6	26.0	26.3	22.3	20.2	23.1	23.0
Iceland	21.8	26.3	25.6	25.0	24.3	22.3	24.4	25.7	24.7	25.2
Ireland	13.5	5.4	4.5	3.4	3.5	5.3	7.1	9.0	9.1	10.5
Israel	17.7	13.8	12.4	13.2	12.2	11.1	10.5	10.3	9.9	10.3
Italy	25.1	22.4	23.3	22.2	22.9	23.2	24.0	24.7	24.9	24.6
Japan	14.9	15.8	15.9	16.4	16.5	16.3	15.1	16.0	17.8	18.0
Korea	8.0	8.6	9.0	9.5	9.8	9.3	9.8	9.9	10.4	10.7
Luxembourg	12.6	10.0	10.7	12.1	12.4	11.6	12.3	14.0	13.7	15.0
Mexico	-0.6	1.9	2.3	3.2	2.5	3.2	3.4	6.0	6.4	6.6
Netherlands	30.0	28.3	26.4	26.3	26.8	24.9	24.9	25.0	24.9	24.2
New Zealand	19.0	19.6	15.9	16.1	15.6	14.7	13.8	13.2	14.7	15.8
Norway	24.4	24.0	24.2	24.7	24.9	24.7	24.8	25.1	25.0	25.1
Poland	27.3	27.8	28.2	23.0	20.4	20.1	20.4	20.8	21.0	21.1
Portugal	17.0	15.9	17.5	16.8	16.1	14.8	16.4	18.6	18.9	21.7
Slovak Republic	12.9	13.0	13.6	14.4	15.4	13.2	13.5	15.0	15.0	15.0
Slovenia	25.1	23.5	23.6	23.8	23.7	23.6	23.3	23.5	23.7	23.8
Spain	15.6	16.5	16.8	16.4	14.8	15.5	17.8	18.2	18.8	18.9
Sweden	28.3	26.1	25.0	21.8	21.2	20.0	19.3	19.4	19.6	19.8
Switzerland	12.2	12.2	11.7	12.1	10.5	11.1	11.3	11.1	10.7	10.4
Turkey[1]	28.1	30.1	29.9	30.0	27.9	27.3	27.9	28.2	28.5	28.7
United Kingdom	21.4	22.7	22.0	22.6	21.3	20.7	21.1	20.6	20.3	19.5
United States	20.5	18.1	18.4	18.8	16.3	17.7	18.0	17.2	17.4	19.2
Unweighted average										
OECD-Average	**20.5**	**19.8**	**19.6**	**19.4**	**19.0**	**18.6**	**18.8**	**19.3**	**19.6**	**19.9**
OECD-EU 21	**22.9**	**21.8**	**21.8**	**21.3**	**21.1**	**20.7**	**20.7**	**21.4**	**21.6**	**21.9**

1. Wage figures are based on the old definition of average worker (ISIC D, Rev. 3).

StatLink http://dx.doi.org/10.1787/888933007050

Table II.8a. **Income tax plus employee and employer contributions less cash benefits, married couple without children at 100% and 33% of average earnings**

Tax burden as a % of labour costs

	2000	2005	2006	2007	2008	2009	2010	2011	2012	2013
Australia	27.4	25.5	25.1	24.2	23.5	23.1	23.1	22.9	23.4	23.2
Austria	44.6	45.1	45.3	45.5	45.7	44.3	44.5	44.8	45.0	45.2
Belgium	51.2	48.0	47.8	47.9	48.4	48.2	48.6	48.7	48.8	48.5
Canada	30.0	28.8	28.7	28.1	28.1	27.3	27.2	27.5	27.7	27.9
Chile	7.0	7.0	7.0	7.0	7.0	7.0	7.0	7.0	7.0	7.0
Czech Republic	41.4	42.6	40.9	41.3	41.4	39.9	40.0	40.3	40.2	40.2
Denmark	40.8	38.9	38.9	39.0	38.7	38.1	36.8	37.0	37.2	36.9
Estonia	39.8	38.1	37.3	37.6	37.0	38.0	38.8	39.0	39.2	38.7
Finland	44.7	41.3	40.9	40.7	40.5	39.2	38.9	38.9	38.9	39.4
France	45.3	45.0	44.4	44.4	46.0	46.1	46.1	46.2	46.4	44.9
Germany	47.5	47.3	47.4	46.9	46.5	45.9	44.9	45.5	45.5	45.1
Greece	38.9	40.4	41.1	40.9	40.5	40.2	39.4	42.7	42.5	40.6
Hungary	52.7	47.8	48.3	50.7	50.4	49.5	43.8	46.8	47.4	47.7
Iceland	23.8	28.2	28.2	27.0	27.6	26.1	28.6	29.6	28.9	29.0
Ireland	23.5	17.5	16.7	15.5	15.6	17.3	18.2	19.5	19.6	20.1
Israel	24.7	21.5	20.3	20.6	19.0	17.7	17.3	17.3	17.0	17.2
Italy	44.1	42.4	42.7	42.7	43.2	43.5	43.9	44.4	44.6	44.7
Japan	24.0	27.0	28.0	28.4	28.6	28.3	29.4	30.0	30.4	30.8
Korea	15.8	16.7	17.4	18.6	19.0	18.6	19.2	19.5	20.0	20.3
Luxembourg	28.9	27.1	27.5	28.3	26.6	25.9	26.2	28.0	27.5	28.3
Mexico	9.5	12.2	12.7	13.7	13.1	13.5	13.8	16.3	16.6	16.9
Netherlands	38.0	36.9	34.1	34.2	34.7	33.9	34.2	34.1	34.6	33.5
New Zealand	18.6	19.2	19.5	20.1	19.2	16.9	15.9	14.8	15.2	15.7
Norway	36.1	35.4	35.1	35.1	35.1	34.9	34.8	35.1	34.9	34.6
Poland	37.0	37.5	37.8	37.1	33.6	33.1	33.3	33.4	34.7	34.7
Portugal	33.8	32.4	33.1	32.5	32.1	31.8	32.2	32.2	32.6	34.7
Slovak Republic	40.7	35.3	35.7	35.5	36.0	33.2	33.7	35.7	36.6	39.1
Slovenia	44.5	43.3	43.0	41.4	40.4	39.9	40.1	40.2	40.1	40.0
Spain	36.0	36.3	36.4	36.3	35.5	35.7	36.8	37.0	37.4	37.5
Sweden	49.1	46.6	46.2	43.6	43.0	41.5	41.0	41.1	41.1	41.2
Switzerland	20.8	20.2	20.1	20.4	19.7	19.7	19.8	20.2	19.8	19.8
Turkey[1]	39.7	42.4	42.3	42.3	40.0	37.7	38.1	38.3	38.4	38.6
United Kingdom	29.1	30.5	30.6	30.8	29.7	29.1	29.4	28.4	27.9	26.9
United States	28.8	27.7	27.8	28.0	27.7	28.2	28.4	28.0	28.2	29.8
Unweighted average										
OECD-Average	**34.1**	**33.3**	**33.2**	**33.1**	**32.7**	**32.2**	**32.2**	**32.7**	**32.8**	**32.9**
OECD-EU 21	**40.6**	**39.0**	**38.9**	**38.7**	**38.4**	**37.8**	**37.7**	**38.3**	**38.5**	**38.5**

1. Wage figures are based on the old definition of average worker (ISIC D, Rev. 3).

StatLink http://dx.doi.org/10.1787/888933007069

Table II.8b. Income tax, married couple without children at 100% and 33% of average earnings

Tax burden as a % of gross wage earnings

	2000	2005	2006	2007	2008	2009	2010	2011	2012	2013
Australia	22.8	21.0	20.6	19.6	19.0	18.2	18.3	18.3	18.8	18.7
Austria	9.4	11.0	11.3	11.6	11.9	10.8	11.0	11.4	11.7	12.0
Belgium	25.9	23.8	23.9	24.0	24.5	24.2	24.7	24.6	24.5	24.3
Canada	16.3	13.5	13.5	13.0	13.2	12.2	12.2	12.3	12.3	12.4
Chile	0.0	0.0	0.0	0.0	0.0	0.0	0.0	0.0	0.0	0.0
Czech Republic	8.3	10.0	7.7	8.3	8.4	8.5	8.6	9.1	8.9	8.8
Denmark	27.6	26.7	26.8	26.9	26.7	26.1	25.3	33.5	33.6	33.3
Estonia	19.9	16.3	15.8	16.2	15.5	14.9	14.8	15.2	15.5	15.9
Finland	23.4	21.0	20.1	19.8	20.2	19.1	18.4	18.2	17.5	18.2
France	11.9	10.7	9.9	10.0	12.1	12.2	12.2	12.4	12.6	12.6
Germany	16.3	14.9	14.9	15.2	15.4	14.7	13.7	13.9	14.1	14.1
Greece	5.9	7.7	8.6	8.3	7.7	7.4	6.3	10.1	9.6	7.8
Hungary	19.4	15.1	15.7	16.4	16.1	15.9	10.8	14.2	16.5	16.0
Iceland	19.9	23.9	23.9	22.9	23.0	20.7	21.7	22.8	22.6	22.8
Ireland	11.1	5.2	4.4	3.1	3.1	4.0	4.5	8.9	9.0	8.9
Israel	13.5	9.9	9.4	10.0	8.4	7.3	6.8	6.8	6.6	6.6
Italy	15.9	14.1	15.2	14.8	15.5	15.8	16.5	17.1	17.3	17.5
Japan	6.1	5.8	6.3	7.1	7.1	6.9	6.7	6.7	6.7	6.7
Korea	1.7	2.1	2.6	3.5	3.4	3.1	3.4	3.4	3.7	3.9
Luxembourg	7.7	5.5	6.0	6.5	6.4	5.2	5.6	6.1	6.4	7.2
Mexico	-4.3	-1.5	-0.9	0.2	-0.4	0.0	0.3	3.2	3.6	3.9
Netherlands	7.8	8.6	10.2	11.2	11.9	12.7	12.4	12.5	12.9	12.4
New Zealand	18.6	19.2	19.5	20.1	19.2	16.9	15.9	14.8	15.2	15.7
Norway	20.1	19.1	18.7	18.9	19.0	18.7	18.7	18.8	18.5	18.4
Poland	5.3	5.0	5.2	5.5	6.0	5.4	5.6	5.8	5.9	6.0
Portugal	7.1	5.3	6.2	5.4	5.0	4.6	5.1	5.1	5.6	8.3
Slovak Republic	6.2	5.0	5.5	5.1	5.9	2.3	2.9	5.5	5.5	6.7
Slovenia	11.9	10.4	10.5	8.9	8.2	8.1	8.4	8.5	8.4	8.2
Spain	10.1	10.5	10.6	10.7	9.7	10.1	11.5	11.8	12.4	12.4
Sweden	25.3	22.3	21.8	18.2	17.5	16.1	15.4	15.5	15.6	15.7
Switzerland	9.1	9.3	9.2	9.5	8.7	8.8	8.9	8.9	8.5	8.6
Turkey[1]	14.0	15.0	14.9	14.9	12.9	12.4	12.8	13.1	13.3	13.5
United Kingdom	15.1	15.4	15.5	15.6	14.6	14.2	14.3	13.4	13.0	12.0
United States	15.5	14.3	14.4	14.7	14.4	13.0	13.2	14.6	14.7	14.5
Unweighted average										
OECD-Average	**13.1**	**12.2**	**12.3**	**12.2**	**12.1**	**11.5**	**11.4**	**12.2**	**12.4**	**12.5**
OECD-EU 21	**13.9**	**12.6**	**12.6**	**12.5**	**12.5**	**12.0**	**11.8**	**13.0**	**13.2**	**13.3**

1. Wage figures are based on the old definition of average worker (ISIC D, Rev. 3).

StatLink http://dx.doi.org/10.1787/888933007088

Table II.8c. **Income tax plus employee contributions less cash benefits, married couple without children at 100% and 33% of average earnings**

Tax burden as a % of gross wage earnings

	2000	2005	2006	2007	2008	2009	2010	2011	2012	2013
Australia	22.8	21.0	20.6	19.6	19.0	18.2	18.3	18.3	18.8	18.7
Austria	27.5	29.1	29.4	29.7	30.0	28.1	28.4	28.7	29.0	29.3
Belgium	38.1	35.0	34.7	34.8	35.2	35.0	35.5	35.4	35.3	35.0
Canada	22.0	20.6	20.5	19.8	20.0	19.0	19.0	19.1	19.2	19.4
Chile	7.0	7.0	7.0	7.0	7.0	7.0	7.0	7.0	7.0	7.0
Czech Republic	20.8	22.5	20.2	20.8	20.9	19.5	19.6	20.1	19.9	19.8
Denmark	40.9	38.9	38.9	39.0	38.7	38.1	36.8	37.0	37.2	36.9
Estonia	19.9	17.3	16.4	16.8	16.1	16.7	17.6	18.0	18.3	17.9
Finland	30.4	27.2	26.8	26.4	26.3	25.2	25.3	25.2	24.9	25.6
France	25.3	24.3	23.6	23.7	25.8	25.9	25.9	26.0	26.3	26.4
Germany	36.8	36.3	36.6	36.3	36.0	35.3	34.2	34.8	34.8	34.6
Greece	21.8	23.7	24.6	24.3	23.7	23.4	22.3	26.3	26.1	24.3
Hungary	31.9	28.6	30.0	33.4	33.1	32.9	27.8	31.7	35.0	34.5
Iceland	20.1	24.1	24.1	23.1	23.7	21.5	22.4	23.5	23.3	23.5
Ireland	15.0	9.1	8.2	6.9	7.0	8.9	9.9	11.2	11.4	11.9
Israel	21.0	17.1	16.1	16.8	15.3	14.2	13.6	13.7	13.4	13.4
Italy	25.1	23.3	24.3	24.3	25.0	25.3	26.0	26.6	26.8	27.0
Japan	16.1	17.7	18.6	19.2	19.3	19.1	19.7	20.1	20.4	20.6
Korea	8.4	9.2	9.8	10.9	11.0	10.7	11.2	11.4	11.9	12.2
Luxembourg	19.3	17.1	17.6	18.5	18.4	17.4	17.7	19.1	18.6	19.5
Mexico	-2.9	-0.1	0.5	1.5	0.9	1.3	1.6	4.5	4.9	5.2
Netherlands	30.8	29.4	28.0	27.9	28.3	27.7	27.7	27.7	27.9	27.5
New Zealand	18.6	19.2	19.5	20.1	19.2	16.9	15.9	14.8	15.2	15.7
Norway	27.9	26.9	26.5	26.7	26.8	26.5	26.5	26.6	26.3	26.2
Poland	26.5	27.0	27.4	26.5	23.8	23.2	23.4	23.6	23.7	23.8
Portugal	18.1	16.3	17.2	16.4	16.0	15.6	16.1	16.1	16.6	19.3
Slovak Republic	18.2	18.4	18.9	18.5	19.3	15.7	16.3	18.9	18.9	20.1
Slovenia	34.0	32.5	32.6	31.0	30.3	30.2	30.5	30.6	30.5	30.3
Spain	16.5	16.8	16.9	17.0	16.1	16.4	17.9	18.1	18.7	18.8
Sweden	32.3	29.3	28.8	25.3	24.5	23.1	22.4	22.5	22.6	22.7
Switzerland	15.6	15.4	15.3	15.6	14.8	14.9	15.0	15.2	14.8	14.8
Turkey[1]	28.0	30.0	29.9	29.9	27.9	27.4	27.8	28.1	28.3	28.5
United Kingdom	22.7	23.8	23.8	24.0	22.9	22.4	22.6	21.6	21.1	20.1
United States	23.1	22.0	22.1	22.3	20.0	20.6	20.9	20.3	20.3	22.1
Unweighted average										
OECD-Average	**22.9**	**22.2**	**22.2**	**22.2**	**21.8**	**21.3**	**21.3**	**21.8**	**22.0**	**22.1**
OECD-EU 21	**26.3**	**25.0**	**25.0**	**24.8**	**24.6**	**24.1**	**24.0**	**24.7**	**24.9**	**25.0**

1. Wage figures are based on the old definition of average worker (ISIC D, Rev. 3).

StatLink http://dx.doi.org/10.1787/888933007107

Table II.9. Annual average gross and net wage earnings, single individual no children, 2000-13

In US dollars using PPP

	2000		2005		2006		2007		2008		2009		2010		2011		2012		2013	
	Gross	Net	Gross	Net	Gross	Net	Gross	Net	Gross	Net	Gross	Net	Gross	Net	Gross	Net	Gross	Net	Gross	Net
Australia	31 531	23 145	37 866	28 695	39 125	29 743	40 032	30 681	40 783	31 587	44 055	34 337	44 302	34 430	46 261	35 957	49 622	38 266	52 639	40 431
Austria	33 065	22 827	38 385	25 704	41 075	27 340	41 728	27 609	43 705	28 730	44 984	30 235	45 762	30 628	47 821	31 777	49 320	32 582	50 322	33 064
Belgium	35 558	20 265	40 766	23 648	42 711	24 806	43 556	25 234	46 592	26 795	49 296	28 448	50 843	29 124	53 204	30 418	55 108	31 571	56 171	32 252
Canada	29 284	21 933	32 533	24 774	33 333	25 415	34 558	26 509	34 760	26 634	35 351	27 401	36 296	28 170	36 671	28 406	37 887	29 323	38 948	30 088
Chile	9 672	8 995	10 363	9 638	10 998	10 228	11 681	10 864	12 186	11 333	12 519	11 643	15 518	14 432	16 678	15 510	17 863	16 612	18 989	17 660
Czech Rep.	11 336	8 786	15 301	11 623	16 658	12 925	17 964	13 852	19 117	14 598	20 358	15 820	20 593	15 969	21 903	16 846	22 791	17 571	22 460	17 342
Denmark	33 539	18 721	37 287	22 029	39 783	23 475	42 029	24 745	44 844	26 502	47 037	28 446	48 499	29 922	50 259	30 945	51 358	31 562	51 772	31 976
Estonia	8 646	6 749	12 559	10 073	14 347	11 660	16 096	13 087	18 302	15 032	18 167	14 794	18 539	14 928	19 784	15 884	20 536	16 447	21 217	17 086
Finland	26 529	17 541	32 834	22 640	35 347	24 535	37 772	26 284	40 727	28 362	42 730	30 223	43 253	30 526	44 367	31 334	45 920	32 390	46 748	32 651
France	28 479	20 175	33 055	23 512	34 785	25 187	36 267	26 199	38 062	27 487	39 797	28 715	40 493	29 216	42 027	30 288	43 103	30 962	43 984	31 489
Germany	35 618	20 231	44 643	25 797	46 797	26 902	48 236	27 901	50 514	29 374	50 365	29 612	52 407	31 862	55 614	33 507	57 056	34 365	57 818	34 945
Greece	23 175	18 069	30 673	23 078	34 075	25 190	33 220	24 651	34 001	25 471	35 430	26 638	34 426	26 424	33 745	24 646	33 158	24 335	31 892	23 756
Hungary	10 080	6 479	14 121	9 369	15 468	10 017	16 404	10 038	18 049	11 144	19 478	12 123	20 025	13 739	21 397	13 887	22 728	14 743	22 930	15 019
Iceland	32 204	24 012	41 785	30 019	42 925	30 988	44 841	32 810	46 397	33 754	40 763	30 068	39 870	28 866	42 137	30 179	43 231	31 034	44 883	32 168
Ireland	22 907	18 248	28 670	24 298	30 444	25 970	32 510	28 002	34 208	29 438	35 786	29 827	38 327	31 484	39 002	32 043	39 877	32 722	40 175	32 660
Israel	27 811	20 551	27 734	21 841	27 590	21 994	30 356	23 915	30 832	24 889	30 203	24 855	30 591	25 388	31 790	26 371	32 087	26 749	32 419	27 013
Italy	26 404	18 735	28 212	20 310	30 318	21 602	31 560	22 348	34 030	23 981	35 316	24 819	36 184	25 247	37 505	25 975	38 902	26 875	39 430	27 196
Japan	32 179	26 719	38 431	31 322	39 945	32 180	41 468	33 111	42 654	34 021	41 821	33 439	42 772	33 948	44 869	35 433	46 744	36 768	47 771	37 452
Korea	26 623	24 241	36 557	32 944	39 426	35 240	42 074	36 998	42 837	37 635	41 851	36 959	43 873	38 480	43 081	37 703	45 772	39 811	47 075	40 782
Luxembourg	38 217	27 261	44 146	32 718	47 666	35 000	48 920	35 371	51 912	37 692	53 326	39 333	53 557	39 222	55 932	40 043	57 308	41 242	57 591	40 743
Mexico	7 789	7 621	9 734	9 287	10 212	9 704	10 461	9 833	10 885	10 325	11 381	10 764	11 414	10 774	11 862	10 769	12 146	10 988	12 501	11 281
Netherlands	35 782	23 753	43 185	29 145	47 048	31 761	48 942	33 049	51 222	34 401	52 983	36 138	53 233	36 382	55 654	38 009	57 035	38 722	58 252	40 096
New Zealand	24 246	19 550	25 771	20 609	27 509	21 886	28 531	22 518	29 866	23 740	31 969	26 191	31 948	26 520	33 242	27 967	35 409	29 606	36 381	30 237
Norway	32 725	22 679	42 545	30 197	45 817	32 488	47 922	33 765	50 709	35 697	51 133	36 162	52 334	37 019	54 784	38 673	57 617	40 782	59 548	42 166
Poland	12 540	9 054	14 921	10 687	15 889	11 327	17 506	12 642	18 158	13 611	18 777	14 198	20 045	15 136	21 241	16 012	22 127	16 664	22 968	17 284
Portugal	15 628	12 119	20 519	16 049	23 471	18 146	23 545	18 261	24 000	18 727	24 749	19 437	26 175	20 364	25 826	19 815	28 170	21 752	28 696	20 900
Slovak Rep.	9 614	7 714	12 114	9 477	13 377	10 417	14 642	11 375	16 559	12 781	17 758	13 959	18 279	14 322	18 865	14 563	19 282	14 887	19 716	15 227
Slovenia	16 747	10 792	21 225	13 857	22 539	14 685	23 221	15 593	24 858	16 642	25 045	16 795	26 373	17 594	27 777	18 496	29 089	19 418	29 528	19 767
Spain	23 620	18 932	26 953	21 483	28 805	22 905	30 160	23 950	32 288	26 058	34 191	27 422	34 555	27 046	36 169	28 197	37 813	29 169	38 278	29 505
Sweden	28 888	19 145	33 640	23 149	35 775	24 726	37 876	27 424	40 175	29 361	40 791	30 431	40 939	30 798	42 666	32 065	44 598	33 493	45 388	34 044
Switzerland	39 427	32 401	45 686	37 687	48 724	40 246	52 005	42 798	53 651	44 461	55 503	45 925	56 366	46 567	59 753	49 317	63 002	52 250	64 298	53 296
Turkey[1]	19 631	13 990	18 946	13 167	18 483	12 871	19 930	13 866	21 431	15 498	20 590	15 016	23 188	16 780	25 658	18 481	28 300	20 315	29 436	21 042
United Kingdom	39 213	29 093	47 682	34 879	50 187	36 693	51 425	37 534	51 290	38 168	51 101	38 204	49 625	37 024	48 819	36 580	50 572	38 062	51 255	38 918
United States	33 129	24 877	37 637	28 502	39 377	29 765	42 064	31 615	43 196	33 235	44 295	33 966	45 665	34 807	46 895	36 189	47 960	36 972	48 463	36 549
OECD Average	25 348	18 394	30 191	22 124	32 060	23 471	33 494	24 530	35 040	25 773	35 784	26 498	36 571	27 097	37 955	27 957	39 440	29 043	40 221	29 546

1. Turkey wage figures are based on the old definition of average worker (ISIC D, Rev. 3.).

StatLink http://dx.doi.org/10.1787/888933004086

Table II.10. **Annual average gross and net wage earnings, single individual no children, 2000-13 (national currency)**[1]

	2000		2005		2006		2007		2008		2009		2010		2011		2012		2013	
	Gross	Net	Gross	Net	Gross	Net	Gross	Net	Gross	Net	Gross	Net	Gross	Net	Gross	Net	Gross	Net	Gross	Net
Australia	41 322	30 332	52 572	39 840	55 042	41 844	57 120	43 777	60 321	46 720	63 546	49 529	66 724	51 856	69 903	54 334	73 494	56 676	77 530	59 623
Austria	29 732	20 526	34 025	22 784	35 143	23 391	36 228	23 970	37 258	24 492	37 832	25 428	38 504	25 770	39 693	26 376	40 708	26 893	41 693	27 394
Belgium	31 644	18 035	36 673	21 273	37 674	21 880	38 659	22 397	40 698	23 405	42 149	24 324	43 423	24 873	44 636	25 520	45 886	26 288	46 810	26 878
Canada	36 038	26 992	39 483	30 066	40 191	30 644	41 885	32 129	42 907	32 877	42 516	32 955	44 400	34 459	45 469	35 221	46 940	36 329	48 078	37 140
Chile	2 770 353	2 576 428	3 458 172	3 216 100	3 594 042	3 342 459	3 856 095	3 586 168	4 218 584	3 923 283	4 478 647	4 165 142	5 508 104	5 122 537	5 804 093	5 397 806	6 218 613	5 783 310	6 607 476	6 144 953
Czech Rep.	160 922	124 729	219 050	166 403	233 580	181 234	250 710	193 316	272 651	208 198	281 887	219 060	287 320	222 803	294 987	226 886	302 993	233 602	298 770	230 693
Denmark	281 700	157 242	320 300	189 227	330 900	195 259	346 400	203 947	359 300	212 344	367 051	221 974	376 073	232 025	386 457	237 944	392 000	240 901	395 722	244 412
Estonia	3 931	3 068	6 304	5 056	7 456	6 059	8 939	7 268	10 045	8 250	9 492	7 729	9 712	7 820	10 368	8 324	11 004	8 813	11 664	9 393
Finland	26 362	17 431	32 086	22 125	33 543	23 283	35 559	24 744	37 372	26 026	38 444	27 191	39 395	27 804	40 243	28 422	41 662	29 386	42 493	29 679
France	26 712	18 923	30 521	21 710	31 369	22 713	32 413	23 415	33 580	24 250	34 132	24 628	34 693	25 032	35 497	25 582	36 248	26 038	36 980	26 475
Germany	34 400	19 539	38 700	22 363	39 149	22 505	40 100	23 195	41 000	23 842	40 600	23 871	41 736	25 374	43 300	26 088	44 300	26 682	45 170	27 301
Greece	15 693	12 236	21 902	16 478	23 800	17 594	23 893	17 730	23 835	17 856	24 619	18 510	24 156	18 541	23 391	17 084	22 240	16 322	20 604	15 347
Hungary	1 086 240	698 166	1 815 852	1 204 835	1 985 412	1 285 714	2 156 184	1 319 406	2 336 124	1 442 307	2 436 408	1 516 415	2 512 020	1 723 560	2 645 712	1 717 097	2 838 864	1 841 534	2 914 514	1 909 007
Iceland	2 712 000	2 022 102	4 140 000	2 974 230	4 596 000	3 317 884	5 076 000	3 714 076	5 448 000	3 963 490	5 076 000	3 744 125	5 256 000	3 805 407	5 628 000	4 030 857	5 856 000	4 203 829	6 191 179	4 437 244
Ireland	22 008	17 532	28 963	24 547	29 931	25 533	31 185	26 861	32 550	28 011	31 802	26 507	32 308	26 540	32 264	26 508	32 514	26 680	32 381	26 324
Israel	95 664	70 691	103 087	81 180	105 652	84 223	112 986	89 013	119 233	96 250	120 028	98 777	121 581	100 905	125 405	104 026	128 549	107 162	131 033	109 184
Italy	21 550	15 291	24 450	17 602	25 241	17 985	25 805	18 273	26 845	18 918	27 419	19 270	28 230	19 697	28 820	19 960	29 315	20 252	29 704	20 487
Japan	4 987 116	4 140 942	4 978 855	4 057 883	4 979 155	4 011 225	4 988 400	3 983 177	4 983 948	3 975 163	4 828 001	3 860 274	4 773 076	3 788 423	4 821 385	3 807 417	4 893 341	3 848 998	4 901 704	3 842 895
Korea	19 849 729	18 073 190	28 840 599	25 990 086	30 495 639	27 257 957	32 361 506	28 457 420	33 658 172	29 570 496	34 410 564	30 387 885	36 929 183	32 390 144	36 816 740	32 220 027	38 811 570	33 756 834	39 829 650	34 505 328
Luxembourg	35 875	25 591	42 067	31 176	43 540	31 970	45 266	32 729	47 044	34 157	48 185	35 541	49 393	36 172	50 680	36 283	51 752	37 244	52 902	37 426
Mexico	47 469	46 441	69 370	66 184	73 208	69 572	77 145	72 518	81 306	77 124	84 727	80 135	87 324	82 428	91 014	82 627	94 875	85 832	97 941	88 381
Netherlands	31 901	21 176	38 700	26 118	40 800	27 543	42 000	28 362	43 146	28 977	44 412	30 292	45 215	30 901	46 287	31 612	47 075	31 960	48 109	33 114
New Zealand	34 923	28 159	39 559	31 635	40 843	32 495	43 022	33 955	44 521	35 389	46 653	38 221	48 007	39 850	49 395	41 557	51 278	42 875	53 234	44 244
Norway	298 385	206 788	378 498	268 644	397 765	282 046	420 917	296 570	443 812	312 422	456 214	322 642	471 669	333 640	491 547	346 992	504 929	357 401	524 177	371 176
Poland	23 061	16 649	27 889	19 975	29 271	20 867	32 292	23 320	33 711	25 270	34 878	26 372	36 482	27 548	38 731	29 198	40 205	30 278	41 442	31 186
Portugal	10 922	8 470	14 042	10 983	15 517	11 997	15 549	12 060	15 581	12 158	15 613	12 262	16 542	12 870	16 208	12 435	17 040	13 158	17 335	12 626
Slovak Rep.	5 048	4 050	6 856	5 364	7 418	5 776	7 997	6 213	8 820	6 808	9 043	7 108	9 325	7 306	9 592	7 405	9 810	7 574	10 015	7 735
Slovenia	8 894	5 732	12 981	8 475	13 684	8 916	14 625	9 821	15 769	10 557	16 079	10 783	16 915	11 284	17 373	11 568	17 538	11 707	17 611	11 789
Spain	17 319	13 882	20 616	16 433	21 168	16 833	21 989	17 461	23 252	18 765	24 164	19 380	24 786	19 400	25 515	19 892	25 894	19 975	26 027	20 062
Sweden	263 581	174 686	315 492	217 096	324 618	224 362	336 818	243 870	352 470	257 589	362 291	270 277	368 208	277 001	376 309	282 810	387 960	291 356	391 990	294 016
Switzerland	72 910	59 918	79 620	65 679	80 727	66 682	83 325	68 573	83 088	68 856	83 974	69 483	85 068	70 280	86 130	71 086	87 662	72 701	88 161	73 075
Turkey[2]	5 545	3 952	15 737	10 937	15 645	10 895	17 238	11 993	19 074	13 794	18 709	13 644	21 809	15 782	25 323	18 239	29 209	20 967	31 744	22 692
United King.	24 910	18 481	30 334	22 189	31 419	22 971	33 216	24 244	33 382	24 841	33 391	24 964	34 297	25 589	34 083	25 538	34 877	26 250	35 548	26 992
United States	33 129	24 877	37 637	28 502	39 377	29 765	42 064	31 615	43 196	33 235	44 295	33 966	45 665	34 807	46 895	36 189	47 960	36 972	48 463	36 549

1. The annual average gross wage earnings in euro area countries are expressed in euros for all years.
2. Turkey wage figures are based on the old definition of average worker (ISIC D, Rev. 3.).

StatLink http://dx.doi.org/10.1787/888933004105

PART III

Country details, 2013

This part of the publication provides the individual country details for 2013 that lie behind the comparative analysis. For each country, a table of detailed country results is followed by a description of the tax/benefit system.

All thirty country tables in this part of the report have a similar format. The left hand page of each table specifies the tax-benefit position of single persons in four cases, which differ by wage level and the presence of children (0/2). The right hand page of the table specifies the tax-benefit position of married couples, again discerning between four cases, which now differ by wage level, the presence of children (0/2) and one-/two earner situations.

All tables start with gross wage earnings (line 1) and derive taxable income for the personal income tax levied by central government (line 4), taking into account a number of standard tax allowances (line 2) and taxable cash transfers (line 3). Taxable income allows one to determine central government income tax paid (line 7); including reductions in the form of tax credits (line 6). Total payments to general government (line 10) also include state and local income taxes (line 8) and employees' compulsory social security contributions (line 9). Take-home pay (line 12) is calculated as gross wage earnings less all payments to general government, plus universal cash transfers received from general government (line 11).

Line 13 reports employers' compulsory social security contributions (including payroll taxes).

Average tax rate (line 14) are then calculated as:

- *the share of income tax in gross wage earnings;*
- *the share of employees' social security contributions in gross wage earnings;*
- *the share of income tax and employees' social security contributions minus benefits in gross wage earnings; and,*
- *the share of income tax and all social security contributions minus benefits in gross labour costs.*

Marginal tax rates (line 15) are calculated similarly as:

- *the increase in income tax and employees' contributions minus benefits as a share of the related increase in gross wage earnings (both for the principal earner and the spouse); and,*
- *the increase in tax and all social security contributions minus benefits as a share of the related increase in gross labour costs (both for the principal earner and the spouse).*

Taxing Wages 2014
Changes in sructural labour income tax progressivity
over 2000-12 period in OECD member countries

Australia
(2012-13 income tax year)

This chapter includes data on the income taxes paid by workers, their social security contributions, the family benefits they receive in the form of cash transfers as well as the social security contributions and payroll taxes paid by their employers. Results reported include the marginal and average tax burden for eight different family types.

Methodological information is available for personal income tax systems, compulsory social security contributions to schemes operated within the public sector, universal cash transfers as well as recent changes in the tax/benefit system. The methodology also includes the parameter values and tax equations underlying the data.

Australia 2013

The tax/benefit position of single persons

	Wage level (per cent of average wage)	67	100	167	67
	Number of children	none	none	none	2
1.	**Gross wage earnings**	51687	77 530	129 217	51 687
	Principal Gross wage earnings	51 687	77 530	129 217	51 687
	Spouse Gross wage earnings	0	0	0	0
2.	**Standard tax allowances**				
	Basic allowance				
	Married or head of family				
	Dependent children				
	Deduction for social security contributions and income taxes				
	Work-related expenses				
	Other				
	Total	0	0	0	0
3.	**Tax credits or cash transfers included in taxable income**	0	0	0	0
4.	**Central government taxable income (1 - 2 + 3)**	51 687	77 530	129 217	51 687
5.	**Central government income tax liability (exclusive of tax credits)**				
	Income tax	8 345	16 744	35 757	8 345
	Medicare Levy	775	1 163	1 938	775
	Total	9 120	17 907	37 695	9 120
6.	**Tax credits**				
	Basic credit	225	0	0	225
	Married or head of family	0	0	0	0
	Children				
	Other				
	Total	225	0	0	225
7.	**Central government income tax finally paid (5-6)**	8 896	17 907	37 695	8 896
8.	**State and local taxes**	0	0	0	0
9.	**Employees' compulsory social security contributions**	0	0	0	0
10.	**Total payments to general government (7 + 8 + 9)**	8 896	17 907	37 695	8 896
11.	**Cash transfers from general government**				
	For head of family	0	0	0	0
	For two children	0	0	0	13 550
	Total	0	0	0	13 550
12.	**Take-home pay (1-10+11)**	42 791	59 623	91 521	56 341
13.	**Employers' payroll tax**	3 070	4 606	7 676	3 070
14.	**Average rates**				
	Income tax	17.21%	23.10%	29.17%	17.21%
	Employees' social security contributions	0.00%	0.00%	0.00%	0.00%
	Total payments less cash transfers	17.21%	23.10%	29.17%	-9.00%
	Total tax wedge including employer payroll taxes	21.85%	27.41%	33.14%	-2.89%
15.	**Marginal rates**				
	Total payments less cash transfers: Principal earner	35.50%	34.00%	38.50%	55.50%
	Total payments less cash transfers: Spouse	n.a.	n.a.	n.a.	n.a.
	Total tax wedge: Principal earner	39.12%	37.70%	41.95%	58.00%
	Total tax wedge: Spouse	n.a.	n.a.	n.a.	n.a.

Australia 2013

The tax/benefit position of married couples

		100-0	100-33	100-67	100-33
	Wage level (per cent of average wage)	100-0	100-33	100-67	100-33
	Number of children	2	2	2	none
1.	**Gross wage earnings**	77 530	103 373	129 217	103 373
	Principal Gross wage earnings	77 530	77 530	77 530	77 530
	Spouse Gross wage earnings	0	25 843	51 687	25 843
2.	**Standard tax allowances**				
	Basic allowance				
	Married or head of family				
	Dependent children				
	Deduction for social security contributions and income taxes				
	Work-related expenses				
	Other				
	Total	0	0	0	0
3.	**Tax credits or cash transfers included in taxable income**	0	0	0	0
4.	**Central government taxable income (1 - 2 + 3)**	77 530	103 373	129 217	103 373
5.	**Central government income tax liability (exclusive of tax credits)**				
	Income tax	16 744	18 196	25 089	18 196
	Medicare Levy	1 163	1 551	1 938	1 163
	Total	17 907	19 747	27 028	19 359
6.	**Tax credits**				
	Basic credit	0	445	225	445
	Married or head of family	0	0	0	0
	Children				
	Other				
	Total	0	445	225	445
7.	**Central government income tax finally paid (5-6)**	17 907	19 302	26 803	19 302
8.	**State and local taxes**	0	0	0	0
9.	**Employees' compulsory social security contributions**	0	0	0	0
10.	**Total payments to general government (7 + 8 + 9)**	17 907	19 302	26 803	19 302
11.	**Cash transfers from general government**				
	For head of family	0	0	0	0
	For two children	8 620	3 600	0	0
	Total	8 620	3 600	0	0
12.	**Take-home pay (1-10+11)**	68 242	87 671	102 414	84 071
13.	**Employers' payroll tax**	4 606	6 141	7 676	6 141
14.	**Average rates**				
	Income tax	23.10%	18.67%	20.74%	18.67%
	Employees' social security contributions	0.00%	0.00%	0.00%	0.00%
	Total payments less cash transfers	11.98%	15.19%	20.74%	18.67%
	Total tax wedge including employer payroll taxes	16.91%	19.95%	25.19%	23.23%
15.	**Marginal rates**				
	Total payments less cash transfers: Principal earner	51.50%	64.00%	34.00%	34.00%
	Total payments less cash transfers: Spouse	24.82%	50.50%	35.50%	20.50%
	Total tax wedge: Principal earner	54.22%	66.02%	37.70%	37.70%
	Total tax wedge: Spouse	29.04%	53.28%	39.12%	24.96%

The national currency is the Australian dollar (AUD). For the 2012-13 income tax year AUD 1.04 was equal to USD 1. The average worker earned AUD 77 530 in 2012-13.

1. Personal income tax systems

1.1. *Federal income tax*

1.1.1. *Tax unit*

Members of the family are taxed separately.

1.1.2. *Tax allowances and credits*

1.1.2.1. Standard tax reliefs

- *Basic reliefs:* Income earned up to AUD 18 200 by resident taxpayers is subject to tax at a zero rate.
- *Standard marital status reliefs:* A taxpayer may claim a tax credit where he or she contributes to the maintenance of a dependent spouse (legal or *de facto*). For the 2012-13 income year, eligibility for the dependent spouse tax offset has been limited to taxpayers with a dependent spouse who was born before 1 July 1952 or who is genuinely unable to work due to invalidity or carer obligations. For eligible taxpayers during 2012-13, the maximum offset amount was AUD 2 423. The maximum amount reduces by AUD 1 for every AUD 4 by which the spouse's adjusted taxable income exceeds AUD 282. From 1 July 2008, an income test was introduced so that the offset is not available where the primary earner's adjusted taxable income exceeds AUD 150 000.
- *Relief(s) for children:* See Section 4.2 for more detail on the Baby Bonus.
- *Relief for social security contributions* and other taxes: No such contributions are levied.
- *Reliefs for low income earners:* A tax offset worth a maximum of AUD 445 is available for taxpayers whose taxable income was less than AUD 37 000. This offset is reduced by AUD 0.015 for every AUD 1 by which a taxpayer's taxable income exceeds AUD 37 000, and is no longer available once a taxpayer's taxable income exceeds AUD 66 667.
- *Relief for mature age workers:* Taxpayers born before 1 July 1957, and who have net income from working, may be eligible for the Mature Age Worker Tax Offset. It is worth a maximum of AUD 500, and is reduced by AUD 0.05 for every AUD 1 of earned income above AUD 53 000.
- *Relief for recipients of certain social security benefits:* The Beneficiary Tax Offset is available for those who receive certain taxable social security benefits called "rebatable benefits". It is calculated to ensure that a person who receives a rebatable benefit does not pay any tax on that income.
- There are also tax rebates to ensure that taxpayers who are of Age Pension Age (65 for males and 64.5 for females for 2012-13) and recipients of certain taxable social security pensions pay less tax. The Senior Australian and Pensioner Tax Offset is worth up to AUD 2 230 for a single taxpayer, up to AUD 1 602 for each member of a couple not

separated by illness and AUD 2 040 for each member of a couple separated by illness. The offset is withdrawn at the rate of AUD 0.125 for every dollar that a recipient's income exceeds their effective tax-free threshold. For a single taxpayer, this means that the offset is withdrawn from AUD 32 279 and is no longer available once income reaches AUD 50 119. For members of a couple not separated by illness, who each have the same amount of income, the offset for each member is withdrawn from AUD 28 794 and is no longer available once both their incomes reach AUD 41 790.

- *Other:* No other standard relief available.

1.1.2.2. Main non-standard tax reliefs applicable to an average worker include:

- *Relief for superannuation:* Contributions to a low-income spouse's superannuation attract an 18 per cent rebate up to a maximum rebate of AUD 540.
- *Relief for private health insurance:* For the 2012-13 income year, there is a 30 per cent rebate on the cost of cover for eligible private health care for individuals with annual income for surcharge purposes below AUD 84 000.
- *Relief for medical expenses:* Annual net out-of-pocket medical expenses over AUD 2 060 attract a 20 per cent rebate for individuals with annual income for surcharge purposes below AUD 84 000.
- Other non-standard reliefs provided as deductions are:
  - subscriptions paid in respect of membership of a trade, business or professional association or union;
  - charitable contributions of AUD 2 or more to specified funds, authorities and institutions, including public benevolent institutions, approved research institutes for scientific research, building funds for schools conducted by non-profit organisations etc.; and
  - work-related expenses including cost of replacement of tools of trade, cost of provision and of cleaning protective clothing and footwear, travelling between jobs or travelling in the course of employment.

1.1.3. Tax schedule

General rates of tax – resident individuals

Taxable income (AUD)		Tax at general rates on total taxable income
Not less than	Not more than	
0	18 200	NIL
18 201	37 000	NIL + 19c for each AUD in excess of AUD 18 200
37 001	80 000	AUD 3 572 + 32.50c for each AUD in excess of AUD 37 000
80 001	180 000	AUD 17 547 + 37c for each AUD in excess of AUD 80 000
180 001 and over		AUD 54 547 + 45c for each AUD in excess of AUD 180 000

To nominally contribute towards the cost of basic medical and hospital care a Medicare Levy is imposed on the taxable incomes of resident taxpayers. In 2012-13 the levy applies at the rate of 1.5 per cent of the taxable income of an individual.

Certain thresholds are applied before the levy is imposed. In 2012-13, an individual taxpayer does not pay the levy where their taxable income does not exceed AUD 20 542. A taxpayer in a couple or sole parent family who is not receiving Parenting Payment (see

Section 1.2), does not pay the levy if the taxable family income does not exceed AUD 33 693. The threshold is increased by AUD 3 094 for each dependent child. Where an individual's taxable income exceeds AUD 20 542, or a family's income exceeds AUD 33 693 (plus AUD 3 094 for each dependent child), the levy shades in at a rate of 10 per cent of the excess of taxable income over the threshold, until the levy is equal to 1.5 per cent of the individual's or family's taxable income.

For 2012-13, individual senior Australians of Age Pension age do not pay the levy where their taxable income does not exceed AUD 32 279. Where taxable income exceeds AUD 32 279 but does not exceed AUD 37 975, the levy payable is 10 per cent of the excess of taxable income over AUD 32 279. Pensioner families (including couples and sole parents on Parenting Payment) and senior Australian families of Age Pension age, do not pay any Medicare levy until their combined income exceeds AUD 46 000 (plus AUD 3 094 for each dependent child).

Taxpayers who have income for surcharge purposes greater than AUD 84 000 in 2012-13, but who do not have a complying private health care policy, pay a Medicare levy surcharge applied as a flat rate on their taxable income. However, affected taxpayers typically purchase a complying policy as the cost of such a policy is generally less than the surcharge. The surcharge is therefore not included in this publication.

1.2. *State and local income taxes*

In Australia no states or territories levy a tax based on a resident's income.

2. Social security contributions

2.1. *Employees' contributions*

None. There is, however, a Medicare Levy which is based upon taxable income. See Section 1.1.3.

2.2. *Employers' contributions*

No contributions are collected from employers or employees specifically for pensions, sickness, unemployment or work injury benefits, family allowances or other benefits.

Part of Australia's retirement income system is the provision of compulsory employer contributions (the Superannuation Guarantee system). The Superannuation Guarantee requires employers to pay 9 per cent on top of employees' gross ordinary time earnings to an approved superannuation fund, provided they earn more than AUD 450 per month (they may also choose to make contributions for workers earning less than this threshold). This threshold is not indexed. There is also a limit to the Superannuation Guarantee. In each quarter any earnings beyond a threshold are not covered by the Superannuation Guarantee. This threshold is indexed to a measure of average earnings. In the 2012-13 tax year this threshold was AUD 45 750 per quarter.

These contributions are not reflected in the "Taxing Wages" calculations because they are not a form of taxation (they are not an unrequited transfer to general government). While employers are legislatively required to make contributions to approved superannuation funds legislated, superannuation funds are private, although subject to regulation. Employers' contributions are generally made to individual accounts and form part of employees' personal superannuation assets. Some defined benefit schemes for public sector employees and private defined benefit schemes also exist. The employee may take superannuation benefits as either a lump sum payment or pension on retirement. Accordingly, superannuation contributions are reflected in the Non-Tax Compulsory Payment calculations.

3. Other taxes

3.1. *Pay-roll tax*

Australian State Governments levy pay-roll taxes on wages, cash or in kind, provided by larger employers to their employees. The rates of pay-roll tax, thresholds and deductions differ between States. In New South Wales, the State with the largest population, the pay-roll tax rate in 2012-13 was 5.45 per cent for employers with total Australian wages in excess of AUD 689 000. Employers are entitled to an exemption from tax, or a pro-rated pay-roll tax threshold, on wages paid in New South Wales up to a maximum of AUD 689 000. The exempt amount is reduced based on the proportion of the employer's New South Wales pay-roll to its total Australian pay-roll.

4. Universal cash transfers

4.1. *Transfers related to marital status*

There are no cash transfers made on a universal basis to married couples.

4.2. *Transfers related to dependent children*

- Family Tax Benefit (FTB) Part A is paid to a parent, guardian or an approved care organisation to help families meet the costs of raising children. For 2012-13, the base rate of FTB(A) is payable where the combined "adjusted" taxable income of parents does not exceed AUD 94 316 plus AUD 3 96 for each child after the first. The payment shades out at the rate of AUD 0.30 per AUD 1 of income over the ceiling. The base rate of payment is AUD 2 142.55 for a dependent child aged under 18, and for dependent full time students aged 18 to 19. The base rate of payment is AUD 2 624.35 for a dependent child not in full time study aged 18 to 21. (Note from 1 January 2013 eligibility was limited to those under 18 or 19 where the dependant remains in full time secondary school.) The base rate of payment is increased by a Large Family Supplement (LFS) for families with three or more children. The LFS is payable at a rate of AUD 306.60 for the third and each subsequent child.
- A higher FTB(A) benefit is available for lower income earners, and the value of this benefit is dependent on the age and number of children. Families may receive a maximum payment of AUD 5 150.15 for each child aged under 13 years and AUD 6 478.75 for each child aged 13 to 15 years for 2012-13, and from 1 January 2012 for each child aged 16-19 in full time secondary school. Families can receive up to AUD 2 142.55 for children aged 16-17 and AUD 2 624.35 for those aged 18-21 who are not in secondary school. The higher benefit is also boosted by the LFS for families with three or more children. For 2012-13, the higher benefit tapers out at the rate of AUD 0.20 for each dollar of income over AUD 47 815 until the base payment is reached. However, people receiving any social security allowances or pensions automatically qualify for the maximum higher benefit. The attached calculations assume each dependant is between 5 and 12 years of age.
- Family Tax Benefit Part B [FTB(B)] is targeted at single income couple and sole parent families. Eligibility for FTB(B) is contingent upon the existence of at least one dependent child under the age of 16 or a qualifying dependent full-time student up to and including

the age of 18. There are two separate income tests applied to the parent(s). The parent earning the higher amount (or the sole parent, in the case of single parent families) must earn AUD 150 000 or less for the financial year for the family to be eligible. A secondary earner income threshold is also applied to the parent earning the lower amount. For 2012-13, this threshold is AUD 5 037, above which the entitlement is reduced by AUD 0.20 for each dollar of income. There is no secondary earner income test applied to sole parents. For 2012-13, the maximum payment is AUD 2 978.40 if the youngest dependent child is aged between 5 and 18 years, and AUD 4 117.20 if there is a child under 5 years. The attached calculations assume each dependant is between 5 and 12 years of age.

- Recipients of the Family Tax Benefit may elect to receive the benefit in fortnightly instalments or as an end of year lump sum payment.
- A one-off Baby Bonus is paid to families for each baby born. The value of the payment in 2012-13 is AUD 5 000. Baby Bonus is payable to families with a combined income of AUD 75 000 or less in the six months following the birth.
- On 1 January 2011 the Australia's first Paid Parental Leave (PPL) scheme commenced. PPL provides the primary carer of a child with 18 weeks' pay at the national minimum wage (AUD 606.50 per week before tax in 2012-13), in the year following the child's birth or adoption. The primary carer must have worked for at least 10 of the 13 months prior to the birth or adoption, and for at least 330 hours in that 10 month period. The primary carer's adjusted taxable income must be AUD 150 000 or less in the financial year prior to the date of claim or date of birth or adoption. PPL and Baby Bonus cannot be paid for the same child. A person cannot claim FTB(B) or the dependent spouse, child housekeeper and housekeeper tax offsets while they are receiving PPL.
- Child Care Benefit (CCB) is a means-tested payment which assists families with the cost of approved child care. In 2012-13 CCB is payable to eligible families with incomes up to AUD 142 426 for one child in care, with the income limit rising for each additional child in care. Families with annual incomes under AUD 41 026 receive the maximum rate of CCB, which is AUD 3.90 per hour for a non-school child. CCB is payable for a maximum of 50 hours per week. To receive more than 24 hours of CCB per week both parents must be participating in work, training or study activities for at least 15 hours per week. The attached calculations assume no child care usage.
- Child Care Rebate (CCR) is an additional payment aimed at promoting workforce participation. CCR is not means tested. It pays 50 per cent of out-of-pocket child care expenses (after any CCB), up to an annual cap of AUD 7 500 per child in 2012-13. Families have to participate in work related commitments at some time during a week or have an exemption. No minimum number of hours is required.
- Parenting Payment is a taxable payment payable to partnered and sole parents for low income families with a qualifying child under six and eight years of age respectively. In 2012-13 the maximum annual amount of Parenting Payment (Partnered) [PP(P)] was AUD 11 574. Only one parent in a couple can be entitled to PP(P). The maximum annual amount of Parenting Payment (Single) [PP(S)] was AUD 17 303.60. These payments are subject to income and assets tests. The Parenting Payment (Partnered) tapers out at a rate of AUD 0.50 per AUD 1 of income over AUD 1 612 up to AUD 6 500 and reduces at a rate of AUD 0.60 per AUD 1 for income over AUD 6 500. Under the PP(P) income test, a spouse receives a reduced Parenting Payment, tapering at a rate of AUD 0.60, when the higher earning partner's income exceeds AUD 21 717. If the spouse has little or no

income (less than AUD 1 612 per annum), he or she would not receive any Parenting Payment when the higher earning partner's income exceeds AUD 41 007. PP(S) reduces by AUD 0.40 for each AUD 1 of income above AUD 4 591.60 plus AUD 639.60 for each child other than the first. A sole parent with two qualifying dependants may be entitled to some taxable PP(S) in 2012-13 where private income does not exceed AUD 48 490. The attached calculations assume dependants are aged six and seven.

- The Newstart allowance is a taxable payment payable to single persons and partnered individuals who are unemployed. It is also payable to a member of a couple if their youngest child is aged six years or more and to single parents if their youngest child is aged eight years or more. It is conditional on recipients fulfilling a personal Employment Pathway Plan, which typically involves taking part in activities such as job seeking and training. In 2012-13 the Newstart allowance for singles without dependants was AUD 12 821 and for partnered individuals was AUD 11 574. These payments taper out at a rate of AUD 0.50 per AUD 1 for incomes between AUD 1 612 and AUD 6 500, and reduce at a rate of AUD 0.60 per AUD for incomes over AUD 6 500. The Newstart allowance for partnered individuals reduces by AUD 0.60 for each AUD 1 of their partner's income above AUD 21 717. For single principal carers with dependent child(ren), it reduces at a rate of AUD 0.40 per AUD 1 for incomes over AUD 1 612.
- A non-taxable supplementary payment called Pharmaceutical Allowance (PA) is payable to eligible persons; for example, persons who receive the PP(S). PA is added to the maximum basic rate of PP(S) before a person's PP(S) entitlement is calculated. Anyone with a PP(S) entitlement, after PA has been added, receives the full amount of PA. For 2012-13, the payment is AUD 161.20.
- A Telephone Allowance is available on a quarterly basis to eligible individuals, including individuals who receive PP(S) or PA if their PP(S) entitlement is reduced to 0. The basic rate of the Telephone Allowance is AUD 102.03 for 2012-13, with a higher rate of AUD 153.05 available for recipients of Disability Support Pension who are under the age of 21 and where a home internet service is connected in the individual's or partner's name. The attached calculations assume the standard rate is applicable.

5. Recent changes in the tax/benefit system

5.1. *Introduction of the Clean Energy Future Household Assistance Package*

- In 2012-13 a price on carbon commenced, along with an assistance package to help households meet the effects of a price on carbon. The Household Assistance Package consists of a series of social security payment increases and tax cuts.

Clean Energy Advance and Clean Energy Supplement

- As part of the Household Assistance Package, a one-off non-taxable Clean Energy Advance was paid to eligible families and parents, seniors and individuals during May and June 2012.
- From 20 March 2013, most pensioners and recipients of social security benefits began receiving an ongoing non-taxable Clean Energy Supplement as part of their regular benefit, equivalent to 1.7 per cent of the maximum rate of the benefit.

Single Income Family Supplement

- The Single Income Family Supplement (SIFS) is a non-taxable payment for households with one main income earner.

- The SIF phases in at a rate of AUD 0.025 for every 1 AUD above AUD 68 000 until it reaches AUD 300. Once the main earner's income exceeds AUD 120 000 the SIFS reduces by AUD 0.01 for every 1 AUD. If there is a secondary earner, every AUD of their income above AUD 16 000, reduces the SIFS by AUD 0.15.

Tax cuts

- As part of the Household Assistance Package, the tax free threshold was increased from AUD 6 000 to AUD 18 200 from 1 July 2012.
- Individuals with a taxable income of less than AUD 80 000 received a tax cut. Most were expected to receive a tax cut of around AUD 300 a year.
- Refer to 1.13.

5.2. *Schoolkids Bonus*

- From 2012-13, the Schoolkids Bonus replaced the Education Tax Refund. The Schoolkids Bonus is a payment to help families meet the costs of primary and secondary school studies.
- Parents or carers eligible for FTB Part A are eligible to receive Schoolkids Bonus. In 2012-13, the Bonus was worth AUD 410 for each child in primary school and $820 for each child in secondary school.

5.3. *Income Support Bonus*

- In 2012-13, the Income Support Bonus, a non-taxable payment made to recipients of eligible social security benefits, was introduced. In 2012-13, single persons received AUD 105 and each member of a couple received AUD 87.50.

6. Memorandum items

6.1. *Identification of an average worker*

The source of the information used in replying to the questionnaire was the Australian Bureau of Statistics publication *Average Weekly Earnings – Australia*, catalogue number 6302.0. The survey is now conducted on a biannual basis (it was previously conducted on a quarterly basis up to the June 2012 quarter) and is based on a representative sample of employers in each industry. As a result of this change in frequency, average weekly earnings for the 2012-13 income tax year have been calculated as the average of the two biannual figures (November 2012 and May 2013 [released in August 2013]). If this methodology was adopted for previous income tax years (that is, if the annual average weekly earnings figures were estimated by taking the average of the November and May quarters, rather than the average of all four quarters), average weekly earnings would be 0.6% higher on average for the previous five income tax years.

In August 2009 the Australian Bureau of Statistics redesigned the survey and replaced the industry classification based on the 1993 edition of the Australian and New Zealand Standard Industrial Classification (ANZSIC), which had been in use since 1994, with the 2006 edition of ANZSIC. The 2006 edition of ANZSIC was developed to provide a more contemporary industrial classification system, taking into account issues such as changes in the structure and composition of the economy, changing user demands and compatibility with major international classification standards. Accordingly, the average wage figure for 2010 and later years is inconsistent with that provided for previous years.

All wage and salary earners who received pay for the reference period are represented in the Survey of Average Weekly Earnings (AWE), except:

- members of the Australian permanent defence forces;
- employees of enterprises primarily engaged in agriculture, forestry and fishing;
- employees of private households;
- employees of overseas embassies, consulates, etc.;
- employees based outside Australia; and
- employees on workers' compensation who are not paid through the payroll.

Also excluded are the following persons who are not regarded as employees for the purposes of this survey:

- casual employees who did not receive pay during the reference period;
- employees on leave without pay who did not receive pay during the reference period;
- employees on strike, or stood down, who did not receive pay during the reference period;
- directors who are not paid a salary;
- proprietors/partners of unincorporated businesses;
- self-employed persons such as subcontractors, owner/drivers, consultants;
- persons paid solely by commission without a retainer; and
- employees paid under the Paid Parental Leave Scheme.

The sample for the AWE survey, like most ABS business surveys, is selected from the ABS Business Register which is primarily based on registrations with the Australian Taxation Office's (ATO) Pay As You Go Withholding (PAYGW) scheme (and prior to 1 June 2000 the Group Employer (GE) scheme). The population is updated quarterly to take account of:

- new businesses;
- businesses which have ceased employing;
- changes in employment levels;
- changes in industry; and
- other general business changes.

Earnings comprise weekly ordinary time earnings and weekly overtime earnings.

Weekly ordinary time earnings refers to one week's earnings of employees for the reference period attributable to award, standard or agreed hours of work. It is calculated before taxation and any other deductions (e.g. superannuation, board and lodging) have been made. Included in ordinary time earnings are award, workplace and enterprise bargaining payments, and other agreed base rates of pay, over award and over agreed payments, penalty payments, shift and other allowances; commissions and retainers; bonuses and similar payments related to the reference period; payments under incentive or piecework; payments under profit sharing schemes normally paid each pay period; payment for leave taken during the reference period; all workers' compensation payments made through the payroll; and salary payments made to directors. Excluded are overtime payments, retrospective pay, pay in advance, leave loadings, severance, termination and redundancy payments, and other payments not related to the reference period.

Weekly overtime earnings refers to payment for hours in excess of award, standard or agreed hours of work.

6.2. Employers' contribution to private health and pension scheme

In Australia very few employers make any contributions towards health schemes for their employees, especially where the employee is at a wage level comparable to that of an average production worker.

From a survey of employment benefits conducted by the Australian Bureau of Statistics, the findings of which were published in 2001 as *Superannuation, Australia 2000* (ABS Catalogue No. 6360.0), it was estimated that 98 per cent of all employed persons with leave entitlements were covered by a superannuation scheme.

2013 parameter values

Average earnings/yr	Ave_earn	77 530	Secretariat estimate
Dependant Spouse Tax Offset	spouse_cr	0	
income limit	sp_lim	282	
withdrawal rate	sp_redn	0.25	
income limit (primary earner)	sp_lim_p	150 000	
Low Income Tax Offset	low_inc_cr	445	
	low_inc_lim	37 000	
	low_inc_redn	0.015	
Tax schedule	tax_sch	0	18 200
		0.19	37 000
		0.325	80 000
		0.37	180 000
		0.45	
Medicare levy	medic_rate	0.015	
exemption limits	sing_lim	20 542	
married	m_lim	33 693	
sing parent receiving PPS	SAPTO_lim	46 000	
+ per child	ch_lim	3 094	
shading-in rate	shade_rate	0.1	
Part A FTB max	FTB_A_max	5 150.15	
Part A FTB basic	FTB_A_base	2 142.55	
part A income limit 1	FTB_A_lim1	4 7815	
part A income limit 2	FTB_A_lim2	9 4316	
reduction rate 1	FTB_A_taper1	0.2	
reduction rate 2	FTB_A_taper2	0.3	
additional limit2 per extra child	FTB_A_child	3 796	
Large family supplement	FTB_A_large	306.6	
Part A FTB Clean Energy Advance (CEA) max	FTB_A_CEA_max	87.55	
Part A FTB CEA basic	FTB_A_CEA_basic	36.42	
Part B FTB	FTB_B	2 978.4	
part B partner income limit	FTB_B_lim	5 037	
reduction rate	FTB_B_taper	0.2	
income limit (primary earner)	FTB_B_lim_p	150 000	
Part B FTB CEA no child < 5 years old	FTB_B_CEA_5	50.63	
Single Income Family Supplement max rate	SIFS_max	300	
Single Income Family Supplement phase-in threshold	SIFS_in_lim_pr	68 000	
Single Income Family Supplement taper in Rate – primary earner	SIFS_in_taper_pr	0.025	
Single Income Family Supplement phase-out threshold (primary earner)	SIFS_out_lim_pr	120 000	
Single Income Family Supplement taper out rate (primary earner)	SIFS_out_taper_pr	0.01	
Single Income Family Supplement phase out threshold (secondary earner)	SIFS_out_lim_sec	16 000	
Single income family supplement phase out taper – secondary earner	SIFS_out_taper_sec	0.15	
Parenting payment single	PPS	17 303.52	
reduction rate	PPS_taper	0.4	
income limit	PPS_lim	4 591.6	
additional limit per child	PPS_ch_lim	639.6	
Parenting payment single CEA	PPS_CEA	210	
Parenting payment single Clean Energy Supplement (CES)	PPS_CES	81.12	
Pharmaceutical allowance	PA	161.2	
State pay-roll tax rate (NSW)	Pay_roll_rate	0.0545	
Additional parameters			
Newstart allowance single rate	NSAS	12 821.12	
Newstart allowance single CEA	NSAS_CEA	160	
Newstart allowance single CES	NSAS_CES	58.76	
Newstart allowance partnered rate	NSAP	11 573.9	
Newstart allowance partnered CEA	NSAP_CEA	150	
Newstart allowance partnered CES	NSAP_CES	53.3	
reduction rate 1	NSA_taper1	0.5	
reduction rate 2	NSA_taper2	0.6	
income limit 1	NSA_lim1	1 612	
income limit 2	NSA_lim2	6 500	
Senior Australian and Pensioner Tax Offset	SAPTO	2 230	
Senior Australian and Pensioner Tax Offset single threshold	SAPTO_thresh	32 279	
Senior Australian and Pensioner Tax Offset taper rate	SAPTO_taper	0.125	
Schoolkids Bonus	SKB	410	
Telephone allowance	Tele_A	102.04	
Flood levy	tax_flo		
Income Support Bonus – Single	ISB_s	105	
Income Support Bonus – partnered	ISB_p	87.5	

2013 tax equations

The equations for the Australian system in 2013 are mostly repeated for each individual of a married couple. However, the spouse credit is relevant only to the calculation for the principal earner and the calculation of the Medicare levy uses shading-in rules which depend on the levels of earnings of the spouses. The basis of calculation is shown by the Range indicator in the table below.

The functions which are used in the equations (Taper, MIN, Tax, etc.) are described in the technical note about tax equations. Variable names are defined in the table of parameters above, within the equations table, or are the standard variables "married" and "children". A reference to a variable with the affix "_total" indicates the sum of the relevant variable values for the principal and spouse. And the affixes "_princ" and "_spouse" indicate the value for the principal and spouse respectively. Where the calculation for one earner takes into account variables for the other earner, the affix "_oth" is used. Equations for a single person are as shown for the principal, with "_spouse" values taken as 0.

Line in country table and intermediate steps		Variable name	Range	Equation
1.	Earnings	earn		
2.	Allowances	tax_al	B	0
3.	Credits in taxable income:			
	Credits in taxable income of principal	taxbl_cr_princ	P	IF(AND(Children>0,Married=0),Taper(PPS,earn_princ,PPS_lim+PPS_ch_lim*(Children-1),PPS_taper),IF(AND(Children=0,Married=0),taper2(NSAS,earn_princ,NSA_lim1,NSA_lim2,NSA_taper1,NSA_taper2),IF(Married>0,taper3(NSAP,earn_princ,earn_spouse,NSA_lim1,NSA_lim2,NSA_taper1,NSA_taper2,NSAP_CES),,0)))
	Credits in taxable income of spouse	taxbl_cr_spouse	S	IF(AND(Children>0,Married=0),0,IF(AND(Children=0,Married=0),0,IF(Married>0,taper3(NSAP,earn_spouse,earn_princ,NSA_lim1,NSA_lim2,NSA_taper1,NSA_taper2,NSAP_CES),0)))
4.	CG taxable income	tax_inc	B	earn+taxbl_cr
5.	CG tax before credits			
	Medicare Levy	med_levy	B	medicare(tax_inc,sing_lim,m_lim,SAPTO_lim,ch_lim,shade_rate,medic_rate,Married,tax_inc_oth,Children)
	Tax liability	liab	P	Tax(tax_inc, tax_sch)
6.	Tax credits :			
	Spouse credit	spouse_cr	P	Taper(IF(Children>0,0,spouse_cr*Married),earn_spouse+taxbl_cr_spouse,sp_lim,sp_redn)
	Low income credit	low_cr	B	Taper(low_inc_cr,tax_inc,low_inc_lim,low_inc_redn)
	Senior Australian and Pensioner Tax Offset	sap_cr	P	IF(AND(taxbl_cr_princ>0,NOT(AND(Children>0,Married=0))),Tax(taxbl_cr_princ,tax_sch),IF(taxbl_cr_princ>0,Taper(SAPTO,tax_inc,SAPTO_thresh,SAPTO_taper),0)
	Beneficiary tax offset	ben_cr	B	IF(AND(taxbl_cr>0, NOT(AND(Children>0, Married=0))), Tax(taxbl_cr, tax_sch), 0)
	Total	tax_cr	B	spouse_cr+low_cr+sap_cr+ben_cr
7.	CG tax	CG_tax	B	Positive(liab-tax_cr) + med_levy
8.	State and local taxes	local_tax	B	0
9.	Employees' soc security	SSC	B	0
11.	Cash transfers:			
	Family Tax Benefit (Part A)	ftbA	P	IF(PA>0,(FTB_A_max*Children+IF(Children>2,(Children-2)*FTB_A_large,0)),MAX((FTB_A_max*Children+IF(Children>2,(Children-2)*FTB_A_large,0)-Positive((princ_earn+taxbl_cr+spouse_earn+taxbl_cr_spouse)-FTB_A_lim1)*FTB_A_taper1),Positive(FTB_A_base*Children+IF(Children>2,(Children-2)*FTB_A_large,0)-Positive((princ_earn+taxbl_cr+spouse_earn+taxbl_cr_spouse)-(FTB_A_lim2+(Positive(Children-1))*FTB_A_child))*FTB_A_taper2)))

Line in country table and intermediate steps		Variable name	Range	Equation
	Family Tax Benefit (Part B)	ftbB	J	IF(earn_princ<FTB_B_lim_p,IF(Children>0,Taper(FTB_B, earn_spouse+taxbl_cr_spouse,FTB_B_lim,FTB_B_taper),0),0)
	Pharmaceutical Allowance	PA	J	AND(Children>0,Married=0)*IF(Taper(PPS+PA,earn_princ, PPS_lim+PPS_ch_lim*(Children-1),PPS_taper)>0,PA,0)
	Clean Energy Advance	CEA	J	IF(AND(Children>0,Married=0,Taper(PPS+PPS_CES,earn_princ,PPS_lim+PPS_ch_lim*(Children-1),PPS_taper)>0),PPS_CEA,IF(AND(Children=0,Married=0,taper2(NSAS+NSAS_CES,earn_princ,NSA_lim1,NSA_lim2,NSA_taper1,NSA_taper2)>0),NSAS_CEA,IF(AND(Married>0,taper3(NSAP,earn_spouse,earn_princ,NSA_lim1,NSA_lim2,NSA_taper1,NSA_taper2,NSAP_CES)>0),NSAP_CEA)))+IF(AND(taxbl_cr_princ>0,Married>0,taper2(NSAP+NSAP_CES,earn_princ,NSA_lim1,NSA_lim2,NSA_taper1,NSA_taper2)>0),NSAP_CEA,0)+IF(AND(ftbA>0,ftbA>FTB_A_base*Children+IF(Children>2,(Children-2)*FTB_A_large,0)),FTB_A_CEA_max*Children,0)+ IF(AND(ftbA>0,ftbA<=FTB_A_base*Children+IF(Children>2,(Children-2)*FTB_A_large,0)),FTB_A_CEA_basic*Children,0)+IF(ftbB>0,FTB_B_CEA_5,0)
	Clean Energy Supplement	CES	J	IF(AND(Children>0,Married=0,Taper(PPS+PPS_CES,earn_princ,PPS_lim+PPS_ch_lim*(Children-1),PPS_taper)>0),PPS_CES,IF(AND(Children>0,Married=0,Taper(PPS+PPS_CES,earn_princ,PPS_lim+PPS_ch_lim*(Children-1),PPS_taper)=0),0,IF(AND(Children=0,Married=0,taper2(NSAS+NSAS_CES,earn_princ,NSA_lim1,NSA_lim2,NSA_taper1,NSA_taper2)>0),taper2(NSAS+NSAS_CES,earn_princ,NSA_lim1,NSA_lim2,NSA_taper1,NSA_taper2)-taper2(NSAS,earn_princ,NSA_lim1,NSA_lim2,NSA_taper1,NSA_taper2),IF(AND(Married>0,taper3(NSAP,earn_spouse,earn_princ,NSA_lim1,NSA_lim2,NSA_taper1,NSA_taper2,NSAP_CES)>0),taper3(NSAP,earn_spouse,earn_princ,NSA_lim1,NSA_lim2,NSA_taper1,NSA_taper2,NSAP_CES)-taper3(NSAP,earn_spouse,earn_princ,NSA_lim1,NSA_lim2,NSA_taper1,NSA_taper2,NSAP_CES-NSAP_CES)))))+IF(AND(Married>0,taxbl_cr_princ>0,taper2(NSAP+NSAP_CES,earn_princ,NSA_lim1,NSA_lim2,NSA_taper1,NSA_taper2)>0),NSAP_CES,0)
	Schoolkids Bonus	SKB	J	IF(ftbA>0,SKB*Children,0)
	Single Income Family Supplement	SIFS	J	sifs(tax_inc_princ,tax_inc_spouse,ftbA+ftbB,SIFS_max,SIFS_in_lim_pr,SIFS_in_taper_pr,SIFS_out_lim_pr,SIFS_out_taper_pr,SIFS_out_lim_sec,SIFS_out_taper_sec)
		cash_trans	J	ftbA+ftbB+taxbl_cr_princ+PA+taxbl_cr_spouse+Tele_A +CEA=CES+SKB+SIFS
13.	Employer's State pay-roll tax	tax_empr	B	earn*Pay_roll_rate

Key to range of equation B calculated separately for both principal earner and spouse P calculated for principal only (value taken as 0 for spouse calculation) J calculated once only on a joint basis. Key refers to an optimisation of benefits i.e. Parenting payment for principal and Newstart allowance for spouse versus Parenting payment for spouse and Newstart allowance for principal.

Taxing Wages 2014
Changes in sructural labour income tax progressivity
over 2000-12 period in OECD member countries

Austria

This chapter includes data on the income taxes paid by workers, their social security contributions, the family benefits they receive in the form of cash transfers as well as the social security contributions and payroll taxes paid by their employers. Results reported include the marginal and average tax burden for eight different family types.

Methodological information is available for personal income tax systems, compulsory social security contributions to schemes operated within the government sector, universal cash transfers as well as recent changes in the tax/ benefit system. The methodology also includes the parameter values and tax equations underlying the data.

Austria 2013

The tax/benefit position of single persons

	Wage level (per cent of average wage)		67	100	167	67
	Number of children		none	none	none	2
1.	**Gross wage earnings**		27795	41693	69488	27795
2.	**Standard tax allowances**					
	Basic allowance		60	60	60	60
	Married or head of family					
	Dependent children		0	0	0	440
	Deduction for social security contributions and income taxes		5019	7529	11224	5019
	Work-related expenses		132	132	132	132
	Other		620	620	620	620
		Total	5831	8341	12036	6271
3.	**Tax credits or cash transfers included in taxable income**		0	0	0	0
4.	**Central government taxable income (1 - 2 + 3)**		21964	33352	57452	21524
5.	**Central government income tax liability (exclusive of tax credits)**		3188	7115	16239	3028
6.	**Tax credits**					
	Basic credit		0	0	0	0
	Married or head of family		0	0	0	669
	Children					
	Other		345	345	345	345
		Total	345	345	345	1014
7.	**Central government income tax finally paid (5 - 6)**		2843	6770	15894	2014
8.	**State and local taxes**		0	0	0	0
9.	**Employees' compulsory social security contributions**					
	Gross earnings		5019	7529	11224	5019
	Taxable income					
		Total	5019	7529	11224	5019
10.	**Total payments to general government (7 + 8 + 9)**		7862	14298	27118	7033
11.	**Cash transfers from general government**					
	For head of family					
	For two children		0	0	0	4897
		Total	0	0	0	4897
12.	**Take-home pay (1-10+11)**		19933	27394	42370	25659
13.	**Employer's wage dependent contributions and taxes**					
	Employer's compulsory social security contributions		6012	9018	13444	6012
	payroll taxes		2085	3127	5212	2085
		Total	8096	12145	18656	8096
14.	**Average rates**					
	Income tax		10.2%	16.2%	22.9%	7.2%
	Employees' social security contributions		18.1%	18.1%	16.2%	18.1%
	Total payments less cash transfers		28.3%	34.3%	39.0%	7.7%
	Total tax wedge including employer's social security contributions		44.5%	49.1%	51.9%	28.5%
15.	**Marginal rates**					
	Total payments less cash transfers: Principal earner		44.4%	49.1%	37.9%	44.4%
	Total payments less cash transfers: Spouse		n.a.	n.a.	n.a.	n.a.
	Total tax wedge: Principal earner		56.9%	60.6%	42.2%	56.9%
	Total tax wedge: Spouse		n.a.	n.a.	n.a.	n.a.

Austria 2013

The tax/benefit position of married couples

			100-0	100-33	100-67	100-33
		Wage level (per cent of average wage)	100-0	100-33	100-67	100-33
		Number of children	2	2	2	none
1.	**Gross wage earnings**		41693	55590	69488	55590
2.	**Standard tax allowances**					
	Basic allowance		60	120	120	120
	Married or head of family					
	Dependent children		440	440	528	0
	Deduction for social security contributions and income taxes		7529	9621	12548	9621
	Work-related expenses		132	264	264	264
	Other		620	1240	1240	1240
		Total	8781	11685	14700	11245
3.	**Tax credits or cash transfers included in taxable income**		0	0	0	0
4.	**Central government taxable income (1 - 2 + 3)**		32912	43905	54788	44345
5.	**Central government income tax liability (exclusive of tax credits)**		6925	6925	10093	7115
6.	**Tax credits**					
	Basic credit		0	0	0	0
	Married or head of family		669	0	0	0
	Children					
	Other		345	690	690	690
		Total	1014	690	690	690
7.	**Central government income tax finally paid (5 - 6)**		5911	6470	9403	6660
8.	**State and local taxes**		0	0	0	0
9.	**Employees' compulsory social security contributions**					
	Gross earnings		7529	9621	12548	9621
	Taxable income					
		Total	7529	9621	12548	9621
10.	**Total payments to general government (7 + 8 + 9)**		13439	16091	21950	16281
11.	**Cash transfers from general government**					
	For head of family					
	For two children		4897	4897	4897	0
		Total	4897	4897	4897	0
12.	**Take-home pay (1-10+11)**		33150	44396	52435	39309
13.	**Employer's wage dependent contributions and taxes**					
	Employer's compulsory social security contributions		9018	12023	15029	12023
	Payroll taxes		3127	4169	5212	4169
		Total	12145	16193	20241	16193
14.	**Average rates**					
	Income tax		14.2%	11.6%	13.5%	12.0%
	Employees' social security contributions		18.1%	17.3%	18.1%	17.3%
	Total payments less cash transfers		20.5%	20.1%	24.5%	29.3%
	Total tax wedge including employer's social security contributions		38.4%	38.2%	41.6%	45.2%
15.	**Marginal rates**					
	Total payments less cash transfers: Principal earner		49.1%	49.1%	49.1%	49.1%
	Total payments less cash transfers: Spouse		19.1%	15.1%	44.4%	15.1%
	Total tax wedge: Principal earner		60.6%	60.6%	60.6%	60.6%
	Total tax wedge: Spouse		37.3%	34.2%	56.9%	34.2%

The Austrian currency is the euro (EUR). In 2013, EUR 0.75 was equal to USD 1. In that year, the average worker in Austria earned EUR 41 693 (Secretariat estimate).

1. Personal income tax

1.1. Central government income tax

1.1.1. Tax unit

Each person is taxed separately.

1.1.2. Tax allowances

1.1.2.1. Standard tax reliefs

- Work related expenses: a minimum allowance of EUR 132 is available to all employees.
- Minimum allowance for special expenses of EUR 60.
- Social security contributions and connected contributions (see Section 2).
- Children allowance of EUR 220 for one or EUR 132 for both parents per child. The parents have the choice between these opportunities.

1.1.2.2. Non-standard tax reliefs

- Mainly work-related expenses ("Werbungskosten").
- Traffic relief according to the distance between home/address and working place.

The following allowances are deductible from income (EUR per year):

	Public transport	
	Available	Not available
more than 2 km	0	372
more than 20 km	696	1 476
more than 40 km	1 356	2 568
more than 60 km	2 016	3 672

- Special expenses allowance ("Sonderausgaben"): some personal expenses (for example, life insurance premiums, and expenses for the purchase of residence including repayments of housing loans) are partly deductible from income. The allowance is limited to EUR 2 920 per taxpayer or EUR 5 840 for sole earners or parents. A quarter of "Sonderausgaben" can be deducted up to a taxable income of EUR 36 400, whereas between EUR 36 400 and EUR 60 000 the deductible amount is (linearly) reduced to EUR 60. Unless higher special expenses can be proved, a standard deduction for "Sonderausgaben" of EUR 60 is granted (see Section 1.1.2.1). Grants to non-profit charitable organisations up to 10 per cent of taxable income are deductible. Additionally, contributions to the church are deductible up to an amount of EUR 400.

- Tax-free supplements exist for dirty, hard, dangerous, night, weekend and holiday work and overtime. The supplement for 10 hours of overtime up to EUR 86 per month is tax free, the other supplements are tax free up to EUR 360 (EUR 540 for night workers) per month.

1.1.3. *Rate schedule*

The new tax schedule has a zero-zone up to EUR 11 000 and shows tax formulas for three tax brackets. The effective marginal tax rates resulting from these formulas are:

Income (EUR) up to	Marginal rate %
11 000	0
25 000	36.5
60 000	43.21429
Above	50

There is a special taxation other than the normal tax schedule for Christmas and leave bonus to the extent that their sum does not exceed two average monthly payments (1/6 of current income). If these bonuses before deduction of SSC are below EUR 2 100 p.a., no tax is calculated. Otherwise the tax amount is calculated according to the following formula:

Income from Christmas and leave bonus (EUR) up to	Marginal rate %
620	0
25 000	6
50 000	27
83 333	37.5
Above	50

In case of bonuses up to EUR 25 000 the tax amount is 30% of the bonus (net of SSC) exceeding EUR 2 000 instead of the formula above, if this results to a lower tax amount. So the break-even is at EUR 2 345 a month.

1.1.4. *Tax credits*

Tax credits are available as follows:

- Employee's tax credit of EUR 54. In the overall tax calculation, negative tax is possible where the amount paid to the taxpayer would equal the gross tax minus tax credits but is limited to 10 per cent of social security contributions to a maximum of EUR 110. For employees with a traffic allowance (see 1.12.2) the maximum is EUR 400 and the percentage increases to 18 per cent.
- Traffic (commuting) tax credit EUR 291.
- Additional traffic tax credit in case of entitlement to traffic relief according to the distance between home/address and working place (see 1.12.2). In this case employees are entitled to an additional traffic tax credit of EUR 2 per km distance from home to working place.
- Sole earner's and sole parent's tax credit for families with children. The sole earner's credit is not given when a spouse's income exceeds EUR 6 000. This tax credit is EUR 494

for one child and increases by EUR 175 for the second and by EUR 220 for the third and every additional child. This tax credit is non-wastable and can be paid out as a negative income tax (in addition to the negative tax permitted in respect of the Employee's tax credit).

- Children's tax credit EUR 700.8 (58.40 per month) per child. As this tax credit is paid together with children allowances and not connected with income tax assessment, it is treated as a transfer in this Report (similar treatment as in *Revenue Statistics*).
- Tax credit for retired persons. The tax credit amounts to EUR 764 for sole earners with income up to EUR 19 930 and if the spouse's income does not exceed EUR 2 200. Otherwise the tax credit is EUR 400. The tax credit is linearly reduced to 0 between EUR 17 000 (EUR 19 930 for sole earners) and EUR 25 000 of income.

1.2. State and local income taxes

None.

2. Compulsory social security contributions to schemes operated within the government sector

2.1. Employee and employer social security contributions

	Ceilings (EUR)		Rates (%)	
	Regular wage per month	Christmas and leave bonus	Employee[2]	Employer[3]
Health insurance	4 440	8 880	3.95	3.70
Unemployment insurance	4 440	8 880	[4]	3.00
Pension insurance	4 440	8 880	10.25	12.55
Accident insurance	4 440	8 880	–	1.40
Contribution to the labour chamber	4 440	[1]	0.50	–
Contribution for the promotion of residential building	4 440	[1]	0.50	0.50
Addition to secure wage payments in the case of bankruptcy	4 440	8 880	–	0.55

1. No contributions on Christmas and leave bonus. In *Revenue Statistics*, the contribution to the labour chamber is accounted under Taxes on Income of Individuals (1110) the total of the contribution for the promotion of residential buildings is included in Taxes on payroll (3000).
2. There is a threshold for employee contributions of EUR 386.8 per month.
3. A new program has been introduced as of 1 January, 2004 for severance payments. Employers are required to pay 1.53 per cent of gross wages to the Social Health Security Fund ("Krankenkassen") for those whose employment starts after 1 January, 2003 or where the employer and employee opt to participate in the new program. This contribution is seen as a non-tax compulsory wage-related payment.
4. Employees' unemployment insurance rate is reduced for low earnings. In 2013, it is zero for monthly earnings up to EUR 1 219, 1% up to EUR 1 330, 2% up to EUR 1 497and 3% above.

2.2. Payroll taxes

There are two payroll taxes which are levied on employers for all private sector employees with a monthly gross wage total of more than EUR 1 095: the contribution to the Family Burden Equalisation Fund (4.5 per cent) and the Community Tax (3 per cent). The wage-dependant part of the contribution to the Entrepreneurs' Chamber (listed under heading 1 000, taxes on profits, in the *Revenue Statistics*) which is levied, together with the contributions to the Family Burden Equalisation Fund, at different rates depending upon the Länder Chamber (the average rate is approximately 0.4 per cent) is not taken into account. The contribution for the promotion of residential buildings (listed under heading 3000, taxes on payroll, in *Revenue Statistics*) is included in the social security contributions shown above as it is levied by the Health Insurance Companies on monthly income (current) along with the other social security contribution amounts.

3. Universal cash transfers

3.1. *Amount for marriage*

No recurrent payments.

3.2. *Amount for children*

A family allowance is granted for each child. The monthly payment is EUR 105.40 for the first child, EUR 118.20 for the second, EUR 140.40 for the third and EUR 155.40 for each subsequent child. It is increased by EUR 7.30 for children above 3 years, EUR 25.50 for children above 10 years of age and by EUR 47.30 for students (above 19). Parents of children under the age of 3 years are entitled to a childcare transfer, introduced in 2002. Beginning 2010, the flexibility of the childcare transfer was increased significantly. The entitled parent can choose between following alternatives: EUR 14.53 per day until the 36th month of birth, EUR 20.80 (24 months), EUR 26.60 (18 months) or EUR 33.00 (14 months). Additionally instead of the fix amounts the entitled person can opt for 80% of the last net-earning, limited to EUR 2 000 a month (14 months). The children's tax credit (EUR 50.90 monthly, see § 1.14) is paid out together with the family allowance and therefore treated as a transfer.

There is a supplement to the family allowance of EUR 20.00 per month for the third and every additional child, if the family taxable income (i.e. the sum of the tax base for the progressive income tax schedule) of the preceding year did not exceed EUR 55 000. This supplement is paid out on application after an assessment of the very year.

An additional family allowance ("13th allowance") of EUR 100 is given for children in the age between 6 and 16 every September.

4. Main changes in tax/benefit systems since 1994

In 1994, a major tax reform took effect. Most measures concerned the taxation of firms. For employees the following points are important. The general tax credit was increased by ATS 3 840, i.e. ATS 320 per month. For employees with low income a negative income tax option was introduced (the negative income tax is limited to the wage earners tax credit, but it cannot exceed 10 per cent of social security contributions).

In 1995, family allowances were reduced by ATS 100 per month (ATS 1 200 per year).

In 1996, a consolidation package was introduced, some measures of which took effect already in 1996. The deductibility of special expenses was reduced (half to quarter) and abolished for incomes exceeding ATS 700 000. Tax free overtime supplements were limited to ATS 590 per month. The general tax credit was linearly reduced to zero for income between ATS 200 000 and ATS 500 000 and there was a change in the deductibility of social security contributions on non-current wages and salaries.

The family package of 1998 brought an increase of ATS 1 500 in the family allowances and the children's tax credits each in 1999. A supplement of ATS 2 400 in 1999 and ATS 4 800 in 2000 for the 3rd etc. child for families earning less than ATS 504 000 was introduced. The sole earner's or sole parent's tax credit negative tax limit was abolished. For 2000 and the following years, there was an additional increase in the sum of family allowances and children's tax credits of ATS 3 000, but the differentiation according to the number of children was transferred to the allowances, i.e. from 2000 onwards there is a unique annual tax credit of ATS 8 400 per child.

The tax reform of 1999, effective from the beginning of 2000, brought a reduction in the tax schedule and an increase of the general tax credit leading to a (linearly increasing) tax reduction between ATS 4 000 and 7 000 p.a. The maximum reduction is reached at a gross income near the ceiling for social security contributions. The reform also included a number of other measures which concerned mainly enterprise taxation.

The budget consolidation measures for 2001 included an abolition of the general tax credit for incomes exceeding ATS 487 400, the halving of the employee's tax credit to ATS 750 and a phasing-out of the pensioner's tax credit for income between ATS 230 000 and 300 000. The adaptation of the tax laws to the euro did not bring any substantive changes. In 2004 (effective), the family allowances for children above three years of age were increased by EUR 7.30 per month.

In 2004, the first step of a comprehensive tax reform came into force. The general tax credit was increased from EUR 887 to EUR 1 264 and the phasing-out rules were considerably simplified and made uniform for all groups of taxpayers.

The tax reform in 2005 brought a new income tax schedule. Apart from the top rate of 50 per cent for income exceeding EUR 51 000, it shows the average rates for two amounts of income. The tax amounts for incomes between these amounts have to be calculated by linear interpolation. The formulas that have to be applied are shown in the tax law. The tax reform included some measures which were made retrospective for 2004. These measures are the increase of the sole earner and the single parent tax credit depending on the number of children (together with a higher earnings limit for the spouse of a single earner) and an increase of the traffic reliefs by about 15 per cent. The maximum deductible amount for church contributions was increased as well. In 2006, the traffic reliefs were again increased by about 10 per cent.

In 2007, the traffic allowances were increased by 10 per cent (effective from 1 July), the maximum negative tax for employees with traffic allowances was increased from EUR 110 to EUR 240 (for 2008 and 2009). For 2008, the family allowances for the third and subsequent children were increased. In 2008, the unemployment insurance contributions of low-earning employees were reduced (effective from 1 July). In 2008 up to monthly earnings of EUR 1 100 the rate was zero, for earnings below EUR 1 200 the contribution was 1 per cent, below EUR 1 350 2 per cent and above the current rate of 3 per cent. These income limits are increased according to the raise of the ceiling levels of social security contributions every year.

In September 2008, the parliament decided some measures to compensate for the strong increase of food and energy prices: inter alia, the tax exemption of overtime supplements was increased and a 13th payment of children allowances introduced.

The tax reform 2009 (effective from 1 January) brought an increase of the zero bracket (from EUR 10 000 to EUR 11 000), a reduction of the income tax rates (except the top rate), an upward shift of the top rate bracket (from EUR 51 000 to EUR 60 000) and several measures for families with children: children allowance (EUR 220 or EUR 132 each parent p.a.), deductibility of cost for child care (up to EUR 2 300 p.a. per child), tax-free payments (up to EUR 500 p.a.) from employers to their employees for child care and an increase of the children tax credit.

For the period 2013 to 2016 a progressive rate schedule is applied to Christmas and leave bonus instead of a flat rate regime of 6% (see 1.13).

5. Memorandum items

5.1. Calculation of earnings data

- Sector used: All private employees except apprentices employed full-time for the whole year
- Geographical coverage: Whole country
- Sex: Male and Female
- Earnings base:
  - Items excluded: – Unemployment compensation
    - – Sickness compensation
  - Items included: – Vacation payments
    - – Overtime payments
    - – Recurring cash payments
    - – Fringe benefits (taxable value)
- Basic method of calculation used: Average annual earnings
- Income tax year ends: 31 December

  Period to which the earnings calculation refers to: one year.

2013 parameter values

Average earnings/yr	Ave_earn	41 693	Secretariat estimate
Non current income as %	non_cur_pc	14.286%	
Tax free inc on non-current	Bonus	620	
Ceiling for taxing non-current income	nonc_ceil	2 000	
Tax schedule for nci exc. 25000	nci_sch	0	25 000
		0.21	50 000
		0.2975	83 333
		0.44	
Work related	work_rel	132	
Allowance f."Special expenses"	Basic_al	60	
Children allowance for 2 earning parents	Child_al_2	132	
Children allowance for sole earner/parent	Child_al_1	220	
Tax free inc.	tax_free	0%	
Basic tax credit	basic_cr		
Employee's tax credit	wage_cr	54	
Max. neg. employee's tax credit	neg_wage_cr	110	
Traffic (commuting) tax credit	traffic_cr	291	
Sole earner's (parent's) tax credit	sole_cr	0	
Children suppl.to SETC: 1st child	dsole1_cr	494	
2nd child	dsole2_cr	175	
3rd+ child	dsole3_cr	220	
Spouse income not more than	sole_lim0	0	
Spouse with children	sole_lim1	6 000	
Tax on non-current income	non_cur_rate	6%	
Altern.tax on non-current income	alt_nonc_rate	30%	
Income tax schedule	Tax_sch	0	11 000
		0.365	25 000
		0.43214	60 000
		0.5	
Ceiling f. soc. security contributions	SSC_ceil	4 440	
lower limit	SSC_low	386.80	
Employees' contr. rates	health_rate	3.95%	
	unemp_rate	0%	1 219
		1%	1 330
		2%	1 497
		3%	
	Pension_rate	10.25%	
Sum without unempl. and others	empl_14	14.20%	
	others_rate	1%	
Employers' contr.rates	health_empr	3.70%	
	unemp_empr	3%	
	Pension_empr	12.55%	
	accident_empr	1.40%	
	payinsur_empr	0.55%	
Sum without others	empr_14	21.20%	
	others_empr	0.50%	
Payroll taxes	payroll_rate	7.50%	
Child benefit: 1st child	CB_1	1 264.8	
2nd child	CB_2	1 418.4	
3rd child	CB_3	1 684.8	
4th+ child	CB_4	1 864.8	
suppl. > 3years	CB03sppl	87.6	
suppl. > 10years	CB10sppl	306.0	
suppl > 19years	CB19sppl	567.6	
5 years < suppl < 17years	CB5to17	100.0	
Child tax credit	child_cr_1	700.8	

2013 tax equations

The equations for the Austrian system are, in principle, on an individual basis. The only variable which is dependent on the marital status is the head of family (sole earner) tax credit which is also given to single people with children. For the Christmas and leave bonus (both amounting to one monthly wage or salary) there are special rules for the calculation of social security contributions (separate ceilings and slightly lower rate) and wage tax (reduced flat rate). The income tax schedule and the tax credits are applied only for "current pays". The children tax credit is in principle given to the mother (as a negative tax together with "family allowances" = transfer for children). The sole earner and the employee tax credit are connected with negative income tax rules. Therefore, the tax finally paid may be different from tax liability minus tax credits.

Bn	Variable	Code for docn equations	Excel-Function
3	earnings (%AW)	per cent	0, 1/3, 2/3, 1 or 5/3 in Taxing Wages output tables (but model can be applied to all earnings levels)
4	number of children	child	0 or 2 in Taxing Wages output tables
5	Gross earnings	earn	=Ave_earn*per cent
6	Current income	cearn	=(1-non_cur_pc)*earn
7	Basic allowance	allow	=(earn>14*SSC_low)*Basic_al
8	SSC on curr.inc.	SSCc	=(empl_14+unemp(earn,unemp_rate)+others_rate)* MIN(12*SSC_ceil;cearn)*(cearn>12*SSC_low)
9	Work related expenses	work_rel	=work_rel
10	Tax-free income	taxfrinc	=tax_free*earn
11	Child allowance	Child_al_princ	IF(cearn_spouse-allow_spouse-SSCc_spouse-work_rel_spouse-taxfrinc_spouse-11945<0,Child_al_1, Child_al_2)*child
		Child_al_spouse	IF(Child_al_princ=child*Child_al_2, Child_al_2, 0)*Child
12	Tax base for schedule	ctbase	=(earn>14*SSC_low)*(cearn-allow-SSCc-work_rel-taxfrinc-child_al*child)
13	Gross tax on current income	gtaxcur	=Tax(ctbase;tax_sch)
14	Basic tax credit	btaxcr	=0
15	Married or head of family	headcr	=(earn_sp<IF(child>0;sole_lim1;sole_lim0))*(sole_cr+(child>0)*dsole1_cr+(child>1)*dsole2_cr+(child>2)*(child-2)*dsole3_cr
16	Other	othcr	=min(wage_cr;10%*SSC)+traffic_cr
17	Interm. tax on current income	itcur	=gtaxcur-btaxcr-headcr-othcr
18	Net tax on current income	ntaxcur	=IF(itcur>-headcr; itcur;MAX(-0,1*SSC-(child>0)*headcr; -neg_wage_cr-(child>0)*headcr))
19	Non current income	ncearn	=earn-cearn
20	SSC on non-curr. inc.	SSCnc	=(health_rate+unemp(earn,unemp_rate)+pension_rate)* MIN(2*SSC_ceil;ncearn)*(ncearn>2*SSC_low)
21	Non current income-SSC	ncearn_adj1	=ncearn-SSCnc
22	of which tax free	taxfree	=MIN(bonus;ncearn_adj)
23	Non-curr. tax base	ncearn_adj2	=ncearn_adj-taxfree
24	Tax schedule for nci exc. 25000	nci_sch	=Positive(MINA(ncearn_adj1-nonc_ceil)*alt_nonc_rate;ncearn_adj2*non_cur_rate))+MAX(0;Tax(ncearn_adj1;nci_sch))
25	Taxable income	taxinc	=ctbase+ncearn_adj2
26	Tax liability excl. tax credits	inctax_ex	=gtaxcur+taxnc
27	Income tax finally paid	inctax	=ntaxcur+taxnc
28	Employee's SSC	SSC	=SSCc+SSCnc
29	Employer's SSC	SSCf	=((empr_14+others_empr)*MIN(12*SSC_ceil;cearn)+empr_14*MIN(12*SSC_ceil;ncearn))
30	Pay-roll taxes	payroll	=payroll_rate*earn
31	Cash transfers	cash	=IF(child=0;0;IF(child=2;CB_1+CB_2+child*CB10sppl+child*(child_cr_1+CB5to17)))
32	Take-home pay		=earn-inctax-SSC+cash
33	Wage cost		=earn+SSCf+payroll

unemp is a Visual Basic Function which chooses lower unemployment SSC rates for low earnings

Key to range of equation B calculated separately for both principal earner and spouse P calculated for principal only (value taken as 0 for spouse calculation) J calculated once only on a joint basis.

Taxing Wages 2014
Changes in sructural labour income tax progressivity
over 2000-12 period in OECD member countries

Belgium

This chapter includes data on the income taxes paid by workers, their social security contributions, the family benefits they receive in the form of cash transfers as well as the social security contributions and payroll taxes paid by their employers. Results reported include the marginal and average tax burden for eight different family types.

Methodological information is available for personal income tax systems, compulsory social security contributions to schemes operated within the government sector, universal cash transfers as well as recent changes in the tax/benefit system. The methodology also includes the parameter values and tax equations underlying the data.

Belgium 2013

The tax/benefit position of single persons

	Wage level (per cent of average wage)	67	100	167	67
	Number of children	none	none	none	2
1.	**Gross wage earnings**	31207	46810	78017	31207
2.	**Standard tax allowances**				
	Basic allowance				
	Married or head of family				
	Dependent children				
	Deduction for social security contributions and income taxes	4079	6118	10197	4079
	Work-related expenses	2805	3212	3900	2805
	Other				
	Total	6884	9330	14097	6884
3.	**Tax credits or cash transfers included in taxable income**	0	0	0	0
4.	**Central government taxable income (1 - 2 + 3)**	24323	37481	63921	24323
5.	**Central government income tax liability (exclusive of tax credits)**	8276	14204	27424	8276
6.	**Tax credits**				
	Basic credit	0	0	0	0
	Married or head of family	1818	1748	1748	2199
	Children	0	0	0	1182
	Other				
	Total	1818	1748	1748	3381
7.	**Central government income tax finally paid (5-6)**	6458	12456	25676	4895
8.	**State and local taxes**	478	922	1900	362
9.	**Employees' compulsory social security contributions**				
	Gross earnings	4079	6118	10197	4079
	Taxable income	265	436	731	265
	Total	4344	6555	10928	4344
10.	**Total payments to general government (7 + 8 + 9)**	11280	19933	38505	9601
11.	**Cash transfers from general government**				
	For head of family				
	For two children	0	0	0	3794
	Total	0	0	0	3794
12.	**Take-home pay (1-10+11)**	19927	26878	39513	25399
13.	**Employer's compulsory social security contributions**	8750	14004	23029	8750
14.	**Average rates**				
	Income tax	22.2%	28.6%	35.3%	16.8%
	Employees' social security contributions	13.9%	14.0%	14.0%	13.9%
	Total payments less cash transfers	36.1%	42.6%	49.4%	18.6%
	Total tax wedge including employer's social security contributions	50.1%	55.8%	60.9%	36.4%
15.	**Marginal rates**				
	Total payments less cash transfers: Principal earner	54.9%	59.4%	59.8%	54.9%
	Total payments less cash transfers: Spouse	n.a.	n.a.	n.a.	n.a.
	Total tax wedge: Principal earner	66.3%	69.7%	68.5%	66.3%
	Total tax wedge: Spouse	n.a.	n.a.	n.a.	n.a.

Belgium 2013

The tax/benefit position of married couples

		100-0	100-33	100-67	100-33
	Wage level (per cent of average wage)	100-0	100-33	100-67	100-33
	Number of children	2	2	2	none
1.	**Gross wage earnings**	46810	62414	78017	62414
2.	**Standard tax allowances**				
	Basic allowance				
	Married or head of family				
	Dependent children				
	Deduction for social security contributions and income taxes	6118	6118	10197	6118
	Work-related expenses	3212	5609	6017	5609
	Other				
	Total	9330	11728	16213	11728
3.	**Tax credits or cash transfers included in taxable income**	0	0	0	0
4.	**Central government taxable income (1 - 2 + 3)**	37481	50686	61804	50686
5.	**Central government income tax liability (exclusive of tax credits)**	12253	17835	22479	17835
6.	**Tax credits**				
	Basic credit	0	188	0	188
	Married or head of family	3565	3565	3565	3565
	Children	1066	1066	1066	0
	Other				
	Total	4631	4819	4631	3753
7.	**Central government income tax finally paid (5-6)**	7622	13016	17848	14082
8.	**State and local taxes**	564	977	1321	1056
9.	**Employees' compulsory social security contributions**				
	Gross earnings	6118	6118	10197	6118
	Taxable income	436	608	731	608
	Total	6555	6726	10928	6726
10.	**Total payments to general government (7 + 8 + 9)**	14741	20719	30097	21864
11.	**Cash transfers from general government**				
	For head of family				
	For two children	3794	3794	3794	0
	Total	3794	3794	3794	0
12.	**Take-home pay (1-10+11)**	35863	45489	51714	40550
13.	**Employer's compulsory social security contributions**	14004	16362	22753	16362
14.	**Average rates**				
	Income tax	17.5%	22.4%	24.6%	24.3%
	Employees' social security contributions	14.0%	10.8%	14.0%	10.8%
	Total payments less cash transfers	23.4%	27.1%	33.7%	35.0%
	Total tax wedge including employer's social security contributions	41.0%	42.3%	48.7%	48.5%
15.	**Marginal rates**				
	Total payments less cash transfers: Principal earner	54.9%	59.4%	58.4%	59.4%
	Total payments less cash transfers: Spouse	38.3%	42.0%	53.8%	42.0%
	Total tax wedge: Principal earner	66.3%	69.7%	68.8%	69.7%
	Total tax wedge: Spouse	46.4%	61.3%	65.5%	61.3%

The national currency is the euro. In 2013, EUR 0.75 was equal to USD 1. The Secretariat has estimated that in that same year the average worker earned EUR 46 810 (Secretariat estimate).

1. Personal income tax systems

1.1. *Federal government income tax*

1.1.1. *Tax unit*

Spouses are taxed separately. As from 2004, the principle of separate taxation applies to all categories of income. A non-earning spouse is taxed separately on a notional share of income that can be transferred to him or her (see "non-earning spouse allowance", below). Married couples nonetheless file joint income tax returns.

1.1.2. *Tax allowances*

1.1.2.1. Deduction of social security contributions

Unless stated otherwise, social insurance contributions are deductible from gross income.

1.1.2.2. Work-related expenses

Salaried employees and self-employed professionals are entitled to a standard deduction for work-related expenses. This deduction may under no circumstances exceed EUR 3 900 per spouse and is computed as follows:

Gross earnings less social insurance contributions (EUR)	Rate (%)
Below 5 650	28.7
Between 5 650 and 11 220	10
Between 11 220 and 18 670	5
Above 18 670	3

Paid company directors are also entitled to a standard deduction for work-related expenses; this is equal to 3% of gross income (less social insurance contributions) and may not exceed EUR 2 340 per spouse.

An additional allowance may be granted to wage-earners if their workplace is more than a certain distance from their home.

Actual expenses incurred in order to acquire or retain earned income are deductible if they exceed the standard deduction. The deductibility of certain categories of work-related expenses (cars, clothing, restaurant meals and business gifts) is limited, however. Taxpayers who report actual expenses may deduct EUR 0.15 per kilometre, up to 100 km per single journey, for travel between their home and their workplace by means other than private car.

1.1.2.3. Non-earning spouse allowance (*quotient conjugal*)

A notional amount of income can be transferred between spouses if one of them earns no more than 30 per cent of the couple's combined earned income. In this case, the amount transferred is limited to 30 per cent of aggregate net earned income, less the individual income of the spouse to whom the notional share is transferred. This allowance is limited to EUR 10 090.

1.1.2.4. Exempt income

The base amount is:

Taxable income (S)	Fixed amount	Variable amount
0-25 990	7 270	0
25 990-26 270	6 990	26 270-S
26 270 and up	6 990	0

These amounts vary with regards to the family situation. Additional exemptions for dependent children (a handicapped child counts as two children):

- 1 child 1 490
- 2 children 3 820
- 3 children 8 570
- 4 children 13 860
- > 4 children 5 290 per additional child

Dependent child exemptions in excess of available income give rise to a reimbursable tax credit. This reimbursable tax credit is calculated at the marginal rate for the spouse with the highest income and capped at EUR 430 per dependent child.

Additional special exemptions are also granted for certain household members (in euro):

- Other dependants 1 490
- Handicapped spouse 1 490
- Other handicapped dependants 1 490
- Widow(er) with dependent child(ren) 1 490
- Single father or mother 1 490

These additional exemptions are applied first to the taxable income of the spouse having the most income, with any remainder then being applied to the income of the other spouse.

The basic exemption plus any additional exemptions for dependants and single parents is applied against each bracket from the bottom up; in other words, the lowest brackets are depleted first.

1.1.2.5. Schedule

Taxable income (EUR)	Marginal rate (%)
0-8 590	25
8 590-12 220	30
12 220-20 370	40
20 370-37 330	45
37 330 and above	50

The basic exemption plus any additional exemptions is applied from the bottom up.

1.2. *Local government taxes*

Local taxes are levied as a percentage of federal tax liability before deduction of reimbursable tax credits (for low earned income other than wage income, for low-income workers, for children, for service vouchers and for energy-saving expenses). The rate of this surtax is set by each municipality, and there is no upper limit. The average rate is deemed to be 7.4%.

1.3. *Tax credits*

a) Refundable tax credit for low-income from professional activities

A refundable tax credit is granted for low earned income other than wage income. For wages, the credit is replaced by an "employment bonus" that reduces individual social security contributions (see below). However, civil servants that do not qualify for the "employment bonus", because they are not subject to social security contributions regulations that apply to the private sector, may qualify for the refundable tax credit.

The tax credit is based on the net amount of earned income other than wage income. The net amount is computed after deduction of work-related expenses.

The base for the credit is income before any transfer of notional income between spouses.

Tax credits are granted by spouse according to the following schedule:

Tax credit schedule

Net income brackets (R) in EUR		Amount of tax credit in EUR
L_1	L_2	
	4 910	0
4 910	6 550	$B \times (\mathbf{R} - L_1)/(L_2 - L_1)$
6 550	16 380	B
16 380	21 290	$B \times (L_2 - \mathbf{R})/(L_2 - L_1)$
21 290	and above	0

For 2013 income, the amount of the base (B) was EUR 660. For statutory civil servants, the amount of the base (B), instead of being EUR 660, is EUR 730.

b) Refundable tax credit for low-income workers

A refundable tax credit is intended for low-income workers and company managers (subject to the employees' social security system) entitled to the employment bonus.

The refundable tax credit amounts to 8.95% of the "employment bonus" which is actually granted on remunerations earned during the taxable period. It cannot exceed EUR 188 per taxable period.

1.4. *Rebate on the wage withholding tax*

Employers benefit from a rebate on the wage withholding tax, at the rate of 1%. The rebate does not affect the PIT liability of the employee and the amount of the withholding tax he may credit on its PIT liability: it just reduces the amount of withholding tax paid by the employer to the tax administration. This means that the rebate operates like a wage subsidy, or like a negative payroll tax. The rebate is a standard one: it applies in an unconditional way to any wage earners in Sectors C-K.

2. Compulsory social security contributions to schemes operated within the government sector

2.1. Rates and ceiling

a) Payroll deductions

The rates of employer and employee contributions are set by law. The applicable rates (in %) are as follows (for businesses having 20 or more employees) :

2013	Employee	Employer	Total
Unemployment	0.87	3.16	4.03
Health insurance indemnities	1.15	2.35	3.5
Health care	3.55	3.8	7.35
Placement services		0.05	0.05
Family allowances		7	7
Pensions	7.50	8.86	16.36
Child care		0.05	0.05
Work-related illnesses		1.01	1.01
Work-related accidents		0.32	0.32
Education leave		0.05	0.05
Business closures		0.43	0.43
Wage restraint		7.59	7.59
Total	13.07	34.67	47.74

Vacation pay is not subject to the social security contributions applicable to salaries, but a social security levy of 13.07% is deducted when the money is attributed.

b) Reduction of employer contributions

The schedule applicable as from 01.01.2013 is as follows:

Gross annual earnings (S) in EUR	Fixed amount	Variable amount
0-23 600	1 600	0.162 (23 600 – S)
23 600-49 939.2	1 600	0
49 939.2 and up	1 600	0.06 (S – 49 939.2)

The schedule applicable as from 01.04.2013 is as follows:

Gross annual earnings (S) in EUR	Fixed amount	Variable amount
0-22 303.72	1 810	0.162 (22 303.72 – S)
22 303.72-54 439.20	1 810	0
54 439.20 and up	1 810	0.06 (S – 54 439.20)

c) Reduction of individual social security contributions

A reduction of individual social security contributions is granted monthly for low-income earners, depending on wage level. The schedule below is restated in annual terms.

The schedule applicable as from 01.01.2013 is as follows:

Gross annual salary (S) in EUR	Reduction in euros
0 < S < 18 021.84	2100
18 021.84 < S < 28 624.92	Min (2 100, (2 100 – 0.1981 (S – 18 021.84))
S > 28 624.92	0

The schedule applicable as from 01.04.2013 is as follows:

Gross annual salary (S) in EUR	Reduction in euros
0 < S < 18 021.84	2 208
18 021.84 < S < 28 624.92	Min (2 208, (2 208 – 0.2082 (S – 18 021.84))
S > 28 624.92	0

d) Special social security contribution

All persons totally or partially subject to the social security scheme for salaried workers are liable for this special contribution. In theory, the amount of the contribution is determined according to aggregate household income. Aggregate household income is equal to combined gross earnings less ordinary social security contributions and work-related expenses. The amount of the contribution is as follows:

Taxable income (EUR)	Amount due on the lower limit	% above the lower limit
From 0 to 18 592.02	0	0
From 18 592.02 to 21 070.96	0	9
From 21 070.96 to 60 161.85	223.10	1.3
60 161.85 and above	731.29	0

e) Work accidents

All employers are required to insure their employees against accidents that occur in the workplace or while travelling to or from the workplace. The insurance is written by a private company. The usual premiums are approximately 1% of gross pay for office workers and 3.3% for labourers. The premiums are based on capped gross wages: in 2011 these premiums apply to gross wages (including holiday pay and extra-legal remunerations) with a minimum of EUR 6 068 and a maximum of EUR 37 546 (EUR 5 949 and EUR 36 810 respectively in 2010). Higher rates apply in certain industries in which risks are greater. The premium rate for construction workers, for example, varies between 7% and 8%.

2.2. Deductions according to family status or gender

None.

3. Universal cash transfers

Family allowances are granted for children. The annual amounts of these benefits (in euro) are as follows:

	< 5 years	5-6 years	7-10 years	11-12 years	12-16 years	17-18 years	> 18 years
1st child	1 110.96	1 141.95	1 330.71	1 354.14	1 452.78	1 481.18	1 570.10
2nd child	2 032.2	2 063.19	2 439.51	2 462.94	2 661.66	2 690.06	2 846.18
3rd child	3 020.52	3 051.51	3 427.83	3 451.26	3 649.98	3 678.38	3 834.50

To determine the resources available to the average worker, the *Taxing Wages* calculations assume that one child was between seven and ten years of age and that the other child was between eleven and twelve years of age.

4. Main changes in the tax/benefit system

None.

2013 parameter values

	Ave_earn	46 810	Secretariat estimate		
Work-related expenses	work_rel_max	3 900			
	work_rel_sch	0.287	5 650		
		0.1	11 220		
		0.05	18 670		
		0.03			
Tax credits (exempt income)	single_cr	6 990			
	Married_cr	6 990			
	Supp_cr_base	280			
	supp_cr_thrsh1	25 990			
One child	child_cr1	1 490			
Two children	child_cr2	3 820			
Single parents	s_parent_cr	1 490			
Maximum Child Credit Payment	child_cr_max	430			
Basic Credit	basic_cr_base	0			
	basic_cr_thrsh1	4 910			
	basic_cr_thrsh2	6 550			
	basic_cr_thrsh3	16 380			
	basic_cr_thrsh4	21 290			
Income tax schedule		tax_rate1			
	tax_sch	0.25	8 590		
		0.30	12 220		
		0.40	20 370		
		0.45	37 330		
		0.50			
	quote_max	10 090			
	quote_rate	0.3			
Local tax	local_rate	0.074			
Unemployment	unemp_rate	0.0087			
Medical care	med_rate	0.0115			
Sickness	sickness_rate	0.0355			
Pension	pension_rate	0.0750			
Employee contribution	SSC_rt	0.1307			
	SSC_redn	0	0	2 181	0
	(annual)	18 021.84	18 021.84	2 181	0.2057
		28 624.92	18 021.84	2 181	0.2057
		28 624.92	0	0	0
		99 999 999	0		0
Special annual contribution	SSC_special	0.000	18 592.02		
		0.090	21 070.96		
		0.013	60 161.85		
		0.000			
Employer contributions	SSC_empr_rt	0.3467			
					0.1620
	SSC_empr_redn	0	1 757.50		22627.79
					0
		22 627.79	1 757.50		53 314.20
					-0.06
		53 314.20	1 757.50		53 314.20
		9 999 999	0		0
Structural reduction on the withholding tax on wages	PrP_redn	0.01			
Low-income credit	LIC_rate	0.0895			
	LIC_max	188.00			
Child benefit (age 7-10)	CB_1	1 354.14			
second child (age 7-10)	CB_2	2 439.61			
third child (age 7-10)	CB_3	3 427.83			

2013 tax equations

The equations for the Belgian system in 2013 are mostly calculated on an individual basis. But central government tax for a married couple is calculated on two bases and the lower value is used. One of the bases takes account of the combined income of the couple. Also, tax credits may be used against the tax liability of the secondary earner if the principal earner is unable to use them.

The functions which are used in the equations (Taper, Tax, etc.) are described in the technical note about tax equations. Variable names are defined in the table of parameters above or are the standard variables "married" and "children". A reference to a variable with the affix "_total" indicates the sum of the relevant variable values for the principal and spouse. And the affixes "_princ" and "_spouse" indicate the value for the principal and spouse respectively. Equations for a single person are as shown for the principal with "_spouse" values taken as 0.

	Line in country table and intermediate steps	Variable name	Range	Equation
1.	Earnings	earn		
2.	Allowances:	tax_al	B	MIN(work_rel_max, Tax(earn-SSC, work_rel_sch))+SSC
3.	Credits in taxable income	taxbl_cr	B	0
4.	CG taxable income	tax_inc_int	B	earn-tax_al
	Quote part	Q	J	IF(married, Positive(MIN(tax_inc_int_total*quote_rate, quote_max)-tax_inc_int_spouse), 0)
	CG adjusted taxable income – principal	tax_inc_adj_princ	P	Positive(tax_inc_int_princ – Q)
	CG adjusted taxable income – spouse	tax_inc_adj_spouse	S	Positive(tax_inc_int_spouse + Q)
5.	CG tax before credits	CG_tax_excl	J	Tax(tax_inc_adj, tax_sch)
6.	Calculation of credits			
	Child exemption amount	child_ex_inc	P	(children=1)*child_cr1+(children=2)*child_cr2
	Family exemption amount	fam_ex_inc	B	IF(Married,married_cr,single_cr+(Children>0)*s_parent_cr)+ IF(tax_inc_adj<=0,0,IF(tax_inc_adj<=supp_cr_thrsh1,supp_c r_base,MAX(0,supp_cr_base+supp_cr_thrsh1- tax_inc_adj)))
	Initial exempt income – principal	ex_inc_int_princ	P	child_ex_inc+fam_ex_inc_princ
	Initial exempt income – spouse	ex_inc_int_spouse	S	fam_ex_inc_spouse
	Transferable amount	ex_inc_tran	J	married*IF(ex_inc_int_princ<tax_inc_adj_princ, MIN(MAX((ex_inc_int_spouse-tax_inc_adj_spouse), 0), tax_inc_adj_princ-ex_inc_int_princ), - (MIN(MAX((ex_inc_int_princ-tax_inc_adj_princ), 0), MAX(0, tax_inc_adj_spouse-ex_inc_int_spouse))))
	Final exempt income – principal	ex_inc_fin_princ	P	ex_inc_int_princ+ex_inc_tran
	Final exempt income – spouse	ex_inc_fin_spouse	S	ex_inc_int_spouse-ex_inc_tran
	Tax credits	tax_credits	J	Tax(ex_inc_fin, tax_sch)
	Basic Credit	basic_cr	B	basic_cr_base*IF(tax_inc<=basic_cr_thrsh1, 0, IF(tax_inc<=basic_cr_thrsh2, (tax_inc-basic_cr_thrsh1)/ (basic_cr_thrsh2-basic_cr_thrsh1), IF(tax_inc<=basic_cr_thrsh3, 1, IF(tax_inc<=basic_cr_thrsh4, (basic_cr_thrsh4-tax_inc)/ (basic_cr_thrsh4-basic_cr_thrsh3), 0)))) +IF(tax_inc=0;0;MIN(LIC_rate*(MIN(VLOOKUP(earn, SSC_redn,3), VLOOKUP(earn, SSC_redn, 3)-VLOOKUP(earn, SSC_redn, 4)*(earn-VLOOKUP(earn, SSC_redn, 2)))));LIC_max))
7.	CG tax			
	Tax prior to non-wasteable credits	CG_tax_init	B	Positive(CG_tax_incl-tax_credits)
	Non-wasteable child credit	child_credit_nw	J	MIN(Tax(MIN((children=1)*child_cr1+(children=2)*Paramet ers!child_cr2), (positive(ex_inc_int-tax_inc_int), tax_sch), children*child_cr_max)
	Final CG tax	CG_tax_final	J	CG_tax_init-basic_cr_total-child_credit_nw

	Line in country table and intermediate steps	Variable name	Range	Equation
8.	State and local taxes	local_tax	J	local_rate*CG_tax_init
9.	Employees' soc security	SSC	B	Positive((earn)*SSC_rt-MIN(VLOOKUP(earn, SSC_redn,3), VLOOKUP(earn, SSC_redn, 3)-VLOOKUP(earn, SSC_redn, 4)*(earn-VLOOKUP(earn, SSC_redn, 2))))
		SSC_special	J	positive(Tax(tax_inc_total, SSC_special)
		SSC_total		SSC+SSC_special
11.	Cash transfers	cash_trans	J	(Children>0)*CB_1+(Children>1)*CB_2
13.	Employer's soc security	empr_sch	B	Positive(earn*(SSC_empr_rt- PrP_redn)-(VLOOKUP(earn, SSC_empr_redn, 2)-VLOOKUP(earn, SSC_empr_redn, 3)*(earn-VLOOKUP(earn, SSC_empr_redn, 1))))

Key to range of equation B calculated separately for both principal earner and spouse P calculated for principal only (value taken as 0 for spouse calculation) J calculated once only on a joint basis.

Taxing Wages 2014
Changes in sructural labour income tax progressivity
over 2000-12 period in OECD member countries

Canada

This chapter includes data on the income taxes paid by workers, their social security contributions, the family benefits they receive in the form of cash transfers as well as the social security contributions and payroll taxes paid by their employers. Results reported include the marginal and average tax burden for eight different family types.

Methodological information is available for personal income tax systems, compulsory social security contributions to schemes operated within the government sector, universal cash transfers as well as recent changes in the tax/ benefit system. The methodology also includes the parameter values and tax equations underlying the data.

Canada 2013

The tax/benefit position of single persons

	Wage level (per cent of average wage)	67	100	167	67
	Number of children	none	none	none	2
1.	**Gross wage earnings**	32052	48078	80129	32052
2.	**Standard tax allowances**				
	Basic allowance				
	Married or head of family				
	Dependent children				
	Deduction for social security contributions and income taxes				
	Work-related expenses				
	Other				
	Total	0	0	0	0
3.	**Tax credits or cash transfers included in taxable income**	0	0	0	0
4.	**Central government taxable income (1 - 2 + 3)**	32052	48078	80129	32052
5.	**Central government income tax liability (exclusive of tax credits)**	4808	7528	14579	4808
6.	**Tax credits**				
	Basic credit	1823	1823	1823	1823
	Married or head of family	0	0	0	1656
	Children	0	0	0	670
	Other(CPP & EI)	302	465	487	302
	Total	2126	2288	2310	4452
7.	**Central government income tax finally paid (5-6)**	2682	5240	12269	356
8.	**State and local taxes**	1033	2131	5225	0
9.	**Employees' compulsory social security contributions**				
	Gross earnings	2016	3098	3247	2016
	Taxable income (Provincial Health Care Levy)	300	469	750	300
	Total	2316	3567	3997	2316
10.	**Total payments to general government (7 + 8 + 9)**	6031	10938	21492	2672
11.	**Cash transfers from general government**				
	For head of family	409	0	0	490
	For two children	0	0	0	8275
	Total	409	0	0	8764
12.	**Take-home pay (1-10+11)**	26429	37140	58638	38144
13.	**Employer's compulsory social security contributions**	3818	5796	7506	3818
14.	**Average rates**				
	Income tax	11.6%	15.3%	21.8%	1.1%
	Employees' social security contributions	7.2%	7.4%	5.0%	7.2%
	Total payments less cash transfers	17.5%	22.7%	26.8%	-19.0%
	Total tax wedge including employer's social security contributions	26.3%	31.1%	33.1%	-6.3%
15.	**Marginal rates**				
	Total payments less cash transfers: Principal earner	26%	60.1%	35.4%	55.8%
	Total payments less cash transfers: Spouse	n.a.	n.a.	n.a.	n.a.
	Total tax wedge: Principal earner	33.8%	63.7%	38.4%	60.7%
	Total tax wedge: Spouse	n.a.	n.a.	n.a.	n.a.

Canada 2013

The tax/benefit position of married couples

		100-0	100-33	100-67	100-33
	Wage level (per cent of average wage)	100-0	100-33	100-67	100-33
	Number of children	2	2	2	none
1.	**Gross wage earnings**	48078	64103	80129	64103
2.	**Standard tax allowances**				
	Basic allowance				
	Married or head of family				
	Dependent children				
	Deduction for social security contributions and income taxes				
	Work-related expenses				
	Other				
	Total	0	0	0	0
3.	**Tax credits or cash transfers included in taxable income**	0	0	0	0
4.	**Central government taxable income (1 - 2 + 3)**	48078	64103	80129	64103
5.	**Central government income tax liability (exclusive of tax credits)**	7528	9932	12336	9932
6.	**Tax credits**				
	Basic credit	3479	3647	3647	3647
	Married or head of family	1656	0	0	0
	Children	670	670	670	0
	Other(CPP & EI)	465	603	767	603
	Total	6270	4920	5084	4249
7.	**Central government income tax finally paid (5-6)**	2914	5012	7252	5682
8.	**State and local taxes**	1362	2247	3164	2247
9.	**Employees' compulsory social security contributions**				
	Gross earnings	3098	4019	5114	4019
	Taxable income (Provincial Health Care Levy)	469	469	769	469
	Total	3567	4488	5883	4488
10.	**Total payments to general government (7 + 8 + 9)**	7843	11748	16299	12418
11.	**Cash transfers from general government**				
	For head of family	0	0	0	0
	For two children	3551	2093	1452	0
	Total	3551	2093	1452	0
12.	**Take-home pay (1-10+11)**	43785	54449	65282	51686
13.	**Employer's compulsory social security contributions**	5796	7618	9613	7618
14.	**Average rates**				
	Income tax	8.9%	11.3%	13.0%	12.4%
	Employees' social security contributions	7.4%	7.0%	7.3%	7.0%
	Total payments less cash transfers	8.9%	15.1%	18.5%	19.4%
	Total tax wedge including employer's social security contributions	18.7%	24.1%	27.3%	27.9%
15.	**Marginal rates**				
	Total payments less cash transfers: Principal earner	90.0%	64.1%	64.1%	60.1%
	Total payments less cash transfers: Spouse	33.5%	34.2%	29.5%	30.2%
	Total tax wedge: Principal earner	90.9%	67.3%	67.3%	63.7%
	Total tax wedge: Spouse	40.3%	41.5%	37.3%	37.9%

The national currency is the Canadian dollar (CAD). In 2013, CAD 1.03 was equal to USD 1. In that year, the average worker earned CAD 48 078 (Secretariat estimate).

1. Personal income tax systems

1.1. *Central/federal government income taxes*

1.1.1. *Tax unit*

Under the present system, tax is levied on individuals separately; certain tax reliefs depend on family circumstances.

1.1.2. *Tax allowances and credits*

1.1.2.1. Standard credits

- *Basic personal amount:* All taxpayers qualify for a basic personal tax credit of CAD 1 655.70.
- *Credit for spouse or eligible dependant*: A taxpayer supporting a spouse or other eligible dependant receives a tax credit of CAD 1 655.70 which is reduced by 15 cents for each dollar of the dependant's income.
- *Child tax credit:* A tax credit that provides up to CAD 335.10 of tax relief for each dependent child under the age of 18. The credit can be claimed by either parent.
- *Social security contributions:* Taxpayers are entitled to claim 15 per cent of their contributions to the Canada or Quebec Pension Plans (to a maximum of CAD 2 356.20 for the Canada Pension Plan and to a maximum of CAD 2 427.60 for the Quebec Pension Plan) and their Employment Insurance premiums (to a maximum of CAD 891.12).
- *Working Income Tax Benefit (WITB)*: The WITB provides a non-wastable tax credit equal to 25 per cent of each dollar of earned income in excess of CAD 3 000 to a maximum credit of CAD 989 for single individuals without dependents and CAD 1 797 for families (couples and single parents). The credit will be reduced by 15 per cent of net family income in excess of CAD 11 231 for single individuals and CAD 15 509 for families. This is the default national design; provinces may choose to propose jurisdiction-specific changes to this design, subject to certain principles.
- *Canada employment tax credit:* A tax credit of up to CAD 167.55 on employment income.

1.1.2.2. Main non-standard tax reliefs applicable to an average worker:

A number of non-standard tax reliefs are available to the average worker in Canada. The main ones are:

- *Medical expenses credit:* Taxpayers are entitled to a 15 per cent tax credit for an amount of eligible medical expenses that exceeds the lesser of 3 per cent of net income or CAD 2 152.
- *Charitable donations credit:* The credit is 15 per cent on the first CAD 200 of eligible charitable donations and 29 per cent on eligible donations in excess of CAD 200. Eligible donations are those made to registered charities, to a maximum of 75 per cent of net income.

- *Registered pension plan contributions:* Employees who are members of a registered pension plan are entitled to deduct their contributions to the plan in respect of current and/or past service. Generally, employee contributions to a defined benefit registered pension plan are not subject to any limit; however, limits apply to the benefits that a plan may provide. Individuals can deduct their contributions to a defined contribution registered pension plan up to a limit of 18 per cent of earned income, to a maximum of CAD 24 270.
- *Registered retirement savings plan (RRSP) premiums:* Individuals can deduct their contributions to an RRSP up to a limit of 18 per cent of the previous year's earned income, to a maximum of CAD 23 820 a year, unless they are also accruing benefits under a registered pension plan or a deferred profit sharing plan. Members of those other plans are limited to RRSP contributions of 18 per cent of the previous year's earned income to a maximum of CAD 23 820, minus a pension adjustment amount based on pension benefits accrued in the previous year.
- *Union and professional dues:* Individuals with annual dues paid to a trade union or an association of public servants or paying dues required to maintain a professional status recognised by statute are allowed to deduct such fees in computing taxable income.
- *Moving expenses:* Eligible moving expenses are deductible from income if the taxpayer moves at least 40 kilometres closer to a new place of employment.
- *Child care expenses:* A portion of child care expenses is deductible if incurred for the purpose of earning business or employment income, studying or taking an occupational training course or carrying on research for which a grant is received. The lower-income spouse must generally claim the deduction. The amount of the deduction is limited to the least of:
  1. the expenses incurred for the care of a child;
  2. two-thirds of the taxpayer's earned income; and
  3. CAD 7 000 for each child who is under age seven, and CAD 4 000 per child between seven and sixteen years of age. The amount for a disabled child under seventeen is CAD 10 000.

1.1.3. *Tax schedule*

2013 Federal income tax rates

Taxable income (CAD)	Rate (%)
0-43 561	15
43 561-87 123	22
87 123-135 054	26
135 054 and over	29

1.2. *State and local income taxes*

1.2.1. *General description*

All provinces and territories levy their own personal income taxes. All, with the exception of Quebec, have a tax collection agreement with the federal government, and thus use the federal definition of taxable income. They are free to determine their own tax brackets, rates and credits. Quebec collects its own personal income tax and is free to determine all of the tax parameters, including taxable income. In practice, its definition of taxable income is similar to the federal definition.

1.2.2. *Tax regime selected for this study*

The calculation of provincial tax for the average worker study assumes the worker lives in Ontario, the most populous of the 10 provinces and 3 territories. The main features of the Ontario tax system relevant to this report are summarised below:

Tax schedule

Income bracket	Rate (%)
CAD 0 to CAD 39 723	5.05
CAD 39 723 to CAD 79 448	9.15
CAD 79 448 to CAD 509 000	11.16
Over CAD 509 000	13.16

Surtax

Provincial tax after accounting for wastable credits	Surtax rate
Amounts exceeding CAD 4 289	20% of the excess amount
Amounts exceeding CAD 5 489	36% of the excess amount

Wastable tax credits

- A basic tax credit of CAD 483.49.
- A maximum credit of CAD 410.51 for a dependant spouse or eligible dependant that is withdrawn as the income of the spouse or eligible dependant exceeds CAD 813 and is completely withdrawn when the income of the spouse is at least CAD 8 941.91.
- 5.05 per cent of contributions made to the Canada Pension Plan and of Employment Insurance premiums.

Tax Reduction

An earner is entitled to claim a tax reduction where the initial entitlement is equal to CAD 221 plus CAD 409 for each dependent child under the age of 19. Where someone has a spouse, only the spouse with the higher net income can claim the dependent child tax reduction. If this amount is greater or equal to the liable provincial tax, then no tax is due. If the amount is less than the liable tax, then the actual tax reduction is equal to twice the initial entitlement amount less the liable tax (if this calculation is zero or negative, the reduction is equal to zero).

2. Compulsory social security contributions to schemes operated within the government sector

2.1. Employees' contributions

2.1.1. Pensions

Generally, all employees are eligible for coverage under the Canada Pension Plan (Québec Pension Plan in the province of Québec). For 2013, all employees are required to contribute to the Canada Pension Plan at a rate of 4.95 per cent of income up to a maximum contribution of CAD 2 356.20 (the contribution rate is 5.100 per cent of income for the Québec Pension Plan up to a maximum contribution of CAD 2 427.60). Income subject to contributions is earnings (wages and salaries) less a CAD 3 500 basic exemption. The maximum contribution of CAD 2 356.20 is reached at an earnings level of CAD 51 100 i.e. (CAD 51 100-CAD 3 500) × 0.0495 = CAD 2 356.20. For employees, each contribution to the CPP or QPP gives rise to a tax credit equal to 15 per cent of the contributed amount. Employers are also required to contribute to the Canada Pension Plan on behalf of their employees at the same rate and can deduct their contributions from taxable income (see Section 2.2.1).

Self-employed persons must also contribute to the Canada Pension Plan (Québec Pension Plan in the province of Québec) on their own behalf. However, the self-employed are required to contribute at the combined employer/employee rate of 9.90 per cent of earnings up to a maximum of CAD 4 712.40. The self-employed can deduct the employer portion of their contribution from income, equal to 50 per cent of the total contribution or CAD 2 356.20. The remaining 50 per cent, representing the employee portion, is then claimed as a tax credit at 15 per cent.

2.1.2. *Sickness*

There is no national sickness benefit plan administered by the federal government. However, all provinces have provincially-administered health care insurance plans. Three provinces, Quebec, Ontario, and British Columbia, levy health insurance premiums on individuals separately from the personal income tax to help finance their health programmes.

In the case of Ontario, the premium is determined based on taxable income. Individuals who earn up to CAD 20 000 are exempt. The premium is phased in with a number of different rates to a maximum of CAD 900 for taxable income levels greater than CAD 200 600. The following table provides further details on the structure that is applicable in 2013.

The Ontario Health Premium

Taxable income	Fixed component (CAD)	Variable component
0-CAD 20 000	0	
CAD 20 000-CAD 25 000	0	6% of the taxable income in excess of CAD 20 000
CAD 25 000-CAD 36 000	300	
CAD 36 000-CAD 38 500	300	6% of the taxable income in excess of CAD 36 000
CAD 38 500-CAD 48 000	450	
CAD 48 000-CAD 48 600	450	25% of the taxable income in excess of CAD 48 000
CAD 48 600-CAD 72 000	600	
CAD 72 000-CAD 72 600	600	25% of the amount of taxable income in excess of CAD 72 600
CAD 72 600-CAD 200 000	750	
CAD 200 000-CAD 200 600	750	25% of the amount of taxable income in excess of CAD 200 000
Over CAD 200 600	900	

2.1.3. *Unemployment*

In general, all employees are eligible for employment insurance. Eligibility to receive benefits is determined by insurable hours worked (with a minimum entry threshold of 420 hours). For 2013, employees are required to contribute at the rate of 1.88 per cent of insurable earnings. Insurable earnings are earnings (wages and salaries) up to a maximum of CAD 47 400 per year. The maximum employee contribution is therefore CAD 891.12 per year. Employment insurance contributions give rise to a tax credit equal to 15 per cent of the amount contributed. Employers are also required to contribute to the plan (see Section 2.2.3).

2.1.4. *Work injury*

See Section 2.2.4.

2.2. *Employers' contributions*

2.2.1. *Pensions*

Employers are required to contribute to the Canada Pension Plan on behalf of their employees an amount equal to their employees' contributions. Thus, employers also contribute at the rate of 4.95 per cent of earnings (less the CAD 3 500 earnings exemption) to a maximum of CAD 2 356.20.

2.2.2. *Sickness*

There is no national sickness benefit plan administered by the federal government. However, all provinces have provincially-administered health care insurance plans. Three provinces levy a special tax on employer payrolls to finance health services (Québec and Ontario) or health services and education (Manitoba). These payroll taxes are deductible from the employer's income subject to tax. In the case of the province of Ontario, employers pay a 1.95 per cent Employer Health Tax on the value of their payroll that exceeds CAD 400 000.

2.2.3. *Unemployment*

Employers are required to contribute to the employment insurance scheme. The general employer contribution is 1.4 times the employee contribution, that is, 2.56 per cent of insurable earnings. Premiums are adjusted for employers who provide sick pay superior to payments provided under the employment insurance regime. All employment insurance contributions are deductible from the employer's income subject to tax.

2.2.4. *Work injury*

There is no national work injury benefit plan administered by the federal government. However, employers are required to contribute to a provincial workers' compensation plan which pays benefits to workers (or their families in case of death) for work-related illness or injury. The employer contribution rates, which vary by industry and province, are related to industry experience of work-related illness and injury. Premiums are deductible from the employer's income subject to tax. In the case of Ontario, employers in the C to K industry sector pay, on average, 2.92 per cent of the wages paid to each employee to a maximum of CAD 83 200.

3. Universal cash transfers

3.1. *Transfers related to marital status*

None.

3.2. *Transfers for dependent children*

3.2.1. *Federal*

The Canada Child Tax Benefit (CCTB) provides CAD 1 448 per child under age 18 plus a CAD 101 supplement for the 3rd child and each additional child. This basic benefit is reduced by 4 per cent of family net income in excess of CAD 44 022 for families with two or more children and 2 per cent for families with one child. In addition, a National Child

Benefit supplement (NCBs) is provided to low-income families with children. The maximum NCBs is CAD 2 244 for one child, plus CAD 1 985 for a second child, plus CAD 1 889 for the third and each additional child. The NCBs is phased out based on family net income in excess of CAD 25 629. The reduction rates are 12.2 per cent for families with one child, 23.0 per cent for families with two children and 33.3 per cent for larger families.

The Universal Child Care Benefit (UCCB) provides all families with CAD 1 200 for each child under age six. Amounts received under the UCCB are taxable in the hands of the lower-income spouse but are not used to reduce other income-tested benefits such as the CCTB. In the case of single parents, the UCCB can be taxable in the hands of the eligible dependant. Since the *Taxing Wages* model assumes that children are at least six years old, this benefit is not applicable for these estimates.

The Goods and Services Tax Credit provides a relief of CAD 268 for each adult 19 years of age or older and CAD 141 for each dependent child under the age of 19. Single tax filers without children and with an employment income higher than CAD 8 699 receive an additional CAD 141 that is phased in at a rate of 2 per cent. Single tax filers with children receive an additional CAD 141 that is not subject to phase-in. The credit received for the first dependent child of a single parent is also increased from CAD 141 to CAD 268. The total amount is reduced at a rate of five per cent of net family income over CAD 34 927. The amount is paid directly to families.*

3.2.2. *Provincial*

The province of Ontario announced the creation of the Ontario Child Benefit (OCB) in its 2007 Budget. This measure is replacing the Ontario Child Care Supplement for Working Families (OCCS). For each child under eighteen, qualifying families can receive up to CAD 1 310 from the OCB. The benefit is withdrawn at a rate of 8 per cent of family income that exceeds CAD 20 000.

Qualifying families will receive whichever entitlement is more generous during the transition period. The calculation of the OCCS is as follows: For each child under seven, qualifying two-parent families can receive up to CAD 1 100 annually while qualifying single parent families can receive up to CAD 1 310. The actual OCCS is calculated as being either the greater of qualifying child care expenses or a percentage of the earnings of a family over CAD 5 000. The percentage used depends upon the number of children. For a one child family, the rate is 21 per cent. For a two child family, the rate is 42 per cent. For families with more than two children, the rate is 63 per cent. The OCCS is withdrawn at a rate of 8 per cent of family income that exceeds CAD 20 000. Children born before 1 July, 2009 and under age seven remain eligible for the OCCS in the transition period to the OCB.

Ontario has a Sales Tax Credit that provides a relief of up to CAD 281 for each adult and each child. It is reduced by four per cent of adjusted family net income over CAD 21 637 for single people and over CAD 27 046 for families. The amount is paid directly to families.

* The payments that relate to the 2013 tax year are payable between July 2014 and June 2015. The amounts shown in this Report assume indexation of 1.1% for the 2013 tax year (and 2014-15 benefit year); the actual indexation parameter will be announced in December 2013.

4. Main changes in tax/benefit system since 2009

5. Memorandum items

5.1. *Identification of an average worker*

The earnings data refer to production workers in the industries C to K. To obtain the annual average wage figure, the average weekly earnings for the year for employees (including overtime) are multiplied by 52.

5.2. *Employer contributions to private health and pension schemes*

These do exist but no information is available on the amounts involved.

2013 parameter values

Average earnings/yr	Ave_earn	48 078	Secretariat estimate
Tax credits	Basic_cred	1 655.70	
Spouse	Spouse_cred	1 655.70	
withdrawal rate	Sp_crd_wth	0.15	
threshold	Sp_crd_thrsh	0	
Canada Employment Tax Credit	Empl_crd	167.55	
Child tax credit	Dep_ch_crd	335.10	
Canada Child Tax Benefit	Ch_credit	1 448	
Child under 7	Ch_crd_und7	0	
additional for 3rd+	Ch_crd_3rd	101	
reduction rate: 1 child	Ch_crd_red1	0.02	
reduction. rate: 2 or more	Ch_crd_red2	0.04	
threshold	Ch_crd_thrsh	44 022	
National Child Benefit Supplement	WIS_crd_1st	2 244	
	WIS_crd_2nd	1 985	
	WIS_crd_3rd	1 889	
threshold to start phase-out	WIS_phout_st	25 629	
threshold to end phase-out	WIS_phout_end	44 022	
reduction rate	WIS_redn1	0.122	
	WIS_redn2	0.230	
	WIS_redn3	0.333	
Working Income Tax Benefit	WITB_phzin_thrsh	3 000	
WITB–Phase-in Rate	WITB_phzn_rt	0.25	
WITB–Maximum Credit (per Adult/Equiv.)	WITB_max	989	
WITB–Addl. Maximum Credit (Fam.)	WITB_max_fam	808	
WITB–Reduction Rate	WITB_phzout_rt	0.15	
WITB–Threshold	WITB_phzout_thrsh	11 231	
WITB–Addl. Threshold (Fam.)	WITB_phzn_thrsh_fa m	4 278	
Federal tax schedule	Fed_sch	0.15	43 561
		0.22	87 123
		0.26	13 5054
		0.29	
High-income surtax rate	H_sur_rate	0	
threshold	H_sur_thrsh	18 500	
Canada pension plan rate	CPP_rate	0.0495	
exemption	CPP_ex	3 500	
max contrib.	CPP_max	2 356.20	
Unemployment ins.rate	Unemp_rate	0.0188	
max contrib.	Unemp_max	891.12	
tax credit rate	Unemp_crd_rate	0.15	
employer contrib. mult.	Unemp_emplr	1.4	

GST adult credit	GST_crd_ad	268		
child credit	GST_crd_ch	141		
threshold	GST_crd_thrsh	34 927		
reduction rate	GST_crd_redn	0.05		
single supplement	GST_crd_sgsp	141		
single supplement eligibility threshold	GST_sgsp_thrsh	8 699		
single supplement phase-in rate	GST_sgsp_rate	0.02		
Province: Ontario				
Tax Credits	P_basic_crd	483.49		
Spouse	P_spouse_crd	410.51		
withdrawal rate	P_sp_crd_wd	0.0505		
threshold	P_sp_crd_thr	813		
% of BFT	P_pct_bft	0.375		
Unemployement tax credit rate	P_unem_tc_rt	0.0505		
Surtax rate 1	P_sur_rt1	0.20		
threshold	P_sur_thr1	4 289		
rate 2	P_sur_rt2	0.36		
threshold	P_sur_thr2	5 489		
Tax reduction	P_tax_red	221		
amount per dependent	P_tr_chld	409		
amount per disabled dep	P_tr_dis_ch	409		
Provincial tax schedule	Prov_sch	0.0505	39 723	
		0.0915	79 448	
		0.1116		
		0.1316	509 000	
Ontario Child Care Supplement				
% per child of earnings over threshold				
For 1 Child under 7	P_pct_earn	0.21		
threshold	P_ch_crd_th	5 000		
max per child under 7	P_und7_max	1 100		
single parent sup per ch under 7	P_sps_und7	210		
threshold reduction	P_thrsh_red	20 000		
reduction rate	P_redn_rate	0.08		
Ontario Child Benefit	P_ch_amt	1 310		
amount per child	P_ch_thresh	20 000		
threshold	P_ch_redn_rate	0.08		
reduction rate				
Sales tax credits				
sales tax credit adult	P_sales_cred	281		
sales tax credit child	P_salcr_chd	281		
threshold	P_ps_thresh	21 637		
threshold seniors/families	P_ps_thr_sen	27 046		
reduction rate	P_ps_red_rt	0.04		
reduction rate seniors	P_ps_rr_sen	0.04		
Ontario Health Premium	P_hlth_sch	20 000	0	0
		25 000	0.06	0
		36 000	0	300
		38 500	0.06	300
		48 000	0	450
		48 600	0.25	450
		72 000	0	600
		72 600	0.25	600
		200 000	0	750
		200 600	0.25	750
maximum	P_hlth_max	900		
Employer Health Tax	emp_healthtax	0.0195		
Employer Workers Compensation Levy	emp_workcomp	0.0292		
Employer Workers Compensation Levy Ceiling	emp_workcomp_ceil	83 200		
Maximum number of children under the age of 7	children_und7_max	1		

2013 tax equations

The equations for the Canadian system are mostly repeated for each individual of a married couple. But the spouse credit is relevant only to the calculation for the principal earner and the non-wastable credits are calculated only once. This is shown by the Range indicator in the table below.

The functions which are used in the equations (Taper, MIN, Tax, etc.) are described in the technical note about tax equations. Variable names are defined in the table of parameters above, within the equations table, or are the standard variables "married" and "children". A reference to a variable with the affix "_total" indicates the sum of the relevant variable values for the principal and spouse. And the affixes "_princ" and "_spouse" indicate the value for the principal and spouse, respectively. Equations for a single person are as shown for the principal, with "_spouse" values taken as 0.

	Line in country table and intermediate steps	Variable name	Range	Equation
1.	Earnings	earn		
2.	2Allowances	tax_al	B	0
3.	Credits in taxable income	taxbl_cr	B	0
4.	CG taxable income	tax_inc	B	Earn
5.	CG tax before credits:	Basic_Fed_tax	B	Tax(earn, Fed_sch)
	Basic Federal tax	Basic_Fed_tax	B	Tax(earn, Fed_sch)
6.	Tax credits :			
	Basic credit	basic_cr	B	IF (Earn>0, (Basic_cred + Empl_crd) , Basic_cred)
	Spouse credit	spouse_cr	P	((married+children)>0)*Taper(Spouse_cred, earn_spouse, Sp_crd_thrsh, Sp_crd_wth)
	Unemployment insurance	unemp_cr	B	Unemp_crd_rate*SSC
	Child tax credit	dep_ch_crd	P	IF(Children>0, Children*Dep_Ch_crd, 0)
	Total (wastable) tax credits	tax_cr	B	basic_cr+spouse_cr+unemp_cr+dep_ch_crd
	Working Income Tax Benefit	WITB	P	IF(Married>0,MAX(0,MIN(WITB_max+WITB_max_fam,(WITB_phzn_rt*MAX(0,earn_total-WITB_phzin_thrsh)))-MAX(0,WITB_phzout_rt*MAX(0,earn_total-(WITB_phzout_thrsh+WITB_phzn_thrsh_fam)))), IF(Children>0,MAX(0,MIN(WITB_max+WITB_max_fam,(WITB_phzn_rt*MAX(0,earn_total-WITB_phzin_thrsh)))-MAX(0,WITB_phzout_rt*MAX(0,earn_total-(WITB_phzout_thrsh+WITB_phzn_thrsh_fam)))), MAX(0,MIN(WITB_max,(WITB_phzn_rt*MAX(0,earn_total-WITB_phzin_thrsh)))-MAX(0,WITB_phzout_rt*MAX(0,earn_total-WITB_phzout_thrsh)))))
7.	CG tax	CG_tax	B	Positive(Basic_Fed_tax-tax_cr)-WITB
8.	State and local taxes			
	Liable provincial tax	Prov_tax_sch	B	Tax(earn, Prov_sch)
	Provincial tax credits	Prov_tax_cred	B	P_basic_crd+P_unem_tc_rt*SSC+IF(AND(Married=0, Children>0), P_spouse_crd, Married*Taper(P_spouse_crd, earn_spouse, P_sp_crd_thr, P_sp_crd_wd))
	Provincial surtax	Prov_surtax	B	P_sur_rt1*Positive(Prov_tax_sch-Prov_tax_cred-P_sur_thr1)+P_sur_rt2*Positive(Prov_tax_sch-Prov_tax_cred-P_sur_thr2)
	Provincial tax reduction	Prov_tax_redn	B	MAX(2*(P_tax_red+Children*P_tr_chld)-(Prov_tax_sch-Prov_tax_cred+Prov_surtax), 0)
	Provincial sales tax credit	Prov_tax_stcred	P	Taper(IF(Married=1, 2, 1)*P_sales_cred+Children*P_salcr_chd, earn_total, IF(Married+Children=0, P_ps_thresh,P_ps_thr_sen),P_ps_red_rt)
	Liable provincial tax	Prov_tax	B	Positive(Prov_tax_sch-Prov_tax_cred+Prov_surtax-Prov_tax_redn)
9.	Employees' soc security:			
	Canada Pension Plan	CPP	B	MIN(CPP_rate*Positive((earn-CPP_ex), CPP_max)
	Unemployment insurance	Unemp	B	MIN(Unemp_rate*earn, Unemp_max)

Line in country table and intermediate steps	Variable name	Range	Equation
State health premium	Prov_health	B	MIN(Hstep(tax_inc, P_hlth_sch), P_hlth_max)
Total Employees'soc security	SSC	B	CPP+Unemp+Prov_health
11. Cash transfers (nonwastable)			
Child Tax Benefit	CTB	P	(Children>0)*(Taper(Children*Ch_credit +MAXA((Children-2), 0)*Ch_crd_3rd+MINA(Children, children_und7_max)*Ch_crd_und7, earn_total, Ch_crd_thrsh, IF(Children=1, Ch_crd_red1, Ch_crd_red2)))+MAXA(IF(Children>0, IF(Children<2, WIS_crd_1st, IF(Children<3, WIS_crd_1st+WIS_crd_2nd, WIS_crd_1st+WIS_crd_2nd+(Children-2)* WIS_crd_3rd)), 0)-MAXA((earn_total-WIS_phout_st), 0)*IF(Children=1, WIS_redn1, IF(Children=2, WIS_redn2, WIS_redn3)), 0)
GST Credit – Total	GST_cr	P	Taper((GST_crd_ad+(Married=1)*(GST_crd_ad+Children*GST_crd_ch)+(Married=0)*(Children>0)*(GST_crd_ad+GST_crd_sgsp+Positive(Children-1)*GST_crd_ch)+(Married=0)*(Children=0)*Positive(MIN(GST_crd_sgsp, (earn_total-GST_sgsp_thrsh)*GST_sgsp_rate))), earn_total, GST_crd_thrsh, GST_crd_redn)
GST Credit – Adult	GST_cr_adult	P	Taper((GST_crd_ad+(Married=1)*(GST_crd_ad)+(Married=0)*Positive(MIN(GST_crd_sgsp, (earn_total-GST_sgsp_thrsh)*GST_sgsp_rate))), earn_total, GST_crd_thrsh, GST_crd_redn)
GST Credit – Child	GST_cr_child	P	GST_cr-GST_cr_adult
Ontario child benefit	Prov_child_ben	P	MAX(Taper(MIN(((earn_total)-P_ch_crd_th)*MIN(Children,children_und7_max,3)*P_pct_earn,Positive((P_und7_max+IF(Married=0,P_sps_und7,0))*MIN(Children,children_und7_max))),earn_total,P_thrsh_red,P_redn_rate),Taper(Children*P_ch_amt,(earn_total)),P_ch_thresh,P_ch_redn_rate))
Ontario sales tax credit	Prov_sales_cr	P	Taper(IF(Married=1,2,1)*P_sales_cred+Children*P_salcr_chd,earn_total, IF(Married+Children=0, P_ps_thresh,P_ps_thr_sen),P_ps_red_rt)
Total Cash Transfers	Cash_tran	P	CTB+GST_cr+Prov_child_ben+ Prov_sales_cr
13. Employer's soc security			
Canada Pension Plan	CPP_empr	B	CPP
Unemployment insurance	Unemp_empr	B	Unemp*Unemp_emplr
Ontario Employers Health Tax	Health_empr	B	earn*emp_healthtax
Ontario Workers Compensation	Comp_empr	B	MIN(earn, emp_workcomp_ceil)*emp_workcomp
Total Employer's soc security	SSC_empr	B	CPP_empr+Unemp_empr+Health_empr+Comp_empr

Key to range of equation B calculated separately for both principal earner and spouse P calculated for principal only (value taken as 0 for spouse calculation) J calculated once only on a joint basis.

Taxing Wages 2014
Changes in sructural labour income tax progressivity
over 2000-12 period in OECD member countries

Chile

This chapter includes data on the income taxes paid by workers, their social security contributions, the family benefits they receive in the form of cash transfers as well as the social security contributions and payroll taxes paid by their employers. Results reported include the marginal and average tax burden for eight different family types.

Methodological information is available for personal income tax systems, compulsory social security contributions to schemes operated within the government sector, universal cash transfers as well as recent changes in the tax/benefit system. The methodology also includes the parameter values and tax equations underlying the data

Chile 2013

The tax/benefit position of single persons

	Wage level (per cent of average wage)	67	100	167	67
	Number of children	none	none	none	2
1.	**Gross wage earnings**	4404984	6607476	11012460	4404984
2.	**Standard tax allowances**				
	Basic allowance	3564513	5346770	6605064	3564513
	Married or head of family				
	Dependent children				
	Deduction for social security contributions and income taxes	308349	462523	770872	308349
	Work-related expenses				
	Other	532122	798183	1330305	532122
	Total	4404984	6607476	8706241	4404984
3.	**Tax credits or cash transfers included in taxable income**	0	0	0	0
4.	**Central government taxable income (1 - 2 + 3)**	0	0	2306219	0
5.	**Central government income tax liability (exclusive of tax credits)**	0	0	92249	0
6.	**Tax credits**				
	Basic credit				
	Married or head of family				
	Children	0	0	0	0
	Other				
	Total	0	0	0	0
7.	**Central government income tax finally paid (5-6)**	0	0	92249	0
8.	**State and local taxes**	0	0	0	0
9.	**Employees' compulsory social security contributions**				
	Gross earnings	308349	462523	770872	308349
	Taxable income				
	Total	308349	462523	770872	308349
10.	**Total payments to general government (7 + 8 + 9)**	308349	462523	863121	308349
11.	**Cash transfers from general government**				
	For head of family				
	For two children	0	0	0	39876
	Total	0	0	0	39876
12.	**Take-home pay (1-10+11)**	4096635	6144953	10149339	4136511
13.	**Employer's compulsory social security contributions**	0	0	0	0
14.	**Average rates**				
	Income tax	0.0%	0.0%	0.8%	0.0%
	Employees' social security contributions	7.0%	7.0%	7.0%	7.0%
	Total payments less cash transfers	7.0%	7.0%	7.8%	6.1%
	Total tax wedge including employer's social security contributions	7.0%	7.0%	7.8%	6.1%
15.	**Marginal rates**				
	Total payments less cash transfers: Principal earner	7.0%	7.0%	10.2%	7.0%
	Total payments less cash transfers: Spouse	n.a.	n.a.	n.a.	n.a.
	Total tax wedge: Principal earner	7.0%	7.0%	10.2%	7.0%
	Total tax wedge: Spouse	n.a.	n.a.	n.a.	n.a.

Chile 2013

The tax/benefit position of married couples

		Wage level (per cent of average wage)	100-0	100-33	100-67	100-33
		Number of children	2	2	2	none
1.	**Gross wage earnings**		6607476	8809968	11012460	8809968
2.	**Standard tax allowances**					
	Basic allowance		5346770	7129026	8911283	7129026
	Married or head of family					
	Dependent children					
	Deduction for social security contributions and income taxes		462523	616698	770872	616698
	Work-related expenses					
	Other		798183	1064244	1330305	1064244
		Total	6607476	8809968	11012460	8809968
3.	**Tax credits or cash transfers included in taxable income**		0	0	0	0
4.	**Central government taxable income (1 - 2 + 3)**		0	0	0	0
5.	**Central government income tax liability (exclusive of tax credits)**		0	0	0	0
6.	**Tax credits**					
	Basic credit					
	Married or head of family					
	Children		0	0	0	0
	Other					
		Total	0	0	0	0
7.	**Central government income tax finally paid (5-6)**		0	0	0	0
8.	**State and local taxes**		0	0	0	0
9.	**Employees' compulsory social security contributions**					
	Gross earnings		462523	616698	770872	616698
	Taxable income					
		Total	462523	616698	770872	616698
10.	**Total payments to general government (7 + 8 + 9)**		462523	616698	770872	616698
11.	**Cash transfers from general government**					
	For head of family					
	For two children		0	196440	39876	0
		Total	0	196440	39876	0
12.	**Take-home pay (1-10+11)**		6144953	8389710	10281464	8193270
13.	**Employer's compulsory social security contributions**		0	0	0	0
14.	**Average rates**					
	Income tax		0.0%	0.0%	0.0%	0.0%
	Employees' social security contributions		7.0%	7.0%	7.0%	7.0%
	Total payments less cash transfers		7.0%	4.8%	6.6%	7.0%
	Total tax wedge including employer's social security contributions		7.0%	4.8%	6.6%	7.0%
15.	**Marginal rates**					
	Total payments less cash transfers: Principal earner		7.0%	7.0%	7.0%	7.0%
	Total payments less cash transfers: Spouse		-1.9%	7.0%	7.0%	7.0%
	Total tax wedge: Principal earner		7.0%	7.0%	7.0%	7.0%
	Total tax wedge: Spouse		-1.9%	7.0%	7.0%	7.0%

Chile's national currency is the peso (CLP). For 2013, the average exchange rate was CLP 495.28 to USD 1. That same year, the average worker in Chile earned CLP 6 607 476 (country estimate).

Taxes allowances and tax thresholds for the personal income tax system and upper earnings limits for social security contributions are determined using and expressed in CPI-indexed units. At 31 December, 2013, the following currency values applied to these units:

Major revenue items	Unit	CLP	USD
Social security contributions	Unidad de Fomento[1] (UF)	23 309.56[1]	47.06
Monthly tax thresholds	Unidad Tributaria Mensual (UTM)	40 772	82.32
Annual tax thresholds	Unidad Tributaria Anual (UTA)	489 264	987.85

1. This amount is subject to daily adjustment in line with the CPI and is compared with monthly earnings in the assessment of social security contributions.

1. Personal income tax systems

1.1. *Central/federal government income taxes*

1.1.1. *Tax unit*

Each family member declares and pays taxes separately.

1.1.2. *Tax allowances and credits*

1.1.2.1. Standard tax reliefs

- *A general basic allowance* of UTA 13.5, around CLP 6 605 064 is deductible from income in 2013.
- *Relief for social security contributions:* Employee's compulsory social insurance contributions are deductible for income tax purposes regardless of whether they are paid to government or private health insurers (see Section 2.1 below).

1.1.2.2. Main non-standard tax reliefs

- *Voluntary contributions and APV (Voluntary Pension Fund Savings):* Voluntary contributions to pension funds and voluntary pension savings fund (APV) may be deducted from taxable income, with an annual upper limit of CLP 13 985 736 (UF 600).
- *Mortgage Interest:* Taxpayers whose annual income falls below CLP 44 033 760 (UTA 90) may deduct from their taxable income 100 per cent of interest paid within a year for mortgage loans. This percentage is reduced in the case of taxpayers with higher incomes up to CLP 73 389 600 (UTA 150). This relief cannot be granted along-side the *DFL2 Housing Mortgage Loan Payments* benefit, and cannot exceed CLP 3 914 112 (UTA 8) per annum.

1.1.3. *Tax schedule*

Tax rates are applied on monthly income and these taxes are retained and paid by employers. In order to estimate taxes, tax rates are applied proportionately to annual average income.

On 1 January 2013 a decrease in the personal income tax rates, in all the brackets (except for the top statutory rate) was implemented.

Taxable income (UTA)	Taxable income (CLP thousands)	Tax rates
0-13.5	0-6 605	Exempt
13.5-30	6 605-14 678	4%
30-50	14 678-24 463	8%
50-70	24 463-34 248	13.5%
70-90	34 248-44 034	23%
90-120	44 034-58 712	30.4%
120-150	58 712-73 390	35.5%
150 and over	73 390 and over	40%

1.2. *State and local income taxes*

No taxes apply to income at state or local government level.

2. Compulsory social security contributions to schemes operated within the government sector

2.1. *Employees' contributions*

Employees have mandatorily to contribute 7% of their income to a health insurance plan subject to an upper earnings limit of CLP 19 403 272 (UF 70.3). They are free to choose whether to pay into a government-managed plan or alternatively to a private insurer* (Isapres). The public insurance is based on a joint system that, in general, operates on an equal basis for all its beneficiaries, irrespective of the risk and the amount of the individual contribution. Its financing is partly covered by the contributions and partly by way of a government subsidy. Premiums paid to the plans offered by Isapres are based on the contributors' individual risk and these plans are exclusively financed with the employees' contributions. These contributions are included in the modelling as the majority of employees pay into plans managed by the government sector.

Employee social security contributions in respect of pensions and unemployment are not classified as taxes in this report; though they are included in modelling as deductions for income tax.

- The mandatory contributions to pension funds and unemployment insurance plans are not classified as taxes, since the payments are made to private institutions. In 1980, the public social security system was replaced with a privately managed individual capitalisation system. This system is obligatory to all employees who have joined the labour force since 1983 and free-lance workers since 2012, and of a voluntary nature to all contributing to the former system. The contributions to the old government operated pension fund system are not included in the modelling because they relate to a minority

* Enrollement in the private health system during 2012 amounted to 17.5% of all beneficiaries.

of employees and the system will eventually disappear once the contributions and related benefit payments to those individuals remaining in it have ceased.

- The modelling allows that the contributions to pension funds and unemployment insurance managed by private institutions are deducted from gross income. In the case of their pension funds, these payments amount to 10 per cent of their gross income, with an upper earnings limit of CLP 19 403 272 (UF 70.3). Added to that is an amount that varies depending on the managing company that covers the management of each pension fund account.* The monthly unemployment insurance premium is 0.6 per cent of the employee's gross income, with an upper earnings limit of CLP 29 091 108 (UF 105.4) limit. Employees do not pay the monthly unemployment insurance premium when they have a fixed-term contract.
- There are also mandatory contributions to managed funds by members of the police force and the army which are classified as taxes but are not included in the modelling as they relate to a minority of the overall workforce.
- If the employee has a high risk job, he has to make an additional contribution of up to 2 per cent of his gross income to his pension fund account.

2.2. Employers' contributions

There are four categories of employer social security contribution, none of which are classified as tax revenues in this report.

- Employers make mandatory payments of 0.95 per cent of their employees' gross income for an occupational accident and disease insurance policy subject to an upper earnings limit. For the majority of employees the payments are made to employers' associations of labour security which are private non-profit institutions. Those remaining are made to the Social Security Regularisation Unit (ISL). Although this latter organisation is controlled by the government, the funds are invested on the private institutions market. The employers also pay an additional contribution which depends on the activity and risk associated to the enterprise (it cannot exceed 3.4 per cent of the employees' gross earnings). This additional contribution could be reduced, down to 0 per cent, depending on the safety measures the employer implements in the enterprise. If health and safety conditions at work are not satisfactory, this additional contribution could be applied with a surcharge of up to 100 per cent.
- In addition, employers make payments of 2.4 per cent of each employee's income (3 per cent for fixed-term contracts) to finance unemployment insurance. These funds are managed privately.
- Employers have to pay a disability insurance of 1.26 per cent of the employees' gross income, to the pension fund manager.
- If the employee has a high risk job, the employer has to pay up to 2 per cent of the employee's gross income to his pension fund account.

3. Universal cash transfers

3.1. Marital status-related transfers

No such transfers are paid.

* Average cost in 2013 was 1.48% of gross income.

3.2. *Transfers related to dependent children*

The "Family Allowance" is paid on a monthly basis to any employee making social security contributions who has dependent children. The definition of dependants includes;

- Adopted children as well as those born to the parents;
- Children up to the age of 18 or 24 years provided they are single and are regular students in an elementary, secondary, technical, specialised or higher education establishment and whose income is less than or equal to half the minimum wage.
- The amount of the payment depends on the number of dependent children and the beneficiary's level of income according to the table below. The modelling assumes that the benefit is assessed on the spouse with the lower earning level where both spouses are working.

2013 transfer by dependant

Annual income range (CLP)	Annual payment (CLP)
0-2 537 232	98 220
2 537 232-3 835 560	63 090
3 835 560-5 982 162	19 938
5 982 162 and over	0

4. Memorandum items

4.1. *Identification of an average worker*

- The source of information is a survey conducted by the National Statistics Institute (INE) to determine the Salary and Labour Cost Index. This nationwide survey is carried out on a monthly sample and gathers information on salaries and labour costs. It applies to companies with at least 5-worker payrolls grouped in accordance with UN ISIC Rev. 3 international economic activity standard, covering workers in industry Sectors C – O.*
- The average gross earnings was obtained by multiplying the average hourly wage by the average number of hours worked. Only full-time workers are considered.

4.2. *Employers' contribution to private health and pension schemes*

- In Chile very few employers make any contributions towards health schemes for their employees, and the relevant information is not available.

* L(7522) and L(7523) are not included.

2013 parameter values

Average earnings/yr	Ave_earn	6 607 476	Country estimate
Allowances	Basic_al	6 605 064	
Income tax	Tax_sch	0.04	14 677 920
		0.080	24 463 200
		0.135	34 248 480
		0.23	44 033 760
		0.304	58 711 680
		0.355	73 389 600
		0.4	
Employees SSC	SSC_sch	0.07	19 403 272
Upper threshold		0	
Family allowance	CTR_child	0	98 220
Child element		2 537 232	63 090
		3 835 560	19 938
		5 982 162	0

2013 tax equations

The functions which are used in the equations (Taper, MIN, Tax, etc.) are described in the technical note about tax equations. Variable names are defined in the table of parameters above, within the equations table, or are the standard variables "married" and "children". A reference to a variable with the affix "_total" indicates the sum of the relevant variable values for the principal and spouse. And the affixes "_princ" and "_spouse" indicate the value for the principal and spouse, respectively. Equations for a single person are as shown for the principal, with "_spouse" values taken as 0.

	Line in country table and intermediate steps	Variable name	Range	Equation
1.	Earnings	earn		
2.	Allowances:	Tax_al	B	Min(Basic_al,earn)
3.	Credits in taxable income	taxbl_cr	B	0
4.	CG taxable income	tax_inc	B	Positive(earn-tax_al)
5.	CG tax before credits	CG_tax_excl	B	Tax(tax_inc, tax_sch)
6.	Tax credits :	tax_cr	B	0
7.	CG tax	CG_tax	B	CG_tax_excl
8.	State and local taxes	local_tax	B	0
9.	Employees' soc security	SSC	B	Tax(earn, SSC_sch)
11.	Family allowance	cash_trans	P/S	IF(Children=0,0, IF(earn_spouse>0, VLOOKUP (earn_spouse, CTR_child) , VLOOKUP (earn_princ, CTR_child)) * children)
13.	Employer's soc security	SSC_empr		0

Key to range of equation B calculated separately for both principal earner and spouse P calculated for principal only (value taken as 0 for spouse calculation) J calculated once only on a joint basis.

Taxing Wages 2014
Changes in sructural labour income tax progressivity
over 2000-12 period in OECD member countries

Czech Republic

This chapter includes data on the income taxes paid by workers, their social security contributions, the family benefits they receive in the form of cash transfers as well as the social security contributions and payroll taxes paid by their employers. Results reported include the marginal and average tax burden for eight different family types.

Methodological information is available for personal income tax systems, compulsory social security contributions to schemes operated within the government sector, universal cash transfers as well as recent changes in the tax/ benefit system. The methodology also includes the parameter values and tax equations underlying the data.

Czech Republic 2013

The tax/benefit position of single persons

	Wage level (per cent of average wage)	67	100	167	67
	Number of children	none	none	none	2
1.	**Gross wage earnings**	199180	298770	497950	199180
2.	**Standard tax allowances**				
	Basic allowance	0	0	0	0
	Married or head of family	0	0	0	0
	Dependent children	0	0	0	0
	Deduction for social security contributions and income taxes	0	0	0	0
	Work-related expenses				
	Other				
	Total	0	0	0	0
3.	**Tax credits or cash transfers included in taxable income**	0	0	0	0
4.	**Central government taxable income (1 - 2 + 3 + 13)**	266901	400352	667253	266901
5.	**Central government income tax liability (exclusive of tax credits)**	40035	60053	100088	40035
6.	**Tax credits**				
	Basic credit				
	Married or head of family				
	Children				
	Other	24840	24840	24840	51648
	Total	24840	24840	24840	51648
7.	**Central government income tax finally paid (5-6)**	15195	35213	75248	-11613
8.	**State and local taxes**	0	0	0	0
9.	**Employees' compulsory social security contributions**				
	Gross earnings	21910	32865	54775	21910
	Taxable income				
	Total	21910	32865	54775	21910
10.	**Total payments to general government (7 + 8 + 9)**	37105	68077	130022	10297
11.	**Cash transfers from general government**				
	For head of family				
	For two children	0	0	0	39753
	Total	0	0	0	39753
12.	**Take-home pay (1-10+11)**	162075	230693	367928	228636
13.	**Employer's compulsory social security contributions**	67721	101582	169303	67721
14.	**Average rates**				
	Income tax	7.6%	11.8%	15.1%	-5.8%
	Employees' social security contributions	11.0%	11.0%	11.0%	11.0%
	Total payments less cash transfers	18.6%	22.8%	26.1%	-14.8%
	Total tax wedge including employer's social security contributions	39.3%	42.4%	44.9%	14.3%
15.	**Marginal rates**				
	Total payments less cash transfers: Principal earner	31.1%	31.1%	31.1%	40.7%
	Total payments less cash transfers: Spouse	n.a.	n.a.	n.a.	n.a.
	Total tax wedge: Principal earner	48.6%	48.6%	48.6%	55.7%
	Total tax wedge: Spouse	n.a.	n.a.	n.a.	n.a.

Czech Republic 2013

The tax/benefit position of married couples

	Wage level (per cent of average wage)	100-0	100-33	100-67	100-33
	Number of children	2	2	2	none
1.	**Gross wage earnings**	298770	398360	497950	398360
2.	**Standard tax allowances**				
	Basic allowance	0	0	0	0
	Married or head of family	0	0	0	0
	Dependent children	0	0	0	0
	Deduction for social security contributions and income taxes	0	0	0	0
	Work-related expenses				
	Other				
	Total	0	0	0	0
3.	**Tax credits or cash transfers included in taxable income**	0	0	0	0
4.	**Central government taxable income (1 - 2 + 3 + 13)**	400352	533802	667253	533802
5.	**Central government income tax liability (exclusive of tax credits)**	60053	80070	100088	80070
6.	**Tax credits**				
	Basic credit				
	Married or head of family				
	Children				
	Other	76488	51648	51648	24840
	Total	76488	51648	51648	24840
7.	**Central government income tax finally paid (5-6)**	-16435	8405	23600	35213
8.	**State and local taxes**	0	0	0	0
9.	**Employees' compulsory social security contributions**				
	Gross earnings	32865	43820	54775	43820
	Taxable income				
	Total	32865	43820	54775	43820
10.	**Total payments to general government (7 + 8 + 9)**	16429	52224	78374	79032
11.	**Cash transfers from general government**				
	For head of family				
	For two children	35940	29148	21329	0
	Total	35940	29148	21329	0
12.	**Take-home pay (1-10+11)**	318280	375283	440904	319328
13.	**Employer's compulsory social security contributions**	101582	135442	169303	135442
14.	**Average rates**				
	Income tax	-5.5%	2.1%	4.7%	8.8%
	Employees' social security contributions	11.0%	11.0%	11.0%	11.0%
	Total payments less cash transfers	-6.5%	5.8%	11.5%	19.8%
	Total tax wedge including employer's social security contributions	20.5%	29.7%	33.9%	40.2%
15.	**Marginal rates**				
	Total payments less cash transfers: Principal earner	38.4%	38.4%	38.4%	31.1%
	Total payments less cash transfers: Spouse	42.8%	20.5%	38.4%	11.0%
	Total tax wedge: Principal earner	54.1%	54.1%	54.1%	48.6%
	Total tax wedge: Spouse	57.3%	40.7%	54.1%	33.6%

The national currency is the Czech koruna (CZK). In 2013, CZK 19.56 equal to USD 1. In that year, the average worker earned CZK 298 770 (country estimate).

1. Personal income tax systems

1.1. *Central government income taxes*

1.1.1. *Tax unit*

- The tax unit is the individual.

1.1.2. *Tax allowances and tax credits*

1.1.2.1. Standard reliefs

- *Relief for social and health security contributions.* Employees' social security contributions (see Section 2.1) are not deductible for income tax purposes.

1.1.2.2. Main non-standard tax reliefs applicable to an AW

- *Charitable donations allowance:* A tax allowance of up to 10 per cent of taxable income is available for donations made to municipalities or legal entities for the financing of social, health, cultural, humanitarian, religious, ecological and sport activities. The minimum limit for donations is the lesser of 2 per cent of taxable income or CZK 1 000.
- *Interest payments:* Taxpayers may claim an allowance of up to CZK 300 000 for mortgage interest payments or other interest payments related to the purchase or the improvement of their house. If more than one individual living in the same household apply for this allowance, the sum of their annual deductions is subject to the above-mentioned ceiling, i.e. CZK 300 000.
- *Supplementary pension scheme contributions:* Taxpayers who are members of a registered supplementary private pension scheme are entitled to deduct the individually paid (i.e. paid by employee) annual contributions to a registered pension scheme reduced by CZK 6 000 from the earned income. The maximum allowance is CZK 12 000 a year.
- *Private life insurance premiums:* Taxpayers may claim an allowance of up to CZK 12 000 for premiums paid according to a contract between the taxpayer and an insurance company if the benefit (lump sum or recurrent pension) is paid out 60 months after the signature of the contract and in the year in which the taxpayer reaches the age of 60.

1.1.2.3. Tax schedule

From January 2008, a progressive system of taxation is replaced by a single rate of 15%, levied on gross earnings augmented with employer social security contributions net of non-standard tax reliefs. The non-standard tax reliefs are not included in the tax equations underlying the *Taxing Wages* results.

1.1.2.4. Tax credits

- Credit of CZK 24 840 per taxpayer.

- Credit of CZK 24 840 per spouse (husband or wife) living with a taxpayer in one household provided that the spouse's own income does not exceed CZK 68 000 in the taxable period.
- Credit for children: Payable tax credit of CZK 13 404 (irrespective of the child's own income) if the child satisfies one or more of the following criteria:
  - age below 18;
  - age below 26 and receiving full-time education;
  - age below 26 and physically or mentally disabled provided that the child is not in receipt of a state disability payment.

  Non-standard tax credits:
- Credit of CZK 2 520 if the taxpayer is in receipt of a partial disability pension or is entitled to both an old-age pension and a partial disability pension.
- Credit of CZK 5 040 it the taxpayer is in receipt of a full disability pension, or another type of pension conditional on his full disability pension, or if the taxpayer is entitled to both old-age pension and full disability pension or deemed to be fully disabled under statutory provisions, but his application for a full disability pension was rejected for reasons other than that he was not fully disabled (handicapped)
- Credit of CZK 16 140 if the taxpayer is a "ZTP-P" card holder (ZTP-P means handicapped person requiring an escort).
- Credit of CZK 4 020 if the taxpayer takes part in a systematic educational or training programme under statutory provisions in order to prepare for his future vocation (profession) by means of such studies or prescribed training until completion of his/her 26 or 28 years (Ph.D. programme).

1.2. State and local income tax

There are no regional or local income taxes.

2. Compulsory social security contributions to schemes operated within the government sector

Since 2012, there are two ceilings on social security contributions. In 2013, a separate ceiling set at four times the average annual salary, i.e. CZK 1 242 432 applies to social security contributions. For the 2013-15 tax years, the ceiling on health insurance contributions (six times the average annual salary) is abolished. As of 2015 both employees and the self-employed will pay health insurance contributions at 6.5% of the contribution base.

2.1. Employees' contributions

Compulsory contributions of 11 per cent of gross wages and salaries are paid by all employees into government operated schemes. The total is made up as follows (in %):

Health insurance	4.5
Social insurance	6.5

2.2. Employers' contributions

The total contribution for employers is 34 per cent of gross earnings.

The contribution consists of the health insurance contribution (9 per cent of gross wages and salaries) and social insurance (25 per cent).

3. Universal cash transfers

3.1. *Transfers related to marital status*

None.

3.2. *Transfers for dependent children*

Non-taxable family allowances are paid as follows:

Family income	Up to 2.4 LM
Age of child	Total payment CZK per month
Below 6	500
6-15	610
15-26	700

The central government pays this allowance in respect of each dependent child based on the family income level and provided that family income does not exceed 2.4 times the relevant living minimum (LM). Family income includes the earnings of both parents net of income tax and the employees' social security and health insurance contributions. The monthly LM for the AW-type family with children can be calculated by summing the following amounts (in CZK):

Living minimum	
Basic personal requirement	
Single	3 410
First person in household	3 140
Second and other persons who are not a dependent child	2 830
Child aged below 6	1 740
Child aged between 6 and 15	2 140
Child aged between 15 and 26	2 450
Household expenses	
One person household	3 140
Two person household	5 970
Three person household	7 710
Four person household	9 850
Five person household	12 300

A family is also entitled to a social allowance if there is at least one child in the family and the net monthly income of the family is below two times the LM. The transfer is calculated based on the following formula:

$$\text{child's basic personal requirement} - \frac{\text{child's basic personal requirement * net family income}}{\text{LM * 2}}$$

If the net family income is below the LM, then the LM is to be used in this formula instead of the net family income. The central government pays this allowance monthly.

3.3. *Additional transfers*

An additional allowance is paid by local government to low income families. The amount transferred varies according to the budget capacity and is provided if total family income including family allowances is less than the LM. This allowance is not included in the computation.

4. Main changes in tax/benefit systems since 2013

In 2013, there were no changes that would have a significant effect on the current calculation of *Taxing Wages*.

5. Memorandum items

5.1. *Identification of AW and valuation of earnings*

The Ministry of Finance estimates the average earnings of the AW based on the data supplied by the Czech Statistical Office. The calculation of the average earnings AW is made by CZ-NACE division, which is compatible with ISIC classifications Ver. 4.

5.2. *Employers' contributions to private pension, health and related schemes*

There are supplementary private pension schemes only, but employers' contributions vary. Relevant information is not available.

2013 parameter values

	Ave_earn	298 770	Secretariat estimate
Income tax rate	tax_rate	0.15	
Social security – social insurance	SSs_rate	0.065	
Social security – health insurance	SSh_rate	0.045	
Employers	SSC_empr_rate	0.34	
Child Tax credit	child_ cr	13 404	
Tax credit for individuals	tax_cr_base	24 840	
Tax credit for spouse	tax_cr_spo	24 840	
Tax credit for spouse income ceiling	Tax_cr_spo_inc_ceil	68 000	
Living minimum (LM)			
	basic_adult	3 410	
	basic_household	5 970	
	basic_child	2 140	
	house_exp	1	3 140
		2	5 970
		3	7 710
		4	9 850
		5	12 300
Cash transfers	transf_1	610	
Social security, social insurance – ceiling	soc_sec_si_ceil	1 242 432	

2013 tax equations

The equations for the Czech system are on an individual basis. But the spouse tax credit is relevant only to the calculation for the principal earner and cash transfers are calculated only once. This is shown by the Range indicator in the table below.

The functions which are used in the equations (Taper, MIN, Tax, etc.) are described in the technical note about tax equations. Variable names are defined in the table of parameters above, within the equations table, or are the standard variables "married" and "children". A reference to a variable with the affix "_total" indicates the sum of the relevant variable values for the principal and spouse. And the affixes "_princ" and "_spouse" indicate the value for the principal and spouse, respectively. Equations for a single person are as shown for the principal, with "_spouse" values taken as 0.

	Line in country table and intermediate steps	Variable name	Range	Equation
1.	Earnings	earn	B	
2.	CG taxable income	tax_inc_princ	B	Earn+(earn*SSC_empr_rate)
3.	CG tax before credits			
	CG tax before credits principal	CG_tax_excl_princ	B	Tax(tax_inc_princ, tax_rate)
4.	Tax credits:			
	Tax credit for children	tax_cr_ch	P	children*child_cr
	Basic tax credit	tax_cr_bas	B	tax_cr_bas
	Tax credit for spouse	tax_cr_spouse	P	Married*tax_cr_spo
5.	CG tax			
	CG tax principal	CG_tax_princ	B	Max(CG_tax_excl_princ - tax_cr_bas_princ - tax_cr_spo , 0) - tax_cr_ch
6.	State and local taxes	local_tax	B	0
7.	Employees' social security	SSs SSh	B B	MIN(earn,soc_sec_si__ceil)*SSs_rate earn*SSh_rate
8.	Cash transfers			
	Net family income	net_inc	J	earn_total-CG_tax_total-SSC_total
9.	Living minimum (monthly)	LM	J	(1-Married)*basic_adult+Married*basic_household +Children*basic_child+ VLOOKUP((1+Married+Children), house_exp, 2, FALSE)
10.	Total cash transfers	cash_trans	J	Children*IF(net_inc<=(2.4)*LM*12, transf_1*12) +Children*12*IF(net_inc<LM*12, basic_child*(1/2), IF(net_inc<2*LM*12, basic_child*(1- net_inc/(2*LM*12)),0))
11.	Employer's social security	SSs_empr SSh_empr	B B	MIN(earn,soc_sec_sir_ceil)*SSs_empr_rate earn*SSh_empr_rate

Key to range of equation: B calculated separately for both principal earner and spouse; P calculated for principal only (value taken as 0 for spouse calculation); J calculated once only on a joint basis.

Taxing Wages 2014
Changes in sructural labour income tax progressivity
over 2000-12 period in OECD member countries

Denmark

This chapter includes data on the income taxes paid by workers, their social security contributions, the family benefits they receive in the form of cash transfers as well as the social security contributions and payroll taxes paid by their employers. Results reported include the marginal and average tax burden for eight different family types.

Methodological information is available for personal income tax systems, compulsory social security contributions to schemes operated within the government sector, universal cash transfers as well as recent changes in the tax/ benefit system. The methodology also includes the parameter values and tax equations underlying the data.

Denmark 2013

	The tax/benefit position of single persons				
	Wage level (per cent of average wage)	67	100	167	67
	Number of children	none	none	none	2
1.	**Gross wage earnings**	263815	395722	659536	263815
2.	**Standard tax allowances**				
	Basic allowance				
	Married or head of family				
	Dependent children				
	Deduction for social security contributions and income taxes	21105	31658	52763	21105
	Work-related expenses	10837	10837	10837	10837
	Other				
	Total	31942	42495	63600	31942
3.	**Tax credits or cash transfers included in taxable income**	0	0	0	0
	Earnings tax credit deduction	18335	22300	22300	18335
	Total	-18335	-22300	-22300	-18335
4.	**Central government taxable income (1 - 2 + 3)**	213537	330927	573637	213537
5.	**Central government income tax liability (exclusive of tax credits)**	26899	41018	97366	26899
6.	**Tax credits**				
	Basic credit	4969	4969	4969	4969
	Married or head of family				
	Children				
	Other				
	Total	4969	4969	4969	4969
7.	**Central government income tax finally paid (5-6)**	43036	67707	145160	43036
8.	**State and local taxes**	43965	74052	136258	43965
9.	**Employees' compulsory social security contributions**				
	Gross earnings	10837	10837	10837	10837
	Taxable income				
	Total	10837	10837	10837	10837
10.	**Total payments to general government (7 + 8 + 9)**	97838	152596	292256	97838
11.	**Cash transfers from general government**				
	For head of family				
	For two children	0	0	0	66472
	Green check	1300	1286	0	1900
	Total	1300	1286	0	68372
12.	**Take-home pay (1-10+11)**	167277	244412	367281	234349
13.	**Employer's compulsory social security contributions**	0	0	0	0
14.	**Average rates**				
	Income tax	33.0%	35.8%	42.7%	33.0%
	Employees' social security contributions	4.1%	2.7%	1.6%	4.1%
	Total payments less cash transfers	36.6%	38.2%	44.3%	11.2%
	Total tax wedge including employer's social security contributions	36.6%	38.2%	44.3%	11.2%
15.	**Marginal rates**				
	Total payments less cash transfers: Principal earner	40.3%	49.4%	56.2%	40.3%
	Total payments less cash transfers: Spouse	n.a.	n.a.	n.a.	n.a.
	Total tax wedge: Principal earner	40.3%	49.4%	56.2%	40.3%
	Total tax wedge: Spouse	n.a.	n.a.	n.a.	n.a.

Denmark 2013

The tax/benefit position of married couples

		Wage level (per cent of average wage)	100-0	100-33	100-67	100-33
		Number of children	2	2	2	none
1.	**Gross wage earnings**		395722	527629	659536	527629
2.	**Standard tax allowances**					
	Basic allowance					
	Married or head of family					
	Dependent children					
	Deduction for social security contributions and income taxes		31658	42210	52763	42210
	Work-related expenses		10837	21674	21674	21674
	Other					
		Total	42495	63884	74437	63884
3.	**Tax credits or cash transfers included in taxable income**		0	0	0	0
	Earnings tax credit deduction		22300	22300	22300	22300
		Total	-22300	-22300	-22300	-22300
4.	**Central government taxable income (1 - 2 + 3)**		330927	432277	544464	432277
5.	**Central government income tax liability (exclusive of tax credits)**		41018	54111	67917	54111
6.	**Tax credits**					
	Basic credit		14906	9937	9937	9937
	Married or head of family					
	Children					
	Other					
		Total	14906	9937	9937	9937
7.	**Central government income tax finally paid (5-6)**		62738	86384	110743	86384
8.	**State and local taxes**		63287	89263	118017	89263
9.	**Employees' compulsory social security contributions**					
	Gross earnings		10837	21674	21674	21674
	Taxable income					
		Total	10837	21674	21674	21674
10.	**Total payments to general government (7 + 8 + 9)**		136863	197321	250434	197321
11.	**Cash transfers from general government**					
	For head of family					
	For two children		24324	24324	24324	0
	Green check		3466	3466	3186	2866
		Total	27790	27790	27510	2866
12.	**Take-home pay (1-10+11)**		286649	358098	436613	333174
13.	**Employer's compulsory social security contributions**		0	0	0	0
14.	**Average rates**					
	Income tax		31.8%	33.3%	34.7%	33.3%
	Employees' social security contributions		2.7%	4.1%	3.3%	4.1%
	Total payments less cash transfers		27.6%	32.1%	33.8%	36.9%
	Total tax wedge including employer's social security contributions		27.6%	32.1%	33.8%	36.9%
15.	**Marginal rates**					
	Total payments less cash transfers: Principal earner		49.4%	49.4%	49.4%	49.4%
	Total payments less cash transfers: Spouse		45.8%	40.3%	40.3%	40.3%
	Total tax wedge: Principal earner		49.4%	49.4%	49.4%	49.4%
	Total tax wedge: Spouse		45.8%	40.3%	40.3%	40.3%

The national currency is the kroner (DKK). In 2013, DKK 5.62 was equal to USD 1. In that year, the average worker earned DKK 395 722 (Secretariat estimate), which is calculated on the background of the extrapolated 2012 average worker income with the 2013 growth rate on 0.94946 pct.).

1. Personal income tax systems

In the Danish personal income tax system, the income of the individual taxpayer is split into three categories:

- *Personal income,* which consists of employment income, business income, pensions, unemployment benefits, etc. and with fully deductibility of Labour Market Contributions.
- *Capital income* (e.g. interest income and some capital gains) is calculated as a net amount (the sum of positive and negative capital income net of interest expenses). Dividend income and the property value of owner-occupied dwellings are taxed at different tax rates.
- *Taxable income* – the aggregate of personal income and capital income less deductions (e.g. work-related expenses, etc.).

All three categories are relevant for various tax rates, see Section 1.2.1.

The employees' social security contributions and their payments to labour market supplementary pension schemes (see Section 2.1) are not included in personal income (or taxable income).

Regarding the tax unit, the earned income of each spouse is taxed separately. However, as is mentioned in Section 1.2.1, some unutilised personal allowances can be transferred between them.

1.1. *Tax allowances and tax credits*

1.1.1. *Standard reliefs*

Wage or salary earners who make expenses in order to earn their income (e.g. transport expenses, trade union membership dues, unemployment premiums) can fully deduct these expenses from taxable income. In this Report, contributions to unemployment insurance are therefore regarded as a standard tax allowance (and as a social security contribution).

The tax credit scheme allows the taxpayer to deduct 6.95 per cent of earned income to a maximum of DKK 22 300 in order to calculate taxable income. The effective value of the credit is equal to the municipality tax (24.9 per cent), the church tax rate (0.7 per cent) plus the 6.0 per cent health care tax rate that is paid to the state (31.63 per cent on average) multiplied by the value of the deduction.

1.1.2. *Main non-standard tax reliefs applicable to an AW*

- *Interest payments* are fully deductible from capital income.

- The *non-standard deduction for wage and salary earners:* The actual costs that are made in order to acquire income are deductible from taxable income. The main items are:
  - Contributions paid to trade unions.
  - Transportation costs: Up to 24 km per day: no deduction. 24-120 km.: DKK 2.13 per km. Above 120 km: DKK 1.07 per km as a standard, but transport from municipalities placed in the outskirts of the country gives a credit of DKK 2.13 also above 120 km.
  - Other costs above DKK 5 500.
- *Contributions/premiums* paid to *private pension saving plans* are in general deductible from personal income. From 1999 onwards, contributions/premiums paid to private pension saving plans with sum payments are no longer deductible from income subject to the top tax bracket rate. From 2013 onwards, contributions/premiums paid to private pension saving plans with sum payments are no longer deductible.
- Other reliefs:
  - Alimonies, if according to contract, are deductible from taxable income.
  - Contributions to certain non-profit institutions are deductible from taxable income (limit DKK 14 500).
  - Losses incurred from unincorporated business in earlier years are, in principle, deductible from personal income.

1.1.3. Tax credits

Each individual is granted a personal allowance, which is converted into a wastable tax credit by applying the marginal tax rate of the first bracket of the income tax schedule. For taxpayers who are 18 years of age or are older, the tax credit amounts to:

For central government income tax	5.83 per cent of DKK 42 000 = DKK 2 449
For central government health care tax	6.00 per cent of DKK 42 000 = DKK 2 520
For municipal income tax and church tax (average rate)	25.63 per cent of DKK 42 000 = DKK 11 765

Special personal allowance for an individual younger than 18: DKK 31 500.

If a married person cannot utilise the personal allowance, the unutilised part is transferred to the spouse.

1.2. Central government income taxes

1.2.1. Tax schedule

Individuals pay an 8 per cent Labour Market Contribution (*Arbejdsmarkedsbidrag* in Danish), levied on the gross wage or other income from work before the deduction of any allowance.

Before 2008, the revenue was earmarked for certain social security expenditures through the Labour market Fund, but this system was abolished from 2008, and the tax enters the budget in the same way as any other income taxes. From 2011 the last links regarding social security of the tax were removed making all taxpayers working in Denmark pay the labour market contribution. The labour market contribution is thus treated as a PIT in *Taxing Wages* from 2011.

Low tax bracket to the central government is assessed on the aggregate of personal income and positive net capital income at the rate of 5.83 per cent.

From 2010 and onwards the medium tax bracket was removed.

Top tax bracket to the central government is assessed on the excess of DKK 421 000 of the aggregate of personal income and positive net capital income at the rate of 15 per cent. If a married individual cannot utilise the total allowance of DKK 421 000, the unutilised part is *not* transferred to the spouse.

If the marginal tax rate including local tax but excluding church tax exceeds 51.7 per cent, the top tax bracket rate is reduced by the difference between the marginal tax rate and 51.7 per cent.

1.2.2. Health care tax

Central government levies an additional health care tax of 6 per cent. The tax base is taxable income (see Section 1).

1.3. State and local income taxes

1.3.1. General description

Local income taxes are levied only by the municipalities (and the church). The rates vary across jurisdictions.

1.3.2. Tax base

The tax base is taxable income (see Section 1). Tax credit varies with tax rates. The average amount is given below.

1.3.3. Tax rates

Lowest rate: 22.7 per cent (municipalities)

Highest rate: 27.8 per cent (municipalities)

Average rate: 25.63 per cent (municipalities: 24.907 per cent; church: 0.723 per cent).

The average rate is used in this study. It is applied to the tax base less personal allowances (see Section 1.1).

2. Compulsory social security contributions to schemes operated within the government sector

2.1. Employees' contributions

Employees make a fixed contribution of DKK 10 837 for unemployment insurance. From 1999 onwards, the contribution for unemployment insurance is split into two: one part consists of the contribution for unemployment insurance (DKK 3 840) while the other part consists of a voluntary contribution to an early retirement scheme (DKK 5 604). In addition an administration fee of DKK 1 393 on average is added.

Contributions to the unemployment funds are not mandatory. Nevertheless these payments are defined as social security contributions and classified as taxes in the Danish national accounts because there is no direct link between what members pay to the schemes and what they receive and the funds are subsidized by the state. In this Report, both contributions as well as the administration fee are included.

In addition, there is a compulsory fixed contribution to a general Labour Market Supplementary Pension Scheme of DKK 1 080 for workers who work at least 117 hours per month (for workers who work less than 117 hours but not less than 78 hours, the rate is

DKK 720; for workers who work less than 78 hours but not less than 39 hours, the rate is DKK 360); their employer makes a corresponding contribution that is double this amount. Under this scheme, each employee has a plan and it should be noted that the contribution that is ascribed to this plan is determined by the level of employment and does not necessarily relate to the actual amount described above. The employee contribution of DKK 1 080 is modelled as a standard tax relief from the personal income tax. As the employee and employer contribution is paid to a privately-managed pension scheme, these contributions are not considered to be taxes but rather as non-tax compulsory payments and are therefore not included in the tax calculations.

2.2. Employers' contributions

From 2000 onwards, the social security contribution is zero. The employer only contributes to a Labour Market Supplementary Pension scheme, which in case of a full-time employee corresponds to a fixed amount of DKK 2 160 (being twice the fixed amount of DKK 1 080 mentioned in Section 2.1).

3. Universal cash transfers

The transfers for each dependent child are as follows:

Age group	Quarterly amount (DKK) for each child
0-2	4 299
3-6	3 402
7-17	2 679

The transfer is independent of the parents' income. There are additional special amounts for single parents: the transfer for each dependent child is DKK 5 184 per year and a yearly transfer of DKK 5 284 regardless of the number of children. In addition, there is a state transfer of DKK 13 248 per year for each dependent child in case an "absent parent" does not contribute (this amount) to the family. This transfer is included in this Report's calculations for single parents.

Individuals older than 18 years receive a "green check" of DKK 1 300; this amount is increased with DKK 300 per child for up to two children. Only one partner in a married couple receives the increased "green check" for children. The "green check" is nominally fixed and is phased out at a rate of 7.5 per cent for income above DKK 362 800. If the yearly income of the individuals is lower than DKK 212 000 the individuals receive an "additional green check" of DKK 280.

4. Main changes in tax/benefit systems

From 2000 to 2002, the low tax bracket rate has been reduced from 7 per cent to 5.5 per cent. The low tax bracket is assessed on the aggregate of personal income and positive net capital income.

After the parliamentary elections in 2001, the Conservative/Liberal government adopted a tax freeze policy, which implied that tax rates could not be increased, either in nominal or relative terms, during that government term. Taxes were therefore not increased during the period 2002-05. After the parliamentary elections in February 2005, the Conservative/Liberal government and the tax freeze policy were confirmed.

In order to respect the "tax freeze", the low tax bracket has been reduced by 0.36 per cent from 2004 to 2010 as a compensation for increases in local income taxes from 33.31 per cent in 2004 to 33.66 per cent in 2011.

In the spring of 2003, the government agreed with one of the opposition parties to implement a tax package. The aim of this package was to decrease the level of labour taxation in Denmark, and thereby to reduce the distortions in the labour market and to improve the incentives to work. The package contained two main elements: an increase of the threshold for the medium tax bracket of nearly DKK 50 000 and the introduction of a tax credit scheme whereby the taxpayer can deduct 2.5 per cent of earned income to a maximum of DKK 7 500 (in 2007) in the calculation of taxable income.

Before 2004, a compulsory contribution of 1 per cent of employees' gross earnings was paid to an individual Labour Market Supplementary Pension Scheme established for the employee – this contribution is not considered as a social security contribution but rather as savings being made by the individual. However, from 2004 to 2010, this contribution was suspended and finally abolished and the deposits paid out as of April 2010.

In September 2007, the tax cuts from the 2003-package was extended. The threshold for the medium tax bracket was to be raised with DKK 57 900 in 2009 to meet with the top tax bracket threshold. The deductible tax credit was increased to 4.0 per cent of earned income in 2008 and to 4.25 per cent in 2009; thus raising the maximum to 12 300 in 2008 and to 13 600 in 2009. The effective value of the credit and of the personal income allowance is equal to the local income tax rate, the church tax plus the health care tax rate (31.63 per cent on average in 2013) multiplied by the value of the deduction.

From the 1 January 2007 a Local Government Reform has come into force, which changes the structure of labour taxation. The reform however had only a minimal impact on the overall level of taxation. The number of municipalities has been cut from 270 to 98 and five regions have replaced the 14 counties. The regions will not impose taxes but will be financed through state subsidies and by contributions from the municipalities. The reform implied an increase in the average municipal tax rate from 22.1 per cent in 2006 to 24.577 per cent in 2007. Since then, there has been a further increase in the average municipal tax to 24.907 per cent in 2013. The county tax has been replaced by a new health care tax of 8 per cent which is levied by central government. The health care tax rate is decreased to 6 per cent in 2013. The levels of taxation have thus been reduced from three to two: only the central and local governments now levy taxes.

In the spring of 2009, the government and one of the opposition parties agreed upon a major tax reform to be phased in from 2010 to 2019. The reform aims at reducing the high marginal tax rates on personal income and thus to stimulate labour supply in the medium to long-term. The reform decreases income taxes by DKK 29 billion in 2010. The tax reform is planned to be revenue neutral as a whole, but was underfinanced in the short run (2010-12) in order to stimulate the economy. The main measures taken in 2010 include the reduction of the rate of the bottom tax bracket from 5.26 per cent to 3.67 per cent, abolition of the medium tax bracket with the 6 per cent rate altogether, and increase the top tax bracket threshold by DKK 28 800 to DKK 389 000. The reform will decrease the lowest marginal tax rate from 42.4 per cent to 41.0 per cent and the highest marginal tax rate on labour income from 63.0 per cent to 56.1 per cent. The marginal tax rate on positive net capital income (up to 51.5 after abolition of the middle tax bracket) is further reduced for the vast majority by introduction of an extra allowance of DKK 40 000 (DKK 80 000 for married couples) for positive net capital income in the top bracket tax.

The reform is partly financed by higher energy, transport and environmental taxes to support the energy and climate policy objectives of the government, and also by increases of excise rates on health-related goods (fat, candy, sugary drinks, tobacco). These increases are partly compensated by giving a "green check" to households (see Section 3). The tax reform is also partly financed by base broadening measures. The measures include a gradual reduction from 2012 to 2019 of the tax value (from 33.5 per cent to 25.5 per cent) of assessment oriented deductions and limitations of the tax deductibility of net interest payments over a nominal threshold of DKK 50 000 (DKK 100 000 for married couples). Also the deductibility of payments above DKK 100 000 a year to individual pension insurance schemes with less than life-long coverage has been limited, as well as tightening of the tax treatment of company cars and other fringe benefits. Furthermore, a 6 per cent tax is imposed from 2011 on pension payments exceeding DKK 362 800.

To consolidate the budget, a *Fiscal Consolidation Agreement* was reached in May 2010, somewhat modifying the prescriptions of the Spring Package of 2009.

The specific provisions of the *Fiscal Consolidation Agreement* include:

- The suspension from 2011 until 2013 of automatic adjustments in various tax thresholds (including personal allowances).
- Postponing from 2011 to 2014 the increase of the threshold for the top income tax rate (15 per cent) from DKK 389 900 to 409 100 (EUR 52 316 to 54 892). The increase was an element of the *2009 tax reform*.
- The labour union membership fees' tax deductibility is limited to DKK 3 000 (EUR 403) from the year 2011. The threshold is not adjusted.
- From 2011, the annual amount of child allowance is limited to DKK 35 000 (EUR 4 696), irrespective of the number of children. This was abolished by the new government by 2012. Child allowances will be gradually reduced by 5 per cent until 2013.

As part of the Finance Act 2012 it was decided to introduce an "additional green check" to people beyond 18 years with low income (less than DKK 212 000). The "additional green check" is DKK 280.

In June 2012 a tax reform was reached. Included in the reform were changes in the earned income tax credit and the top tax bracket. The earned income tax credit is gradually raised from 4.40 per cent in 2012 to 10.65 per cent in 2022 (6.95 per cent in 2013) where the maximum limit of earned income tax credit is raised from DKK 14 100 in 2012 to DKK 34 100 in 2022 (DKK 22 300 in 2013). Furthermore, a special earned income tax credit for single parents was decided from 2014. This will be gradually introduced to the amount of 6.25 per cent in 2022 with a maximum limit of DKK 20 000. In The Tax Reform 2012 it was also decided to gradually raise the top tax bracket from DKK 389 900 in 2012 to DKK 467 000 in 2022 (DKK 421 000 in 2013).

As part of the Finance Act 2013 an agreement, The Excise Duty and Competition Package, was reached. This agreement includes a decrease in the excise duty on electricity, an abolition of the fat tax and a planned expansion in the excise duty on sugar, which will reduce expenses of both consumers and companies. This was financed by an increase in the bottom tax rate of 0.19 percentage points and a reduction in the personal allowance by DKK 900 for all persons (under and over 18 years) introduced from the income year 2013. As a consequence the marginal tax ceiling was increased from 51.5 per cent to 51.7 per cent. It is estimated that the abolished excise duties and the increased income taxes will have similar effects on distribution and labour supply.

5. Memorandum items

5.1. *Identification of an AW*

The AW is identified as an average worker employed at firms which are members of the Danish Employers' Confederation.

5.2. *Employers' contribution to private schemes*

The employer must provide his employees with work injuries' insurance.

Employees typically participate in a private occupational (labour market) pension scheme to which both the employee and the employer make contributions. The employee's contribution is deductible for income tax purposes and is treated in this Report as a non-standard tax relief. The employer's contribution is not included in the gross wage income of the employee.

2013 parameter values

Average earnings	Ave_earn	395 722
Central taxes	Health_tax_rate	0.06
	Low_rate	0.0583
	Medium_thrsh	0
	Medium_rate	0
	Top_thrsh	421 000
	Top_rate	0.15
	Marg_rate_ceil	0.517
	Adj_top_rate	0.14963
	Temp_tax_rate	0.00
	Temp_tax_thrsh	0
	Personal_al	42 000
The green check	green_check	1 300
	1 child	300
	child max	600
	Green_check_thrsh	362 800
	Green_check_taper_rate	0.075
	Extra_green_check	280
	Extra_green_check_thrsh	212 000
Local taxes	gener_rate	0.24907
	church_rate	0.00723
total local tax rate	Local_rates	0.2563
Earned income tax credit scheme	earncredit_rate	0.0695
	earncredit_max	22 300
Child transfers	Child_3to6	13 608
	Child_7to17	10 716
for single parents	Sing_par_basic	5 284
	Sing_par_ch	18 432
Individual Labour Market Pension Scheme	Pension_rate	0
Employees soc. security:		
suppl. pension scheme	Pension	1 080
unempl. insurance	Unemp	10 837
Labour Market Contribution	Labour_market_rate	0.08
Employer soc. security:		
suppl. pension scheme	Pension_empr	2 160
refunded by government	Pension_ref	0.00
SSC rate	SSC_empr	0.00

2013 tax equations

The equations for the Danish system in 2013 are mostly on an individual basis but there is an interaction in the calculation of Central Government tax between spouses and the child benefit is calculated only once. This is shown by the Range indicator in the table below.

The functions which are used in the equations (Taper, MIN, Tax, etc.) are described in the technical note about tax equations. Variable names are defined in the table of parameters above, within the equations table, or are the standard variables "married" and "children". A reference to a variable with the affix "_total" indicates the sum of the relevant variable values for the principal and spouse. And the affixes "_princ" and "_spouse" indicate the value for the principal and spouse, respectively. Equations for a single person are as shown for the principal, with "_spouse" values taken as 0.

Line in country table and intermediate steps	Variable name	Range	Equation
1. Earnings	earn		
2. Allowances:	tax_al	B	Labour_market_contr+Pension_rate*earn
	earncredit	B	Min(earn*earncredit_rate, earncredit_max)
3. Credits in taxable income	taxbl_cr	B	0
4. CG taxable income	tax_inc	B	Positive(earn-tax_al-earncredit+taxbl_cr)
Personal income	pers_inc	B	Positive(earn-pension-pension_rate*earn-Labour_market_contr)
5. CG tax before credits	CG_tax_excl_princ	P	Low_rate*tax_inc_princ+Medium_rate*Positive(tax_inc_princ-Medium_thrsh-Married*Positive(Medium_thrsh-pers_inc_spouse))+Adj_top_rate*Positive(tax_inc_princ-Top_thrsh)
	CG_health_tax_excl_princ	P	Health_tax_rate*tax_inc_princ
	CG_tax_excl_spouse	S	Low_rate*tax_inc_spouse+Medium_rate*Positive(tax_inc_spouse-Medium_thrsh)+Adj_top_rate*Positive(tax_inc_spouse-Top_thrsh)
	CG_health_tax_excl_spouse	S	(Married=1)*Health_tax_rate*tax_inc_spouse
6. Tax credits :	tax_cr_princ	P	Personal_al*Low_rate+Married*Positive(Personal_al-pers_inc_spouse)*Low_rate
	health_tax_cr_princ	P	Health_tax_rate*(Personal_al+Married*Positive(Personal_al-tax_inc_spouse))
	tax_cr_spouse	S	Personal_al*Low_rate
	health_tax_cr_spouse	S	(Married=1)*Health_tax_rate*Personal_al
Labour Market Contribution	Labour_market_contr	B	Labour_market_rate*earn
7. CG tax	CG_tax	B	Positive(CG_tax_excl-tax_cr)+Positive(CG_health_tax_excl-health_tax_cr)+Labour_market_contr
8. State and local taxes	local_tax_princ	P	Positive((Local_rates)*(tax_inc_princ-Personal_al-Married*Positive(Personal_al-tax_inc_spouse)))
	local_tax_spouse	S	(Local_rates)*Positive(tax_inc_spouse-Personal_al)
9. Employees' soc security contribution	SSC	B	(earn>0)*Unemp
10. Total payments	tot_payments	J	Positive(CG_tax_total+local_tax_total+SSC_total)
11. Cash transfers	cash_trans	J	(Children>0)*(Child_3to6+(Children>1)*(Children-1)*Child_7to17+(Married=0)*(Sing_par_basic+Children*Sing_par_ch))+IF(Married=1,(Taper(green_check,pers_inc_princ,Green_check_thrsh,Green_check_taper_rate)+Taper(green_check+MIN(Children*_1_child,child_max),pers_inc_spouse,Green_check_thrsh,Green_check_taper_rate)),Taper(green_check+MIN(Children*_1_child,child_max),pers_inc_princ,Green_check_thrsh,Green_check_taper_rate))+IF(Married=1,(IF(pers_inc_princ<Extra_green_check_thrsh,Extra_green_check,0)+IF(pers_inc_spouse<Extra_green_check_thrsh,Extra_green_check,0)),IF(pers_inc_princ<Extra_green_check_thrsh,Extra_green_check,0))
13. Employer's soc security	SSC_empr	B	SSC_empr*earn

Key to range of equation B calculated separately for both principal earner and spouse P calculated for principal only (value taken as 0 for spouse calculation) J calculated once only on a joint basis.

Taxing Wages 2014
Changes in sructural labour income tax progressivity
over 2000-12 period in OECD member countries

Estonia

This chapter includes data on the income taxes paid by workers, their social security contributions, the family benefits they receive in the form of cash transfers as well as the social security contributions and payroll taxes paid by their employers. Results reported include the marginal and average tax burden for eight different family types.

Methodological information is available for personal income tax systems, compulsory social security contributions to schemes operated within the government sector, universal cash transfers as well as recent changes in the tax/benefit system. The methodology also includes the parameter values and tax equations underlying the data.

Estonia 2013

The tax/benefit position of single persons

	Wage level (per cent of average wage)		67	100	167	67
	Number of children		none	none	none	2
1.	**Gross wage earnings**		7776	11664	19439	7776
2.	**Standard tax allowances**					
	Basic allowance		1728	1728	1728	3456
	Married or head of family					
	Dependent children					
	Deduction for social security contributions and income taxes		156	233	389	156
	Work-related expenses		0	0	0	0
	Other					
		Total	1884	1961	2117	3612
3.	**Tax credits or cash transfers included in taxable income**		0	0	0	0
4.	**Central government taxable income (1 - 2 + 3)**		5892	9702	17322	4164
5.	**Central government income tax liability (exclusive of tax credits)**		1237	2037	3638	874
6.	**Tax credits**					
	Basic credit					
	Married or head of family					
	Children		0	0	0	0
	Other					
		Total	0	0	0	0
7.	**Central government income tax finally paid (5-6)**		1237	2037	3638	874
8.	**State and local taxes**		0	0	0	0
9.	**Employees' compulsory social security contributions**					
	Gross earnings		156	233	389	156
	Taxable income					
		Total	156	233	389	156
10.	**Total payments to general government (7 + 8 + 9)**		1393	2271	4027	1030
11.	**Cash transfers from general government**					
	For head of family					
	For two children		0	0	0	921
		Total	0	0	0	921
12.	**Take-home pay (1-10+11)**		6383	9393	15413	7666
13.	**Employer's compulsory social security contributions**		2644	3966	6609	2644
14.	**Average rates**					
	Income tax		15.9%	17.5%	18.7%	11.2%
	Employees' social security contributions		2.0%	2.0%	2.0%	2.0%
	Total payments less cash transfers		17.9%	19.5%	20.7%	1.4%
	Total tax wedge including employer's social security contributions		38.7%	39.9%	40.8%	26.4%
15.	**Marginal rates**					
	Total payments less cash transfers: Principal earner		22.6%	22.6%	22.6%	22.6%
	Total payments less cash transfers: Spouse		n.a.	n.a.	n.a.	n.a.
	Total tax wedge: Principal earner		42.2%	42.2%	42.2%	42.2%
	Total tax wedge: Spouse		n.a.	n.a.	n.a.	n.a.

Estonia 2013

The tax/benefit position of married couples

		Wage level (per cent of average wage)	100-0	100-33	100-67	100-33
		Number of children	2	2	2	none
1.	**Gross wage earnings**		11664	15551	19439	15551
2.	**Standard tax allowances**					
	Basic allowance		5184	5184	5184	3456
	Married or head of family					
	Dependent children					
	Deduction for social security contributions and income taxes		233	311	389	311
	Work-related expenses		0	0	0	0
	Other					
		Total	5417	5495	5573	3767
3.	**Tax credits or cash transfers included in taxable income**		0	0	0	0
4.	**Central government taxable income (1 - 2 + 3)**		6246	10056	13866	11784
5.	**Central government income tax liability (exclusive of tax credits)**		1312	2112	2912	2475
6.	**Tax credits**					
	Basic credit					
	Married or head of family					
	Children		0	0	0	0
	Other					
		Total	0	0	0	0
7.	**Central government income tax finally paid (5-6)**		1312	2112	2912	2475
8.	**State and local taxes**		0	0	0	0
9.	**Employees' compulsory social security contributions**					
	Gross earnings		233	311	389	311
	Taxable income					
		Total	233	311	389	311
10.	**Total payments to general government (7 + 8 + 9)**		1545	2423	3301	2786
11.	**Cash transfers from general government**					
	For head of family					
	For two children		460	460	460	0
		Total	460	460	460	0
12.	**Take-home pay (1-10+11)**		10579	13589	16599	12766
13.	**Employer's compulsory social security contributions**		3966	5287	6609	5287
14.	**Average rates**					
	Income tax		11.2%	13.6%	15.0%	15.9%
	Employees' social security contributions		2.0%	2.0%	2.0%	2.0%
	Total payments less cash transfers		9.3%	12.6%	14.6%	17.9%
	Total tax wedge including employer's social security contributions		32.3%	34.8%	36.3%	38.7%
15.	**Marginal rates**					
	Total payments less cash transfers: Principal earner		22.6%	22.6%	22.6%	22.6%
	Total payments less cash transfers: Spouse		0.0%	22.6%	22.6%	22.6%
	Total tax wedge: Principal earner		42.2%	42.2%	42.2%	42.2%
	Total tax wedge: Spouse		0.0%	42.2%	42.2%	42.2%

The Estonian currency is the euro (EUR). In 2013, EUR 0.75 was equal to USD 1. In 2013, the average worker in Estonia earned EUR 11 664 (country estimate).

1. Personal income tax systems

1.1. Central government income tax

1.1.1. *Tax unit*

The tax unit is the family.

1.1.2. *Tax allowances*

1.1.2.1. Standard tax reliefs

- *A general (basic) allowance* of EUR 1 728 is deductible from individual income in 2013.
- *A child* allowance of EUR 1 728 is also deductible from income for each of the second and any subsequent children up to and including the age of 16.
- *Relief for social security contributions:* Employee's compulsory contributions for unemployment insurance are deductible for income tax purposes.
- *Tax credits:* None for employees

1.1.2.2. Non-standard tax reliefs applicable to income from employment

- *II pillar pension contributions:* In 2013, these represent voluntary payments to private funds for all employees and are paid at a rate of 2% of earnings.
- Occupational accident and illness benefits that are not paid as insurance benefits are deductible from taxable income within the limit of EUR 768 per year.
- *Housing loan interest, educational costs, gifts and donations* are deductible from taxable income within upper limits of EUR 1 920 and 50% of taxable income per year.
- *Voluntary pension contributions (III pillar):* Contributions paid by a resident to the provider of a pension plan based in Estonia or in another EU Member State according to a pension plan that is approved and entered into a special register in accordance with the pension legislation are deductible from taxable income. In 2013 such deductions are subject to an annual limit of a sum equal to 15% and maximum of EUR 6 000 of the employee's, public servant`s or members of legal person management or control body income in a calendar year.

1.1.3. *Tax schedule*

The rate of 21% applies for all levels of taxable income.

1.2. *Regional and local income tax*

There are no regional or local income taxes.

2. Compulsory social security insurance system

The compulsory social security insurance system consists of three schemes as follows:

- pension insurance;
- health insurance;
- unemployment insurance.

2.1. *Employees' contributions*

Employees pay 2.0% of their earnings in contributions for unemployment insurance. The taxable base is the total amount of the gross wage or salary including vacation payments, fringe benefits and remuneration of expenses related to work above a certain threshold. The assessment period is the calendar month.

2.2. *Employers' contributions*

Social security insurance contributions are also paid by employers on behalf of their employees. The taxable base and the assessment period are the same as for employees' contributions. The employers' contribution rates are applied in two parts:

- Unemployment insurance – 1.0% of employee earnings.
- Pension and health insurance – as follows for monthly earnings above EUR 290.

Scheme name	Rate of contribution (%)
Pension insurance	20.00
Health insurance	13.00
Total	**33.00**

In addition there is a lump sum payment for each employee of EUR 95.7 per month (split between pensions and health insurance on a 20:13 basis).

3. Payroll tax

None.

4. Universal cash transfers

4.1. *Transfers related to marital status*

None.

4.2. *Transfers for dependent children*

Estonia's family benefits are designed to provide partial coverage of the costs families incur in caring for, raising and educating their children.

The state pays family benefits to all children until they reach the age of 16. Children enrolled in basic or secondary schools or vocational education institutions operating on the basis of basic education have the right to receive family benefits until the age of 19. Applications for the allowance are made on an annual basis and the payments are not taxable. The values of these benefits in 2011 are shown in the table below. The single parent child allowance is paid for each child.

In addition there are nine other types of family benefits for which payment depends on either the age of the child(ren) and/ or the status of the person(s) looking of them: maternity benefit; childbirth allowance; parental benefit; child care allowance; conscript's child allowance; child's school allowance, child allowance for a child under guardianship or foster care; start in independent life allowance; adoption allowance (single payment). These are not included in the modelling.

Type of benefit	Annual amount of benefit (in EUR)
Child allowance (paid until children turn 16 or until the end of the academic year in which they turn 19 if they continue studying).	
For the first and second child	230.16
For the third and any subsequent children	690.48
Single parent's child allowance	230.16
Parents allowance for families with seven or more children	2 024.88

5. Main changes in tax/benefit system since 2005

- The personal income tax rate was steadily reduced from 24% in 2005 to 21% in 2008.
- The child tax allowance applied for the third and subsequent children for 2005 and the second and subsequent children in 2006 and 2007. It applied to all children in 2008 and then returned to the 2007 position in 2009.
- The employee unemployment contribution rate was reduced from 1% to 0.6% in 2006 and then raised in 2 stages to 2.8% at the end of 2009. The corresponding rates for employers were a reduction from 0.5% to 0.3% in 2006 increasing to 1.4%. In 2013 the employee unemployment contribution rate was reduced from 2.8% to 2.0% and the corresponding rate for employers from 1.4% to 1.0%.
- In addition to existing benefits, from 1 July, 2013 the need-based child benefits were introduced. Need-based family benefit income threshold is based on Statistical Office relative poverty threshold published by the 1st of March in a year before current budget year. In 2013 the need-based threshold is EUR 280 in a month for the first household member. For every other at least 14-years old member the threshold is EUR 140 and for the younger members EUR 84 in a month. Need-based family benefit is from 1 July 2013 until the end of 2014 9.59 in a month for single child family and EUR 19.18 for families with two or more children. From 2015 the benefits will rise to EUR 19.18 and EUR 38.36 respectively.

6. Memorandum items

6.1. *Average gross annual wage earnings calculation*

In Estonia the gross earnings figures cover wages and salaries paid to individuals in formal employment including payment for overtime. They also include bonus payments and other payments such as pay for annual leave, paid leave up to seven days, public holidays, absences due to sickness for up to 30 days, job training, and slowdown through no fault of the person in formal employment.

The average gross wage earnings figures of all adult workers covering industry Sectors B-N by NACE Rev. 2 are estimated with average wage growth rate forecast of Estonian Ministry of Finance.

6.2. Employer contributions to private pension and health schemes

Some employer contributions are made to private health and pension schemes but there is no relevant information available on the amounts that are paid.

2013 parameter values

Average earnings/yr	Ave_earn	11 664	Country estimate
Allowances	Basic_al	1 728	
	Child_al	1 728	
Income tax	Tax_rate	0.21	
Employers SSC	SSC_rate1	0.33	
	Threshold	3 480	
	lump_sum	1 148.4	
	SSC_rate2	0.01	
Employees SSC	SSC_rate3	0.02	
Child allowances			
First & second child	CA_first&second	230.16	
Other children	CA_others	690.48	
Additional for children of lone parents	CA_onepar	230.16	
Need-based child benefits			
one child	CB_1	57.54	
two or more children	CB_2	115.08	
Need-based family threshold			
first member	F_thrsh_1	3 360.00	
other members above 14	F_thrsh_2	1 680.00	
other members under 14	F_thrsh_3	1 008.00	
Days in tax year	numdays	365	

2013 tax equations

The equations for the Estonian system are mostly on an individual basis.

The functions which are used in the equations (Taper, MIN, Tax, etc.) are described in the technical note about tax equations. Variable names are defined in the table of parameters above, within the equations table, or are the standard variables "married" and "children". A reference to a variable with the affix "_total" indicates the sum of the relevant variable values for the principal and spouse. And the affixes "_princ" and "_spouse" indicate the value for the principal and spouse, respectively. Equations for a single person are as shown for the principal, with "_spouse" values taken as 0.

	Line in country table and intermediate steps	Variable name	Range	Equation
1.	Earnings	earn		
2.	Allowances:	tax_al	J	Min(Basic_al*(1+married)+SSC_empee+(children>1)*child_al*(Children-1),earn)
3.	Credits in taxable income	taxbl_cr	B	0
4.	CG taxable income	tax_inc	B	Positive(earn-tax_al)
5.	CG tax before credits	CG_tax_excl	B	Tax_inc*tax_rate
6.	Tax credits :	tax_cr	B	0
7.	CG tax	CG_tax	B	CG_tax_excl-tax_cr
8;	State and local taxes	local_tax	B	0
9.	Employees' soc security	SSC_empee	B	earn*SSC_rate3
11.	Cash transfers	cash_trans	J	IF(Children<3,CA_firstsecond*Children,(2*CA_firstsecond)+(CA_other*(Children-2)))+(Married=0)*Children*CA_onepar+IF((earn_total-CG_tax-SSC_empee)<(F_thrsh_1+ (F_thrsh_2*Married=1)+(F_thrsh_3*Children)),IF(Children>1, CB_2, CB_1),0)
13.	Employer's soc security	SSC_empr	B	IF(earn>0,IF(earn>threshold,earn*SSC_rate1,lump_sum),0)+earn*SSC_rate2

Key to range of equation B calculated separately for both principal earner and spouse P calculated for principal only (value taken as 0 for spouse calculation) J calculated once only on a joint basis.

Taxing Wages 2014
Changes in sructural labour income tax progressivity
over 2000-12 period in OECD member countries

Finland

This chapter includes data on the income taxes paid by workers, their social security contributions, the family benefits they receive in the form of cash transfers as well as the social security contributions and payroll taxes paid by their employers. Results reported include the marginal and average tax burden for eight different family types.

Methodological information is available for personal income tax systems, compulsory social security contributions to schemes operated within the government sector, universal cash transfers as well as recent changes in the tax/ benefit system. The methodology also includes the parameter values and tax equations underlying the data.

Finland 2013

The tax/benefit position of single persons

		Wage level (per cent of average wage)	67	100	167	67
		Number of children	none	none	none	2
1.	**Gross wage earnings**		28329	42493	70822	28329
2.	**Standard tax allowances**					
	Basic allowance					
	Married or head of family					
	Dependent children					
	Deduction for social security contributions and income taxes		1839	2758	4596	1839
	Work-related expenses		620	620	620	620
	Other					
		Total	2459	3378	5216	2459
3.	**Tax credits or cash transfers included in taxable income**		0	0	0	0
4.	**Central government taxable income (1 - 2 + 3)**		25870	39115	65605	25870
5.	**Central government income tax liability (exclusive of tax credits)**		860	3178	8874	860
6.	**Tax credits**					
	Basic credit		970	872	561	970
	Married or head of family					
	Children					
	Other					
		Total	970	872	561	970
7.	**Central government income tax finally paid (5-6)**		140	2446	8453	140
8.	**State and local taxes**		4338	7132	12513	4338
9.	**Employees' compulsory social security contributions**					
	Gross earnings		1839	2758	4596	1839
	Taxable income		291	478	839	291
		Total	2130	3236	5436	2130
10.	**Total payments to general government (7 + 8 + 9)**		6608	12814	26401	6608
11.	**Cash transfers from general government**					
	For head of family					
	For two children		0	0	0	3797
		Total	0	0	0	3797
12.	**Take-home pay (1-10+11)**		21721	29679	44421	25518
13.	**Employer's compulsory social security contributions**		6459	9688	16147	6459
14.	**Average rates**					
	Income tax		15.8%	22.5%	29.6%	15.8%
	Employees' social security contributions		7.5%	7.6%	7.7%	7.5%
	Total payments less cash transfers		23.3%	30.2%	37.3%	9.9%
	Total tax wedge including employer's social security contributions		37.6%	43.1%	48.9%	26.6%
15.	**Marginal rates**					
	Total payments less cash transfers: Principal earner		43.1%	48.0%	48.0%	43.1%
	Total payments less cash transfers: Spouse		n.a.	n.a.	n.a.	n.a.
	Total tax wedge: Principal earner		53.7%	57.6%	57.6%	53.7%
	Total tax wedge: Spouse		n.a.	n.a.	n.a.	n.a.

Finland 2013

The tax/benefit position of married couples

		Wage level (per cent of average wage)	100-0	100-33	100-67	100-33
		Number of children	2	2	2	none
1.	**Gross wage earnings**		42493	56657	70822	56657
2.	**Standard tax allowances**					
	Basic allowance					
	Married or head of family					
	Dependent children					
	Deduction for social security contributions and income taxes		2758	3677	4596	3677
	Work-related expenses		620	1240	1240	1240
	Other					
		Total	3378	4917	5836	4917
3.	**Tax credits or cash transfers included in taxable income**		0	0	0	0
4.	**Central government taxable income (1 - 2 + 3)**		39115	51740	64985	51740
5.	**Central government income tax liability (exclusive of tax credits)**		3178	3178	4038	3178
6.	**Tax credits**					
	Basic credit		872	1724	1842	1724
	Married or head of family					
	Children					
	Other					
		Total	872	1724	1842	1724
7.	**Central government income tax finally paid (5-6)**		2446	2538	2586	2538
8.	**State and local taxes**		7132	7770	11470	7770
9.	**Employees' compulsory social security contributions**					
	Gross earnings		2758	3677.1	4596	3677
	Taxable income		478	521	769	521
		Total	3236	4198	5366	4198
10.	**Total payments to general government (7 + 8 + 9)**		12814	14506	19421	14506
11.	**Cash transfers from general government**					
	For head of family					
	For two children		2632	2632	2632	0
		Total	2632	2632	2632	0
12.	**Take-home pay (1-10+11)**		32311	44783	54032	42151
13.	**Employer's compulsory social security contributions**		9688	12917.9	16147	12918
14.	**Average rates**					
	Income tax		22.5%	18.2%	19.8%	18.2%
	Employees' social security contributions		7.6%	7.4%	7.6%	7.4%
	Total payments less cash transfers		24.0%	21.0%	23.7%	25.6%
	Total tax wedge including employer's social security contributions		38.1%	35.6%	37.9%	39.4%
15.	**Marginal rates**					
	Total payments less cash transfers: Principal earner		48.0%	48.0%	48.0%	48.0%
	Total payments less cash transfers: Spouse		11.9%	23.1%	43.1%	23.1%
	Total tax wedge: Principal earner		57.6%	57.6%	57.6%	57.6%
	Total tax wedge: Spouse		28.3%	37.4%	53.7%	37.4%

The national currency is the euro (EUR). In 2013, EUR 0.75 was equal to USD 1. In that year, the average worker earned EUR 42 493 (Secretariat estimate).

1. Personal income tax systems

1.1. Central government income taxes

1.1.1. Tax unit

Spouses are taxed separately for earned income.

1.1.2. Standard tax allowances and tax credits

1.1.2.1. Standard reliefs

- *Work-related expenses:* A standard deduction for work-related expenses equal to the amount of wage or salary, with a maximum amount of EUR 620 is granted.
- *Tax credit:* An earned income tax credit is granted against the central government income tax. If the credit exceeds the amount of central government income tax, the excess credit is deductible from the municipal income tax and the health insurance contribution for medical care. The credit is calculated on the basis of taxpayers' income from work. The credit amounts to 7.3 per cent of income exceeding EUR 2 500, until it reaches its maximum of EUR 970. The amount of the credit is reduced by 1.1 per cent of the earned income minus work related expenses exceeding EUR 33 000. The credit is fully phased out when taxpayers' income is about EUR 120 000.

1.1.2.2. Main non-standard tax reliefs applicable to an AW

- *Interest:* Interest on loans associated with the earning of taxable income, 80 per cent of the interest on loans for the purchase of owner-occupied dwellings, and student loans guaranteed by the state can be deducted against capital income. Of the excess of interest over capital income, 30 (32 per cent for first-time homebuyers) per cent can be credited against income tax up to a maximum of EUR 1 400.
- *Membership fees:* Membership fees paid to employees' organisations or trade unions.
- *Travelling expenses:* Travelling expenses from the place of residence to the place of employment using the cheapest means in excess of EUR 600 up to a maximum deduction of EUR 7 000.
- *Double housing expenses:* If the place of employment is located too far from home in order to commute (distance > 100 km), the taxpayer can deduct the costs of hiring a second dwelling located near the place of work up to EUR 250 per month. This deduction can be claimed only by one person per household.
- *Other work-related outlays:* Outlays for tools, professional literature, research equipment and scientific literature, and expenses incurred in scientific or artistic work (unless compensated by scholarships).

Travelling expenses and other work-related outlays are deductible only to the extent that their total amount exceeds the amount of the standard deduction for work-related expenses.

1.1.3. Rate schedule

Central government income tax:

Taxable income (EUR)	Tax on lower limit (EUR)	Tax on excess income in bracket (%)
16 100-23 900	8	6.5
23 900-39 100	515	17.5
39 100-70 300	3 175	21.5
70 300-100 000	9 883	29.75
100 000 and more	18 718.75	31.75

1.2. Local income tax

1.2.1. Tax base and tax rates

The tax base of the local income tax is taxable income as established for the income tax levied by central government.

Municipal tax is levied at flat rates. In 2013 the tax rate varies between 16.25 and 22.00 per cent, the average rate being approximately 19.38 per cent.

Municipal tax is not deductible against central government taxes. Work-related expenses and other non-standard deductions are deductible, as for purposes of the central government income tax.

1.2.2. Tax allowances in municipal income taxation

- An earned income tax allowance is calculated on the basis of taxpayer's income from work. The allowance amounts to 51 per cent of income between EUR 2 500 and EUR 7 230, and 28 per cent of the income exceeding EUR 7 230, until it reaches its maximum of EUR 3 570. The amount of the allowance is reduced by 4.5 per cent on earned income minus work related expenses exceeding EUR 14 000.
- A basic tax allowance is granted on the basis of taxable income remaining after the other allowances have been subtracted. The maximum amount, EUR 2 880, is reduced by 20 per cent on income exceeding the aforementioned amount.

2. Compulsory social security contributions to schemes operated within the government sector

2.1. Employee contributions

2.1.1. Rate and ceiling

In 2013, the rate of the health insurance contribution for medical care paid by an employee is 1.30 per cent. The tax base for this contribution is net taxable income for municipal income tax purposes.

In addition there is an employees' pension insurance contribution which amounts to 5.15 per cent of gross salary, an employees' unemployment insurance contribution equal to 0.6 per cent of gross salary and a health insurance contribution for daily allowance equal to 0.74 per cent of gross salary. For employees aged 53 and older, the pension insurance contribution amounts to 6.5 per cent of gross salary. These contributions are deductible for income tax purposes.

2.1.2. *Distinction by marital status or sex*

The rates do not differ.

2.2. *Employers' contributions*

The average rate of the employers' social security contribution in 2013 is 22.8 per cent of gross wage.

3. Universal cash transfers

3.1. *Amount for marriage*

None.

3.2. *Amount for children*

The central government pays in 2013 the following allowances (EUR):

For the first child	1 250.28
For the second child	1 381.56
For the third child	1 762.92
For the fourth child	2 019.24
Fifth and subsequent child	2 275.56

The child subsidy for a single parent is increased by an annual amount of EUR 582.6 for each child.

4. Main changes in tax/benefit system since 2012

In January 2013 a temporary (2013-15) new top bracket was introduced into the central government income tax scales. The new bracket is for taxable earned income of over EUR 100 000/year and the tax rate within the bracket is 31.75%. In 2013 no adjustment for inflation and rise of earnings levels was made to the central government tax brackets.

From the beginning of 2013 an additional tax of 6 percentage points on pension income exceeding EUR 45 000 is collected.

In January 2013 a new public broadcasting tax was introduced to finance the activity of the national public service broadcasting company. The tax is 0.68% on taxable earned income, taxes of min. EUR 50 and max. EUR 140 will be collected.

The maximum amount of the earned income tax credit in state taxation was raised from EUR 945 to EUR 970.

The maximum amount of the basic allowance in municipal taxation was raised from EUR 2 850 to EUR 2 880.

The rate of the employees' health insurance contribution for medical care was increased from 1.22 per cent to 1.30 per cent. Home-loan interest counts at 80 per cent, down from 85 per cent, as deductible/creditable interest.

5. Memorandum items

5.1. Calculation of average gross annual wage

The Finnish figures are generally calculated as follows:

- Gross annual earnings are calculated at an individual level on the basis of the hour's usually worked, average hourly pay for the fourth quarter, and the share of annual periodic bonuses.
- The earnings exclude sickness and unemployment compensations, but include all normal overtime compensations, bonuses, holiday remunerations and remunerations for public holidays.

5.2. Employer contributions to private pension and health schemes

No information is available.

2013 parameter values

Average earnings	Ave_earn	42 493	Secretariat estimate
Expenses	Work_exp_max	620	
	Work_exp_rate	1	
Allowances	al_SSC_rate	0.0649	
State tax	Tax_min	8	
Tax schedule	Tax_sch	0	16 100
		0.065	23 900
		0.175	39 100
		0.215	70 300
		0.2975	100 000
		0.3175	
Earned income tax credit	eitc_thrsh	2 500	
	eitc_rate	0.073	
	eitc_redn_thrsh	33 000	
	eitc_redn_rate	0.011	
	eitc_max	970	
Earned income tax allowance	al_thrsh	2 500	
	al_thrsh2	7 230	
	al_rate	0.51	
	al_rate2	0.28	
	al_redn_thrsh	14 000	
	al_redn_rate	0.045	
	al_max	3 570	
low income	SL_max	2 880	
	SL_rate	0.2	
Local intax	Local_rate	0.1938	
	Church_rate	0	
	Local_tot	0.1938	
Soc sec taxpayer	SSC_rate	0.0130	
soc.sec empr	SSC_empr	0.228	
Cash transfer	ch_1	1 250.28	
	ch_2	1 381.56	
	ch_3	1 762.92	
	ch_4	2 019.24	
	ch_5	2 275.56	
	ch_small	0	
	ch_lone	582.6	

2013 tax equations

The equations for the Finnish system are mostly on an individual basis except for the child benefit which is calculated only once. This is shown by the Range indicator in the table below.

The functions which are used in the equations (Taper, MIN, Tax, etc.) are described in the technical note about tax equations.

Variable names are defined in the table of parameters above, within the equations table, or are the standard variables "married" and "children". A reference to a variable with the affix "_total" indicates the sum of the relevant variable values for the principal and spouse. And the affixes "_princ" and "_spouse" indicate the value for the principal and spouse, respectively. Equations for a single person are as shown for the principal, with "_spouse" values taken as 0.

	Line in country table and intermediate steps	Variable name	Range	Equation
1.	Earnings	earn		
	Work related expenses	work_rel	B	MIN(Work_exp_max, Work_exp_rate*earn)
	SSC deduction	SSC_al	B	earn*al_SSC_rate
2.	Allowances:	tax_al	B	work_rel+SSC_al
3.	Credits in taxable income	taxbl_cr	B	0
4.	CG taxable income	tax_inc	B	Positive(earn-tax_al)
5.	CG tax before credits	CG_tax_excl	B	=Tax(tax_inc, Tax_sch)+Tax_min* (tax_inc>Tax_thrsh)
6.	Tax credits :	tax_cr	B	MINA(eitc_max,eitc_rate*Positive(earn-eitc_thrsh))-MINA(eitc_max,eitc_redn_rate*Positive(earn-work_rel-eitc_redn_thrsh))
7.	CG tax	CG_tax	B	Positive(CG_tax_excl - tax_cr)
	Earned income allowance	earninc_al	B	MIN(al_max, IF(earn>al_thrsh2, al_rate*(al_thrsh2-al_thrsh1)+al_rate2*(earn-al_thrsh2), Positive(earn-al_thrsh)))-MIN(al_max, al_redn_rate* Positive(earn-work_rel-al_redn_thrsh))
	Low income	low_inc	B	Positive(MIN(earn-work_rel-low_al-SSC_al, SL_max)-SL_rate*Positive(earn- work_rel- low_al-SSC_al-SL_max))
	Taxable income (local)	tax_inc_l	B	tax_inc-earninc_al-low_inc
8.	State and local taxes	local_tax	B	Positive(tax_inc_l*Local_tot-(local_tot/(local_tot+SSC_rate))*Positive(Tax_cr-CG_tax_excl))
9.	Employees' soc security	SSC	B	Positive(SSC_rate*tax_inc_l – (SSC_rate/(local_tot+SSC_rate))*Positive(Tax_cr-CG_tax_excl)) + SSC_al
11.	Cash transfers	cash_trans	J	(Children>0)*ch_1+(Children>1)*ch_2+ (Children>2)*ch_3+(Children>3)*ch_4+ Positive(Children-4)*ch_4 +(Married=0)*Children*ch_lone
13.	Employer's soc security	SSC_empr	B	earn*SSC_empr

Key to range of equation B calculated separately for both principal earner and spouse P calculated for principal only (value taken as 0 for spouse calculation) J calculated once only on a joint basis.

Taxing Wages 2014
Changes in sructural labour income tax progressivity
over 2000-12 period in OECD member countries

France

This chapter includes data on the income taxes paid by workers, their social security contributions, the family benefits they receive in the form of cash transfers as well as the social security contributions and payroll taxes paid by their employers. Results reported include the marginal and average tax burden for eight different family types.

Methodological information is available for personal income tax systems, compulsory social security contributions to schemes operated within the government sector, universal cash transfers as well as recent changes in the tax/ benefit system. The methodology also includes the parameter values and tax equations underlying the data.

France 2013

The tax/benefit position of single persons

	Wage level (per cent of average wage)	67	100	167	67
	Number of children	none	none	none	2
1.	**Gross wage earnings**	24653	36980	61633	24653
2.	**Standard tax allowances**				
	Basic allowance				
	Married or head of family				
	Dependent children				
	Deduction for social security contributions and income taxes	4637	6956	11188	4637
	Work-related expenses	2002	3002	5045	2002
	Other				
	Total	6639	9959	16232	6639
3.	**Tax credits or cash transfers included in taxable income**	0	0	0	0
4.	**Central government taxable income (1 - 2 + 3)**	18014	27021	45401	18014
5.	**Central government income tax liability (exclusive of tax credits)**	3110	5402	12854	1938
6.	**Tax credits**				
	Basic credit				
	Married or head of family				
	Children				
	Other	0	0	0	72
	Total	0	0	0	72
7.	**Central government income tax finally paid (5-6)**	3110	5402	12854	1866
8.	**State and local taxes**	0	0	0	0
9.	**Employees' compulsory social security contributions**				
	Gross earnings	3402	5103	8099	3402
	Taxable income				
	Total	3402	5103	8099	3402
10.	**Total payments to general government (7 + 8 + 9)**	6512	10506	20953	5268
11.	**Cash transfers from general government**				
	For head of family (Gross)				
	For two children (Gross)	0	0	0	1546
	CRDS Deducted	0	0	0	-8
	Total	0	0	0	1538
12.	**Take-home pay (1-10+11)**	18141	26475	40680	20924
13.	**Employers' compulsory social security contributions**	8685	14851	27020	8685
14.	**Average rates**				
	Income tax	12.6%	14.6%	20.9%	7.6%
	Employees' social security contributions	13.8%	13.8%	13.1%	13.8%
	Total payments less cash transfers	26.4%	28.4%	34.0%	15.1%
	Total tax wedge including employer's social security contributions	45.6%	48.9%	54.1%	37.2%
15.	**Marginal rates**				
	Total payments less cash transfers: Principal earner	31.9%	43.6%	42.4%	21.7%
	Total payments less cash transfers: Spouse	n.a.	n.a.	n.a.	n.a.
	Total tax wedge: Principal earner	62.9%	59.7%	59.8%	57.3%
	Total tax wedge: Spouse	n.a.	n.a.	n.a.	n.a.

France 2013

The tax/benefit position of married couples

		Wage level (per cent of average wage)	100-0	100-33	100-67	100-33
		Number of children	2	2	2	none
1.	**Gross wage earnings**		36980	49307	61633	49307
2.	**Standard tax allowances**					
	Basic allowance					
	Married or head of family					
	Dependent children					
	Deduction for social security contributions and income taxes		6956	9275	11594	9275
	Work-related expenses		3002	4003	5004	4003
	Other					
		Total	9959	13278	16598	13278
3.	**Tax credits or cash transfers included in taxable income**		0	0	0	0
4.	**Central government taxable income (1 - 2 + 3)**		27021	36029	45036	36029
5.	**Central government income tax liability (exclusive of tax credits)**		3140	4859	7100	6220
6.	**Tax credits**					
	Basic credit					
	Married or head of family					
	Children					
	Other		0	722	0	0
		Total	0	722	0	0
7.	**Central government income tax finally paid (5-6)**		3140	4137	7100	6220
8.	**State and local taxes**		0	0	0	0
9.	**Employees' compulsory social security contributions**					
	Gross earnings		5103	6804	8505	6804
	Taxable income					
		Total	5103	6804	8505	6804
10.	**Total payments to general government (7 + 8 + 9)**		8243	10942	15605	13024
11.	**Cash transfers from general government**					
	For head of family (Gross)					
	For two children (Gross)		1546	1546	1546	0
	CRDS Deducted		-8	-8	-8	0
		Total	1538	1538	1538	0
12.	**Take-home pay (1-10+11)**		30275	39903	47566	36283
13.	**Employers' compulsory social security contributions**		14851	16597	23536	16597
14.	**Average rates**					
	Income tax		8.5%	8.4%	11.5%	12.6%
	Employees' social security contributions		13.8%	13.8%	13.8%	13.8%
	Total payments less cash transfers		18.1%	19.1%	22.8%	26.4%
	Total tax wedge including employer's social security contributions		41.6%	39.5%	44.2%	44.9%
15.	**Marginal rates**					
	Total payments less cash transfers: Principal earner		27.7%	37.0%	31.9%	31.9%
	Total payments less cash transfers: Spouse		21.9%	36.4%	31.9%	31.9%
	Total tax wedge: Principal earner		48.4%	55.1%	51.4%	51.4%
	Total tax wedge: Spouse		31.6%	44.3%	62.9%	40.3%

The national currency is the euro (EUR). In 2013, EUR 0.75 equalled USD 1. In that year, the average worker earned EUR 36 980 (Secretariat estimate).

1. Personal income tax systems

1.1. Tax levied by the central government on 2013 income

1.1.1. *Tax unit*

The tax unit is aggregate family income, but children over 18 are included only if their parents claim them as dependants. Other persons may be fiscally attached on certain conditions: unlike spouses, who are always taxed jointly, children over 18 and other members of the household may opt to be taxed separately. Beginning with the taxation of 2004 income, the law provides for joint taxation of partners in a French civil union (*pacte civil de solidarité*, or PACS), as soon as the PACS is signed. Reporting obligations for "PACSed" partners are similar to those of married couples.

Earned income is reported net of compulsory employer and employee payroll deductions, except for 2.4 percentage points' worth of CSG (*contribution sociale généralisée*) and the 0.5% CRDS (*contribution pour le remboursement de la dette sociale*), which are not deductible from the income tax base.

1.1.2. *Tax reliefs and tax credits*

1.1.2.1. Standard tax reliefs

- Work-related expenses, corresponding to actual amounts or a standard allowance of 10 per cent of net pay (with a minimum of EUR 424 and a ceiling of EUR 12 096 per earner).
- Family status: The "family quotient" (*quotient familial*) system takes a taxpayer's marital status and family responsibilities into account. It involves dividing net taxable income into a certain number of shares [two shares for a married (or "PACSed") couple, one share for a single person, one half-share for each dependent child, an additional half-share for the third and each subsequent dependent child, an additional half-share for single parent, and so on]: the total tax due is equal to the amount of tax corresponding to one share multiplied by the total number of shares. The tax benefit for a half-share is limited, however, to EUR 1 500 as for 2013 income (2 000 for 2012 income) per half-share in excess of two shares for a couple, or one share for a single person, except for the first two half-shares granted for the first child of a single parent, in which case the maximum benefit is EUR 3 540 as for 2013 income (4 040 for 2012 income).

1.1.2.2. Main non-standard reliefs available to the average worker

Certain expenditures to improve or maintain the taxpayer's primary residence, including outlays for heat insulation or heating adjustments, major capital expenditures and money spent to equip a home to produce energy from a renewable source (from 10 per cent to 40 per cent tax credits, subject to a multi-year maximum); compensatory allowances in case of divorce if paid in a lump sum (25 per cent reduction, capped at

EUR 30 500); child care costs for children under seven (50 per cent reduction, up to annual expenditure of EUR 2 300); dependent children attending secondary school or in higher education; donations to charities or other organisations assisting those in needs; trade union dues, etc. The exemption of the employer's participation to the collective contracts of supplementary health cover is abolished in the budget act for 2014 (i.e. income earned in 2013).

1.1.2.3. Refundable tax credit: Employment premium (*prime pour l'emploi*, or PPE)

This is a tax credit for households comprising wage-earners whose equivalent full-time net taxable earned income was between EUR 3 743 and EUR 26 572. The credit is determined in a multi-step calculation. First, the amount of the premium is calculated for each eligible wage-earner, and then the individual amounts are aggregated. The resulting amount may then be increased under certain conditions (dependent children or single-parent wage-earner). It is this final amount that is deducted from the family's tax liability. However, the credit is attributed only if the household's reference taxable income does not exceed the following limits: EUR 16 251 for a single person, EUR 25 231 for a single-parent family with two children, EUR 32 498 for a married or PACSed couple with no children, EUR 41 478 for a married or PACSed couple with two children. The credit was increased sharply, since the maximum individual amount was raised to EUR 960 in 2008. The PPE is not paid if it is less than EUR 30.

In the event of part-time work, the income used to compute the amount of the credit is converted to a full-time equivalent, and the resulting credit is then adjusted to the actual amount of time worked and increased. The increase has been raised: in 2007 (2006 income), the PPE of persons whose work ratio is 50 per cent (persons working half-time all year or full-time for six months) amounts to 92.5 per cent of the PPE of persons working full-time all year, versus 82.5 per cent in 2006.

The following table shows the applicable schedule for computing the employment premium by income level and type of family, as selected by the OECD:

Family status	Full-time equivalent annual earnings between	Amount of employment premium (PPE)	Increase for family responsibilities	
Single person with no children	EUR 3 743 < R <= EUR 12 475	R*7.7%		
	EUR 12 475 < R <= EUR 17 451	(EUR 17 451-R) * 19.3%		
			Childless	Two children
Two-earner couple (married/PACSed)	EUR 3 743 < R <= EUR 12 475	R * 7.7%	-	EUR 72
	EUR 12 475 < R <= EUR 17 451	(EUR 17 451-R) * 19.3%	-	EUR 72
			Childless	Two children
Single-earner couple (married/PACSed)	EUR 3 743 < R <= EUR 12 475	R * 7.7% + EUR 83	-	EUR 72
	EUR 12 475 < R<= EUR 17 451	(EUR 17 451 -R) * 19.3%+ EUR 83	-	EUR 72
	EUR 17 451 < R <= EUR 24 950	EUR 83	-	EUR 36
	EUR 24 950 < R <= EUR 26 572	(EUR 26 572-R) * 5.1%	-	EUR 36
Single-parent family with two children	EUR 3 743 < R <= EUR 12 475	R * 7.7%	EUR 108	
	EUR 12 475 < R <= EUR 17 451	(EUR 17 451-R) * 19.3%	EUR 108	
	EUR 17 451 < R <= EUR 26 572	0	EUR 72	

The PPE is increased for dependants in a household, and whether a married/PACSed couple has one or two earners can also affect the amount of the credit (with the amount for single-earner couples increased by EUR 83). The PPE is increased by EUR 36 for each dependent child, except in special cases (e.g. single-earner married/PACSed PPE recipients in the top two income brackets).

For the sixth consecutive year, the government decided to continue the freeze on the PPE scale for 2013.

Since 2010 personal income tax, the PPE is partly replaced by a new cash transfer benefit implemented in July 2009: the RSA (active solidarity income). This cash transfer ensures households earn a minimum income that increases with the number of hours worked. The RSA is not assessed here because to do so the knowledge of every cash transfer of the households (such as cash transfers for housing, unemployment, etc.) is needed. The RSA is designed to meet three goals:

- encourage people to enter or return to the labour market, by guaranteeing them a lasting improvement in income;
- reduce poverty by providing recipients with a decent income;
- improve social support and occupational reintegration.

The RSA is a new benefit that supersedes two existing basic welfare payments, the so called "revenu minimum d'insertion" (minimum unemployment benefit – RMI) and the so called "allocation de parent isolé" (single-parent allowance – API). It also replaces temporary payments for welfare recipients who return to work ("prime de retour à l'emploi", "prime forfaitaire de retour à l'emploi" bonuses and the "intéressement proportionnel" system of benefits combined with part-time work). However, the eight family types studied here earn too high an income to benefit from this credit.

1.1.3. *Tax schedule*

	Fraction of taxable income (1 share, in euros)	Rate (in %)
1st bracket	Up to 6 011	0
2nd bracket	From 6 011 to 11 991	5.5
3rd bracket	From 11 991 to 26 631	14
4th bracket	From 26 631 to 71 397	30
5th bracket	From 71 397 to 151 200	41
6th bracket	Above 151 200	45

A special rebate for taxpayers with a low tax liability is applied to the amount of tax resulting from the above schedule before reductions and tax credits. To be eligible, the tax on the household's income must be less than EUR 1 016, in which case the rebate is equal to one-half the difference between this ceiling and the amount of tax before the rebate. If the final tax is less than EUR 61, no tax is payable.

1.1.4. *Exceptional contribution on high revenues**

An exceptional contribution on high revenues is based on the reference taxable income ("revenu fiscal de référence"). The tax rates are 3 per cent from EUR 250 000 to EUR 500 0000 (single person), 4 per cent over EUR 500 0000 (single person), 3 per cent from EUR 500 000 to EUR 1 000 000 (married couple or civil union) and 4 per cent over EUR 1 000 000 (married couple or civil unions).

* The contribution was applied for the first time to 2011 income, but it has not been included in the previous editions of the *Taxing Wages*.

1.2. Taxes levied by decentralised authorities

Local taxes levied on working households are:

- Residency tax (*taxe d'habitation*), which is set by local authorities;
- Property taxes on developed and undeveloped land;
- There are common rules for each type of tax, to which certain municipalities make certain adjustments.

These local taxes, the rates of which vary widely, depending on the municipality, are not assessed here.

1.3. Universal social contribution (contribution sociale généralisée, or CSG)

The universal social contribution (CSG) was introduced on 1 February 1991. Since 1 January 1998, the rate of CSG has been 7.5 per cent. This rate has been applied to a base of 98.25 per cent as of 1 January 2012. The CSG is deductible against taxable income, but at a lower rate of 5.1 per cent.

1.4. Contribution to the reimbursement of social debt (contribution au remboursement de la dette sociale, or CRDS)

The contribution to the reimbursement of social debt has been in effect since 1 February 1997. Like the universal social contribution, its base has passed to 98.25 per cent of gross pay as of 1 January 2012. The rate is set at 0.5 per cent. Unlike social security contributions, CRDS payments are not deductible from taxable income.

2. Compulsory social security contributions to schemes operated within the government sector

Some contributions are levied on a capped portion of monthly earnings. Since 1997, this ceiling has been adjusted once a year on 1 January. In January 2013, the ceiling was EUR 3 086 (or EUR 37 032 per year).

2.1. Employee contributions

2.1.1. Pension

- 6.75 per cent on earnings up to the ceiling (6.67 per cent in 2012).
- 0.10 per cent on total earnings.

2.1.2. Illness, pregnancy, disability, death

- 0.75 per cent on total earnings.

2.1.3. Unemployment

- 2.4 per cent on earnings up to 4 times the ceiling.

2.1.4. Others

- Supplemental pension* for non-managers: minimum 3 per cent up to the ceiling and 8 per cent between one and three times the ceiling; for managers, 3 per cent up to the ceiling and 7.7 per cent between one and four times the ceiling.

* The social protection scheme is named ARRCO for non-managers and AGGIRC for managers.

- The AGFF (Association pour la gestion du fonds de financement) contribution replaces ASF (Association pour la gestion de la structure financière), which had previously been included in "unemployment" levies. The rate of this contribution for non-managerial workers is 0.8 per cent of earnings up to the social security ceiling plus 0.9 per cent of any income in excess of the ceiling but not exceeding triple the amount of the ceiling.

2.2. Employer contributions

2.2.1. Pensions

8.4 per cent (8.32 per cent in 2012) of gross pay, up to the ceiling, plus a 1.6 per cent levy on total pay.

2.2.2. Illness, pregnancy, disability, death

12.8% of total earnings.

An additional contribution of 0.3 per cent (contribution de solidarité autonomie – CSA) is levied on total salary.

2.2.3. Unemployment

4 per cent of earnings (4.5 per cent, 5.5 per cent or 7 per cent for some temporary contracts), up to four times the ceiling; in addition, 0.3 per cent up to four times the ceiling to endow the salary guarantee fund (AGS).

2.2.4. Work-related accidents

Contribution rates for work-related accidents vary by line of business and are published annually in the official gazette (*Journal officiel de la République française*). In 2013, the average rate is 2.43 per cent. The rates increased by 0.05 percentage points in 2013.

2.2.5. Family allowances

5.4 per cent of total pay.

2.2.6. Others

- Supplemental pension: For non-managers, 4.5 per cent up to the ceiling and 12 per cent between one and three times the ceiling; for managers, 4.5 per cent up to the ceiling and 12.6 per cent between one and four times the ceiling.*
- The AGFF contribution is 1.2 per cent for non-managers or managers up to the ceiling, 1.2 per cent for non-managers between one and three times the ceiling and 1.3 per cent for managers between one and four times the ceiling. In the table, this is combined with the rates for supplemental pensions.
- Others (construction, housing, apprenticeship, further training): 3.23 per cent of pay (for enterprises with more than 20 employees). The transport tax is not included because it varies geographically.

2.2.7. Reduction of employer-paid social insurance contributions

Act No. 2003-47 of 17 January 2003 on salaries, working time and the development of employment (the "Fillon Act") amended how the reduction of contributions is calculated.

* Between four and eight times the ceiling, the rate of the AGFF contribution is not nationaly decided.

As a result, since 1 July 2005 the maximum reduction has been 26 per cent (in companies with more than 20 employees) for a worker paid the minimum wage. It then declines gradually to zero at 160 per cent of the annual minimum wage. It applies irrespective of the number of hours worked.

The Budget Act for 2007 (Article 41 V) bolsters this measure for very small enterprises with effect from 1 July 2007. For employers with between 1 and 19 employees, the maximum deduction was raised to 28.1 per cent at the minimum wage, declining gradually – here too – to zero at 160 per cent of the minimum wage.

In 1 January 2011 the "Fillon act" was modified and included an annualized calculation of the general tax reliefs of employer contributions. For part-time wage-earners, the relief is computed using an equivalent full-time salary and is then adjusted proportionally to the number of hours paid.

The gross annual minimum wage (for 1 820 hours) in 2013 was an estimated EUR 17 163.

2.2.8. *Competitive tax credit (CICE – Crédit d'impôt pour la compétitivité et l'emploi)*

As for 2013, the competitive tax credit (CICE – Crédit d'impôt pour la compétitivité et l'emploi) will benefit all businesses, regardless of their legal status or economic sector, that employ salaried workers and be liable for either corporation tax or income tax, based on actual profits.

The CICE is based on all wages paid to salaried employees in a given calendar year up to 2.5 times the minimum wage (without taking into account any overtime or additional hours worked). For part-time employees and seasonal workers, the minimum wage corresponding to the working hours stipulated in the contract shall be taken into account.

The rate of the tax credit shall be 4 per cent for wages paid in 2013 (rising to 6 per cent as from 2014).

3. Universal cash transfers

Main family benefits (in respect of dependent children)

- Family allowances: monthly base for family allowances (BMAF) = EUR 403.79 as of 1 April 2013 (EUR 399 as of 1 April 2012, 402.59 in average over 2013). Rate: two children: 32 per cent; per additional child: 41 per cent.
- ARS (Allocation de Rentrée Scolaire): The amount payable depends on the age of the child to reflect needs. The allowance is payable to families or persons with children aged 6 to 18 attending school, and whose income is below a certain level (not incorporated into the model).

Age of the child	Percentage of the BMAF at 1 January 2013
6-10 years	89.72
11-14 years	94.67
15-18 years	97.95

- Family supplement: 41.65 per cent of the BMAF at 1 January 2013. Subject to revenue ceilings, this is paid to families as of the third child (not incorporated into the model).

- The CRDS is levied on family allowances at a rate of 0.5 per cent (no deduction).

4. Main changes in the tax system and social benefits regime since the taxation of 2012 income

- Tax system (2013 income)
  - for the "family quotient" system, the tax benefit for an additional half-share is limited to EUR 1 500;
  - end of the tax reductions for dependent children attending secondary school or in higher education;
  - end of the exemption on overtime work (August 2012);
  - end of the exemption of the employer's participation to the collective contracts of supplementary health cover;
  - end of the freeze of the tax schedule (applying since 2011 income) and increase of the special rebate for lower taxpayers;
  - competitive tax credit.
- Social benefits regime
  - increase of 2% of the "RSA" in September of 2013;
  - employer and employee contributions to the basic pension scheme rose by 0.1 percentage point;
  - contribution rates for work-related accidents increased (+0.05 percentage point in the average national rate).

5. Memorandum items

To assess the degree of comparability between countries, the following additional information should be taken into account:

- Coverage is of the private and semi-public sectors of NACE Sections C to K up to 2007 and NACE Rev. 2 Sections B to N from 2008.
- The category "employees" encompasses all full-time dependent employees (excluding apprentices and interns).
- The figures presented are obtained by applying income tax and social contribution scales to gross salaries as listed in annual social data reports (DADS) in NACE.

2013 parameter values

APW earnings	Ave_earn	36 980	Secretariat estimate
Work expenses	work_rel_fl	424	
	work_rel_ceil	12 096	
	work_rel_rate	0.1	
Tax schedule	tax_sch	0	6 011
		0.055	11 991
		0.14	26 631
		0.3	71 397
		0.41	151 200
		0.45	
	limit_demipart	1 500	
	limit_sp_demipart1	3 540	
Décote value	decote	1 016	
	tax_min	61	
Prime Pour l'Emploi	rev_ref_sing	16 251	
	rev_ref_mar	32 498	
	maj_dem_part	4 490	
	rate1	0.077	
	rate2	0.193	
	extra_pers	36	
	rate3	0.051	
	seuil1	3 743	
	seuil2	12 475	
	seuil3	17 451	
	seuil4	24 950	
	seuil5	26 572	
	seuil_min	30	
	ppe_mar_1earn	83	
	maj_tp_seuil	0.5	
	maj_tp	0.85	
CEHR	cehr_rate1	0.03	
	cehr_rate2	0.04	
	cehr_ceil1	250 000	
	cehr_ceil2	500 000	
CSG+CRDS	CSG_CRDS_abat	0.0175	
	CSG_rat_noded	0.0240	
	CRDS_rat_noded	0.0050	
	CSG_CRDS_rat_noded	0.0290	
	CSG_rat_ded	0.0510	
	CRDS_special	0.0050	
Social security contributions	SSC_ceil	37 032.0	
	pension_rate	0.0675	
	pension_rate2	0.0010	
	sickness_rate	0.0075	
	unemp_rate	0.0240	
Extra pension (non-cadres) (incl. AGFF)	pens_rate_ex	0.0380	
	pens_rate_ex2	0.0890	
Employer contributions	pens_empr1	0.084	
	pens_empr2	0.0160	
Authonomous Solidarity Contribution	sickness_empr	0.1280	
	CSA	0.0030	
Unemployment (incl. "garantie de salaire")	unemp_empr	0.0430	
Accidents	accidents_empr	0.0243	
	SMIC	17 162.6	
Family Allowance	fam_empr	0.054	
Extra pension (incl. AGFF)	pens_empr_ex	0.057	

	pens_empr_ex2	0.133
Others	others_empr	0.0323
	others_empr2	0.0323
Transitory Empl. SSC reduction rate	SSC_empr_redrate1	0
Employer SSC reduction rate	SSC_empr_redrate2	0.6
Employer SSC reduction maximum	SSC_empr_red_max	0.26
Employer SSC reduction SMIC reference	SSC_empr_SMIC_ref	1.6
Child benefit (second child) before CRDS	CB_2	1 545.95
third & subsequent before CRDS	CB_3	1 980.74
Derivation of minimum income	SMIC_horaire	9.43
	SMIC_heures	1 820
	minrevtp	17 163
Taux de réduction CICE	cice_red	0.04
	cice_max	2.5

2013 tax equations

The equations for the French system are mostly calculated on a family basis.

Variable names are defined in the table of parameters above, within the equations table, or are the standard variables "married" and "children". A reference to a variable with the affix "_total" indicates the sum of the relevant variable values for the principal and spouse. And the affixes "_princ" and "_spouse" indicate the value for the principal and spouse, respectively. Equations for a single person are as shown for the principal, with "_spouse" values taken as 0.

	Line in country table and intermediate steps	Variable name	Range	Equation
1.	Earnings	earn		
	Quotient for tax calculation	quotient	J	1+Married+IF(Children<3, Children/2, Children-1)+0.5*(Married=0)*(Children>0)
2.	Allowances:			
	CSG deductible	CSG_ded	B	CSG_rat_ded*((1-CSG_CRDS_abat)*MIN(earn;4*SSC_ceil)+Positive(earn-4*SSC_ceil))
	Salary net	earn_dec	B	earn-SSC-CSG_ded
	Work related	work_exp	B	MIN(work_rel_ceil, MAX(work_rel_rate* earn_dec, MIN(work_rel_fl, earn_dec)))
	Basic	basic_al	B	0
3.	Credits in taxable income	taxbl_cr	B	0
4.	CG taxable income	tax_inc	J	Positive(earn_dec_total-work_exp)
5.	CG tax before credits			
	Calculation according to schedule	sch_tax	J	MAX(quotient*Tax(tax_inc/quotient, tax_sch), IF(Married, 2*Tax(tax_inc/2, tax_sch)-limit_demipart*(quotient-2), Tax(tax_inc, tax_sch)-(Children>0)*(limit_sp_demipart1+limit_demipart*(quotient-2))))++cehr_rate1*MIN((cehr_ceil2-cehr_ceil1)*(1+Married);MAX(tax_inc-cehr_ceil1*(1+Married);0))+cehr_rate2 * MAX(tax_inc-cehr_ceil2*(1+Married);0)
	Adjusted for decote	adj_tax	J	Positive(MIN(1.5*sch_tax-decote/2, sch_tax))
	Tax liable	inc_tax	J	(adj_tax>=tax_min)*adj_tax
	CSG+CRDS (non-deductible)	CSG_CRDS_noded	B	CSG_CRDS_rat_nod*((1-CSG_CRDS_abat)*MIN(earn;4*SSC_ceil)+Positive(earn-4*SSC_ceil))
	CSG deductible	CSG_ded	B	CSG_rat_ded*((1-CSG_CRDS_abat)*MIN(earn;4*SSC_ceil)+Positive(earn-4*SSC_ceil))

	Line in country table and intermediate steps	Variable name	Range	Equation
6.	Tax credits :			
	Prime pour l'emploi	PPE_main_princ	P	seuilMin(IF(tax_inc<((Married=0)*rev_ref_sing+(Married=1)*rev_ref_mar+maj_dem_part*Children),1,0)*IF(earn_dec_princ>=seuil1,(Married=1)*(earn_dec_spouse<seuil1)*IF(earn_dec_princ*MAX(minrevtp/earn_princ,1)>seuil4,Positive(seuil5-earn_dec_princ*MAX(minrevtp/earn_princ,1))*rate3*(((earn_princ/minrevtp)>=1)+((earn_princ/minrevtp)<=maj_tp_seuil)*MIN(earn_princ/minrevtp,1)*(1+maj_tp)+((earn_princ/minrevtp)>maj_tp_seuil)*((earn_princ/minrevtp)<1)*((1-maj_tp)*MIN(earn_princ/minrevtp,1)+maj_tp)),ppe_mar_1earn)+(earn_dec_princ*MAX(minrevtp/earn_princ,1)<seuil2)*rate1*earn_dec_princ*MAX(minrevtp/earn_princ,1)*(((earn_princ/minrevtp)>=1)+((earn_princ/minrevtp)<=maj_tp_seuil)*MIN(EARN_PRINC/minrevtp,1)*(1+maj_tp)+((EARN_PRINC/minrevtp)>maj_tp_seuil)*((earn_princ/minrevtp)<1)*((1-maj_tp)*MIN(earn_princ/minrevtp,1)+maj_tp))+(earn_dec_princ*MAX(minrevtp/earn_princ,1)>=seuil2)*Positive(seuil3-earn_dec_princ*MAX(minrevtp/earn_princ,1))*rate2*(((earn_princ/minrevtp)>=1)+((earn_princ/minrevtp)<=maj_tp_seuil)*MIN(earn_princ/minrevtp,1)*(1+maj_tp)+((earn_princ/minrevtp)>maj_tp_seuil)*((earn_princ/minrevtp)<1)*((1-maj_tp)*MIN(earn_princ/minrevtp,1)+maj_tp)),0),seuil_min)
		PPE_main_spouse	S	seuilMin(IF(tax_inc<((Married=0)*rev_ref_sing+(Married=1)*rev_ref_mar+maj_dem_part*Children),1,0)*IF(earn_dec_spouse>=seuil1,(Married=1)*(earn_dec_princ<seuil1)*IF(earn_dec_spouse*MAX(minrevtp/earn_spouse,1)>seuil4,Positive(seuil5-earn_dec_spouse*MAX(minrevtp/earn_spouse,1))*rate3*(((earn_spouse/minrevtp)>=1)+((earn_spouse/minrevtp)<=maj_tp_seuil)*MIN(earn_spouse/minrevtp,1)*(1+maj_tp)+((earn_spouse/minrevtp)>maj_tp_seuil)*((earn_spouse/minrevtp)<1)*((1-maj_tp)* MIN(earn_spouse/minrevtp,1)+maj_tp)),ppe_mar_1earn)+(earn_dec_spouse*MAX(minrevtp/earn_spouse,1)<seuil2)*rate1*earn_dec_spouse*MAX(minrevtp/earn_spouse,1)*(((earn_spouse/minrevtp)>=1)+((earn_spouse/minrevtp)<=maj_tp_seuil)*MIN(earn_spouse/minrevtp,1)*(1+maj_tp)+((earn_spouse/minrevtp)>maj_tp_seuil)*((earn_spouse/minrevtp)<1)*((1-maj_tp)*MIN(earn_spouse/minrevtp,1)+maj_tp))+(earn_dec_spouse*MAX(minrevtp/earn_spouse,1)>=seuil2)*Positive(seuil3-earn_dec_spouse*MAX(minrevtp/earn_spouse,1))*rate2*(((earn_spouse/minrevtp)>=1)+((earn_spouse/minrevtp)<=maj_tp_seuil)*MIN(earn_spouse/minrevtp,1)*(1+maj_tp)+((earn_spouse/minrevtp)>maj_tp_seuil)*((earn_spouse/minrevtp)<1)*((1-maj_tp)*MIN(earn_spouse /minrevtp,1)+maj_tp)),0),seuil_min)

	Line in country table and intermediate steps	Variable name	Range	Equation
	Additional flat rate allowance	add_all	J	IF(tax_inc<((Married=0)*rev_ref_sing+(Married=1)*rev_ref_mar+maj_dem_part*Children),1,0)*OR((earn_dec_princ>=seuil1),(earn_dec_spouse>=seuil1))*(IF(OR(IF(earn_dec_princ>0,AND(earn_dec_princ>=seuil1,earn_dec_princ*MAX(minrevtp/earn_princ,1)<=seuil3),0),IF(earn_dec_spouse>0,AND(earn_dec_spouse>=seuil1,earn_dec_spouse*MAX(minrevtp/earn_spouse,1)<=seuil3),0)),extra_pers*Children,IF(OR(IF(earn_dec_princ>0,AND(seuil3<earn_dec_princ*MAX(minrevtp/earn_princ,1),earn_dec_princ*MAX(minrevtp/earn_princ,1)<=seuil5,earn_dec_spouse<seuil1),0),IF(earn_dec_spouse>0,AND(seuil3<earn_dec_spouse*MAX(minrevtp/earn_spouse,1),earn_dec_spouse*MAX(minrevtp/earn_spouse,1)<=seuil5,earn_princ<seuil1),0)),extra_pers*(Children>0),0))+(Married=0)*(Children>0)*extra_pers)
	Total NWTC	tax_cr	J	PPE_main_princ+PPE_main_spouse+add_all
7.	CG tax	CG_tax	J	inc_tax+CSG_CRDS_noded+CSG_ded-tax_cr
8.	State and local taxes	local_tax	J	0
9.	Employees' soc security	SSC	B	pension_rate*MINA(earn, SSC_ceil)+(sickness_rate+pension_rate2)*earn+unemp_rate1*MINA(earn, SSC_ceil)+(earn>SSC_ceil)*unemp_rate2*MINA(earn-SSC_ceil, 3*SSC_ceil)+pens_rate_ex*MINA(earn, SSC_ceil)+(earn>SSC_ceil)*pens_rate_ex2*MINA(earn-SSC_ceil, 3*SSC_ceil-SSC_ceil)
11.	Cash transfers	cash_transf_gross	J	IF(Children<2, 0, CB_2+(Children-2)*CB_3)
		crds_cash_transf	J	cash_transf_gross*-1*CRDS_special
		cash_transf_net	J	cash_transf_gross+crds_cash_transf
13.	Employer's soc security	SSC_empr_gross	B	(sickness_empr + CSA + pens_empr2 + fam_empr + accidents_empr)*earn + pens_empr1*MINA(earn;SSC_ceil) + pens_empr_ex*MINA(earn;SSC_ceil) + pens_empr_ex2*MAX(MIN(earn;3*SSC_ceil) - SSC_ceil;0) + unemp_empr*MIN(earn;4*SSC_ceil) + others_empr*MINA(earn;SSC_ceil) + others_empr2*MAX(earn-SSC_ceil;0)
		SSC_empr_reduction	B	IF(OR(earn>SSC_empr_SMIC_ref*SMIC,earn=0),0,-MIN(SSC_empr_red_max*earn,(SSC_empr_red_max/SSC_empr_redrate2)*(SSC_empr_SMIC_ref*minrevtp/earn-1)*earn)) -IF(earn<cice_max*minrevtp;earn*cice_red)
		SSC_empr_final	B	SSC_empr_gross+SSC_empr_reduction
	Memorandum item: Non-wastable tax credit			
	tax expenditure component	taxexp	P	tax_cr-transfer
	cash transfer component	transfer	P	IF(CG_tax<0,-CG_tax,0)

Key to range of equation B calculated separately for both principal earner and spouse P calculated for principal only (value taken as 0 for spouse calculation) J calculated once only on a joint basis.

Taxing Wages 2014
Changes in sructural labour income tax progressivity
over 2000-12 period in OECD member countries

Germany

This chapter includes data on the income taxes paid by workers, their social security contributions, the family benefits they receive in the form of cash transfers as well as the social security contributions and payroll taxes paid by their employers. Results reported include the marginal and average tax burden for eight different family types.

Methodological information is available for personal income tax systems, compulsory social security contributions to schemes operated within the government sector, universal cash transfers as well as recent changes in the tax/benefit system. The methodology also includes the parameter values and tax equations underlying the data.

Germany 2013

The tax/benefit position of single persons

		Wage level (per cent of average wage)	67	100	167	67
		Number of children	none	none	none	2
1.	**Gross wage earnings**		30114	45170	75284	30114
2.	**Standard tax allowances**					
	Basic allowance					
	Married or head of family		0	0	0	1308
	Dependent children		0	0	0	0
	Deduction for social security contributions and income taxes		4235	6352	7743	4159
	Work-related expenses		1000	1000	1000	1000
	Other		36	36	36	36
		Total	5271	7388	8779	6503
3.	**Tax credits or cash transfers included in taxable income**		0	0	0	0
4.	**Central government taxable income (1 - 2 + 3)**		24843	37782	66505	23611
5.	**Central government income tax liability (exclusive of tax credits)**		4257	8644	20821	3680
6.	**Tax credits**					
	Basic credit					
	Married or head of family					
	Children		0	0	0	4416
	Other					
		Total	0	0	0	4416
7.	**Central government income tax finally paid (5-6)**		4257	8644	20821	-736
8.	**State and local taxes**		0	0	0	0
9.	**Employees' compulsory social security contributions**					
	Gross earnings		6151	9226	12098	6075
	Taxable income					
		Total	6151	9226	12098	6075
10.	**Total payments to general government (7 + 8 + 9)**		10408	17870	32920	5339
11.	**Cash transfers from general government**					
	For head of family					
	For two children		0	0	0	0
		Total	0	0	0	0
12.	**Take-home pay (1-10+11)**		19706	27301	42364	24774
13.	**Employers' compulsory social security contributions**		5804	8707	11555	5804
14.	**Average rates**					
	Income tax		14.1%	19.1%	27.7%	-2.4%
	Employees' social security contributions		20.4%	20.4%	16.1%	20.2%
	Total payments less cash transfers		34.6%	39.6%	43.7%	17.7%
	Total tax wedge including employer's social security contributions		45.1%	49.3%	51.2%	31.0%
15.	**Marginal rates**					
	Total payments less cash transfers: Principal earner		46.9%	52.2%	44.3%	44.8%
	Total payments less cash transfers: Spouse		n.a.	n.a.	n.a.	n.a.
	Total tax wedge: Principal earner		55.5%	60.0%	44.3%	53.7%
	Total tax wedge: Spouse		n.a.	n.a.	n.a.	n.a.

Germany 2013

The tax/benefit position of married couples

		Wage level (per cent of average wage)	100-0	100-33	100-67	100-33
		Number of children	2	2	2	none
1.	**Gross wage earnings**		45170	60227	75284	60227
2.	**Standard tax allowances**					
	Basic allowance					
	Married or head of family		0	0	0	0
	Dependent children		0	0	0	0
	Deduction for social security contributions and income taxes		6239	8318	10398	8469
	Work-related expenses		1000	2000	2000	2000
	Other		72	72	72	72
		Total	7311	10390	12470	10541
3.	**Tax credits or cash transfers included in taxable income**		0	0	0	0
4.	**Central government taxable income (1 - 2 + 3)**		37859	49837	62814	49686
5.	**Central government income tax liability (exclusive of tax credits)**		4780	8350	12528	8516
6.	**Tax credits**					
	Basic credit					
	Married or head of family					
	Children		4416	4416	4416	0
	Other					
		Total	4416	4416	4416	0
7.	**Central government income tax finally paid (5-6)**		364	3934	8112	8516
8.	**State and local taxes**		0	0	0	0
9.	**Employees' compulsory social security contributions**					
	Gross earnings		9113	12151	15189	12301
	Taxable income					
		Total	9113	12151	15189	12301
10.	**Total payments to general government (7 + 8 + 9)**		9477	16084	23300	20817
11.	**Cash transfers from general government**					
	For head of family					
	For two children		0	0	0	0
		Total	0	0	0	0
12.	**Take-home pay (1-10+11)**		35693	44143	51984	39410
13.	**Employers' compulsory social security contributions**		8707	11609	14511	11609
14.	**Average rates**					
	Income tax		0.8%	6.5%	10.8%	14.1%
	Employees' social security contributions		20.2%	20.2%	20.2%	20.4%
	Total payments less cash transfers		21.0%	26.7%	30.9%	34.6%
	Total tax wedge including employer's social security contributions		33.8%	38.6%	42.1%	45.1%
15.	**Marginal rates**					
	Total payments less cash transfers: Principal earner		43.0%	46.6%	49.3%	46.9%
	Total payments less cash transfers: Spouse		43.9%	46.6%	49.3%	46.9%
	Total tax wedge: Principal earner		52.2%	55.2%	57.5%	55.5%
	Total tax wedge: Spouse		52.9%	55.2%	57.5%	55.5%

The national currency is the euro (EUR). In 2013, EUR 0.75 was equal to USD 1. The average worker earned EUR 45 170 (Secretariat estimate).

1. Personal income tax systems

1.1. *Central/federal government income taxes*

1.1.1. Tax unit

Spouses are generally assessed jointly. They however have the option of being assessed separately. The income of dependent children is not assessable with that of the parents. The calculations in this Report assume joint taxation of the income of the spouses.

1.1.2. Tax allowances and tax credits:

1.1.2.1. Standard reliefs and work-related expenses

- *Basic reliefs:* None.
- *Standard marital status reliefs:* In the case of joint assessment, specific allowances are doubled. The income tax liability is computed by applying the income splitting method.
- *Relief(s) for children:* As of 1 January 2010, there are increased tax credits of EUR 2 208 for the first and the second child, of EUR 2 280 for the third child and of EUR 2 580 for the fourth and subsequent children. There is a tax allowance of EUR 2 184 for the subsistence of a child and an additional EUR 1 320 for minding and education or training needs (EUR 3 504). The amount of this allowance is doubled in case of jointly assessed parents. If the value of the tax credit is less than the relief calculated applying the tax allowances, the taxpayer obtains the tax allowance instead of the tax credit. It is also doubled for lone parents in cases where the other parent does not pay alimony. This is the assumption in the calculations presented in this Report.
- *Relief for lone parents:* Taxpayers who live alone with at least one child that entitles them to the tax allowances or tax credits for children, receive an additional allowance of EUR 1 308.
- *Reliefs for social security contributions and life insurance contributions:* Social security contributions and other expenses incurred in provision for the future (e.g. life insurance) are deductible up to specific ceilings. In 2005, a new calculation scheme came into force:

  Step 1: all contributions made to pension funds (i.e. both employee's and employer's contributions) are added up. Step 2: the resulting amount is limited to EUR 20 000. Step 3: a certain percentage is applied to this amount (starting from 60 per cent in 2005, this percentage will be increased by 2 percentage points each year; it will reach 100 per cent in 2025). Step 4: the resulting amount, diminished by the (tax-free) contributions of the employer, is deductible from income.

  The tax treatment of social security expenses (health, unemployment and care insurance) changed as of 1 January 2010. Employees' annual contributions to statutory health insurance excluding sickness benefit (assumed to amount to 96 per cent of statutory health contributions) and employees' contributions to mandatory long-term care insurance are deductible from the tax base. In case these contributions do not exceed EUR 1 900/3 800 (single/married couples), contributions to unemployment insurance and other insurances premiums can be deducted in addition up to this ceiling.

If the resulting sum of deductible amounts according the legislation in force since 2005 is lower than the allowance calculated under the scheme that was valid up to 2004, the former regulations are applied in favour of the taxpayer (for more details on the old scheme: see 2005 edition and Section 4. of this Report).

- *Work-related expenses:* EUR 1 000 lump-sum allowance per gainfully-employed person.
- *Special expenses:* Lump sum allowance (EUR 36/72 (singles/couples)) for special expenses, e.g. for tax accountancy. The actual expenses will be fully deductible from taxable income if the taxpayer proves that these expenses exceed the lump sum allowance.

1.1.2.2. Main non-standard tax reliefs applicable to an AW

- *Contributions to pensions, life insurance, superannuation schemes:* Other expenses than the compulsory contributions to social security are deductible as reliefs for (voluntary) social security contributions up to specific ceilings (see Section 1.1.2.1).
- *Medical expenses:* Partially deductible if not covered by insurance.
- *Other:* Work-related expenses that exceed the lump-sum allowance are fully deductible (no ceiling).

1.1.3. *Tax schedule*

The German tax schedule is formula-based. Taxable income is rounded down (to the EUR).

- X is the taxable income,
- T is the income tax liability,
- As of 1 January 2013 the following definitions are used in the income tax liability formulas:

$$Y = \frac{X - 8130}{10000}$$

$$Z = \frac{X - 13469}{10000}$$

The income tax liability (amounts in EUR) is calculated as follows:

1. T = 0 for X ≤ 8 130
2. T = (933.70 Y + 1 400) Y for 8 131 ≤ X ≤ 13 469
3. T = (228.74 Z + 2 397) Z + 1 014 for 13 470 ≤ X ≤ 52 881
4. T = 0.42 X – 8 196 for 52 882 ≤ X ≤ 250 730
5. T = 0.45 X – 15 718 for 250 731 ≤ X

These formulas are used to calculate the income tax for single individuals.

The income tax liability for spouses who are assessed jointly is computed as follows: the income tax is calculated with respect to one-half of the joint taxable income. The resulting amount is doubled to obtain the income tax liability of the family (splitting method).

1.1.4. Solidarity surcharge

The solidarity surcharge is levied at 5.5 per cent of the income tax liability subject to an exemption limit of EUR 972/1 944 (singles/couples). The income tax liability is calculated applying the tax allowance for children. If the income tax liability exceeds the exemption limit, the solidarity surcharge will be phased in at a higher rate of 20 per cent of the difference between the income tax liability and the exemption limit until it equals 5.5 per cent of the total liability.

1.2. State and local income taxes

None.

2. Compulsory social security contributions to schemes operated within the government sector

The amount of social security contributions depends on the wage and the insurance contribution rate. All contributions are subject to a contribution ceiling, i.e. the maximum income for which statutory insurance contributions are calculated. The contribution rates for pension, health, care and unemployment insurances are fixed by the government.

2.1. Employees' contributions

In general, earnings up to EUR 4 800 per year were free of employee social security contributions until 31 December 2012. As of 1 January 2013, some essential changes came into effect concerning minimally paid employment. The earnings limit increased from EUR 400 to EUR 450 per month. Persons whose mini-job started before 2013 and do not exceed the previous earnings limit of EUR 400 stay contribution-free in all classes of social insurance. Otherwise, persons who take up a new mini-job are generally subject to mandatory insurance coverage in the statutory pension scheme with the full pension contribution rate of 18.9 per cent (in 2013). If the earnings are below the amount of EUR 175 (minimum contribution limit), a minimum contribution of EUR 33.08 has to be paid (18.9 per cent of EUR 175). The employer's share amounts to 15 per cent of the whole pay whereas the employee's part adds up to 3.9 per cent (or the difference between minimum contribution and employer share). By applying for an exemption from obligatory insurance coverage the mini-job holder may reduce his share to EUR 0.

As of 1 April 2003, there was an additional concession for employees with monthly income between EUR 400.01 and EUR 800 per month (the so-called "sliding pay scale", EUR 4 800.12 and EUR 9 600 per year). Due to the new regulations mentioned above the earnings limits shifted to EUR 450.01 and EUR 850.00 per month (EUR 5 400.12 and EUR 10 200 per year). If the employee's income falls within this range, part of the income will be exempt from social insurance contributions. However, employers are still required to pay the regular contributions on the employee's earnings. The arrangement is purely intended to relieve the financial burden on employees. The employees' contributions to social insurance rise on a straight-line basis over the income band reaching the full rate at EUR 850 per month. Details on social security contributions for workers earning more than EUR 10 200 per year are provided below.

2.1.1. *Pensions*

Employers and employees pay each half of the contribution rate of 18.9 per cent in 2013, that is 9.45 per cent of the employee's gross wage earnings, up to a contribution ceiling of EUR 69 600.

2.1.2. *Sickness*

As of 1 January 2011, the rate remains on the level of 7.3 per cent for employers and 8.2 per cent for employees. The contribution ceiling in 2013 is EUR 47 250. While all calculations shown in this Report assume membership in the public health insurance, workers with earnings above the contribution ceiling may opt out of the mandatory public health insurance system and may choose a private insurance provider instead (those opting for a private health insurance provider are required to obtain private long-term care insurance as well).

2.1.3. *Unemployment*

Employees pay half of the insurance contributions; the employer pays the other half. In 2013, the contribution rate is 3.0 per cent of assessable income. Employee and employer each pay 1.5 per cent. The contribution ceiling is EUR 69 600.

2.1.4. *Care*

A long-term care insurance (a 1 per cent contribution rate) went into effect on 1 January 1995. The rate was raised to 1.7 per cent of the gross wage when home nursing care benefits were added six months later. As of 1 July 2008, the rate was increased to 1.95 per cent. As of 1 January 2013, the contribution rate amounts to 2.05 per cent. The employers pay half of the contributions for long-term care insurance. In other words, employers and employees both pay a rate of 1.025 per cent. The assessable income is scaled according to the gross wage earnings but there is a contribution ceiling of EUR 47 250 in 2013.

As from 1 January 2005, child-raising is given special recognition in the law relating to statutory long-term care insurance. Childless contribution payers are required to pay a supplement of 0.25 per cent, raising the contribution rate paid by a childless employee from 0.975 per cent to 1.225 per cent as of 1 July 2008. In 2013, the contribution rate of a childless employee adds up to 1.275 per cent.

2.1.5. *Work injury*

Employer only.

2.1.6. *Family allowances*

None.

2.1.7. *Others*

None.

2.2. *Employers' contributions*

See Section 2.1.

2.2.1-2.2.4. (Pensions, sickness, unemployment, care):

See Section 2.1.

2.2.5. Work injury

Germany has established a statutory occupational accident insurance. It is provided by industrial, agricultural and public-sector employers' liability insurance funds. This insurance protects employees and their families against the consequences of accidents at work and occupational illnesses. It is funded through the contributions paid by employers only. The amount of the employer's contributions depends on the sum total of employee's annual pay and the employer's respective hazard level. As it is not possible to identify a representative contribution rate, these amounts are not considered in this Report.

2.2.6. Family allowances

None.

2.2.7. Others

None.

3. Universal cash transfers

3.1. Transfers related to marital status

None.

3.2. Transfers for dependent children

None.

4. Main changes in tax/benefit systems since 1997

The following table shows changes in the tax credit and the tax allowance for children since 1997:

	Child credit				Child allowance
	First child	Second child	Third child	Fourth and subsequent children	
1997	1 350	1 350	1 841	2 147	3 534
1999	1 534	1 534	1 841	2 147	3 534
2000	1 657	1 657	1 841	2 147	5 080
2002	1 848	1 848	1 848	2 148	5 808
2009[1]	1 968	1 968	2 040	2 340	6 024
2010	2 208	2 208	2 280	2 580	7 008

1. plus EUR 100 one-off child credit payment for each child.

Up to 2004, the calculation of the relief for social security contributions and other expenses proceeded in three steps. First, EUR 3 068/6 136 (singles/couples) was deducted. These amounts were, however, lowered by 16 per cent of gross wages (serving as a proxy for employers' social security contributions). This deduction was provided as a partial compensation for the self-employed which do not receive tax-free employers' social security contributions. Second, the remaining expenses were deductible up to

EUR 1 334/2 668 (singles/couples). Third, half of the remaining expenses were deductible up to EUR 667/1 334 (singles/couples).

In 2004, the tax rate was reduced and the formula for calculating the income tax was changed. The relief for lone parents was reduced to EUR 1 308, the lump sum allowance for work related expenses was reduced to EUR 920.

As from 1 January 2005, the final stage of the 2000-tax reform came into effect. The bottom and top income tax rates were further reduced to 15 per cent and 42 per cent. Since 1998, both the bottom and top income tax rate have been reduced by about 11 percentage points while the personal allowance has been raised from EUR 6 322 to EUR 7 664. The tax cuts reduce the tax burden for all income taxpayers, affording the greatest relief to employees and families with low and medium incomes as well as to small- and medium-sized unincorporated businesses.

On 1 January 2005, the law regulating the taxation of pensions and pension expenses entered into force. The law provides a gradual transition to ex-post taxation of pensions paid by the statutory pensions insurance. In the long run, the tax treatment of capital-based employee pension schemes based on a contract between employer and employee will be reformed in the same way as the tax treatment in respect of the state pension scheme. In addition to the increased deductibility of contributions to the state and certain private pension schemes, the law contains rules which are intended to increase the attractiveness of private capital-based pension schemes and to encourage individuals to invest privately for their old-age pension.

Up to 30 June of 2005, employees paid half of the sickness insurance contributions; the employer paid the other half. As from 1 July 2005, members of the statutory health insurance scheme also pay an income-linked contribution of 0.9 per cent to which employers do not contribute. As from 1 July 2005, all statutory health insurance funds have reduced their contribution rates by 0.9 percentage points.

In 2007, a new top income tax rate of 45 per cent was introduced for taxable income above EUR 250 000 (EUR 500 000 for jointly assessed spouses).

In 2009, the bottom income tax rate was reduced to 14 per cent. The basic allowance was increased to EUR 7 834. All thresholds were increased by EUR 400.

Since 1 January 2010, the basic allowance has been augmented to EUR 8 004 and all thresholds have been increased by EUR 330. Furthermore, new legislation improves the tax treatment of expenditure on health insurance and long-term care insurance. As of 1 January 2013, the basic allowance raises to EUR 8 130.

5. Memorandum items

5.1. *Average gross annual earnings calculation*

- Source of calculation: Federal Statistical Office.
- Excluding sickness and unemployment, including normal overtime and bonuses.

5.2. *Employer's contributions to private pension, etc., schemes*

No information available, though such schemes do exist.

2013 parameter values

Average earnings/yr	Ave_earn	45 315	Secretariat estimate
Tax allowances	Child_al	7 008	
Lone Parents	Lone_al	1 308	
Work related	Work_rel_al	1 000	
SSC allowance	SSC_dn	2 100	
	SSC_dn_rt	0.16	
	SSC_dn_lim	1 334	
	SSC_dn_lump_rt	0.2	
Allow. for special expenses	SE_al	36	
Church tax rate	Ch_tax_rt	0	
Tax formula	Tax_rate2	0.42	
	Tax_rate3	0.45	
	Tax_thrsh1	8 130	
	Tax_thrsh2	13 469	
Top Rate Tax Reduction	Reduction	8 196	
	Reduction2	15 718	
Tax Equation Rates			
tax_eqn_rates	Squared	Single	Constant
z	228.74	2 397	
			1014
y		1 400	0
	933.70		
Income tax rate stage	tax_first_stage	8 130	
	tax_second_stage	13 469	
	tax_third_stage	52 881	
	tax_fourth_stage	250 730	
Solidarity Surcharge	surcharge	0.055	
Solidarity Exemption Limit	surcharge_limit	972	
Alternative Surcharge Rate	surcharge_alt	0.2	
Child credit	Ch_cred		
	1. ch.	2 208	
	2. ch.	2 208	
	3.ch.	2 280	
	4.ch.	2 580	

Social security	Sickness	Pension	Unemployment	Care	Alternative employer rate	SSC Factor F
period_1	12	12	12	12	12	12
period_2	0					
sum (Month's)	12	12	12	12	12	12
employer_1	0.073	0.0945	0.015	0.01025	0.3	0.7605
employer_2	0					
employee_1	0.082	0.0945	0.015	0.01025	0.039	0.7605
employee_2	0					
childless_1	0.082	0.0945	0.015	0.01275	0.039	0.7605
childless_2	0					
ceil	47 250	69 600	69 600	47 250	2 100	
SSC Floor	SSC_floor	10 200				
Intermediate SSC Ceiling	SSC_floor1	5 400				

2013 tax equations

The equations for the German system in 2013 are mostly calculated on a family basis.

The standard functions which are used in the equations are described in the technical note about tax equations. The function acttax carry out a rounded calculation for the tables but the unrounded version purtax is used in calculating the marginal rates.

For a taxpayer with children, either the child allowance is given in the tax calculation or the cash transfer is given if this is more beneficial. In practice, therefore, it is necessary to make two calculations – with and without the child allowance. Nevertheless, the calculation of solidarity surcharge is always based on the calculation which does assume that the child tax allowance is given.

Variable names are defined in the table of parameters above, within the equations table, or are the standard variables "married" and "children". The affixes "_princ" and "_spouse" on Variable names in functions indicate that the values have to be calculated for the principal and spouse, respectively. The parameter year in function SSC_Allowance is the year for which you calculate the Allowance.

	Line in country table and intermediate steps	Variable name	Range	Equation
1.	Earnings	earn		
	Quotient for tax calculation	quotient	J	1+Married
2.	Allowances:			
	Children	children_al	J	Children*Child_al
	Lone parent	lone_allce	J	Lone_al*(Children>0)*(Married=0)
	Soc sec contributions	SSC_al	J	Function: SSC_Allowance(earn_princ, earn_spouse , SSC_princ + SSC_spouse , Quotient, SSC_dn, SSC_dn_rt, SSC_dn_lim, SSC_dn_lump_rt, If(Children>0; "employee"; "childless"), year, rounded)
	Work related	work_al	J	Work_rel_al+MIN(earn_spouse,Work_rel_al)
	Allow. for special expenses	SE_al	J	SE_al*quotient
	Total	tax_al	J	children_al+SSC_al+work_al+ lone_allce + SE_al
3.	Credits in taxable income	taxbl_cr	J	0
4.	CG taxable income	tax_inc	J	earn-tax_al
5.	CG tax before credits			
	adjusted taxable income	adj	J	tax_inc/quotient
	Formula based tax schedule	tax_formula	J	Function: acttax(taxinc, rate, reduction, threshold1, threshold2, threshold3, equationrate, tax_first_stage, tax_second_stage, tax_third_stage, tax_fourth_stage, rate2, reduction2)
	Adjust for the quotient	tax_adj	J	Quotient*tax_formula
	Include solidarity surcharge	sol_surch	J	MIN(tax_adj * surcharge, Positive(tax_adj - surcharge_limit*Quotient) * surcharge_alt)
	Tax paid	CG_tax_excl	J	tax_adj+sol_surch
6.	Tax credits :	tax_cr	J	0
7.	CG tax	CG_tax	J	CG_tax_excl
8.	State and local taxes	local_tax	J	0
9.	Employees' soc security	SSC	B	Function: SSC (earn_princ, If(Children>0; "employee"; "childless"), rounded) + SSC (earn_spouse, If(Children>0; "employee"; "childless"), rounded)
11.	Cash transfers	Cash_tran	J	Children*ch_cred
13.	Employer's soc security	SSC_empr	B	Function: SSC (earn_princ, "employer", rounded) + SSC (earn_spouse, "employer", rounded)

Key to range of equation.
B calculated separately for both principal earner and spouse.
P calculated for principal only (value taken as 0 for spouse calculation).
J calculated once only on a joint basis.

Taxing Wages 2014
Changes in sructural labour income tax progressivity
over 2000-12 period in OECD member countries

Greece

This chapter includes data on the income taxes paid by workers, their social security contributions, the family benefits they receive in the form of cash transfers as well as the social security contributions and payroll taxes paid by their employers. Results reported include the marginal and average tax burden for eight different family types.

Methodological information is available for personal income tax systems, compulsory social security contributions to schemes operated within the government sector, universal cash transfers as well as recent changes in the tax/ benefit system. The methodology also includes the parameter values and tax equations underlying the data.

Greece 2013

The tax/benefit position of single persons

	Wage level (per cent of average wage)	67	100	167	67
	Number of children	none	none	none	2
1.	**Gross wage earnings**	13736	20604	34340	15109
2.	**Standard tax allowances**				
	Basic allowance				
	Married or head of family				
	Dependent children				
	Deduction for social security contributions and income taxes	2266	3400	5666	2493
	Work-related expenses				
	Other				
	Total	2266	3400	5666	2493
3.	**Tax credits or cash transfers included in taxable income**	0	0	0	0
4.	**Central government taxable income (1 - 2 + 3)**	11469	17204	28674	12616
5.	**Central government income tax liability (exclusive of tax credits)**	2523	3785	6676	2776
6.	**Tax credits**				
	Basic credit	2100	2100	800	2100
	Married or head of family				
	Children				
	Other				
	Total	2100	2100	800	2100
7.	**Central government income tax finally paid (5-6)**	423	1857	6449	802
8.	**State and local taxes**	0	0	0	0
9.	**Employees' compulsory social security contributions**				
	Gross earnings	2266	3400	5666	2493
	Taxable income				
	Total	2266	3400	5666	2493
10.	**Total payments to general government (7 + 8 + 9)**	2690	5257	12115	3295
11.	**Cash transfers from general government**				
	For head of family				
	For two children	0	0	0	0
	Total	0	0	0	0
12.	**Take-home pay (1-10+11)**	11046	15347	22225	11815
13.	**Employer's compulsory social security contributions**	3772	5658	9430	4149
14.	**Average rates**				
	Income tax	3.1%	9.0%	18.8%	5.3%
	Employees' social security contributions	16.5%	16.5%	16.5%	16.5%
	Total payments less cash transfers	19.6%	25.5%	35.3%	21.8%
	Total tax wedge including employer's social security contributions	36.9%	41.6%	49.2%	38.7%
15.	**Marginal rates**				
	Total payments less cash transfers: Principal earner	34.9%	35.7%	44.9%	35.7%
	Total payments less cash transfers: Spouse	n.a.	n.a.	n.a.	n.a.
	Total tax wedge: Principal earner	48.9%	49.6%	56.8%	49.6%
	Total tax wedge: Spouse	n.a.	n.a.	n.a.	n.a.

Greece 2013

The tax/benefit position of married couples

			100-0	100-33	100-67	100-33
	Wage level (per cent of average wage)		100-0	100-33	100-67	100-33
	Number of children		2	2	2	none
1.	**Gross wage earnings**		24725	32966	41208	30219
2.	**Standard tax allowances**					
	Basic allowance					
	Married or head of family					
	Dependent children					
	Deduction for social security contributions and income taxes		4080	5439	6799	4986
	Work-related expenses					
	Other					
		Total	4080	5439	6799	4986
3.	**Tax credits or cash transfers included in taxable income**		0	0	0	0
4.	**Central government taxable income (1 - 2 + 3)**		20645	27527	34408	25233
5.	**Central government income tax liability (exclusive of tax credits)**		4542	6056	7570	5551
6.	**Tax credits**					
	Basic credit		1800	3900	3900	4100
	Married or head of family					
	Children					
	Other					
		Total	1800	3900	3900	4100
7.	**Central government income tax finally paid (5-6)**		3155	3155	4220	2353
8.	**State and local taxes**		0	0	0	0
9.	**Employees' compulsory social security contributions**					
	Gross earnings		4080	5439	6799	4986
	Taxable income					
		Total	4080	5439	6799	4986
10.	**Total payments to general government (7 + 8 + 9)**		7234	8594	11020	7339
11.	**Cash transfers from general government**					
	For head of family					
	For two children		0	0	0	0
		Total	0	0	0	0
12.	**Take-home pay (1-10+11)**		17490	24372	30188	22880
13.	**Employer's compulsory social security contributions**		6789	9052	11316	8298
14.	**Average rates**					
	Income tax		12.8%	9.6%	10.2%	7.8%
	Employees' social security contributions		16.5%	16.5%	16.5%	16.5%
	Total payments less cash transfers		29.3%	26.1%	26.7%	24.3%
	Total tax wedge including employer's social security contributions		44.5%	42.0%	42.5%	40.6%
15.	**Marginal rates**					
	Total payments less cash transfers: Principal earner		36.5%	36.5%	36.5%	35.7%
	Total payments less cash transfers: Spouse		16.5%	16.5%	35.7%	16.5%
	Total tax wedge: Principal earner		50.2%	50.2%	50.2%	49.6%
	Total tax wedge: Spouse		34.5%	34.5%	49.6%	34.5%

The national currency is the euro (EUR). In 2013, EUR 0.75 was equal to USD 1. In 2013, the estimated gross earnings of the average worker are EUR 20 604 (Secretariat estimate).

1. Personal income tax systems

1.1. Central government income tax

1.1.1. Tax unit

Individuals are subject to national income tax. Every individual who derives income from sources in Greece is subject to tax irrespective of his nationality, place of domicile or residence. Moreover, every individual with domicile in Greece (more than 183 days) is subject to tax on his/her worldwide income irrespective of the individual's nationality. Due consideration is given to bilateral conventions designed to obviate double taxation. From 2013 onwards, all Individuals who have completed 18 years of age are obliged to file a tax return regardless of having taxable income or not. The minimum imputed income, which is required to cover the taxpayer's main living expenses is EUR 3 000 for a single individual and EUR 5 000 for spouses. Spouses file a joint return but each spouse is liable for the tax payable on his or her share of the joint income. Losses incurred by one spouse may not be set off against the income of the other spouse. Deductible personal expenses concerning both spouses and tax credits are apportioned to each spouse according to the income earned by each one of them. Income of children under the age of 18 is, in principle, added and taxed with the income of their parents.

1.1.2. Tax allowances and tax credits

1.1.2.1. Standard tax reliefs

- Social security contributions: All compulsory social security contributions and optional contributions to legally constituted funds are fully deductible from taxable gross income.

1.1.2.2. Deductions from the payable amount of tax, as calculated on the basis of the scale (Non-Standard tax credits):

A. As from 2013 onwards, the previously existing tax-free threshold of EUR 5 000 was replaced with a system of tax deductions. Specifically, the tax arising by the tax scale for employees and pensioners is reduced as following:

- by EUR 2 100 for annual income up to EUR 21 000,
- by the amount of EUR 100 per each EUR 1 000 of income and up to EUR 2 100 for annual income exceeding the amount of EUR 21 000.

The above tax deduction is granted under the condition of the on time submission of receipts/invoices for the purchase of goods and services equal to 25 per cent of the taxable income and up to the amount of EUR 10 500. Should the value of invoices is less than the one required, a 22 per cent penalty is imposed on the remaining amount.

B. The following tax credits are deducted from the payable amount of tax, as calculated on the basis of the scale after applying the above tax allowance:

1. 10 per cent of the expenses of medical and hospital care of the taxpayer and his/her dependents, provided they are not covered by Social Security Funds and they exceed 5 per cent of the taxable income. The total credit cannot exceed EUR 3 000. Hospital expenses in respect of unmarried or widowed children who suffer from an incurable disease, who are mentally retarded or are blind and whose total annual income does not exceed EUR 6 000 are also included.
2. 10 per cent of the amount of alimony that is paid to a spouse and is adjudicated by the Court. The tax reduction cannot exceed EUR 1 500.
3. a. 10 per cent of the total amount of donations to the State, municipalities and communities, state universities, the church, the monasteries of Mount Athos, the World Patriarchate of Constantinople, the Patriarchate of Alexandria and Jerusalem, the Sacred Monastery of Mountain Sinai, the state and municipal nursing homes and hospitals which are subsidized from State budget and the Archaeological Resources Fund.

   b. 10 per cent of the total amount of donations to public or private non-profit legal entities which have been or are being legally constituted for cultural purposes.

   c. 10 per cent of the amounts donated to philanthropic institutions, non-profit making bodies which provide educational services or grant scholarships, Greek legal entities governed by private or public law which have been or are being set up for philanthropic purposes.

   Note: The amounts of the above donations are taken into account only if they have been deposited in a bank account in Greece, created for this purpose
4. 10 per cent of the value of medical equipment and ambulances donated to the state and municipal nursing homes and private hospitals which are subsidized from the State budget.

Note: The total amount of all the above donations (case 3 and 4) cannot exceed 5 per cent of the total income that is taxed by the general provisions and the deduction can be up to EUR 100.

C. The amount of tax derived on the basis of all scales is reduced by EUR 200 provided that the taxpayer himself or the people living with him and dependent upon him are handicapped (invalidity over 67%) or are invalid soldiers or military personnel injured in the course of their duties or receive pension by the State as war victims.

Note: Taxpayers who reside abroad but derive taxable income from sources in Greece are not eligible for these deductions, with the exemptions of residents of the EU member States who derive at least 90 per cent of their total income from sources in Greece.

Spouses:

When the wife derives income taxable on the basis of the scale, then the following are deducted from her own payable amount of tax:

a) deductions related to medical and hospital expenses, donations and the lump sum of EUR 200 of the spouse;

b) deductions related to medical and hospital expenses of the spouse's children from a former marriage, her children born out of wedlock, her parents and orphaned relatives of first and second degree of kin;

If from the joint tax return submitted by the spouses no tax obligation arises for one of them, or the payable amount of tax is less than the sum of the deductions (medical and hospital expenses, lump sum of EUR 200) then the whole amount of the deductions or the ensuing difference is attributed to the payable tax of the other spouse.

1.1.2.3. Exemptions

Some forms of income, specified by Law (art. 6 of Law No. 2238/1994, as amended) are exempt from the tax.

Examples:

- on condition of reciprocity, income of all kinds derived abroad by foreign ambassadors and diplomatic representatives;
- on condition of reciprocity, income from salaried services derived by consuls, consulate agents and employees of embassies and consulates that have the nationality of the represented State;
- gross imputed income from residence of self-owned house (for income effected from 1.1.2003);
- imputed income deriving from the gratuitous granting of the use of house up to 200 square meters total by parents to children and vice-versa, provided that the house will be used as residence;
- profits from the operation of ships under the Greek flag, where such profits are subject to the special taxation on ship owners' profits;
- all forms of pensions and relief provided to war victims and their families, as well as to soldiers and military personnel injured in the course of their duties in times of peace;
- salaries, pensions, etc., paid to totally blind individuals or to heavily (over 80%) mobility impaired individuals. Also non-institutional relief and the additional amount of pension paid to blind individuals and persons totally dependent for their care on others because of invalidity;
- the amount of grants and scholarships lawfully awarded by the Greek State, public entities or private charitable funds as specified by Law, provided that they are proven to be pursuing objectives beneficial to the Nation, or religious, educational, artistic, philanthropic etc. ones; also grants and scholarships paid by foreign States, organisations and funds to Greek citizens;
- money awards paid by the State, the Academy of Athens or the Organisation of the "Music Hall" ("Megaro Mousikis") to reward scientific, artistic and generally intellectual performance;
- financial aid to recognised political refugees residing temporarily in Greece as well as to persons that have submitted the relevant application to the competent Greek authorities, paid by bodies carrying out refugee aid schemes financed by the UN, the EU or the Greek State;
- subsidies paid to young professionals and entrepreneurs within the framework of employment programmes of the National Employment Organisation (OAED), as specified by Law;
- subsidies paid to young professionals and entrepreneurs;
- benefits for third child or more.

1.1.2.4. Tax calculation

For income tax purposes, there are six categories of taxable income: income from immovable property (category A-B), income from movable property (category C), income from business (category D), income from agriculture (category E), income from employment (category F) and income from professional services or other sources (category G).

Net income is computed separately within each category with tax rules that vary across income categories. Total taxable income is computed as the aggregate of the net results of all categories. Losses in one category may be set off against income of another category. If the declared income is not accepted as the base for the tax assessment, the tax authorities can base the assessment on the presumptive income, which is the minimum amount of income required to cover the taxpayer's main living expenses.

Employment income (category F) is subject to withholding tax. The tax is withheld by the employer and is calculated by applying the taxpayer's progressive income tax schedule. The employer calculates the withholding tax on the basis of the taxpayer's annual net salary (net of social security contributions). The withholding tax is then reduced by 1.5 per cent of the total amount of taxes due. The resulting tax is the annual tax due, 1/14 of which constitutes the monthly withholding tax for the private sector's employees (every employee in the private sector receives 14 monthly salaries per year, i.e. 12 monthly wages plus 1 salary as Christmas bonus, 1/2 salary as Easter bonus and 1/2 salary as summer vacation bonus). For the employees of the public sector, the monthly withholding tax is calculated as 1/12 of the annual tax due, because of the fact that bonuses in the public sector have been eliminated. If the taxpayer's final tax liability (derived from the annual declared income) exceeds the aggregate of the amounts already withheld or prepaid, the remaining tax is generally payable in three equal bimonthly instalments. Any excess tax paid or withheld will be refunded.

1.1.3. Rate schedule

Law 4141/2013 introduced three different tax schedules for each category of Personal income earned in 2013:

a) Income Tax schedule for Salaried persons (employees and pensioners)

b) Income Tax schedule for Non-Salaried persons (Self-Employed and personal businesses)

c) Income Tax schedule for immovable property and securities

a) Tax schedule for employees and pensioners

Income bracket (EUR)	Tax rate (%)	Tax bracket (EUR)	Total amount	
			Income (EUR)	Tax (EUR)
25 000	22	5 500	25 000	5 500
17 000	32	5 440	42 000	10 940
Excess	42			

The previously existing tax-free threshold of EUR 5 000 was abolished and replaced with a system of tax deductions. Specifically, the tax derived by the above tax scale is reduced as following:

- by EUR 2 100 for annual income up to EUR 21 000,

- by the amount of EUR 100 per each EUR 1 000 of income and up to EUR 2 100 for annual income exceeding the amount of EUR 21 000.

The above tax deduction is granted under the condition of the on time submission of receipts/invoices for the purchase of goods and services equal to 25% of the taxable income and up to the amount of EUR 10 500. Should the value of invoices is less than the one required, a 22% penalty is imposed on the remaining amount.

Special categories of taxpayers (prisoners, mentally handicapped living in psychiatric Institutions, old people living in nursing homes, etc.) are exempt by the obligation of submitting receipts.

b) Tax schedule for self employed and personal businesses

Income bracket (EUR)	Tax rate (%)	Tax bracket (EUR)	Total amount	
			Income (EUR)	Tax (EUR)
50 000	26	13 000	50 000	13 000
Excess	33			

For new personal business or new self-employed who started their entrepreneurship after 1 January 2013, the tax rate of the first income bracket of the above scale is decreased by 50% for income up to EUR 10 000 for the first three years of their business activity.

c) Tax schedule for Immovable property and securities

Income bracket (EUR)	Tax rate (%)	Tax bracket (EUR)	Total amount	
			Income (EUR)	Tax (EUR)
12 000	10	1 200	12 000	1 200
Excess	33			

The gross income derived by real estate is subject to an additional tax of 1.5%. The rate is raised to 3% where the surface area of such residence is greater than 300 square meters. The amount of additional tax may not be greater than the amount payable on the taxpayer's total net income.

Note: Married persons must submit a joint return, but taxes, duties and levies are calculated separately on the income declared by each spouse

Moreover, a special solidarity contribution was introduced with the art. 29 of Law 3986/2011 for annual income exceeding EUR 12 000 and varied from 1% to 4% on the actual or imputed, taxable or tax exempt reported income. The special solidarity contribution is imposed on net income earned in the years 2010-14 (financial years 2011-15), according to the following schedule:

Note: The tax rate is imposed on the total net income and not progressively according to scale (steps). The net income is defined as individual gross income minus social security contributions.

e.g.: Net income EUR 50 000 * 2% = EUR 1 000 for special solidarity contribution.

Net income (EUR)	Tax rate (%)
12 000-20 000	1
20 000-50 000	2
50 000-100 000	3
Above 100 000	4

1.2. State and local income taxes

There are no local income taxes in Greece. Municipalities (the local authorities) receive 20 per cent of the national income tax revenues.

2. Compulsory social security contributions to schemes operated within the government sector

The great majority of individuals who are employed in the private sector and render dependent personal services are principally, directly and compulsorily insured in the Social Insurance Organisation (IKA). Apart from the main contribution, IKA compulsorily collects contributions for other minor Funds created for the employee's benefit (Unemployment Benefits Funds, etc.). A subsidiary Social Insurance Fund (ETEAM) for employees who are principally insured in IKA has been established since 1983.

The average rates of contributions payable by white-collar employees as a percentage of gross earnings are as follows (%) (since the beginning of 2003):

	Employer	Employee	Total
1. Social Insurance Organisation (IKA)	18.43	9.22	27.65
2. Subsidiary Social Insurance Fund (ETEAM)	3.00	3.00	6.00
3. Other Funds	6.03	4.28	10.31
Total	**27.46**	**16.50**	**43.96**

Higher contributions are due (19.95 per cent paid by the employee and 30.71 per cent paid by the employer) in case of blue-collar workers who are engaged in heavy work (unhealthy, dangerous, etc., work) as they are entitled to a pension five years earlier than the other workers. In the industrial sector, the employer pays an additional occupational risk contribution at a rate of 1 per cent because these workers are more vulnerable to labour accidents and occupational diseases.

Contributions are calculated on the basis of the monthly salary or wages paid but within the limits specified in the National General Collective Employment Agreement. Monthly gross remuneration includes salaries and wages, fringe benefits and bonuses and any profit distributions to employees. From 2013 onwards, an equalized ceiling of EUR 5 546.80 applies for all categories of employees

Self-employed individuals must make monthly compulsory lump-sum contributions to OAEE (Free Professional Social Insurance Organisation); these contributions depend on the number of years that the self-employed has been insured (for more details, see the explanatory annex to Table III.3 of the OECD's *Tax Database*).

All of these social security contributions are fully deductible for income tax purposes.

3. Universal cash transfers

3.1. *Transfers related to marital status*

Employees working in the private sector, according to the relevant Collective Labour Agreement or arbitrary decision, are granted by their employers a benefit representing 10 per cent of their gross basic salary (excluding any other cash transfers), independently of their spouse's income status. For public servants no marriage benefit is granted.

3.2. *Transfers for dependent children*

Benefits for dependent children are determined by the worker's Collective Labour Agreement. The benefits are usually equal to 5 per cent of the gross basic monthly salary of each spouse per child. When a relevant Collective Labour Agreement does not exist, the rules of the National General Collective Labour Agreement apply. The latter agreement works as a safety net; it provides a benefit related to marital status but not related to dependent children.

Benefits for dependent children are granted for each child starting either from the 1st, 2nd or the 3rd child, depending on the provisions of the relative Collective Labour Agreement that is in force. Examples of industries whose workers receive benefits for each and every child are the insurance industry (7.5 per cent), the accountants (5 per cent) and the shipping industry (6 per cent). For public servants, this benefit is limited to a flat gross monthly amount of EUR 18 for each of the first two children (a different amount applies for the 3rd and additional children).

If no benefit for dependent children is provided by the worker's Collective Labour Agreement, a very small yearly subsidy is provided by the Manpower Employment Organisation (OAED) under certain circumstances and depending on the employees' income and family status. Only one of the spouses is entitled to this OAED cash transfer.

3.3. *State benefits for having more than 2 children*

Law 1892/1990 determines the benefits for having more than two children. For 2012 the monthly state benefit for a family that has a 3rd child is EUR 177. This benefit is tax-free and is given during the first 6 years of the child's life. In addition, families with more than 3 children receive a tax free monthly allowance of EUR 44 for each of every unmarried child under the age of 23. The Law also provides for a multi-children pension of EUR 102 that is given to the mother who no longer is the beneficiary of the monthly multi-children allowance of EUR 44. Law 3454/2006 provides for a lump sum amount of EUR 2 000 for all mothers for every of their 3rd and any additional child.

4. Main changes in tax/benefit system since 2012

In the year 2013, a lot of changes have been introduced.

- Three different tax schedules were introduced replacing the previous one, for the following income categories: a) Employees & Pensioners with three tax brackets (instead of the previous eight) of 22%, 32% and 42% for income up to EUR 25 000, EUR 42 000 end excess respectively, b) Self-employed and personal businesses with two applicable rates, 26% for income up to EUR 50 000 and 33% for the excess, c) income from rentals and securities with two rates, 10% for income up to EUR 12 000 and 33% for the excess.

- The previously existing tax free threshold of EUR 5 000 was abolished for all income categories but especially for employees & pensioners it was replaced with a system of tax deductions (credits).
- Most remaining income tax credits, such as expenses for rent, tuition fees, mortgage loan interest for primary residence and life or medical insurance premiums were abolished. The tax credits that are still granted are subject to specific conditions.
- Social Security Contributions of self-employed which in 2012 were partially deductible (10%) from the tax, they qualify now as expenses of the self-employed, which are fully deducted from the gross income.
- The way of taxation of personal businesses, partnerships, joint ventures and other entities has changed. Those which maintain single-entry books are now taxed similarly with the self-employed (26% and 33%) whereas the entities with double entry books are taxed at the level of the entity according to the CIT tax rate. The entrepreneurial fee is abolished.
- Income tax rate on interest deriving from any form of saving accounts was increased to 15% (from 10%)
- The previously existing distinction of SSC ceilings for those who started their employment before or after 1/1/1993 has been abolished and a unified ceiling of EUR 5 546.80 applies for all categories of employees.
- A United Fund for supplementary insurance (ETEA) was set up by the unification of the former supplementary pension funds of workers in the private, public and broader public sector, banks and utilities.

5. Memorandum items

5.1. Identification of an AW and method of calculations used

Methodological note for the estimation of the average annual earnings per employee, for the period 2000-13

Terminology and coverage

The average annual earnings below refer to full time employees for Sectors C to N of ISIC Rev. 3.1, before 2008, and for Sectors B to N including Division 95 and excluding Divisions 37, 39 and 75 of ISIC Rev. 4, for 2008 onwards.

Data sources

In the estimation procedure of the average annual earnings per employee, for the period 2000-13 the following data are taken into account:

- Annual earnings and number of employees, as derived from the **Structure of Earnings Survey** (SES), of the years 2002, 2006 and 2010.
- Hours worked and annual average number of employees, as derived from the **Labour Force Survey** (LFS), of the years 2000-13.*
- Average annual earnings indices, as derived from the Indices on **Quarterly Labour Cost Survey**, of the years 2000-13.

* Data only for the first two quarters of 2013.

Annual gross earnings per full time employee 2000-13 Greece

Year	NACE Rev. 2 classification
2000	15 693
2001	15 688
2002	**17 359**
2003	19 339
2004	21 669
2005	21 902
2006	**23 800**
2007	23 893
2008	23 835
2009	24 619
2010	**24 156**
2011	23 391
2012	22 240
2013	19 558

1. The average gross annual earnings per full time employee for the period 2000 to 2012 **includes**:
- the special payments for shift and night work, as well as work during weekends and holidays;
- the total annual bonuses as well as those that are regularly paid on a monthly basis, the 13th salary (Christmas salary) and 14th salary (Easter and vacation payments);
- the annual bonuses based on productivity;
- the education and working time allowance;
- the marriage and children allowance;

and **excludes**:
- the annual payments in kind: foods, drinks, footwear, clothes, accommodation, business cars provided, mobile phone, etc.;
- the annual premiums related to profit-sharing schemes.

2. The data for 2011 and onwards will be revised when the final results of the SES 2014 will be available.
3. Estimates for 2013 will be revised when the final results of the SES 2014 will be available and with the most recent data from LFS and CLI.

Source: ELSTAT.

5.2. *Main employers' contributions to private pension, health, and related schemes*

Contributions to private pension and sickness schemes made by employers are not added to employees' gross earnings for tax purposes and are therefore not subject to tax. Since these contributions are not obligatory for employers, no data is provided by the National Statistical Service of Greece. Very few employers have adopted such additional insurance schemes.

2013 parameter values

Average earnings/yr	Ave_earn	20 604	Secretariat estimate
Tax credit	Child_cred	0	
Rates of family subsidies			
paid by employers	Wife_sub	0.1	
children (up to 3)	Child_sub	0.05	
Income tax schedule	Tax_sch	0.22	25 000
		0.32	42 000
		0.42	
Tax deduction	Tax_cred	2 100	
	Tax_cred_thrsh	21 000	
	Tax_red	100	
Solidarity contribution	Solidarity_sch	0	12 000
		0.01	20 000
		0.02	50 000
		0.03	100 000
		0.04	
Social security contributions	SSC_rate	0.165	
	SSC_rate_empr	0.2746	
	SSC_ceil	77 655.20	
	SSC_ceil_use	0	

2013 tax equations

The equations for the Greek system in 2013 are mostly on an individual basis. The level of gross earnings for the principal earner is increased by the spouse and child subsidy paid by the employer.

The functions which are used in the equations (Taper, MIN, Tax, etc.) are described in the technical note about tax equations. Variable names are defined in the table of parameters above, within the equations table, or are the standard variables "married" and "children". A reference to a variable with the affix "_total" indicates the sum of the relevant variable values for the principal and spouse. And the affixes "_princ" and "_spouse" indicate the value for the principal and spouse, respectively. Equations for a single person are as shown for the principal, with "_spouse" values taken as 0.

	Line in country table and intermediate steps	Variable name	Range	Equation
1.	Earnings	earn_princ	P	Ave_earn*(1+Married*Wife_sub+ MIN(Children,3)*Child_sub)
		earn_spouse	S	Ave_earn*(1+Married*Wife_sub+ MIN(Children,3)*Child_sub)
2.	Allowances:	tax_al	B	SSC
3.	Credits in taxable income	taxbl_cr		0
4.	CG taxable income	tax_inc	B	Positive(earn-tax_al)
5.	CG tax before credits	CG_tax_excl	B	Tax(tax_inc,tax_sch)-Low_rate*Positive(MIN(Effect_low_band-Low_thrsh,tax_inc-Low_thrsh))
	Solidarity contribution	sol_contr	B	=Solidarity(earn-SSC, Solidarity_sch)
6.	Tax credits :	tax_cr	**B**	=Positive(tax_cred-(INT(Positive(earn-tax_cred_thrsh)/ 1000)*tax_cred_red))
7.	CG tax	CG_tax	B	Positive(CG_tax_excl-tax_cr)+sol_contr
8.	State and local taxes	local_tax	B	0
9.	Employees' soc security	SSC	B	IF(SSC_ceil_use=1,SSC_rate*MIN(earn,SSC_ceil),SSC_rate*earn)
11.	Cash transfers	cash_trans	B	0
13.	Employer's soc security	SSC_empr	B	IF(SSC_ceil_use=1,SSC_rate_empr*MIN(earn,SSC_ceil),SSC_rate_empr*earn)

Key to range of equation B calculated separately for both principal earner and spouse P calculated for principal only (value taken as 0 for spouse calculation) J calculated once only on a joint basis.

Taxing Wages 2014
Changes in sructural labour income tax progressivity
over 2000-12 period in OECD member countries

Hungary

This chapter includes data on the income taxes paid by workers, their social security contributions, the family benefits they receive in the form of cash transfers as well as the social security contributions and payroll taxes paid by their employers. Results reported include the marginal and average tax burden for eight different family types.

Methodological information is available for personal income tax systems, compulsory social security contributions to schemes operated within the government sector, universal cash transfers as well as recent changes in the tax/ benefit system. The methodology also includes the parameter values and tax equations underlying the data.

Hungary 2013

The tax/benefit position of single persons

	Wage level (per cent of average wage)	67	100	167	67
	Number of children	none	none	none	2
1.	**Gross wage earnings**	1943009	2914514	4857524	1943009
2.	**Standard tax allowances**				
	Basic allowance				
	Married or head of family				
	Dependent children	0	0	0	1500000
	Deduction for social security contributions and income taxes				
	Work-related expenses				
	Other				
	Total	0	0	0	1500000
3.	**Tax credits or cash transfers included in taxable income**	0	0	0	0
4.	**Central government taxable income (1 - 2 + 3)**	1943009	2914514	4857524	443009
5.	**Central government income tax liability (exclusive of tax credits)**				
	Central government income tax liability (exclusive of tax credits)	310882	466322	777204	70882
	Total	310882	466322	777204	70882
6.	**Tax credits**				
	Basic credit	0	0	0	0
	Married or head of family				
	Children				
	Other				
	Total	0	0	0	0
7.	**Central government income tax finally paid (5-6)**	310882	466322	777204	70882
8.	**State and local taxes**	0	0	0	0
9.	**Employees' compulsory social security contributions**				
	Gross earnings	359457	539185	898642	359457
	Taxable income				
	Total	359457	539185	898642	359457
10.	**Total payments to general government (7 + 8 + 9)**	670338	1005507	1675846	430338
11.	**Cash transfers from general government**				
	For head of family				
	For two children	0	0	0	355200
	Total	0	0	0	355200
12.	**Take-home pay (1-10+11)**	1272671	1909007	3181678	1867871
13.	**Employer's wage dependent contributions and taxes**				
	Employer's compulsory social security contributions	524613	786919	1311531	524613
	Payroll taxes	29145	43718	72863	29145
	Total	553758	830637	1384394	553758
14.	**Average rates**				
	Income tax	16.0%	16.0%	16.0%	3.6%
	Employees' social security contributions	18.5%	18.5%	18.5%	18.5%
	Total payments less cash transfers	34.5%	34.5%	34.5%	3.9%
	Total tax wedge including employer's social security contributions	49.0%	49.0%	49.0%	25.2%
15.	**Marginal rates**				
	Total payments less cash transfers: Principal earner	34.5%	34.5%	34.5%	34.5%
	Total payments less cash transfers: Spouse	n.a.	n.a.	n.a.	n.a.
	Total tax wedge: Principal earner	49.0%	49.0%	49.0%	49.0%
	Total tax wedge: Spouse	n.a.	n.a.	n.a.	n.a.

Hungary 2013

The tax/benefit position of married couples

		Wage level (per cent of average wage)	100-0	100-33	100-67	100-33
		Number of children	2	2	2	none
1.	**Gross wage earnings**		2914514	3886019	4857524	3886019
2.	**Standard tax allowances**					
	Basic allowance					
	Married or head of family					
	Dependent children		1500000	1500000	1500000	0
	Deduction for social security contributions and income taxes					
	Work-related expenses					
	Other					
		Total	1500000	1500000	1500000	0
3.	**Tax credits or cash transfers included in taxable income**		0	0	0	0
4.	**Central government taxable income (1 - 2 + 3)**		1414514	2386019	3357524	3886019
5.	**Central government income tax liability (exclusive of tax credits)**					
	Central government income tax liability (exclusive of tax credits)		226322	381763	537204	621763
		Total	226322	381763	537204	621763
6.	**Tax credits**					
	Basic credit		0	0	0	0
	Married or head of family					
	Children					
	Other					
		Total	0	0	0	0
7.	**Central government income tax finally paid (5-6)**		226322	381763	537204	621763
8.	**State and local taxes**		0	0	0	0
9.	**Employees' compulsory social security contributions**					
	Gross earnings		539185	718914	898642	718914
	Taxable income					
		Total	539185	718914	898642	718914
10.	**Total payments to general government (7 + 8 + 9)**		765507	1100677	1435846	1340677
11.	**Cash transfers from general government**					
	For head of family					
	For two children		319200	319200	319200	0
		Total	319200	319200	319200	0
12.	**Take-home pay (1-10+11)**		2468207	3104542	3740878	2545342
13.	**Employer's wage dependent contributions and taxes**					
	Employer's compulsory social security contributions		786919	919526	1311531	919526
	Payroll taxes		43718	58290	72863	58290
		Total	830637	977816	1384394	977816
14.	**Average rates**					
	Income tax		7.8%	9.8%	11.1%	16.0%
	Employees' social security contributions		18.5%	18.5%	18.5%	18.5%
	Total payments less cash transfers		15.3%	20.1%	23.0%	34.5%
	Total tax wedge including employer's social security contributions		34.1%	36.2%	40.1%	47.7%
15.	**Marginal rates**					
	Total payments less cash transfers: Principal earner		34.5%	34.5%	34.5%	34.5%
	Total payments less cash transfers: Spouse		34.5%	34.5%	34.5%	34.5%
	Total tax wedge: Principal earner		49.0%	49.0%	49.0%	49.0%
	Total tax wedge: Spouse		43.1%	55.9%	49.0%	55.9%

The national currency is the forint (HUF). In 2013, HUF 223.58 was equal to USD 1. In that year, the average worker earned HUF 2 914 514 (Secretariat estimate).

1. Personal income tax systems

1.1. *Central/federal government income taxes*

1.1.1. *Tax unit*

The tax unit is, in all cases, the separate individual. In exceptional cases, the employer can become subject to personal income tax, for instance in the case of benefits in kind.

1.1.2. *Tax allowances and tax credits*

1.1.2.1. Standard reliefs

- *Basic reliefs:* None.
- *Standard marital status reliefs:* None.
- *Employee Tax credit:* Since 1 January 2012 there is no employee tax credit.
- *Family tax allowance:* For families having children, the basis of income tax can be reduced by the family tax allowance, which amounts to HUF 62 500 per month/each dependent (for families having one or two children), or HUF 206 250 per month/each dependent (for families having at least three children). This tax allowance can be applied by a pregnant woman (or her husband) as from the 91st day after conception until birth of the child. The tax allowance may be claimed by one spouse or be split between the spouses.

1.1.2.2. Main non-standard tax reliefs

- *Trade Union membership dues:* Membership dues and contributions paid to trade unions and other corporate bodies of employees are deductible without any restriction.
- Tax credits are made available for physical disability or agricultural activities. Tax deduction is available for those having income from abroad.

1.1.3. *Tax schedule*

The rate of personal income tax amounts to 16 per cent.

1.2. *State and local income taxes*

In Hungary there is no local personal income tax system supplementing the central one.

2. Compulsory social security contributions to schemes operated within the government sector

2.1. *Employees' contributions*

2.1.1. *Pensions*

The rate of pension contribution amounts to 10 per cent of gross earnings.

2.1.2. Sickness

The rate of health security contribution amounts to 7 per cent of gross earnings.

2.1.3. Unemployment

The worker must pay, as employees' contribution, 1.5 per cent of gross earnings.

2.1.4. Others

None. The average worker does not have any obligation to pay other contributions than the above mentioned. However, the contribution rates may be different for certain types of income or for certain groups of income recipients (e.g. employees with pensioner status). None of these exceptions are applicable to the workers taken into consideration in this report.

2.2. Employers' contributions

2.2.1. Pensions

None.

2.2.2. Sickness

None.

2.2.3. Unemployment

None.

2.2.4. Others

From 2012 the employers' social security contributions were merged into the new payroll tax, called social contribution tax. This change is of legal nature, the combined rate remains 27% while the revenue is divided among the pension, health care and labour – market funds in the same proportion as the separate SSCs were until 2011 (24% for pensions, 2% for health care, 1% for unemployment).

The employer contributions also include a payroll tax: the training levy amounts to 1.5 per cent of gross earnings.

From 1 January 2013, the Job Protection Act (JPA) introduced new targeted reliefs in the employers' contributions (social contribution tax and training levy) to incentivise the employment of the most disadvantageous groups on the labour market. This measure reduces the standard rate of the employers' contributions up to a cap of HUF 100 000 per month. The JPA introduced a permanent reduction of the employers' tax rate by 14.5% for:

- employees under 25 years of age,
- employees over 55 years of age,
- employees working in elementary occupations.

It also introduced temporary reductions (28.5% in the first two years of the employment, and 14.5% in the third year) for:

- long term unemployed re-entering the labour market,
- people returning to work after child-care leave,
- career starters.

The new targeted reliefs in the employers' contributions are not considered in the *Taxing Wages* model.

The SSC deduction related to the wage compensation scheme adopted in 2012 still remains in force in 2013, albeit at a lower rate: the rate of reduction is 16%, tapered by 20% above HUF 75 000/month. In 2014, the compensation scheme will be phased out completely.

Social security contributions will have to be paid on other benefits than gross earnings (e.g., grants in kind) and payments (e.g., certain kind of contracts).

3. Universal cash transfers

3.1. *Transfers related to marital status*

None.

3.2. *Transfers for dependent children*

Effective from 1 January 2008:

Type of family	HUF per month
For a couple with one child	12 200
For a single earner with one child	13 700
For a couple with two children, per child	13 300
For a single earner with two children, per child	14 800
For a couple with 3 or more children, per child	16 000
For a single earner with 3 or more children, per child	17 000
For a couple with permanently sick and disabled child	23 300
For a single earner with permanently sick and disabled child	25 900

4. Main changes in the tax/benefit system since 2010

- The tax base correction was phased out in two steps.
- The employee tax credit was abolished.
- The employees' health care contribution was increased.
- The employers' social security contributions were merged into the social contribution tax (legal change only, rates and base remained unchanged).
- Health contributions on benefits in kind were increased.
- As a temporary measure, a wage compensation scheme was introduced in form of an employers' SSC credit.
- Targeted employment incentives to boost the employment levels of groups at the margin of the labour force.

5. Memorandum items

5.1. *Employer contributions to private social security arrangements*

In Hungary the law dealing with the voluntary mutual insurance funds (like pension funds) was enacted on 6 December 1993. Based on the rules for 2011, the monthly contribution paid to a voluntary mutual pension fund by the employer of a private worker who participates in a voluntary mutual pension fund, limited to an amount below half of the mandatory minimum wage, is taxable according to an effective personal income tax rate of 19.04 (the nominal tax rate of 16 per cent multiplied by 1.19) per cent. In the case of employers' contributions paid to health or mutual aid funds, the applicable limit is 30 per cent of the mandatory minimum wage. Contributions in excess of these limits are taxable at an effective personal income tax rate of 19.04 per cent and a health contribution of 27 per cent is also payable on these amounts. Sponsor's donations paid by the employer to its employees' voluntary mutual insurance fund are taxable as well. In addition, employees can apply a 20 per cent tax credit (with a limit of HUF 100 000 or 130 000 per year; in the case of payments simultaneously made to pension, health or mutual aid funds, the limit is HUF 120 000 or 150 000 per year) on these taxable payments. The tax authority pays the tax credit directly to a voluntary mutual insurance fund.

In general, insurance premiums (on the basis of which an employee is named as the recipient/beneficiary of insurance services) paid by the employer are taxable, and social security contributions plus training contribution are also payable. At the same time insurance premiums related to life insurance policy for accidental death, injury liability, or medical care insurance for full and permanent incapacity to work are exempted from taxation and any contributions.

As from 2008 employer pension institutions can be established. Based on the rules for 2011, the monthly contribution paid to an employer pension institution by the employer of a private worker, limited to an amount below half of the mandatory minimum wage, is taxable according to an effective personal income tax rate of 19.04 per cent. Contributions in excess of this limit are taxable at an effective personal income tax rate of 19.04 per cent and a health contribution of 27 per cent is also payable on these amounts.

2013 parameter values

Average earnings/yr	Ave_earn	2 914 514	Secretariat estimate		
Child allowance (per child)	child_al	1	750 000		
		2	750 000		
		3	2 475 000		
		4	2 475 000		
Income tax schedule	tax_sch	0.16			
Social security contributions	SSC_unemp	0.015			
	SSC_p	0.1			
	SSC_h	0.07			
Wage Compensation Scheme	SSC_red_lim	900 000			
(employer SSC deduction)	SSC_red_rate	0.16			
	SSC_red_taper	144000			
	SSC_red_taper_rate	0.20			
Payroll taxes	SSC_empr	0.27			
	payroll_rate	0.015			
		# of children	1	2	3+
Transfers for children	CB_rates	0	12 200	13 300	16 000
(monthly)		1	13 700	14 800	17 000

2013 tax equations

The equations for the Hungarian system in 2013 are mostly on an individual basis. But the child allowance is relevant only to the calculation for the principal earner and cash transfers are calculated only once. This is shown by the Range indicator in the table below.

The functions which are used in the equations (Taper, MIN, Tax, etc.) are described in the technical note about tax equations. Variable names are defined in the table of parameters above, within the equations table, or are the standard variables "married" and "children". A reference to a variable with the affix "_total" indicates the sum of the relevant variable values for the principal and spouse. And the affixes "_princ" and "_spouse" indicate the value for the principal and spouse, respectively. Equations for a single person are as shown for the principal, with "_spouse" values taken as 0.

Line in country table and intermediate steps		Variable name	Range	Equation
1.	Earnings	earn		
2.	Allowances:			
	Children	child_al	P	IF(Children>0, Children*VLOOKUP(Children, child_al, 2), 0)
	Total	tax_al	B	child_al
3.	Credits in taxable income	taxbl_cr	B	0
4.	CG taxable income	tax_inc	B	MAX(0,earn -tax_al)
5.	CG tax before credits	CG_tax_excl	B	tax_inc*tax_sch
7.	CG tax	CG_tax	B	CG_tax_excl-tax_cr
8.	State and local taxes	local_tax	B	0
9.	Employees' soc security	SSC	B	earn*(SSC_unemp+ SSC_h+SSC_p)
11.	Cash transfers	cash_trans	J	Children*(VLOOKUP((1-Married), CB_rates, MIN(Children, 3)+1)*12)
13.	Employer's soc security	SSC_empr	B	earn*SSC_empr
	Final employer's social security		B	IF(earn<SSC_red_lim,SSC_empr-earn*SSC_red_rate,SSC_empr-MAX(0,SSC_red_taper-(earn-SSC_red_lim)*SSC_red_taper_rate))
	Employer's payroll taxes	Payroll	B	earn*payroll_rate

Key to range of equation B calculated separately for both principal earner and spouse P calculated for principal only (value taken as 0 for spouse calculation) J calculated once only.

Taxing Wages 2014
Changes in sructural labour income tax progressivity
over 2000-12 period in OECD member countries

Iceland

This chapter includes data on the income taxes paid by workers, their social security contributions, the family benefits they receive in the form of cash transfers as well as the social security contributions and payroll taxes paid by their employers. Results reported include the marginal and average tax burden for eight different family types.

Methodological information is available for personal income tax systems, compulsory social security contributions to schemes operated within the government sector, universal cash transfers as well as recent changes in the tax/ benefit system. The methodology also includes the parameter values and tax equations underlying the data.

Iceland 2013

The tax/benefit position of single persons

	Wage level (per cent of average wage)	67	100	167	67
	Number of children	none	none	none	2
1.	**Gross wage earnings**	4127453	6191179	10318632	4127453
2.	**Standard tax allowances**				
	Basic allowance				
	Married or head of family				
	Dependent children				
	Deduction for social security contributions and income taxes	165098	247647	412745	165098
	Work-related expenses				
	Other				
	Total	165098	247647	412745	165098
3.	**Tax credits or cash transfers included in taxable income**	0	0	0	0
4.	**Central government taxable income (1 - 2 + 3)**	3962355	5943532	9905887	3962355
5.	**Central government income tax liability (exclusive of tax credits)**	938254	1449398	2533592	938254
6.	**Tax credits**				
	Basic credit	581820	581820	581820	581820
	Married or head of family				
	Children				
	Other				
	Total	581820	581820	581820	581820
7.	**Central government income tax finally paid (5-6)**	356434	867578	1951772	356434
8.	**State and local taxes**	571372	857057	1428429	571372
9.	**Employees' compulsory social security contributions**				
	Gross earnings	29300	29300	29300	29300
	Taxable income				
	Total	29300	29300	29300	29300
10.	**Total payments to general government (7 + 8 + 9)**	957106	1753935	3409501	957106
11.	**Cash transfers from general government**				
	For head of family				
	For two children	0	0	0	540387
	Total	0	0	0	540387
12.	**Take-home pay (1-10+11)**	3170347	4437244	6909131	3710734
13.	**Employer's compulsory social security contributions**	317401	476102	793503	317401
14.	**Average rates**				
	Income tax	22.5%	27.9%	32.8%	22.5%
	Employees' social security contributions	0.7%	0.5%	0.3%	0.7%
	Total payments less cash transfers	23.2%	28.3%	33.0%	10.1%
	Total tax wedge including employer's social security contributions	28.7%	33.4%	37.8%	16.5%
15.	**Marginal rates**				
	Total payments less cash transfers: Principal earner	38.6%	38.6%	44.4%	46.3%
	Total payments less cash transfers: Spouse	n.a.	n.a.	n.a.	n.a.
	Total tax wedge: Principal earner	43.0%	43.0%	48.3%	50.1%
	Total tax wedge: Spouse	n.a.	n.a.	n.a.	n.a.

Iceland 2013

The tax/benefit position of married couples

			Wage level (per cent of average wage)	100-0	100-33	100-67	100-33
			Number of children	2	2	2	none
1.	**Gross wage earnings**			6191179	8254906	10318632	8254906
2.	**Standard tax allowances**						
		Basic allowance					
		Married or head of family					
		Dependent children					
		Deduction for social security contributions and income taxes		247647	330196	412745	330196
		Work-related expenses					
		Other					
			Total	247647	330196	412745	330196
3.	**Tax credits or cash transfers included in taxable income**			0	0	0	0
4.	**Central government taxable income (1 - 2 + 3)**			5943532	7924709	9905887	7924709
5.	**Central government income tax liability (exclusive of tax credits)**			1449398	1903088	2387652	1903088
6.	**Tax credits**						
		Basic credit		1163640	1035510	1163640	1035510
		Married or head of family					
		Children					
		Other					
			Total	1163640	1035510	1163640	1035510
7.	**Central government income tax finally paid (5-6)**			285758	867578	1224012	867578
8.	**State and local taxes**			857057	1014613	1428429	1014613
9.	**Employees' compulsory social security contributions**						
		Gross earnings		29300	58600	58600	58600
		Taxable income					
			Total	29300	58600	58600	58600
10.	**Total payments to general government (7 + 8 + 9)**			1172115	1940791	2711041	1940791
11.	**Cash transfers from general government**						
		For head of family					
		For two children		375536	217042	111725	0
			Total	375536	217042	111725	0
12.	**Take-home pay (1-10+11)**			5394600	6531157	7719316	6314115
13.	**Employer's compulsory social security contributions**			476102	634802	793503	634802
14.	**Average rates**						
	Income tax			18.5%	22.8%	25.7%	22.8%
	Employees' social security contributions			0.5%	0.7%	0.6%	0.7%
	Total payments less cash transfers			12.9%	20.9%	25.2%	23.5%
	Total tax wedge including employer's social security contributions			19.1%	26.5%	30.5%	29.0%
15.	**Marginal rates**						
	Total payments less cash transfers: Principal earner			46.3%	46.3%	43.4%	38.6%
	Total payments less cash transfers: Spouse			44.9%	43.5%	43.4%	35.8%
	Total tax wedge: Principal earner			50.1%	50.1%	47.5%	43.0%
	Total tax wedge: Spouse			48.9%	47.5%	47.5%	40.4%

The national currency is the króna (plural: krónur) (ISK). In 2013, ISK 122.17 was equal to USD 1. In 2013, the average worker is expected to earn ISK 6 191 179 (Secretariat estimate).*

1. Personal income tax systems

1.1. *Central government income taxes*

1.1.1. *Tax unit*

Income is taxed on an individual basis, except for capital income of married couples which is taxed jointly.

1.1.2. *Tax allowances and credits*

1.1.2.1. Standard reliefs

- *Basic tax credit:* A fixed tax credit, amounting to ISK 581 820 in 2013, is granted to all individuals 16 years and older, regardless of their marital status. The tax credit is deducted from levied central and local government taxes. Unutilised tax credits or portions thereof are wastable, i.e. non-refundable and non-transferable between tax years.
- *Standard marital status relief:* Married couples may utilise up to 100 per cent of each spouses' unutilised portion of his/her basic tax credit.
- *Relief(s) for children:* None.
- *Relief(s) for compulsory pension contributions:* The compulsory payment to pension funds amounts to 4 per cent of wages and is deductible. In addition, an optional payment of up to 2 per cent of wages may also be deducted. As the additional 2 per cent contribution is optional, it is viewed as a non-standard relief in this Report.

1.1.2.2. Main non-standard tax reliefs applicable to an AW

- *Interest payment relief:* A fully refundable tax credit is granted to purchasers of personal dwellings (homes) to recuperate a part of mortgage-related interest expenses. The maximum tax-related interest credit in 2012 is ISK 400 000 for a single person, ISK 500 000 for a single parent and ISK 600 000 for a married couple. The following constraints apply to interest rebates: 1) they cannot exceed 7.0 per cent of the remaining debt balance incurred in buying a home for one's own use. 2) the maximum amount of interest payments that qualify for an interest rebate calculation is ISK 800 000 for an individual, ISK 1 000 000 for a single parent and ISK 1 200 000 for a couple. 3) eight per cent of taxable income is subtracted from the interest expense. 4) The rebates begin to be curtailed at a net worth threshold of ISK 4 000 000 for a single individual and a single parent and ISK 6 500 000 for a couple and are eliminated altogether at a 60 per cent higher amount, or ISK 6 400 000 and 10 400 000, respectively. (These amounts are based

* The definition of average worker in Iceland includes workers in five categories. See Section 5.1.

on income in the year 2013 but are paid out in 2014. These numbers are estimates; final figures will be available once the 2014 budget has been passed.)

- Fishermen are entitled to a special credit against income tax of ISK 246 per day at sea in 2013.

1.1.3. Tax schedule

The income tax base is composed of *personal income* (e.g. wages, salaries, fringe benefits, pensions, etc.), which is taxed on an individual basis, and *capital income* which is taxed jointly for married couples.

The tax on personal income is triple-rated. The central government income tax rate in 2013 is 22.90 per cent for income up to ISK 241 475 per month. A 25.8 per cent tax rate applies to the next ISK 498 034 or up to ISK 739 509. For income exceeding ISK 739 509 the tax rate is 31.8 per cent. The income tax rate applies to all personal income in excess of ISK 135 330 per month (ISK 1 623 960 per year). Tax relief is provided by the basic credit described in Section 1.1.2.1.

The tax on capital income is 20 per cent. It is levied on all capital income of individuals, such as interest, dividends, rents etc. Interest income up to ISK 100 000 per year and 30 per cent of income from rent of residential property is tax free.

1.2. Local government income tax

The local government income tax base is the same as the central government's personal income tax base.

The local governments' income tax is single-rated, but the rate varies between 12.44 and 14.48 per cent between municipalities. The average rate in 2013 is 14.42 per cent.

2. Compulsory social security contributions to schemes operated within the government sector

2.1. Employees' contributions

Fee to the Retiree Investment Fund: 16 to 70 year-old individuals are subject to a fixed tax of ISK 9 900 in 2013, provided the individual's taxable income is at least ISK 1 559 003 for the year. This tax will be collected in 2014.

Fee to the broadcast media: 16 to 70 year-old individuals with taxable income over ISK 1 559 003 for the year are subject to a fixed tax of ISK 19 400 in 2013, which will be collected in 2014.

These amounts are estimates and thus subject to change as the fees are payable in 2014.

2.2. Employers' contributions

Employers have to pay a social security tax on total wages of 7.69 per cent. In addition, 0.65 per cent is levied on the wages of fishermen as a premium for their government accident insurance. Furthermore, a new financial activities tax was introduced in 2012, which requires financial and insurance companies to pay an additional 6.75 per cent payroll tax in 2013.

3. Universal cash transfers

3.1. *Marital status related transfers*

None.

3.2. *Transfers for dependent children*

Child benefits are granted for each child, subject to income thresholds. In 2013 they are as follows (in ISK per year):

For each child under the age of seven:	100 000
Children under the age of eighteen at the end of 2013:	
First child	167 564
Each additional child	199 455
Benefits for single parents:	
First child	279 087
Each additional child	286 288
Income threshold for benefit curtailment:	
For couples	4 800 000
For a single parent	2 400 000
Curtailment of benefits (children under the age of seven only):	
For each child	3 per cent
Curtailment of benefits (all children under the age of eighteen):	
For one child	3 per cent
For two children	5 per cent
For three children or more	7 per cent

Note that child benefits in this Report are based on income in the year 2013 but are paid out in 2014 (see also Section 4.4). These numbers are estimates and thus subject to change.

4. Main changes in tax/benefit system since 1998

4.1. *The deductibility of the payment to pension funds*

All employees are required to participate in pension funds. The employee contribution is generally 4 per cent of wages and the employer contribution was 6 per cent, and increased to 8 per cent as of beginning 2007. Both contributions are deductible from income before tax. In some cases, the contributions of employees and employers are higher. An optional, additional payment from employees of up to 4 per cent of wages is also deductible and goes into an individual retirement account. However, in 2012-14, this additional payment has been temporarily set at 2%.

This voluntary pension savings option was first introduced in 1999 in order to encourage personal saving. At the time the contribution rate was 2 per cent for employees and 0.2 per cent for employers. In May 2000 these rates were doubled to 4 and 0.4 per cent, respectively, as noted above. In addition, some employers, such as the central government, have increased their employer counter-contribution by agreement with employees. The central government contributed 1 per cent against a voluntary employee contribution of 4 per cent in 2001 and 2 per cent as of the beginning of 2002. All such contributions are tax-deductible, both with the employer and the employee at the time the contribution is made. The actual pension is taxed as personal income when it is drawn. As of the beginning of 2004, the employer option of deducting the above 0.4 per cent against the social security tax was abolished. Since such employer counter-contributions had become part of wage agreements in most cases, it was no longer felt that such a tax incentive was needed.

4.2. Central and local income tax rates in 1997-2007

In 1997-2007, the Government pursued a policy of reducing the marginal tax rate, as can been seen in the table below. This development was reversed in 2009 when income tax was raised by 1.35 percentage points in response to the Treasury's rising debt burden brought on by the economic crisis. At the beginning of 2010 the tax system was changed from single rated to triple rated. The tax rate was set at 24.1 per cent for the first monthly ISK 200 000 but it was raised by 2.9 per cent for the next ISK 450 000 and again by 6 per cent for income in excess of ISK 650 000. In 2013, the rates are 22.9%, 25.8% and 31.8%, and the corresponding income thresholds are ISK 241 475 and 739 509 per month; see Section 1.1.3 for further details. From 1998 onwards, the central government and average local government personal income tax rates have been as follows:

	Central government general tax rate (%)	Municipal tax rate (%)	Total tax rate (%)	Central government surtax (%)
1998	27.41	11.61	39.02	7.00
1999	26.41	11.93	38.34	7.00
2000	26.41	11.96	38.37	7.00
2001	26.08	12.68	38.76	7.00
2002	25.75	12.79	38.54	7.00
2003	25.75	12.80	38.55	5.00
2004	25.75	12.83	38.58	4.00
2005	24.75	12.98	37.73	2.00
2006	23.75	12.97	36.72	0
2007	22.75	12.97	35.72	0
2008	22.75	12.97	35.72	0
2009	24.10	13.10	37.20	0
2010	24.10	13.12	37.32	2.90/6.00
2011	22.90	14.41	37.31	2.90/6.00
2012	22.90	14.44	37.34	2.90/6.00
2013	22.90	14.42	37.32	2.90/6.00

4.3. A special tax on higher income

In 1998, the special tax on higher income was raised by 2 percentage points, from 5 to 7 per cent. For 2003-income, it was reduced back to 5 per cent. It was reduced to 4 per cent for 2004 income and to 2 per cent for 2005-income. In the fiscal year 2006, the tax was abolished. In the latter half of 2009 the special tax on higher income was introduced again at 8 per cent. In 2010 the tax system changed to triple-rated; see Sections 4.2 and 1.13.

4.4. A revision of child benefit system

Child benefits are granted for each child, subject to income thresholds. The amendments to tax legislation that came into effect in 2004 included a schedule for raising child benefits. As from 2007, the child benefits will be paid for children up to 18 years instead of 16 years. For 2006-13, benefits are as follows (in ISK per year):

	2006	2007	2008	2009	2010	2011	2012	2013
For all children under the age of seven	56 096	57 891	61 191	61 191	61 191	61 191	100 000	100 000
Children under the age of eighteen:								
First child	139 647	144 116	152 331	152 331	152 331	152 331	167 564	167 564
Each additional child	166 226	166 226	171 545	181 323	181 323	181 323	199 455	199 455
Benefits for single parents:								
First child	232 591	232 591	240 034	253 716	253 716	253 716	279 087	279 087
Each additional child	238 592	238 592	246 227	260 262	260 262	260 262	286 288	286 288
Income threshold for benefit curtailment:								
For couples	1 859 329	2 231 195	2 880 000	3 600 000	3 600 000	3 600 000	4 800 000	4 800 000
For a single parent	929 665	1 115 598	1 440 000	1 800 000	1 800 000	1 800 000	2 400 000	2 400 000
Curtailment of benefits under the age of seven:								
For each child						3%	3%	3%
Curtailment of benefits under the age of eighteen:								
For one child	3%	2%	2%	2%	2%	3%	3%	3%
For two children	7%	6%	5%	5%	5%	5%	5%	5%
For three children or more	9%	8%	7%	7%	7%	7%	7%	7%

The data for 2013 is subject to change as the benefits are not payable until 2014.

4.5. *A revision of interest rebates*

In 2004, the interest rebate was cut by 10 per cent, effective for that year only. The ceiling on interest payments that qualify for the interest rebate was reduced from 7 per cent to 5.5 per cent in 2005 and the interest rate cut was reduced from 10 per cent to 5 per cent. As of the beginning of 2006, the ceiling was further reduced to 5 per cent. In 2005 and again in 2007 the net worth ceiling was lifted considerably in reaction to the increase in net worth due to the house price boom in 2005-07. In 2008, as mortgage-related interest expenses surged, the ceiling on interest payments was raised back to 7 per cent and the maximum rebate amount increased by 37 per cent. These measures stayed in effect in 2009. In 2010 the maximum rebate amount increased by 47-62 per cent and the net worth ceiling was reduced significantly. The rate of taxable income which is subtracted from the interest expense was increased from 6 per cent to 8 per cent. These measures still apply in 2013. In addition to the ordinary interest payment relief, a temporary interest cost rebate was in effect in 2010-11; see Section 1.1.2.2.

4.6. *Transferability of basic tax credit between spouses*

The basic tax credit was made transferable between spouses in stages; see Section 1.1.2.1 above. In fiscal year 2001, 90 per cent of the credit became transferable, rising to 95 per cent in 2002 and 100 per cent in 2003.

5. Memorandum items

5.1. *Identification of AW (only five categories) and valuation of earnings*

The data on average earnings refers to average workers in five categories according to the NACE Rev. 1 classification which corresponds to the ISIC Rev. 3 system. The categories are D – production, F – construction, G – wholesale and retail trade, repair of motor vehicles, motorcycles and personal and household goods, I – transport, storage and communication, and J – financial intermediation. Public sector employees are not included. Together, these five categories comprise approximately 80% of Iceland's private sector labour force. This classification system corresponds with the NACE Rev. 2 classification system, which corresponds with the ISIC Rev. 4 system (Sectors B-N).

The original data are obtained from a monthly survey among Icelandic firms with 10 or more employees.

5.2. *Employer contributions to private pension funds, health and related schemes*

By law, all employees and employers must contribute to pension funds. These funds are private, generally linked to unions and employee associations. The private pension funds are not part of the government-run social security system, to which a payroll tax is paid as described under Section 2.2 above. Compulsory and voluntary payments to such funds are described in Section 4.1 above.

2013 parameter values

Average earnings/yr	Ave_earn	6 191 179	Secretariat estimate
Pension rate for tax allowance	pension_rate	0.04	
Tax credit	Basic_crd	581 820	
	Married_propn	1	
Central income tax	tax_sch	0.229	2 897 700
		0.258	8 874 108
		0.318	
Special tax	special_rate	0	
threshold	special_thrsh		
Local tax	local_rate	0.1442	
Church tax	church_tax	0	
Social Security Contr.	SSC_fixed	29 300	
	SSC_thrsh	1 559 003	
Employer SSC	SSC_empr	0.0769	
General child allowance:			
child allowance	CA	100 000	
Maximum number of children under 7	max_child_under7	1	
Supplement child allowance:			
Married couple case			
first child	SA_first_m	167 564	
other children	SA_others_m	199 455	
income threshold	SA_tresh_m	4 800 000	
Single parent case			
first child	SA_first_s	279 087	
other children	SA_others_s	286 288	
income threshold	SA_tresh_s	2 400 000	
reduction rate (one child)	SA_redn_1	0.03	
reduction rate (two children)	SA_redn_2	0.05	
reduction rate (tree or more children)	SA_redn_3	0.07	

2013 tax equations

The equations for the Iceland system are mostly on an individual basis. But the tax credit for married couples is relevant only to the calculation for the principal earner and child benefit is calculated only once. This is shown by the Range indicator in the table below.

The functions which are used in the equations (Taper, MIN, Tax, etc.) are described in the technical note about tax equations. Variable names are defined in the table of parameters above, within the equations table, or are the standard variables "married" and "children". A reference to a variable with the affix "_total" indicates the sum of the relevant variable values for the principal and spouse. And the affixes "_princ" and "_spouse" indicate the value for the principal and spouse, respectively. Equations for a single person are as shown for the principal, with "_spouse" values taken as 0.

	Line in country table and intermediate steps	Variable name	Range	Equation
1.	Earnings	earn		
2.	Allowances:	tax_al	B	earn*pension_rate
3.	Credits in taxable income	taxbl_cr	B	0
4.	CG taxable income	tax_inc	B	earn-tax_al
5.	CG tax before credits	CG_tax_excl	B	tax(tax_inc, tax_sch)
6.	Tax credits :	tax_cr	P	MIN(CG_tax_excl_princ,Basic_crd+MAX(Married*Basic_crd-CG_tax_excl_spouse-(tax_inc_spouse*local_rate),0))
			S	MIN(Married*Basic_crd, CG_tax_excl_spouse)
		special_tax	J	0
7.	CG tax	CG_tax	B	CG_tax_excl-tax_cr+special_tax
8.	State and local taxes	local_tax	P	MAX(tax_inc_princ*local_rate-MAX(Basic_crd+Max(Married*Basic_crd-CG_tax_excl_spouse-(tax_inc_spouse*local_rate),0)-CG_tax_excl_princ,0),0)
			S	MAX(tax_inc_spouse*local_rate-MAX(Married*Basic_crd-CG_tax_excl_spouse,0),0)
9.	Employees' soc security	SSC	B	SSC_fixed*(earn>SSC_thrsh)
11.	Cash transfers:			
	Total family income	inc_tot	J	earn_total
	Child allowance	cash_trans	J	Positive(MIN(Children,max_child_under7)*CA-Positive(inc_total*(1-pension_rate)-IF(Married,SA_tresh_m,SA_tresh_s))*SA_redn_1) +(Children>0)*(IF(Married,SA_first_m+ Positive(Children-1)*SA_others_m,SA_first_s+ Positive(Children-1)*SA_others_s) -Positive(inc_tot*(1-pension_rate)-IF(Married,SA_tresh_m,SA_tresh_s))*IF(Children=1, SA_redn_1,IF(Children=2,SA_redn_2,SA_redn_3)))
13.	Employer's soc security	SSC_empr	B	earn*SSC_empr_rate

Key to range of equation B calculated separately for both principal earner and spouse P calculated for principal only (value taken as 0 for spouse calculation) J calculated once only on a joint basis.

Taxing Wages 2014
Changes in sructural labour income tax progressivity
over 2000-12 period in OECD member countries

Ireland

This chapter includes data on the income taxes paid by workers, their social security contributions, the family benefits they receive in the form of cash transfers as well as the social security contributions and payroll taxes paid by their employers. Results reported include the marginal and average tax burden for eight different family types.

Methodological information is available for personal income tax systems, compulsory social security contributions to schemes operated within the government sector, universal cash transfers as well as recent changes in the tax/benefit system. The methodology also includes the parameter values and tax equations underlying the data.

Ireland 2013

The tax/benefit position of single persons

	Wage level (per cent of average wage)	67	100	167	67
	Number of children	none	none	none	2
1.	**Gross wage earnings**	21587	32381	53968	21587
2.	**Standard tax allowances**	0	0	0	0
3.	**Tax credits or cash transfers included in taxable income**	0	0	0	0
4.	**Central government taxable income (1 - 2 + 3)**	21587	32381	53968	21587
5.	**Central government income tax liability (exclusive of tax credits)**	4317	6476	15239	4317
6.	**Tax credits**				
	Basic credit	1650	1650	1650	1650
	Single, head of family	0	0	0	1650
	Children				
	Other	1650	1650	1650	1650
	Total	3300	3300	3300	4950
7.	**Central government income tax finally paid (5-6)**	1847	4762	15036	830
8.	**State and local taxes**	0	0	0	0
9.	**Employees' compulsory social security contributions**				
	Gross earnings	863	1295	2159	863
	Taxable income				
	Total	863	1295	2159	863
10.	**Total payments to general government (7 + 8 + 9)**	2711	6057	17194	1693
11.	**Cash transfers from general government**				
	For head of family	0	0	0	6846
	For two children	0	0	0	3120
	Total	0	0	0	9966
12.	**Take-home pay (1-10+11)**	18876	26324	36774	29860
13.	**Employer's compulsory social security contributions**	2321	3481	5802	2321
14.	**Average rates**				
	Income tax	8.6%	14.7%	27.9%	3.8%
	Employees' social security contributions	4.0%	4.0%	4.0%	4.0%
	Total payments less cash transfers	12.6%	18.7%	31.9%	-38.3%
	Total tax wedge including employer's social security contributions	21.0%	26.6%	38.5%	-24.9%
15.	**Marginal rates**				
	Total payments less cash transfers: Principal earner	31.0%	31.0%	52.0%	64.4%
	Total payments less cash transfers: Spouse	n.a.	n.a.	n.a.	n.a.
	Total tax wedge: Principal earner	37.7%	37.7%	56.7%	67.9%
	Total tax wedge: Spouse	n.a.	n.a.	n.a.	n.a.

Ireland 2013

The tax/benefit position of married couples

	Wage level (per cent of average wage)	100-0	100-33	100-67	100-33
	Number of children	2	2	2	none
1.	**Gross wage earnings**	32381	43175	53968	43175
2.	**Standard tax allowances**	0	0	0	0
3.	**Tax credits or cash transfers included in taxable income**	0	0	0	0
4.	**Central government taxable income (1 - 2 + 3)**	32381	43175	53968	43175
5.	**Central government income tax liability (exclusive of tax credits)**	6476	8635	10794	8635
6.	**Tax credits**				
	Basic credit	3300	3300	3300	3300
	Single, head of family	0	0	0	0
	Children				
	Other	2460	3300	3300	3300
	Total	5760	6600	6600	6600
7.	**Central government income tax finally paid (5-6)**	2302	3851	6609	3851
8.	**State and local taxes**	0	0	0	0
9.	**Employees' compulsory social security contributions**				
	Gross earnings	1295	1295	2159	1295
	Taxable income				
	Total	1295	1295	2159	1295
10.	**Total payments to general government (7 + 8 + 9)**	3597	5147	8768	5147
11.	**Cash transfers from general government**				
	For head of family	1512	0	0	0
	For two children	3120	3120	3120	0
	Total	4632	3120	3120	0
12.	**Take-home pay (1-10+11)**	33416	41148	48320	38028
13.	**Employer's compulsory social security contributions**	3481	4398	5802	4398
14.	**Average rates**				
	Income tax	7.1%	8.9%	12.2%	8.9%
	Employees' social security contributions	4.0%	3.0%	4.0%	3.0%
	Total payments less cash transfers	-3.2%	4.7%	10.5%	11.9%
	Total tax wedge including employer's social security contributions	6.8%	13.5%	19.2%	20.1%
15.	**Marginal rates**				
	Total payments less cash transfers: Principal earner	72.4%	31.0%	31.0%	31.0%
	Total payments less cash transfers: Spouse	28.4%	24.0%	31.0%	24.0%
	Total tax wedge: Principal earner	75.1%	37.7%	37.7%	37.7%
	Total tax wedge: Spouse	34.0%	30.0%	37.7%	30.0%

The national currency is the euro (EUR). In 2013, EUR 0.75 was equal to USD 1. In that year, the average production worker earned EUR 32 381 (Secretariat estimate).

1. Personal income tax systems

1.1. *Central/ federal government income taxes*

1.1.1. *Tax unit*

Tax is levied on the combined income of both spouses. Either spouse may, however, opt for separate assessment, in which case the tax payable by both spouses must be the same as would be payable under joint taxation. A further option allows either spouse to opt for assessment as single persons in which case they are treated as separate units. The calculations presented in this Report are based on family taxation.

1.1.2. *Tax credits*

1.1.2.1. Standard reliefs:

- *Basic reliefs:* The single person's credit is EUR 1 650 per year.
- *Standard marital status reliefs:* The married person's credit is EUR 3 300 per year (i.e. twice the basic credit of EUR 1 650).
- *Employee credit:* With the exception of certain company directors and their spouses and the spouses of partners in partnership cases, all employees, including (subject to certain conditions) children who are full-time employees in the business of their parents, are entitled to an employee credit of EUR 1 650.
- *Single-Parent Family Relief:* The single parent family credit is EUR 1 650.

1.1.2.2. Main non-standard tax reliefs applicable to an APW

- *Interest on qualifying loans:* A qualifying loan in respect of the purchase, repair or improvement of the principal private residence. This relief is subject to the following overall limits in 2012

	First time mortgage holders	Other mortgage holders
Married Couple	EUR 8 000	EUR 5 079
Widowed Person	EUR 8 000	EUR 5 079
Single Person	EUR 4 000	EUR 2 539

- *Medical Insurance:* Relief at the taxpayer's standard rate of tax is available for taxpayers who make a payment to an authorised insurer under a contract which provides for the payment of medical expenses resulting from sickness of the person, his wife, child or other dependants. This *relief is now granted at source and is paid to the insurance provider.*
- *Mortgage Interest Relief:* Mortgage interest relief is discontinued for any mortgage over 7 years from 1 May 2009.

- *Work-related Expenses:* These are relieved to the extent that they are wholly, exclusively and necessarily incurred in the performance of the duties of an employment.
- *Home Carers Allowance:* This is a tax credit of EUR 810 f or families where one spouse works at home to care for children, the aged or incapacitated persons, where the carer spouse's income does not exceed EUR 5 079. A reduced measure of relief is granted for income between EUR 5 080 and EUR 6 620: if the income exceeds EUR 5 080 the tax credit is reduced by one half of the income of the Home Carer that exceeds this limit. This credit and the increased standard rate tax band for two income couples (see tax schedule below) are mutually exclusive but the person may opt for whichever is the more beneficial. If the Home Carer earns income of up to EUR 5 080 in his/her own right for the tax year, the full tax credit may be claimed. For the purposes of this tax credit, income means any taxable income such as income from a part-time job, dividends, etc., but does not include the Carer's Allowance payable by the Department of Social and Family Affairs.

1.1.3. *Tax schedule*

Band of taxable income (EUR)				Rate (%)
Single/widow(er)	Married couple (one income)	Married couple (two Incomes)	One-parent families	
Up to 32 800	Up to 41 800	Up to the lesser of: 65 600; 41 800 plus the amount of the lowest income	36 800	20
Balance	Balance	Balance	Balance	41

1.1.4. *Low income exemption and marginal relief tax*

Where total income is less than or equal to the income exemption limit that income is exempt from tax.

Exemption limits:

	EUR
Single/Widowed	
Under 65	5 210
65 and over	17 000
Married	
Under 65	10 420
65 and over	34 000
Children	
One or two children (each)	575
Subsequent children	830

The marginal relief rate of tax applies where liability to tax at the marginal relief rate is less than that which would be chargeable under the normal tax schedule and where total income is less than twice the relevant exemption limit, otherwise tax is charged under the normal tax schedule.

Marginal relief tax is charged, where applicable, at a rate of 40 per cent on the difference between total income and the relevant exemption limit.

1.1.5. *Universal Social Charge (USC)*

In 2011, the Universal Social Charge (USC) replaced the Income and Health Levies that were introduced in 2009 in the income tax. The USC applies at a low rate on a broad base.

The USC is charged on an individualised basis on gross income at 2 per cent on income up to and including EUR 10 036, at 4 per cent for income in excess of EUR 10 036 but not greater than EUR 16 016 and at 7 per cent above that level. Those aged over 70 year do not pay this higher rate. The lower exemption threshold has been increased from EUR 4 004 to EUR 10 036.

The USC does not apply to social welfare payments, including contributory and non-contributory social welfare State pensions.

Individuals in possession of full medical card, including a Health Amendment Act card, will only pay USC at a max rate of 4% irrespective of the level of their income. However, when an individual has self-employment income in excess of EUR 100 000 for a tax year, the max rate is 7% on the amount of the excess. Non-medical card holders are subject to a maximum rate of 10% on such income.

USC rates for individuals aged 70 years and over and individuals who hold FULL medical cards: The 4% rate applies to all income over EUR 10 036. There is a surcharge of 3% on individuals who have income from self-employment that exceeds EUR 100 000 in a year, regardless of age. Where such individuals are aged over 70 years or hold a full medical card, a rate of 7% applies.

1.2. *State and local income taxes*

No State or local income taxes exist in Ireland.

2. Compulsory social security contributions to schemes operated within the government sector.

2.1. *Employees' contributions*

Contributions are payable at a rate of 4 per cent of an employee's gross earnings less allowable superannuation contributions. No distinction is made by marital status or sex. Those earning less than EUR 352 per week are exempt. The following is a breakdown of the 2012 rate of contribution together with ceilings where applicable:

Description	Rate	Threshold (EUR)	Ceiling (EUR)
Pension and social insurance	4.00	352 per week	

2.2. *Employers' contributions*

Like employees' contributions, employers' contributions are payable as a percentage of gross employee earnings less allowable superannuation contributions. The following is a breakdown of the 2012 rate of contribution:

Description	Rate (%)
Occupational injuries	0.50
Redundancy contribution	0.40
Pension and social insurance	9.85
TOTAL	10.75

The employers' contribution is reduced from 10.75 per cent to 8.5 per cent in respect of employees earning less than EUR 356 per week.

3. Universal cash transfers

3.1. *Transfers related to marital status*

None.

3.2. *Transfers for dependent children*

These are payable to all children under the age of 16 (or under 19 years, if the child is undergoing full-time education by day or is incapacitated and likely to remain so for a prolonged period). These payments do not depend on any insurance or on the means of the claimant. Entitlements to higher rate for the third and subsequent child are being phased out over two years. The amounts payable in 2012 are as follows:

Period	Monthly rate per child	
January 2013 to December 2013	First to second child: EUR 130.00	Subsequent children: EUR 130.00

3.3. *Transfers for low income families*

A non-taxable family income supplement is payable to low income families where either the principal earner and/or the spouse are in full-time employment. Full-time employment is defined as working nineteen hours per week or more. The hours worked by the principal and the spouse can be aggregated for the purposes of this definition. When calculating income for the purposes of the relief superannuation payments, social welfare payments, tax payments, health and employment and training levies are all subtracted to arrive at disposable income.

The level of payment is dependent on the amount of family income and the number of children. The supplement payable is 60 per cent of the difference between the family income and the income limit applicable to the family. A minimum of EUR 20 per week is payable to eligible families. No supplement is payable to families with income in excess of the relevant income limit.

The income limit for a family with two children in 2013 is EUR 602 per week.

One Parent Family Payment: This new non-taxable payment is available for men and women who for a variety of reasons are bringing up a child or children without the support of a partner. The payment which is means tested is payable in full where the persons earnings does not exceed EUR 7 618. Where earnings are between EUR 7 618 and EUR 22 100 a reduced payment is received. The amount of the full payment for 2013 is EUR 6 552 plus EUR 1 550 for each child. Because of the complex means testing system this type of person is excluded from the AW examples.

4. Other main changes in tax/benefit system since 2010

4.1-4.2. *Universal Social Charge (USC)*

In 2011, the Universal Social Charge (USC) replaced the Income and Health Levies that were introduced in 2009 in the income tax. The USC applies at a low rate on a broad base.

5. Memorandum items

5.1. *Employer contributions to private social security arrangements*

Information not available, although such schemes do exist.

2013 parameter values

Average earnings/yr		Ave_earn	32 381	Secretariat estimate
Tax allowances				
Tax Credits		Basic_al_at_standard rate	1 650	
		Married_al_at_standardrate	1 650	
		Empl_al_at_standard rate	1 650	
		Singleparent_at_standardrate	1 650	
		Carers_allow	810	
		Carers_thrsh1	5 080	
		Carers_thrsh2	6 620	
		Carers_taper_rt	0.5	
Exemption amount		Single_ex	5 210	
		Married_ex	5 210	
		Child_ex	575	
		Child_ex_3	830	
Marginal relief limit		Single_MR	10 420	
		Married_MR	10 420	
		Child_MR	1 150	
		Child_MR_3	1 660	
Marginal relief		marg_rel_rate	0.4	
Income tax		Single_sch	0.2	32 800
			0.41	
		Single_sch_child	0.2	36 800
			0.41	
		Married_sch_oneinc	0.2	41 800
			0.41	
		Married_sch_twoinc	0.2	65 600
			0.41	
Universal Social Charge	USC		0.02	10 036
			0.04	16 016
			0.07	
	USC_sch_med_card		0.02	10 036
			0.04	
	USC threshold		4 004	
Maximum increase in first band		Band_increase_lim	27 400	
Social security contributions		SSC_thresh	18 304	
Employees		pension_rate	0.04	
		pension_ceil	0	
		Non_cum_Allc	0	
Employers		Empr_rate	0.1075	
		Empr_lower_rate	0.085	
		Empr_thrsh	18 512	
Child benefit		Ch_ben	1 560	
		Ch_ben_3	1 560	
Family income supplement		FIS_pay_limit	31 304	
		FIS_min	1 040	
		FIS_rate	0.6	
Medical card		single_med_card	9 568	
		married_med_card	13 858	
		child_add_med_card	1 976	

2013 tax equations

The equations for the Irish system in 2013 are mostly on a family basis using mainly a tax credit system for the first time. But social security contributions are calculated separately for each spouse. This is shown by the Range indicator in the table below.

The functions which are used in the equations (Taper, MIN, Tax, etc.) are described in the technical note about tax equations. Variable names are defined in the table of parameters above, within the equations table, or are the standard variables "married" and "children". A reference to a variable with the affix "_total" indicates the sum of the relevant variable values for the principal and spouse. And the affixes "_princ" and "_spouse" indicate the value for the principal and spouse, respectively. Equations for a single person are as shown for the principal, with "_spouse" values taken as 0.

	Line in country table and intermediate steps	Variable name	Range	Equation
1.	Earnings	earn		
2.	Allowances:			(provided at standard rate (tax credit equivalent))
3.	Credits in taxable income	taxbl_cr	J	0
4.	Taxable income	tax_inc	J	earn
	New carers allowance (provided as a tax credit)	career_allow		IF((Married*Children)>0, IF(earn_spouse<=Carers_thrsh1, Carers_allow, IF(earn_spouse>Carers_thrsh2, 0, Positive (Carers_allow-Carers_taper_rt*(earn_spouse-Carers_thrsh1)))), 0)
	Preliminary Tax Liable (including carers allowance)	tax_prel	J	IF(Married=0, IF(Children=0, Tax(tax_inc, Single_sch), Tax(tax_inc, Single_sch_child)), IF(AB7=0, Tax(tax_inc, Married_sch_oneinc)-AG7, Tax(earn_principal+Positive(earn_spouse-Band_increase_lim), Married_sch_oneinc)+Tax(MIN(earn_spouse, Band_increase_lim), Married_sch_oneinc)))
5.	Tax before credits (but including carers allowance)	_tax_excl	J	IF((Married*earn_spouse)>0, MINA(tax_prel, (Tax(tax_inc, Married_sch_oneinc)-career_allow)), tax_prel)
	Universal social charge	USG	J	IF(earn>USC_threshold,IF(med_crd_fac=1,Tax(earn,USC_sch),Tax(earn,USC_sch_med_card)),0)
6.	Tax credits :	basic_cr	J	Basic_al_at_standardrate+(Married*Married_al_at_standardrate)
		single_par_cr		IF(Married=0, IF(Children>0, Singleparent_at_standardrate, 0), 0)
		other_cr		Empl_al_at_standardrate+ (IF(earn_spouse>0, Empl_al_at_standardrate, 0))
		tax_cr		basic_cr+single_par_cr+other_cr
	Exemption amount	exemp_amt	J	Single_ex+Married*Married_ex+Child_ex*MIN(2, Children)+ (Children>2)*(Children-2)*Child_ex_3
	Marginal relief limit	MRL	J	Single_MR+Married*Married_MR+Child_MR*MIN(2, Children)+ (Children>2)*(Children-2)*Child_MR_3
7.	Net tax	CG_tax	J	If(earn_total<=MRL, MIN(marg_rel_rate*positive(earn_total-exem_amt), positive(_tax_excl-tax_cr)), positive(_tax_excl-tax_cr))+USG
8.	State and local taxes	local_tax	J	0
	Employees' soc security weekly allowance	weekly_allce	B	IF(earn=0,0,MINA(Non_cum_Allc,earn))
	Medical card factor	Med_crd_fac	J	(single_med_card+Married*(married_med_card-single_med_card) +child_add_med_card*Children<earn_princ+earn_spouse)
	employees' soc security	SSC	B	IF(earn>SSC_thresh, pension_rate*Positive(earn-weekly_allce), 0)
11.	Cash transfers			
		Child_benefit	J	Children*Ch_ben+(Children>2)*(Children-2)*(Ch_ben_3-Ch_ben)
		FIS	J	(Children>0)*IF((earn-_tax-SSC)<=FIS_pay_limit , MAXA((FIS_pay_limit-(earn-_tax-SSC))*FIS_rate, FIS_min), 0)
	Total cash transfers	cash_trans		Child_benefit+FIS
13.	Employer's soc security	SSC_empr	B	IF(earn<=Empr_thrsh, Empr_lower_rate, Empr_rate)* MIN(earn, Empr_ceil)

Key to range of equation:
B calculated separately for both principal earner and spouse.
P calculated for principal only (value taken as 0 for spouse calculation).
J calculated once only on a joint basis.

Taxing Wages 2014
Changes in sructural labour income tax progressivity
over 2000-12 period in OECD member countries

Israel

This chapter includes data on the income taxes paid by workers, their social security contributions, the family benefits they receive in the form of cash transfers as well as the social security contributions and payroll taxes paid by their employers. Results reported include the marginal and average tax burden for eight different family types.

Methodological information is available for personal income tax systems, compulsory social security contributions to schemes operated within the government sector, universal cash transfers as well as recent changes in the tax/benefit system. The methodology also includes the parameter values and tax equations underlying the data.

Israel 2013

The tax/benefit position of single persons

	Wage level (per cent of average wage)		67	100	167	67
	Number of children		none	none	none	2
1.	**Gross wage earnings**		87356	131033	218389	87356
2.	**Standard tax allowances**					
	Basic allowance		0	0	0	0
	Married or head of family					
	Dependent children					
	Deduction for social security contributions and income taxes					
	Work-related expenses		0	0	0	0
	Other					
		Total	0	0	0	0
3.	**Tax credits or cash transfers included in taxable income**		0	0	0	0
4.	**Central government taxable income (1 - 2 + 3)**		87356	131033	218389	87356
5.	**Central government income tax liability (exclusive of tax credits)**		9695	17414	40798	9695
6.	**Tax credits**					
	Basic credit		5886	5886	5886	7194
	Married or head of family		0	0	0	2616
	Children		0	0	0	5232
	EITC		0	0	0	0
	Unused wastable tax credits		0	0	0	5347
		Total	5886	5886	5886	15042
7.	**Central government income tax finally paid (5-6)**		3809	11528	34912	0
8.	**State and local taxes**		0	0	0	0
9.	**Employees' compulsory social security contributions**					
	Gross earnings		5080	10321	20804	5080
	Taxable income					
		Total	5080	10321	20804	5080
10.	**Total payments to general government (7 + 8 + 9)**		8889	21849	55715	5080
11.	**Cash transfers from general government**					
	For head of family					
	For two children		0	0	0	7522
		Total	0	0	0	7522
12.	**Take-home pay (1-10+11)**		78466	109184	162673	89798
13.	**Employer's compulsory social security contributions**		3739	6578	12257	3739
14.	**Average rates**					
	Income tax		4.4%	8.8%	16.0%	0.0%
	Employees' social security contributions		5.8%	7.9%	9.5%	5.8%
	Total payments less cash transfers		10.2%	16.7%	25.5%	-2.8%
	Total tax wedge including employer's social security contributions		13.9%	20.7%	29.5%	1.4%
15.	**Marginal rates**					
	Total payments less cash transfers: Principal earner		26.0%	33.0%	43.0%	12.0%
	Total payments less cash transfers: Spouse		n.a.	n.a.	n.a.	n.a.
	Total tax wedge: Principal earner		30.5%	37.1%	46.5%	17.4%
	Total tax wedge: Spouse		n.a.	n.a.	n.a.	n.a.

Israel 2013

The tax/benefit position of married couples

	Wage level (per cent of average wage)	100-0	100-33	100-67	100-33
	Number of children	2	2	2	none
1.	**Gross wage earnings**	131033	174711	218389	174711
2.	**Standard tax allowances**				
	Basic allowance	0	0	0	0
	Married or head of family				
	Dependent children				
	Deduction for social security contributions and income taxes				
	Work-related expenses	0	0	0	0
	Other				
	Total	0	0	0	0
3.	**Tax credits or cash transfers included in taxable income**	0	0	0	0
4.	**Central government taxable income (1 - 2 + 3)**	131033	174711	218389	174711
5.	**Central government income tax liability (exclusive of tax credits)**	17414	21782	27110	21782
6.	**Tax credits**				
	Basic credit	5886	13080	13080	13080
	Married or head of family	0	0	0	0
	Children	0	5232	5232	0
	EITC	0	1479	0	0
	Unused wastable tax credits	0	8058	2731	2826
	Total	5886	19791	18312	13080
7.	**Central government income tax finally paid (5-6)**	11528	10049	11528	11528
8.	**State and local taxes**	0	0	0	0
9.	**Employees' compulsory social security contributions**				
	Gross earnings	10321	11850	15401	11850
	Taxable income				
	Total	10321	11850	15401	11850
10.	**Total payments to general government (7 + 8 + 9)**	21849	21899	26929	23378
11.	**Cash transfers from general government**				
	For head of family				
	For two children	4466	4466	4466	0
	Total	4466	4466	4466	0
12.	**Take-home pay (1-10+11)**	113650	157278	195926	151333
13.	**Employer's compulsory social security contributions**	6578	8085	10318	8085
14.	**Average rates**				
	Income tax	8.8%	5.8%	5.3%	6.6%
	Employees' social security contributions	7.9%	6.8%	7.1%	6.8%
	Total payments less cash transfers	13.3%	10.0%	10.3%	13.4%
	Total tax wedge including employer's social security contributions	17.4%	14.0%	14.3%	17.2%
15.	**Marginal rates**				
	Total payments less cash transfers: Principal earner	33.0%	67.5%	33.0%	33.0%
	Total payments less cash transfers: Spouse	0.1%	38.0%	12.0%	3.5%
	Total tax wedge: Principal earner	37.1%	69.5%	37.1%	37.1%
	Total tax wedge: Spouse	3.4%	40.1%	17.4%	6.7%

The Israeli currency is the Israeli shekel (ILS). In 2013, ILS 3.61 was equal to USD 1. In that year, the average worker in Israel earned ILS 131 033 (Secretariat estimate).

1. Personal income tax systems

1.1. *Central government income tax*

1.1.1. *Tax unit*

In general, spouses are taxed separately on their earned income, subject to the condition that its sources are independent. The household is taxed jointly if their earned income is deemed to be interdependent. The conditions for interdependence involve situations where one spouse works in a business which the other spouse either owns or has certain levels of capital or management/voting rights.

1.1.2. *Tax allowances and credits*

1.1.2.1. Standard tax credits

The standard tax credits are given in the form of credit points subtracted from the tax liability. Each point is worth ILS 2 616 in 2013.

- *Basic credit:* Every resident taxpayer is entitled to 2.25 credit points (ILS 5 886 in 2013).
- *Additional credit for women:* Women are entitled to a further half credit point (ILS 1 308 in 2013).
- *Child credit:* Working mothers (and fathers in one parent families) with children aged under 18 are entitled to one additional credit point per child (ILS 2 616 in 2013). In 2012 this credit was increased to 2 credit points per child aged under 5 (ILS 5 232 in 2013). Since 2012, married working fathers with children aged under 2 are also entitled to 2 credit points per child.
- *Single parent credit:* Single parents (male or female) are entitled to one additional credit point (ILS 2 616 in 2013).

1.1.2.2. Non-standard tax credits applicable to income from employment

- Tax credits are awarded for contributions to approved pension schemes, up to a ceiling which varies according to the employee's circumstances.
- Employees living in certain development areas or in conflict zones receive credits as a percentage of their income up to ceiling. In 2013 the credits range from 10% in the lowest category to 24% in the highest category with ceilings of ILS 157 680 and 236 760 respectively. About 9% of the population lives in these areas.
- New immigrants are entitled to three additional credit points in their first eighteen months in Israel, two additional credit points in the following year, and one credit point in the year after.
- Discharged soldiers receive 2 credit points for three years after the completion of at least 23 months of service or 1 credit point for a shorter service.

- Graduates of academic studies receive 1 credit point for three years after the completion of a B.A. degree (or after the completion of 1 700 study hours that led to a professional certificate) and 0.5 credit point for two years after the completion of a M.A. degree.

1.1.3. *Tax schedule*

The tax schedule for earned income in 2013 is as follows:

Taxable income (ILS)	Tax rate (%)
0-63 360	10
63 360-108 120	14
108 120-168 000	21
168 000-240 000	31
240 000-501 960	34
501 960-811 560	48
Above 811 560	50

1.2. *Regional and local income tax*

There are no regional or local income taxes.

2. Compulsory social security insurance system

Social security contributions are made up of a combination of those for National Insurance and Health Insurance. The tax rates paid by employees and employers are applied in two brackets:

- A reduced rate for income up to a level of 60% of the average wage per employee post (ILS 5 297 per month in 2013).
- A full rate for income exceeding 60% of the average wage per employee post and up to a level of around 5 times the average wage per employee post (ILS 42 435 per month in 2013).

2.1. *Employees' contributions*

The taxable base for social security insurance contributions paid by employees is the total amount of the gross wage or salary including fringe benefits. The assessment period is the calendar month. The effective employees' contribution rates in 2013 are as follows:

Insurance branch	Full rate contribution (%)	Reduced rate contribution (%)
Total for National Insurance branches	7.00	0.40
Health	5.00	3.10
Total contributions	12.00	3.50

2.2. *Employers' contributions*

Social security insurance contributions are also paid by employers on behalf of their employees. These relate to National Insurance only – employers do not pay any contributions for health insurance.

The employers' contribution rates in 2013 are as follows:

Insurance branch	Full rate contribution (%)	Reduced rate contribution (%)
Total for National Insurance branches	6.50	3.45
Health	-	-
Total contributions	6.50	3.45

3. Payroll taxes

The following payroll taxes exist in Israel but neither of them is included in the modelling as they have limited coverage:

- Wage tax on the non-profit institutions: the VAT law imposes a 7.5 per cent on the wage-bill on the non-profit sector including government.
- Wage tax on the financial institutions: the VAT law also imposes a 17.58 per cent tax on the wage-bill of the financial institutions. **The tax rate was 17 per cent until "May" and was increased to 18 per cent in June.**

4. Universal cash transfers

4.1. *Transfers related to marital status*

None.

4.2. *Transfers for dependent children*

A monthly child allowance is paid to the parent (usually the mother) of unmarried children aged up to 18. The amount of the entitlement for each child depends on the date of birth of the child. Between August 2003 and June 2009, all children born after 1 June 2003 received the same benefit as the first child. But, according to the Coalition agreement signed in March 2009, the benefits for the second, third and fourth child (including those born after June 2003) were increased gradually over a period of four years (i.e. from 2009 to 2012). In August 2013 the allowance for all children will be decreased to ILS 40 per month per child.

In 2013 the monthly payments per child are shown in the following table. The "average" figure is used in the modelling.

	Children born before 1 June 2003			Children born on or after 1 June 2003		
	Average	Jan.-July	Aug.-Dec.	Average	Jan.-July	Aug.-Dec.
First child	160.42	175	140	160.42	175	140
Second child	211.75	263	140	211.75	263	140
Third child	230.42	295	140	211.75	263	140
Fourth child	326.08	459	140	211.75	263	140
Fifth child and above	285.25	389	140	160.42	175	140

In addition a Study Grant is paid to lone parents with children aged 6 to 14. The grant is paid in one instalment, usually in September at the beginning of the school year. In 2013, the rates of grant per child were 1 528 ILS and 849 ILS respectively for children aged 6-11 and 12-14.

5. Main changes in the tax and benefit systems since 2002

- There has been a policy of gradually reducing the level of personal income taxes since 2003. This policy was expected to continue till 2016 but came to an end in 2012 with the top tax bracket increasing from 4% to 48% although the rate of one middle income tax bracket was further decreased from 23% to 21%. The rates were further increased in 2013 and will increase again in 2014. In 2013 the ceiling of some brackets were reduced and a surtax of 2% was imposed on total income above ILS 811 560, effectively increasing the top marginal rate to 50%.
- The full contribution rate for employee social security contributions was increased gradually from 9.7% in 2002 to 12% in 2006. The reduced contribution rate was lowered

from 5.76% in 2002 to 3.5% in 2006. The upper threshold for contributions was removed in July 2002 but re-instated one year later. In August 2009, as a temporary measure until December 2011, it was increased to 10 times the average wage per employee post until December 2010 and to 9 times the average wage per employed post until December 2011.

- Prior to July 2005, there was only one contribution rate for employer social security contributions and this was set at 5.93% between July 2002 and June 2005. The upper threshold for contributions was removed in July 2002 but was re-instated one year later. The current system of two tax brackets was introduced in July 2005 with a reduced contribution rate of 5.33% and a full rate of 5.68%. There has been a lowering of rates in each year between 2006 and 2009. In August 2009, as a temporary measure until March 2011, the reduced rate was increased from 3.45% to 3.85%. In April 2011 the regular rate was increased to 5.9%. It was increased again to 6.5% in January 2013.
- The Employers tax on wage bill of the non-profit sector excluding government was abolished in 2008.
- In the period between August 2003 and June 2009, all children that were born on or after 1 June 2003 received the same level of benefit payment as the first child. The 2009 Coalition agreement introduced a gradual increase in the benefit payments for the second, third and fourth children in all families (including those where children were born after June 2003) over a period of four years from July 2009 to April 2012. In August 2013 the allowance for all children will be decreased to ILS 140 per month per child.

6. Memorandum items

6.1. *Average gross annual wage earnings calculation*

The average wage figures represent the amount earned for a full time post by employees working 35 hours per week or more. This information is available from the Israeli Income Survey for the years up to 2011 with an estimate for 2012 and 2013. As to the economic classification, Israel uses a modified version of ISIC 3 where the B-I industries (see Table below) are a very close equivalent of C-K industries in ISIC 3.1. Israel's Central Bureau of Statistics adopted ISIC 4 in 2012 but the Average Wage used in the modelling isn't available yet.

A	Agriculture.
B	Manufacturing.
C	Electricity and water supply.
D	Construction (building and civil engineering projects).
E	Wholesale and retail trade and repairs.
F	Accommodation services and restaurants
G	Transport, storage and communication.
H	Banking, insurance and other financial institutions.
I	Business activities.
J	Public administration.
K	Education.
L	Health, welfare and social work services.
M	Community, social, personal and other services.

6.2. *Employer contributions to private pension*

Until 2007 employers were not legally obliged to pay into a pension plan for their employees. Pension rights were guaranteed in collective agreements that covered less than half of the labour force. About one million employees in Israel had no pension arrangement (mainly those earning a relatively low wage, temporary workers and those working for subcontractors).

In 2008, a compulsory employment pension was introduced for employees with a period of employment of at least 6 months. The minimum rate of contributions in 2013 is 15.0 per cent of the employee's salary (up to the level of the average wage of ILS 8 828 per month), one third to be paid by the employee and two thirds by the employer. The minimum contribution rate will increase by 2.5 per cent of the employee's salary in 2014, reaching 17.5 per cent.

6.3. *Earned income tax credit*

A non-wastable earned income tax credit was implemented in 2008 in selected geographical areas of Israel covering 15% of the population. Entitlement to this credit is established based on earnings in the previous year. The tax credit was extended to all areas of Israel in 2012 (based on the earnings in 2011 and therefore we already included it in the 2011 version of the model). For mothers of children up to the age of 2 and for single parents the full coverage started in 2011 (based on earnings in 2010).

Under the law, workers aged 23 or more who are parents of one or two children aged less than 18 (or workers aged 55 or more even without children), and earn at least ILS 2 070 per month (about 45 per cent of the minimum wage) but not more than ILS 6 240 per month are eligible for a monthly increment of up to ILS 330. The corresponding figure for a family with 3 or more children is ILS 480. These sums were increased by 50% in 2013 (based on earnings in 2012), for working mothers and fathers in one-parent family. Families in which both parents work, and their joint income does not exceed ILS 12 000, will be entitled to these benefits for each wage-earner. The grant will is paid four times a year directly into the account of the eligible persons.

2013 parameter values

Average earnings/yr	Ave_earn	131 033	Secretariat estimate
Income tax	Tax_sch	0.1	63 360
		0.14	108 120
		0.21	168 000
		0.31	240 000
		0.34	501 960
		0.48	811 560
		0.50	
Employees SSC	SSC_sch	0.035	63 564
		0.12	509 220
		0	
Employers SSC	SSC_rate2	0.0345	63 564
		0.065	509 220
		0.0000	
Child benefit	CB_firstchild	1 925	
	CB_secondchild	2 541	
	Studygrant_rate	1 528	
Wastable tax credits			
Basic element	WTC_Basic	5 886	
Lone parent	WTC_lone	2 616	
Parents/per child	WTC_Child	2 616	
Women	WTC_woman	1 308	
Negative Income tax			
Family with 1 or	NIT_sch1	0	24 840
2 children		0.161	43 188
		3.831	43 200
		0	57 600
		-0.23	74 880
Family with 3 or	NIT_sch2	0	24 840
more children		0.235	43 188
		0.685	43 200
		0	57 600
		-0.235	82 080
	NIT_basic1	960	
	NIT_basic2	1 440	
	NIT_min	240	
	NIT_MinIncome	24 840	
	NIT_MaxIncome	144 000	
	Nit_AddIncome	17 780	
	NIT_Bonus	1.50	
Days in tax year	numdays	366	

2013 tax equations

	Line in country table and intermediate steps	Variable name	Range	Equation
1.	Earnings	earn		
2.	Allowances:	Tax_al	B	0
3.	Credits in taxable income	taxbl_cr	B	0
4.	CG taxable income	tax_inc	B	Earn
5.	CG tax before credits	CG_tax_excl	B	Tax(tax_inc, tax_sch)
6.	Tax credits (nonwastable):			
	Principal	tax_cr_princ	B	(earn>0)*(wtc_basic+(IF(married=0)*(children>0),wtc_woman+wtc_lone+(wtc_child*children))
	Spouse	tax_cr_spouse	B	(earn>0)*(wtc_basic+wtc_woman+(wtc_child*children))
	Tax credits (nonwastable)	NIT_princ	B	NIT=+MAX(0, MAX(0,+IF(princ_earnings<NIT_MinIncome,0,IF(Children=0,0,IF(Children<3,NIT_basic1+Tax(princ_earnings,NIT_sch1),NIT_basic2+Tax(princ_earnings,NIT_sch2)))))+NIT_sch1_rate5*MAX(0,+(princ_earnings + spouse_earnings)-NIT_MaxIncome-MIN(MAX(princ_earnings - NIT_sch1_inc4,0),(NIT_AddIncome))-MIN(MAX(spouse_earnings - NIT_sch1_inc4,0),(NIT_AddIncome)))) IF(NIT<NIT_min,NIT=0,NIT)*NIT_Bonus
		NIT_spouse	B	NIT=+MAX(0, MAX(0,+IF(spouse_earnings<NIT_MinIncome,0,IF(Children=0,0,IF(Children<3,NIT_basic1+Tax(spouse_earnings,NIT_sch1),NIT_basic2+Tax(spouse_earnings,NIT_sch2)))))+NIT_sch1_rate5*MAX(0,+(princ_earnings + spouse_earnings)-NIT_MaxIncome-MIN(MAX(princ_earnings - NIT_sch1_inc4,0),(NIT_AddIncome))-MIN(MAX(spouse_earnings - NIT_sch1_inc4,0),(NIT_AddIncome)))) IF(NIT<NIT_min,NIT=0,NIT)*NIT_Bonus
7.	CG tax	CG_tax	B	Positive(CG_tax_excl-tax_cr)-NIT
8.	State and local taxes	local_tax	B	0
9.	Employees' soc security	SSC	B	Tax(earn, SSC_sch)
11.	Cash transfers	cash_trans	J	IF(children=1,CB_firstchild,IF(Children=2,CB_firstchild+CB_secondchild)+(IF(married=0)*(children>0),Studygrant_rate*children)
13.	Employer's soc security	SSC_empr	B	Tax(earn, SSC_rate2)

Key to range of equation B calculated separately for both principal earner and spouse P calculated for principal only (value taken as 0 for spouse calculation) J calculated once only on a joint basis.

Taxing Wages 2014
Changes in sructural labour income tax progressivity
over 2000-12 period in OECD member countries

Italy

This chapter includes data on the income taxes paid by workers, their social security contributions, the family benefits they receive in the form of cash transfers as well as the social security contributions and payroll taxes paid by their employers. Results reported include the marginal and average tax burden for eight different family types.

Methodological information is available for personal income tax systems, compulsory social security contributions to schemes operated within the government sector, universal cash transfers as well as recent changes in the tax/benefit system. The methodology also includes the parameter values and tax equations underlying the data.

Italy 2013

The tax/benefit position of single persons

		Wage level (per cent of average wage)	67	100	167	67
		Number of children	none	none	none	2
1.	**Gross wage earnings**		19802	29704	49506	19802
2.	**Standard tax allowances**					
	Basic allowance					
	Married or head of family					
	Dependent children					
	Deduction for social security contributions and income taxes		1879	2819	4738	1879
	Work-related expenses					
	Other					
		Total	1879	2819	4738	1879
3.	**Tax credits or cash transfers included in taxable income**		0	0	0	0
4.	**Central government taxable income (1 - 2 + 3)**		17923	26885	44768	17923
5.	**Central government income tax liability (exclusive of tax credits)**		4239	6659	13332	4239
6.	**Tax credits**					
	Basic credit		1240	969	342	1240
	Married or head of family		0	0	0	0
	Children		0	0	0	1590
	Other					
		Total	1240	969	342	2831
7.	**Central government income tax finally paid (5-6)**		2999	5690	12990	1409
8.	**State and local taxes**		471	707	1177	471
9.	**Employees' compulsory social security contributions**					
	Gross earnings		1879	2819	4738	1879
	Taxable income					
		Total	1879	2819	4738	1879
10.	**Total payments to general government (7 + 8 + 9)**		5350	9216	18905	3759
11.	**Cash transfers from general government**					
	For head of family					
	For two children		0	0	0	2671
		Total	0	0	0	2671
12.	**Take-home pay (1-10+11)**		14453	20487	30601	18714
13.	**Employer's compulsory social security contributions**		6353	9529	15882	6353
14.	**Average rates**					
	Income tax		17.5%	21.5%	28.6%	9.5%
	Employees' social security contributions		9.5%	9.5%	9.6%	9.5%
	Total payments less cash transfers		27.0%	31.0%	38.2%	5.5%
	Total tax wedge including employer's social security contributions		44.7%	47.8%	53.2%	28.4%
15.	**Marginal rates**					
	Total payments less cash transfers: Principal earner		39.3%	39.4%	49.9%	40.9%
	Total payments less cash transfers: Spouse		n.a.	n.a.	n.a.	n.a.
	Total tax wedge: Principal earner		54.1%	54.1%	62.0%	55.3%
	Total tax wedge: Spouse		n.a.	n.a.	n.a.	n.a.

Italy 2013

The tax/benefit position of married couples

		Wage level (per cent of average wage)	100-0	100-33	100-67	100-33
		Number of children	2	2	2	none
1.	**Gross wage earnings**		29704	39605	49506	39605
2.	**Standard tax allowances**					
	Basic allowance					
	Married or head of family					
	Dependent children					
	Deduction for social security contributions and income taxes		2819	3758	4698	3758
	Work-related expenses					
	Other					
		Total	2819	3758	4698	3758
3.	**Tax credits or cash transfers included in taxable income**		0	0	0	0
4.	**Central government taxable income (1 - 2 + 3)**		26885	35846	44808	35846
5.	**Central government income tax liability (exclusive of tax credits)**		6659	8720	10898	8720
6.	**Tax credits**					
	Basic credit		969	2740	2209	2740
	Married or head of family		690	0	0	0
	Children		1436	1436	1513	0
	Other					
		Total	3094	4175	3722	2740
7.	**Central government income tax finally paid (5-6)**		3565	4545	7176	5980
8.	**State and local taxes**		707	943	1178	943
9.	**Employees' compulsory social security contributions**					
	Gross earnings		2819	3758	4698	3758
	Taxable income					
		Total	2819	3758	4698	3758
10.	**Total payments to general government (7 + 8 + 9)**		7091	9246	13053	10682
11.	**Cash transfers from general government**					
	For head of family					
	For two children		1644	932	861	0
		Total	1644	932	861	0
12.	**Take-home pay (1-10+11)**		24257	31290	37314	28923
13.	**Employer's compulsory social security contributions**		9529	12705	15882	12705
14.	**Average rates**					
	Income tax		14.4%	13.9%	16.9%	17.5%
	Employees' social security contributions		9.5%	9.5%	9.5%	9.5%
	Total payments less cash transfers		18.3%	21.0%	24.6%	27.0%
	Total tax wedge including employer's social security contributions		38.2%	40.2%	42.9%	44.7%
15.	**Marginal rates**					
	Total payments less cash transfers: Principal earner		41.0%	41.0%	40.2%	39.4%
	Total payments less cash transfers: Spouse		29.0%	39.2%	40.1%	39.2%
	Total tax wedge: Principal earner		55.3%	55.3%	54.7%	54.1%
	Total tax wedge: Spouse		46.2%	54.0%	54.7%	54.0%

The national currency is the euro (EUR). In 2013, EUR 0.75 was equal to USD 1. In that year the average worker earned EUR 29 704 (Secretariat estimate).

1. Personal income tax

1.1. Central government income tax

1.1.1. Tax unit

Spouses are taxed separately.

1.1.2. Tax allowances and tax credits

1.1.2.1. Tax allowances

- Social security contributions due by law

1.1.2.2. Tax credits

All the tax credits in Italy are non-refundable

- Standard tax credits

The PAYE tax credit is defined as a function of net income:

Taxable income (EUR)	PAYE tax credit (EUR)
Up to 8 000	1 840
From 8 001 to 15 000	Maximum tax credit + 502 *(15 000 – taxable income)/7 000
From 15 001 to 55 000	Maximum tax credit *(55 000 – taxable income)/40 000
More than 55 000	0

The maximum value for the tax credit depends on the level of taxable income:

Level of taxable income (EUR)	Maximum tax credit (EUR)
From 8 001 to 15 000	1 338
From 15 001 to 23 000	1 338
From 23 001 to 24 000	1 348
From 24 001 to 25 000	1 358
From 24 001 to 26 000	1 368
From 26 001 to 27 700	1 378
From 27 701 to 28 000	1 363
From 28 001 to 55 000	1 338

- Tax credits for family dependents

The tax credits for family dependants, which have replaced the former tax allowances, are as follows:

Family tax credit (EUR)[1]	Amount (EUR)
Spouse	800 decreasing to 0 for net income over 80 000
Children	
Under three years of age	1 220 decreasing to 0 for net income over 95 000
Over three years of age	950 decreasing to 0 for net income over 95 000
Other dependent relatives	750 decreasing to 0 for net income over 80 000

1. Tax credits are granted for family dependents earning less than EUR 2 840.51.

The spouse tax credit is calculated as a function of net income:

Level of taxable income (EUR)	Amount of tax credit (EUR)
Up to 15 000	800 – 110 * taxable income/15 000
From 15 001 to 29 000	690
From 29 001 to 29 200	700
From 29 201 to 34 700	710
From 34 701 to 35 000	720
From 35 001 to 35 100	710
From 35 101 to 35 200	700
From 35 201 to 40 000	690
From 40 001 to 80 000	690*(80 000 – taxable income)/40 000
More than 80 000	0

The child tax credit is calculated as a function of net income:

- for families with only one child: 950 * (95 000 – taxable income)/95 000;
- for families with more than one child the amount of 95 000 is increased by 15 000 for each child other than the first, for every children (including the first one).

Families with more than 3 children receive an additional tax credit of EUR 200 per child.

A lone parent receives an actual tax credit for the first child equal to the maximum of the spouse tax credit and the child tax credit.

Tax credits for children have to be equally shared between the parents; different shares are no longer allowed.

If the spouse's tax liable net of the PAYE tax credit is less than his/her share (50 per cent) in the child tax credit, the entire child tax credit is provided to the principal earner.

1.1.2.3. Main non-standard tax allowances and tax credits

- Other compulsory contributions.
- Periodical benefits allowed to the spouse fixed by judicial authority.
- Charitable donations to certain religious institutions (up to EUR 1 032.91).
- Medical and assistance expenses incurred by handicapped persons.
- Expenses to restore one's own residence at 36 per cent (50 per cent as from June 2012) of full expenses up to EUR 48 000 (up to EUR 96 000 as from June 2012), apportioned into 5 or 10 annual allowances of the same amount.

- Expenses for energy requalification of buildings at 55 per cent (65 per cent as from June 2012) of full expenses (up to EUR 100 000) apportioned into 3 annual allowances of the same amount.
- Expenses for the replacement of covers, windows and shutters and for the installation of solar panels at 55 per cent of full expenses (up to EUR 60 000).

For the following expenses, a tax credit of 19 per cent of each incurred expense is allowed:

- Mortgage loan interest (up to EUR 4 000).
- Most medical expenses that exceed EUR 129.11.
- Payments to insurance funds up to EUR 1 291.14.
- Expenses to attend secondary school and university courses; in case such courses are private, the expenses allowed cannot exceed those foreseen for State courses.
- Expenses for nursery school (up to EUR 632 for each child).
- Rents paid by out of town students (up to EUR 2 633).
- Funeral charges up to EUR 1 549.37.
- Expenses for disabled persons.
- Donations to political parties (ranging from EUR 51.65 to EUR 103 291.38).
- Payments to foundations (up to EUR 2 065.83).
- Expenses related to sport activities for children between 5 and 18 years of age (up to EUR 210 per child).

1.1.3. *Tax schedule*

The following tax schedule is applied to taxable income:

Bracket (EUR)	Rate (%)
Up to 15 000	23
Over 15 000 up to 28 000	27
Over 28 000 up to 55 000	38
Over 55 000 up to 75 000	41
Over 75 000	43

Decree-Law No. 138 of 13 August 2011 introduced the "Contributo di Solidarietà" for the 2011-13 tax periods, that is a 3% "solidarity contribution" on the portion of income higher than EUR 300 000 (the amount paid is deductible from PIT base).

1.2. *State and local taxes*

These surcharges are due only by taxpayers who pay individual income tax IRPEF (imposta sul reddito delle persone fisiche).

Regional surcharge tax

This surcharge tax has been introduced in 1997. The tax is levied by each region on resident taxpayers' total taxable income at a discretionary rate, which must fall within an established range. As from the year 2000 this range is 0.9 per cent-1.4 per cent.

In December 2011, with the DL 201/2011, the minimum state rate has been increased from 0.9% to 1.23%.

The figure given in the 2013 parameter values table under the heading "Regional and local tax" includes the regional surcharge tax paid in the most representative city which is Rome (Lazio); the rate is 1.73 per cent in 2013.

Local surcharge tax

This surcharge tax has been introduced in 1999. The tax may be levied by each local government at an initial rate that cannot exceed 0.2 per cent. If the tax is levied, the local government can increase the initial rate, on a yearly basis, up to a maximum of 0.5 per cent. Each yearly increase cannot exceed 0.2 per cent. As from 2012, municipalities can increase the rate up to 0.8. A 0.9 special rate can be introduced by Roma Capitale Local Government.

The figure given in the 2013 parameter values table under the heading "Regional and local tax" includes the local surcharge tax paid in the most representative city which is Rome; the rate is 0.9 per cent in 2013.

Starting from 2011, exemption is provided to taxpayers whose total income consists of retirement income not exceeding EUR 8 000, income from land not exceeding EUR 185.92, and income from primary residence. The ordinary rate is applied if any one of these limits is passed.

The surcharge rates can be adjusted above the fixed roof because of the health care losses.

2. Compulsory social security

2.1. *Employee contributions*

- Rate and ceiling
  - The average rate is 9.49 per cent on earnings up to EUR 45 530.
  - The average rate is 10.49 per cent on earnings over EUR 45 530 and up to EUR 99 034.
  - For earnings exceeding EUR 96 149, the employee pays a fixed amount given by (0.0949 × 45 530) + 0.1049 × (99 034 – 44 204).
- Distinction by marital status or sex
  - None.

2.2. *Employer contributions*

- Contributions equal 32.08 per cent on earnings up to EUR 99 034. For earnings exceeding EUR 99 034, the employer pays a fixed amount given by 0.3208 × 99 034.

3. Universal cash transfers

3.1. *Amount for spouse and for dependent children*

Cash transfers are granted for family income that is:

- composed of at least 70 per cent wage and/or pension income;
- below a given threshold set by law each year.

Family income is the sum of the incomes of all individuals comprising the family.

Cash transfers are determined each year by INPS (Istituto Nazionale di Previdenza Sociale), the public body that collects and manages the social security contributions for dependent workers for the period beginning in July of that year (t) to June in the following year (t + 1) and relate to family income earned in the previous year (t –1).

As such, the transfers granted in any given year t are determined by the family income in the previous two years. The following table provides a description of the calculations.

Transfer granted in year t	Relevant amounts as given in INPS tables
January-June	The amount of cash transfers is that given in the INPS table published in July t – 1. The transfers are granted with reference to family income earned in year t – 2.
July-December	The amount of cash transfers is that given in the INPS table published in July t. The transfers are granted with reference to family income earned in year t – 1.

For the purposes of *Taxing Wages*, the cash transfers that are calculated represent those amounts that would be received by the family based on their incomes for that year even though these amounts would only begin to be paid in July of the following year.

4. Main changes

The “extraordinary bonus” for low income families has been abolished.

5. Memorandum Item

5.1. *Identification of an AW*

The data refer to the annual earnings of average workers.

5.2. *Contributions by employers to private pension, health, etc., schemes*

In addition to the mandatory social security contributions employers may pay contributions to private pension schemes (currently about forty pension funds). Employer’s contributions are included in the taxable income of the employee.

Employees may also choose to contribute to the pension funds with all or part of the retirement allowance that is otherwise withheld by the employers. In this case the employee can deduct from his taxable income an amount equal to twice the amount of the contribution paid to fund.

Employer’s contributions to private health insurance schemes are not included in the taxable income of the employee up to the limit of EUR 3 615.20.

2013 parameter values

Average earnings/yr	Ave_earn	29 704	Secretariat estimate
Tax schedule	tax_sch	0.23	15 000.00
		0.27	28 000.00
		0.38	55 000.00
		0.41	75 000.00
		0.43	999 999 999.99
Sloidarity contribution	sol_tax	0.03	
	sol_inc_limit	300 000	
Tax credits			
Employment			
	emp_add	0	1 840.00
		8 000	1 338.00
		15 000	1 338.00
		23 000	1 348.00
		24 000	1 358.00
		25 000	1 368.00
		26 000	1 378.00
		27 700	1 363.00
		28 000	1 338.00
		55 000	0.00
Spouse	Spouse_cred	0	800.00
		15 000	690.00
		29 000	700.00
		29 200	710.00
		34 700	720.00
		35 000	710.00
		35 100	700.00
		35 200	690.00
		40 000	690.00
		80 000	0
limit	Sp_crd_lim	2 840.51	
Child credit	Child_credit	950	
Additional child credit	add_child	200	
Regional and local tax	reg_rt	0.0263	
Social security contributions	SSC_sch	0.0949	45 530
		0.1049	99 034
		0.00	999 999 999.99
Employer contributions	Empr_sch	0.3208	96 149
		0.00	999 999 999.99
Cash transfers:			
family allowance schedule (t)			
married couple	trans_sch	Table is too long to be included	
single parent	Trans_sch_sp	Table is too long to be included	

2013 tax equations

The equations for the Italian system in 2012 are mostly repeated for each individual of a married couple. But the spouse credit is relevant only to the calculation for the principal earner and any child credit which the spouse is unable to use is transferred to the principal. This is shown by the Range indicator in the table below.

The functions which are used in the equations (Taper, MIN, Tax, etc.) are described in the technical note about tax equations. Variable names are defined in the table of parameters above, within the equations table, or are the standard variables "married" and "children". A reference to a variable with the affix "_total" indicates the sum of the relevant variable values for the principal and spouse. And the affixes "_princ" and "_spouse" indicate the value for the principal and spouse, respectively. Equations for a single person are as shown for the principal, with "_spouse" values taken as 0.

	Line in country table and intermediate steps	Variable name	Range	Equation
1.	Earnings	earn		
2.	Allowances:	tax_al	B	SSC
		Sol_tax	B	sol_tax*Positive(Gross-sol_inc_limit)
3.	Credits in taxable income	taxbl_cr	B	0
4.	CG taxable income	tax_inc	B	earn-tax_al1-sol_tax
5.	CG tax before credits	CG_tax_excl	B	Tax(tax_inc, tax_sch)
6.	Tax credits :			
	Employment credit	emp_cr_max	P	VLOOKUP(tax_inc, emp_add, 2))
		emp_cr_max_spouse	S	IF(tax_inc_spouse=0,0,(VLOOKUP(tax_inc_spouse,emp_add,2)))
		emp_cr	P	MIN(CG_tax_excl, IF(tax_inc<=8000,emp_cr_max, IF(tax_inc<=15000,emp_cr_max+502*(15000-tax_inc)/7000, IF(tax_inc>55000,emp_cr_max,emp_cr_max*(55000-tax_inc)/40000))))
			S	MIN(CG_tax_excl_spouse, IF(tax_inc_spouse<=8000,emp_cr_max_spouse, IF(tax_inc_spouse<=15000,emp_cr_max_spouse+502*(15000-tax_inc_spouse)/7000, IF(tax_inc_spouse>55000,emp_cr_max_spouse,emp_cr_max_spouse*(55000-tax_inc_spouse)/40000))))
	Spouse credit	spouse_cr	P	IF(Married=1, IF(tax_inc_spouse>Sp_crd_lim,0, IF(tax_inc>80000,0, IF(tax_inc<15000,800-110*tax_inc/15000, IF(tax_inc>40000,690*(80000-tax_inc)/40000,VLOOKUP(tax_inc,Spouse_cred,2))))),0)
	Child credit	child_cr_princ	P	IF(Children=0,0,IF(Married=1,(800*(95000-tax_inc)/95000+(Children-1)*800*(110000-tax_inc)/110000)*(1-child_crpct_spouse), MAX(800*(95000-tax_inc)/95000, IF(tax_inc>80000,0,IF(tax_inc<15000,800-110*tax_inc/15000, IF(tax_inc>40000,690*(80000-tax_inc)/40000, VLOOKUP(tax_inc,Spouse_cred,2)))))+(Children-1)*800*(110000-tax_inc)/110000))
		child_crfull_spouse	S	IF(Children=0,0,(spouse_cr=0)*Married*(800*(95000-tax_inc_spouse)/95000+(Children-1)*800*(110000-tax_inc_spouse)/110000))
		child_crpct_spouse	S	IF(child_crfull_spouse>0,IF((CG_tax_excl_spouse-emp_cr_spouse)/child_crfull_spouse<0.5,0,0.5),0)
		child_cr_spouse	S	child_crfull_spouse*child_crpct_spouse
	Total	tax_cr	B	MIN(emp_cr+spouse_cr+child_cr, CG_tax_excl)
7.	CG tax	CG_tax	B	Positive(CG_tax_excl-tax_cr)+sol_tax
8.	State and local taxes	reg_rt	B	IF(CG_tax=0, 0, tax_inc*reg_rt)
9.	Employees' soc security	SSC	B	Tax(earn, SSC_sch)
11.	Cash transfers		J	IF(Children=0,0,12*VLOOKUP(earn_total, IF(Married,trans_sch,trans_sch_sp),1+Children))
13.	Employer's soc security	SSC_empr	B	Tax(earn, Empr_sch)

Key to range of equation B calculated separately for both principal earner and spouse P calculated for principal only (value taken as 0 for spouse calculation) J calculated once only on a joint basis.

Taxing Wages 2014
Changes in sructural labour income tax progressivity
over 2000-12 period in OECD member countries

Japan

This chapter includes data on the income taxes paid by workers, their social security contributions, the family benefits they receive in the form of cash transfers as well as the social security contributions and payroll taxes paid by their employers. Results reported include the marginal and average tax burden for eight different family types.

Methodological information is available for personal income tax systems, compulsory social security contributions to schemes operated within the government sector, universal cash transfers as well as recent changes in the tax/ benefit system. The methodology also includes the parameter values and tax equations underlying the data.

Japan 2013

The tax/benefit position of single persons

	Wage level (per cent of average wage)	67	100	167	67
	Number of children	none	none	none	2
1.	**Gross wage earnings**	3267803	4901704	8169507	3267803
2.	**Standard tax allowances:**				
	Basic allowance	380000	380000	380000	380000
	Married or head of family	0	0	0	0
	Dependent children	0	0	0	0
	Deduction for social security contributions and income taxes	455597	683396	1077408	455597
	Work-related expenses	1160341	1520341	2016951	1160341
	Other				
	Total	1995938	2583736	3474358	1995938
3.	**Tax credits or cash transfers included in taxable income**	0	0	0	0
4.	**Central government taxable income (1 - 2 + 3)**	1271865	2317968	4695149	1271865
5.	**Central government income tax liability (exclusive of tax credits)**	64929	137117	522272	64929
6.	**Tax credits**				
	Basic credit				
	Married or head of family				
	Children				
	Other				
	Total	0	0	0	0
7.	**Central government income tax finally paid (5-6)**	64929	137117	522272	64929
8.	**State and local taxes**	133686	238297	476015	133686
9.	**Employees' compulsory social security contributions**				
	Gross earnings	455597	683396	1077408	455597
	Taxable income				
	Total	455597	683396	1077408	455597
10.	**Total payments to general government (7 + 8 + 9)**	654212	1058809	2075694	654212
11.	**Cash transfers from general government**				
	For head of family				
	For two children	0	0	0	240000
	Total	0	0	0	240000
12.	**Take-home pay (1-10+11)**	2613591	3842895	6093813	2853591
13.	**Employer's compulsory social security contributions**	480106	720158	1138679	480106
14.	**Average rates**				
	Income tax	6.1%	7.7%	12.2%	6.1%
	Employees' social security contributions	13.9%	13.9%	13.2%	13.9%
	Total payments less cash transfers	20.0%	21.6%	25.4%	12.7%
	Total tax wedge including employer's social security contributions	30.3%	31.6%	34.5%	23.9%
15.	**Marginal rates**				
	Total payments less cash transfers: Principal earner	22.4%	27.3%	31.2%	22.4%
	Total payments less cash transfers: Spouse	n.a.	n.a.	n.a.	n.a.
	Total tax wedge: Principal earner	32.3%	36.6%	35.3%	32.3%
	Total tax wedge: Spouse	n.a.	n.a.	n.a.	n.a.

Japan 2013

The tax/benefit position of married couples

		Wage level (per cent of average wage)	100-0	100-33	100-67	100-33
		Number of children	2	2	2	none
1.	**Gross wage earnings**		4901704	6535606	8169507	6535606
2.	**Standard tax allowances**					
	Basic allowance		380000	760000	760000	760000
	Married or head of family		380000	0	0	0
	Dependent children		0	0	0	0
	Deduction for social security contributions and income taxes		683396	911194	1138993	911194
	Work-related expenses		1520341	2173901	2680682	2173901
	Other					
		Total	2963736	3845096	4579674	3845096
3.	**Tax credits or cash transfers included in taxable income**		0	0	0	0
4.	**Central government taxable income (1 - 2 + 3)**		1937968	2690510	3589833	2690510
5.	**Central government income tax liability (exclusive of tax credits)**		98933	156135	202046	156135
6.	**Tax credits**					
	Basic credit					
	Married or head of family					
	Children					
	Other					
		Total	0	0	0	0
7.	**Central government income tax finally paid (5-6)**		98933	156135	202046	156135
8.	**State and local taxes**		204695	282051	371983	282051
9.	**Employees' compulsory social security contributions**					
	Gross earnings		683396	911194	1138993	911194
	Taxable income					
		Total	683396	911194	1138993	911194
10.	**Total payments to general government (7 + 8 + 9)**		987024	1349380	1713022	1349380
11.	**Cash transfers from general government**					
	For head of family					
	For two children		240000	240000	240000	0
		Total	240000	240000	240000	0
12.	**Take-home pay (1-10+11)**		4154680	5426225	6696485	5186225
13.	**Employer's compulsory social security contributions**		720158	960211	1200264	960211
14.	**Average rates**					
	Income tax		6.2%	6.7%	7.0%	6.7%
	Employees' social security contributions		13.9%	13.9%	13.9%	13.9%
	Total payments less cash transfers		15.2%	17.0%	18.0%	20.6%
	Total tax wedge including employer's social security contributions		26.1%	27.6%	28.5%	30.8%
15.	**Marginal rates**					
	Total payments less cash transfers: Principal earner		27.2%	27.3%	27.3%	27.3%
	Total payments less cash transfers: Spouse		22.2%	20.9%	22.4%	20.9%
	Total tax wedge: Principal earner		36.5%	36.6%	36.6%	36.6%
	Total tax wedge: Spouse		32.1%	31.0%	32.3%	31.0%

The national currency is the yen (JPY). In 2013 JPY 97.60 was equal to USD 1. In that year, the average worker is assumed to earn JPY 4 901 704 (Secretariat estimate). In Japan, the central government income tax year is a calendar year and the local government income tax year is from April to March. The calculations in this report are based on the tax rules and rates, which are applicable the 1 April.

1. Personal income tax systems

1.1. *Central government income tax*

1.1.1. *Tax unit*

Each individual is taxed separately.

1.1.2. *Allowances and tax credits*

1.1.2.1. Standard reliefs

- *Basic allowance:* A taxpayer may deduct JPY 380 000 as a basic allowance from his or her income.
- *Allowance for spouse:* Allowance equal to JPY 380 000 is given to a resident taxpayer who lives with a spouse whose income does not exceed JPY 380 000.
- *Special allowance for spouse:* The allowance included in the following table is given to a resident taxpayer who lives with a spouse:

Spouse's income	Amount
0-380 000	0
380 001-399 999	380 000
400 000-449 999	360 000
450 000-499 999	310 000
500 000-549 999	260 000
550 000-599 999	210 000
600 000-649 999	160 000
650 000-699 999	110 000
700 000-749 999	60 000
750 000-759 999	30 000
760 000 or more	0

- *Allowance for dependents:* If a resident taxpayer has children and other relatives whose income does not exceed JPY380 000 and who are over 15 years old, an allowance of JPY 380 000 is given for each dependent.
- *Special allowance for dependents:* If a resident taxpayer has dependents whose income does not exceed JPY 380 000 and who are between 19 and 22 years old, an allowance of JPY 630 000 is given for each dependent instead of the allowances for dependents mentioned above.

- *Deduction for social insurance premiums:* The amount of social insurance premiums for a resident taxpayer or his/her dependents shall be deducted from his/her income without any ceiling.
- *Employment income deduction:* The following amounts may be deducted from employment income in calculating taxable income:
  - If gross employment income does not exceed JPY 1 800 000, the deduction is 40 per cent of salaries (etc.), but the minimum amount deductible is JPY 650 000.
  - If gross employment income exceeds JPY 1 800 000, but not JPY 3 600 000, the deduction is JPY 180 000 plus 30 per cent of salaries.
  - If gross employment income exceeds JPY 3 600 000, but not JPY 6 600 000, the deduction is JPY 540 000 plus 20 per cent of salaries.
  - If gross employment income exceeds JPY 6 600 000, but not JPY 10 000 000, the deduction is JPY 1 200 000 plus 10 per cent of salaries.
  - If gross employment income exceeds JPY 10 000 000, but not JPY 15 000 000, the deduction is JPY 1 700 000 plus 5 per cent of salaries.
  - If gross employment income exceeds JPY 15 000 000, the deduction will be fixed at JPY 2 450 000.

1.1.2.2. Main non-standard tax reliefs applicable to an AW

- *Credit for housing loans:* A resident taxpayer who constructs, purchases, enlarges or rebuilds a house and finances the cost by means of a housing loan and uses the property as his or her own dwelling is entitled to an income tax credit up to the amount described below for 10 years [or 15 years] after the first use of the house, provided that the floor space is not less than 50 m^2 and that at least half of the floor space is used as the owner-occupied dwelling. The base of the tax credit equals the balance of the housing loan debt amount, calculated at the end of each year, consisting of the loan obtained not only from private financial institutions but also from public institutions. This tax credit cannot be claimed by those whose total income is more than JPY 30 million.

  The rates of the tax credits correspond to the year in which residence in the house commenced. The rates are as follows :

Residence starts:	From 1 January 2005 to 31 December 2005	From 1 January 2006 to 31 December 2006	From 1 January 2007 to 31 December 2007
Tax credit rate	If the remaining housing loan balance at the end of year (R.H.L.B). is JPY 40 million or less: The R.H.L.B. x 1.0% (for first 8 years) The R.H.L.B. x 0.5% (for last 2 years)	If the R.H.L.B. is JPY 30 million or less: The R.H.L.B. x 1.0% (for first 7 years) The R.H.L.B. x 0.5% (for last 3 years)	If the R.H.L.B. is JPY 25 million or less: The R.H.L.B. x 1.0%[or 0.6%] (for first 6 years [or 10 years]) The R.H.L.B. x 0.5%[or 0.4%] (for last 4 years [or 5 years])
Maximum tax credit amount (for each year)	JPY 400 000 JPY 200 000 (for last 2 years)	JPY 300 000 JPY 150 000 (for last 3 years)	JPY 250 000 [or 150 000] JPY 125 000 [or 100 000] (for last 4 years [or 5 years])
Maximum tax credit amount (for the deductible period in total)	JPY 3.6 million	JPY 2.55 million	JPY 2 million

Residence starts:	From 1 January 2008 to 31 December 2008	From 1 January 2009 to 31 December 2010	From 1 January 2011 to 31 December 2011
Tax credit rate	If the R.H.L.B. is JPY 20 million or less: The R.H.L.B. x 1.0%[or 0.6%] (for first 6 years [or 10 years]) The R.H.L.B. x 0.5%[or 0.4%] (for last 4 years [or 5 years])	If the R.H.L.B. is JPY 50 million or less: The R.H.L.B. x 1.0%	If the R.H.L.B. is JPY 40 million or less: The R.H.L.B. x 1.0%
Maximum tax credit amount (for each year)	JPY 200 000 [or 120 000] JPY 100 000 [or 80 000] (for last 4 years [or 5 years])	JPY 500 000	JPY 400 000
Maximum tax credit amount (for the deductible period in total)	JPY 1.6 million	JPY 5 million	JPY 4 million

Residence starts:	From 1 January 2012 to 31 December 2012	From 1 January 2013 to 31 March 2014	From 1 April 2014 to 31 December 2017
Tax credit rate	If the R.H.L.B. is JPY 30 million or less: The R.H.L.B. x 1.0%	If the R.H.L.B. is JPY 20 million or less: The R.H.L.B. x 1.0%	If the R.H.L.B. is JPY 40 million or less: The R.H.L.B x 1.0%
Maximum tax credit amount (for each year)	JPY 300 000	JPY 200 000	JPY 400 000
Maximum tax credit amount (for the deductible period in total)	JPY 3 million	JPY 2 million	JPY 4 million

- *Deduction for life insurance premiums and personal pension plan premiums:* If a resident taxpayer pays insurance premiums on life insurance contracts and the recipient of the insurance proceeds is the taxpayer, his/her spouse or other relatives living with him/her, the portion of these insurance premiums which does not exceed the maximum prescribed below, is deductible from ordinary income, retirement income or timber income.

In addition, if a resident taxpayer pays insurance premiums for a "qualified personal pension plan (insurance type)", and the recipient of the pension payment is the taxpayer or his/her spouse under a specific condition, the portion of such premiums which does not exceed the maximum prescribed below, is deductible from ordinary income, retirement income, or timber income.

Annual Premium Paid (JPY)		Deduction
Over	Not over	
	25 000	Total amount of premiums paid (1)
25 000	50 000	(1) x 1/2 + JPY 12 500
50 000	100 000	(1) x 1/4 + JPY 25 000
100 000	-	JPY 50 000

- The insurance premiums of this type of pension plan are not considered as the life insurance premiums described above. Thus, a resident tax payer can claim the deduction up to JPY 100 000 in total. For the insurance contracts made on or after 1 January 2012 the maximum deduction will be increased to JPY 120 000 from JPY 100 000. A resident taxpayer can claim the deduction up to JPY 40 000 for life insurance premiums, personal pension plan premiums and long-term care insurance premiums respectively.

- *Deduction for medical expenses:* If a resident taxpayer pays bills for medical or dental care for himself/herself or for his/her spouse or other relatives living with him/her and the amount of such expenses (excluding those recovered by insurance) exceeds the lesser of JPY 100 000 or 5 per cent of the total of his/her ordinary income, retirement income and timber income, the excess amount is deductible from his/her ordinary income, retirement income or timber income. The maximum deduction is JPY 2 million.
- *Deduction for earthquake insurance premiums:* Earthquake insurance premiums up to JPY 50 000 can be deducted from income. Although the income deduction for casualty insurance premiums was basically abolished, the deduction for long-term casualty insurance premiums remains available if contracted before 31 December 2006. The maximum deduction for long-term casualty insurance premiums is JPY 15 000. If an individual applies for both a deduction for earthquake insurance premiums and a deduction for long-term casualty premiums, the maximum deductible amount is JPY 50 000 in total.

1.1.3. *Tax schedule*

Taxable income (JPY)[1]		Tax rate (%)	Deductible amounts for each bracket (JPY)
Over	Not over	(A)	(B)
	1 950 000	5	-
1 950 000	3 300 000	10	97 500
3 300 000	6 950 000	20	427 500
6 950 000	9 000 000	23	636 000
9 000 000	18 000 000	33	1 536 000
18 000 000		40	2 796 000

1. The fraction of taxable income that is less than JPY 1 000 is rounded down.

Tax liability is obtained by multiplying the taxable income by tax rate (A) and deducting the amount (B). For example, income tax due on taxable income of JPY 7 million is:

7 000 000 × 0.23 (A) – 636 000 (B) = JPY 974 000.

In addition, a taxpayer is required to file tax returns and make tax payments for additional 2.1% of the base income taxes from 2013 through 2037 annually together with the regular income tax of respective years.

1.2. *State and local income taxes*

1.2.1. *General description of the system*

State and local income taxes in Japan consist of prefectural inhabitant's tax levied by prefectures and municipal inhabitant's tax levied by cities, towns and villages. The prefectural inhabitant's tax is collected together with the municipal inhabitant's tax by cities, towns and villages.

1.2.2. *Tax base*

Basically, prefectural and municipal inhabitants' taxes (local taxes) consist of two parts; one is proportional taxable income and the other is a fixed per capita amount. The way to compute the taxable income of local taxes is similar to that of the previous year's national income tax. The main difference is the amount of reliefs. For example, the amount of Basic Allowance, Allowance for Spouse, Allowance for Dependants is JPY 330 000, the amount of Special Allowance for dependants is JPY 450 000, etc. Allowance for Dependents is available for dependents 16 years or older excluding the specified dependents described below. Special Allowance for dependents is available for the specified dependents (between 19 and 22 years old).

1.2.3. *Tax rate*

- The standard fixed (annual) per-capita amount of Prefectural inhabitants tax is JPY 1 000.
- The standard fixed (annual) per-capita amount of Municipal inhabitants tax is JPY 3 000.
- The standard rate of the local taxes equals a proportional rate of 10 per cent (Prefectural inhabitant's tax: 4 per cent, Municipal inhabitant's tax: 6 per cent).*

(*) The local tax rate and the central government income tax rate were changed in the FY2006 tax reform. Also a new local income tax credit regime was introduced in order to alleviate the tax burden increase arising from the changes in the tax rates and from the difference between the personal reliefs (Basic Allowance, Allowance for Spouse, Allowance for Dependents, Special Allowance for dependents, etc.) for national income tax purposes and for inhabitant tax purposes.

Taxable income for local income tax purposes	The tax credit
JPY 2 000 000 or less	5 per cent of the lesser of: • total amount of differences in personal reliefs between those for national income tax purposes and for local income tax purposes; or • taxable income for local income tax purposes
More than JPY 2 000 000	((total amount of differences in personal reliefs between those for national income tax purposes and for local income tax purposes) – (taxable income for local income tax purposes – JPY 2 000 000)) * 5%. The minimum credit is JPY 2 500

Note: Local authorities do not levy the per-capita rate and the proportional rate on a taxpayer whose previous year's income does not exceed a certain amount. For example, in special wards of Tokyo, this threshold is calculated as follows:

- Per-capita rate: (1 + number of spouse and dependent(s) qualified for the allowance for spouse/dependents) * 350 000 (+ 210 000 in case the taxpayer has a qualified spouse or dependent(s)).
- Proportional rate: (1 + number of spouse and dependent(s) qualified for the allowance for spouse/dependents) * 350 000 (+ 320 000 in case the taxpayer has a qualified spouse or dependent(s)).

1.2.4. *Tax rate selected for this study*

Country-wide rates as described above. The local income tax rates chosen for the purpose of this Report represent a country-wide average.

* The local tax rate and the central government income tax rate were changed in the FY2006 tax reform. Also a new local income tax credit regime was introduced in order to alleviate the tax burden increase arising from the changes in the tax rates and from the difference between the personal reliefs (Basic Allowance, Allowance for Spouse, Allowance for Dependents, Special Allowance for dependents, etc.) for national income tax purposes and for inhabitant tax purposes.

2. Compulsory social security contribution to schemes operated within the government sector

2.1. Employees' contributions

2.1.1. Pension

8.383 per cent (8.560 per cent as from September 2013) of total remuneration (standard remuneration and bonuses). The insurable ceiling of the monthly amount of pensionable remuneration is JPY 620 000 and the insurable ceiling of the standard amount of bonus is JPY 1 500 000.

2.1.2. Sickness

As from April 2012 about 5.00 per cent (about 4.75 per cent before March 2012), of total remuneration, (standard remuneration and bonuses), up to the insurable ceiling of JPY 1 210 000 (monthly).

2.1.3. Unemployment

0.5 per cent of total remuneration.

2.1.4-1.5. Work injury and family allowance

None.

2.2. Employers' contributions

2.2.1. Pensions

8.383 per cent (8.560 per cent as from September 2013) of total remuneration. The insurable ceiling of the monthly amount of pensionable remuneration is JPY 620 000 and the insurable ceiling of the standard amount of bonus is JPY 1 500 000.

2.2.2. Sickness

As from April 2012, about 5.00 per cent (about 4.75 per cent before March 2012) of total remuneration up to the insurable ceiling of JPY 1 210 000 (monthly).

2.2.3. Unemployment

0.85 per cent of total remuneration.

2.2.4. Work injury

0.25 per cent to 8.9 per cent of total remuneration, the contribution rate depending on each industry's accident rate over the last three years and other factors. There are thirty rates for fifty-five industrial categories at present.

2.2.5. Family allowance

0.15 per cent of total remuneration.

3. Universal cash transfers

3.1. Transfers related to marital status

Not available.

3.2. Transfers for dependent children

From April 2012 (Income caps are applied beginning from June 2012 payments):

a) For persons earning incomes below the income cap

JPY 15 000 (per month) is paid to parents/guardians for each child who is under 3 years old or for the third or subsequent child from 3 years old until he/she graduates from elementary school.

JPY 10 000 (per month) is paid to parents/guardians for each child who is for the first or second child from 3 years old until he/she graduates from elementary school or who is a junior high school student.

b) For persons earning incomes no less than the income cap

JPY 50 00 (per month) is paid to parents/guardians for each child until he/she graduates from junior high school as the Special Interim Allowances.

The income cap is set at JPY 6 220 000 (the principal's gross earnings net of certain deductions, plus JPY 380 000 per dependent).

4. Main changes in tax/benefit systems since 1998

As part of the Fiscal Year 1999 tax reform, the highest marginal rate of the personal income tax imposed by the central government was reduced from 50 per cent to 37 per cent. The top rate of the local inhabitants' tax was reduced from 15 per cent to 13 per cent. A proportional tax reduction was granted with respect to the national income tax and the local inhabitants tax. The amount is equal to the lesser of 20 per cent (local inhabitants tax: 15 per cent) of the amount of tax before reduction or JPY 250 000 (local inhabitants tax: JPY 40 000).

As part of the FY 2005 tax reform, the rate of the reduction was reduced from 20 per cent to 10 per cent (local inhabitants tax: from 15 per cent to 7.5 per cent) and the ceiling was reduced from JPY 250 000 to JPY 125 000 (local inhabitants' tax from JPY 40 000 to JPY 20 000) as from 2006 (local inhabitants tax: FY 2006). And as part of the FY 2006 tax reform, the reduction was abolished as from 2007 (local inhabitants tax: FY 2007).

As part of the FY 2006 tax reform, the progressive rate structure of national income tax was reformed into a 6 brackets structure with tax rates ranging from 5 per cent to 40 per cent, and the rate of local inhabitants' tax became proportional at a rate of 10 per cent.

Eligible age for transfers for dependent children was raised from three to six as from 1 June 2001, from six to nine as from 1 April 2004 and from nine to twelve as from 1 April 2006. It has been doubled to JPY 10 000 for the first and second child under the age of three as from 1 April, 2007.

As from 2010, JPY 13 000 per month is paid to parents/guardians regardless of their income for each child until he/she graduates from junior high school.

As from April 2012 (Income caps are applied beginning from June 2012 payments):

a) For persons earning incomes below the income cap

JPY 15 000 (per month) is paid to parents/guardians for each child who is under 3 years old or for the third or subsequent child from 3 years old until he/she graduates from elementary school.

JPY 10 000 (per month) is paid to parents/guardians for each child who is for the first or second child from 3 years old until he/she graduates from elementary school or who is a junior high school student.

b) For persons earning incomes no less than the income cap

JPY 5 000 (per month) is paid to parents/guardians for each child until he/she graduates from junior high school as the Special Interim Allowances.

As part of the FY 2012 tax reform, the upper limit on employment income deduction (JPY 2 450 000) was set for those who earn employment income more than JPY 15 000 000 as from 2013 (local inhabitants tax: FY2014).

5. Memorandum Item

5.1. *Average gross annual wage earnings calculation*

The source of calculation is the *Basic Survey on Wage Structure,* published by the Ministry of Health, Labour and Welfare. This survey covers establishments with ten or more regular employees over the whole country, and contains statistical figures for monthly contractual cash earnings in June and annual special cash earnings (such as bonuses) received by various categories of workers. Male and female workers of the manufacturing, mining and quarrying, construction, wholesale and retail trade, accommodation and food service activities, financial and insurance activities, real estate activities sector are the point of departure. Their gross annual earnings have been calculated by multiplying monthly contractual cash earnings by 12 and adding any annual special cash earnings. In the *Basic Survey*, sickness and unemployment compensations are excluded from cash earnings, but average overtime and bonuses are included.

As far as the *Basic Survey* is concerned, it covers the whole country, and no special assumption is made regarding the place of residence of the average worker.

5.2. *Employer contributions to private pension and health schemes*

No information available.

2013 parameter values

Average earnings/yr	Ave_earn	4 901 704	Secretariat estimate
Allowances for central tax	basic_al	380 000	
	spouse_al	380 000	
	Spouse_al_sp	0	0
		380 001	380 000
		400 000	360 000
		450 000	310 000
		500 000	260 000
		550 000	210 000
		600 000	160 000
		650 000	110 000
		700 000	60 000
		750 000	30 000
		760 000	0
spouse_al_ceil		380 000	
	child_al	0	
Employment income deduction	emp_inc_min	650 000	
	emp_inc_sch	0.4	1 800 000
		0.3	3 600 000
		0.2	6 600 000
		0.1	10 000 000
		0.05	
	emp_inc_max	2 450 000	
Central gov't tax schedule	tax_sch	0.05	1 950 000
		0.10	3 300 000
		0.20	6 950 000
		0.23	9 000 000
		0.33	18 000 000
		0.40	
	surtax	1.021	
Allowances for state/local tax	s_basic_al	330 000	
	s_spouse_al	330 000	
	s_spouse_al_sp	0	0
		380 001	330 000
		450 000	310 000
		500 000	260 000
		550 000	210 000
		600 000	160 000
		650 000	110 000
		700 000	60 000
		750 000	30 000
		760 000	0
	S_spouse_al_ceil	380 000	
	s_child_al	0	
Prefectural tax	pref_per_cap	1 000	
Municipal tax	mun_per_cap	3 000	
	local_sch	0.1	
Social security contributions	SSC_pens	0.08442	
	pens_ceil	7 440 000	
	SSC_sick	0.05	
	sick_ceil	14 520 000	
	SSC_unemp	0.0050	
Employer contribution proportion	SSC_empr_unemp	0.0085	
	SSC_empr_oth	0.0040	
Child transfer	Child_transfer	120 000	
	Child_transfer2	90 000	
	Child_transfer_lim	6 220 000	
	Child_transfer_lim_incr	380 000	

2013 tax equations

The equations for the Japanese system are mostly on an individual basis. But the tax allowances for the spouse and for children are relevant only to the calculation for the principal earner. This is shown by the Range indicator in the table below.

The functions which are used in the equations (Taper, MIN, Tax, etc.) are described in the technical note about tax equations. Variable names are defined in the table of parameters above, within the equations table, or are the standard variables "married" and "children". A reference to a variable with the affix "_total" indicates the sum of the relevant variable values for the principal and spouse. And the affixes "_princ" and "_spouse" indicate the value for the principal and spouse, respectively. Equations for a single person are as shown for the principal, with "_spouse" values taken as 0.

	Line in country table and intermediate steps	Variable name	Range	Equation
1.	Earnings	earn		
2.	Allowances:			
		tax_al	P	basic_al + Married*(earn_princ - (earn_princ>0)*MIN(emp_inc_max,MAX(emp_inc_min,Tax(earn_princ, emp_inc_sch)))<=spouse_al_ceil)*spouse_al + Married*VLOOKUP(Positive(earn_princ - (earn_princ>0)*MAX(emp_inc_min,Tax(earn_princ, emp_inc_sch))),spouse_al_sp,2,TRUE) + Children*child_al + MAX(emp_inc_min,Tax(earn_princ,emp_inc_sch)) + SSC_princ
			S	MIN(earn_spouse, basic_al + MAX(emp_inc_min, Tax(earn, emp_inc_sch)) + SSC_spouse)
3.	Credits in taxable income	taxbl_cr	B	0
4.	CG taxable income	tax_inc	B	Positive(earn-tax_al)
5.	CG tax before credits	CG_tax_excl	B	Positive(Tax(tax_inc, tax_sch))
6.	Tax credits :	tax_cr	B	0
7.	CG tax	CG_tax	B	CG_tax_excl*surtax
8.	State and local taxes			
	Local taxable income	local_tax_inc	P	Positive(earn_princ- (s_basic_al+Married*((earn_spouse-(earn_spouse>0)*MAX(emp_inc_min,Tax(earn_spouse,emp_inc_sch))<=s_spouse_al_ceil)*s_spouse_al+VLOOKUP(Positive(earn_spouse-(earn_spouse>0)*MAX(emp_inc_min,Tax(earn_spouse,emp_inc_sch))),s_spouse_al_sp,2,TRUE))+Children*s_child_al+MAX(emp_inc_min,Tax(earn_princ,emp_inc_sch))+SSC_princ))
			S	Positive(earn_spouse-(s_basic_al+(earn_spouse>0)*MAX(emp_inc_min,Tax(earn_spouse,emp_inc_sch))+SSC_spouse))
	Local tax	local_tax	P	(earn_princ-MAX(emp_inc_min,Tax(earn_princ,emp_inc_sch))>350000+(Married*(earn_princ -(earn_princ>0)*MAX(emp_inc_min,Tax(earn_princ, emp_inc_sch))<=s_spouse_al_ceil)+Children>0)*((Married*(earn_princ -(earn_princ>0)*MAX(emp_inc_min,Tax(earn_princ, emp_inc_sch))<=s_spouse_al_ceil)+Children)*350000+210000))*(pref_per_cap+mun_per_cap)+(earn_princ-MAX(emp_inc_min,Tax(earn_princ,emp_inc_sch))>350000+(Married*(earn_princ -(earn_princ>0)*MAX(emp_inc_min,Tax(earn_princ, emp_inc_sch))<=s_spouse_al_ceil)+Children>0)*((Married*(earn_princ -(earn_princ>0)*MAX(emp_inc_min,Tax(earn_princ, emp_inc_sch))<=s_spouse_al_ceil)+Children)*350000+320000))*Positive(Tax(Positive(earn_spouse-tax_al_spouse),local_sch)-IF(Positive(earn_spouse-tax_al_spouse)>2000000,MAXA(2500,((Positive(earn_spouse-tax_al_spouse)-MAX(emp_inc_min,Tax(earn_princ,emp_inc_sch)))-(Positive(earn_spouse-tax_al_spouse)-2000000))*5%),MINA((Positive(earn_spouse-tax_al_spouse)-MAX(emp_inc_min,Tax(earn_princ,emp_inc_sch))),Positive(earn_spouse-tax_al_spouse))*5%))

Line in country table and intermediate steps		Variable name	Range	Equation
			S	(earn_spouse - (earn_spouse>0)*MAX(emp_inc_min,Tax(earn_spouse, emp_inc_sch))>350000)*(pref_per_cap+mun_per_cap+Positive(Tax(local_tax_inc_spouse,local_sch)-IF(local_tax_inc_spouse>2000000,MAXA(2500,((local_tax_inc_spouse-tax_inc_spouse)-(local_tax_inc_spouse-2000000))*5%),MINA((local_tax_inc_spouse-tax_inc_spouse),local_tax_inc_spouse)*5%)))
9.	Employees' soc security	SSC	B	SSC_pens*MIN(earn, pens_ceil)+SSC_sick*MIN(earn, sick_ceil)+SSC_unemp*earn
11.	Cash transfers	cash_trans	B	IF(Children>0,IF(Positive(princ_inc - princ_empl_inc)<Child_transfer_lim+(Child_transfer_lim_incr*Children), Child_transfer,Child_transfer2)*Children,0)
13.	Employer's social security	SSC_empr	B	SSC_pens*MIN(earn, pens_ceil)+SSC_sick*MIN(earn, sick_ceil)+(SSC_empr_unemp+SSC_empr_oth)*earn

Key to range of equation B calculated separately for both principal earner and spouse P calculated for principal only (value taken as 0 for spouse calculation).

Taxing Wages 2014
Changes in sructural labour income tax progressivity
over 2000-12 period in OECD member countries

Korea

This chapter includes data on the income taxes paid by workers, their social security contributions, the family benefits they receive in the form of cash transfers as well as the social security contributions and payroll taxes paid by their employers. Results reported include the marginal and average tax burden for eight different family types.

Methodological information is available for personal income tax systems, compulsory social security contributions to schemes operated within the government sector, universal cash transfers as well as recent changes in the tax/benefit system. The methodology also includes the parameter values and tax equations underlying the data.

Korea 2013

The tax/benefit position of single persons

		Wage level (per cent of average wage)	67	100	167	67
		Number of children	none	none	none	2
1.	**Gross wage earnings**		26553100	39829650	66382750	26553100
2.	**Standard tax allowances**					
	Basic allowance					
	Married or head of family					
	Dependent children					
	Deduction for social security contributions and income taxes					
	Work-related expenses					
	Other					
		Total	14433659	17034006	19982848	20433659
3.	**Tax credits or cash transfers included in taxable income**		0	0	0	0
4.	**Central government taxable income (1 - 2 + 3)**		12119441	22795645	46399902	6119441
5.	**Central government income tax liability (exclusive of tax credits)**		737916	2339347	5915977	367166
6.	**Tax credits**					
	Basic credit		346375	500000	500000	201942
	Married or head of family					
	Children					
	Other					
		Total	346375	500000	500000	201942
7.	**Central government income tax finally paid (5-6)**		391541	1839347	5415977	165225
8.	**State and local taxes**		39154	183935	541598	16522
9.	**Employees' compulsory social security contributions**					
	Gross earnings		2200694	3301041	4663711	2200694
	Taxable income					
		Total	2200694	3301041	4663711	2200694
10.	**Total payments to general government (7 + 8 + 9)**		2631389	5324322	10621285	2382441
11.	**Cash transfers from general government**					
	For head of family					
	For two children					
		Total	0	0	0	0
12.	**Take-home pay (1-10+11)**		23921711	34505328	55761466	24170659
13.	**Employer's compulsory social security contributions**		2718479	4077719	5958174	2718479
14.	**Average rates**					
	Income tax		1.6%	5.1%	9.0%	0.7%
	Employees' social security contributions		8.3%	8.3%	7.0%	8.3%
	Total payments less cash transfers		9.9%	13.4%	16.0%	9.0%
	Total tax wedge including employer's social security contributions		18.3%	21.4%	22.9%	17.4%
15.	**Marginal rates**					
	Total payments less cash transfers: Principal earner		17.1%	21.8%	27.9%	10.6%
	Total payments less cash transfers: Spouse		n.a.	n.a.	n.a.	n.a.
	Total tax wedge: Principal earner		24.8%	29.0%	31.8%	18.9%
	Total tax wedge: Spouse		n.a.	n.a.	n.a.	n.a.

Korea 2013

The tax/benefit position of married couples

	Wage level (per cent of average wage)	100-0	100-33	100-67	100-33
	Number of children	2	2	2	none
1.	**Gross wage earnings**	39829650	53106200	66382750	53106200
2.	**Standard tax allowances**				
	Basic allowance				
	Married or head of family				
	Dependent children				
	Deduction for social security contributions and income taxes				
	Work-related expenses				
	Other				
	Total	23534006	33769725	36967664	28769725
3.	**Tax credits or cash transfers included in taxable income**	0	0	0	0
4.	**Central government taxable income (1 - 2 + 3)**	16295645	19336475	29415086	24336475
5.	**Central government income tax liability (exclusive of tax credits)**	1364347	1681797	2286513	2431797
6.	**Tax credits**				
	Basic credit	500000	550847	834150	550847
	Married or head of family				
	Children				
	Other				
	Total	500000	550847	834150	550847
7.	**Central government income tax finally paid (5-6)**	864347	1130949	1452363	1880949
8.	**State and local taxes**	86435	113095	145236	188095
9.	**Employees' compulsory social security contributions**				
	Gross earnings	3301041	4401387	5501734	4401387
	Taxable income				
	Total	3301041	4401387	5501734	4401387
10.	**Total payments to general government (7 + 8 + 9)**	4251822	5645431	7099334	6470431
11.	**Cash transfers from general government**				
	For head of family				
	For two children				
	Total	0	0	0	0
12.	**Take-home pay (1-10+11)**	35577828	47460769	59283417	46635769
13.	**Employers' compulsory social security contributions**	4077719	5436958	6796198	5436958
14.	**Average rates**				
	Income tax	2.4%	2.3%	2.4%	3.9%
	Employees' social security contributions	8.3%	8.3%	8.3%	8.3%
	Total payments less cash transfers	10.7%	10.6%	10.7%	12.2%
	Total tax wedge including employer's social security contributions	19.0%	18.9%	19.0%	20.3%
15.	**Marginal rates**				
	Total payments less cash transfers: Principal earner	21.8%	21.8%	21.8%	21.8%
	Total payments less cash transfers: Spouse	10.5%	9.6%	11.8%	9.6%
	Total tax wedge: Principal earner	29.0%	29.0%	29.0%	29.0%
	Total tax wedge: Spouse	18.8%	18.0%	20.0%	18.0%

The national currency is the won (KRW). In 2013, KRW 1 094.93 was equal to USD 1, (2 Jan. 2013). In this year, the average worker is expected to earn KRW 39 829 650 (Secretariat estimate).

1. Personal income tax systems

1.1. Central government income tax system

1.1.1. Tax unit

Each individual is taxed on his/her own income.

Non-taxable wage income includes the:

- national pension, medical insurance, unemployment insurance and work injury insurance that are borne by employer;
- overtime payment to productive workers: up to KRW 2 400 000 of overwork payment of productive workers in manufacturing and mining sectors whose monthly wage is less than KRW 1 500 000 and whose yearly wage is less than 25 000 000.

1.1.2. Allowances and tax credits

1.1.2.1. Standard reliefs

- *Employment income deduction:* The following deduction from gross income is provided to wage and salary income earners:

Salary	Deduction
Up to KRW 5 000 000	80%
KRW 5 000 000 to KRW 15 000 000	KRW 4 000 000 plus 50% of the salary over KRW 5 000 000
KRW 15 000 000 to KRW 30 000 000	KRW 9 000 000 plus 15% of the salary over KRW 15 000 000
KRW 30 000 000 to KRW 45 000 000	KRW 11 250 000 plus 10% of the salary over KRW 30 000 000
Over KRW 45 000 000	KRW 12 750 000 plus 5% of the salary over KRW 45 000 000

- *Basic allowance:* A taxpayer can deduct KRW 1 500 000 from his/her income for each person who meets one of following conditions:
  - the taxpayer him/herself;
  - the taxpayer's spouse whose taxable income (gross earnings net of employment income deduction) is less than KRW 1 000 000;
  - the taxpayer's (including the spouse's) dependents (parents, siblings, children) within the same household whose income after accounting for the employment income deduction is less than KRW 1 000 000 and whose age is:

    1. parents: 60 years or older;
    2. brother/sister: 60 years or older or 20 years or younger;

3. children: 20 years or younger (if both partners in the household earn wage-income, this Report assumes that the principal wage earner will claim the allowance).

- *Additional allowance:* A taxpayer can deduct KRW 1 000 000 (500 000 in the case of (c), KRW 2 000 000 in the case of (b) and (e)) from his/her gross income when the taxpayer or his/her dependents fall into one of the following categories (for this report, only cases (c) and (d) are modelled):
  - a person aged 70 years or older (a);
  - a handicapped person (b);
  - a female wage earner who is the head of a household with dependents (but without spouse) or a female wage earner with spouse (in this Report,* any female wage earner is entitled to this allowance) (c);
  - a child aged 6 years or younger (in this Report, the allowance of KRW 1 000 000 is claimed by the principal wage earner in a household with children) (d);
  - Lineal descendants who are born or adopted during the concerned taxable year (the allowance is KRW 2 000 000 per child) (e);
  - a single parent with lineal descendants or adopted children who are eligible for basic exemption**(f);
- *Extra allowance for multiple children*: An income earner with two or more dependent children eligible for basic allowance may deduct from gross income KRW 1 000 000 if there are (at least) 2 children plus an additional KRW 2 000 000 for every additional child.
- *National pension deduction*: Employees can deduct 100 per cent of their National Pension contributions.
- *Tax credits*: Wage and salary income earners obtain the following tax credit:

Calculated tax	Amount of tax credit
Up to KRW 500 000	55% of calculated tax
Over KRW 500 000	KRW 275 000 plus 30% of the calculated tax over KRW 500 000 (maximum credit: KRW 500 000)

1.1.2.2. Main non-standard tax reliefs

Wage and salary income earners may deduct from gross income the expenses for the following items during the tax year:

- *Insurance premiums* (a): The general insurance premium up to KRW 1 000 000, as well as the Medical insurance premium and the Unemployment insurance premium can be entirely (100 per cent) deducted from taxable income.
- *Medical expenses* (b): Up to KRW 7 000 000. Full deductions are allowed for medical expenses exceeding 3 per cent of taxable income for the taxpayer himself, taxpayer's dependents who are aged 65 years or older and handicapped persons.
- *Educational expenses* (c): Tuition fees for pre-school, elementary, middle school and college (but the graduate school fee deduction is allowed only for the taxpayer himself),

* The calculations for Korea assume that the husband is the principal and that the wife is the spouse.

** Overlapping deductions for (c) and (f) are not allowed. If a resident belongs to both of the classes, he/she shall be deemed to belong to class (f) only.

either for the taxpayer himself or his/her dependents (including the taxpayer's spouse, children, and siblings), can be deducted from gross income. The deductible amount is 100 per cent for the taxpayer himself. For the taxpayer's dependents, the maximum deductions are as follows:

- for pre-school: up to KRW 3 000 000 per child;
- for elementary, middle and high school: up to KRW 3 000 000 per student;
- for college/university: up to KRW 9 000 000 per student.

- *Saving/Payment for housing* (d): The full amount of the interest paid on a long-term mortgage loan for buying a house which is not more than $85m^2$ in area and KRW 300 million in value; 40 per cent of the amount contributed to a savings account for housing by a non-homeowner; 50 per cent of the monthly rent or the principal and interest of a loan for leasing a house paid or repaid by a non-homeowner. The sum of the deductible amounts above shall not exceed KRW 15 million.
- *Charities* (e):
  - donations to a government body, donations for national defence, natural disaster, and certain charitable associations: total amount up to gross income is deductible;
  - donations to public welfare or religious associations: up to thirty per cent of gross income.
- *Credit card purchases* (f): Employees may deduct 15 per cent of their credit card (30 per cent of their debit card, prepaid card or cash receipt) purchases that exceed 25 per cent of their total income to a maximum of the lesser of KRW 3 000 000 or 20 per cent of their total income. However, for expenditures spent for traditional markets and public transportation, the allowed deduction is equivalent to 30 per cent of the expenditure and the ceiling is raised by an additional KRW 1 000 000 for each.
- Insurance premiums, medical expenses, education expenses, loans for house, designated donations, saving deposits for housing subscription, investment in employee stock ownership associations or in associations for investment in start-ups, and credit cards are allowed income deduction with a ceiling at KRW 25 000 000 in total. However, for the amount of designated donations exceeding the ceiling, deduction can be carried forward for 5 years.
- *Lump-sum tax relief*: Any taxpayer whose total deductible expense for (a), (b), (c), (d) and (e) is not over KRW 1 000 000 may deduct KRW 1 000 000 from gross income as a lump-sum tax relief.

1.1.3. *Tax schedule*

Over (KRW)	Not more than (KRW)	Marginal tax rate (%)
0	12 000 000	6
12 000 000	46 000 000	15
46 000 000	88 000 000	24
88 000 000	300 000 000	35
300 000 000		38

1.2. *Local income tax*

1.2.1. *Tax base*

The local income tax base is the income tax paid to the central government.

1.2.2. *Tax rate*

A uniform rate of 10 per cent is applied. However, the local government can adjust the rate between the lower limit of 5 per cent and the upper limit of 15 per cent.

1.2.3. *Tax rate (selected for this study)*

A country-wide rate of 10 per cent is used in this Report.

2. Compulsory social security contribution to schemes operated within the government sector

2.1. Employees' contribution

2.1.1. *National pension*

The National pension contribution rate is 4.5 per cent of the standardised average monthly wage income as of 2013.

The scope of the standardised average monthly wage income is from KRW 250 000 to KRW 3 980 000 as of 1 July 2013.

2.1.2. *Medical insurance*

The Medical insurance premium, which has a rate of 3.1378975 per cent (Health insurance: 2.945%, Long term care insurance: 6.55% of Health insurance premium rate), is levied on average monthly wage income as of 1 January 2013.

The scope of the average monthly wage income is from KRW 280 000 to KRW 78 100 000.

2.1.3. *Unemployment insurance*

0.65 per cent of gross income.

2.1.4. *Industrial accident compensation insurance (premiums)*

Compulsory application, premiums paid only by employers.

2.2. Employers' contribution

2.2.1. *National pension*

The national pension contribution rate is 4.5 per cent of the standardised average monthly wage income as of 2013.

The scope of the standardised average monthly wage income is from KRW 250 000 to KRW 3 980 000 as of 1 July 2013.

If the average monthly wage income of a person is less than KRW 250 000, the average monthly wage income of the person is regarded as KRW 250 000 and the rate (0.045) is applied. If the average monthly wage income of a person is more than KRW 3 980 000, the average monthly wage income of the person is regarded as KRW 3 980 000 and the rate (0.045) is applied; so the maximum of the national pension contribution per year is KRW 2 149 200 (= KRW 3 980 000 x 0.045 x 12 months).

2.2.2. *Medical insurance*

The Medical insurance premium, which has a rate of 3.1378975 per cent (Health insurance: 2.945%, Long term care insurance: 6.55% of Health insurance premium rate), is levied on average monthly wage income as of 1 January 2013.

The scope of the average monthly wage income is from KRW 280 000 to KRW 78 100 000.

2.2.3. *Unemployment insurance*

- the insurance premium is between 0.9 per cent and 1.5 per cent of total wage;
- the insurance premium selected for this study is 0.9 per cent.

2.2.4. *Work injury insurance*

- the insurance premium consists of an industry-specific rate which is set by the Ministry of Employment and Labour multiplied by total wage;
- the average rate of all industries (selected for this study) is 1.70 per cent.

3. Universal cash transfers

- Child benefit

Child benefit is paid every month to those who have children aged 5 years or younger: KRW 200 000 for a child aged 12 months or younger, KRW 150 000 for a child aged 1 to 2 years and KRW 100 000 for a child aged 2 to 5 years.

If a child attends a nursery or pre-school, childcare benefit is paid instead every month: KRW 394 000 for a child aged 0, KRW 347 000 for a child aged 1 year, KRW 286 000 for a child aged 2 years and KRW 220 000 for a child aged 3 to 5 years.

The above child benefits are not included in the *Taxing Wages* calculations that consider children aged between 6 and 11 inclusive.

4. Main changes in tax/benefit system since 2000

2000	Contribution to National Pension are to be deductible from 2001, upper cap of employment income deduction limit (KRW 12 000 000) is abolished from 2001
2001	Personal income tax rates are lowered by 10% (10, 20 ,30, 40% were reduced to 9, 18, 27, 36%, respectively) from 2002
2002	Limits of deduction for education fees are expanded from 2003. For pre-school: from KRW 1 000 000 to KRW 1 500 000. For elementary, middle school and high school: from KRW 1 500 000 to KRW 2 000 000. For college and university: from KRW 3 000 000 to KRW 5 000 000. Limit of deduction for interest of long-term mortgage loan for housing is expanded from KRW 3 000 000 to KRW 6 000 000 from 2003
2003	Employment income deduction and tax credit applicable to low income are increased. The deduction rate for the taxable wage income range of KRW 5 000 000 to KRW 15 000 000 is increased from 45 per cent to 47.5 per cent. The tax credit rate for calculated tax below KRW 500 000 is increased from 45% to 50% and the maximum tax credit is increased from KRW 400 000 to KRW 450 000.
2004	Limits of deduction for education fees are expanded. For pre-school: from KRW 1 500 000 to KRW 2 000 000. For college and university: from KRW 5 000 000 to KRW 7 000 000. Limit of deduction for interest on long-term mortgage loan for housing is expanded from KRW 6 000 000 to KRW 10 000 000. The marginal deduction rate for the taxable wage income range from KRW 5 000 000 to KRW 15 000 000 is increased from 47.5 per cent to 50 per cent. The tax credit rate for tax amounts below KRW 500 000 is increased from 50% to 55% and the maximum permitted tax credit goes up from KRW 450 000 to KRW 500 000.
2005	Personal income tax rates are lowered by 1% point (9, 18, 27, 36% were reduced to 8, 17, 26, 35%, respectively). Lump-sum tax relief are expanded from KRW 600 000 to KRW 1 000 000.

2007	Eligibility for the extra allowance amount has been changed. Previously, an income earner with a small number of dependents (e.g., spouse, child) eligible for basic allowance was eligible for an allowance of up to KRW 1 000 000 depending on the number of dependents. As from 2007, however, an income earner with two or more dependent children eligible for basic allowance is eligible for an allowance equivalent to KRW 500,000 if there are 2 children plus an additional KRW 1 000 000 for every additional child (e.g. 2 children: KRW 500 000; 3 children: KRW 1 500 000; 4 children: KRW 2 500 000, etc.).
2008	Tax schedule has been changed: from KRW 10 000 000, KRW 40 000 000 , KRW 80 000 000 to KRW 12 000 000, KRW 46 000 000, KRW 88 000 000; New items have been added to the additional allowance with respect to lineal descendants who are born or adopted during the concerned taxable year; Credit card purchase deduction has been changed : Employees may deduct 20 per cent (previously 15%) of their credit/debit card purchases that exceed 20 per cent (previously 15%) of their total income; Deduction for donations to public welfare or religious associations has been increased up to 15% of gross income. Previously, the limit was 10% of gross income.
2009	Personal income tax rates have been changed: from 8%, 17%, 26%, 35% to 6%, 16%, 25%, and 35%. Employment income deduction has been changed: from 100%, 50%, 15% and 10%, 5% to 80%, 50%, 15% and 10%, 5%.
2010	Personal income tax rates have been changed: from 6%, 16%, 25%, 35% to 6%, 15%, 24%, and 35%.
2012	Personal income tax rates have been changed: from 6%, 15%, 24%, and 35% to 6%, 15%, 24%, 35% and 38%.
2013	• A new additional allowance is added: a single parent with lineal descendants or adopted children who are eligible for basic exemption can deduct KRW 1 000 000. • Insurance premiums, medical expenses, education expenses, loans for house, designated donations, saving deposits for housing subscription, investment in employee stock ownership associations or in associations for investment in start-ups, and credit cards are allowed income deduction with a ceiling at KRW 25 000 000 in total. However, for the amount of designated donations exceeding the ceiling, deduction can be carried forward for 5 years.

5. Memorandum Item

5.1. *Identification of the Average Worker (AW)*

Sectors used: Industry Sectors B-N with reference to the International Standard Industrial Classification of All Economic Activities, Revision 4 (ISIC Rev. 4).

Geographical coverage: Whole country

Type of workers: Wage workers (male and female).

5.2. *Method to calculate wages*

Report on Labour Force Survey at Establishments covering data in 2013 by the Ministry of Employment and Labour is used to calculate the annual wages of the AW. The statistics were obtained through a sample survey of 12 000 firms with five or more permanent employees throughout the whole country.

Basic method of calculation used: average monthly wages multiplied by 12.

5.3. *Employer's reserve for employee's retirement payment*

An employer should pay to a retiree the retirement payment which is not less than 30 days' wage and salary per one year of service (about 8.3 per cent of gross income or more). An employer can contribute to the Retirement Payment Reserve Fund established within the company or Retirement Insurance Fund established outside the company to prepare for the retirement payment. Such contribution is treated as business expense under certain constraints. Because contribution to the Retirement Fund is not compulsory, this survey does not include such contribution except the contribution converted to employer's contribution to the national pension plan (see Section 2.2.1).

2013 parameter values

Average earnings/yr	Ave_earn	39 829 650	Secretariat estimate
Tax allowances	basic_al	1 500 000	
spouse	spouse_al	1 500 000	
dependents including children	dep_al	1 500 000	
extra allowance 1	ext1_all	1 000 000	
extra allowance 2	ext2_all	2 000 000	
additional allowance	add_all	500 000	
additional allowance 2	add2_all	1 000 000	
additional allowance 3	Add3_all	1 000 000	
Main non-standard tax relief	lump_sum	1 000 000	
max number of kids permitted to be under 6	child_und 6 _max	1	
Employment income deduction	empdedsch	0	0.8
		5 000 000	0.5
		15 000 000	0.15
		30 000 000	0.1
		45 000 000	0.05
Tax credit threshold	tax_thresh	500 000	
maximum credit	cred_max	500 000	
tax credit rate 1	cred_rate1	0.55	
tax credit rate 2	cred_rate2	0.3	
Tax schedule	tax_sch	0.06	12 000 000
		0.15	46 000 000
		0.24	88 000 000
		0.35	300 000 000
		0.38	
Local tax rate	local_rate	0.1	
Social security contributions	SSC_pens	0.045	
	SSC_pens_max	2 149 200	
	SSC_sick	0.031379	
	SSC_sick_max	29 408 375	
	SSC_unemp	0.0065	
Employer contributions	emp_pens	0.045	
	emp_sick	0.031379	
	emp_unemp	0.009	
	emp_inj	0.0170	

2013 tax equations

The equations for the Korean system are independent between spouses except that the principal earner has tax allowances for the spouse and for any children.

The functions which are used in the equations (Taper, MIN, Tax, etc.) are described in the technical note about tax equations. Variable names are defined in the table of parameters above, within the equations table, or are the standard variables married and children. A reference to a variable with the affix total indicates the sum of the relevant variable values for the principal and spouse. And the affixes princ and spouse indicate the value for the principal and spouse, respectively. Equations for a single person are as shown for the principal, with spouse values taken as 0.

Line in country table and intermediate steps		Variable name	Range	Equation
1.	Earnings	earn		
2.	Allowances:			
	employment income	emp_al	B	Empincded(earn, empincdedsch)
	basic	bas_al	B	basic_al
	spouse	sp_al	P	Married*spouse_al*(earn_spouse-emp_al_spouse<=spouse_al)
	dependents	dp_al	P	Children*dep_al
	extra and additional allowances	ext_al_princ	P	IF(Children=2,ext1_all,IF(Children>=3,ext1_all+(Children-2)*ext2_all,0))+(Children>0)*add2_all+
		!!!!!!voir chngt ligne!!!!!!!		MIN(Chidren, child_und6_max1)*add2_all + IF(AND(Married=0,Children>0), add3_all,0)
	extra and additional allowances	ext_al_spouse	S	(earn_spouse>0)*add_all
	national pension deduction	np_de	B	Min(earn*SSC_pens, SSC_pens_max)
	lump-sum	lump_sum	B	IF(earn*(SSC_sick+SSC_unemp)>lump_sum,earn*(SSC_sick+SSC_unemp),lump_sum)
	Total	tax_al	B	emp_al+bas_al+sp_al+dp_al+ext_al+np_al+lump_sum
3.	Credits in taxable income	taxbl_cr	B	0
4.	CG taxable income	tax_inc	B	Positive(earn-tax_al)
5.	CG tax before credits	CG_tax_excl	B	Tax(tax_inc, tax_sch)
6.	Tax credits :	tax_cr	B	IF(CG_tax_excl<=tax_thresh, cred_rate1* CG_tax_excl, MIN((cred_rate1*tax_thresh+ cred_rate2*(CG_tax_excl-tax_thresh)), cred_max))
7.	CG tax	CG_tax	B	CG_tax_excl-tax_cr
8.	State and local taxes	local_tax	B	local_rate*CG_tax
9.	Employees' soc security	SSC	B	MIN(earn*(SSC_pens),SSC_pens_max)+MIN(earn*(SSC_sick),SSC_sick_max)+earn*(SSC_unemp)
11.	Cash transfers	cash_trans	J	
13.	Employer's soc security	SSC_empr	B	MIN(earn*(SSC_pens),SSC_pens_max)+MIN(earn*(emp_sick),SSC_sick_max)+earn*(emp_unemp+emp_inj)

Key to range of equation:
B calculated separately for both principal earner and spouse.
P calculated for principal only (value taken as 0 for spouse calculation).
S calculated for spouse only.
J calculated once only on a joint basis.

Taxing Wages 2014
Changes in sructural labour income tax progressivity
over 2000-12 period in OECD member countries

Luxembourg

This chapter includes data on the income taxes paid by workers, their social security contributions, the family benefits they receive in the form of cash transfers as well as the social security contributions and payroll taxes paid by their employers. Results reported include the marginal and average tax burden for eight different family types.

Methodological information is available for personal income tax systems, compulsory social security contributions to schemes operated within the government sector, universal cash transfers as well as recent changes in the tax/ benefit system. The methodology also includes the parameter values and tax equations underlying the data.

Luxembourg 2013

The tax/benefit position of single persons

	Wage level (per cent of average wage)	67	100	167	67
	Number of children	none	none	none	2
1.	**Gross wage earnings**	35268	52902	88170	35268
2.	**Standard tax allowances**				
	Basic allowance	480	480	480	480
	Married or head of family				
	Dependent children				
	Deduction for social security contributions and income taxes	3897	5846	9743	3897
	Work-related expenses	540	540	540	540
	Other	0	0	0	0
	Total	4917	6866	10763	4917
3.	**Tax credits or cash transfers included in taxable income**	0	0	0	0
4.	**Central government rounded taxable income (1 - 2 + 3)**	30350	46000	77400	30350
5.	**Central government income tax liability (exclusive of tax credits)**	3472	9269	22372	1653
6.	**Tax credits**				
	Basic credit	300	300	300	300
	Married or head of family				
	Children				
	Other	0	0	0	750
	Total	300	300	300	1050
7.	**Central government income tax finally paid (5-6)**	3172	8969	22072	603
8.	**State and local taxes**	0	0	0	0
9.	**Employees' compulsory social security contributions**				
	Gross earnings	4312	6508	10898	4312
	Taxable income				
	Total	4312	6508	10898	4312
10.	**Total payments to general government (7 + 8 + 9)**	7484	15476	32970	4915
11.	**Cash transfers from general government**				
	For head of family				
	For two children	0	0	0	7522
	Total	0	0	0	7522
12.	**Take-home pay (1-10+11)**	27784	37426	55200	37875
13.	**Employer's compulsory social security contributions**	4341	6512	10854	4341
14.	**Average rates**				
	Income tax	9.0%	17.0%	25.0%	1.7%
	Employees' social security contributions	12.2%	12.3%	12.4%	12.2%
	Total payments less cash transfers	21.2%	29.3%	37.4%	-7.4%
	Total tax wedge including employer's social security contributions	29.9%	37.0%	44.3%	4.4%
15.	**Marginal rates**				
	Total payments less cash transfers: Principal earner	39.1%	49.6%	49.6%	41.0%
	Total payments less cash transfers: Spouse	n.a.	n.a.	n.a.	n.a.
	Total tax wedge: Principal earner	45.8%	55.1%	55.1%	47.5%
	Total tax wedge: Spouse	n.a.	n.a.	n.a.	n.a.

Luxembourg 2013

The tax/benefit position of married couples

			100-0	100-33	100-67	100-33
	Wage level (per cent of average wage)		100-0	100-33	100-67	100-33
	Number of children		2	2	2	none
1.	**Gross wage earnings**		52902	70536	88170	70536
2.	**Standard tax allowances**					
	Basic allowance		480	960	960	960
	Married or head of family					
	Dependent children					
	Deduction for social security contributions and income taxes		5846	7794	9743	7794
	Work-related expenses		540	1080	1080	1080
	Other		0	4500	4500	4500
		Total	6866	14334	16283	14334
3.	**Tax credits or cash transfers included in taxable income**		0	0	0	0
4.	**Central government rounded taxable income (1 - 2 + 3)**		46000	56200	71850	56200
5.	**Central government income tax liability (exclusive of tax credits)**		3308	5707	10518	5707
6.	**Tax credits**					
	Basic credit		300	600	600	600
	Married or head of family					
	Children					
	Other		0	0	0	0
		Total	300	600	600	600
7.	**Central government income tax finally paid (5-6)**		3008	5107	9918	5107
8.	**State and local taxes**		0	0	0	0
9.	**Employees' compulsory social security contributions**					
	Gross earnings		6508	8624	10820	8624
	Taxable income					
		Total	6508	8624	10820	8624
10.	**Total payments to general government (7 + 8 + 9)**		9515	13731	20737	13731
11.	**Cash transfers from general government**					
	For head of family					
	For two children		7522	7522	7522	0
		Total	7522	7522	7522	0
12.	**Take-home pay (1-10+11)**		50908	64327	74955	56805
13.	**Employer's compulsory social security contributions**		6512	8683	10854	8683
14.	**Average rates**					
	Income tax		5.7%	7.2%	11.2%	7.2%
	Employees' social security contributions		12.3%	12.2%	12.3%	12.2%
	Total payments less cash transfers		3.8%	8.8%	15.0%	19.5%
	Total tax wedge including employer's social security contributions		14.3%	18.8%	24.3%	28.3%
15.	**Marginal rates**					
	Total payments less cash transfers: Principal earner		31.5%	35.3%	42.9%	35.3%
	Total payments less cash transfers: Spouse		25.6%	35.3%	42.9%	35.3%
	Total tax wedge: Principal earner		39.0%	42.4%	49.2%	42.4%
	Total tax wedge: Spouse		33.7%	42.4%	49.2%	42.4%

The national currency is the euro (EUR). In 2013, EUR 0.75 equalled USD 1. The Secretariat has estimated that in that same year the average worker earned EUR 52 902 (Secretariat estimate).

1. Personal income tax systems

1.1. *Taxes levied by central government*

1.1.1. *Tax unit*

Spouses and partners are taxed jointly on their income. The income of minor children is included in determining the couple's taxable income. However, any earned income that children may derive from work is excluded from joint taxation.

1.1.2. *Tax reliefs and tax credits*

1.1.2.1. Standard reliefs in the form of deductions from income

- Wage-earners are entitled to a standard minimum deduction of EUR 540 for work-related expenses other than travel, unless their actual deductible expenses are higher. This deduction is doubled for spouses taxed jointly.
- The first 4 distance units (i.e. 4 * 99 = EUR 396 per year) of the lump sum deduction for travel expenses between a taxpayer's home and his working places are abolished. The maximum deduction will be limited to EUR 2 574 per year.
- Like other taxpayers, wage-earners having no special expenses (interest charges, insurance premiums or contributions other than for social security) may take a standard deduction of EUR 480 for special expenses. Actual insurance premiums are deductible up to the limit set by law.
- If both spouses have earned income and are taxed jointly, they qualify for an earned income allowance of EUR 4 500.
- Social security contributions: contributions paid to compulsory health insurance and pension schemes are deductible in full.
- Dependency insurance: the dependency contribution is not deductible for income tax purposes.

1.1.2.2. Standard reliefs in the form of tax credits

- Wage-earners and pensioners receive a refundable tax credit of EUR 300 per annum.
- Single-parents receive a refundable tax credit of EUR 750 per annum.

1.1.2.3. Non-standard allowances deductible from taxable income

- Interest charges are deductible insofar as they are not considered operating expenses or acquisition expenses, and provided they are unrelated economically to the exempt income. However, the deduction of interest charges is capped at EUR 336 per year. This ceiling is increased by EUR 336 for the taxpayer's spouse/partner and for each child.

- Taxpayers may deduct premiums paid to insurers licensed in an EU country in respect of life, death, accident, disability, illness or liability insurance, as well as dues paid to recognised mutual assistance companies. However, deductions are capped at EUR 672 per year.
- Payments to an insurance company or credit institution in respect of an individual retirement scheme are deductible. These payments are capped according to the subscriber's age and must meet certain investment policy constraints. The ceiling varies between EUR 1 500 and EUR 3 200. Each spouse/partner may take out such a contract and qualify for the respective ceilings.
- Contributions to building society savings are deductible up to the limit of EUR 672.
- Interest charges in respect of the rental value of owner-occupied housing are deductible only up to an annual ceiling. During the first five years, the ceiling is EUR 1 500; for the following five years it is EUR 1 125; thereafter it is EUR 750. These ceilings are increased by an equal amount for the taxpayer's spouse/partner, and for each qualifying child.
- As from 1 January 2009, the maximal deduction of premium related to the mortgage life insurance on the taxpayer's principal residence is EUR 6 000. This ceiling is increased by an equal amount for the taxpayer's spouse/partner and by 1 200 for each qualifying child. For taxpayers over the age of 30, the allowable deduction of EUR 6 000 is increased by 8% for each year over 30, with a ceiling of 160%.
- Upon request, taxpayers may be granted exemptions for extraordinary expenses that are unavoidable, and that considerably reduce their ability to pay taxes (e.g. uninsured health care costs, support for needy relatives, uninsured funeral costs beyond the taxpayer's means, domestic or childcare expenses, expenses for children outside the taxpayer's household, or expenses for children in a single-parent household).

1.1.3. *Tax schedule reliefs*

Income tax is determined on the basis of the following schedule (amounts in Euros):

0% for the portion of income between 11 265
8% for the portion of income between 11 265 and 13 173
10% for the portion of income between 13 173 and 15 081
12% for the portion of income between 15 081 and 16 989
14% for the portion of income between 16 989 and 18 897
16% for the portion of income between 18 897 and 20 805
18% for the portion of income between 20 805 and 22 713
20% for the portion of income between 22 713 and 24 621
22% for the portion of income between 24 621 and 26 529
24% for the portion of income between 26 529 and 28 437
26% for the portion of income between 28 437 and 30 345
28% for the portion of income between 30 345 and 32 253
30% for the portion of income between 32 253 and 34 161
32% for the portion of income between 34 161 and 36 069
34% for the portion of income between 36 069 and 37 977
36% for the portion of income between 37 977 and 39 885
38% for the portion of income between 39 885 and 41 793
39% for the portion of income between 41 793 and 100 000
40% for the portion exceeding 100 000

The income tax liability of *single* taxpayers is determined by applying the above schedule to taxable income.

The income tax liability of *married* taxpayers and partners corresponds to double the amount obtained if the above schedule is applied to half of their income (class 2).

For widow(er)s, taxpayers with a dependent child allowance and persons over 64 years of age (class 1a), tax is calculated as follows: the schedule is applied to adjusted taxable income reduced by half of the difference between that amount and EUR 45 060, with the marginal tax rate capped at 40%.

Income tax as determined by the applicable schedules is subject to a 7% "solidarity" surtax to finance the employment fund. The rate is 9% for the taxable income exceeding EUR 150 000 (tax classes 1 and 1a), respectively EUR 300 000 (tax class 2).

1.1.4. *Income exemptions*

A taxpayer may claim a deduction for a dependent child under 21 years of age who is not part of the household. This deduction is allowed for expenses actually incurred but may not exceed EUR 3 480.

1.2. *Local (municipal) taxes*

No particular income tax is levied by municipalities, which receive a direct share of the income tax revenue collected by the State. This share is equal to 18% of tax revenue.

2. Compulsory social security contributions to schemes operated within the government sector

	Employer's share (%)	Employee's share (%)	Ceiling on contributions (in euros)
a) Pension and disability insurance	8	8	112 451.28
b) Health insurance	3.05	3.05	112 451.28
c) Dependency insurance		1.4	Monthly allowance 468.55[1]
d) Health in the workplace	0.11		
e) Accident insurance	1.15		

1. (Monthly allowance: EUR 468.55 = 0.25* social minimum salary/12). The social minimum salary in 2013 is equal to EUR 22 490.28.

No distinction is made according to family status or gender.

As from 1 January 2009 the differences in social security contributions between workers and employees are abolished.

3. Universal cash transfers

3.1. *For married persons*

None.

3.2. *For dependent children*

Every child raised in the Grand Duchy entitles the person on whom the child is dependent to a monthly family allowance. Family allowances are adjusted regularly for the cost of living. For 2013, the amounts are:

Effective date	As of 1 July 2006
1 eligible child	EUR 185.60
2 eligible children	EUR 440.72
3 eligible children	EUR 802.74

Starting with the fourth eligible child, the allowance is raised by EUR 361.82 per child.

The amounts indicated above are increased by EUR 16.17 for children aged 6 to 11 and by EUR 48.52 for those aged 12 years or older.

Additionally, a child bonus amounting to EUR 76.88 per child per month is paid in cash irrespective of the taxable income of the parents as from 1 January 2009. This amount is paid by the National Family Benefits Administration.

4. Main changes since 2008

4.1. *Partnerships*

The Act of 9 July 2004 introduced the notion of partnerships into tax law. The Act construes the term "partnership" as a relationship between two persons, called "partners", of opposite sex or the same sex, who live together as a couple and declare themselves as such.

As from 1 January 2008, the fiscal treatment of the partnerships is modified. The deduction for extraordinary expenses is replaced by the joint taxation of partners as it already exists for spouses.

4.2. *Introduction of tax credits*

The following changes were made as of 1 January 2009:

- Four tax allowances have been replaced by refundable tax credits. Instead of reducing their taxable income by EUR 600, wage-earners get a tax credit of EUR 300 per annum. A similar tax credit is allowed for pensioners.
- The tax exemption of EUR 1 920 for single-parent households is replaced by a tax credit of EUR 750 per annum.
- A tax credit of EUR 300 per annum is granted to self-employed persons deriving income from trade or business, income from agriculture and forestry or income from self-employment. This tax credit substitutes the allowance for business income and the agricultural allowance.

5. Memorandum item

5.1. *Identification of the average worker*

Average gross hourly wages by industry and by gender are determined on the basis of biannual surveys on industry wages and working hours. These surveys cover gross compensation for regular hours (working hours + leave time) plus overtime pay. Hourly wages include bonuses and allowances such as premiums for output, production or productivity. In contrast, non-periodic compensation (bonuses, profit-sharing) that is not paid systematically in each pay period is not included. Nevertheless, in order to allow for comparisons between countries, gross annual pay is adjusted on the basis of average non-periodic compensation as calculated from triennial surveys of labour costs.

Regarding working hours, the time taken into account is the time effectively offered, including regular working hours, overtime, night shifts and work on Sunday.

2013 parameter values

Average earnings/yr	Ave_earn	52 902	Secretariat estimate
Tax allowances: general	gen_dedn	480	
professional expenses	prof_exp	540	
travel expenses	travel_exp	0	
extra if both spouses earning	extra_dedn	4 500	
Low earner allowance	allow_1		
Low earner allowance (couples)	allow_2		
Class 1a limit	cl_1a_lim	45 060	
Tax schedule	tax_sch	0	11 265
		0.08	13 173
		0.1	15 081
		0.12	16 989
		0.14	18 897
		0.16	20 805
		0.18	22 713
		0.2	24 621
		0.22	26 529
		0.24	28 437
		0.26	30 345
		0.28	32 253
		0.3	34 161
		0.32	36 069
		0.34	37 977
		0.36	39 885
		0.38	41 793
		0.39	100 000
		0.40	
Child credit maximum	ch_cred	0	
Social Minimum Salary	min_salary	22 490.28	
Multiplier for unemployment	unemp_rate_1	1.07	
	Unemp_rate_2	1.09	
	Unemp_lim	150 000	
Social security contributions	SSC_rate	0.1105	
	SSC_ceil	112 451.28	
	infirm	0.014	
	infirm_abatement	0.25	
Employer contributions	workhealth	0.0011	
	SSC_empr	0.1105	
	SSC_acc	0.0115	
Child benefit (1 child)	CB_1	185.6	
2 children	CB_2	440.72	
extra age 6-11	CB_ex	16.17	
Child bonus	ch_bonus	922.50	
Worker tax credit	worker_credit	300	
Single parent tax credit	cr_monoparent	750	
Class 1a Discount	discount	0.5	
Maximum Marginal Rate	max_rate	0.40	

2013 tax equations

The equations for the Luxembourg system are on a joint basis except for social security contributions.

The functions which are used in the equations (Taper, MIN, Tax, etc.) are described in the technical note about tax equations. Variable names are defined in the table of parameters above, within the equations table, or are the standard variables "married" and "children". A reference to a variable with the affix "_total" indicates the sum of the relevant variable values for the principal and spouse. And the affixes "_princ" and "_spouse" indicate the value for the principal and spouse, respectively. Equations for a single person are as shown for the principal, with "_spouse" values taken as 0.

	Line in country table and intermediate steps	Variable name	Range	Equation
1.	Earnings	earn		
2.	Allowances:			
	Basic	basic	J	IF(earn_spouse=0, 1, 2)*gen_dedn
	work-related	work_rel	J	IF(earn_spouse=0, 1, 2)*(prof_exp)
	Other	other_al	J	(earn_spouse>0)*extra_dedn
	Total	tax_al	J	min(basic+work_rel+other_al+SSC_ded_total, earn)
3.	Credits in taxable income	taxbl_cr	J	0
	family quotient	quotient	J	1+Married
4.	CG taxable income unadjusted taxable income	tax_inc	J	earn-tax_al
5.	CG tax before credits	tax_excl	J	((Children=0)*IF(Married=0,Tax(tax_inc, tax_sch), quotient*Tax(tax_inc/quotient, tax_sch)) + (Children>0)*IF(Married=0, Taxclass1a(tax_inc, tax_sch, discount, cl_1a_lim, max_rate), quotient*Tax(tax_inc/quotient, tax_sch)))*IF(tax_inc>unemp_lim*(1+Married,unemp_rate_2,unemp_rate_1)
6.	Tax credits :	worker_cr	J	IF(earn_spouse=0,1,2)*worker_credit
		monoparent_cr	J	cr_monoparent*(AND(Married=0,Children>0))
		tax_cr	J	worker_cr+monoparent_cr
7.	CG tax	CG_tax	J	tax_excl-tax_cr
8.	State and local taxes	local_tax	J	0
9.	Employees' soc security	SSC	B	SSC_rate*MIN(earn, SSC_ceil)+infirm*Positive(earn-infirm_abatement*min_salary)
	deductible portion	SSC_ded	B	SSC_rate*MIN(earn, SSC_ceil)
11.	Cash transfers	cash_trans	J	((Children=1)*(CB_1+CB_ex)+(Children=2)*(CB_2+2*CB_ex))*12+Children*ch_bonus
13.	Employer's soc security	SSC_empr	B	(SSC_empr+workhealth)*MIN(earn, SSC_ceil)+SSC_acc*MIN(earn, SSC_ceil)

Key to range of equation B calculated separately for both principal earner and spouse P calculated for principal only (value taken as 0 for spouse calculation) J calculated once only on a joint basis.

Taxing Wages 2014
Changes in sructural labour income tax progressivity
over 2000-12 period in OECD member countries

Mexico

This chapter includes data on the income taxes paid by workers, their social security contributions, the family benefits they receive in the form of cash transfers as well as the social security contributions and payroll taxes paid by their employers. Results reported include the marginal and average tax burden for eight different family types.

Methodological information is available for personal income tax systems, compulsory social security contributions to schemes operated within the government sector, universal cash transfers as well as recent changes in the tax/ benefit system. The methodology also includes the parameter values and tax equations

Mexico 2013

The tax/benefit position of single persons

	Wage level (per cent of average wage)	67	100	167	67
	Number of children	none	none	none	2
1.	**Gross wage earnings**	65294	97941	163235	65294
2.	**Standard tax allowances**				
	Basic allowance	2162	2296	2564	2162
	Married or head of family				
	Dependent children				
	Deduction for social security contributions and income taxes				
	Work-related expenses				
	Other				
	Total	2162	2296	2564	2162
3.	**Tax credits or cash transfers included in taxable income**	0	0	0	0
4.	**Central government taxable income (1 - 2 + 3)**	63132	95645	160671	63132
5.	**Central government income tax liability (exclusive of tax credits)**	4338	8227	21010	4338
6.	**Tax credits**				
	Basic credit	3898	0	0	3898
	Married or head of family				
	Children				
	Other	0	0	0	0
	Total	3898	0	0	3898
7.	**Central government income tax finally paid (5-6)**	440	8227	21010	440
8.	**State and local taxes**	0	0	0	0
9.	**Employees' compulsory social security contributions**				
	Gross earnings	816	1332	2410	816
	Taxable income				
	Total	816	1332	2410	816
10.	**Total payments to general government (7 + 8 + 9)**	1256	9560	23420	1256
11.	**Cash transfers from general government**				
	For head of family				
	For two children	0	0	0	0
	Total	0	0	0	0
12.	**Take-home pay (1-10+11)**	64038	88381	139815	64038
13.	**Employers' compulsory social security contributions**	9053	11466	16415	9053
14.	**Average rates**				
	Income tax	0.7%	8.4%	12.9%	0.7%
	Employees' social security contributions	1.3%	1.4%	1.5%	1.3%
	Total payments less cash transfers	1.9%	9.8%	14.3%	1.9%
	Total tax wedge including employer's social security contributions	13.9%	19.2%	22.2%	13.9%
15.	**Marginal rates**				
	Total payments less cash transfers: Principal earner	12.1%	17.6%	22.9%	12.1%
	Total payments less cash transfers: Spouse	n.a.	n.a.	n.a.	n.a.
	Total tax wedge: Principal earner	17.4%	23.4%	28.4%	17.4%
	Total tax wedge: Spouse	n.a.	n.a.	n.a.	n.a.

Mexico 2013

The tax/benefit position of married couples

		100-0	100-33	100-67	100-33
	Wage level (per cent of average wage)	100-0	100-33	100-67	100-33
	Number of children	2	2	2	none
1.	**Gross wage earnings**	97941	130588	163235	130588
2.	**Standard tax allowances**				
	Basic allowance	2296	3772	4458	3772
	Married or head of family				
	Dependent children				
	Deduction for social security contributions and income taxes				
	Work-related expenses				
	Other				
	Total	2296	3772	4458	3772
3.	**Tax credits or cash transfers included in taxable income**	0	0	0	0
4.	**Central government taxable income (1 - 2 + 3)**	95645	126816	158777	126816
5.	**Central government income tax liability (exclusive of tax credits)**	8227	9955	12566	9955
6.	**Tax credits**				
	Basic credit	0	4882	3898	4882
	Married or head of family				
	Children				
	Other	0	0	0	0
	Total	0	4882	3898	4882
7.	**Central government income tax finally paid (5-6)**	8227	5073	8667	5073
8.	**State and local taxes**	0	0	0	0
9.	**Employees' compulsory social security contributions**				
	Gross earnings	1332	1740	2149	1740
	Taxable income				
	Total	1332	1740	2149	1740
10.	**Total payments to general government (7 + 8 + 9)**	9560	6814	10816	6814
11.	**Cash transfers from general government**				
	For head of family				
	For two children	0	0	0	0
	Total	0	0	0	0
12.	**Take-home pay (1-10+11)**	88381	123774	152419	123774
13.	**Employers' compulsory social security contributions**	11466	18403	20519	18403
14.	**Average rates**				
	Income tax	8.4%	3.9%	5.3%	3.9%
	Employees' social security contributions	1.4%	1.3%	1.3%	1.3%
	Total payments less cash transfers	9.8%	5.2%	6.6%	5.2%
	Total tax wedge including employer's social security contributions	19.2%	16.9%	17.1%	16.9%
15.	**Marginal rates**				
	Total payments less cash transfers: Principal earner	17.6%	17.6%	17.6%	17.6%
	Total payments less cash transfers: Spouse	-8.4%	7.4%	12.1%	7.4%
	Total tax wedge: Principal earner	23.4%	23.4%	23.4%	23.4%
	Total tax wedge: Spouse	10.6%	13.0%	17.4%	13.0%

The national currency is the peso (MXN). In 2013, MXN 12.77 is equal to USD 1. In 2013, the estimated earnings of the average worker are MXN 97 941 (Secretariat estimate).

1. Personal income tax

1.1. *Central government income tax*

1.1.1. *Tax unit*

Each person is taxed separately.

1.1.2. *Tax allowances and tax credits*

1.1.2.1. Standard tax reliefs

There are two basic allowances, a yearly holiday bonus and an end-of-year bonus.

- *Holiday Bonus:* Mexico's Labour Law stipulates a minimum holiday bonus of 25 per cent of six days of the worker's wage. The maximum exemption according to Tax Law is equivalent to 15 days of the minimum wage (the minimum wage for the whole country).* Given these two restrictions, the allowance is estimated as the minimum established by the Labour Law, up to the amount that is exempt according to Tax Law.
- *End-of-year bonus:* The minimum end-of-year bonus established in the Labour Law is 15 days of the worker's wage. Tax Law exempts end-of-year-bonuses up to 30 days of the minimum wage (the amount for the whole country). The allowance is estimated as the minimum established by the Labour Law, up to the amount that is exempt according to Tax Law.

1.1.2.2. Main non-standard tax reliefs

Deductions:

- Compulsory school transportation costs.
- Medical expenses (doctor and dental fees and hospital expenses): An unlimited deduction is allowed for the taxpayer's medical expenses. For those made by the taxpayer, on behalf of his or her spouse and straight line relatives, the deduction is allowed only if the person, for whom the taxpayer makes the expense, earns less than the minimum annual wage of his geographical area.
- Complementary contributions of certain retirement accounts are considered eligible as long as they do not exceed 10 per cent of taxable income and MXN 115 194 (five annual minimum wages).
- Funeral charges: for the spouse and straight-line relatives up to a minimum annual wage of the taxpayer's geographical area.

* There are two minimum wage rates established in Mexico depending upon geographical location (in Zone A the minimum wage is equal to MXN 64.76 on a daily basis and in Zone B it is MXN 61.38. For the purposes of this Report, the calculations are either based on the minimum wage that applies within the Federal District of Mexico City (Zone A) or a representative value for the country as a whole (the average minimum wage is equal to MXN 63.12). The latter is used in the evaluation of the holiday bonus and the end-of-year bonus.

- Charitable donations made to institutions such as:
  - Federal, state, and municipal governments.
  - Non-profit organisations involved in the fields of social beneficence, education, culture and research and technology.
- Deposits on special savings accounts, payments of insurance premium of pension plans and for the acquisition of shares of investment societies as long as they do not exceed MXN 152 000.
- Health insurance premiums for individuals, if the beneficiary is the taxpayer, and/or his family.
- Real interest expenditure for the payment of mortgage loans for housing purposes that do not exceed MXN 7 378 969. Real interest expenditure is considered the excess of interest expense over the inflation rate.*
- Deduction of taxpayer's educational expenditures for himself, on behalf of his/her spouse, parents or children, among others, for the following educational levels.

Educational level	Maximum annual deduction (MXN)
Kinder garden	14 200
Primary education	12 900
Secondary education	19 900
Technical profession	17 100
High school	24 500

1.1.2.3. Employment subsidy credit

The employment subsidy credit is assigned through a table and this amount is decreasing in the level of income obtained by each worker. For monthly income higher than MXN 7 382, no employment subsidy credit is given. Employees with an income tax lower than the credit receive in cash the difference along with their salary. The rest of the workers that receive the credit are entitled to a reduction in their tax burden. The employment subsidy credit is paid by the employers who may credit it against their tax liabilities; the credit therefore represents a fiscal cost for the government.

1.1.3. Tax schedule and other tables

1.1.3.1. Tax schedule**

Taxable income (MXN)		Fixed quota (MXN)	Tax on the amount in excess of the lower limit (%)[1]
Lower limit	Upper limit		
0	5 952.84	0	1.92
5 952.85	50 524.92	114.24	6.40
50 524.93	88 793.04	2 966.76	10.88
88 793.05	103 218.00	7 130.88	16.00
103 218.01	123 580.20	9 438.60	17.92
123 580.21	249 243.48	13 087.44	21.36
249 243.49	392 841.96	39 929.04	23.52
392 841.97	And over	73 703.40	30.00

1. In 2012 and 2013 the rate of the highest income bracket is 30 per cent (as shown in the Table 1.1.3.1); however, for 2014 the highest rate will be 29 per cent and in 2015 it will be 28 per cent. The rates of the sixth and seventh brackets will decrease in the same proportion.

* Since 2010, this exemption is applicable only if in the immediate previous five years the taxpayer has not sold any other house for which he/she obtained this exemption.

** The income tax schedule and the employment subsidy credit table are updated every time the accumulated inflation reaches 10 per cent.

1.1.3.2. Employment subsidy credit table

For taxable income in a certain income range, the employment subsidy credit is given in the third column of the following table:

Lower limit (MXN)	Upper limit (MXN)	Tax credit (MXN)
0.0	21 227.52	4 884.24
21 227.53	31 840.56	4 881.96
31 840.57	41 674.08	4 879.44
41 674.09	42 454.44	4 713.24
42 454.45	53 353.80	4 589.52
53 353.81	56 606.16	4 250.76
56 606.17	64 025.04	3 898.44
64 025.05	74 696.04	3 535.56
74 696.05	85 366.80	3 042.48
85 366.81	88 587.96	2 611.32
88 587.97	And Over	0.00

1.2. State and local income taxes

States do not levy taxes on income.

1.3. Payroll taxes

Mexico does not have a Federal pay-roll tax. However, most States apply a state pay-roll tax with an average rate of 2.13 per cent. These taxes are not considered in this Report since there are a wide range of practices with respect to the definition of the tax base that does not allow obtaining a reliable estimation.

2. Compulsory social security contributions to schemes operated within the government sector

2.1. Employees' contributions

Social security contributions are divided as follows:

For sickness and maternity insurance, 0.625 per cent of the workers monthly wage, plus 0.40 per cent of the amount in excess of three times the minimal legal wage (the amount that applies within the Federal District of Mexico City MWFD). For disability and life insurance, 0.625 per cent of the monthly wage.

In 2013 a ceiling of 25 MWFD applies to the salary that is used to calculate the social security contributions.

2.2. Employers' contributions

- For sickness and maternity 20.40 per cent of the MWFD, plus 1.10 per cent of the amount in excess of three times the MWFD, plus 1.75 of the monthly wage.
- For disability and life insurance, 1.75 per cent of worker's monthly wage.
- For social services and nursery, 1 per cent of worker's monthly wage.
- For insurance for work injuries of employees, 1.98 per cent of worker's monthly wage.*

* The amount of the work injury fee depends on the risk level in which the company is classified. The Mexican Institute of Social Security provided a weighted average rate that considers the economic activities from C to K of the International Standard Classification.

In 2013 a ceiling of 25 MWDF applies to the salary that is used to calculate the social security contributions.

3. Universal cash transfers

3.1. *Transfers related to marital status*

None.

3.2. *Transfers for dependent children*

None.

4. Main changes in tax/benefit system since 1995

The Social Security Law enacted in July 1997 changed fundamentally the financing of non-government employees' social security, which shifted from a pay-as-you-go scheme to funded individual accounts. The government does not manage these accounts; new private financial institutions were created specifically for this purpose. However, the contractual obligation is between the workers and the government, not with the private administrator of the fund, because legally they are still considered as contributions to social security, independently of who manages the fund. It should be noted that the federal government also contributes to each pension account, and guarantees a minimum pension to every beneficiary of the social security system, again independently of the administration of the fund.

5. Memorandum items

5.1. *Method used to identify an average worker and to calculate his gross earnings*

The income data refer to average workers. It should be noted that in the sample used for this survey, medium and large size firms are over-represented. In Mexico, there are no state or local government income taxes. Information on non-standard tax reliefs is not available.

Figures for 1999 and subsequent years cannot be compared with preliminary figures from previous editions of this publication for two reasons: first, the wage level of the average worker is now based on observed data instead of being estimated; second, social security contributions taken into account no longer include contributions made by employers and employees to privately managed individual accounts. Contributions no longer included in the calculation of social security contributions are specified in the table below.

5.2. *Main employees' and employers' contributions to private pension, health, etc. schemes*

	Account	Per cent of workers' monthly wage
Employers' contributions	Retirement	2.00
	Discharge and old age insurance	3.15
	Housing Fund (INFONAVIT)	5.00
Employees' contributions	Discharge and old age insurance	1.125

2013 parameter values

Average earnings/yr	Ave_earn	97 941		Secretariat estimate
(general min wage per day)	min_wage	63.12		
(general min wage per day for the Federal District of Mexico City)	min_wage_FD	64.76		
Income tax	tax_table	0.00	0	0.0192
		5 952.85	114.24	0.0640
		50 524.93	2 966.76	0.1088
		88 793.05	7 130.88	0.1600
		103 218.01	9 438.60	0.1792
		123 580.21	13 087.44	0.2136
		249 243.49	39 929.04	0.2352
		392 841.97	73 703.40	0.3000
Tax credit basic	Basic_crd	0.0	4 884.24	
		21 227.53	4 881.96	
		31 840.57	4 879.44	
		41 674.09	4 713.24	
		42 454.45	4 589.52	
		53 353.81	4 250.76	
		56 606.17	3 898.44	
		64 025.05	3 535.56	
		74 696.05	3 042.48	
		85 366.81	2 611.32	
		88 587.97	0.00	
Employees SSC	SSC_rate	0.0125		
	SSC_rate_sur	0.0040		
Employers SSC	SSC_empr	0.0648		
	SSC_empr_min	0.2040		
	SSC_empr_sur	0.0110		

2013 tax equations

The equations for the Mexican system in 2013 are on an individual basis.

The functions which are used in the equations (Taper, MIN, Tax, etc.) are described in the technical note about tax equations. Variable names are defined in the table of parameters above, within the equations table, or are the standard variables "married" and "children". A reference to a variable with the affix "_total" indicates the sum of the relevant variable values for the principal and spouse. And the affixes "_princ" and "_spouse" indicate the value for the principal and spouse, respectively. Equations for a single person are as shown for the principal, with "_spouse" values taken as 0.

	Line in country table and intermediate steps	Variable name	Range	Equation
1.	Earnings	earn		
2.	Allowances	tax_al	B	MIN(earn, MIN(earn*(6/365)*0.25, min_wage*15)+ MIN(earn*(15/365), min_wage*30))
3.	Credits in taxable income	taxbl_cr	B	0
4.	CG taxable income	tax_inc	B	Positive(earn-tax_al)
5.	CG tax before credits	CG_tax_excl	B	Tax(tax_inc, Tax_sch)
6.	Tax credits	tax_cr	B	VLOOKUP(tax_inc, Basic_crd, 2)
7.	CG tax	CG_tax	B	CG_tax_excl-tax_cr
8.	State and local taxes	local_tax	B	0
9.	Employees' soc security	SSC	B	MIN(earn*ssc_rate, min_wage_FD*25*365*ssc_rate)+MIN(Positive(earn-(3*365*min_wage_FD))*ssc_rate_sur, min_wage_FD*(25-3)*365*ssc_rate_sur)
11.	Cash transfers	cash_trans	B	0
13.	Employer's soc security	SSC_empr	B	MIN(earn*ssc_empr, min_wage_FD*25*365*ssc_empr)+365*min_wage_FD*ssc_empr_min +MIN(Positive(earn-(3*365*min_wage_FD))*ssc_empr_sur, min_wage_FD*(25-3)*365*ssc_empr_sur)
	Memorandum item: Non-wastable tax credit			
	tax expenditure component	taxexp	B	tax_cr-transfer
	cash transfer component	transfer	B	IF(CG_tax<0, -CG_tax, 0)

Key to range of equation B calculated separately for both principal earner and spouse P calculated for principal only (value taken as 0 for spouse calculation).

Taxing Wages 2014
Changes in sructural labour income tax progressivity
over 2000-12 period in OECD member countries

Netherlands

This chapter includes data on the income taxes paid by workers, their social security contributions, the family benefits they receive in the form of cash transfers as well as the social security contributions and payroll taxes paid by their employers. Results reported include the marginal and average tax burden for eight different family types.

Methodological information is available for personal income tax systems, compulsory social security contributions to schemes operated within the government sector, universal cash transfers as well as recent changes in the tax/benefit system. The methodology also includes the parameter values and tax equations.

Netherlands 2013

The tax/benefit position of single persons

			67	100	167	67
	Wage level (per cent of average wage)		67	100	167	67
	Number of children		none	none	none	2
1.	**Gross wage earnings**		32073	48109	80182	32073
2.	**Standard tax allowances:**					
	Basic allowance					
	Married or head of family					
	Dependent children					
	Deduction for social security contributions and income taxes		0	0	0	0
	Work-related expenses					
	Other					
		Total	0	0	0	0
3.	**Tax credits or cash transfers included in taxable income**		2413	3590	3941	2413
4.	**Central government taxable income (1 - 2 + 3)**		31129	46328	76727	31129
5.	**Central government income tax liability (exclusive of tax credits)**		2395	8083	22924	2395
6.	**Tax credits :**					
	Basic credit					
	Married or head of family					
	Children					
	Other					
		Total	589	550	403	1355
7.	**Central government income tax finally paid (5-6)**		1806	7533	22521	1040
8.	**State and local taxes**		0	0	0	0
9.	**Employees' compulsory social security contributions**					
	Gross earnings		0	0	0	0
	Taxable income (net of credits)		6562	7462	8245	2985
		Total	6562	7462	8245	2985
10.	**Total payments to general government (7 + 8 + 9)**		8368	14995	30766	4025
11.	**Cash transfers from general government**					
	For head of family					
	For two children		0	0	0	3035
		Total	0	0	0	3035
12.	**Take-home pay (1-10+11)**		23705	33114	49416	31083
13.	**Employers' compulsory social security contributions**		2862	4405	4864	2862
14.	**Average rates**					
	Income tax		5.6%	15.7%	28.1%	3.2%
	Employees' social security contributions		20.5%	15.5%	10.3%	9.3%
	Total payments less cash transfers		26.1%	31.2%	38.4%	3.1%
	Total tax wedge including employer's social security contributions		32.1%	36.9%	41.9%	11.0%
15.	**Marginal rates**					
	Total payments less cash transfers: Principal earner		39.8%	43.6%	49.3%	47.0%
	Total payments less cash transfers: Spouse		n.a.	n.a.	n.a.	n.a.
	Total tax wedge: Principal earner		45.1%	48.5%	49.3%	51.7%
	Total tax wedge: Spouse		n.a.	n.a.	n.a.	n.a.

Netherlands 2013

The tax/benefit position of married couples

	Wage level (per cent of average wage)	100-0	100-33	100-67	100-33
	Number of children	2	2	2	none
1.	**Gross wage earnings**	48109	64146	80182	64146
2.	**Standard tax allowances:**				
	Basic allowance				
	Married or head of family				
	Dependent children				
	Deduction for social security contributions and income taxes	0	0	0	0
	Work-related expenses				
	Other				
	Total	0	0	0	0
3.	**Tax credits or cash transfers included in taxable income**	3590	4825	6003	4825
4.	**Central government taxable income (1 - 2 + 3)**	46328	62258	77457	62258
5.	**Central government income tax liability (exclusive of tax credits)**	8083	9015	10478	9015
6.	**Tax credits :**				
	Basic credit				
	Married or head of family				
	Children				
	Other				
	Total	761	1296	1467	1064
7.	**Central government income tax finally paid (5-6)**	7322	7719	9011	7951
8.	**State and local taxes**	0	0	0	0
9.	**Employees' compulsory social security contributions**				
	Gross earnings	0	0	0	0
	Taxable income (net of credits)	6339	8453	12275	9689
	Total	6339	8453	12275	9689
10.	**Total payments to general government (7 + 8 + 9)**	13661	16172	21286	17640
11.	**Cash transfers from general government**				
	For head of family				
	For two children	1880	1861	1861	0
	Total	1880	1861	1861	0
12.	**Take-home pay (1-10+11)**	36328	49835	60757	46505
13.	**Employers' compulsory social security contributions**	4405	5751	7267	5751
14.	**Average rates**				
	Income tax	15.2%	12.0%	11.2%	12.4%
	Employees' social security contributions	13.2%	13.2%	15.3%	15.1%
	Total payments less cash transfers	24.5%	22.3%	24.2%	27.5%
	Total tax wedge including employer's social security contributions	30.8%	28.7%	30.5%	33.5%
15.	**Marginal rates**				
	Total payments less cash transfers: Principal earner	50.8%	43.6%	43.6%	43.6%
	Total payments less cash transfers: Spouse	15.8%	16.8%	36.0%	20.6%
	Total tax wedge: Principal earner	55.1%	48.5%	48.5%	48.5%
	Total tax wedge: Spouse	22.3%	23.0%	41.6%	26.5%

The national currency is the euro (EUR). In 2013, EUR 0.75 was equal to USD 1. In that year, the average worker earned EUR 48 109 (Secretariat estimate).*

1. Personal income tax systems (central government)

1.1. *Central government income tax*

There are three categories ("boxes") of taxable income:

- Taxable income from work and owner-occupied housing.
- Taxable income from a substantial interest in a limited liability company.
- Taxable income from savings and investments.

This description is limited to the most relevant aspects of taxable income from the first category, "taxable income from work and owner-occupied housing", because of its relevance for the AW.

1.1.1. *Tax unit*

Husbands and wives are taxed separately on their personal income, which includes income from business, profession and employment, pensions and social security benefits. Certain parts of income may be freely split between husbands and wives, such as the net-income from owner-occupied housing and the income from savings and investments.

1.1.2. *Tax allowances*

1.1.2.1. Standard allowances

Related to wage earnings:

- Employees' social security contributions (see Section 2.1) are deductible, whereas the health insurance contribution is not deductible and is not a part of the *Taxing Wages* model (for more information, see the Special Feature on "non-tax compulsory payments" in the 2009 edition of the *Taxing Wages* Report). In the *Taxing Wages* model the employers' income dependant health insurance contribution was subject to income tax for the employee. In 2013 the income base for SSC and Income-Tax is harmonised. Standardising or harmonisation of the income tax base for levying SSC and Taxes is introduces in 2013 and is called the Law "WUL" i.e. Harmonising the income base for SSC and Taxes... (see publication CPB the Netherlands). So the income tax base is since 2013 exclusive the income dependant health care contribution and employees will no longer have to pay taxes over income dependant health care contributions, instead they pay a higher tax rate in the first tax bracket and mainly Work credit is adjusted. The tax rate in the first tax bracket has been increased from 1.95% till 5.85% and the Work credit is

* The Dutch labour market is characterized by a substantial share of part-time employees. As explained in the methodological section of this volume, the average wage measure used in the tax burden calculations refer to full-time employees only. If the wages of part-timers were taken into account, the average wage would be substantially lower.

reduced for employees with a higher income such that the effect of this harmonisation is budgetary neutral.

1.1.2.2. Non-standard allowances applicable to AW

Related to wage earnings:

- For distances of more than 10 km between home and work, fixed amounts for travel expenses with public transportation are deductible. The maximum deduction for employees who travel by public transport is EUR 1 951 for distances of more than 80 km. If the travel expenses are reimbursed or the employer provides transport, there is no deduction; the reimbursement is untaxed (also for employees who travel by car) if it is below certain specified amounts;
- Employee contributions to private (company provided) pension schemes.

Related to owner-occupied housing:

- Excess of mortgage interest over net imputed rent.

Related to personal circumstances:

- Medical expenses and other exceptional expenses:
  - Fiscal deduction of exceptional health expenses will be reduced to the specific costs as a result of the chronic illness. As specific costs are seen diet costs, special medicine described by a doctor and transportation costs. Visual tools and insurance premiums are not seen as specific costs and are therefore no longer deductible.
  - For a single person: the specific expenses in excess of 1.65 per cent of income are deductible if income exceeds EUR 7 457 and is below EUR 39 618. If income is lower than or equal to EUR 7 457, the non-deductible limit is EUR 125. For a person with a partner: the joint income is used to determine the non-deductible amounts and the non-deductible limit is EUR 250.
  - If income exceeds EUR 39 618 the specific expenses in excess of 1.65 per cent of EUR 39 618 increased with 5.75 per cent of income above EUR 39 618 are deductible.
- Some educational expenses: in direct connection with vocational education. Expenses above the threshold of EUR 500 are deductible. Expenses above EUR 15 000 are not deductible;
- Donations to certain institutions (charity) that serve the public good are deductible if in excess of 1 per cent of the income and in excess of EUR 60. No more than 10 per cent of the income may be deducted in this way.

1.1.3. *Tax schedule*

The tax schedule for income from work and owner-occupied housing is as follows:

Taxable income (EUR)	Tax rate (%)	Social security contributions	
		< 65 years	> 65 years
0-19 645	5.85	31.15	13.25
19 645-33 363	10.85	31.15	13.25
33 363-55991	42	-	-
55 991 and over	52	-	-

The contributions for the general social security schemes are levied on income from work and owner-occupied housing in the first and second income tax bracket. These social security contributions are not deductible for income tax purposes. Individuals of 65 years and older pay 13.25 per cent, (for widows and orphans pensions, and exceptional medical expenses). Individuals younger than 65 years pay 31.15 per cent (for widows and orphans pensions, exceptional medical expenses, and old age income provision). For further information see Section 2.1.

1.1.4. *Tax credits*

1.1.4.1. Standard tax credits

The tax credits are deducted partly from the income tax liability and partly from the contributions that are made to the general social security schemes (see Section 1.1.3). For most families, the share of the credit attributed to tax is related to the ratio of the tax rate to the sum of the tax rate and the social security contributions rate in the *first* bracket of the tax schedule. In 2013, this ratio was 15.81 per cent (= 5.85%/(5.85% + 31.15%), implying that 15.81 per cent of the (tax) credit is attributed to the personal income tax and the remaining 84.19 per cent to social security contributions. If the individual's total tax credit is higher than the total tax and social security contributions levied on the first tax bracket, the shares of the residual amount of the tax credit that are attributed to the personal income tax and social security contributions are based on the rates of deduction in the second tax bracket in order that the employee can benefit from the full amount of the credit where the level of income allows it. As a result, the ratio of the tax rate to the sum of the tax rate and social security contribution rates is increased to 25.83% for the residual amount in 2013 (i.e. 10.85%/[31.15%+10.85%]).

For example in 2013, the total tax credit of a single parent with 2 children earning 67 per cent of the average wage amounts to rounded off EUR 8 000. The total tax and social security contributions levied on the first tax bracket equals EUR 7 268.65 (= 19 645 * (31.15% + 5.85%). The residual tax credit equals EUR 731.35.

The first tax ratio of 15.81 per cent is applied on EUR 7 268.65 and the second tax ratio of 25.83 per cent is applied on EUR 731.35. Then the part of the total tax credit that is attributed to personal income tax is EUR 1 338.08. The remaining EUR 6 661.92 is attributed to the social security contributions.

Division of credits for tax and social security contributions is essential in the OECD publications. In the Netherlands no division is made in the general tax scheme between tax and SSC.

Note that the tax/benefit position tables show the total amount of social security contributions net of the credits that are claimed.

- *General tax credit:* This credit amounts to EUR 2 001 and is mainly reduced due to harmonising income base for levying Taxes and SSC; the transfer of the general tax credit of the spouse to the principal will diminish with 6.67 per cent per year in the period 2009-24, such that in 15 year time the general tax credit for a non-working spouse cannot be capitalised against the tax paid by the principal. This reduction of the transfer of the general tax credit started in 2009. In 2024 the general tax credit can only be capitalised against the tax and premiums paid on own earned income. In 2012 a reduction of the general tax credit for non-working spouses born after 31 December 1962 and before 1 January 1972 is introduced. The reduction will be equal to the reduction of non-working spouses born before 1 January 1963 in year 2015. For Household types in de *Taxing Wages* model no difference is made between year of birth before 1963 or after 1963, idem before or after 1972. For that reason the additional reduction of the general tax credit is not added to the *Taxing Wages* model.

- *Work credit:* This credit is strongly reduced due to harmonisation of the income base for levying Tax and SSC and such that the harmonisation is budgetary neutral. The Work credit is the sum of 1.827 per cent of taxable income from work with a maximum of EUR 161 and 15.274 per cent of taxable income from work with a franchise of EUR 8 816. The work credit is income dependent and will be reduced by 4 per cent of taxable income above EUR 40 248; the reduction will be maximised till EUR 1 173; so the reduction stops at a taxable income of EUR 69 573. The maximum work credit before it is reduced is EUR 1 723; the maximum reduced work credit is EUR 550.
- *Combination credit:* The combination credit is abolished in 2009.
- *Income dependant combination credit:* The additional combination credit is replaced with the income dependent combination credit. A taxpayer who is either a single parent or the partner with the lowest income, who has children below the age of 12 and has his/her taxable income from work exceeding EUR 4 814, is entitled to an income dependent combination credit of EUR 1 024 plus an extra combination credit of 4 per cent of taxable income above EUR 4 814. The maximum total combination credit is EUR 2 133.
- *Single parent credit:* A single parent under certain conditions is entitled to the single parent credit of EUR 947.
- *Additional single parent credit:* A single parent who is entitled to the single parent credit receives an additional credit of 4.3 per cent of his or her income from work, with a maximum of EUR 1 319.

The amount of the tax credit is limited to the amount of tax and premiums payable (non-refundable tax credit). If, however, a taxpayer with insufficient income to fully exploit his/her tax credit has a partner with a surplus of tax and premiums payable over his/her own tax credit, the tax credit of the former taxpayer is increased by (at most) the surplus tax and premiums payable by his/her fiscal partner. As a consequence, the tax credit of the former taxpayer will exceed tax and premiums payable, resulting in a payout of the residual tax credit to the taxpayer by the tax authority.

1.2. State and local income taxes

None.

2. Compulsory social security contributions to schemes operated within the government sector

2.1. Employees' contributions

Schemes for employees:

- Unemployment: 0 per cent of the gross earnings between EUR 17 501 and EUR 50 853 (this contribution is only for the general unemployment fund); employees do not have to pay an unemployment premium in order to reduce administration costs. Employers pay both an unemployment premium and a premium for invalidity for their employees (see Section 2.2).

- For basic health insurance each adult pays an average amount of EUR 1 250 a year to a self-chosen private health insurance company. This premium is a non-tax compulsory payment and is not included in the *Taxing Wages* calculations but only in the NTCP calculations. Employees might obtain compensation for this nominal contribution, depending on the household's personal situation and taxable income. This is called the health care benefit. This benefit is included in the NTCP calculations as it compensates for the basic health insurance premium of on average EUR 1 250. Also 7.75 per cent of gross earnings net of employees' pension premiums and unemployment social security contributions is paid for health care until a maximum of net earnings of EUR 50 853. Since 2013 employers contribute the Health care Fund directly for the health care of their employees, these costs remain labour costs in the *Taxing Wages* model. These Health care costs for employers are no longer included in the taxpayer's taxable income. t. The income dependent health care contribution itself, however, is not modelled (as an employer SSC) in *Taxing Wages* because it is seen as a Non-Tax Compulsary Payment.
- Employees might obtain compensation for the nominal contribution of on average EUR 1 250 for the basic health insurance, depending on the household's personal situation and taxable income. This is called the health care benefit. The care benefit is calculated as follows:

  Single parent households: 1483 – 2.195 per cent * 19 043 – 8.713 per cent * (taxable income – 19 043)

  Married couples: number of adults * 1 483 – 4.695 per cent * 19 043 – 8.713 per cent * (taxable income principal and spouse – 19 043).

  This health care benefit is a non-tax compulsory payment and is not included in the *Taxing Wages* calculations but only in the "non-tax compulsory payment" calculations (see *www.oecd.org/ctp/taxingwages* for more details on non-tax compulsory payments as well as the Special Feature in the 2009 edition of the *Taxing Wages* Report).
- Old age pension: The age is adjusted such that elderly will receive Old Age (state) pension at the age of 66 years old in 2018 and at 67 years old in 2021. The Old age premium percentage is 17.9 per cent of taxable income in the first and second tax bracket. This scheme does not apply to individuals aged 65 and one month(and in future aged 66 or 67) or older;
- Widows and orphans pension: 0.60 per cent of taxable income in the first and second tax bracket;
- Exceptional medical expenses and disability: 12.65 per cent of taxable income in the first and second tax bracket.

2.2. Employers' contributions

Schemes for employees:

- Unemployment: 1.70 per cent of gross earnings between EUR 17 501 and EUR 50 853 for the general unemployment fund and a contribution of 3.26 per cent of gross earnings below EUR 50 853 for the industrial insurance associations redundancy payments fund;
- Invalidity: 5.19 per cent of gross earnings below EUR 50 853;
- For medical care employers contribute 7.75 per cent of gross earnings net of employees' pension premiums and unemployment social security contributions until a maximum of gross earnings of EUR 50 853. The premium itself, however, is not modelled (either as an

employee or employer SSC) in *Taxing Wages*. Instead, it is modelled as a NTCP from the employer to a public-managed health insurance fund. The spending of this fund mainly compensates private insurance companies for their (public) obligation to insure individuals with a high health risk.

3. Universal cash transfers

3.1. *Transfers related to marital status*

None.

3.2. *Transfers for dependent children*

Families with children receive a tax free benefit, depending on the number and age of the children. For a family with two children in the age group of 6 to 12 years, the total benefit amounts to EUR 1 861 a year. Indexation of the child benefits was frozen for three years (period 2009-11).

An additional income dependent child benefit was introduced in 2008. As of 2009, this benefit also depends on the number of children per family. A family can only claim the extra child benefit when it has children under the age of 18 years old for whom it also receives the tax free and income independent child benefit. Indexation of the extra child benefit was frozen until 2011 and has still a maximum value of EUR 1 017 per year for families with one child. The child credit increases to EUR 1 553 a year for families with two children. The benefit is reduced at a rate of 7.6 per cent per euro when the family's yearly taxable income exceeds EUR 26 147 and is completely withdrawn for families with two children when the taxable income is at least EUR 46 581.

4. Main changes in tax/benefit systems since 2000

In 2001, the tax system was changed thoroughly. The tax rates have been lowered; the basic allowance and its supplements have been transformed into tax credits. The deduction for labour costs has also been replaced by a tax credit. Certain other deductions have been reduced or abolished. Extra tax credits for households with children were introduced.

In 2002 and 2003 the tax system was only slightly changed. The additional combination credit was introduced in 2004. The various child credits were integrated and streamlined in 2006.

Public insurance for medical care has been reformed in 2006. A new standard health insurance system was introduced. Until 2005, no public health insurance contributions were levied on income in excess of EUR 33 000. However, taxpayers earning more than EUR 33 000 were obliged to take a private insurance. These private health insurance contributions were not included in the *Taxing Wages* calculations because they were made to a privately-managed fund (and are therefore not taxes). Since 2006, every individual contributes a nominal contribution to a privately-managed fund (on average EUR 1 064, depending on the competition between insurance companies, a year in 2009) and, in addition for employees, a percentage of gross income (6.9 per cent) net of employees' pension premiums and unemployment social security contributions until a maximum of gross income of EUR 32 369 (in 2009). For this last contribution, the employee receives mandatory compensation of his employer for the same amount. The premium itself, however, is not modelled (either as an employee or employer SSC) in *Taxing Wages*. Instead it is modelled as a non-tax compulsory payment from the employer to a public-managed health insurance fund. The spending of this fund mainly compensates private insurance companies for their (public) obligation to insure individuals with a high health risk. Taxpayers might obtain compensation for the nominal contribution to the private insurance company of on average EUR 1 064 in 2009, depending on the households personal situation and taxable income. This is called the health care benefit and is part of the NTCP (see Section 2.1).

In 2007, the tax system has not been changed, except for some parameter updates. In 2008, the child credit has been replaced by an extra child benefit.

In 2009 the general tax credit will be reduced for non-working spouses in order to cut down the capitalization of this tax credit in 2024. A non-working spouse can in 2024 capitalise the general tax credit only against his/her own earned income. In 2009 the employment credit is extended for income exceeding EUR 42 509. This credit will be reduced by maximum EUR 24, whereas the employment credit is increased for lower incomes. The income dependant combination credit is introduced in order to promote the labour participation of single parents or partners of married workers. The income-dependent combination credit has been increased considerably. The extra child benefit depends on the total income of the family and the number of children per family. The income-dependent child benefit is higher when more children under the age of 18 years are member of the family. As from 2009 onwards, employees do not have to pay an unemployment premium mainly to reduce administration costs for employers. Employers pay now both an unemployment premium and a premium for invalidity for their employees (see also Section 2.2).

In 2013 the income base for SSC and Income-Tax is harmonised. Standardising or harmonisation of the income tax base for levying SSC and Taxes is introduces in 2013 and is called the Law "WUL" i.e. Harmonising the income base for SSC and Taxes (see publication CPB the Netherlands). So the income tax base is since 2013 exclusive the income dependant health care contribution and employees will no longer have to pay taxes over income dependant health care contributions, instead they pay a higher tax rate in the first tax bracket and mainly Work credit is adjusted. The tax rate in the first tax bracket has been increased from 1.95 per ent till 5 85 per cent and the Work credit is reduced for employees with a higher income such that the effect of this harmonisation is budgetary neutral.

5. Memorandum items

5.1. *Identification of the AW and calculation of the AW's gross earnings*

The calculation of the annual gross earnings of an AW is based upon data on gross earnings of full-time workers in industry C-K. These data have been obtained through a yearly sample survey carried out by the Central Bureau of Statistics. Included in the AW annual salary are irregular payments, such as holiday allowances, loyalty payments and bonuses. Payments for working overtime are not included. However, the CBS has stopped carrying out the "employment and wages" survey in July 2006 due to new legislation. On Inquiry at the Central Bureau of Statistics (CBS) the information from the wage declarations by employers, delivered nowadays at the tax department, will be implemented by the CBS for the new survey about employment and wages. These changes produced a delay in delivery of the information on wages and employment for 2006.

As the AW figure for 2005 and 2006 are not available, the 2004 figure was taken and adjusted for the wage increases in 2005, 2006 and 2007 by the OECD Secretariat based on wage increase estimates from the most recent issue of the *OECD Economic Outlook*. On the base of new information on wages per industry sector, the AW is delivered to EUROSTAT in November 2009 by the CBS for years 2006 and 2007. The standard classification NACE Rev. 1 for industrial Sectors C-K is used.

The new classification NACE Revision 2 (Sectors B-N) will be applicable as from 2008 onwards. The estimation of the AW for 2008 according to the new classification is applicable at the beginning of May 2010. The AW for 2009 is available since November 2010. For 2008 the average annual gross earnings (full-time Nace Rev. 2) comes to EUR 43 146, for 2009 EUR 44.412, and EUR 45 215 in 2010. The latest information according to Eurostat is an AW in 2011 of EUR 46 287 (Nace Rev. 2).

5.2. *Main employers' contributions to private pension, health and related schemes*

In addition to the obligatory contributions of employees to private insurance companies, all employers pay contributions to a public-managed health fund. More information is included in the Special Feature where the contributions to the public-managed health funds are also presented.

Employers have to pay at least 70 per cent of the gross wage of their sick employees for two years. Many employers have insured themselves privately for the risks of their employees being sick. This insurance for illness of their employees is not compulsory.

2013 parameter values

	Ave_earn	48 109	Secretariat estimate
Social security contributions	SSC_ceil	50853	
Employees' schemes	Unemp_rate1	0.0	
	Unemp_franchise1	17 501	
Medical care	Med_rate	0.0775	
	Med_limit	999 999	
	Med_ceil	50 853	
	Med_adult	1 250	
	Med_child	0	
	Med_compensation1	0.02195	
	Med_compensation2	0.08713	
	Med_compensation3	0.04695	
	Med_compensation4	0.08713	
	Med_key	19 043	
	Med_aldult for care benefit	1 483	
General schemes	Old_rate	0.179	
	Wid_rate	0.006	
	Ex_med_rate	0.1265	
	Gen_Schemes_thrsh	33 363	
	Unemp_empr1	0.017	
	Unemp_empr2	0.0326	
	Unemp_unempr_franchise1	17 501	
	Unemp_unempr_franchise2	0	
	Inv_empr_rate	0.0519	
	Inv_empr_franchise	0	
	Med_empr	0.0775	
	Med_franchise	0	
Tax schedule	Tax_sch	0.0585	19 645
	"tax_sch_lowest"	0.1085	33 363
	"tax_thrsh_1"	0.42	55 991
		0.52	
Tax credits	Gen_credit	2 001	
	Red_gen_credit	1 334	
	Emp_credit1	161	
	Emp_credit2	1 562	
	Emp_credit3	389	
	Emp_credit1_thr	8 816	
	Emp_credit2_thr	19 043	
	Emp_credit3_thr	40 248	
	Emp_credit4_thr	69 573	
	Comb_credit	Nvt	
	Comb_credit_franchise	4 814	
	add_comb_credit	Nvt	
	Income_dependant_comb_comb_credit1	1 024	
	Income_dependant_comb_credit_max	2 133	
	Income_dependant_comb_par_credit_per	0,04	
	Sing_par_credit	947	
	Ex_sing_par_credit_per	0.043	
	Ex_sing_par_credit_max	1 319	
Family cash transfers	Ch1_trans	931	
	Ch2_trans	1 861	
	Child_ben_1child	1 017	
	Child_ben_2children	1 553	
	Child_ben_redn	0.076	
	Child_ben_ceil	26 147	

2013 tax equations

The equations for the tax system in the Netherlands in 2013 are repeated for each individual of a married couple. Tax credits, except a part of the general credit of the spouse, depend also on the tax paid by the principal if the spouse's income is zero or very low, and the cash transfers are calculated only once. The functions which are used in the equations (Taper, MIN, Tax, etc.) are described in the technical note on the tax equations. Due to the adjustment of the employment credit in 2009, the function Emp_credit(Value) was altered in 2009; no changes were made in 2010 till 2012. Variable names are defined in the table of parameters above, within the equations table, or are the standard variables "married" and "children". A reference to a variable with the affix "_total" indicates the sum of the relevant variable values for the principal and spouse. And the affix "_spouse" indicates the value for the spouse. No affix is used for the principal values. Equations for a single person are as shown for the principal, with "_spouse" values taken as 0.

	Line in country table and intermediate steps	Variable name	Range	Equation
1.	Earnings (gross)	gr_earn		
	Earnings (net)	earn	B	gr_earn
2.	Social security contributions	SSC_al	B	SSC_f(earn,Unemp_rate1,SSC_ceil,Unemp_franchise1)
3.	Credits in taxable income	taxbl_cr	B	MIN(earn-SSC_al, Med_ceil)*Med_rate
4.	CG taxable income	tax_inc	B	earn-SSC_al
5.	CG tax before credits	CG_tax_excl / tax_liable	B	Tax(tax_inc,Tax_sch)
6.	Tax credits	tax_cr	P	MIN(CG_tax_excl+SSC_taxinc,Gen_credit+Emp_credit(tax_inc) +IF(AND(Children>0,earn>Comb_credit_franchise),IF(Married=0,Comb_credit +add_comb_credit,Comb_credit),0) +IF(AND(Children>0,Married=0),Sing_par_credit+MIN(Ex_sing_par_credit_m ax,Ex_sing_par_credit_per*tax_inc),0))
		tax_cr_spouse	S	IF(Married>0,MIN(CG_tax_excl_spouse+SSC_taxinc_spouse+ CG_tax_excl+SSC_taxinc-tax_cr,Gen_credit +Emp_credit(tax_inc_spouse)+IF(AND(Children>0,earn_spouse>Comb_credit _franchise),Comb_credit+add_comb_credit,0)),0)
		tax_cr_inc	B	IF(tax_cr>Tax_thrsh_1*SUM(Old_rate+Wid_rate+Ex_med_rate+tax_sch_lowe st),(tax_sch_2/SUM(Old_rate+Wid_rate+Ex_med_rate+tax_sch_2))*(tax_cr-(SUM(Old_rate+Wid_rate+Ex_med_rate+tax_sch_lowest)*Tax_thrsh_1))+(tax _sch_lowest/ SUM(Old_rate+Wid_rate+Ex_med_rate+tax_sch_lowest))*(Tax_thrsh_1*SUM (Old_rate+Wid_rate+Ex_med_rate+tax_sch_lowest)),tax_sch_lowest/ SUM(Old_rate+Wid_rate+Ex_med_rate+tax_sch_lowest)*tax_cr)
7.	CG tax	CG_tax	B	tax_liable-tax_cr_inc
8.	State and local taxes	local_tax	B	0
9.	Employees' soc security' based on earnings	SSC_earn	P	SSC_f(earn,Unemp_rate1,SSC_ceil,Unemp_franchise1)
		SSC_earn_spouse	S	SSC_f(earn_spouse,Unemp_rate1,SSC_ceil,Unemp_franchise1)
	Based on taxable income	SSC_taxinc	B	(Old_rate+Wid_rate+Ex_med_rate)*MINA(tax_inc,Gen_Schemes_thrsh)
	Total employees' soc security	SSC_liable	J	SSC_earn+SSC_taxinc+SSC_earn_spouse+SSC_taxinc_spouse

Line in country table and intermediate steps		Variable name	Range	Equation
		tax_cr_SSC	B	IF(tax_cr>Tax_thrsh_1*SUM(Old_rate+Wid_rate+Ex_med_rate+tax_sch_lowest),((Old_rate+Wid_rate+Ex_med_rate)/ SUM(Old_rate+Wid_rate+Ex_med_rate+tax_sch_2))*(tax_cr-(SUM(Old_rate+Wid_rate+Ex_med_rate+tax_sch_lowest)*Tax_thrsh_1))+((Old_rate+Wid_rate+Ex_med_rate)/ SUM(Old_rate+Wid_rate+Ex_med_rate+tax_sch_lowest))*(Tax_thrsh_1*SUM(Old_rate+Wid_rate+Ex_med_rate+tax_sch_lowest)),SUM(Old_rate+Wid_rate+Ex_med_rate)/ SUM(Old_rate+Wid_rate+Ex_med_rate+tax_sch_lowest)*tax_cr)
	Total	SSC	J	SSC_liable-tax_cr_SSC
10.	Total payments	total_payments	J	CG_tax+local_tax+SSC
11.	Cash transfers	cash_trans	J	IF(Children=1,Ch1_trans,IF(Children=2,Ch2_trans,0))+ (Children>0)*(IF((tax_inc+tax_inc_spouse)<Child_ben_ceil, Child_ben, Positive(Child_ben – Child_ ben_redn*(tax_inc+tax_inc_spouse – Child_ben_ceil))))

13.	Employer's soc security	SSC_empr	B	If Value <= 0 Then
				Emp_credit = 0
				ElseIf Value <= Range("Emp_credit1_thr").Value Then
				Emp_credit = (Value / Range("Emp_credit1_thr").Value) * Range("Emp_credit1").Value
				ElseIf Value <= Range("Emp_credit2_thr").Value Then
				Emp_credit = Range("Emp_credit1").Value + ((Value - Range("Emp_credit1_thr").Value) / (Range("Emp_credit2_thr").Value - Range("Emp_credit1_thr").Value)) * Range("Emp_credit2").Value
				ElseIf Value <= Range("Emp_credit3_thr").Value Then
				Emp_credit = Range("Emp_credit1").Value + Range("Emp_credit2").Value
				ElseIf Value <= Range("Emp_credit4_thr").Value Then
				Emp_credit = Range("Emp_credit1").Value + Range("Emp_credit2").Value - ((Value - Range("Emp_credit3_thr").Value) / (Range("Emp_credit4_thr").Value - Range("Emp_credit3_thr").Value)) * (Range("Emp_credit2").Value - Range("Emp_credit3").Value)
				Else
				Emp_credit = Range("Emp_credit1").Value + Range("Emp_credit3").Value
				End If

Key to range of equations B calculated separately for both principal earner and spouse P calculated for principal only (value taken as 0 for spouse calculation) J calculated once only on a joint basis.

Taxing Wages 2014
Changes in sructural labour income tax progressivity
over 2000-12 period in OECD member countries

New Zealand (2013-14 income tax year)

This chapter includes data on the income taxes paid by workers, their social security contributions, the family benefits they receive in the form of cash transfers as well as the social security contributions and payroll taxes paid by their employers. Results reported include the marginal and average tax burden for eight different family types.

Methodological information is available for personal income tax systems, compulsory social security contributions to schemes operated within the government sector, universal cash transfers as well as recent changes in the tax/ benefit system. The methodology also includes the parameter values and tax equations underlying the data.

New Zealand 2013

The tax/benefit position of single persons

		Wage level (per cent of average wage)	67	100	167	67
		Number of children	none	none	none	2
1.	**Gross wage earnings**		35489	53234	88723	35489
2.	**Standard tax allowances:**					
	Basic allowance					
	Married or head of family					
	Dependent children					
	Deduction for social security contributions and income taxes					
	Work-related expenses					
	Other					
		Total	0	0	0	0
3.	**Tax credits or cash transfers included in taxable income**		0	0	0	0
4.	**Central government taxable income (1 - 2 + 3)**		35489	53234	88723	35489
5.	**Central government income tax liability (exclusive of tax credits)**		5231	8990	20199	5231
6.	**Tax credits :**					
	Basic credit		520	0	0	0
	Married or head of family					
	Children					
	Other					
		Total	520	0	0	0
7.	**Central government income tax finally paid (5-6)**		4711	8990	20199	5231
8.	**State and local taxes**		0	0	0	0
9.	**Employees' compulsory social security contributions**					
	Gross earnings		0	0	0	0
	Taxable income					
		Total	0	0	0	0
10.	**Total payments to general government (7 + 8 + 9)**		4711	8990	20199	5231
11.	**Cash transfers from general government**					
	For head of family					
	For two children		0	0	0	11293
		Total	0	0	0	11293
12.	**Take-home pay (1-10+11)**		30779	44244	68525	41552
13.	**Employer's compulsory social security contributions**		0	0	0	0
14.	**Average rates**					
	Income tax		13.3%	16.9%	22.8%	14.7%
	Employees' social security contributions		0.0%	0.0%	0.0%	0.0%
	Total payments less cash transfers		13.3%	16.9%	22.8%	-17.1%
	Total tax wedge including employer's social security contributions		13.3%	16.9%	22.8%	-17.1%
15.	**Marginal rates**					
	Total payments less cash transfers: Principal earner		17.5%	30.0%	33.0%	17.5%
	Total payments less cash transfers: Spouse		n.a.	n.a.	n.a.	n.a.
	Total tax wedge: Principal earner		17.5%	30.0%	33.0%	17.5%
	Total tax wedge: Spouse		n.a.	n.a.	n.a.	n.a.

New Zealand 2013

The tax/benefit position of married couples

		Wage level (per cent of average wage)	100-0	100-33	100-67	100-33
		Number of children	2	2	2	none
1.	**Gross wage earnings**		53234	70979	88723	70979
2.	**Standard tax allowances:**					
	Basic allowance					
	Married or head of family					
	Dependent children					
	Deduction for social security contributions and income taxes					
	Work-related expenses					
	Other					
		Total	0	0	0	0
3.	**Tax credits or cash transfers included in taxable income**		0	0	0	0
4.	**Central government taxable income (1 - 2 + 3)**		53234	70979	88723	70979
5.	**Central government income tax liability (exclusive of tax credits)**		8990	11116	14221	11116
6.	**Tax credits :**					
	Basic credit		0	0	0	0
	Married or head of family					
	Children					
	Other					
		Total	0	0	0	0
7.	**Central government income tax finally paid (5-6)**		8990	11116	14221	11116
8.	**State and local taxes**		0	0	0	0
9.	**Employees' compulsory social security contributions**					
	Gross earnings					
	Taxable income					
		Total	0	0	0	0
10.	**Total payments to general government (7 + 8 + 9)**		8990	11116	14221	11116
11.	**Cash transfers from general government**					
	For head of family					
	For two children		7705	3934	164	0
		Total	7705	3934	164	0
12.	**Take-home pay (1-10+11)**		51949	63798	74666	59863
13.	**Employer's compulsory social security contributions**		0	0	0	0
14.	**Average rates**					
	Income tax		16.9%	15.7%	16.0%	15.7%
	Employees' social security contributions		0.0%	0.0%	0.0%	0.0%
	Total payments less cash transfers		2.4%	10.1%	15.8%	15.7%
	Total tax wedge including employer's social security contributions		2.4%	10.1%	15.8%	15.7%
15.	**Marginal rates**					
	Total payments less cash transfers: Principal earner		51.3%	51.3%	51.2%	30.0%
	Total payments less cash transfers: Spouse		33.2%	38.8%	38.7%	17.5%
	Total tax wedge: Principal earner		51.3%	51.3%	51.2%	30.0%
	Total tax wedge: Spouse		33.2%	38.8%	38.7%	17.5%

The national currency is the New Zealand dollar (NZD). In 2013, NZD 1.22 was equal to USD 1. In that year the average worker earned NZD 53 234 (country estimate).

1. Personal income tax systems

1.1. *Central/federal government income taxes*

1.1.1. *Tax unit*

Members of the family are taxed separately.

1.1.2. *Tax allowances and tax credits*

1.1.2.1. Standard reliefs

- The Transitional Tax Allowance is available to persons with income under NZD 9 880. The rebate is NZD 728, reduced by 20 cents on each dollar earned over NZD 6 240. Therefore the rebate is fully abated once income reaches NZD 9 800. This rebate is limited to those in full-time employment or who would have been in full-time employment but for sickness or accident. However, the Transitional Tax Allowance is not available if the taxpayer receives an income tested benefit or if any of the universal cash transfers apply. In addition, the amount of the rebate depends on the proportion of weeks in the year where more than 20 hours have been worked. The Transitional Tax Allowance was repealed on 24 May 2012 but is grandparented for some taxpayers in certain circumstances for the 2012/13 tax year.
- Children: No credit to parents. A child under 15 years of age, or under 18 and attending an educational institution, may claim the child rebate against their own earnings. The rebate is calculated as 13.75 per cent of gross earnings from employment, up to a maximum allowance of NZD 321.75 on NZD 2 340 of income. Investment earnings are excluded from the calculation of this rebate.

1.1.2.2. Main non-standard tax reliefs applicable to an AW

None.

1.1.3. *Schedule*

- Rates of income tax for individuals:
  - On so much of the income as does not exceed NZD 14 000: 10.5 per cent.
  - On so much of the income as exceeds NZD 14 000 but does not exceed NZD 48 000: 17.5 per cent.
  - On so much of the income as exceeds NZD 48 000 but does not exceed NZD 70 000: 30 per cent.
  - On so much of the income as exceeds NZD 70 000: 33 per cent.

1.2. *State and local income taxes*

New Zealand has no state or local income tax.

2. Compulsory social security contributions to schemes operated within the government sector

New Zealand has no Compulsory social security contributions to schemes operated within the government sector.

It should be noted that there is an accident compensation scheme administered by the Accident Compensation Corporation for residents and temporary visitors to New Zealand. This scheme is funded in part by premiums paid by employees and employers. For employees, the premium represents 1.7 per cent of their gross earnings. For employers and the self-employed, the premiums are based on a percentage of the total payroll and the applicable rate varies depending upon the associated accident risk (the average rate is 1.15%). This scheme is not considered as a compulsory social security contribution for the purposes of the Report.

3. Universal cash transfers

3.1. *Amount for marriage*

None.

3.2. *Amount for children*

The Parental Tax Credit provides NZD 150 per week for the first eight weeks of each child's life. This tax credit abates under the same regime as the Family Tax Credit, although it is unaffected until both the Family Tax Credit and In Work Tax Credit have been abated to zero.

3.3. *Family Tax Credit*

For an eldest child aged 16-18, the rate of the Family Tax Credit is NZD 5 303 per year, while the rate of NZD 4 822 applies if the eldest child is younger than 16. For subsequent children the rate depends on the age of the child; NZD 4 745 per year for 16-18 year-olds, NZD 3 822 per year for 13-15 year-olds and NZD 3 351 per year for children under 13 years of age. The total credit is abated by 21.25 cents on each dollar earned over NZD 36 350. The abatement is based on the combined income of the parents.

3.4. *In Work Tax Credit*

The In Work Tax Credit is available to families with dependent children who are not receiving an income-tested benefit, veteran's pension, New Zealand Superannuation or student allowance. The level of assistance it provides is NZD 3 120 per family per year, plus an additional NZD 780 per year for fourth and subsequent children. It is only available to couple families working a total of 30 hours or more per week, or to sole parents working 20 hours or more per week. It is also affected by the abatement regime used with the Family Tax Credit, although it is unaffected until the latter has been abated to zero.

3.5. *Minimum Family Tax Credit*

The Minimum Family Tax Credit is a scheme that ensures a guaranteed minimum family net income for all full-time earners with dependent children. The guaranteed minimum after-tax income is NZD 22 724 per year plus the Family Tax Credit and In Work Tax Credit.

3.6. *Independent Earner Tax Credit*

The Independent Earner Tax Credit of NZD 520 is available to individuals with annual net income between NZD 24 000 and NZD 48 000 that do not receive other forms of tax credits or benefits. It is abated by 13 cents on each dollar earned over NZD 44 000.

4. Main changes in tax/benefit systems over 2011/12

The rates for the Minimum Family Tax Credit changed on 1 April 2013.

5. Memorandum items

5.1. *Method used to identify AW and to calculate the AW's gross earnings*

The Annual Earnings figure is derived from the *Quarterly Employment Survey* for those employees in the B-N industry groups. The annual earnings figure for the average worker is the sum of the four quarterly earnings figures, with each quarterly figure calculated by taking the average total weekly earnings and multiplying it by 13 weeks per quarter.

5.2. *Employer's contributions to private pension, health schemes, etc.*

No information available.

2013 parameter values

	Ave_earn	53234	Country estimate
Income tax schedule	Tax_sch	0.105	14 000
		0.175	48 000
		0.3	70 000
		0.33	
Family tax credit	Fam_sup_eld	4 822	
	Fam_sup_oth	3 351	
	Fam_sup_thrsh	36 350	
	Fam_sup_rate	0.2125	
In-work tax credit	In_work_children123	3 120	
	In_work_children4plus	780	
Minimum Family Tax Credit	Min_inc	22 724	
Independent Earner Tax Credit	IETC	520	
	IETC_thrsh1	24 000	
	IETC_thrsh2	44 000	
	IETC_rate	0.13	

2013 tax equations

The equations for the New Zealand system in 2013 are mostly repeated for each individual of a married couple. But the cash transfer is calculated only once. This is shown by the Range indicator in the table below. The functions which are used in the equations (Taper, MIN, Tax, etc.) are described in the technical note about tax equations. Variable names are defined in the table of parameters above, within the equations table, or are the standard variables "married" and "children". A reference to a variable with the affix "_total" indicates the sum of the relevant variable values for the principal and spouse. And the affixes "_princ" and "_spouse" indicate the value for the principal and spouse, respectively. Equations for a single person are as shown for the principal, with "_spouse" values taken as 0.

	Line in country table andintermediate steps	Variable name	Range	Equation
1.	Earnings	earn		
2.	Allowances	tax_al	B	0
3.	Credits in taxable income	taxbl_cr	B	0
4.	CG taxable income	tax_inc	B	earn
5.	CG tax before credits	CG_tax_excl	B	Tax(tax_inc, Tax_sch)
6.	Tax credits :			
	Guaranteed minimum income	GMI	J	(Children>0)*Min_inc
	Independent Earner Tax Credit	IETC_rebate	B	=AND(Children=0,earn>IETC_thrsh1)*Taper(IETC,earn,IETC_thrsh2,IETC_rate)
6.	Tax credits:	tax_cr	B	IETC_rebate
7.	CG tax	CG_tax	B	CG_tax_excl-tax_cr
8.	Local tax	local_tax	B	0
9.	Employees' soc security	SSC	B	0
11.	Cash transfers:			
	Family tax credit (unabated)	fam_tax_cr	J	Fam_sup_eld*(Children>0)+ Fam_sup_oth*Positive(Children-1)
	In-work tax credit (unabated)	in_work_tax_cr	J	(Children>0)*(In_work_children123+Positive(Children-3)*In_work_children4plus)
	Tax credits abated	tax_cr_ab	J	Taper(fam_tax_cr+in_work_tax_cr, earn_total, Fam_sup_thrsh1, Fam_sup_rate1)
	Minimum Family tax credit	min_fam_tax_cr	J	Positive(GMI-(earn_total-CG_tax_excl_totall))
	Cash transfers	cash_trans	J	tax_cr_ab + min_fam_tax_cr
13.	Employer's soc security	SSC_empr	B	0

Key to range of equation B calculated separately for both principal earner and spouse P calculated for principal only (value taken as 0 for spouse calculation) J calculated once only on a joint basis.

Taxing Wages 2014
Changes in sructural labour income tax progressivity
over 2000-12 period in OECD member countries

Norway

This chapter includes data on the income taxes paid by workers, their social security contributions, the family benefits they receive in the form of cash transfers as well as the social security contributions and payroll taxes paid by their employers. Results reported include the marginal and average tax burden for eight different family types.

Methodological information is available for personal income tax systems, Compulsory social security contributions to schemes operated within the government sector, universal cash transfers as well as recent changes in the tax/benefit system. The methodology also includes the parameter values and tax equations underlying the data.

Norway 2013

The tax/benefit position of single persons

	Wage level (per cent of average wage)	67	100	167	67
	Number of children	none	none	none	2
1. Gross wage earnings		349451	524177	873628	349451
2. Standard tax allowances					
Basic allowance					
Married or head of family					
Dependent children					
Deduction for social security contributions and income taxes					
Work-related expenses					
Other					
	Total	128450	128450	128450	175600
3. Tax credits or cash transfers included in taxable income		0	0	0	0
4. Central government taxable (ordinary) income (1 - 2 + 3)		221001	395727	745178	173851
5. Central government income tax liability (ordinary + personal)		30388	55724	136584	23905
6. Tax credits (applicable against local tax)					
Basic credit					
Married or head of family					
Children		0	0	0	0
Other					
	Total	0	0	0	0
7. Central government income tax finally paid (5-6)		30388	55724	136584	23905
8. State and local taxes (net of tax credits)		31493	56391	106188	24774
9. Employees' compulsory social security contributions					
Gross earnings		27257	40886	68143	27257
Taxable income					
	Total	27257	40886	68143	27257
10. Total payments to general government (7 + 8 + 9)		89137	153001	310915	75935
11. Cash transfers from general government					
For head of family					
For two children		0	0	0	34920
	Total	0	0	0	34920
12. Take-home pay (1-10+11)		260314	371176	562713	308436
13. Employer's compulsory social security contributions		45429	68143	113572	45429
14. Average rates					
Income tax		17.7%	21.4%	27.8%	13.9%
Employees' social security contributions		7.8%	7.8%	7.8%	7.8%
Total payments less cash transfers		25.5%	29.2%	35.6%	11.7%
Total tax wedge including employer's social security contributions		34.1%	37.3%	43.0%	21.9%
15. Marginal rates					
Total payments less cash transfers: Principal earner		35.8%	44.8%	47.8%	35.8%
Total payments less cash transfers: Spouse		n.a.	n.a.	n.a.	n.a.
Total tax wedge: Principal earner		43.2%	51.2%	53.8%	43.2%
Total tax wedge: Spouse		n.a.	n.a.	n.a.	n.a.

Norway 2013

The tax/benefit position of married couples

		100-0	100-33	100-67	100-33
	Wage level (per cent of average wage)	100-0	100-33	100-67	100-33
	Number of children	2	2	2	none
1.	**Gross wage earnings**	524177	698902	873628	698902
2.	**Standard tax allowances**				
	Basic allowance				
	Married or head of family				
	Dependent children				
	Deduction for social security contributions and income taxes				
	Work-related expenses				
	Other				
	Total	175600	245490	256900	245490
3.	**Tax credits or cash transfers included in taxable income**	0	0	0	0
4.	**Central government taxable (ordinary) income (1 - 2 + 3)**	348577	453412	616728	453412
5.	**Central government income tax liability (ordinary + personal)**	49241	63656	86112	63656
6.	**Tax credits (applicable against local tax)**				
	Basic credit				
	Married or head of family				
	Children	0	0	0	0
	Other				
	Total	0	0	0	0
7.	**Central government income tax finally paid (5-6)**	49241	63656	86112	63656
8.	**State and local taxes (net of tax credits)**	49672	64611	87884	64611
9.	**Employees' compulsory social security contributions**				
	Gross earnings	40886	54514	68143	54514
	Taxable income				
	Total	40886	54514	68143	54514
10.	**Total payments to general government (7 + 8 + 9)**	139799	182782	242139	182782
11.	**Cash transfers from general government**				
	For head of family				
	For two children	23280	23280	23280	0
	Total	23280	23280	23280	0
12.	**Take-home pay (1-10+11)**	407658	539401	654769	516121
13.	**Employer's compulsory social security contributions**	68143	90857	113572	90857
14.	**Average rates**				
	Income tax	18.9%	18.4%	19.9%	18.4%
	Employees' social security contributions	7.8%	7.8%	7.8%	7.8%
	Total payments less cash transfers	22.2%	22.8%	25.1%	26.2%
	Total tax wedge including employer's social security contributions	31.2%	31.7%	33.7%	34.6%
15.	**Marginal rates**				
	Total payments less cash transfers: Principal earner	44.8%	44.8%	44.8%	44.8%
	Total payments less cash transfers: Spouse	24.6%	24.6%	35.8%	24.6%
	Total tax wedge: Principal earner	51.2%	51.2%	51.2%	51.2%
	Total tax wedge: Spouse	33.3%	33.3%	43.2%	33.3%

The national currency is the kroner (NOK). In 2013, NOK 5.88 was equal to 1 USD. In that year the average worker earned NOK 524 177 (Secretariat estimate).

1. Personal income tax systems

The personal income tax has two tax bases: *personal income* and *ordinary income*. Personal income is defined as income from labour and pensions. Personal income is a gross income base from which no deductions are made. Ordinary income includes all types of taxable income from labour, pensions, business and capital. Certain costs and expenses, including interest paid on debt, are deductible in the computation of ordinary income.

1.1. Central government income tax

1.1.1. Tax unit

The tax unit is in most cases the individual (tax class 1), but joint taxation (tax class 2) is also possible. Single parents are entitled to a special allowance that provides a tax benefit equivalent to being taxed under the tax class 2 schedule. Children aged below 17 are generally taxed together with their parents, but they may be taxed individually. All other income earners are taxed on an individual basis (class 1).

1.1.2. Tax allowances applicable to an AW

There are no tax allowances applicable to an AW under the central government income tax (surtax). The tax base is personal income from which no deductions are allowed. As part of the overall tax rate of 28 per cent on ordinary income, 13.75 per cent is considered to be the central government income tax.

1.1.3. Rate schedule (surtax)

Rate (%)	NOK
0	0-509 600
9.0	509 600-828 300
12.0	828 300 and over

1.2. Local government income tax

The overall tax rate on ordinary income is 28 per cent. The local government (municipal and county) income tax is 14.25 per cent points of the overall rate. Tax on ordinary income is levied after taking into account a standard allowance of NOK 47 150 (class 1) and NOK 94 300 (class 2) in 2013. The deductions in the computation of ordinary income are:

1.2.1. *Standard reliefs*

- Basic allowance: each individual receives a minimum allowance equal to 40 per cent of personal income, with a minimum of NOK 4 000 and a maximum of NOK 81 300. For wage income each individual can choose a separate allowance of NOK 31 800 instead of the basic allowance. Hence, wage earners would opt to choose this separate allowance as long as it exceeds the basic allowance to which they are entitled.

1.2.2. *Non-standard reliefs*

The main non-standard allowances deductible from ordinary income are:

- Parent allowance: Documented expenses for child care limited to:
  - maximum NOK 25 000 for one child
  - plus NOK 15 000 for each subsequent child.

The allowance applies in general to the spouse who has the highest income. Unused parent allowance may be transferred to the other spouse. The allowance is also applicable to single parents.

- Travel expenses related to work exceeding NOK 13 950.
- Labour union fees up to NOK 3 850.
- Donations to voluntary organisations up to NOK 12 000.
- Contributions to individual pension agreement schemes, maximum NOK 15 000.
- Premiums and contributions to occupational pension schemes in the private and public sector, unlimited.
- Unlimited deduction for interest payments.

The main non-standard tax credits are:

- Home savings scheme (BSU): The BSU scheme aims to encourage young people (under 34 years old) to save for a future home purchase. A wastable *tax credit* of 20 per cent of annual savings up to NOK 20 000 in special accounts is granted. Total savings may not exceed NOK 150 000.

2. Social security contributions

2.1. Contributions to the national insurance scheme

2.1.1. *Employees' contributions*

Employees' contributions to the National Insurance Scheme generally amount to 7.8 per cent of personal wage income. Employees do not make contributions if their wage income is less than NOK 39 600. Once wage income exceeds this floor, an alternative calculation is made where the contributions equal 25 per cent of the wage income in excess of the floor. The actual contributions made would represent the minimum between the alternative calculation and 7.8 per cent of the total wage income.

Contributions from the self-employed are 11.0 per cent of personal income attributable to labour.

2.1.2. *Employers' contributions*

Employer's social security contributions are due for all employees in both the private and the public sector. The contribution is geographically differentiated according to the municipality where the work-place is. The standard rates are 14.1, 10.6, 7.9, 6.4, 5.1 or 0 per cent of gross wages. The highest rate applies to central parts of southern Norway. Lower rates may apply under certain circumstances. The weighted average rate is approximately 13 per cent.

3. Universal cash transfers

3.1. *Transfers related to marital status*

None.

3.2. *Transfers for dependent children (child support)*

The following transfers are available:

NOK 11 640 per child aged 0-18 years.

Single parents receive transfers for one more child than their actual number of children. Families living in the northernmost parts of Norway receive extra child support of NOK 3 840 per year for each child aged 18 or younger.

4. Main changes in tax/benefit systems since 2002

- Most important changes in 2013:
  - The personal allowance for labour income was increased for low income earners (below NOK 213 950) by 2 percentage points from 38 to 40 per cent of their labour income.
  - The taxable value of second homes and commercial property for the purposes of net wealth tax was increased from 40 per cent to 50 per cent of estimated market value.
  - The basic allowance in the net wealth tax was increased from NOK 750 000 to NOK 870 000. Married couples will thus have a total basic allowance of NOK 1 740 000.
  - The current class 2 for sole providers was replaced by a special allowance for ordinary income which provides an equivalent tax benefit.
  - The maximum deduction for labour union fees was increased from NOK 3 750 to NOK 3 850.
- Most important changes in 2012:
  - The personal allowance for labour income was increased for low income earners (below NOK 217 000) by 2 percentage points from 36 to 38 per cent of their labour income.
  - For self-employed the wage allowance was abolished to eliminate residual discrimination between sole proprietorships with employees and limited companies.
  - In the deduction for travel expenses for travels between home and work the deduction rate per kilometre was increased for tax payers travelling between 35 000 km and 50 000 km per year.
  - The maximum deduction for labour union fees was increased by NOK 90 to NOK 3 750.
- In 2011 changes to the tax system was made to provide better incentives for people to work when drawing a pension. The tax limitation rule for early-retirement and old-age pensioners was replaced by a new tax allowance for pension income. The allowance ensures that people who only receive the minimum pension will continue not to pay income tax. The allowance is scaled down against pension income, so that the marginal

tax on earned income is reduced to the same level as for wage earners. The marginal tax on capital for low-income pensioners is also reduced to the same level as for other taxpayers. The new tax allowance is determined regardless of the spouse's income and married early-retirement and old-age pensioners will each have their own allowance. In addition, the pension income social security contribution is increased and the special allowance for age is discontinued.

- In 2010 a new formula-based system for determining the tax-assessed value of homes was introduced. The new tax-assessed value will be determined by multiplying the floor space of the dwelling by a square metre price based on the geographical location (neighbourhood, municipality, sparsely populated vs. densely populated area), size, age and type (detached, semi-detached, terraced, flat) of the property. For *primary homes* (owner-occupied), the per square metre rate will be set at 25 per cent of the estimated sale price per square metre, whereas the rate for second homes, i.e. any other dwellings in addition to the primary home that are not defined as business or recreational properties, will be set at 40 per cent of the estimated sale price per square metre. The current "safety valve" system is being continued so that taxpayers can appeal and have the tax-assessed value reduced to 30 per cent of the documented fair market value (60 per cent for second homes). In addition, the tax-assessed values of recreational properties are increased by 10 per cent.
- Most important changes in 2009 were the abolition of the 80 per cent rule, which primarily reduced the wealth tax of the richest. The wealth tax on equities for those who fall within the scope of the 80 per cent rule has been more than doubled since 2005.
- The home savings scheme (BSU) was expanded in 2009 by increasing the annual savings amount to NOK 20 000 and the maximum aggregate savings amount to NOK 150 000.
- The rates of the inheritance tax were reduced and the exempted amount was increased in 2009. The instalment scheme for family businesses was expanded through the abolition of the upper limit, and the payment period was increased from 7 to 12 years.

Other changes in the personal tax base in 2009:

- The fishermen's allowance was increased from NOK 115 000 to NOK 150 000.
- The reindeer husbandry allowance was increased to the same level as the agriculture allowance.
- The allowance for labour union fees was increased by NOK 450 to NOK 3 600.
- The rate of the travel allowance was increased from NOK 1.40 per km to NOK 1.50 per km.
- The tax-free net income thresholds under the tax limitation rule were increased such as to ensure that singles and couples who receive the minimum state pension will still not be paying tax following the favourable social security settlement they benefited from in 2008.
- A tax favoured contributions to individual pension agreement schemes was reintroduced as of 2008.
- From 1 January 2008 the employees' SSC rate for self-employed was increased from 10.7 per cent to 11.0 per cent.
- The upper threshold in the surtax schedule was substantially reduced from 2006 to 2007.

- The surtax rates were reduced in 2005 and 2006, as part of a reform of the dual income tax system. The basic allowance has been substantially increased.
- From 1 January 2006 the supplementary employer's social security contribution at 12.5 per cent for gross wage income that exceeds 16 times "G" (average "G" is estimated to be NOK 74 721 in 2010) was removed.
- From 1 January 2006 the class 2 in the surtax was removed.
- From 1 January 2005 the ceiling in the parent allowance for two and more children was removed, and the maximum allowance was increased with NOK 5 000 for each child after the first. From 2008 the maximum allowance will be increased with NOK 15 000 for each child after the first.
- The additional child support of NOK 7 884 for children aged 1 and 2 years was abolished as of 1 August 2003.
- An allowance of maximum NOK 6 000 for donations to voluntary organisations was introduced as of 1 January 2003. Previously this allowance was co-ordinated with the allowance for labour union fees (with a combined maximum allowance). The allowance was increased to NOK 12 000 as of 1 January 2005.
- As of 1 July 2002 the employer's social security contribution rates for employees aged 62 years or older were reduced by 4 percentage points, although not below zero per cent. From 2007 the reduction was abolished.

5. Memorandum items

5.1. *Identification of an AW and calculation of earnings*

The wage series used refers to full time employees in the B-N industry group (ISIC Rev. 4).

The calculation of annual wage earnings is as follows:

- Weighted average monthly wage plus overtime times 12.

The average monthly wage is agreed payment for a wage earner working a normal agreed working-year. It includes bonus payments and other allowances, but not payments for overtime, sick leave, and an establishment's indirect wage costs. The sum is weighted with the number of persons employed in the different industry groups.

5.2. *Employers' contributions to private health and pension schemes*

No information available.

2013 parameter values

Average earnings/yr	Ave_earn	524 177	Secretariat estimate
Central rate (pers)	Tax1_sch	0	509 600
class 1		0.09	828 300
		0.12	
class 2	Tax2_sch	0	509 600
		0.09	828 300
		0.12	
Central rate (ord)	Cent_rate_ord	0,1375	
Local rate (ord)	Local_rate	0.1425	
Allowances	Class_al_1	47 150	
	Class_al_2	94 300	
Basic relief	Basic_min	4 000	
	Basic_max	81 300	
	Basic_rel_rate	0.4	
	Basic_min_wage	31 800	
Soc security contribs	SSC_rate	0.078	
Employer	SSC_empr	0.13	
Trygd. low.lim	SSC_low_lim	39 600	
pct.rate	SSC_low_rate	0.25	
Ref. Income "G"	SSC_G	84 204	
Child cash transfer	Child_sup	11 640	

2013 tax equations

The equations for the system for Norway in 2012 may be calculated on an individual or joint basis for married couples. Social security contributions are calculated on an individual basis. The calculation for Class 2 is always chosen for single parents and is chosen for married couples whenever this gives a lower value of tax than the corresponding Class 1 calculations. The functions which are used in the equations (Taper, MIN, Tax, etc.) are described in the technical note about tax equations. Variable names are defined in the table of parameters above, within the equations table, or are the standard variables "married" and "children". A reference to a variable with the affix "_total" indicates the sum of the relevant variable values for the principal and spouse. And the affixes "_princ" and "_spouse" indicate the value for the principal and spouse, respectively. Equations for a single person are as shown for the principal, with "_spouse" values taken as 0.

	Line in country table and intermediate steps	Variable name	Range	Equation
1.	Earnings	earn		
2.	Allowances:	tax_al	J	IF(class=1, tax1_al_princ+tax1_al_spouse, tax2_al)
	Class 1 tax allowance (ordinary)	tax1_al_princ	P	MIN(MAX(Basic_min_wage, MIN(earn_princ*Basic_rel_rate, Basic_max)) +Class_al_1, earn_princ)
	Class 1 tax allowance (ordinary)	tax1_al_spouse	S	MIN(MAX(Basic_min_wage, MIN(earn_spouse*Basic_rel_rate, Basic_max)) +Class_al_1, earn_spouse)
	Class 2 tax allowance (ordinary)	tax2_al	J	MIN(MAX(Basic_min_wage, MIN(earn_princ*Basic_rel_rate, Basic_max)), earn_princ)+MIN(MAX(Basic_min_wage, MIN(earn_spouse* Basic_rel_rate, Basic_max)), earn_spouse)+Class_al_2
3.	Credits in taxable income	taxbl_cr	J	0
4.	CG taxable income (ordinary)			
	Class 1 taxable income	tax1_inc	B	Positive(earn-tax1_al)
	Class 2 taxable income	tax2_inc	J	Positive(earn_total-tax2_al)
5.	CG tax	CG_tax		IF(class=1, CG1_tax, CG2_tax)
	Class 1 tax (personal+ordinary)	CG1_tax	B	Tax(earn, Tax1_sch)+Cent_rate_ord*tax1_inc
	Class 2 tax (personal+ordinary)	CG2_tax	J	Tax(earn_p, Tax2_sch)+ Tax(earn_s, Tax2_sch)+Cent_rate_ord*tax2_inc
6.	Tax credits :	tax_cr	P	0
7.	CG tax	CG_tax	B	CG_tax
8.	State and local taxes	local_tax	J	IF(class=1, local1_tax_total, local2_tax)
	Class 1 local tax	local1_tax	B	(Local_rate*(tax1_inc_princ+tax1_inc_spouse))-tax_cr
	Class 2 local tax	local2_tax	J	(Local_rate*tax2_inc)-tax_cr
	Favourable class	class	J	1+((CG2_tax_excl+local2_tax)<(CG1_tax_excl_total+local1_tax_total))
9.	Employees' soc security	SSC	B	MIN(earn*SSC_rate, Positive(SSC_low_rate*(earn-SSC_low_lim)))
11.	Cash transfers	cash_trans	J	(children>0)*Child_sup
13.	Employer's soc security	SSC_empr	B	earn*SSC_empr

Key to range of equation B calculated separately for both principal earner and spouse P calculated for principal only (value taken as 0 for spouse calculation) J calculated once only on a joint basis.

Taxing Wages 2014
Changes in sructural labour income tax progressivity
over 2000-12 period in OECD member countries

Poland

This chapter includes data on the income tax paid by workers, their social security contributions, the family benefits they receive in the form of cash transfers as well as the social security contributions and payroll taxes paid by their employers. Results reported include the marginal and average tax burden for eight different family types.

Methodological information is available for personal income tax systems, Compulsory social security contributions to schemes operated within the government sector, universal cash transfers as well as recent changes in the tax/benefit system. The methodology also includes the parameter values and tax equations underlying the data.

Poland 2013

The tax/benefit position of single persons

		Wage level (per cent of average wage)	67	100	167	67
		Number of children	none	none	none	2
1.	**Gross wage earnings**		27628	41442	69071	27628
2.	**Standard tax allowances**					
	Basic allowance					
	Married or head of family					
	Dependent children					
	Deduction for social security contributions and income taxes		2779	4169	6948	2779
	Work-related expenses		1335	1335	1335	1335
	Other					
		Total	4114	5504	8283	4114
3.	**Tax credits or cash transfers included in taxable income**		0	0	0	0
4.	**Central government taxable income (1 - 2 + 3)**		22505	34426	58266	22505
5.	**Central government income tax liability (exclusive of tax credits)**		4051	6197	10488	4051
6.	**Tax credits**					
	Basic credit		556	556	556	1112
	Married or head of family					
	Children		0	0	0	2224
	Other (health insurance)		1848	2771	4619	1848
		Total	2404	3327	5175	5184
7.	**Central government income tax finally paid (5-6)**		1647	2869	5313	0
8.	**State and local taxes**		0	0	0	0
9.	**Employees' compulsory social security contributions**					
	Gross earnings		2779	4169	6948	2779
	Taxable income		2146	3218	5364	2146
		Total	4925	7387	12312	4925
10.	**Total payments to general government (7 + 8 + 9)**		6572	10257	17625	4925
11.	**Cash transfers from general government**					
	For head of family					
	For two children		0	0	0	0
		Total	0	0	0	0
12.	**Take-home pay (1-10+11)**		21056	31186	51445	22703
13.	**Employers' compulsory social security contributions**		4636	6954	11590	4636
14.	**Average rates**					
	Income tax		6.0%	6.9%	7.7%	0.0%
	Employees' social security contributions		17.8%	17.8%	17.8%	17.8%
	Total payments less cash transfers		23.8%	24.7%	25.5%	17.8%
	Total tax wedge including employer's social security contributions		34.7%	35.6%	36.2%	29.6%
15.	**Marginal rates**					
	Total payments less cash transfers: Principal earner		26.7%	26.7%	26.7%	17.8%
	Total payments less cash transfers: Spouse		n.a.	n.a.	n.a.	n.a.
	Total tax wedge: Principal earner		37.2%	37.2%	37.2%	29.6%
	Total tax wedge: Spouse		n.a.	n.a.	n.a.	n.a.

Poland 2013

The tax/benefit position of married couples

		100-0	100-33	100-67	100-33
	Wage level (per cent of average wage)	100-0	100-33	100-67	100-33
	Number of children	2	2	2	none
1.	**Gross wage earnings**	41442	55257	69071	55257
2.	**Standard tax allowances**				
	Basic allowance				
	Married or head of family				
	Dependent children				
	Deduction for social security contributions and income taxes	4169	5559	6948	5559
	Work-related expenses	1335	2670	2670	2670
	Other				
	Total	5504	8229	9618	8229
3.	**Tax credits or cash transfers included in taxable income**	0	0	0	0
4.	**Central government taxable income (1 - 2 + 3)**	34426	45011	56931	45011
5.	**Central government income tax liability (exclusive of tax credits)**	6197	8102	10248	8102
6.	**Tax credits**				
	Basic credit	1112	1112	1112	1112
	Married or head of family				
	Children	2224	2224	2224	0
	Other (health insurance)	2771	3695	4619	3695
	Total	6108	7031	7955	4807
7.	**Central government income tax finally paid (5-6)**	89	1071	2292	3295
8.	**State and local taxes**	0	0	0	0
9.	**Employees' compulsory social security contributions**				
	Gross earnings	4169	5559	6948	5559
	Taxable income	3218	4291	5364	4291
	Total	7387	9850	12312	9850
10.	**Total payments to general government (7 + 8 + 9)**	7477	10921	14605	13145
11.	**Cash transfers from general government**				
	For head of family				
	For two children	0	0	0	0
	Total	0	0	0	0
12.	**Take-home pay (1-10+11)**	33966	44336	54466	42112
13.	**Employers' compulsory social security contributions**	6954	9272	11590	9272
14.	**Average rates**				
	Income tax	0.2%	1.9%	3.3%	6.0%
	Employees' social security contributions	17.8%	17.8%	17.8%	17.8%
	Total payments less cash transfers	18.0%	19.8%	21.1%	23.8%
	Total tax wedge including employer's social security contributions	29.8%	31.3%	32.5%	34.7%
15.	**Marginal rates**				
	Total payments less cash transfers: Principal earner	26.7%	26.7%	26.7%	26.7%
	Total payments less cash transfers: Spouse	24.9%	26.7%	26.7%	26.7%
	Total tax wedge: Principal earner	37.2%	37.2%	37.2%	37.2%
	Total tax wedge: Spouse	35.7%	37.2%	37.2%	37.2%

The national currency is the zloty (PLN). In 2013, PLN 3.16 was equal to USD 1. In that year, the average worker earned PLN 41 442 (Secretariat Estimate).

1. Personal income tax systems

An individual being a tax resident in Poland is liable to tax on the basis of world-wide income, irrespective of the source and origin of that income. (The term "residency" is understood similarly to Article 4 paragraph 2 point a) of the *OECD Model Tax Convention on Income and Capital*).

1.1. Central government income tax

1.1.1. Tax unit

Individuals are taxed on their own income, but couples married during the whole calendar year* can opt to be taxed on their joint income. In the latter case, the "splitting" system applies: the tax bill for a couple is twice the income tax due on half of joint income, provided the joint income does not include capital income taxed at the flat 19 per cent rate. Single individuals with dependent children are also entitled to use the splitting system (their family quotient is two). For the purpose of this report, it is assumed that married couples are taxed on joint income.

1.1.1.1. Tax base

1.1.1.1.1.Gross employment income

For taxation purposes, taxable gross employment income in Poland includes both cash income and the value of benefits in kind. More specifically, gross employment income includes base salary, overtime payments, bonuses, awards, compensation for unused holidays, and costs that are paid in full or in part by the employer on behalf of the employee.

1.1.2. Tax allowances and tax credits

1.1.2.1. Standard reliefs

- Basic relief: A non-refundable tax credit of PLN 556.02 per person.
- Marital status relief: None.
- Relief for children: Yes.**

A taxpayer can deduct from the due tax decreased by the amount of health contributions specified in the PIT Act, the amount, which is equal for *each month* of raising a child:

- PLN -92.67 (annually PLN 1 112.04) for the first child, if the income received by parents (married or single parent, who meets special requirements) doesn't exceed in the tax year the amount of PLN 112 000. For other parent the threshold of income is PLN 56 000,

* However, a widowed spouse is entitled to apply the join income taxation.

** It concerns a child of 18 years old or younger or a child up to 25 years old provided they are students or a disabled child irrespective of their age. The actual description in Section 4.

- PLN -92.67 (annually PLN 1 112.04) for the second child,
- PLN -139.01 (annually PLN 1 668.12) for the third child,
- PLN -185.34 (annually PLN 2 224.08) for the fourth and every next child.
- Relief for health insurance contributions: A tax credit is almost equal to health insurance contribution paid to the National Health Fund. The contribution is 9 per cent of the calculation basis whereas the tax credit is 7.75 per cent of this basis.
- Relief for other social security contributions: An allowance is provided for all social insurance contributions paid by the taxpayer.
- Relief for selected work-related expenses: Standard deductions depend on the number of workplaces and on whether place of residence and workplace are within the same town/city or not. The annual amounts in PLN (deductible from income) are:

	One workplace	Two/more workplaces
Workplace in the same town/city as place of residence	1 335.00[1]	2 002.05
Workplace in different town/city as place of residence	1 668.72	2 502.56

Note: If the actual commuting expenses exceed standard deduction, relief can be determined by the actual expenses incurred solely on personal season tickets.

1. For the purpose of the calculations in this publication, it is assumed that the worker has the same town/city as place of residence.

1.1.2.2. Main non-standard tax reliefs applicable to an average worker

Allowances:

- Expenses for the purpose of rehabilitation incurred by a taxpayer who is a disabled person, or a taxpayer, who supports the disabled.
- Equivalent of blood donations, donations made for the purposes of public benefit activity and of religious practice – in the amount of donation, no more than 6 per cent of income.
- Donations made for charity church care – in the amount of the donation.
- Expenses incurred for the use of the Internet – a taxpayer is entitled to deduct the Internet tax allowance within the next two years, providing that during the phase preceded this period he did not deduct Internet for the use of the Internet (up to PLN 760);
- Abolished allowance (since 2007 continued on the acquired right basis) for interests payments on mortgage loans raised no later than in 2006 on acquisition of housing property on the primary market – up to the amount of interests related to the part of loan not exceeding PLN 325 990 for investments finished in 2012. The limit in 2013 will be known at the end of the year but will not be less than the limit for the year 2012.

Tax credits:

- Donation made to public benefit organizations – up to 1 per cent of due tax.*
- Abolished tax credits (continued on the acquired rights basis), i.e. expenses for saving with the aim of buying a house or flat, the amount of social contributions paid on income of an unemployed person hired by a taxpayer in order to take care of their children and/or house.

* This relief is distinct from an allowance for donations deducted from income.

1.1.3. *Tax schedule*

The tax schedule is as follows:

Tax base (in PLN)		Tax amount
Over	Below	
0	85 528	18% of the tax base, less a basic tax credit of PLN 556.02
85 528		PLN 14 839.02 + 32% of surplus over PLN 85 528

1.2. *State and local income tax*

There are no regional or local income taxes.

1.3. *Wealth tax*

There is no wealth tax.

2. Social Security Contributions

2.1. *Employees' contributions*

Employees pay 13.71 per cent of the gross wage. This contribution includes:

- Pension insurance contribution – 9.76 per cent of the gross wage.
- Disability insurance contribution – 1.5 per cent of the gross wage.
- Sickness/maternity insurance contribution – 2.45 per cent of the gross wage.
- 14.34 per cent of the old age insurance contribution (1.4 percentage points*) are transferred by ZUS to a privately-managed fund, which is called an "open pension fund (OPF)" where the savings accumulate at a market conform rate. These pension savings are paid out if the taxpayer dies before reaching the pension age. These pension savings are not included in the *Taxing Wages* calculations as they are "non-tax compulsory payments"; more information can be found in the online *OECD Tax Database* (*www.oecd.org/ctp/taxdatabase*).
- In case of pension and disability insurance, contributions are not paid on the part of the wage that exceeds PLN 111 390.**

2.2. *Employers' contributions*

In respect of income paid under an employment contract with a Polish entity, employers have an obligation to pay social security contributions equal to 20.43 per cent of gross wage. This value consists of:

- 9.76 percentage points are aimed for pension insurance.
- 6.5 percentage points are aimed for disability insurance.

* From May 2011 2.3 per cent of gross earnings (which is 11.78 per cent of old age contribution paid both by employee and employer). This percentage will increase in future years.

** The contribution ceiling of pension and disability insurance funds for a given calendar year may not exceed thirty times the amount of the projected average monthly remuneration in the national economy for that year, as set forth in the Budgetary Act.

- 4.17 percentage points are aimed for other insurances i.e. 1.62 percentage points (on average) accident insurance, 2.45 percentage points for Labour Found and 0.1 percentage points for the Guaranteed Employee Benefit Fund.
- 14.34 per cent of the old age insurance contributions (1.4 percentage points*) are transferred by ZUS to a privately-managed fund, which is called an "open pension fund (OPF)"; where the savings accumulate at a market conform rate. These pension savings are paid out if the taxpayer dies before reaching the pension age. These pension savings are not included in the *Taxing Wages* calculation as they are "non-tax compulsory payments"; more information can be found in the online *OECD Tax Database* (*www.oecd.org/ctp/taxdatabase*).
- In case of pension and disability insurance, contributions are not paid on the part of the wage that exceeds PLN 111 390.

3. Universal cash transfers

3.1. Transfers related to marital status

None.

3.2. Transfers for dependent children

From 1st of November 2012 families where the average monthly income per household member for the previous period is no greater than PLN 539 or PLN 623 when there are one or more disabled children in the household) are entitled to family allowances. From 1st of November 2014 the income criteria will be as high as PLN 574 and PLN 664. Families receive PLN 77 monthly for a child no older than 5 years, PLN 106 monthly for a child of 5 up to 18 years old, and PLN 115 monthly for a child of 18 up to 24 years old. The calculations in this Report are based on the assumption that the children are aged between 5 and 18 years.

Single parents are entitled to a supplement of PLN 170 for each child up to a maximum of PLN 340 for all children (and PLN 250 for a disabled child up to a maximum of PLN 500 for all children).

There are several supplements to family allowances:

- for large families – PLN 80 monthly for the 3rd and next children in the family;
- for education of disabled children – PLN 60 monthly for children not older than 5 years and PLN 80 for children older than 5 years.

4. Main changes in tax/benefit systems since 2012

There have been the following changes in tax system concerning tax allowances and relieves since 2012.

On the basis of the last amendment of the Act on Personal income tax, that has been in force since 1 January 2013:

- Deduction of the expenses on the Internet has been limited; now the tax relief will refer to the taxpayers who did not benefit from this tax relief in the previous years, moreover the deduction will apply to the expenses incurred through 2 years following one another.

* See previous footnote.

- Changes in the child relief have been introduced; they involve:
  - increasing the child relief for families with three and more children (for the third child monthly amount of deduction will be PLN 139.01/PLN 1 668.12 annually/, for the fourth and every next child the monthly amount of deduction will be PLN 185.34/PLN 2 224.08 annually);
  - changes in the tax relief for families with one child by introducing the limit of income received by parents.

For taxpayers who have two or more children the child relief will apply regardless of the income received during the tax year.

There have been the following changes in Social Security Contributions since 2012.

- Adjustment in the transfers for dependent children.
- Amount of pension contributions transferred by ZUS to a privately-managed fund "open pension fund (OPF)" has been changed from 2.3 per cent up to 2.8 per cent.

From the 1st of January 2013 the retirement age is increasing by a month in January, May and September each year until it receives 67 for both sexes (women – 2040, men – 2020).

5. Memorandum items

5.1. *Identification of AW and valuation of earnings*

The Polish Central Statistical Office calculates average monthly wages and salaries for employees on the basis of reports of enterprises. The figures include overtime and bonus payments and also include information for part-time employees converted to full-time equivalents. Male and female workers are included. The information, which includes estimates for different sectors, is published in the monthly *Statistical Bulletin*.

5.2. *Employers' contributions to private pension, health and related schemes*

No information provided.

2013 parameter values

Average earnings/yr	Ave_earn		41 442	Secretariat Estimate
Work expenses	work_exp		1 335.00[1]	
Income tax schedule	tax_sch		0.18	85 528
			0.32	
Tax credits				
Basic credit	basic_cr		556.02	
Health insurance	health_ins		0.09	
	health_ins_credit		0.0775	
Children	Child_cr		1 112.04	
	Child_cr_lim		112 000	
Social security contributions				
Employers	SSC_empr	0.2043		
old-age pension and disability pension insurance	SSC_old	0.097676		
	SSC_old_ZUS	0.061097676		
	SSC_old_ZUSII		0.0225	
	SSC_old_OPF		0.014	
	SSC_dis		0.065	
other insurances	SSC_a		0.0417	
Employees	SSC		0.1371	
old-age pension and disability pension insurance	SSC_old_e		0.0976	
	SSC_old_e_ZUS		0.0610976	
	SSC_old_e_ZUSII		0.0225	
	SSC_old_e_OPF		0.014	
	SSC_dis_e		0.015	
sickness insurance	SSC_s		0.0245	
Contribution ceiling	SSC_c		111 390	
Family benefit	fam_ben		1 272	
single parent additional family benefit	fam_ben_Spsup		170	
single parent additional family benefit ceiling	fam_ben_Spsup_lim		340	
income limit	fam_ben_lim		6 468	
income limit for single parent	fam_ben_lim_sp		6 468	

1. Lump-sum annual work expenses for an employee having one workplace and living in the place (town, city) where the workplace is; employees living outside the city (town) where their workplace is may deduct 1668,72 PLN annually.

2013 tax equations

The equations for the Polish system are mostly calculated on a family basis.

The standard functions which are used in the equations (Taper, MIN, Tax, etc.) are described in the technical note about tax equations. Two additional functions (Tax93 and ftax) have been incorporated to carry out an iterative calculation for central government tax. These allow for the fact that the church tax is calculated as 9 per cent of Central Government tax and is also allowed as a deduction when calculating taxable income. Variable names are defined in the table of parameters above, within the equations table, or are the standard variables "married" and "children". A reference to a variable with the affix "_total" indicates the sum of the relevant variable values for the principal and spouse. And the affixes "_princ" and "_spouse" indicate the value for the principal and spouse, respectively. Equations for a single person are as shown for the principal, with "_spouse" values taken as 0.

	Line in country table and intermediate steps	Variable name	Range	Equation
1.	Earnings	earn		
	Quotient for tax calculation	quotient	J	1+MAX(Married,(Children>0))
2.	Allowances:	tax_al	J	work_exp+MIN(earn_spouse,work_exp)+SSC+SSC_old_e_OPF*MIN(earn, SSC_c)
3.	Credits in taxable income	taxbl_cr	J	0
4.	CG taxable income	tax_inc	J	Positive(earn-tax_al)
5.	CG tax before credits	CG_tax_excl	J	quotient*Tax(tax_inc/quotient,tax_sch)
6.	Tax credits :			
	Basic credit	basic_cr	J	basic_cr*quotient
	Health insurance	health_ins_cr	B	health_ins_credit*(earn-SSC-SSC_old_e_OPF*MIN(earn, SSC_c))
	Child credit	child_cr	J	If(earn_total<Child_cr_lim,children*child_cr,0)
	Total tax credits	tax_cr	J	basic_cr+health_ins_cr+child_cr
7.	CG tax	CG_tax	J	Positive(CG_tax_excl-tax_cr)
8.	State and local taxes	local_tax	J	0
9.	Employees' soc security	health_ins	B	(earn-(MIN(earn, SSC_c)*(SSC_old_e+SSC_dis_e)+earn*SSC_s))*health_ins
.		SSC	B	(SSC_old_e_ZUS+SSC_dis_e)*MIN(earn,SSC_c)+SSC_s*earn
11.	Cash transfers	cash_tran	J	((earn_total/(1+Married+Children))<(Married*fam_ben_lim+(1-Married)*fam_ben_lim_sp))*(Children*fam_ben+(1-Married)*(Children>0)*MIN(fam_ben_Spsup*Children;fam_ben_Spsup_lim))
13.	Employer's soc security	SSC_empr	B	(SSC_old_ZUS+SSC_dis)*MIN(earn,SSC_c)+SSC_a*earn

Key to range of equation:
B calculated separately for both principal earner and spouse,
P calculated for principal only (value taken as 0 for spouse calculation),
J calculated once only on a joint basis.

Taxing Wages 2014
Changes in sructural labour income tax progressivity
over 2000-12 period in OECD member countries

Portugal

This chapter includes data on the income taxes paid by workers, their social security contributions, the family benefits they receive in the form of cash transfers as well as the social security contributions and payroll taxes paid by their employers. Results reported include the marginal and average tax burden for eight different family types.

Methodological information is available for personal income tax systems, Compulsory social security contributions to schemes operated within the government sector, universal cash transfers as well as recent changes in the tax/ benefit system. The methodology also includes the parameter values and tax equations underlying the data.

Portugal 2013

The tax/benefit position of single persons

	Wage level (per cent of average wage)	67	100	167	67
	Number of children	none	none	none	2
1.	**Gross wage earnings**	11557	17335	28892	11557
2.	**Standard tax allowances**				
	Basic allowance	4104	4104	4104	4104
	Married or head of family				
	Dependent children				
	Deduction for social security contributions and income taxes				
	Work-related expenses	0	0	0	0
	Other				
	Total	4104	4104	4104	4104
3.	**Tax credits or cash transfers included in taxable income**	0	0	0	0
4.	**Central government taxable income (1 - 2 + 3)**	7453	13231	24788	7453
5.	**Central government income tax liability (exclusive of tax credits)**	1144	2791	6492	1144
6.	**Tax credits**				
	Basic credit	214	214	214	333
	Married or head of family				
	Children	0	0	0	428
	Other				
	Total	214	214	214	760
7.	**Central government income tax finally paid (5-6)**	954	2803	6908	384
8.	**State and local taxes**	0	0	0	0
9.	**Employees' compulsory social security contributions**				
	Gross earnings	1271	1907	3178	1271
	Taxable income				
	Total	1271	1907	3178	1271
10.	**Total payments to general government (7 + 8 + 9)**	2225	4710	10086	1655
11.	**Cash transfers from general government**				
	For head of family				
	For two children	0	0	0	841
	Total	0	0	0	841
12.	**Take-home pay (1-10+11)**	9332	12626	18806	10742
13.	**Employer's compulsory social security contributions**	2745	4117	6862	2745
14.	**Average rates**				
	Income tax	8.3%	16.2%	23.9%	3.3%
	Employees' social security contributions	11.0%	11.0%	11.0%	11.0%
	Total payments less cash transfers	19.3%	27.2%	34.9%	7.0%
	Total tax wedge including employer's social security contributions	34.7%	41.1%	47.4%	24.9%
15.	**Marginal rates**				
	Total payments less cash transfers: Principal earner	43.0%	43.0%	51.5%	39.5%
	Total payments less cash transfers: Spouse	n.a.	n.a.	n.a.	n.a.
	Total tax wedge: Principal earner	53.9%	53.9%	60.8%	51.1%
	Total tax wedge: Spouse	n.a.	n.a.	n.a.	n.a.

Portugal 2013

The tax/benefit position of married couples

	Wage level (per cent of average wage)	100-0	100-33	100-67	100-33
	Number of children	2	2	2	none
1.	**Gross wage earnings**	17335	23114	28892	23114
2.	**Standard tax allowances**				
	Basic allowance	4104	8208	8208	8208
	Married or head of family				
	Dependent children				
	Deduction for social security contributions and income taxes				
	Work-related expenses	0	0	0	0
	Other				
	Total	4104	8208	8208	8208
3.	**Tax credits or cash transfers included in taxable income**	0	0	0	0
4.	**Central government taxable income (1 - 2 + 3)**	13231	14906	20684	14906
5.	**Central government income tax liability (exclusive of tax credits)**	1919	2288	3935	2288
6.	**Tax credits**				
	Basic credit	428	428	428	428
	Married or head of family				
	Children	428	428	428	0
	Other				
	Total	855	855	855	428
7.	**Central government income tax finally paid (5-6)**	1064	1433	3080	1907
8.	**State and local taxes**	0	0	0	0
9.	**Employees' compulsory social security contributions**				
	Gross earnings	1907	2543	3178	2543
	Taxable income				
	Total	1907	2543	3178	2543
10.	**Total payments to general government (7 + 8 + 9)**	2970	3976	6258	4450
11.	**Cash transfers from general government**				
	For head of family				
	For two children	701	637	0	0
	Total	701	637	0	0
12.	**Take-home pay (1-10+11)**	15065	19775	22634	18664
13.	**Employer's compulsory social security contributions**	4117	5490	6862	5490
14.	**Average rates**				
	Income tax	6.1%	6.2%	10.7%	8.3%
	Employees' social security contributions	11.0%	11.0%	11.0%	11.0%
	Total payments less cash transfers	13.1%	14.4%	21.7%	19.3%
	Total tax wedge including employer's social security contributions	29.8%	30.9%	36.7%	34.7%
15.	**Marginal rates**				
	Total payments less cash transfers: Principal earner	25.5%	39.5%	39.5%	43.0%
	Total payments less cash transfers: Spouse	18.5%	39.5%	39.5%	43.0%
	Total tax wedge: Principal earner	39.8%	51.1%	51.1%	53.9%
	Total tax wedge: Spouse	34.1%	51.1%	51.1%	53.9%

The national currency is the euro (EUR). In 2013, EUR 0.75 equalled USD 1. The Secretariat has estimated that in that same year the average worker earned EUR 17 335 (Secretariat estimate).

1. Personal income tax systems

1.1. *Taxes levied by central government*

1.1.1. *Tax unit*

The tax unit is the family. Family income includes the income of any dependent children. Tax is computed on aggregate net income in the various categories of income, i.e. after the deductions specific to each category and standard and non-standard reliefs.

1.1.2. *Standard and non-standard reliefs and tax credits*

1.1.2.1. Standard reliefs

Standard deduction of 72 per cent of 12 times the Social Benefit Index per taxpayer (the 2010 highest monthly minimum wage until the index reaches this value).* If compulsory contributions to social protection schemes and statutory sub-schemes for health care exceed that limit, the deduction will equal the amount of those contributions.

1.1.2.2. Non-standard reliefs

For income received from 1 January 1999 onwards, the majority of the standard reliefs have been replaced by tax credits (see Section 1.1.4).

Non-standard reliefs still in effect:

- A deduction is provided for the portion of trade union dues not constituting consideration for benefits in the realm of health care, education, assistance for the elderly, housing, insurance or social security, up to 1 per cent of the taxpayer's gross income, increased by 50 per cent. These dues are not taken into account in the calculations underlying this Report.

1.1.3. *Social security contributions*

Social security contributions are totally deductible if they exceed EUR 4 104.00 per taxpayer, in which case the deduction for the contributions replaces the standard earned income deduction (see Section 1.1.2.1).

1.1.4. *Tax credits*

Basic credits:

- EUR 213.75 for each unmarried taxpayer or for each spouse;
- EUR 332.5 for a taxpayer in a single-parent family;

* The corresponding amount equals EUR 4 104.00 (72 per cent x 12 x EUR 475.00).

- EUR 213.75 for each dependent child. This tax credit is doubled for dependent children whose age does not exceed 3 years old.
- EUR 261.25 for each ascendant whose income does not exceed the minimum pension benefit. When there is only one ascendant, the tax credit is EUR 403.75.

Other tax credits

- Non-reimbursed health care costs, not covered by Social Security: 10 per cent of health care costs plus interest on loans contracted to meet them, with a limit of EUR 838.44 (2 times the Social Benefit Index); for households with three or more dependents with health expenses the limit is raised by EUR 125.77 (30% of SBI), per dependent.
- Expenditures for educating the taxpayer or the taxpayer's dependants: 30 per cent of outlays, up to 160 per cent of the social benefits index (EUR 760.00; 160 per cent of 2010 highest minimum wage until this index reaches that value). For households having three or more dependants, the limit is raised by 30 per cent of the social benefits reference value (EUR 142.50; 30 per cent of 2010 highest minimum wage until this index reaches that value) for each dependant, if each of them incurs education costs.
- Costs for sanatoria or retirement homes for taxpayers, their ascendants and collaterals up to the third degree whose income does not exceed the national minimum wage: 25 per cent of expenses up to EUR 403.75.
- Costs for the acquisition, construction or improvement of the taxpayers' primary, permanent residence, or for renting out property for a permanent residence: 15 per cent of interest up to EUR 296.00. Rent paid by a tenant, for his permanent residence under an agreement typified by the law, up to EUR 502.00. This credit is applicable to contracts up to 31.12.2011. These limits are also increased by 50 per cent for taxpayers in the first tax rate bracket, by 20 per cent for taxpayers in the second tax rate bracket. This credit is to be phased out until 2016 (interests) and 2018 (rents).
- 20 per cent of alimony payments compulsory under court order or court-approved agreement, up to a monthly limit of EUR 419.22 (SBI).

Tax credits from tax benefits

- Individual Retirement Savings Plans (PPRs): 20 per cent of amounts invested, for unmarried taxpayers or for each spouse, up to:
  - EUR 400 for taxpayers under 35;
  - EUR 350 for taxpayers over 35 and under 50;
  - EUR 300 for taxpayers over 50.
- Social Security Individual Accounts: 20 per cent of amounts invested, for unmarried taxpayers or for each spouse, up to a limit of EUR 350.
- Donations granted on the conditions stated in the statutes governing charities (grants to central, regional or local government, special "social solidarity institutions", museums, libraries, schools, institutes, educational or research associations, public administrative bodies, etc.): 25 per cent of donations, limited in certain cases to 15 per cent of the donor's tax liability.
- 15 per cent of VAT paid for certain services (restaurants, lodging, hairdressers, and auto-repair) up to a limit of EUR 250. This benefit is not included on the limits referred to on the next page.

However the total of tax credits related to health care costs, education and formation, alimony, retirement homes and house expenses cannot exceed the values of the following amounts:

Taxable income (EUR) (R)	Limit
Up to 7 000	Without limit
Over 7 000 up to 20000	EUR 1 250
Over 20 000 up to 40 000	EUR 1 000
Over 40 000 up to 80 000	EUR 500
Over 80 000	EUR 0 (no tax credit)

Limits are increased in 10 per cent for each dependent.

And the total of tax credits from tax benefits (which include the tax credits related to Individual Retirement Savings Plans, Social Security Individual Accounts and donations) cannot exceed the following amounts:

Taxable income (EUR) (R)	Limit
Up to 7000	Without limit
Over 7000 up to 20000	EUR 100
Over 20000 up to 40000	EUR 80
Over 40000 up to 80000	EUR 60
Over 80 000	EUR 0 (no tax credit)

1.1.5. *Family status*

To take the taxpayer's family status into account, joint taxation of the family unit was introduced, with the use of an income-splitting system to obtain taxable income.

1.1.5.1. Determination of taxable income

To determine taxable income, to which the rates listed in the tax schedule are applied, income is divided by 2.

1.1.6. *Tax rate schedule (applicable to 2012 income)*

Taxable income (EUR) (R)	Marginal tax rate (%) (T)	Amount to deduct (EUR) (K)
Up to 7 000	14.50	–
Over 7 000 up to 20 000	28.50	980
Over 20 000 up to 40 000	37.00	2 680
Over 40 000 up to 80 000	45.00	5 880
Over 80 000	48.00	8 280

In the case of taxpayers whose income stems primarily from dependent employment (earned income), disposable income after application of the tax rates to taxable income may not be less than 120 per cent of the national minimum wage, (EUR 8 148.00 in 2013), nor may it result in income tax of which the taxable base after application of the conjugal quotient is EUR 1 911 or less.

For residents in the Autonomous Regions of the Azores, reduced tax rates are applicable. Tax calculation formula (I = Income tax due):

- Unmarried taxpayers: I = R × T – K – C

Married taxpayers (with one or two earned incomes/see Section 1.1.5.1):

- I ={[(R : 2) × T – K] × 2 } – C

Where:

R = Taxable income, after deduction of standard and non-standard reliefs (see Sections 1.1.2 and 1.1.5.1)

T = Tax rate corresponding to the taxable income bracket

K = Amount to be deducted from each bracket

C = Tax credits (see Section 1.1.4)

Surtax:

A surtax was introduced by the 2012 State Budget and is *applicable on highest income* bracket. The surtax is now 2.5 per cent applicable to taxable income between EUR 80 000 and EUR 250 000 and 5 per cent for taxable income above EUR 250 000. Furthermore, a 3.5 per cent surtax was reintroduced, for taxable income above the annual national minimum wage (EUR 6 790), with a tax credit of 2.5 per cent of the annual minimum wage per dependent (EUR 169.75).

1.1.7. *Special family situations*

1.1.7.1. Handicapped taxpayer/spouse, with a disability rating of 60 per cent or more:

- A tax credit corresponding to 4 times the 2010 minimum wage (EUR 1 900) is granted for each taxpayer or spouse.

1.1.7.2. Handicapped dependent children, with a disability rating of 60 per cent or more:

- A tax credit corresponding to 1.5 times the social benefits index (EUR 712.50) is granted for each dependent child.

1.1.7.3. Handicapped taxpayer/spouse or dependent children, with a disability rating of 90 per cent or more:

- An additional tax credit corresponding to 4 times the 2010 minimum wage (EUR 1 900) is granted for each taxpayer or spouse or dependent child.

1.1.8. *Non liable income*

- Lawfully granted family allowances;
- Living expenses per diem, up to the limits established for national civil servants;
- Meal allowances, up to the amount established for national civil servants, increased by 20 per cent or 60 per cent in the event of a meal allowance in the form of meal vouchers.

2. Compulsory social security contributions to schemes operated within the government sector

Rates and ceilings: social security contributions are levied on gross pay and are not subject to any ceiling.

2.1. *Employee contributions*

As a rule, the rate of employee contributions is 11 per cent of gross pay, with no ceiling.

2.2. *Employer contributions*

The employer's rate of social security contributions is 23.75 per cent of gross pay, with no ceiling.

2.3. *Areas of social protection*

- Health (sickness, disability, work accidents, work-related illness).
- Old age, survival.
- Maternity.
- Family (family allowances).
- Unemployment.

3. Universal cash benefits

3.1. *Benefits for dependent children*

The basic principle is to grant higher monthly social benefits to lower-income households.

There are six different levels of monthly allowances for dependent children, depending on the family's reference income. This reference income is determined by dividing the family's annual gross income, including vacation and Christmas allowances, by the number of dependent children plus one:

- Level 1: Families whose reference income is under 50 per cent of 14 times the reference value (i.e. under EUR 2 934.54).
- Level 2: Families whose reference income is over 50 per cent and under 100 per cent of 14 times the reference value(i.e. over EUR 2 934.54 and under EUR 5 869.08).
- Level 3: Families whose reference income is over 100 per cent and under 150 per cent of 14 times the reference value (i.e. over EUR 5 869.08 and under EUR 8 803.62).
- Level 4: Families whose reference income is over 150 per cent (i.e. over EUR 8 803.62).

Each level is also divided according to the age of the dependent child. Benefits are higher during the first 12 months of a child's life.

Monthly social benefits per child are as follows:

	Child under 12 months	Child over 12 months old	Additional benefit per child over 12 months and under 36 months in a family with 2 children	Additional benefit per child over 12 months and under 36 months in a family with 3 or more children
Level 1	140.76	35.19	35.19	70.38
Level 2	116.74	29.19	29.19	58.38
Level 3	92.29	26.54	26.54	53.08
Level 4	0	0	0	0

Monthly social benefits per child in a single-parent family are increased by 20 per cent.

In September, families with dependent school children aged between 6 and 16 years receiving child benefits in level 1 receive an additional amount equal to the regular monthly benefit.

An amount equal to the cash benefits for dependent children under 12 months is attributed for each unborn child after the first month following that of the 13th week of gestation.

3.2. *Benefits for handicapped dependent children*

There is also a special family allowance scheme for handicapped children.

The above cash benefits (in Sections 3.1 and 3.2) are not taxable.

4. Main changes in tax/benefit system since 2006

- The relief for disabled taxpayers was restructured. Former partial exemptions and allowances were replaced by tax credits.
- Tax credits for higher income households were limited or abolished;
- The fiscal autonomy of local authorities (municipalities) increased. They may set the level of their share in the revenue from personal income tax, up to 5 per cent of their resident taxpayers' tax liability. If this rate is set below 5 per cent, the difference will be credited against the taxpayers' tax liability.
- Tax credits for handicapped taxpayers and dependants were increased.
- Social benefits for dependent children were increased for low income families, single-parent families and families with 2 or more children.
- Introduction of social benefits for unborn children.

5. Memorandum items

5.1. *Method used to identify and compute gross wages of the average worker*

The operative concept of monthly compensation is that of amounts paid to full time staff before deductions for tax and compulsory contributions. It therefore includes wages and basic salaries of staff paid by the hour, by the job, or by tasks; benefits in kind or housing, if they are considered an integral part of compensation; cash subsidies for meals, housing or transport; bonuses for regular night shifts and seniority, as well as incentive pay and rewards for diligence and productivity; family allowances, compensation for overtime and work on holidays. Benefits, subsidies and bonuses are taken into account only if paid regularly at each pay period.

Payments in kind are incorporated into the concept of compensation. The statistics record such advantages in kind at their taxable value.

All managerial and supervisory workers are included in the computations.

Average annual pay is based on the average of monthly earnings for April and October multiplied by an adjustment coefficient representing the share of annual bonuses and allowances (including vacation subsidies and the Christmas allowance), which is provided by the labour cost survey.

The following formula is applied:

- Average annual pay = Average monthly pay adjusted by the coefficient × 12.

5.2. *Description of the employer's main contributions to private retirement, health insurance schemes, etc.*

Outside the social security system, employers are required to insure their employees against work-related accidents (with private insurance companies). They may also provide their employees with life insurance, although this is optional.

2013 parameter values

Average earnings/yr	Ave_earn	17 335	Secretariat estimate	
Tax allowances	perc	1		
	max_al	4 104		
Tax credits				
Married (basic)	married_cred	213.75		
Single (basic)	single_cred	213.75		
Single parent	singlepar_cred	332.5		
Each child credit	child_cred	213.75		
Tax schedule	tax_sch	0.145	7 000	
		0.285	20 000	
		0.37	40 000	
		0.45	80 000	
		0.48		
	tax_floor	1 911		
Surtax	surtax_rate	0.025		
	surtax_rate2	0.05		
	surtax_thrs	250 000		
	add_surtax_rate	0.035		
	add_surtax_cred	0.025		
Social security contributions	SSC_rate	0.11		
ceiling	SSC_empr	0.2375		
Child benefit – Schedule	ch_ben_sch	0	457.47	1st echelon
		2 934.54	350.28	2nd echelon
		5 869.08	318.48	3rd echelon
		8 803.62	0	4th echelon
Extra child benefit for lone parents	ch_ben_lone	0.2		
Minimum Wage	MW	6 790		
Minimum Disposable Income	MinDispY	8 148		

2013 tax equations

The equations for the Portuguese system in 2012 are mostly calculated on a family basis.

The functions which are used in the equations (Taper, MIN, Tax, etc.) are described in the technical note about tax equations. Variable names are defined in the table of parameters above, within the equations table, or are the standard variables "married" and "children". A reference to a variable with the affix "_total" indicates the sum of the relevant variable values for the principal and spouse. And the affixes "_princ" and "_spouse" indicate the value for the principal and spouse, respectively. Equations for a single person are as shown for the principal, with "_spouse" values taken as 0.

	Line in country table and intermediate steps	Variable name	Range	Equation
1.	Earnings	earn		
	Divisor for tax calculation	divisor	J	1+Married
2.	Allowances:	tax_al	J	MAX((MIN(perc*earn_princ, max_al)+MIN(perc* earn_spouse, max_al)), SSC_princ+SSC_spouse)
3.	Credits in taxable income	taxbl_cr	J	0
4.	CG taxable income	tax_inc	J	earn-tax_al
5.	CG tax before credits	CG_tax_excl	J	IF(tax_inc/divisor>tax_floor, Tax(tax_inc/divisor, tax_sch)*(1+Married), 0)
6.	Tax credits :		J	
	Basic credit	basic_cr	J	IF(Married, 2*married_cred, IF(children, singlepar_cred, single_cred))
	Child credit	child_cr	J	Children*child_cred
	Total	tax_cr	J	basic_cr+child_cr
	Surtax	surtax	J	IF(taxable income/Divisor>surtax_thrs,(surtax_rate*(surtax_thrs-TopIncBracket)+surtax_rate2*(taxable income/Divisor -surtax_thrs))*Divisor, surtax_rate*Positive(taxable income/Divisor -TopIncBracket)*Divisor)+Positive((add_surtax_rate*Positive(taxable income/Divisor –Annual Minimum Wage)*Divisor)-(add_surtax_cred*Annual Mimimum Wage*Children))
7.	CG tax	CG_tax	J	IF(earn-CG-tax-excl> MinDispY,Positive(CG_tax_excl-tax_cr),0)+surtax
8.	State and local taxes	local_tax	J	0
9.	Employees' soc security	SSC	B	earn*SSC_rt
11.	Cash transfers	cash_trans	J	=IF(Married=0, VLOOKUP(earn/(Children+1),ch_ben_sch,2,1)*Children*(1+ch_ben_lone), VLOOKUP(earn/(Children+1),ch_ben_sch,2,1)*Children)
13.	13. Employer's soc security	SSC_empr	B	earn*SSC_empr

Key to range of equation B calculated separately for both principal earner and spouse P calculated for principal only (value taken as 0 for spouse calculation) J calculated once only on a joint basis.

Taxing Wages 2014
Changes in sructural labour income tax progressivity
over 2000-12 period in OECD member countries

Slovak Republic

This chapter includes data on the income taxes paid by workers, their social security contributions, the family benefits they receive in the form of cash transfers as well as the social security contributions and payroll taxes paid by their employers. Results reported include the marginal and average tax burden for eight different family types.

Methodological information is available for personal income tax systems, compulsory social security contributions to schemes operated within the government sector, universal cash transfers as well as recent changes in the tax/benefit system. The methodology also includes the parameter values and tax equations underlying the data.

Slovak Republic 2013

The tax/benefit position of single persons

	Wage level (per cent of average wage)	67	100	167	67
	Number of children	none	none	none	2
1.	**Gross wage earnings**	6677	10015	16692	6677
2.	**Standard tax allowances**				
	Basic allowance	3736	3736	3736	3736
	Married or head of family	0	0	0	0
	Dependent children	0	0	0	0
	Deduction for social security contributions and income taxes	895	1342	2237	895
	Work-related expenses				
	Other				
	Total	4631	5078	5973	4631
3.	**Tax credits or cash transfers included in taxable income**	0	0	0	0
4.	**Central government taxable income (1 - 2 + 3)**	2046	4937	10720	2046
5.	**Central government income tax liability (exclusive of tax credits)**	389	938	2037	389
6.	**Tax credits**				
	Basic credit	0	0	0	0
	Married or head of family	0	0	0	0
	Children	0	0	0	509
	Other (ETC)	0	0	0	0
	Total	0	0	0	509
7.	**Central government income tax finally paid (5-6)**	389	938	2037	-120
8.	**State and local taxes**	0	0	0	0
9.	**Employees' compulsory social security contributions**				
	Gross earnings	895	1342	2237	895
	Taxable income				
	Total	895	1342	2237	895
10.	**Total payments to general government (7 + 8 + 9)**	1283	2280	4273	774
11.	**Cash transfers from general government**				
	For head of family				
	For two children	0	0	0	554
	Total	0	0	0	554
12.	**Take-home pay (1-10+11)**	5393	7735	12419	6457
13.	**Employers' compulsory social security contributions**	2083	3125	5208	2083
14.	**Average rates**				
	Income tax	5.8%	9.4%	12.2%	-1.8%
	Employees' social security contributions	13.4%	13.4%	13.4%	13.4%
	Total payments less cash transfers	19.2%	22.8%	25.6%	3.3%
	Total tax wedge including employer's social security contributions	38.4%	41.1%	43.3%	26.3%
15.	**Marginal rates**				
	Total payments less cash transfers: Principal earner	29.9%	29.9%	29.9%	29.9%
	Total payments less cash transfers: Spouse	n.a.	n.a.	n.a.	n.a.
	Total tax wedge: Principal earner	46.5%	46.5%	46.5%	46.5%
	Total tax wedge: Spouse	n.a.	n.a.	n.a.	n.a.

Slovak Republic 2013

The tax/benefit position of married couples

			Wage level (per cent of average wage)	100-0	100-33	100-67	100-33
			Number of children	2	2	2	none
1.	**Gross wage earnings**			10015	13354	16692	13354
2.	**Standard tax allowances**						
		Basic allowance		3736	6627	7472	6627
		Married or head of family		3736	0	0	0
		Dependent children		0	0	0	0
		Deduction for social security contributions and income taxes		1342	1789	2237	1789
		Work-related expenses					
		Other					
			Total	8814	8416	9709	8416
3.	**Tax credits or cash transfers included in taxable income**			0	0	0	0
4.	**Central government taxable income (1 - 2 + 3)**			1201	4937	6984	4937
5.	**Central government income tax liability (exclusive of tax credits)**			228	938	1327	938
6.	**Tax credits**						
		Basic credit		0	0	0	0
		Married or head of family		0	0	0	0
		Children		509	509	509	0
		Other (ETC)		0	43	0	43
			Total	509	552	509	43
7.	**Central government income tax finally paid (5-6)**			-281	386	818	895
8.	**State and local taxes**			0	0	0	0
9.	**Employees' compulsory social security contributions**						
		Gross earnings		1342	1789	2237	1789
		Taxable income					
			Total	1342	1789	2237	1789
10.	**Total payments to general government (7 + 8 + 9)**			1061	2175	3054	2685
11.	**Cash transfers from general government**						
		For head of family					
		For two children		554	554	554	0
			Total	554	554	554	0
12.	**Take-home pay (1-10+11)**			9509	11733	14192	10669
13.	**Employers' compulsory social security contributions**			3125	4166	5208	4166
14.	**Average rates**						
	Income tax			-2.8%	2.9%	4.9%	6.7%
	Employees' social security contributions			13.4%	13.4%	13.4%	13.4%
	Total payments less cash transfers			5.1%	12.1%	15.0%	20.1%
	Total tax wedge including employer's social security contributions			27.6%	33.0%	35.2%	39.1%
15.	**Marginal rates**						
	Total payments less cash transfers: Principal earner			29.9%	29.9%	29.9%	29.9%
	Total payments less cash transfers: Spouse			33.4%	13.4%	29.9%	13.4%
	Total tax wedge: Principal earner			46.5%	46.5%	46.5%	46.5%
	Total tax wedge: Spouse			49.2%	34.0%	46.5%	34.0%

As from 1.1.2009 Slovakia has joined the Euro zone; the national currency became the Euro (EUR). In 2013, EUR 0.75 is equal to USD 1. In that year, the average worker earned EUR 10 015 (Secretariat estimate).

1. Personal income tax systems

1.1. Central government income taxes

1.1.1. Tax unit

The tax unit is the individual.

1.1.2. Tax allowances and tax credits

1.1.2.1. Standard reliefs

- *Basic relief:* An allowance for all taxpayers is set at 19.2 times the minimum living standard (MLS) for a basic adult as of 1 January 2013 (EUR 3 735.94). In 2013, the basic personal allowance for taxpayers with gross earnings net of employee social security contributions in excess of the threshold of EUR 19 458 per year (19 458 = 100 × MLS, which is approximately equal to an employee's monthly gross wage of EUR 1 873) is gradually withdrawn. If gross earnings net of employee social security contributions exceed EUR 19 458, the personal allowance is calculated as 44.2 times the minimum living standard minus 0.25 times gross earnings net of employee social security contributions. The basic personal allowance reaches 0 if the gross earnings net of employee social security contributions amount to EUR 34 401.74 per year (employee's monthly gross wage of approximately EUR 3 311). The value of the basic tax allowance cannot become negative.

  The degressive tax allowance is taken into account only once a year (when the tax return is filed or when the annual clearing is performed). Monthly tax prepayments during the year are therefore not affected.

- *Marital status relief:* An additional allowance is given to the principal earner in respect of a spouse living in a common household if the spouse earns no more than EUR 3 735.9. As from 1 January 2007 the value of the spouse allowance depends on the gross earnings net of employee social security contributions of both principal and spouse. As of 2013, to be entitled to spouse allowance one of the following conditions should be met:

  - spouse is taking care of (not necessarily personally) children up to 3 years (or up to 6 years if child is disabled), or
  - spouse is unemployed, or
  - spouse is receiving nursing allowance, or
  - spouse is disabled.

  If the principal's gross earnings net of employee social security contributions in 2013 are lower or equal to EUR 34 401.74 (= 176.8 times MLS) and the spouse's gross earnings net of employee social security contributions are lower than EUR 3 735.94, the spouse allowance is calculated as the difference between 19.2 times MLS and the spouse's gross earnings net of employee social security contributions. If the gross earnings net of employee social security contributions of the spouse exceed EUR 3 735.94, the spouse allowance is 0. If the principal's gross earnings net of employee social security contributions exceed EUR 34 401.74 (= 176.8 times MLS), the spouse allowance is calculated as 63.4 times MLS minus 0.25 times the principal's gross earnings net of employee social security contributions. This amount is reduced by the spouse's gross earnings net of employee social security contributions. The value of the spouse allowance cannot become negative.

The digressive tax allowance is taken into account only once a year (when the tax return is filed or when the annual clearing is performed). Monthly tax prepayments during the year are therefore not affected.

For the purposes of this Report, only families with unemployed spouse are entitled to spouse allowance (spouse income does not influence any equations of spouse allowance as of 2013). Child care up to 3 years does not affect the calculation of tax wedges as according to the Taxing wages methodology any children in the household are assumed to be aged between six and eleven inclusive.

- *Relief for children:* The prior allowance for children has been replaced by a non-wastable tax credit as from January 2004. As from July 2007, the monthly tax credit is indexed as result of a new indexation rule. The tax credit is automatically indexed by MLS growth and is effective as from the 1st of July when also the new amount of MLS comes into force. During the period from 1 January to 30 June 2013 monthly tax credit was EUR 21.03 per child, from 1 July 2013 the amount of tax credit is EUR 21.41 (the annual amount will be EUR 254.64). The tax credit for each dependent child is deducted from the tax liability; if the credit exceeds the tax liability, the excess will be paid to the taxpayer. In order to receive this credit, the parent must annually earn at least 6 times the minimum monthly wage, which for 2013 is set at EUR 337.7 (the total annual earnings must therefore be at least EUR 2 026.2). The credit can be taken only by one partner. It can be taken by one partner for part of the tax period (year) and by the other partner for the rest of the tax period (year); this choice will have to hold for all dependent children. (For the purposes of this Report, it is assumed that the credit is claimed by the principal wage earner.)
- *Relief for social and health security contributions:* Employee's social security contributions (see Section 2.1) are deductible for income tax purposes.

1.1.2.2. Main non-standard tax reliefs applicable to an average wage worker

- Supplementary pension insurance, special-purpose savings and life insurances repealed as from January 2011.
- As of 2013 voluntary contributions to the privately managed fully funded pillar up to 2% of gross earnings net of employee social security contributions are tax-deductible. Maximum yearly limit for this tax relief is calculated as: 2% × 60 × AW(t-2), where AW(t-2) average wage two years ago. It is legislated that this relief will be automatically abolished as of 2017.

1.1.2.3. Non-wastable tax credit: Employee tax credit (ETC/zamestnanecká prémia)

The employee tax credit is effective as from 2009 and is targeted at low-income workers whose wages are subject to the payment of social and health insurance contributions. The amount of tax credit depends upon the employee's earnings and the number of months worked.

In order to receive this tax credit, the employee must fulfil the entitlement criteria which are:

- the employee's earnings over the tax period must be at least 6 times higher than the minimum wage, which for 2013 is set at EUR 337.7 per month,
- the employee must have worked for at least 6 months over the tax period (the conditions of month worked is considered to be fulfilled when only one hour is worked during that month).

The ETC is a non-wastable tax credit as is the child tax credit. The value of the ETC depends on the level of the employee's earnings. If earnings are between at least 6 times of the minimum wage and 12 times of the minimum wage, the credit is calculated as 19 per cent of the difference between the basic allowance (EUR 3 735.94) and the tax base (gross earnings net of employee SSC), evaluated at the level of the minimum wage (EUR 3 509.76). If earnings exceed 12 times the minimum wage, then the ETC is calculated as 19 per cent of the difference of the basic allowance and the tax base (gross earnings net of employee SSC). The tax credit is zero when the tax base (gross earnings net of employee SSC) is equal to or higher than the basic allowance.

The highest value of the employee tax credit amounts to EUR 42.98 per year; this maximum value is received by employees with income between one half of the minimum wage and the full minimum wage, provided that the employee has worked for 12 months. As the employee tax credit is designed to benefit working individuals, its amount is adequately reduced for employees that have worked less months in the calendar year. Due to extensive paperwork it was decided that the tax credit will be paid within the framework of the annual clearing of the tax advances or when a tax return is filed.

1.1.3. *Tax schedule*

As from 2013 the previous flat tax rate of 19 per cent was replaced by new tax schedule with two tax brackets. The ceiling for the first bracket is set out as 176.8 times MLS (equal to EUR 34 401.74) what secure its automatic indexation. The tax schedule is as follows:

Annual taxable income (EUR)[1]	Rate (%)
0-34 401.74	19
34 401.74 and over	25

1. Employee's social security contributions (see 1.12.) are deductible for income tax purposes.

1.2. *State and local income tax*

No separate state and local income tax exist. As from 2012 the share of distribution of PIT revenue has changed. Out of the total revenue from the personal income tax (PIT) collected by the central government, 65.4 per cent of PIT is transferred into the budget of the municipalities and 21.9 per cent of PIT is transferred into the budget of the self-governing regions. The remaining revenue of the state budget is 12.7 per cent of PIT.

2. Compulsory social security contributions to schemes operated within the government sector

2.1. Employees' contributions

Compulsory contributions of 13.4 per cent of gross wages and salaries are paid by all employees into government operated schemes. The total is made up as follows:

Health insurance		4.0 per cent
Social insurance		9.4 per cent
of which:		
Sickness	1.4 per cent	
Retirement	4.0 per cent	
Disability	3.0 per cent	
Unemployment	1.0 per cent	

There are maximum assessment bases MSSAB (maximum threshold for contributions to apply) that apply to social security contributions. From 2004 these MSSAB are no longer fixed values but depend upon the average wages (AW). The latest amendment of the Social insurance Law and the Health insurance Law, which is valid from 1January 2013 unified formulae for calculation of all maximum assessment bases. Monthly MSSAB for social security contributions are calculated as: 5 × AW(t-2), where AW(t-2) is the average wage two years ago. The average wage (AW) is determined by the Statistical Office of the Slovak Republic – for 2011 it was EUR 786 per month.

2.2. Employers' contributions

The total contribution for employers is 35.2 per cent of gross wages and salaries. The contribution comprises the health insurance contribution (10 per cent of gross wages and salaries) and the social insurance contribution (25.2 per cent). The social insurance rate reflects contributions to sickness insurance (1.4 per cent), disability insurance (3 per cent), retirement insurance (14 per cent), the Guaranteed Fund (0.25 per cent), accident insurance (0.8 per cent), for unemployment (1 per cent) and to the Reserve Fund (4.75 per cent). All contributions are rounded down on two decimal places.

Since January 2005, Slovakia has introduced the privately managed fully funded pillar. This means that a given proportion (9 percentage points) of social contributions paid by the employer for retirement insurance flew directly to the private pension funds and not to the Social insurance agency as in previous years. As from September 2012 pension sharing scheme has been changed. Employer's retirement contribution rate to the fully funded pillar has been reduced from 9 per cent to 4 per cent (for more see pension contribution sharing scheme table below). The effective employer's retirement contribution rate will therefore increase from 5 per cent in 2011 to 10 per cent in 2013. Private pension funds are treated outside of general government; these contributions are therefore not taken into account in the calculations of average and marginal tax rates. For the purposes of this Report, the total contribution rate for employers in 2013 is 31.2 per cent.

The MSSAB also applies to the employer's SSC. The next table presents the annual values of MSSAB:

	Formula for MSSAB	Value of MSSAB
Health insurance	5.0 x AW (t-2)	47 160.00
Social insurance		
of which		
Sickness, retirement, unemployment, disability, Guarantee fund, Reserve fund	5.0 x AW (t-2)	47 160.00
Accident		No limit

SSC: Pension – contribution sharing in case of II. Pillar participation

Period	Percentage of gross earnings		
	I Pillar	II Pillar	Total
Previous system (up to September 2012)	9% (5% employer + 4% employee contribution)	9% (employer contribution)	18%
Current system (from September 2012)[1]	14% (10% employer + 4% employee contribution)	4% (employer contribution)	18%

1. As from 2017 contribution rate to the II. pillar will automatically increase by 0.25 p.p. per year (i.e. contribution rate to the I. pillar will decrease in the same volume), stopping at 6 per cent in 2024.

3. Universal cash transfers

3.1. *Transfers related to marital status*

None.

3.2. *Transfers for dependent children*

The central government pays an allowance in respect of each dependent child in the amount of EUR 23.10 per month in 2013. In January 2008 an extra allowance for dependent children whose parents are not eligible for the non-wastable child tax credit was introduced. The monthly amount of this allowance is EUR 10.83. For the purpose of the tax wedge calculations this allowance is not relevant, as only non-workers and taxpayers with annual earnings lower than six times the minimum monthly wage (which is the condition for eligibility for the non-wastable child tax credit) are entitled to the extra allowance.

The non-wastable tax credit mentioned in Section 1.1.2.1 is part of the social support for families with dependent children. However, it is not considered as a transfer for the purposes of this Report.

3.3. *Transfers related to social status*

To determine the claim to state social benefits (for example the allowance for housing costs), the minimum living standard amounts are relevant as they form the basis of the income test. For 2013, these amounts are:

	MLS monthly (1.1.2013- 30.6.2013)	MLS monthly (1.7.2013- 31.12.2013)
First adult	194.58	198.09
Second adult	135.74	138.19
Child	88.82	90.42

A family is entitled to a social allowance if the total combined net monthly income of the family is less than the calculated MLS for this family. The allowance varies with the family type.

The benefits available to a family in material need (valid on the 1st of January 2013) are:

- EUR 60.50 per month for an individual.
- EUR 115.10 per month for an individual with between one and four children.
- EUR 105.20 per month for a couple without children.

- EUR 157.60 per month for a couple with between one and four children.
- EUR 168.20 per month for an individual with more than four children.
- EUR 212.30 per month for a couple with more than four children.

If one family member is pregnant, the social benefits described above are increased by EUR 13.50. The entitlement for this additional benefit arises from the 4th month of the pregnancy and lasts until the child's age of 1 year (benefit for children until age of 1 year does not affect the calculations in this Report).

- Activation allowance: EUR 63.07 per month – for people who become active either by accepting qualifying employment opportunities or participating in retraining courses.
- Housing allowance: EUR 55.80 per month for individual in material need, EUR 89.20 for a household in material need (if household has more than 1 person).
- Protection allowance: EUR 63.07 per month for an individual in material need where employment is not possible due to such circumstances as a disability or old age.
- Health care allowance: EUR 2.00 per month.

4. Main changes in tax/benefit systems since 2012

The main changes relate to the abolition of the flat tax rate of 19 per cent by introduction of the second personal income tax rate of 25 per cent, limitation of spousal allowance, unification of monthly maximum assessment bases for social and health security contributions at the level of 5 times average wage two years ago and introduction of the new main non-standard tax relief for voluntary contribution to the second pension pillar. Also previously lowered contribution to the second pension pillar will be applicable for the whole year.

5. Memorandum items

5.1. *Identification of AW and valuation of earnings*

The Ministry of Finance of the Slovak republic estimates the average earnings of the AW based on the data supplied by the Statistical Office of the Slovak republic, Labour Force Survey data (LFS). Earnings data covering also self-employees are based on average wage definition including industries falling under categories B to N inclusive, with reference to International Standard Industrial Classification of All Economic Activities, Revision 4.

2013 parameter values

Average earnings/yr	Ave_earn	10 015	Secretariat estimate
Minimum living standard (MLS) 2013	basic_adult	194.58	
	basic_adult1	135.74	
	basic_child	88.82	
Basic allowance	basic_al_mult	19.2	
	basic_al	3 735.94	
	basic_al_mult1	100	
	basic_al_mult2	44.2	
	basic_al_redn	0.25	
Spouse allowance	spouse_al_limit	3 735.94	
	spouse_al_mult1	176.8	
	spouse_al_mult2	63.4	
	spouse_al_redn	0.25	
Income tax rate	Tax_sch/tax_rate	0.19	34 401.744
		0.25	
Tax credits – nonwastable	tax_cr	254.64	
	min_wage	337.7	
	minwage_mult	6	
	etc_thresh	3 509.76	
Employee social security contributions	SSC_rate	0.134	
	SSC_sick	0.014	
	SSC_ret	0.04	
	SSC_dis	0.03	
	SSC_unemp	0.01	
	SSC_health	0.04	
Employer social security contributions	SSC_empr	0.304	
	SSC_empsick	0.014	
	SSC_empret	0.1	
	SSC_empdis	0.03	
	SSC_empunemp	0.01	
	SSC_emphealth	0.1	
	SSC_gua	0.0025	
	SSC_acc	0.008	
	SSC_fund	0.0475	
Maximum assessment base	MSSAB	47 160	
Cash transfers	transf_1	277.2	
	transf_indiv	726.00	
	transf_indiv_child	1 381.20	
	transf_couple	1 262.40	
	transf_couple_child	1 891.20	
	transf_hous_indiv	669.60	
	transf_hous_couple	1070.40	
	transf_activ	756.84	
	transf_health	24.00	

2013 tax equations

	Line in country table and intermediate steps	Variable name	Range	Equation
1.	Earnings	earn		
2.	Allowances:			
	Basic	basic_allce	B	IF(earn-SSC<=basic_al_mult1*basic_adult, basic_al,MAXA(basic_al_mult2*basic_adult-basic_al_redn*(earn-SSC),0))
	Spouse	spouse_allce	P	IF(earn_spouse=0,1,0)*Married*Positive(IF(earn_princ-SSC_princ<=spouse_al_mult1*basic_adult, basic_al_mult*basic_adult,spouse_al_mult2*basic_adult-spouse_al_redn*(earn_princ-SSC_princ)))
	Social security contributions	SSC_al	B	SSC
	Total	tax_al	B	basic_allce+spouse_allce+SSC_al
3.	Credits in taxable income	taxbl_cr	B	0
4.	CG taxable income	tax_inc	B	Positive(earn-tax_al)
5.	CG tax before credits	CG_tax_excl	B	Tax(tax_inc,tax_sch)
6.	Tax credits:			
	Employee tax credit	etc_cr	B	IF(earn>=min_wage*minwage_mult, tax_rate*Positive(basic_al-MAX(etc_thresh, earn-SSC)), 0)
	Children	child_cr	P	(earn>=min_wage*minwage_mult)*Children*tax_cr
	Total	tax_cr	B	etc_cr+child_cr
7.	CG tax	CG_tax	B	CG_tax_excl-tax_cr
8.	State and local taxes	local_tax	B	0
9.	Employees' soc security	SSC	B	MINA(earn,MSSAB)*SSC_rate
11.	Cash transfers	cash_trans	J	Children*transf_1+Positive(IF(0,75*((earn-SSC-CG_tax_excl)/12)<(basic_adult+Married*basic_adult1+ Children*basic_child); ((1-Married)*(IF(Children>0;transf_indiv_child;transf_indiv))+ Married*(IF(Children>0;transf_couple_child;transf_couple))+IF((Married+Children)>0;transf_hous_couple;transf_hous_indiv)+((1+Married+Children)*transf_health)+IF(A7>0;transf_activ;0)+IF(B7>0;transf_activ;0)-0,75*(earn-SSC-CG_tax_excl));0))
13.	Employer's soc security	SSC_empr	B	MINA(earn,MSSAB)*SSC_empr earn*SSC_acc+

Key to range of equation B calculated separately for both principal earner and spouse P calculated for principal only (value taken as 0 for spouse calculation) J calculated once only on a joint basis.

Taxing Wages 2014
Changes in sructural labour income tax progressivity
over 2000-12 period in OECD member countries

Slovenia

This chapter includes data on the income taxes paid by workers, their social security contributions, the family benefits they receive in the form of cash transfers as well as the social security contributions and payroll taxes paid by their employers. Results reported include the marginal and average tax burden for eight different family types.

Methodological information is available for personal income tax systems, compulsory social security contributions to schemes operated within the government sector, universal cash transfers as well as recent changes in the tax/benefit system. The methodology also includes the parameter values and tax equations underlying the data.

Slovenia 2013

The tax/benefit position of single persons

		Wage level (per cent of average wage)	67	100	167	67
		Number of children	none	none	none	2
1.	**Gross wage earnings**		11740	17611	29351	11740
2.	**Standard tax allowances**					
	Basic allowance		4419	3303	3303	4419
	Married or head of family					
	Dependent children					5086
	Deduction for social security contributions and income taxes		2595	3892	6487	2595
	Work-related expenses		0	0	0	0
	Other					
		Total	7013	7195	9789	12099
3.	**Tax credits or cash transfers included in taxable income**		0	0	0	0
4.	**Central government taxable income (1 - 2 + 3)**		4727	10416	19562	0
5.	**Central government income tax liability (exclusive of tax credits)**		756	1930	4483	0
6.	**Tax credits**					
	Basic credit					
	Married or head of family					
	Children		0	0	0	0
	Other					
		Total	0	0	0	0
7.	**Central government income tax finally paid (5-6)**		756	1930	4483	0
8.	**State and local taxes**		0	0	0	0
9.	**Employees' compulsory social security contributions**					
	Gross earnings		2595	3892	6487	2595
	Taxable income					
		Total	2595	3892	6487	2595
10.	**Total payments to general government (7 + 8 + 9)**		3351	5822	10970	2595
11.	**Cash transfers from general government**					
	For head of family					
	For two children		0	0	0	2716
		Total	0	0	0	2716
12.	**Take-home pay (1-10+11)**		8389	11789	18381	11862
13.	**Employer's wage dependent contributions and taxes**		1890	2835	4725	1890
	Employer's compulsory social security contributions		1890	2835	4725	1890
	Payroll taxes		0	0	0	0
14.	**Average rates**					
	Income tax		6.4%	11.0%	15.3%	0.0%
	Employees' social security contributions		22.1%	22.1%	22.1%	22.1%
	Total payments less cash transfers		28.5%	33.1%	37.4%	-1.0%
	Total tax wedge including employer's social security contributions		38.5%	42.3%	46.1%	13.0%
15.	**Marginal rates**					
	Total payments less cash transfers: Principal earner		34.6%	43.1%	54.0%	22.1%
	Total payments less cash transfers: Spouse		n.a.	n.a.	n.a.	n.a.
	Total tax wedge: Principal earner		43.6%	51.0%	60.4%	32.9%
	Total tax wedge: Spouse		n.a.	n.a.	n.a.	n.a.

Slovenia 2013

The tax/benefit position of married couples

			Wage level (per cent of average wage)	100-0	100-33	100-67	100-33
			Number of children	2	2	2	none
1.	**Gross wage earnings**			17611	23481	29351	23481
2.	**Standard tax allowances**						
	Basic allowance			3303	7876	7721	7876
	Married or head of family						
	Dependent children			5086	5086	5086	
	Other dependent family member			2437			
	Deduction for social security contributions and income taxes			3892	5189	6487	5189
	Work-related expenses			0	0	0	0
			Total	14718	18151	19294	13065
3.	**Tax credits or cash transfers included in taxable income**			0	0	0	0
4.	**Central government taxable income (1 - 2 + 3)**			2893	5330	10057	10416
5.	**Central government income tax liability (exclusive of tax credits)**			463	853	1609	1930
6.	**Tax credits**						
	Basic credit						
	Married or head of family						
	Children			0	0	0	0
	Other						
			Total	0	0	0	0
7.	**Central government income tax finally paid (5-6)**			463	853	1609	1930
8.	**State and local taxes**			0	0	0	0
9.	**Employees' compulsory social security contributions**						
	Gross earnings			3892	5189	6487	5189
	Taxable income						
			Total	3892	5189	6487	5189
10.	**Total payments to general government (7 + 8 + 9)**			4355	6042	8096	7119
11.	**Cash transfers from general government**						
	For head of family						
	For two children			2469	1509	1124	0
			Total	2469	1509	1124	0
12.	**Take-home pay (1-10+11)**			15725	18948	22379	16362
13.	**Employer's wage dependent contributions and taxes**			2835	3780	4725	3780
	Employer's compulsory social security contributions			2835	3780	4725	3780
	Payroll taxes			0	0	0	0
14.	**Average rates**						
	Income tax			2.6%	3.6%	5.5%	8.2%
	Employees' social security contributions			22.1%	22.1%	22.1%	22.1%
	Total payments less cash transfers			10.7%	19.3%	23.8%	30.3%
	Total tax wedge including employer's social security contributions			23.1%	30.5%	34.3%	40.0%
15.	**Marginal rates**						
	Total payments less cash transfers: Principal earner			34.6%	34.6%	34.6%	43.1%
	Total payments less cash transfers: Spouse			45.1%	22.1%	34.6%	22.1%
	Total tax wedge: Principal earner			43.6%	43.6%	43.6%	51.0%
	Total tax wedge: Spouse			52.7%	32.9%	43.6%	32.9%

The Slovenian currency is the euro (EUR). In 2013, EUR 0.75 was equal to USD 1. In that year, the average worker in Slovenia earned EUR 17 611 (Secretariat estimate).

1. Personal income tax systems

1.1. Central government income tax

1.1.1. Tax unit

The tax unit is the individual.

1.1.2. Tax allowances

1.1.2.1. Standard tax reliefs

- A *general (basic) allowance* of EUR 3 302.70 is deductible from income in 2013. For lower income groups an additional general allowance of EUR 3 217.12 is deductible when taxable income is lower than EUR 10 866.37 and of EUR 1 115.94 when taxable income is between EUR 10 866.37 and EUR 12 570.89.
- *Family allowances* are also deductible from the tax base in the same way as for the general allowance. The allowances for 2013 are as follows:
  - EUR 2 436.92 for the first dependent child;
  - EUR 2 649.24 for the second child;
  - EUR 4 418.54 for the third child;
  - EUR 6 187.85 for the fourth child;
  - EUR 7 957.14 for the fifth child;
  - EUR 1 769.30 for the sixth and all additional maintained children relative to the level of relief for the preceding maintained child;
  - EUR 8 830.00 for a dependent child who requires special care;
  - EUR 2 436.92 for any other dependent family member.
- *Relief for social security contributions:* Employee's compulsory contributions for the social insurance system are deductible for income tax purposes.
- *Tax credits:* None for employees.

1.1.2.2. Non-standard tax reliefs applicable to income from employment

- *Additional voluntary pension insurance premiums:* Premiums paid by a resident to the provider of a pension plan based in Slovenia or in another EU member state according to a pension plan that is approved and entered into a special register in accordance with the pension legislation are deductible from taxable income. In 2013 such deductions are subject to an annual limit of EUR 2 819.09 or a sum equal to 24% of the employee's contribution for compulsory pension and disability insurance if that is a lower figure.
- *Reimbursement of expenses associated with work,* such as in-work meals, transport to and from work, in-the-field supplements (per diem when an employee works outside his or

her working place) and compensation for being away from home, are exempt subject to statutory conditions and upper limits.

- *Reimbursement of expenses associated with business travel* such as: Per diem allowances, transport costs (including the use of the employee's private vehicle for work purposes), and the costs of overnight accommodation, are exempt subject to statutory conditions and upper limits.
- The cost of purchasing and maintaining uniforms and personal protection work equipment defined in special regulations is exempt from income tax.
- *Compensation for the use of an employee's own tools* and other equipment (except private vehicles) necessary for the performance of work at the work place, is exempt up to a level of 2% of the monthly wage or salary of the employee, subject to an upper limit of 2% of the average gross monthly wage (AGMW).
- Long service bonuses, severance pay upon retirement and payments related to accidents, long term sickness and other unexpected events are exempt subject to statutory conditions and upper limits.
- *Severance pay* on redundancy is exempt subject to an upper limit of ten times the AGMW.
- *Compensation for the use of an employee's own possessions and property when working at home* in accordance with statutory regulations is exempt up to a level of 5% of the monthly wage or salary of the employee, subject to an upper limit of 5% of the AGMW.

1.1.3. Tax schedule

The tax schedule for 2013 is as follows:

Taxable income (EUR)	Tax rate (%)
Up to 8 021.34	16
8 021.34-18 960.28	27
18 960.28-70 907.20	41
Above 70 907.20	50

1.2. Regional and local income tax

There are no regional or local income taxes.

2. Compulsory social security insurance system

The compulsory social security insurance system consists of four schemes as follows:

- pension and disability insurance;
- health insurance;
- unemployment insurance;
- parental leave insurance.

2.1. Employees' contributions

The taxable base for social security insurance contributions paid by employees is the total amount of the gross wage or salary including vacation payments, fringe benefits and remuneration of expenses related to work above a certain threshold. The assessment period is the calendar month. Employees contribute an amount as a percentage of their remuneration as follows:

Scheme name	Rate of contribution (%)
Pension insurance	15.50
Health insurance	6.36
Unemployment insurance	0.14
Parental leave insurance	0.10
Total	22.10

2.2. *Employers' contributions*

Social security insurance contributions are also paid by employers on behalf of their employees. The taxable base and the assessment period are the same as for employees' contributions. The employers' contribution rates are as follows:

Scheme name	Rate of contribution (%)
Pension insurance	8.85
Health insurance	7.09
Unemployment insurance	0.06
Parental leave insurance	0.10
Total	16.10

The only change to these rates since 1996 has been the 0.2 per cent increase in the employers' contribution rates for health insurance in 2002.

3. Payroll tax

None.

4. Universal cash transfers

4.1. *Transfers related to marital status*

None.

4.2. *Transfers for dependent children*

On 1.1.2012 the Exercise of Rights to Public Funds Act (*ZUPJS-A*) entered into force. Regarding to a new act child allowance is a supplementary benefit for maintenance, care and education of children when the family income per family member does not exceed statutorily defined per cent of the average net wage in the previous year.

The new legislation changes family income which is the basis for the income classes from gross family income to net family income. Income includes taxable income and non-taxable income defined by the Personal income tax Act as for instance social benefits. Income is defined as gross income plus social benefits received but excluding the normalized cost and actual cost recognized under the law governing income tax, taxes and mandatory social security contributions levied on such income.

The new legislation also reduces the age of a child's entitlement. The right to a child benefit is held only until the child reaches 18 years. Besides, the child benefit is higher for eligible students included in higher secondary education (aged less than 18 years and with an income per family member below the average net wage).

Applications for the allowance are made on an annual basis and the payments are not taxable.

- The amount of the allowance is calculated for each child separately according to the level of net family income per family member as a percentage of the average net wage and the ranking of the child in the family. Each family is assigned to one of 8 income classes on this basis as follows:

Income class	Net family income per family member as a percentage of the average net wage
1	Up to 18%
2	18%-30%
3	30%-36%
4	36%-42%
5	42%-53%
6	53%-64%
7	64%-82%
8	82%-99%

- The relevant income is the average monthly income per family member in the calendar year prior to the claim (or one year previous if the claim is made in the month of January, February or March).
- Each child is allocated in one of 3 ranking levels (the level of payments increases with the ranking level – the lowest for the first child, higher for the second child and the highest for the third and any subsequent child). When a child lives in a one-parent family, the amount of the allowance is increased by 10%. When a pre-school child does not attend kindergarten, the amount of the allowance is increased by 20%.
- The details for the calculation of the net income per family member was prescribed by the Minister, as follows:

  All income and receipts, namely net disposable income (after deduction of the normalized cost and actual cost recognized under the law governing income tax, taxes and mandatory social security contributions levied on such income) are taken into account, except those that are designed to cover the specific needs (such as allowance and attendance allowance, a large family, etc.). Property is also taken into account like immovable property, cars and other vehicles, watercraft, etc. Property is assigned a value and then it is calculated the amount of interest that would be received within one year from the value of assets deposited in a bank account in the form of time deposits.
- On 1.6.2012 the Public Finance Balance Act entered into force. Regarding to the Act the amounts of transfers for a children in fifth and sixth income classes are reduced for 10%. Moreover, transfers for children in the seventh and eighth income classes are abolished. This is a temporary measure, which applies up to the year following the year in which economic growth exceeds 2.5 per cent of gross domestic product.
- The monthly amounts of transfers for a child **from birth to the end of primary school** in a two-parent family according to the Exercise of Rights to Public Funds Act and Public Finance Balance Act were the following for the year 2013:

Net family income per family member as a percentage of the average net wage	1st child	2nd child	3rd child
	Monthly (EUR)	Monthly (EUR)	Monthly (EUR)
00	114.31	125.73	137.18
2 141.46	97.73	108.04	118.28
3 569.10	74.48	83.25	91.98
4 282.92	58.75	67.03	75.47
4 996.74	43.24	50.45	57.63
6 305.41	27.40	34.29	41.14

In 2013, the maximum annual benefit levels for children in a two-parent family were the following:

- EUR 1 371.72 for the first child;
- EUR 1 508.76 for the second child;
- EUR 1 646.16 for the third or subsequent child.

The amounts decline as the level of income per family member increases. The benefit ceases according to the Public Finance Balance Act to be available for families where the average income per member is higher than 64% of the average net wage for the year 2013.

5. Main changes in tax/benefit system since 2005

- In 2006 the taxation of income of individuals changed from global tax to a kind of a dual income tax system. Active income (from employment, business, basic agriculture and forestry, rents, royalties and other income) is taxed aggregated at progressive rates and taking into account the allowances and deductions; capital income (interest, dividends and capital gains) is taxed at proportionate rates on a scheduler basis.
- In 2007 the number of income tax brackets was reduced from five to three. At the same time, some non-standard tax reliefs for certain expenses and for interest paid on loans for housing were abolished.
- In 2008 additional general allowances were introduced for people on low incomes.
- The payroll tax was phased out at the start of 2009.
- The Exercise of Rights to Public Funds Act entered into force on 1.1.2012. changes family income which is the basis for the income classes from gross family income to net family income, which also includes social benefits received.
- Regarding to the Public Finance Balance Act which entered into force on 1.6.2012, the amounts of transfers for children in fifth and sixth income classes are reduced for 10%. Transfers for children in the seventh and eighth income classes are abolished.
- In 2013 the second bracket in the PIT schedule was broadened according to the Public Finance Balance Act. For the years 2013 and 2014 also the threshold for the third bracket (with the rate 41%) was increased and a new, top bracket with a rate 50% was introduced.

6. Memorandum items

6.1. Average gross annual wage earnings calculation

In Slovenia the gross earnings figures cover wages and salaries paid to individuals in formal employment including payment for overtime. They also include bonus payments and other payments such as pay for annual leave, paid leave up to seven days, public holidays, absences due to sickness for up to 30 days, job training, and slowdown through no fault of the person in formal employment.

The average gross wage earnings figures of all adult workers covering industry sectors B-N are provided by the Statistical Office of the Republic of Slovenia.

6.2. Employer contributions to private pension and health schemes

Some employer contributions are made to private health and pension schemes but there is no relevant information available on the amounts that are paid.

2013 parameter values

Average earnings/yr	Ave_earn	17 611	Secretariat estimate					
Average earnings/yr-1	Ave_earn_1	17 538						
Average net earnings/yr-1	Ave_net_earnfam	11 897						
Family allowances								
Allowances	Basic_al	0	6 519.82					
		10 866.37	4 418.64					
		12 570.89	3 302.70					
	Child_al1	2 436.92						
	Child_al2	5 086.16						
	Child_al3	9 504.70						
	Child_al4	15 692.55						
	Child_al5	23 649.69						
	Depend_al	2 436.92						
Income tax	Tax_sch	0.16	8 021.34					
		0.27	18 960.28					
		0.41	70 907.20					
		0.50						
Employees SSC	SSC_rate1	0.221						
Employers SSC	SSC_rate2	0.161						
			Ist child monthly	2nd child monthly	3rd child monthly	1 child-total annual	2 children-total annual	3 children-total annual
Family allowances	Fam_allow_mc	0	114.31	125.73	137.18	1 371.72	2 880.48	4 526.64
Married couples		2 141.46	97.73	108.04	118.28	1 172.76	2 469.24	3 888.60
		3 569.100	74.48	83.25	91.98	893.76	1 892.76	2 996.52
		4 282.92	58.75	67.03	75.47	705.00	1 509.36	2 415.00
		4 996.74	43.24	50.45	57.63	518.88	1 124.28	1 815.84
		6 305.41	27.40	34.29	41.14	328.80	740.28	1 233.96
		7 614.08	0.00	0.00	0.00	0.00	0.00	0.00
Family allowances								
Single parent uplift	Fam_allow_spup	0.1						
			Ist child monthly	2nd child monthly	3rd child monthly	1 child-total annual	2 children-total annual	3 children-total annual
Family allowances	Fam_allow_sp	0	125.74	138.30	150.90	1508.89	3168.53	4979.30
Single parents		2 141.46	107.50	118.84	130.11	1290.04	2 716.16	4 277.46
		3 569.1	81.93	91.58	101.18	983.14	2 082.04	3 296.17
		4 282.92	64.63	73.73	83.02	775.50	1 660.30	2 656.50
		4 996.74	47.56	55.50	63.39	570.77	1 236.71	1 997.42
		6 305.41	30.14	37.72	45.25	361.68	814.31	1 357.36
		7 614.08	0.00	0.00	0.00	0.00	0.00	0.00
	numdays	365						

2013 tax equations

	Line in country table and intermediate steps	Variable name	Range	Equation
1.	Earnings			
	Current year	earn		
	Net earnings Year-1	net_earn_1		
2.	Allowances:			
	Principal	tax_al_princ	P	VLOOKUP(earn;Basic_al;2)+SSC+IF(children=0,0,IF(children=1,child_al1,IF(children=2,child_al2,child_al3)+IF(Married=0,0,IF(S_earn=0,Depend_al,0))
	Spouse	Tax_al_ spouse	S	MINA(VLOOKUP(earn;Basic_al;2), earn)+SSC
3.	Credits in taxable income	taxbl_cr	B	0
4.	CG taxable income	tax_inc	B	Positive(earn-tax_al)
5.	CG tax before credits	CG_tax_excl	B	Tax(tax_inc, tax_sch)
6.	Tax credits (nonwastable)	Tax_cr	B	0
7.	CG tax	CG_tax	B	CG_tax_excl
8.	State and local taxes	local_tax	B	0
9.	Employees' soc security	SSC	B	earn* SSC_rate1
11.	Cash transfers	cash_trans	J	IF(Children=0,0;VLOOKUP((net_earn_1)/(1+married+children),IF(Married=0;Fam_allow_sp,Fam_allow_mc),IF(Children=1,5,IF(Children=2,6,7))))
13.	Employer's wage dependent contributions and taxes			
	Employer's soc security	SSC_empr	B	earn*SSC_rate2

Key to range of equation B calculated separately for both principal earner and spouse P calculated for principal only (value taken as 0 for spouse calculation) J calculated once only on a joint basis.

Taxing Wages 2014
Changes in sructural labour income tax progressivity
over 2000-12 period in OECD member countries

Spain

This chapter includes data on the income taxes paid by workers, their social security contributions, the family benefits they receive in the form of cash transfers as well as the social security contributions and payroll taxes paid by their employers. Results reported include the marginal and average tax burden for eight different family types.

Methodological information is available for personal income tax systems, compulsory social security contributions to schemes operated within the government sector, universal cash transfers as well as recent changes in the tax/benefit system. The methodology also includes the parameter values and tax equations underlying the data.

Spain 2013

The tax/benefit position of a single persons

	Wage level (per cent of average wage)	67	100	167	67
	Number of children	none	none	none	2
1.	**Gross wage earnings**	17351	26027	43378	17351
2.	**Standard tax allowances:**				
	Basic allowance				
	Married or head of family	0	0	0	2150
	Dependent children				
	Deduction for social security contributions and income taxes	1102	1653	2610	1102
	Work-related expenses	2652	2652	2652	2652
	Other				
	Total	3754	4305	5262	5904
3.	**Tax credits or cash transfers included in taxable income**	0	0	0	0
4.	**Central and state government taxable income (1 - 2 + 3)**	13597	21722	38116	11447
5.	**Central and state government income tax liability (exclusive of tax credits)**	3365	5587	11016	2833
6.	**Central and state government tax credits**				
	Basic credit	1275	1275	1275	2289
	Married or head of family				
	Children				
	Other				
	Total	1275	1275	1275	2289
7.	**Central government income tax finally paid**	1077	2243	5147	253
8.	**State income tax finally paid**	1014	2069	4594	290
9.	**Employees' compulsory social security contributions**				
	Gross earnings	1102	1653	2610	1102
	Taxable income				
	Total	1102	1653	2610	1102
10.	**Total payments to general government (7 + 8 + 9)**	3192	5965	12351	1646
11.	**Cash transfers from general government**				
	For head of family				
	For two children	0	0	0	0
	Total	0	0	0	0
12.	**Take-home pay (1-10+11)**	14159	20062	31027	15706
13.	**Employer's compulsory social security contributions**	5188	7782	12291	5188
14.	**Average rates**				
	Income tax	12.0%	16.6%	22.5%	3.1%
	Employees' social security contributions	6.35%	6.35%	6.02%	6.35%
	Total payments less cash transfers	18.4%	22.9%	28.5%	9.5%
	Total tax wedge including employer's social security contributions	37.2%	40.7%	44.3%	30.3%
15.	**Marginal rates**				
	Total payments less cash transfers: Principal earner	29.5%	34.4%	40.0%	38.9%
	Total payments less cash transfers: Spouse	n.a.	n.a.	n.a.	n.a.
	Total tax wedge: Principal earner	45.7%	49.5%	40.0%	53.0%
	Total tax wedge: Spouse	n.a.	n.a.	n.a.	n.a.

Spain 2013

The tax/benefit position of married couples

		Wage level (per cent of average wage)	100-0	100-33	100-67	100-33
		Number of children	2	2	2	none
1.	**Gross wage earnings**		26027	34703	43378	34703
2.	**Standard tax allowances**					
	Basic allowance					
	Married or head of family		3400	0	0	0
	Dependent children					
	Deduction for social security contributions and income taxes		1653	2204	2755	2204
	Work-related expenses		2652	6732	5304	6732
	Other					
		Total	7705	8936	8059	8936
3.	**Tax credits or cash transfers included in taxable income**		0	0	0	0
4.	**Central and state government taxable income (1 - 2 + 3)**		18322	25767	35320	25767
5.	**Central and state government income tax liability (exclusive of tax credits)**		4567	6588	8952	6588
6.	**Central and state government tax credits**					
	Basic credit		2234	2756	3509	2276
	Married or head of family					
	Children					
	Other					
		Total	2234	2756	3509	2276
7.	**Central government income tax finally paid**		1205	1996	2826	2243
8.	**State income tax finally paid**		1128	1836	2617	2069
9.	**Employees' compulsory social security contributions**					
	Gross earnings		1653	2204	2755	2204
	Taxable income					
		Total	1653	2204	2755	2204
10.	**Total payments to general government (7 + 8 + 9)**		3986	6036	8198	6516
11.	**Cash transfers from general government**					
	For head of family					
	For two children		0	0	0	0
		Total	0	0	0	0
12.	**Take-home pay (1-10+11)**		22041	28666	35180	28187
13.	**Employer's compulsory social security contributions**		7782	10376	12970	10376
14.	**Average rates**					
	Income tax		9.0%	11.0%	12.5%	12.4%
	Employees' social security contributions		6.35%	6.35%	6.35%	6.35%
	Total payments less cash transfers		15.3%	17.4%	18.9%	18.8%
	Total tax wedge including employer's social security contributions		34.8%	36.4%	37.6%	37.5%
15.	**Marginal rates**					
	Total payments less cash transfers: Principal earner		34.4%	34.4%	34.4%	34.4%
	Total payments less cash transfers: Spouse		23.6%	6.4%	29.5%	6.4%
	Total tax wedge: Principal earner		49.5%	49.5%	49.5%	49.5%
	Total tax wedge: Spouse		41.2%	27.9%	45.7%	27.9%

The national currency is the euro (EUR). In 2013, EUR 0.75 was equal to USD 1. In that year the average worker earned EUR 26 027 (Secretariat estimate).

1. Personal income tax systems

1.1. Central government income tax

1.1.1. Tax unit

As a general rule, the tax unit is the individual. Nevertheless, families have the options of being taxed:

- As married couples filing jointly on the combined income of both spouses and dependents.
- As heads of households (only unmarried or separated individuals with dependents).

1.1.2. Tax allowances and tax credits

1.1.2.1. Standard reliefs

- *Basic reliefs:* Married couples filing jointly may claim an allowance of EUR 3 400. This figure amounts to EUR 2 150 for heads of households.
- *Maternity tax credit:* Anon-wastable tax credit addressed to working females with children under 3 years of age up to EUR 1 200.
- *Relief for social security contributions:* All social security payments are fully deductible.
- *Work related expenses:* Net work income (gross income less employee social security contributions) may be reduced according to the following rules:
  - Taxpayers with net employment income equal or less than EUR 9 180: EUR 4 080.
  - Taxpayers with a net employment income between EUR 9 180.01 and EUR 13 260: EUR 4 080 less the result of multiplying by 0.35 the difference between net income and EUR 9 180.
  - Taxpayers with net income over EUR 13 260 or non-employment income over EUR 6 500: EUR 2 652.
- *Extending labour market participation allowance:* Taxpayers extending their labour market participation beyond the retirement age (65 years) may increase the work-related expense allowance by 100 per cent.
- *Geographic mobility allowance:* Unemployed taxpayers accepting a job in a different location may also increase the work related allowance by 100 per cent.
- *Disabled workers allowance:* An allowance of EUR 3 264 for disabled salary earners. Those with reduced mobility may claim an augmented allowance of EUR 7 242.

  As a result of the application of the above rules, net income cannot become negative.
- *Work related tax deduction:* Working taxpayers with a tax base under EUR 8 000 may deduct EUR 400. The amount is phased-out as taxpayer's tax base increases according to

the following formula: EUR 400 – 0.1 * (tax base – EUR 8 000.01), reaching a zero value when taxpayer's tax base reaches EUR 12 000. Prior amount will not exceed the result of applying the average tax rate to net work income less work related expenses allowance.

1.1.2.2. Main non-standard reliefs applicable to an AW

- *Contributions to approved Mutual, Superannuation Funds and Mutual Insured Plans.* Contributions made by each member of the household may reduce taxable income up to a maximum of the following amounts:
  - 30 per cent of net income; 50 per cent of net income for taxpayers aged over 50 years;
  - EUR 10 000; EUR 12 500 for taxpayers aged over 50 years.

Moreover, those households whose second earner has net labour income below EUR 8 000 may reduce taxable income up to a maximum of EUR 2 000 on a yearly basis if the principal earner contributes to a Pension Fund for the spouse.

- *Relief for subscriptions paid in respect of membership* of a trade union and business or professional associations (last item is limited to mandatory membership) up to EUR 500.
- *Relief for expenses made for the legal defence* of the taxpayer for labour-related conflicts up to a maximum limit of EUR 300.

Other non-standard reliefs provided as deductions are:

- *Investment in the acquisition and rehabilitation of own-housing:* As a general rule, up to 1 January 2013, taxpayers were allowed to deduct from their tax liability 15 per cent of the investment made during the year, up to a maximum of EUR 9 040.
- Furthermore, disabled taxpayers were also allowed to deduct from their tax liability 20% of the investment expenses incurred in the repairs carried out for housing adaptation to the handicapped personal needs according up to a maximum of EUR 12 080.
- With effect from 1 January 2013, the above tax credit has been abolished. Nevertheless, grandfathering rules apply for those taxpayers who before 1 January 2013 had acquired their main residence; had made some payments for it to be built; had made some payments for restoration/enlargement of their main residence or had made some payments to carry out the adaptation of the main residence of disabled people. However, in the latter two cases the works performed should be completed before 1 January 2017. For these taxpayers, the above tax credit can still be applied in accordance with the rules set up above.

  Unused payments may be carried forward up to four years within the same above limits.
- *Renting out property for own-housing:* Taxpayers with a tax base below EUR 24 107.20 may deduct a 10.05 per cent of the payments made by renting out property to be used as a permanent residence, on a yearly basis. The maximum amount to be deducted is:
  - EUR 9 040 where taxpayer's the tax base is equal or below EUR 17 707.20;
  - EUR 9 040 less the result of multiplying by 1.4125 the difference between taxpayer's tax base and EUR 17 707.20.
- *Gifts:* 10 per cent of the amounts donated to foundations and associations declared of public benefit. 25 per cent if these amounts are donated to some special legally approved foundations and associations and other private and public institutions.
- *Investments and expenses in goods of cultural interest:* 15 per cent of the amounts granted to the importation, restoration, exhibition, etc. of certain goods listed in the General Register of Goods of Cultural Interest.

Each of these last two amounts cannot exceed 10 per cent of taxable income.

1.1.2.3. Exempt income

- The base amount is EUR 5 151 per taxpayer. The same amount is granted for family units filing jointly. Taxpayers aged over 65 years may add EUR 918 to the former amount. Those aged over 75 years may claim additionally EUR 1 122.
- Dependent children (under 25 years): EUR 1 836 for the first dependent child; EUR 2 040 for the second one; EUR 3 672 for the third, and EUR 4 182 for the fourth child.
- Child care allowance: an additional allowance of EUR 2 244 for each of the above dependent children under 3 years of age.
- In case of disabled workers and additional amount of EUR 2 316 also applies. In case of great disability prior amount reaches EUR 7 038.

Child allowances have to be shared equally between spouses when they file separately.

1.1.3. *Tax schedule*

General rates of tax – resident individuals:

Taxable income (EUR)	Tax at the lower limit (EUR)	Tax rate on taxable income in excess of the lower limit (%)
0-17 707.20	0	12.75
17 707.20-33 007.20	2 257. 67	16.00
33 007.20-53 407.20	4 705.67	21.50
53 407.20-120 000.20	9 091.67	25.50
120 000.20-175 000.20	26 072.88	27.50
175 000.20-300 000.20	41 197.88	29.50
Over 300 000.20	78 072.88	30.50

1.2. *State and local income taxes*

Regional rates of tax – resident individuals: (in case that Regional Governments do not exercise its rights to set their own tax rates.

Taxable income (EUR)	Tax at the lower limit (EUR)	Tax rate on taxable income in excess of the lower limit (%)
0-17 707.20	0	12.00
17 707.20-33 007.20	2 124.86	14.00
33 007.20-53 407.20	4 266.86	18.50
Over 53 407.20	8 040.86	21.50

2. Compulsory social security contributions to schemes operated within the government sector

Social Security contributions are assessed on the basis of employees' gross earnings taking into account certain ceilings of gross employment income. In 2012, these ceilings are:

- Lower ceiling: EUR 9 036.
- Upper Ceiling: EUR 41 108.4.

These ceilings are based on a full-time job. For part-time workers, ceilings are proportional to the real hours worked (the tax equations used for this Report do not take into account the lower ceiling).

2.1. *Employees' contributions*

• Old age pension/sickness and disability	4.7 per cent
• Unemployment	1.55 per cent
• Professional training	0.1 per cent

2.2. *Employers' contributions*

• Old age pension/sickness and disability	23.6 per cent
• Unemployment/work injuries	5.50 per cent
• Wages fund	0.2 per cent
• Professional training	0.6 per cent

3. Universal cash transfers

3.1. *Transfers related to marital status*

None.

3.2. *Transfers for dependent children*

EUR 291 for 1-child families with annual gross earnings below EUR 11 490.43; the child transfer decreases with income between EUR 11 490.43 and EUR 11 757.18; the value is 0 for gross earnings exceeding EUR 11 757.18. EUR 582 for families with 2 children with annual gross earnings below EUR 13 213.99; the child transfer decreases with income between EUR 13 213.99 and EUR 13 747.49; the value is 0 for gross earnings exceeding EUR 13 747.49.

4. Main changes in tax/benefit systems in 2013

In 2013 the following changes apply:

- Spain has implemented temporary and supplementary increases (for 2012 and 2013) in the Central Government tax rates. The new rates that apply to personal income are as follows: up to EUR 17 707.20: 12.00% + 0.75% = 12.75%; up to EUR 33 007.20: 14.00% + 2.00% = 16.00%; up to EUR 53 407.20: 18.50% + 3.00% = 21.00%; up to EUR 120 000: 21.50% + 4% = 25.50%; up to EUR 175 000.20: 22.50% + 5.00% = 27.50%; and two new tax brackets; up to EUR 300 000.20: 23.50% + 6.00% = 29.50%, and over EUR 300 000.20: 23.50% + 7.00% = 30.50%.
- Since January 2010 the Work related tax credit is entirely granted for working taxpayers under EUR 8 000, and then it is phased-out up to a working taxpayer's taxable base of EUR 12 000.
- 15% tax credit for acquisition/restoration of taxpayers own dwelling has been abolished (see above).

5. Memorandum items

5.1. *Identification of an AW and calculation of earnings*

Refer to the information provided in the Annex of this Report.

2013 parameter values

Average earnings/yr	Ave_earn	26 027	Secretariat estimate	
Work related allowance	wr_rate	0.35		
	wr_lim_max	13 260		
	wr_lim_min	9 180		
	wr_lim_min_1	9 180.01		
	wr_allow_max	4 080		
	wr_allow_min	2 652		
Personal & family exempt income	Per_fam_exempt_inc	5 151		
Joint taxation allowance	Joint_tax_allow_fam 1	3 400		
	Joint_tax_allow_fam 2	2 150		
Dependent children	dep_child	1 836		
	dep_child2	2 040		
	dep_child3	3 672		
	dep_child4	4 182		
Tax Rebate (new)	TC_NUEVO	400		
	tc_rate	0.1		
	Tc_lim_max	12 000		
	Tc_lim_min	8 000		
Tax schedule	tax_sch_sg	0	0	12.75%
		17 707.2	2 257.67	16.%
		33 007.2	4 705.67	21.50%
		53 407.2	9 091.67	25.50%
		120 000.2	26 072.88	27.50%
		175 000.2	411 997.88	29.50%
		300 000.2	78 072.88	30.50%
	tax_sch_sa	0	0	12.00%
		17 707.2	2 124.86	14.00%
		33 007.2	4 266.86	18.50%
		53 407.2	8 040.86	21.50%
Social security contributions				
Employee:				
Pension	pension_rate	0.047		
Unemployment	unemp_rate	0.0155		
Other	oth_rate	0.001		
Employer				
Pension	pension_empr	0.236		
Unemployment	unemp_empr	0.055		
Other	oth_empr	0.008		
Ceiling and Floor	min_lim	0	9036	
	top_lim	41 108.4		
Child benefit	SS_child_benefit	291		
	SS_child_table	1	11 490.43	11 757.18
		2	13 213.99	13 747.49
		3	17 293.82	18 094.07
		4	20 094.94	21 161.94
		5	22 896.06	24 229.81

2013 tax equations

The functions which are used in the equations (Taper, MIN, Tax, etc.) are described in the technical note about tax equations. Variable names are defined in the table of parameters above, within the equations table, or are the standard variables "married" and "children". A reference to a variable with the affix "_total" indicates the sum of the relevant variable values for the principal and spouse. And the affixes "_princ" and "_sp" indicate the value for the principal and spouse, respectively. Equations for a single person are as shown for the principal, with "_sp" values taken as 0.

	Line in country table and intermediate steps	Variable name	Range	Equation
1.	Earnings	earn	B	for individual taxation: earn=earn_princ, or earn=earn_sp for joint (family) taxation: earn=earn_princ+earn_sp
2.	Allowances:			
	Work related, individual	work_ind	B	IF(earn-SSC<=wr_lim_min, wr_allow_max, IF(earn-SSC<=wr_lim_max, wr_allow_max-wr_rate*((earn-SSC)-(wr_lim_min_1)), wr_allow_min))
	Work related, family	work_fam	J	IF(AND(earn_sp=0, Married=0, Children=0), 0, IF(earn_total-SSC_fam<=wr_lim_min, wr_allow_max, IF(earn_total-SSC_fam<=wr_lim_max, wr_allow_max-wr_rate*((earn_total-SSC_fam)-(wr_lim_min_1)), wr_allow_min)))
	Joint taxation allowance	joint_allow_fam	J	IF(AND(Married=0,Children=0),0,IF(AND(Married=0,Children>0),joint_tax_allow_fam2,joint_tax_allow_fam1))
	Personal and family exempt income, individual	ex_inc_ind	B	per_fam_exempt_inc
	Personal and family exempt income, family	ex_inc_fam	J	IF(AND(Married=0,Children=0),0,per_fam_exempt_inc)
	Children exempt income, individual	child_ex_inc_ind	P	IF(earn_sp=0, (children>0)*(dep_child+(children>1)*dep_child2+(children>2)*dep_child3+(children>3)*(children-3)*dep_child4), (children>0)*(dep_child+(children>1)*dep_child2+(children>2)*dep_child3+(children>3)*(children-3)*dep_child4)/2)
			S	IF(earn_sp=0, 0, (children>0)*(dep_child+(children>1)*dep_child2+(children>2)*dep_child3+(children>3)*(children-3)*dep_child4)/2)
	Children exempt income, family	child_ex_inc_fam	J	(children>0)*(dep_child+(children>1)*dep_child2+(children>2)*dep_child3+(children>3)*(children-3)*dep_child4)
3.	Credits in taxable income	taxbl_cr	B, J	0
4.	CG taxable income	tax_inc	B, J	IF(AND(Married=0, Children=0), tax_inc_princ, MINA(tax_inc_princ+tax_inc_sp, tax_inc_fam))
		tax_inc_ind	B	Positive(earn-(work_ind+SSC))
		tax_inc_fam	J	IF(AND(Married=0, Children), 0, Positive(earn-(work_fam+joint_allow_fam+SSC_princ+SSC_sp)))
5.	CG tax before credits	CG_tax_ind_excl	B	MAXA(0, VLOOKUP(tax_inc_ind, tax_sch_sg, 2)+(tax_inc_ind-VLOOKUP(tax_inc_ind, tax_sch_sg, 1))*VLOOKUP(tax_inc_ind, tax_sch_sg, 3))
		CG_tax_fam_excl	J	MAXA(0, VLOOKUP(tax_inc_fam, tax_sch_sg, 2)+(tax_inc_fam-VLOOKUP(tax_inc_fam, tax_sch_sg, 1))*VLOOKUP(tax_inc_fam, tax_sch_sg, 3))
6.	CG tax credits :	CG_tax_cr_ind	B	MAXA(0,VLOOKUP(ex_inc_ind+child_ex_inc_ind,tax_sch_sg,2)+((ex_inc_ind+child_ex_inc_ind)-VLOOKUP(ex_inc_ind+child_ex_inc_ind,tax_sch_sg,1))*VLOOKUP(ex_inc_ind+child_ex_inc_ind,tax_sch_sg,3)+IF(earn>0,MINA(taper(TC_NUEVO,tax_inc_ind, tc_lim_min, tc_rate),CG_tax_ind_excl),0))

	Line in country table and intermediate steps	Variable name	Range	Equation
		CG_tax_cr_fam	J	MAXA(0,VLOOKUP(ex_inc_fam+child_ex_inc_fam,tax_sch_sg,2)+((ex_inc_fam+child_ex_inc_fam)-VLOOKUP(ex_inc_fam+child_ex_inc_fam,tax_sch_sg,1))*VLOOKUP(ex_inc_fam+child_ex_inc_fam,tax_sch_sg,3)+IF(AND(married=1,earn_sp>0),(MINA(taper(TC_NUEVO,tax_inc_fam, tc_lim_min, tc_rate),CG_tax_fam_excl))
7.	CG tax	CG_tax_ind	B	Positive(CG_tax_ind_excl-CG_tax_cr_ind)
		CG_tax_fam	J	Positive(CG_tax_fam_excl-CG_tax_cr_fam)
8.	State and local tax before credits	local_tax_ind_excl	B	MAXA(0, VLOOKUP(tax_inc_ind, tax_sch_sa, 2)+(tax_inc_ind-VLOOKUP(tax_inc_ind, tax_sch_sa, 1))*VLOOKUP(tax_inc_ind, tax_sch_sa, 3))
		local_tax_fam_excl	J	MAXA(0, VLOOKUP(tax_inc_fam, tax_sch_sa, 2)+(tax_inc_fam-VLOOKUP(tax_inc_fam, tax_sch_sa, 1))*VLOOKUP(tax_inc_fam, tax_sch_sa, 3))
	local tax credits	local_tax_cr_ind	B	MAXA(0,VLOOKUP(ex_inc_ind+child_ex_inc_ind,tax_sch_sa,2)+((ex_inc_ind+child_ex_inc_ind)-VLOOKUP(ex_inc_ind+child_ex_inc_ind,tax_sch_sa,1))*VLOOKUP(ex_inc_ind+child_ex_inc_ind,tax_sch_sa,3))
		local_tax_cr_fam	J	MAXA(0,VLOOKUP(ex_inc_fam+child_ex_inc_fam,tax_sch_sa,2)+((ex_inc_fam+child_ex_inc_fam)-VLOOKUP(ex_inc_fam+child_ex_inc_fam,tax_sch_sa,1))*VLOOKUP(ex_inc_fam+child_ex_inc_fam,tax_sch_sa,3))
	State and local tax	local_tax_ind	B	Positive(local_tax_ind_excl-local_tax_cr_ind)
		local_tax_fam	J	Positive(local_tax_fam_excl-local_tax_cr_fam)
9.	Employees' soc security	SSC	B	IF(AND(earn>0, earn<=min_lim), min_lim*(pension_rate+unemp_rate+oth_rate), IF(earn>=top_lim, top_lim*(pension_rate+unemp_rate+oth_rate), earn*(pension_rate+unemp_rate+oth_rate)))
		SSC_fam	J	SSC_princ+SSC_sp
11.	Cash transfers	Child_transf		IF(Children=0,0,IF(earn<=VLOOKUP(Children, SS_child_table,2),SS_child_benefit*Children, IF(earn<=VLOOKUP(Children, SS_child_table, 3), VLOOKUP(Children, SS_child_table, 3)-earn, 0)))
13.	Employer's SSC	SSC_empr		IF(AND(earn>0, earn<=min_lim), min_lim*(pension_empr+unemp_empr+oth_umpr), IF(earn>=top_lim, top_lim*(pension_empr+unemp_empr+oth_empr), earn*(pension_empr+unemp_empr+oth_empr)))

Key to range of equation B calculated separately for both principal earner and spouse P calculated for principal only S calculated for spouse only J calculated once only on a joint basis.

Taxing Wages 2014
Changes in sructural labour income tax progressivity
over 2000-12 period in OECD member countries

Sweden

This chapter includes data on the income taxes paid by workers, their social security contributions, the family benefits they receive in the form of cash transfers as well as the social security contributions and payroll taxes paid by their employers. Results reported include the marginal and average tax burden for eight different family types.

Methodological information is available for personal income tax systems, compulsory social security contributions to schemes operated within the government sector, universal cash transfers as well as recent changes in the tax/benefit system. The methodology also includes the parameter values and tax equations underlying the data.

Sweden 2013

The tax/benefit position of single persons

	Wage level (per cent of average wage)	67	100	167	67
	Number of children	none	none	none	2
1.	**Gross wage earnings**	261326	391990	653316	261326
2.	**Standard tax allowances**				
	Basic allowance	22000	13100	13100	22000
	Married or head of family				
	Dependent children				
	Deduction for social security contributions and income taxes	0	0	0	0
	Work-related expenses				
	Other				
	Total	22000	13100	13100	22000
3.	**Tax credits or cash transfers included in taxable income**	0	0	0	0
4.	**Central government taxable income (1 - 2 + 3)**	239300	378800	640200	239300
5.	**Central government income tax liability (exclusive of tax credits)**	0	0	47830	0
6.	**Tax credits**				
	Basic credit				
	Married or head of family				
	Children				
	Other	36176	49619	54219	36176
	Total	36176	49619	54219	36176
7.	**Central government income tax finally paid (5-6)**	-36176	-49619	-6389	-36176
8.	**State and local taxes**	75929	120193	203135	75929
9.	**Employees' compulsory social security contributions**				
	Gross earnings	18300	27400	32000	18300
	Taxable income				
	Total	18300	27400	32000	18300
10.	**Total payments to general government (7 + 8 + 9)**	58053	97974	228746	58053
11.	**Cash transfers from general government**				
	For head of family				
	For two children	0	0	0	27000
	Total	0	0	0	27000
12.	**Take-home pay (1-10+11)**	203273	294016	424570	230273
13.	**Employer's wage dependent contributions and taxes**				
	Employer's compulsory social security contributions	56289	84435	140724	56289
	payroll taxes	25819	38728	64547	25819
	Total	82108	123163	205271	82108
14.	**Average rates**				
	Income tax	15.2%	18.0%	30.1%	15.2%
	Employees' social security contributions	7.0%	7.0%	4.9%	7.0%
	Total payments less cash transfers	22.2%	25.0%	35.0%	11.9%
	Total tax wedge including employer's social security contributions	40.8%	42.9%	50.6%	32.9%
15.	**Marginal rates**				
	Total payments less cash transfers: Principal earner	28.7%	31.7%	56.7%	28.7%
	Total payments less cash transfers: Spouse	n.a.	n.a.	n.a.	n.a.
	Total tax wedge: Principal earner	45.8%	48.1%	67.1%	45.8%
	Total tax wedge: Spouse	n.a.	n.a.	n.a.	n.a.

Sweden 2013

The tax/benefit position of married couples

		100-0	100-33	100-67	100-33
	Wage level (per cent of average wage)	100-0	100-33	100-67	100-33
	Number of children	2	2	2	none
1.	**Gross wage earnings**	391990	522653	653316	522653
2.	**Standard tax allowances:**				
	Basic allowance	13100	47400	35100	47400
	Married or head of family				
	Dependent children				
	Deduction for social security contributions and income taxes	0	0	0	0
	Work-related expenses				
	Other				
	Total	13100	47400	35100	47400
3.	**Tax credits or cash transfers included in taxable income**	0	0	0	0
4.	**Central government taxable income (1 - 2 + 3)**	378800	475100	618100	475100
5.	**Central government income tax liability (exclusive of tax credits)**	0	0	0	0
6.	**Tax credits**				
	Basic credit				
	Married or head of family				
	Children				
	Other	49619	68752	85795	68752
	Total	49619	68752	85795	68752
7.	**Central government income tax finally paid (5-6)**	-49619	-68752	-85795	-68752
8.	**State and local taxes**	120193	150748	196122	150748
9.	**Employees' compulsory social security contributions**				
	Gross earnings	27400	36500	45700	36500
	Taxable income				
	Total	27400	36500	45700	36500
10.	**Total payments to general government (7 + 8 + 9)**	97974	118496	156027	118496
11.	**Cash transfers from general government**				
	For head of family				
	For two children	27000	27000	27000	0
	Total	27000	27000	27000	0
12.	**Take-home pay (1-10+11)**	321016	431157	524289	404157
13.	**Employer's wage dependent contributions and taxes**				
	Employer's compulsory social security contributions	84435	112580	140724	112580
	payroll taxes	38728	51637	64547	51637
	Total	123163	164217	205271	164217
14.	**Average rates**				
	Income tax	18.0%	15.7%	16.9%	15.7%
	Employees' social security contributions	7.0%	7.0%	7.0%	7.0%
	Total payments less cash transfers	18.1%	17.5%	19.7%	22.7%
	Total tax wedge including employer's social security contributions	37.7%	37.2%	38.9%	41.2%
15.	**Marginal rates**				
	Total payments less cash transfers: Principal earner	31.7%	31.7%	31.7%	31.7%
	Total payments less cash transfers: Spouse	15.7%	28.7%	28.7%	28.7%
	Total tax wedge: Principal earner	48.1%	48.1%	48.1%	48.1%
	Total tax wedge: Spouse	35.9%	45.8%	45.8%	45.8%

The national currency is the Swedish Kroner (SEK). In 2013, SEK 6.51 was equal to USD 1. In that year, the average worker earned SEK 391 990 (Secretariat estimate).

1. Personal income tax systems

1.1. Central government income taxes

1.1.1. Tax unit

Spouses are taxed separately.

1.1.2. Tax allowances and tax credits

1.1.2.1. Standard reliefs

- *Basic reliefs:* A basic allowance is given for assessed earned income and varies between SEK 13 100 and SEK 34 300, depending on income. When individuals pay central government income tax, the basic allowance is at its lowest level, which equals SEK 13 100. The basic allowance depends on the assessed earned income and the basic amount, which equals SEK 44 500.

Assessed-Earned-Income (SEK) Relative to Basic Amount (BA)	Share of BA at lower bracket	For exceeding income
-0.99	0.423	
0.99-2.72	0.423	+0.2
2.72-3.11	0.77	
3.11-7.88	0.77	-0.1
7.88-	0.293	

- *Standard marital status reliefs:* None.
- *Relief(s) for children:* None.
- *Work-related expenses:* None.
- *Other:* None.

1.1.2.2. Main non-standard tax reliefs applicable to an AW

- Interest on qualifying loans: Interest payments are offset against capital income. The resulting net capital income is the tax base. A tax credit is given in the case of negative capital income.
- Contributions to pensions, life insurance, superannuation schemes: A deduction of maximum SEK 12 000 can be claimed for premiums paid to private pension arrangements. Medical expenses: None.
- Other allowances are given for:
  - ❖ the amount of commuting expenses exceeding SEK 10 000;

- other types of work-related expenses exceeding SEK 5 000; examples are the costs of tools, work-related phone calls using the taxpayer's private telephone;
- increased living expenses while on business trips, e.g. such as the use of a private car if these costs are not reimbursed by the employer;
- double housing expenses due to *temporary* work at other geographical locations (too far from home for commuting), or if the family for some reason can't move, even if the job is of a *permanent* nature;
- travelling expenses for travelling home if the taxpayer works in another place than his/her place of residence.

1.1.3. *Tax schedule*

Taxable income (SEK)	Tax (SEK) at lower bracket	For exceeding income, %
0-413 200	0	0
413 200-591 600	0	20
Over 591 600	35 680	25

1.1.4. *Tax credits*

A tax credit equal to 100 per cent of the compulsory social security contributions paid by the employee is granted.

For a person aged under 65, an annual Earned Income Tax Credit (EITC) worth up to SEK 22 268 at the average local tax rate is granted on labour income. For those aged 65 or more, a higher credit worth up to SEK 30 000 is granted. For a person aged under 65 the EITC is calculated as follows: EITC = (Special Amount – Basic Allowance) * local tax rate. For those older than 65 a simplified EITC was introduced in 2009 so that it is no longer connected to the local tax rate, the basic allowance or the basic amount. The Basic Allowance is determined in Section 1.1.2.1; the local tax rate is discussed in Section 1.2. The Basic Amount (BA) in 2012 is SEK 44 500. The Special Amount is based on the taxpayer's (gross) earned income.

For taxpayers younger than 65, the Special Amount is calculated as follows:

Earned income (EI)	Special amount
-0.91 BA	EI
0.91 BA-2.72 BA	0.91 BA + 0.304 * (EI-0.91 BA)
2.72 BA-7.00 BA	1.461 BA + 0.095 * (EI-2.72 BA)
7.00 BA-	1.868 BA

BA = SEK 44 500.

For taxpayers older than 65, the EITC is calculated differently:

Earned income (EI)	EITC
-100 000 SEK	0.2 * EI
100 001-300 000 SEK	15 000 SEK + 0.05*EI
300 001 SEK-	30 000 SEK

1.2. Local government income taxes

1.2.1. General description of the systems

Sweden has both a central government and a local government personal income tax. They are completely co-ordinated in the assessment process and refer to the same period, i.e. the income year coincides with the calendar year.

1.2.2. Tax base

The tax base is the same as for the central government income tax. The basic allowance for individuals paying local government tax varies between SEK 13 100 and SEK 34 300; it depends on the taxpayer's income. For a taxpayer earning the AW, this basic allowance amounts to SEK 13 100 (based on an AW equal to SEK 399 211 – subject to revision with the AW).

1.2.3. Tax rates

The local government personal income tax is proportional and differs between municipalities. The average rate amounts to 31.73 per cent in 2013, with the maximum and minimum rates being 36.24 per cent and 29.73 per cent, respectively.

2. Compulsory social security contributions to schemes operated within the government sector

2.1. Employees' contributions

A general pension contribution of 7 per cent of personal income is paid by employees and the self-employed when income is equal to or greater than 42.3 per cent of the basic amount underlying the basic allowance (see Section 1.1.2.1). The contribution cannot exceed SEK 32 000 since the general pension contributions are not paid for income over SEK 456 700 (= 8.07 * 56 600). The employees' contribution is offset with a tax credit.

2.2. Employers' contributions

The employers' contributions are calculated as a percentage of the total sum of salaries and benefits in a year. For the self-employed, the base is net business income. The rates for 2013 are listed below.

Program	Employer (%)	Self-employed (%)
Retirement pension	10.21	10.21
Survivor's pension	1.17	1.17
Parental insurance	2.60	2.60
Health insurance	4.35	4.44
Labour market	2.91	0.37
Occupational health	0.30	0.30
General wage tax	9.88	9.88
Total	31.42	28.97

In certain regions, a reduction of 10 per cent of the base, maximum SEK 7 100 per month, is granted (SEK 18 000 per year for self-employed) (it is not included in the calculations underlying this Report). For employees aged under 26 a reduced SSC rate of 15.49 per cent is applied (14.88 per cent for self-employed). For employees who are over 65 years old and born after 1937 only the retirement pension contribution (10.21 per cent) is applicable. For persons born in 1937 or earlier no employers' social security contributions are applied. On premiums for occupational pensions paid by the employer a reduced SSC rate (24.26 per cent) is applied.

For self-employed a general reduction of 5 per cent on the SSC is applicable if the income exceeds SEK 40 000 per year. The maximal reduction is SEK 10 000 per year.

3. Universal cash transfers

3.1. *Transfers related to marital status*

None.

3.2. *Transfers for dependent children*

The transfers are tax exempt and independent of the parents' income. The transfers for each child are as follows:

First child	12 600
Second child	14 400
Third child	18 048
Fourth child	24 720
Fifth and subsequent child	27 600

4. Main changes in tax/benefit systems since 1998

A tax credit of SEK 1 320 was introduced for low- and average income earners in 1999. The credit is reduced by 1.2 per cent of taxable income above SEK 135 000. This reduction was abolished in 2003 and was replaced by an increase in the basic allowance.

A tax credit of 25 per cent of the social security contribution paid by employees and the self-employed was introduced in 2000. The tax credit has been gradually increased to 100 per cent in 2006.

In 2004, a special tax credit equal to SEK 200 was provided for the statutory minimum local income tax. The special tax credit was abolished in 2005 as was the statutory minimum state income tax (a lump sum tax) of SEK 200. The central government income tax bracket is indexed with the consumer price index plus 2 per cent. In order to reduce the number of people paying the central income tax, there have been additional increases of the tax bracket in 2009. However, in 2004, 2005 and 2006 the central government income tax bracket was restricted to be indexed with the consumer price index plus 1 per cent.

The child allowance was raised by SEK 1 200 per year in 2000, 2001 and 2006.

Maximum fee for childcare was introduced in 2002.

The basic allowance has been increased in 2001, 2002, 2003, 2005 and 2006.

The maximum number of days with unemployment benefit was increased from 564 to 580 days in 1998. The maximum number of days with unemployment benefit was set to 300 days (450 days for persons with children under the age of 18) in 2007. The unemployment benefit was raised in 2001 by SEK 100 to SEK 680 per day. The compensation in the sick leave was raised from 75 to 80 per cent in 1998. In 2003 the compensation was lowered to 77.6 per cent and, at the same time, the number of days for which the employer is responsible was increased from 14 to 21 days. In 2005 the compensation in the sick leave and the number of days for which the employer is responsible were set to their before-2003 level.

The lowest level compensation in the parental leave was raised on 1 July 2006 from SEK 60 to SEK 180 per day.

An earned income tax credit was introduced in 2007 with the purpose of making work economically more rewarding relative to unemployment or inactivity. The earned income tax credit was increased in 2008, 2009 and 2010.

In 2007, the social security contributions for 18-24-year-old employees and self-employed were reduced. In 2009 the reduction were increased and expanded to include all aged under 26. A special wage tax for persons older than 65 was abolished in 2007 for persons born after 1937 and in 2008 for persons born in 1937 or earlier.

An increased basic allowance for persons older than 65 was introduced in 2009 and extended in 2010 and 2011.

5. Memorandum items

5.1. *Identification of an AW and calculation of earnings*

Basic data for gross earnings are taken from the series *Official Statistics of Sweden*, published by Statistics Sweden. The calculation is based upon total average monthly or hourly earnings, primarily in September of the calendar year. To arrive at the annual earnings, data have been multiplied by the normal amount of hours worked during the year or the stipulated monthly salary has been multiplied by a factor of 12.2. The figures are representative for the country as a whole. The branch classification is NACE Rev. 2 B-N according to the OECD recommendation.

5.2. *Employer contributions to private health, pension, etc., schemes*

There are a handful of widespread private social security schemes. The employers' contributions to these systems for the blue-collar workers in the private sector equalled to 6.3 per cent of wage earnings in 2007. For white-collar workers in the private sector the employers' contributions to private social security schemes was 14 per cent in 2007. These figures are based on the statistics of labour costs in the private sector, published by Statistics Sweden.

2013 parameter values

Average earnings/yr	Ave_earn	391 990	Secretariat estimate
Central income tax			
	tax_rate	0.2	
	tax_rate2	0.05	
	tax_thrsh	413 200	
	tax_thrsh2	591 600	
Basic Allowance			
	gr1	0.99	
	gr2	2.72	
	gr3	3.11	
	gr4	7.88	
	gp1	0.423	
	gp2	0.2	
	gp3	0.1	
	gp4	0.293	
	gp5	0.77	
Local income tax			
	local_rate	0.3160	
	min_taxl	0	
Soc. security amount			
	basic_amt	44 500	
	basic_ant	56 600	
Soc. security contributions			
employee	SSC_rate	0.07	
employer	SSC_empr	0.3142	
ceiling	SSCC	8.07	
Child benefit			
	Child 1	12 600	
	Child 2	14 400	
	CB	13 500	
Tax credits			
	TC1	0	
	TC1gr1	0	
	TC1gp1	0	
	TC2gp1	1	
EITC	er_1	0.91	
	er_2	2.72	
	er_3	7.00	
	ep_1	1.461	
	ep_2	0.304	
	ep_3	0.095	
	ep_4	1.868	
Employer payroll tax	PRT	0.0988	

2013 tax equations

The equations for the Swedish system are mostly repeated for each individual of a married couple. But the cash transfer is calculated only once. This is shown by the Range indicator in the table below.

The functions which are used in the equations (Taper, MIN, Tax, etc.) are described in the technical note about tax equations. Variable names are defined in the table of parameters above, within the equations table, or are the standard variables "married" and "children". A reference to a variable with the affix "_total" indicates the sum of the relevant variable values for the principal and spouse. And the affixes "_princ" and "_spouse" indicate the value for the principal and spouse, respectively. Equations for a single person are as shown for the principal, with "_spouse" values taken as 0.

	Line in country table and intermediate steps	Variable name	Range	Equation
1.	Earnings	earn		
		truncearn	B	TRUNC(earn, -2)
2.	Allowances:	basic_al	B	IF(truncearn<=gr_2*basic_amt, MINA(ROUNDUP(MAXA(gp_1*basic_amt, (gp_1+gp_2*(gr_2-gr_1))*basic_amt-gp_2*MAXA(gr_2*basic_amt-truncearn, 0)), -2), truncearn), MINA(ROUNDUP(MAXA(gp_4*basic_amt, gp_5*basic_amt-gp_2*MAXA(gr_2*basic_amt-truncearn, 0)-gp_3*MAXA(truncearn-gr_3*basic_amt, 0)), -2), truncearn))
		ssc_al	B	0
	Total	tax_al	B	basic_al+ssc_credit
3.	Credits in taxable income	taxbl_cr	B	0
4.	CG taxable income	tax_inc	B	Positive(earn-basic_al-ssc_credit)
5.	CG tax before credits	CG_tax_excl	B	tax_rate*Positive(tax_inc-tax_thrsh)+ tax_rate2* Positive(tax_inc-tax_thrsh2)
6.	Tax credits :	ssc_credit	B	Trunc(SSC, -2)
		localtax_credit	B	0
		eitc	B	=TRUNC(MAX((((TRUNC(IF(earned_income>er_2*basic_amt; IF(earned_income>er_3*basic_amt;ep_4*basic_amt;ep_1*basic_amt+ep_3 *(earned_income-er_2*basic_amt));MIN(earned_income;er_1*basic_amt+ep_2*(earned_income-er_1*basic_amt)));0))-basic_allowance)*local_rate);0);0)
		tax_cr	B	ssc_credit+localtax_credit+eitc
7.	CG tax	CG_tax	B	CG_tax_excl-tax_cr
8.	State and local taxes	local_tax	B	IF(tax_inc>0, TRUNC(local_rate*tax_inc, 0)+min_taxl, 0)
9.	Employees' soc security	SSC	B	(truncearn>=gp_1*basic_amt)*MINA(ROUNDSSC(truncearn*SSC_rate), ROUNDSSC(SSCC*basic_ant*SSC_rate))
11.	Cash transfers	cash_trans	J	Children*CB
13.	Employer's contributions		B	
	Employer's SSC	SSC_empr	B	TRUNC(earn*SSC_empr)-Payroll_empr
	Employer's payroll tax	Payroll_empr	B	TRUNC(earn*PRT)
	Total	Cont_empr	B	SSC_empr+Payroll_empr

Key to range of equation B calculated separately for both principal earner and spouse P calculated for principal only (value taken as 0 for spouse calculation) J calculated once only on a joint basis.

Taxing Wages 2014
Changes in sructural labour income tax progressivity
over 2000-12 period in OECD member countries

Switzerland

This chapter includes data on the income taxes paid by workers, their social security contributions, the family benefits they receive in the form of cash transfers as well as the social security contributions and payroll taxes paid by their employers. Results reported include the marginal and average tax burden for eight different family types.

Methodological information is available for personal income tax systems, compulsory social security contributions to schemes operated within the government sector, universal cash transfers as well as recent changes in the tax/ benefit system. The methodology also includes the parameter values and tax equations underlying the data.

Switzerland 2013

The tax/benefit position of single persons

	Wage level (per cent of average wage)	67	100	167	67
	Number of children	none	none	none	2
1.	**Gross wage earnings**	58774	88161	146934	58774
2.	**Standard tax allowances**				
	Basic allowance				
	Married or head of family	0	0	0	0
	Dependent children	0	0	0	13000
	Deduction for social security contributions and income taxes	6310	10413	18492	6310
	Work-related expenses	2000	2480	4000	2000
	Other	1700	1700	1700	3100
	Total	10010	14592	24192	24410
3.	**Tax credits or cash transfers included in taxable income**	0	0	0	6000
4.	**Central government taxable income (1 - 2 + 3)**	48700	73500	122700	40300
5.	**Central government income tax liability (exclusive of tax credits)**	411	1155	4792	120
6.	**Tax credits**				
	Basic credit				
	Married or head of family				
	Children	0	0	0	502
	Other				
	Total	0	0	0	502
7.	**Central government income tax finally paid (5-6)**	411	1155	4792	0
8.	**State and local taxes**	4257	8420	18466	1314
9.	**Employees' compulsory social security contributions**				
	Gross earnings	3673	5510	9058	3673
	Taxable income				
	Total	3673	5510	9058	3673
10.	**Total payments to general government (7 + 8 + 9)**	8341	15086	32316	4987
11.	**Cash transfers from general government**				
	For head of family				
	For two children	0	0	0	6000
	Total	0	0	0	6000
12.	**Take-home pay (1-10+11)**	50432	73075	114618	59786
13.	**Employer's compulsory social security contributions**	3673	5510	9058	3673
14.	**Average rates**				
	Income tax	7.9%	10.9%	15.8%	2.2%
	Employees' social security contributions	6.3%	6.3%	6.2%	6.3%
	Total payments less cash transfers	14.2%	17.1%	22.0%	-1.7%
	Total tax wedge including employer's social security contributions	19.2%	22.0%	26.5%	4.3%
15.	**Marginal rates**				
	Total payments less cash transfers: Principal earner	21.7%	25.8%	32.2%	13.8%
	Total payments less cash transfers: Spouse	n.a.	n.a.	n.a.	n.a.
	Total tax wedge: Principal earner	26.3%	30.1%	35.9%	18.9%
	Total tax wedge: Spouse	n.a.	n.a.	n.a.	n.a.

Switzerland 2013

The tax/benefit position of married couples

	Wage level (per cent of average wage)		100-0	100-33	100-67	100-33
	Number of children		2	2	2	none
1.	**Gross wage earnings**		88161	117547	146934	117547
2.	**Standard tax allowances**					
	Basic allowance					
	Married or head of family		2600	15375	16000	15375
	Dependent children		13000	13000	13000	0
	Deduction for social security contributions and income taxes		10413	14621	18723	14621
	Work-related expenses		2480	2480	2480	2480
	Other		4900	4900	4900	3500
		Total	33392	50376	55103	35976
3.	**Tax credits or cash transfers included in taxable income**		6000	6000	6000	0
4.	**Central government taxable income (1 - 2 + 3)**		60700	73100	97800	81500
5.	**Central government income tax liability (exclusive of tax credits)**		445	817	1858	1131
6.	**Tax credits**					
	Basic credit					
	Married or head of family					
	Children		502	502	502	0
	Other					
		Total	502	502	502	0
7.	**Central government income tax finally paid (5-6)**		0	315	1356	1131
8.	**State and local taxes**		3867	6697	10748	8935
9.	**Employees' compulsory social security contributions**					
	Gross earnings		5510	7347	9183	7347
	Taxable income					
		Total	5510	7347	9183	7347
10.	**Total payments to general government (7 + 8 + 9)**		9377	14359	21288	17413
11.	**Cash transfers from general government**					
	For head of family					
	For two children		6000	6000	6000	0
		Total	6000	6000	6000	0
12.	**Take-home pay (1-10+11)**		84783	109189	131647	100135
13.	**Employer's compulsory social security contributions**		5510	7347	9183	7347
14.	**Average rates**					
	Income tax		4.4%	6.0%	8.2%	8.6%
	Employees' social security contributions		6.3%	6.3%	6.3%	6.3%
	Total payments less cash transfers		3.8%	7.1%	10.4%	14.8%
	Total tax wedge including employer's social security contributions		9.5%	12.6%	15.7%	19.8%
15.	**Marginal rates**					
	Total payments less cash transfers: Principal earner		17.2%	21.5%	25.0%	22.3%
	Total payments less cash transfers: Spouse		17.0%	20.6%	25.6%	21.0%
	Total tax wedge: Principal earner		22.1%	26.1%	29.4%	26.9%
	Total tax wedge: Spouse		21.8%	25.3%	30.0%	25.7%

The national currency is the Swiss franc (CHF). In 2013, CHF 0.93 equalled USD 1. The Secretariat has estimated that in that same year the average worker earned CHF 88 161 (Secretariat estimate).

Cantonal and communal income taxes are very substantial in relation to direct federal tax. Here, the canton and commune of Zurich have been selected as an example of the tax system of the 26 cantons. Local income tax is not deductible when calculating federal income tax.

1. Personal income tax systems

1.1. Income tax collected by the federal government (Confederation)

1.1.1. Tax unit

The income of spouses living together is taxed jointly, regardless of the property regime under which they were married. Income of children living under parental authority is added to the income of their custodian. Children's labour income is taxed separately and in some cases, as in Zurich, is exempt from tax.

1.1.2. Tax reliefs and tax credits

1.1.2.1. Standard reliefs for "postnumerando" taxation [i.e. annual taxation on the basis of actual earned income, assessed at the end of the year].

- Basic deduction

There is a basic deduction of CHF 2 600 for married couples for direct federal tax.

- Deduction for children

A CHF 6 500 deduction is allowed for each child under 18 years of age; the deduction is allowed for older children if they are apprentices or still in school.

- Tax credit for children

A CHF 251 deduction from the tax liability is allowed for each child under 18 years, the deduction is allowed for older children if they are apprentices or still in school.

- Deductions for social insurance contributions and other taxes

Premiums for old age and disability insurance (5.15% of gross earned income) and for unemployment insurance (1.1% for income up to CHF 12-6 000, 0.5% for income between CHF 126 000 and CHF 315 000) are deductible in full. Compulsory contributions of approximately 7.65% to private pension funds are also fully deductible. Health and life insurance premiums are deductible from federal income tax up to CHF 3 500 for married persons and CHF 1 700 for taxpayers who are widow(er)s, divorced or single (such premiums are not considered social contributions). These amounts are increased by CHF 700 for each dependent child.

- Work-related expenses

Taxpayers are allowed a deduction corresponding to 3% of net income (i.e. gross income less contributions for old age and disability insurance, unemployment insurance and work-related provident funds). This deduction may be no less than CHF 2 000 and no more than CHF 4 000.

- Deduction for two-income couples

50% of the smaller income can be deducted, but no less than CHF 8 100 and no more than CHF 13 400.

1.1.2.2. Main non-standard reliefs available to the average worker

- Interest payments on qualifying loans

This is the main non-standard relief available to the average worker. It is allowed for all sorts of loans.

- Medical expenses

Expenses incurred as a result of illness, accidents or disability of the taxpayer or one of its dependants are deductible if the taxpayer bears the expenses personally and they exceed 5% of his or her net income.

1.1.3. *Tax base*

Allowable deductions from gross income	Single taxpayer (CHF)	Married taxpayer, 2 children (CHF)
Work-related expenses[1]	2 000-4 000	2 000-4 000
Personal deduction	–	2 600
Deduction for 2 dependent children	–	13 000 (6 500 * 2)
Social contributions		
Old age insurance	5.05%	5.05%
Unemployment insurance	1.1%[2]	1.1%[2]
Pension fund	7.8%	7.8%
Maximum deductions for health insurance premiums and loan interest[3]	1 700 plus 700 per child	3 500 plus 700 per child
Deduction for two-income couples[4]		8 100-13 400

1. 3% of net income, minimum CHF 2 000, maximum CHF 4 000.
2. 1.1% of income up to CHF 126 000; 0.5% of income between CHF 126 000 and CHF 315 000.
3. For the purposes of this publication, taxpayers are assumed to always receive the relevant maximum deduction.
4. 50% of smaller income, minimum the lower of CHF 8 100 or adjusted smaller income, maximum CHF 13 400.

In addition, for the married taxpayer with 2 children, there is a tax credit for 2 dependent children amounting to CHF 502, thus reducing the tax liability by CHF 502.

1.1.4. *Tax schedules*

1.1.4.1. Rates for persons living alone

Taxable income (CHF)[1]	Base amount (CHF)	Plus % of excess (CHF)	
Up to 14 500	–		–
14 500 to 31 600		0.77	14 500
31 600 to 41 400	131.65	0.88	31 600
41 400 to 55 200	217.90	2.64	41 400
55 200 to 72 500	582.20	2.97	55 200
72 500 to 78 100	1 096.00	5.94	72 500
778 100 to 103 600	1 428.60	6.60	78 100
103 600 to 134 600	3 111.60	8.80	103 600
134 600 to 176 000	5 839.60	11.00	134 600
176 000 to 755 200	10 393.60	13.20	176 000
Over 755 200[2]	–	11.5 of total income	

1. Fractions of less than CHF 100 are disregarded.
2. The calculation model disregards this part of the schedule.

1.1.4.2. Rates for spouses living together and for widowed, separated, divorced taxpayers or unmarried taxpayers living with their own children.

Taxable income (CHF)[1]	Base amount (CHF)	Plus % of the excess (CHF)	
Up to 28 300	–	–	–
28 300 to 50 900		1	28 300
50 900 to 58 400	223	2	50 900
58 400 to 75 300	373	3	58 400
75 300 to 90 300	877	4	75 300
90 300 to 103 400	1 477	5	90 300
103 400 to 114 700	2 127	6	103 400
114 700 to 124 200	2 799	7	114 700
124 200 to 131 700	3 457	8	124 200
131 700 to 137 300	4 057	9	131 700
137 300 to 141 200	4 552	10	137 300
141 200 to 143 100	4 942	11	141 200
143 100 to 145 000	5 151	12	143 100
145 000 to 895 800	5 379	13	145 000
For 895 900	103 028.50		
Over 895 900[2]	–	11.5 of total income	

1. Fractions of less than CHF 100 are disregarded.
2. The calculation model disregards this part of the schedule.

1.2. Taxes levied by decentralised authorities (Canton and commune of Zurich)

1.2.1. General description of the system

The system of cantonal and communal taxation has the same features as that of direct federal tax.

The tax base is comprised of income from all sources.

Once the basic amount of tax is set, cantons, communes and churches levy their taxes by applying a multiple, which may change from year to year. In 2012, for example, the canton applied a multiple of 1.0, the commune of Zurich 1.19 and the reformed church 0.10. The basic amount of tax is therefore multiplied by a total of 2.29. However, following the decision no longer to include church tax in *Revenue Statistics*, it is no longer included in the calculations for *Taxing Wages*. The basic amount of tax is therefore multiplied by a total of 2.19.

1.2.2. *Tax base*

Allowable deductions from gross income	Single taxpayer (CHF)	Married taxpayer, 2 children (CHF)
Work-related expenses[1]	2 000-4 000	2 000-4 000
Personal deduction	–	–
Deduction for 2 dependent children	–	18 000 (9 000 * 2)
Social contributions		
Old age insurance	5.15%	5.15%
Unemployment insurance	1.1%[2]	1.1%[2]
Pension fund	7.8%	7.8%
Maximum deductions for health insurance premiums and loan interest[3]	2 600 plus 1 300 per child	5 200 plus 1 300 per child
Deduction for two-income couples		5 900

1. 3% of net income, minimum CHF 2 000 CHF, maximum CHF 4 000.
2. 1.1% of income up to CHF 126 000; 0.5% of income between CHF 126 000 and CHF 315 000.
3. For the purposes of this publication, taxpayers are assumed to always receive the relevant maximum deduction.

1.2.3. *Postnumerando tax rates*

Cantonal income tax (Zurich)

a) Basic income tax rates for married, divorced, widowed or single taxpayers living with children:

Taxable income (CHF)[1]	Base amount (CHF)	Plus % of the excess (CHF)	
Up to 13 500	–	0	–
13 500 to 19 600	–	2	13 500
19 160 to 27 300	122	3	19 600
27 300 to 36 700	353	4	27 300
36 700 to 47 400	729	5	36 700
47 400 to 61 300	1 264	6	47 400
61 300 to 92 100	2 098	7	61 300
92 100 to 122 900	4 254	8	92 100
122 900 to 169 300	6 718	9	122 900
169 300 to 224 700	10 984	10	169 300
224 700 to 284 800	16 434	11	224 700
284 800 to 354 100	23 045	12	284 800
Over 354 100	31 361	13	354 100

1. Fractions below CHF 100 are disregarded.

b) Basic income tax rates for other taxpayers (single without children):

Taxable income (CHF)[1]	Base amount (CHF)	Plus % of the excess (CHF)	
Up to 6 700	–	0	–
6 700 to 11 400	–	2	6 700
11 400 to 16 100	94	3	11 400
16 100 to 23 700	235	4	16 100
23 700 to 33 000	539	5	23 700
33 000 to 43 700	1 004	6	33 000
43 700 to 56 100	1 646	7	43 700
56 100 to 73 000	2 514	8	56 100
73 000 to 105 500	3 866	9	73 000
105 500 to 137 700	6 791	10	105 500
137 700 to 188 700	10 011	11	137 700
188 700 to 254 900	15 621	12	188 700
Over 254 900	23 565	13	254 900

1. Fractions below CHF 100 are disregarded.

c) Annual multiple as a percentage of basic tax rates:

Canton of Zurich	100
Commune of Zurich	119
Roman Catholic church tax	10 (for info.)
Reformed Church tax	10 (for info.)

A personal tax of CHF 24 is added.

1.2.4. *Tax rates used for this study*

This study uses the rates of tax levied by the federal, cantonal and communal tax authorities.

2. Compulsory social security contributions to schemes operated within the government sector

2.1. *Employee contributions*

2.1.1. *Retirement pensions*

5.15% of gross income for old age insurance.

2.1.2. *Health insurance*

–

2.1.3. *Unemployment*

1.1% on the portion of income up to CHF 126 000; 0.5% for income between CHF 126 000 and CHF 315 000.

2.1.4. *Work-related accidents*

–

2.1.5. *Family allowances*

–

2.1.6. *Other*

–

2.2. *Employer contributions*

2.2.1. *Retirement pensions*

5.15% of gross income for old age insurance.

2.2.2. *Health insurance*

–

2.2.3. *Unemployment*

1.1% on the portion of income up to CHF 126 000; 0.5% for income between CHF 126 000 and CHF 315 000.

2.2.4. *Work-related accidents*

–

2.2.5. *Family allowances*

The employer pays a benefit for dependent children of an employee. The effective benefits paid depend on the Canton of residence and the respective employer. As of 1 January 2009, a new Swiss-wide minimum amount of CHF 2 400 (for children up to 16 years of age and CHF 3 000 for children in education between 16 and 25 years of age) has been established. In most cases, the benefit paid exceeds this minimum. The average family benefit is estimated to amount to CHF 3 000 per child per year.

This benefit is taxable along with other components of income.

The family allowance contributions are not included in the *Taxing Wages* results either as they are paid to a privately-managed fund. These contributions therefore qualify as non-tax compulsory payments (see also Section 5.3).

2.2.6. *Other*

–

3. Universal cash benefits

3.1. *Benefits linked to marital status*

No such benefits are paid.

3.2. *Benefits for dependent children*

The employer pays a benefit of, on average, approximately CHF 3 000 per year for each dependent child of an employee. This benefit is taxable along with other components of income. See 2.25.

4. Main changes in tax/benefit system since 1998

On 1 January 1999, the canton of Zurich switched from biennial praenumerando taxation to annual postnumerando taxation on individual income. As a result, the direct federal tax is based on annual postnumerando taxation as well.

As of 1 January 2008, the basic deduction for married couples and the deduction for two-income couples were introduced. These measures are intended to minimise the marriage penalty and to reduce the high taxation of secondary earners, thereby increasing labour force participation of skilled secondary earners.

As of 1 January 2012, the tax credit for children reduces the tax liability by CHF 251 per child.

5. Memorandum item

5.1. *Identification of the average worker*

The population includes men and women working in industry, arts and crafts. The stated income is for the average of workers in the same sector. The geographical scope is the entire country, whereas the amount of tax is computed in respect of the canton and commune of Zurich.

5.2. *Method of calculation used*

- Unemployment benefits: Not included.
- Sick leave payments: Not included.
- Paid leave allowances: Included.
- Overtime: Included.
- Periodic cash bonuses: Included.
- Fringe benefits: Not included.
- Basic method used for calculation: Monthly wages are multiplied by 12.
- Close of the income tax year: 31 December.
- Reference period for computing wages: From 1 January to 31 December of the year in question.

5.3. *Calculation of non-tax compulsory payments*

Switzerland imposes some important non-tax compulsory payments (NTCPs). These NTPCs are not included in the *Taxing Wages* models except when they qualify as standard personal income tax reliefs. Compulsory payments indicators, which combine the effect of taxes and NTCPs, are calculated by the OECD Secretariat and presented in the *OECD Tax Database* (see: *www.oecd.org/ctp/taxdatabase*). Switzerland levies the following employee and/ or employer NTCPs:

- Contributions to the second pillar of the pension system (occupational pension funds): Occupational pension funds are mandatory for salaried persons earning at least CHF 21 060 annually. Old age insurance is based on individual savings. The savings assets accumulated by the insured person on his individual savings account over the years serve to finance the old age pension. The constituted capital is converted into an annual old age pension on the basis of a conversion factor. Contribution rates depend on the occupation and the pension fund. An estimated representative rate amounts to 7.8% for employees and 10.3% for employers in 2013.
- Health insurance is compulsory for all persons domiciled in Switzerland. Every family member is insured individually, regardless of age. Health insurance contributions are lump sum contributions per capita depending on age, sex, canton of residence and insurer. The national average rates for 2013 amount to CHF 4 652 for adults and CHF 1 072 for children per year. Health insurance premiums can be reduced depending on the contributor's income level and his family situation. Each canton has its own definition of the income thresholds and the reduction regime. The health insurance premium and reduction rates of the Canton of Zurich are used in the calculations.
- Family allowance: Employers have to make family allowance contributions. The contribution rates differ among cantons and family contribution funds. A representative rate has to be estimated, for 2013 it amounts to 1.2%.
- Accident insurance: Accident insurance is compulsory for every employee. Employees are automatically insured by their employer, whereas the employers are more or less automatically assigned to a particular insurance company depending on their branch of trade. The risk and associated costs of the respective business activity determines the insurance premiums. A representative rate would have to be estimated.

2013 parameter values

Average earnings/yr	Ave_earn	88 161	Secretariat estimate
Tax allowances	fed_child_al	6 500	
Tax credit	fed_child_cred	251	
Partner Allowance	partner_rate_fed	0.5	
	partner_min_fed	8 100	
	partner_max_fed	13 400	
Basic deduction for married couples	Married_ded_fed	2 600	
Partner income local	partner_local	5 900	
Single parent	sing_par_al	0	
Workrelated	work_exp	0.03	
	work_exp_min	2 000	
	work_exp_max	4 000	
Allowances for local tax	local_basic	0	
	local_child	9 000	
Federal tax	IFD_min_s	-	
Single	IFD_sch_s	0	14 500
		0.0077	31 600
		0.0088	41 400
		0.0264	55 200
		0.0297	72 500
		0.0594	78 100
		0.066	103 600
		0.088	134 600
		0.11	176 000
		0.132	752 200
		0.132	
Married	IFD_min_m	-	
	IFD_sch_m	0	28 300
		0.01	50 900
		0.02	58 400
		0.03	75 300
		0.04	90 300
		0.05	103 400
		0.06	114 700
		0.07	124 200
		0.08	131 700
		0.09	137 300
		0.1	141 200
		0.11	143 100
		0.12	145 000
		0.13	895 900
		0.13	
Cantonal tax	Zurich_min	24	
Single	Zurich_sch_s	0	6 700
		0.02	11 400
		0.03	16 100
		0.04	23 700
		0.05	33 000
		0.06	43 700
		0.07	56 100
		0.08	73 000
		0.09	105 500
		0.1	13 770
		0.11	188 700
		0.12	254 900
		0.13	

Married	Zurich_sch_m	0	13 500
		0.02	19 600
		0.03	27 300
		0.04	36 700
		0.05	47 400
		0.06	61 300
		0.07	92 100
		0.08	122 900
		0.09	169 300
		0.1	224 700
		0.11	284 800
		0.12	354 100
		0.13	
Canton and Commune Tax Mutiple	statetax_mult	2.19	
Social security contributions	old_age	0.0515	
Pension	pension_rate	0	
Pillar 2 pension	NTCP_old_age_max	28 080	
	NTCP_pension_ee	0.0771	
Unemployment	unemp_rate	0.011	
	unemp_rate2	0.005	
income ceiling	unemp_ciel	126 000	
	unemp_ciel2	315 000	
Cantonal deductible limit	local_dedn	2 600	
deductible extra for child	local_dedn_c	1 300	
Max other insurance deduction			
single	max_dedn_s	1 700	
married couples	max_dedn_m	3 500	
child	max_dedn_c	700	
Child cash transfer	child_ben	3 000	

2013 tax equations

The equations for the Swiss system in 2013 are mostly calculated on a family basis.

Variable names are defined in the table of parameters above, within the equations table, or are the standard variables "married" and "children". A reference to a variable with the affix "_total" indicates the sum of the relevant variable values for the principal and spouse. And the affixes "_princ" and "_spouse" indicate the value for the principal and spouse, respectively. Equations for a single person are as shown for the principal, with "_spouse" values taken as 0.

	Line in country table and intermediate steps	Variable name	Range	Equation
1.	Earnings	earn		
2.	Allowances:	partner_al	J	IF(earn_spouse-work_al_spouse-SSC_spouse>partner_min_fed,(Married*MAX(partner_min_fed,MIN(partner_max_fed,partner_rate_fed*(earn_spouse-work_al_spouse-SSC_spouse)))),earn_spouse-work_al_spouse-SSC_spouse)+Married*Married_ded_fed
	Children	children_al	J	Children*fed_child_al+ (Children>0)*(Married=0)*sing_par_al
	Soc sec contributions	SSC_al	B	SSC + NTCP_pension_ee*IF(earn_princ>0.75*NTCP_old_age_max,MAX(0.125*NTCP_old_age_max,earn_princ-0.875*NTCP_old_age_max),0)+NTCP_pension_ee*IF(earn_spouse>0.75*NTCP_old_age_max,MAX(0.125*NTCP_old_age_max,earn_spouse-0.875*NTCP_old_age_max),0)
	Work related	work_al	B	IF(earn-SSC>work_exp_min,MAX(work_exp_min,MIN(work_exp_max,work_exp*(earn-SSC))),earn-SSC)
	Other	oth_al	J	IF(Married,IF(Children>0,max_dedn_m+Children*fed_dedn_c,max_dedn_m),IF(Children>0,max_dedn_s+Children*fed_dedn_c,max_dedn_s))
	Total	tax_al	J	partner_al+children_al+SSC_al+work_al+oth_al
3.	Credits in taxable income	taxbl_cr	J	Cash_tran
4.	CG taxable income	tax_inc	J	positive(earn_total-tax_al+taxbl_cr)
5.	CG tax before credits	CG_tax_excl	J	IF(Married+Children=0, Tax(tax_inc, IFD_sch_s)+IFD_min_s*(Tax(tax_inc, IFD_sch_s)>0), Tax(tax_inc, IFD_sch_m)+IFD_min_m*(Tax(tax_inc, IFD_sch_m)>0))
6.	Tax credits :	Children_cred	J	Child_cred*Children
7.	CG tax	CG_tax	J	Positive(CG_tax_excl- Children_cred)
8.	State and local taxes	local_tax_inc	J	MAX(earn_total+taxbl_cr-local_basic*(1+Married)-Children*local_child-work_al_total-SSC_total-(local_dedn*(1+Married)+Children*local_dedn_c)-(earn_spouse>0)*partner_local,0)
		local_tax		IF((Married+Children)>0, Tax(local_tax_inc, Zurich_sch_m)*statetax_mult+(1+Married)*Zurich_min*(Tax(local_tax_inc, Zurich_sch_m)>0), Tax(local_tax_inc, Zurich_sch_s)*statetax_mult+(Tax(local_tax_inc, Zurich_sch_s)>0)*Zurich_min)
9.	Employees' soc security	SSC	B	(old_age)*earn+IF(earn<=unemp_ciel, earn*unemp_rate, IF(earn<=unemp_ciel2, unemp_ciel*unemp_rate+(earn-unemp_ciel)*unemp_rate2, unemp_ciel*unemp_rate+unemp_ciel2*unemp_rate2))
11.	Cash transfers	Cash_tran	J	Children*child_ben
13.	Employer's soc security	SSC_empr	B	SSC

Key to range of equation B calculated separately for both principal earner and spouse P calculated for principal only (value taken as 0 for spouse calculation) J calculated once only on a joint basis.

Taxing Wages 2014
Changes in sructural labour income tax progressivity
over 2000-12 period in OECD member countries

Turkey

This chapter includes data on the income taxes paid by workers, their social security contributions, the family benefits they receive in the form of cash transfers as well as the social security contributions and payroll taxes paid by their employers. Results reported include the marginal and average tax burden for eight different family types.

Methodological information is available for personal income tax systems, compulsory social security contributions to schemes operated within the government sector, universal cash transfers as well as recent changes in the tax/benefit system. The methodology also includes the parameter values and tax equations underlying the data.

Turkey 2013

The tax/benefit position of single persons

	Wage level (per cent of average wage)	67	100	167	67
	Number of children	none	none	none	2
1.	**Gross wage earnings**	21163	31744	52907	21163
2.	**Standard tax allowances**				
	Basic allowance	0	0	0	0
	Married or head of family				
	Dependent children				
	Deduction for social security contributions and income taxes	3174	4762	7936	3174
	Work-related expenses				
	Other				
	Total	3174	4762	7936	3174
3.	**Tax credits or cash transfers included in taxable income**	0	0	0	0
4.	**Central government taxable income (1 - 2 + 3)**	17988	26983	44971	17988
5.	**Central government income tax liability (exclusive of tax credits)**	3063	4930	9787	3063
	Stamp tax	161	241	402	161
	Total	3223	5171	10189	3223
6.	**Tax credits**				
	Basic credit	881	881	881	1145
	Married or head of family				
	Children				
	Other				
	Total	881	881	881	1145
7.	**Central government income tax finally paid (5-6)**	2343	4290	9308	2078
8.	**State and local taxes**	0	0	0	0
9.	**Employees' compulsory social security contributions**				
	Gross earnings	3174	4762	7936	3174
	Taxable income				
	Total	3174	4762	7936	3174
10.	**Total payments to general government (7 + 8 + 9)**	5517	9052	17244	5253
11.	**Cash transfers from general government**				
	For head of family				
	For two children	0	0	0	0
	Total	0	0	0	0
12.	**Take-home pay (1-10+11)**	15646	22692	35663	15910
13.	**Employer's compulsory social security contributions**	3492	5238	8730	3492
14.	**Average rates**				
	Income tax	11.1%	13.5%	17.6%	9.8%
	Employees' social security contributions	15.0%	15.0%	15.0%	15.0%
	Total payments less cash transfers	26.1%	28.5%	32.6%	24.8%
	Total tax wedge including employer's social security contributions	36.5%	38.6%	42.1%	35.5%
15.	**Marginal rates**				
	Total payments less cash transfers: Principal earner	32.8%	38.7%	38.7%	32.8%
	Total payments less cash transfers: Spouse	n.a.	n.a.	n.a.	n.a.
	Total tax wedge: Principal earner	42.3%	47.4%	47.4%	42.3%
	Total tax wedge: Spouse	n.a.	n.a.	n.a.	n.a.

Turkey 2013

The tax/benefit position of married couples

		Wage level (per cent of average wage)	100-0	100-33	100-67	100-33
		Number of children	2	2	2	none
1.	**Gross wage earnings**		31744	42326	52907	42326
2.	**Standard tax allowances**					
	Basic allowance		0	0	0	0
	Married or head of family					
	Dependent children					
	Deduction for social security contributions and income taxes		4762	6349	7936	6349
	Work-related expenses					
	Other					
		Total	4762	6349	7936	6349
3.	**Tax credits or cash transfers included in taxable income**		0	0	0	0
4.	**Central government taxable income (1 - 2 + 3)**		26983	35977	44971	35977
5.	**Central government income tax liability (exclusive of tax credits)**		4930	6279	7993	6279
	Stamp tax		241	241	241	241
		Total	5171	6520	8234	6520
6.	**Tax credits**					
	Basic credit		1321	1145	1145	881
	Married or head of family					
	Children					
	Other					
		Total	1321	1145	1145	881
7.	**Central government income tax finally paid (5-6)**		3850	5456	7250	5720
8.	**State and local taxes**		0	0	0	0
9.	**Employees' compulsory social security contributions**					
	Gross earnings		4762	6349	7936	6349
	Taxable income					
		Total	4762	6349	7936	6349
10.	**Total payments to general government (7 + 8 + 9)**		8612	11805	15186	12069
11.	**Cash transfers from general government**					
	For head of family					
	For two children		0	0	0	0
		Total	0	0	0	0
12.	**Take-home pay (1-10+11)**		23132	30521	37721	30257
13.	**Employer's compulsory social security contributions**		5238	6984	8730	6984
14.	**Average rates**					
	Income tax		12.1%	12.9%	13.7%	13.5%
	Employees' social security contributions		15.0%	15.0%	15.0%	15.0%
	Total payments less cash transfers		27.1%	27.9%	28.7%	28.5%
	Total tax wedge including employer's social security contributions		37.4%	38.1%	38.8%	38.6%
15.	**Marginal rates**					
	Total payments less cash transfers: Principal earner		38.7%	38.7%	38.7%	38.7%
	Total payments less cash transfers: Spouse		28.5%	28.5%	32.8%	28.5%
	Total tax wedge: Principal earner		47.4%	47.4%	47.4%	47.4%
	Total tax wedge: Spouse		38.6%	38.6%	42.3%	38.6%

The national currency unit is the "Turkish lira" (TL). In 2013, TL 1.90 was equal to USD 1. For 2013, the average production worker earned TL 31 744.19 (country estimate).

1. Personal income tax systems

1.1. *Central government income tax*

1.1.1. *Tax unit*

Spouses are taxed separately on earned income. This rule has been applied since 1 January 1999.

1.1.2. *Tax allowances and tax credits*

1.1.2.1. Standard reliefs:

- *Reliefs for social security contributions:* Employee's social security contributions are deductible from gross earnings. These contributions are 15 per cent of gross income as stated by the Social Insurance Act. The contribution to the unemployment fund is included in this amount and equals 1 per cent of gross income.
- Contributions to public pension funds established by law are deductible.
- *Work-related expenses:* None.
- *Minimum Living Relief:* The calculation of the minimum living allowance is based on the annual gross amount of the minimum wage for employees older than 16 at the beginning of the calendar year in which the income is obtained multiplied by the following rates:
  - 50 per cent for the taxpayer him or herself;
  - 10 per cent for the spouse who neither works nor has an income;
  - 7.5 per cent for each of the first two children;
  - 5 per cent for each additional child.

  This total amount is then multiplied by the rate (15 per cent) which is applied to the first income bracket of PIT Schedule stated in Article 103 of PIT Law, and then minimum living relief is calculated by offsetting 1/12 of the allowance amount against monthly calculated tax due on employment income. Any excess is non-refundable.
- *Reliefs for disabled:* Law 4842 regulates tax relief for disabled persons. The employee who lost his/her working capacity with at least 80 per cent is considered to be disabled in the 1st degree; employees are disabled in the 2nd respectively 3rd degree if they lost their working capacity with at least 60 respectively 40 per cent. In these cases, the following amounts are deductible from monthly wages:
  - Disabled in the 1st degree: TL 800.
  - Disabled in the 2nd degree: TL 400.
  - Disabled in the 3rd degree: TL 190.

1.1.2.2. Main non-standard tax reliefs applicable to an APW

- Legal deductions for public institutions such as OYAK (Social Aid Institution for Military Officers).
- Contributions to private pension funds and premiums paid by the wage-earner for himself (or herself), the spouse and dependent children to personal insurance schemes covering death, illness, accident, disablement, maternity, birth and education, provided that the insurance is contracted with a company established in or with a main office in Turkey. The total amount of deductible contributions to the private pension funds cannot exceed 15 per cent of the wage that is earned in the month when the premiums or contributions are actually paid. The annual amount cannot exceed the annual minimum wage either.
- Membership payments made to labour unions.

1.1.3. *Tax schedule*

The tax schedule in 2013 is as follows:

Taxable income (TL)	Tax on lower threshold (TL)	Tax on excess amount above lower threshold (%)
Up to 10 700		15
10 700 up to 26 000	1 605	20
26 000 up to 94 000	4 665	27
Over 94 000	23 025	35

1.2. *State and local income taxes*

Income tax is levied only by the central government.

1.3. *Stamp tax*

The stamp tax base is gross earnings. The tax rate is 0.759 per cent in 2013.

2. Compulsory social security contributions to schemes operated within the government sector

2.1. *Employees' contributions*

2.1.1. Pensions (disability, old age and death insurance): 9 per cent

2.1.2. Sickness: 5 per cent

2.1.3. Unemployment: 1 per cent

2.2. *Employers' contributions*

2.2.1. Pensions (disability, old age and death insurance): 11 per cent

2.2.2. Sickness: 7.5 per cent

2.2.3. Unemployment: 2 per cent

2.2.4. Work injury: Short term insurance branches premium rate shall be determined by the Institution pursuant to Article 83 of law No. 5510, between 1% and 6.5% depending on the gravity of the danger of the work in terms of work accident and occupational disease. All of this premium shall be paid by the employer. However, with Article 9 of Law No. 6385, short-term insurance branches premium rate were fixed to 2% which will be implemented from 01.09.2013. (As shown in the above table, social security contributions, except for short-term rates, have not changed.)

If disability, old age and death insurance premiums paid regularly by employers as stated law 5510 article of 81 (Social Security and General Health Insurance Law) 5 per cent of total 11 per cent premiums are paid by state on behalf of employers. (5 per cent discount applied in employers share).

There is no distinction by marital status or sex and the contributions apply to gross earnings. Compulsory social security contributions of employees and their employers are calculated according to the schemes presented above.

For employees whose gross earnings are below the base or above ceiling earnings, which are determined at least twice in a year, these contribution rates are applied to the base or ceiling amounts respectively. In 2013, the base amount is TL 12 001 and the ceiling amount is TL 78 005. Under the Law No. 5510 (Social Security and General Health Insurance Law), the base wage for social security contributions is equal to the minimum wage. Because employees cannot earn less than the minimum wage, the base wage is not considered in this publication. However, the ceiling earnings are considered for the purposes of this Report.

3. Universal cash transfers

Employees obtain universal cash transfers according to the collective labour agreements that are signed between their employer and the labour union(s). These agreements vary with the bargaining power of the different parties in the different sectors in the economy. This explains why there is no standard amount reflecting these general transfers.

4. Main changes in tax/benefit system since 2004

Personal income tax Law (No. 193) which is about income tax, Social Security and General Health Insurance Law (No. 5510) which is about social security contributions and Unemployment Insurance Law (No. 4447) which is about unemployment insurance fund are the main laws about tax/benefit system.

The main changes have been made to the following laws 5615, 6009 and 6327 which are as follows:

- According to Act No. 5615, the new application "Minimum Living Relief" began to be implemented. (see the Section 1.1.2).
- According to Act No. 6009, the taxation of the wages are differentiated than the taxation of the other taxable revenue resources like trading income, income from immovable property or income from investments. By this way, it is ensured that wages (comparative to other income items) are later entered into the 3rd bracket on the income tax schedule.
- According to Act No. 6327, (published in the *Official Gazette* issue 28338 on 29 June 2012.) there are important amendments in the Private Pension System Regulations. According to this law, any citizen of the Republic of Turkey will have the right for state subsidy for his/her paid contributions to the Private Pension Account. The contribution upper limit

to favour this incentive is the annual amount of minimum wage 25% of this amount shall be transferred to the account of the insured party as a state subsidy. The state subsidy shall be earned in proportion to the amount of time within the system.

5. Memorandum items

5.1. *Identification of an APW*

The earnings figure refers to all production workers in the manufacturing sector. The APW figure has been calculated by using quarterly industrial gross wages-salaries index which is published by the Turkish Statistical Institute. If this data is not available for calculation, officially published increasing rates of minimum wages are used for estimation.

5.2. *Contribution to private pension and health schemes*

Business enterprises (employers) are permitted to make additional contributions for pension savings of their employees. However, these amounts of additional premiums are limited by main tax laws. Such additional pension arrangements, which are optional, are not widely used.

2013 parameter values

Average earnings/yr	Ave_earn	31 744	Country estimate
Income tax	Tax_sch	0.15	10 700
		0.20	26 000
		0.27	94 000
		0.35	
Stamp tax	Stamp_rate	0.00759	
Employees SSC	SSC_rate	0.15	
	SSC_ceil	78 005	
Employers SSC	SSC_empr	0.165	
Minimum living relief	credit_rate	0.15	
	basic_allow	0.5	
	spouse_allow	0.1	
	child_allow	0.075	
	add_child_allow	0.05	
	min_wage	11 743	

2013 tax equations

The equations for the Turkish system are on an individual basis.

The functions which are used in the equations (Taper, MIN, Tax, etc.) are described in the technical note about tax equations. Variable names are defined in the table of parameters above, within the equations table, or are the standard variables "married" and "children". A reference to a variable with the affix "_total" indicates the sum of the relevant variable values for the principal and spouse. And the affixes "_princ" and "_spouse" indicate the value for the principal and spouse, respectively. Equations for a single person are as shown for the principal, with "_spouse" values taken as 0.

	Line in country table and intermediate steps	Variable name	Range	Equation
1.	Earnings	earn		
2.	Allowances:	tax_al	B	SSC
3.	Credits in taxable income	taxbl_cr	B	0
4.	CG taxable income	tax_inc	B	Positive(earn-tax_al)
	Stamp tax	stamp_tax	B	earn*stamp_rate
5.	CG tax before credits	CG_tax_excl	B	Tax(tax_inc,tax_sch)
6.	Tax credits :	tax_cr	B	credit_rate*min_wage*(basic_allow+spouse_allow*(IF(Wife=0,Married,0))+IF(OR(Children=1,Children=2),Children*child_allow,0)+IF(Children>2,2*child_allow+(Children-2)*add_child_allow,0))
7.	CG tax	CG_tax	B	positive(CG_tax_excl-tax_cr)+stamp_tax
8.	State and local taxes	local_tax	B	0
9.	Employees' soc security	SSC	B	Min(earn,SSC_ceil)*SSC_rate
11.	Cash transfers	cash_trans	B	0
13.	Employer's soc security	SSC_empr	B	Min(earn,SSC_ceil)*SSC_empr

Key to range of equation B calculated separately for both principal earner and spouse P calculated for principal only (value taken as 0 for spouse calculation) J calculated once only on a joint basis.

Taxing Wages 2014
Changes in sructural labour income tax progressivity
over 2000-12 period in OECD member countries

United Kingdom (2013-14 income tax year)

This chapter includes data on the income taxes paid by workers, their social security contributions, the family benefits they receive in the form of cash transfers as well as the social security contributions and payroll taxes paid by their employers. Results reported include the marginal and average tax burden for eight different family types.

Methodological information is available for personal income tax systems, compulsory social security contributions to schemes operated within the government sector, universal cash transfers as well as recent changes in the tax/benefit system. The methodology also includes the parameter values and tax equations underlying the data.

United Kingdom 2013

The tax/benefit position of single persons

		Wage level (per cent of average wage)	67	100	167	67
		Number of children	none	none	none	2
1.	**Gross wage earnings**		23699	35548	59247	23699
2.	**Standard tax allowances**					
	Basic allowance		9440	9440	9440	9440
	Married or head of family					
	Dependent children					
	Deduction for social security contributions and income taxes					
	Work-related expenses					
	Other					
		Total	9440	9440	9440	9440
3.	**Tax credits or cash transfers included in taxable income**		0	0	0	0
4.	**Central government taxable income (1 - 2 + 3)**		14259	26108	49807	14259
5.	**Central government income tax liability (exclusive of tax credits)**		2852	5222	13521	2852
6.	**Tax credits**					
	Basic credit					
	Married or head of family					
	Children		0	0	0	3596
	Other					
		Total	0	0	0	3596
7.	**Central government income tax finally paid (5-6)**		2852	5222	13521	-744
8.	**State and local taxes**		0	0	0	0
9.	**Employees' compulsory social security contributions**					
	Gross earnings		1913	3335	4399	1913
	Taxable income					
		Total	1913	3335	4399	1913
10.	**Total payments to general government (7 + 8 + 9)**		4765	8557	17920	1170
11.	**Cash transfers from general government**					
	For head of family					
	For two children		0	0	0	1757
		Total	0	0	0	1757
12.	**Take-home pay (1-10+11)**		18934	26992	41327	24287
13.	**Employer's compulsory social security contributions**		2208	3844	7114	2208
14.	**Average rates**					
	Income tax		12.0%	14.7%	22.8%	-3.1%
	Employees' social security contributions		8.1%	9.4%	7.4%	8.1%
	Total payments less cash transfers		20.1%	24.1%	30.2%	-2.5%
	Total tax wedge including employer's social security contributions		26.9%	31.5%	37.7%	6.3%
15.	**Marginal rates**					
	Total payments less cash transfers: Principal earner		32.0%	32.0%	42.0%	73.0%
	Total payments less cash transfers: Spouse		n.a.	n.a.	n.a.	n.a.
	Total tax wedge: Principal earner		40.2%	40.2%	49.0%	76.3%
	Total tax wedge: Spouse		n.a.	n.a.	n.a.	n.a.

United Kingdom 2013

The tax/benefit position of married couples

		Wage level (per cent of average wage)	100-0	100-33	100-67	100-33
		Number of children	2	2	2	none
1.	**Gross wage earnings**		35548	47398	59247	47398
2.	**Standard tax allowances**					
	Basic allowance		9440	18880	18880	18880
	Married or head of family					
	Dependent children					
	Deduction for social security contributions and income taxes					
	Work-related expenses					
	Other					
		Total	9440	18880	18880	18880
3.	**Tax credits or cash transfers included in taxable income**		0	0	0	0
4.	**Central government taxable income (1 - 2 + 3)**		26108	28518	40367	28518
5.	**Central government income tax liability (exclusive of tax credits)**		5222	5704	8073	5704
6.	**Tax credits**					
	Basic credit					
	Married or head of family					
	Children		0	0	0	0
	Other					
		Total	0	0	0	0
7.	**Central government income tax finally paid (5-6)**		5222	5704	8073	5704
8.	**State and local taxes**		0	0	0	0
9.	**Employees' compulsory social security contributions**					
	Gross earnings		3335	3827	5248	3827
	Taxable income					
		Total	3335	3827	5248	3827
10.	**Total payments to general government (7 + 8 + 9)**		8557	9530	13322	9530
11.	**Cash transfers from general government**					
	For head of family					
	For two children		1757	1757	1757	0
		Total	1757	1757	1757	0
12.	**Take-home pay (1-10+11)**		28749	39625	47683	37868
13.	**Employer's compulsory social security contributions**		3844	4417	6052	4417
14.	**Average rates**					
	Income tax		14.7%	12.0%	13.6%	12.0%
	Employees' social security contributions		9.4%	8.1%	8.9%	8.1%
	Total payments less cash transfers		19.1%	16.4%	19.5%	20.1%
	Total tax wedge including employer's social security contributions		27.0%	23.5%	27.0%	26.9%
15.	**Marginal rates**					
	Total payments less cash transfers: Principal earner		32.0%	32.0%	32.0%	32.0%
	Total payments less cash transfers: Spouse		8.2%	32.0%	32.0%	32.0%
	Total tax wedge: Principal earner		40.2%	40.2%	40.2%	40.2%
	Total tax wedge: Spouse		12.4%	40.2%	40.2%	40.2%

The national currency is the Pound Sterling (GBP). In 2013, GBP 0.64 was equal to USD 1. In 2013-14, the Average Worker is estimated to earn GBP 35 548 (Secretariat estimate).

1. Personal income tax systems

1.1. Central government income taxes

1.1.1. Tax unit

The tax unit is the individual, but certain reliefs depend on family circumstances (see Section 1.1.2.1).

1.1.2. Tax allowances and tax credits

All figures shown are those applying at the start of the tax year in April.

1.1.2.1. Standard reliefs

- *Basic reliefs:* A personal allowance of GBP 9 440 is granted to each individual with income below GBP 100 000. The personal allowance is then tapered away by GBP 1 for every GBP 2 of income above GBP 100 000.
- Standard marital status reliefs: None.
- Working Tax Credit (WTC): A non-wastable tax credit available to low income families with or without children. It is available for families with children where one person works at least 16 hours a week. It is also available for people with a disability who work at least 16 hours a week and for families without children where one person works at least 30 hours a week. The amount depends upon the hours worked, the ages of children, eligible childcare costs, and gross income. A family with a child 16 or under where the claimant (or, where applicable, their partner, or both claimants jointly) works at least 30 hours a week, would get a maximum credit of GBP 4 680 per year before taking into account eligible childcare costs*. This credit is reduced by 41 pence for each GBP 1 of net income above a threshold of GBP 6 420 per year. Extra amounts are available where one or, where applicable, both claimants are disabled. WTC was introduced on 6th April 2003.
- Relief for social security contributions and other taxes: None.
- Child Tax Credit (CTC): A non-wastable tax credit available to low and middle income families with children. It provides support for children until 1 September following their 16th birthday, and beyond that date to the age of 19 for those who continue in full-time non-advanced education. The amount depends on gross income and the number and age of the children. A family with two children would get a maximum credit GBP 5 985 per year, which is reduced by 41 pence for each GBP 1 of gross income above a threshold of GBP 15 995 if the family is not working. A higher threshold applies if the family is

* The amount of credit received is calculated by dividing separately each element of the credit by the number of days in the tax year and rounding up to the nearest penny to give a daily rate. These daily rates are then multiplied by the number of days in the relevant period (for the purposes of this Report, the tax year) and added together.

working; their CTC is reduced at the same rate once their WTC has been tapered to zero. CTC was introduced on 6th April 2003.

1.1.2.2. Main non-standard tax reliefs applicable to an AW

- Work-related expenses: Flat rate expenses for tools and special clothing are allowed to certain occupational categories. Since this provision is not applicable to all manufacturing occupations, and hence average workers, and because the rates vary slightly across categories, this relief is considered here as non-standard;
- Contributions to approved superannuation schemes or personal pension schemes are deducted when calculating taxable income. Premiums on approved life assurance policies payable to life assurance companies attract 12.5 per cent tax relief for policies entered into force before 13 March 1984.

1.1.3. *Tax schedule*

In 2013-14 all taxpayers are liable on taxable income other than savings and dividend income at the basic rate of 20 per cent on the first GBP 32 010, 40 per cent over the basic rate limit of GBP 32 010 and 45 per cent over the higher rate limit of GBP 150 000. (Taxable Income is defined as gross income for income tax purposes less allowances and reliefs available at the marginal rate.) Dividend income is charged at 10 per cent up to the basic rate limit of GBP 32 010, 32.5 per cent above GBP 32 010 and 37.5 per cent above GBP 150 000. Savings income is charged at 10 per cent up to the starting rate limit on the first GBP 2 790, at 20 per cent up to GBP 32 010, 40 per cent above GBP 32 010 and 45 per cent above GBP 150 000.

Taxable income (GBP)	Rate %
0-32 010	20
32 010-150 000	40
Over 150 000	45

1.2. *State and local income tax*

There are no regional or local income taxes.

2. Compulsory social security contributions to schemes operated within the government sector

2.1. *Employees' contributions*

National Insurance contributions are payable by employees earning more than GBP 149 in any week. These are 12 per cent of earnings between GBP 149 and GBP 797 and 2 per cent of earnings above GBP 797 for employees not contracted out of the state second pension scheme (additional state pension which supplements the basic retirement pension). For employees who are contracted out, there is a rebate of 1.4 per cent on earnings between GBP 109 and GBP 770. Depending on eligibility, members of the National Insurance scheme qualify for pensions, sickness, industrial injury, unemployment benefits, etc. All employees earning under GBP 149 per week have no National Insurance contribution liability but a notional contribution will be deemed to have been paid in respect of earnings between GBP 109 and GBP 149 to protect benefit entitlement.

2.2. *Employers' contributions*

Employer's contributions are not payable for employees earning less than GBP 148 per week. The rate of employers' contributions for employees not contracted out of the additional (earnings related) scheme is 13.8 per cent of earnings above GBP 148 per week. For employees who are contracted out, there is a rebate of 3.4 per cent on earnings between GBP 109 and GBP 770 per week.

3. Universal cash transfers

3.1. *Transfers related to marital status*

None (widows' benefit is covered by the government pensions scheme noted above).

3.2. *Transfers for dependent children*

A child benefit of GBP 20.30 per week is paid in respect of the first child in the family up to the age of 19 (if the child aged 16-19 is in education or training) with GBP 13.40 per week paid for each subsequent child.

From January 2013, a new tax charge will be introduced for a taxpayer who has income over GBP 50 000 and either they or their partner are in receipt of Child Benefit. For those with income between GBP 50 000 and GBP 60 000, the amount of the charge will be 1% of the Child Benefit for every GBP 100 of income over GBP 50 000. For those with income over GBP 60 000, the amount of the charge will equal the amount of Child Benefit.

4. Memorandum items

4.1. *Identification of AW and valuation of earnings*

A new Annual Survey of Hours and Earnings (ASHE) has been developed to replace the New Earnings Survey (NES) (results of which are published in *Labour Market Trends*) and shows the average weekly earnings of full-time employees in April each year. It covers men and women at adult rates in the United Kingdom (excluding Northern Ireland). The annual figure used for the gross earnings of the AW in the United Kingdom is the annual equivalent of the arithmetic average of the weekly earnings figures for April at the beginning and end of the fiscal year, as published in *Labour Market Trends*.

The earnings figures exclude the earnings of those whose pay was affected by absence (due to sickness, etc.). They include overtime, payment by results and shift payments. But they do not include benefits in kind (which could in some circumstances be included in the employee's taxable income in the United Kingdom).

4.2. *Employers' contributions to private pension, health, etc., schemes*

In 2008, there were 9.0 million active members of occupational pension schemes with two or more members in the UK, of whom 3.6 million were in the private sector and 5.4 million in the public sector.

2013 parameter values

Average earnings/yr	Ave_earn	35 548	Secretariat Estimate	
Allowances	Basic_al	9 440		
	PA taper start	100 000		
	Married_al	0		
	Married_rate	0		
Income tax	Tax_sch	0.2	32 010	
		0.4	150 000	
		0.45		
Employees SSC				
Primary threshold	SSC_sch	0	7 755	PT
Upper earnings limit		0.12	41 450	UEL
		0.02		
Employers SSC	SSC_rate2	0.138		
	ST	7696		
Child benefit (first)	CB_first	20.30		
Child benefit (others)	CB_others	13.40		
	CB_1st_thres	50 000.00		
	CB_2nd_thres	60 000.00		
	CB_taper1	0.01		
	CB_taper2	100.00		
NEW TAX CREDITS				
WTC				
Basic element	WTC_Basic	1 920		
Couple/Lone parent	WTC_couple_or_lone	1 970		
30 Hour element	WTC_30hr	790		
CTC				
Family element	CTC_family	545		
Child element	CTC_child	2720		
Baby element	CTC_baby			
Threshold	NTC_1st_thres	6 420		
	NTC_1st_taper	0.41		
Days in tax year	Numdays	365		

2013 tax equations

The equations for the UK system are mostly on an individual basis. But Child and Working tax credits are calculated on a family basis and child benefit is calculated only once. This is shown by the Range indicator in the table below.

The functions which are used in the equations (Taper, MIN, Tax, etc.) are described in the technical note about tax equations. Variable names are defined in the table of parameters above, within the equations table, or are the standard variables "married" and "children". A reference to a variable with the affix "_total" indicates the sum of the relevant variable values for the principal and spouse. And the affixes "_princ" and "_spouse" indicate the value for the principal and spouse, respectively. Equations for a single person are as shown for the principal, with "_spouse" values taken as 0.

	Line in country table and intermediate steps	Variable name	Range	Equation
1.	Earnings	Earn		
2.	Allowances:	tax_al	B	Tax_al =IF(earn<PA_taper,Basic_al,IF(earn>(PA_taper+(Basic_al*2)),0,MAX(0,(Basic_al-((earn-PA_taper)/2)))))
2.	PA Start	PA_taper	B	IF(earn<PA_taper,Basic_al,IF(AA7>(PA_taper+(Basic_al*2)),0,MAX(0,(Basic_al-((AA7-PA_taper)/2)))))
3.	Credits in taxable income	taxbl_cr	B	0
4.	CG taxable income	tax_inc	B	Positive(earn-tax_al)
5.	CG tax before credits	CG_tax_excl	B	Tax(tax_inc, tax_sch)
6.	Tax credits (nonwastable)	tax_cr	J	IF(Children>0, (Taper(ROUNDUP(CTC_family/numdays, 2)*numdays+Children*ROUNDUP(CTC_child/numdays, 2)*numdays+ROUNDUP(WTC_Basic/numdays, 2)*numdays+ROUNDUP(WTC_30hr/numdays, 2)*numdays+ROUNDUP(WTC_couple_or_lone/numdays, 2)*numdays, earn_total, NTC_1st_thres, NTC_1st_taper), Taper(ROUNDUP(WTC_Basic/numdays, 2)*numdays+ROUNDUP(WTC_30hr/numdays, 2)*numdays+IF(Married=1, ROUNDUP(WTC_couple_or_lone/numdays, 2)*numdays, 0), earn_total, NTC_1st_thres, NTC_1st_taper))
7.	CG tax	CG_tax	B	CG_tax_excl-tax_cr
8.	State and local taxes	local_tax	B	0
9.	Employees' soc security	SSC	B	Tax(earn, SSC_sch)
11.	Cash transfers	cash_trans	J	=IF(princ_earn>CB_1st_thres,IF(princ_earn>CB_2nd_thres,0,((1-(AA7-CB_1st_thres)/(CB_taper2/CB_taper1)))*(numdays/7*((Children>0)*CB_first+CB_others*Positive(Children-1)))),(numdays/7*((Children>0)*CB_first+CB_others*Positive(Children-1))))
13.	Employer's soc security	SSC_empr	B	(earn>ST)*(earn-ST)*SSC_rate2
	Memorandum item: Non-wastable tax credit			
	tax expenditure component	Taxexp	J	Tax_cr-transfer
	cash transfer component	Transfer	J	IF(CG_tax_excl<0, -CG_tax_excl, 0)

Key to range of equation B calculated separately for both principal earner and spouse P calculated for principal only (value taken as 0 for spouse calculation) J calculated once only on a joint basis.

Taxing Wages 2014
Changes in sructural labour income tax progressivity
over 2000-12 period in OECD member countries

United States

This chapter includes data on the income taxes paid by workers, their social security contributions, the family benefits they receive in the form of cash transfers as well as the social security contributions and payroll taxes paid by their employers. Results reported include the marginal and average tax burden for eight different family types.

Methodological information is available for personal income tax systems, compulsory social security contributions to schemes operated within the government sector, universal cash transfers as well as recent changes in the tax/ benefit system. The methodology also includes the parameter values and tax equations underlying the data.

United States 2013

The tax/benefit position of single persons

		Wage level (per cent of average wage)	67	100	167	67
		Number of children	none	none	none	2
1.	**Gross wage earnings**		32309	48463	80772	32309
2.	**Standard tax allowances**					
	Basic allowance		10000	10000	10000	12850
	Married or head of family					
	Dependent children		0	0	0	7800
	Deduction for social security contributions and income taxes					
	Work-related expenses					
	Other					
		Total	10000	10000	10000	20650
3.	**Tax credits or cash transfers included in taxable income**		0	0	0	0
4.	**Central government taxable income (1 - 2 + 3)**		22309	38463	70772	11659
5.	**Central government income tax liability (exclusive of tax credits)**		2900	5545	13622	1166
6.	**Tax credits**					
	Basic credit		0	0	0	2260
	Married or head of family					
	Children		0	0	0	2000
	Other		378	378	378	378
		Total	378	378	378	4638
7.	**Central government income tax finally paid (5-6)**		2522	5167	13244	-3472
8.	**State and local taxes**		1966	3041	5189	1466
9.	**Employees' compulsory social security contributions**					
	Gross earnings		2472	3707	6179	2472
	Taxable income					
		Total	2472	3707	6179	2472
10.	**Total payments to general government (7 + 8 + 9)**		6960	11915	24612	466
11.	**Cash transfers from general government**					
	For head of family					
	For two children		0	0	0	0
		Total	0	0	0	0
12.	**Take-home pay (1-10+11)**		25349	36549	56160	31843
13.	**Employer's compulsory social security contributions**		3523	4759	7231	3523
14.	**Average rates**					
	Income tax		13.9%	16.9%	22.8%	-6.2%
	Employees' social security contributions		7.7%	7.7%	7.7%	7.7%
	Total payments less cash transfers		21.5%	24.6%	30.5%	1.4%
	Total tax wedge including employer's social security contributions		29.3%	31.3%	36.2%	11.1%
15.	**Marginal rates**					
	Total payments less cash transfers: Principal earner		29.3%	39.3%	39.3%	46.6%
	Total payments less cash transfers: Spouse		n.a.	n.a.	n.a.	n.a.
	Total tax wedge: Principal earner		34.3%	43.6%	43.6%	50.4%
	Total tax wedge: Spouse		n.a.	n.a.	n.a.	n.a.

United States 2013

The tax/benefit position of married couples

		Wage level (per cent of average wage)	100-0	100-33	100-67	100-33
		Number of children	2	2	2	none
1.	**Gross wage earnings**		48463	64618	80772	64618
2.	**Standard tax allowances**					
	Basic allowance		20000	20000	20000	20000
	Married or head of family					
	Dependent children		7800	7800	7800	0
	Deduction for social security contributions and income taxes					
	Work-related expenses					
	Other					
		Total	27800	27800	27800	20000
3.	**Tax credits or cash transfers included in taxable income**		0	0	0	0
4.	**Central government taxable income (1 - 2 + 3)**		20663	36818	52972	44618
5.	**Central government income tax liability (exclusive of tax credits)**		2207	4630	7053	5800
6.	**Tax credits**					
	Basic credit		0	0	0	0
	Married or head of family					
	Children		2000	2000	2000	0
	Other		378	378	378	378
		Total	2378	2378	2378	378
7.	**Central government income tax finally paid (5-6)**		-171	2252	4675	5422
8.	**State and local taxes**		2494	3568	4642	3933
9.	**Employees' compulsory social security contributions**					
	Gross earnings		3707	4943	6179	4943
	Taxable income					
		Total	3707	4943	6179	4943
10.	**Total payments to general government (7 + 8 + 9)**		6030	10763	15497	14298
11.	**Cash transfers from general government**					
	For head of family					
	For two children		0	0	0	0
		Total	0	0	0	0
12.	**Take-home pay (1-10+11)**		42433	53854	65276	50320
13.	**Employer's compulsory social security contributions**		4759	7047	8283	7047
14.	**Average rates**					
	Income tax		4.8%	9.0%	11.5%	14.5%
	Employees' social security contributions		7.7%	7.7%	7.7%	7.7%
	Total payments less cash transfers		12.4%	16.7%	19.2%	22.1%
	Total tax wedge including employer's social security contributions		20.3%	24.9%	26.7%	29.8%
15.	**Marginal rates**					
	Total payments less cash transfers: Principal earner		29.3%	29.3%	29.3%	29.3%
	Total payments less cash transfers: Spouse		29.3%	29.3%	29.3%	29.3%
	Total tax wedge: Principal earner		34.3%	34.3%	34.3%	34.3%
	Total tax wedge: Spouse		38.1%	34.3%	34.3%	34.3%

The national currency is the dollar (USD). In 2013, the average worker earned USD 48 463 (Secretariat estimate).

1. Personal income tax systems

1.1. *Central/federal government income taxes*

1.1.1. *Tax unit*

Families are generally taxed in one of three ways:

- as married couples filing jointly on the combined income of both spouses;
- as married individuals filing separately and reporting actual income of each spouse; or
- as heads of households (only unmarried or separated individuals with dependents).

All others, including dependent children with sufficient income, file as single individuals.

1.1.2. *Tax allowances and tax credits*

1.1.2.1. Standard reliefs

- *Basic reliefs:* In 2013 a married couple filing a joint tax return is entitled to a standard deduction of USD 12 200. The standard deduction is USD 8 950 for heads of households and USD 6 100 for single individuals. This relief is indexed for inflation. More liberal standard deductions are available for taxpayers who are age 65 or older and taxpayers who are blind. Special rules apply to children who have sufficient income to pay tax and are also claimed as dependents by their parents.
- In addition to the standard deduction, in 2013 a USD 3 900 *personal exemption* is given to every taxpayer (including both husband and wife filing a joint return). The personal exemption is indexed annually for inflation. In 2013, there is a phase out for personal exemptions.
- Personal exemption phase out: Personal exemptions are phased out in 50 steps for taxpayers with incomes in excess of certain amounts. All of a taxpayer's exemptions are phased out simultaneously. For each USD 2 500 or fraction thereof by which income exceeds the beginning of the phase out range, personal exemptions are phased down by two percentage points.

Filing status	Beginning of phase out range (USD)
Single	250 000
Joint return	300 000
Head of household	275 000

- *Standard marital status reliefs:* Married couples generally benefit from a more favourable schedule of tax rates for joint returns of spouses (see Section 1.1.3). There are no other general tax reliefs for marriage.

- *Relief for children:* For each child and other person claimed as a dependent on a taxpayer's return, the taxpayer is entitled to a dependency exemption of USD 3 900 in 2013. Low income workers with dependents are allowed a refundable (non-wastable) earned income credit. For taxpayers with one child, the credit is 34 per cent of up to USD 9 560 of earned income in 2013. The credit phases down when income exceeds USD 17 530 (22 870 for married taxpayers) and phases out when it reaches USD 37 870 (42 210 for married taxpayers). The earned income threshold and the phase-out threshold are indexed for inflation. For taxpayers with two children, the credit is 40 per cent of up to USD 13 430 of earned income in 2013. The credit phases down when income exceeds USD 17 530 (22 870 for married taxpayers) and phases out when it reaches USD 43 038 (48 378 for married taxpayers). For taxpayers with three or more children the credit is 45 per cent of up to USD 13 430 of earned income. The credit phases down when income exceeds USD 17 530 (22 870 for married taxpayers) and phases out when it reaches USD 46 227 (51 567 for married taxpayers).

  Since 1998, taxpayers are permitted a tax credit for each qualifying child under the age of 17. In 2013 the maximum credit is USD 1 000. The maximum credit is reduced for taxpayers with income in excess of certain thresholds. The credit is reduced by USD 50 for each USD 1 000 of income in excess of USD 110 000 for married taxpayers (USD 75 000 for single and head of household taxpayers). These threshold amounts are not indexed for inflation. The child credit is refundable (non-wasteable) to the extent of 15 per cent of earned income in excess of USD 3 000. A taxpayer with three or more qualifying children may be allowed a supplemental refundable (non-wasteable) child credit, subject to certain restrictions. The refundable credit is the excess of the taxpayer's share of social security (including Medicare) taxes over his earned income tax credit for the year not used to offset income tax liability.

- *Relief for low income workers without children:* In 1994 and thereafter, low income workers without children are eligible for the earned income credit. In 2013 low income workers without children are permitted a non-wastable earned income credit of 7.65 per cent of up to USD 6 370 of earned income. The credit phases down when income exceeds USD 7 970 (13 310 for married taxpayers) and phases out when income reaches USD 14 340 (19 680 for married taxpayers). This credit is available for taxpayers at least 25 years old and under 65 years old.

- *Relief for social security and other taxes:* In 2013, the withholding rate for Social Security taxes for employees is increased from 4.2 per cent to 6.2 per cent. The earned income credits described above are sometimes considered an offset to social security contributions made by eligible employees. Furthermore, only a portion of social security benefits are subject to tax.

1.1.2.2. Main non-standard reliefs applicable to an AW

- The basic non-standard relief is the deduction of certain expenses to the extent that, when itemised, they exceed in aggregate the standard deduction. For the purposes of this Report, it is assumed that workers claim the standard deduction. The principal itemised deductions claimed by individuals where the standard deduction is not being claimed are:

- *medical and dental expenses that exceed* 7.5 per cent of income;

- state and local income taxes, real property taxes, and personal property taxes. Home mortgage interest;

- investment interest expense up to investment income with an indefinite carry forward of disallowed investment interest expense;
- contributions to qualified charitable organisations (including religious and educational institutions);
- *casualty and theft losses* to the extent that each loss exceeds USD 100 and that all such losses combined exceed 10 per cent of income; and
- miscellaneous expenses such as non-reimbursed employee business expenses (union dues, work shoes, etc.), investment expenses, tax return preparation fees and educational expenses required by employment, to the extent that, in aggregate; they exceed 2 per cent of income.

In 2010, the most recent year for which such statistics are available, the 36 per cent of taxpayers with income between USD 40 000 and USD 50 000 (the AW range) who itemised their deductions claimed average deductions as follows: medical expenses, USD 3 359; taxes paid, USD 1 831; charitable contributions, USD 2 310; interest expense, USD 7 951.

- *Contributions to pension and life insurance plans.* No relief is provided for employee contributions to employer sponsored pension plans or for life insurance premiums. However, tax relief is provided for certain retirement savings.

1.1.3. *Tax schedule*

Federal income tax rates

Taxable income bracket (USD)[1]			Marginal tax rate (%)
Single individual	Joint return of married couple	Head of household	
0 to 8 925	0 to 17 850	0 to 12 750	10
8 925 to 36 250	17 850 to 72 500	12 750 to 48 600	15
36 250 to 87 850	72 500 to 146 400	48 600 to 125 450	25
87 850 to 183 250	146 400 to 223 050	125 450 to 203 150	28
183 250 to 398 350	223 050 to 398 350	203 150 to 398 350	33
398 350 to 400 000	398 350 to 450 000	398 350 to 425 000	35
400 000 and over	450 000 and over	425 000 and over	39.6

1. The taxable income brackets are indexed for inflation.

In addition starting in 2013, there is a 3.8 per cent tax on certain net investment income of individuals if their income exceeds USD 200 000 (USD 250 000 for joint returns). Net investment income includes interest, dividends, capital gains, rental and royalty income, and income from businesses trading financial instruments.

1.2. *State and local income taxes*

1.2.1. *General description of the system*

The District of Columbia and 41 of the 50 States impose some form of individual income tax. In addition, some local governments (cities and counties) impose an individual income tax, although this is not generally the case. State individual income tax structures are usually related to the federal tax structure by the use of similar definitions of taxable income, with some appropriate adjustments. This linkage is not a legal requirement but a practical convention that functions for the convenience of the taxpayer who must fill out both federal and State income tax returns.

The AW calculations assume that the average worker lives in Detroit, Michigan. The state of Michigan permits a personal exemption of USD 3 950 for the taxpayer, the taxpayer's spouse and each child, and taxes income at the rate of 4.25 per cent. Michigan allows taxpayers who are eligible to claim the federal earned income tax credit to claim a Michigan earned income tax credit. The Michigan earned income tax credit is a refundable (non-wasteable) credit equal to 6 per cent of the federal earned income tax credit.

The city of Detroit permits a personal exemption of USD 600 and taxes income at the rate of 2.4 per cent.

2. Compulsory social security contributions to schemes operated within the government sector

2.1. Employees' contributions

2.1.1. Pensions

In 2013, the rate for employee contributions is 7.65 per cent (6.2 per cent for old age, survivors, and disability insurance, and 1.45 per cent for old age hospital insurance). The 6.2 per cent rate applies to earnings up to USD 113 700. Beginning in 1994, there is no limit on the amount of earnings subject to the 1.45 per cent rate. Beginning in 2013, there is an additional 0.9 per cent tax on employee wages and salaries that exceed USD 200 000 (USD 250 000 for joint returns) as the additional hospital insurance tax on high-income taxpayers. The additional tax on wages and salaries is subject to withholding (but without regard to the earnings of the spouse) when wages from a particular job exceed USD 200 000 per year. These thresholds are not indexed for inflation.

There is no distinction by marital status or sex.

2.1.2. Other

No compulsory employee contributions exist.

2.2. Employers' contributions

2.2.1. Pensions

The rate for employers' contributions is 6.2 per cent on earnings up to USD 113 700 and 1.45 per cent of all earnings (without limit).

2.2.2. Unemployment

Employers are required by the federal government to pay unemployment tax of 6 per cent on earnings up to USD 7 000. Taxes are also paid to various state-sponsored unemployment plans which may generally be credited against the required federal percentage. In 2012 the average unemployment insurance tax rate in Michigan was 6.65 per cent of the first USD 9 500 of wages. The model considers that the Federal government allows employers to take a credit for state unemployment taxes of up to 5.4 per cent, resulting in a net Federal tax of 0.6 per cent on earnings up to USD 7 000.

3. Universal cash transfers

3.1. Transfers related to marital status

None.

3.2. *Transfers for dependent children*

No general cash transfers exist, although low-income mothers qualifying for categorical welfare grants may receive cash transfers.

4. Principal Changes since 2011

None.

5. Memorandum items

5.1. *Identification of an AW at the wage calculation*

- The AW is identified from monthly data compiled from establishment questionnaires covering more than 40 million non-agricultural full- and part-time workers. Beginning in March 2006, data on average weekly hours and average hourly earnings cover all employees rather than solely production or non-supervisory workers. To obtain average annual wages, the product of average weekly hours (including overtime) and average hourly earnings (including overtime) is multiplied by 52 and is adjusted to reflect a full-time equivalent worker. The AW wage is estimated to be USD 47 960 for 2012.

5.2. *Employer contributions to private social security arrangements*

Employers commonly contribute to private pension plans, health insurance and life insurance. Data for these contributions are available only on a total workforce basis. It is not possible to state with accuracy the levels applicable to the AW. The following are estimates for 2012 for employees in private industry:

	Pension	Health	Life
Per cent of workers covered	48	51	56
USD per covered employee	n.a.	10 292 (family) 4 276 (single)	n.a.

2013 parameter values

APW earnings	Ave_earn	48 463	Secretariat estimate			
Standard deductions	Married_al	12 200				
	hh_al	8 950				
	single_al	6 100				
Personal exemption	pers_ex	3 900				
Dependency exemption	dep_ex	3 900				
Federal tax schedules	Fed_sch_s	0.1	8 925			
		0.15	336 250			
Single individuals		0.25	87 850			
		0.28	183 250			
		0.33	398 350			
		0.35	400 000			
		0.396				
Married filing jointly	Fed_sch_m	0.1	17 850			
		0.15	72 500			
		0.25	146 400			
		0.28	223 050			
		0.33	398 350			
		0.35	450 000			
		0.396				
Head of household	Fed_sch_h	0.1	12 750			
		0.15	48 600			
		0.25	125 450			
		0.28	203 150			
		0.33	398 350			
		0.35	425 000			
		0.396				
Earned income credit	EIC_sch	rate	income limit	threshold	thresh-married	phase-out
	no children	0.0765	6 210	7 770	12 980	0.0765
	1 child	0.34	9 320	17 090	22 300	0.1598
	2 children	0.4	13 090	17 090	22 300	0.2106
	3 or more children	0.45	13 090	17 090	22 300	0.2106
Child credit	chcrd_max	1 000				
	chcrd_rdn	50				
	chcrd_thrsh_m	110 000				
	chcrd_thrsh_oth	75 000				
	chcrd_ref_perct	0.15				
	chcrd_ref_thresh	3 000				
Detroit	Detroit_ex	600				
	Detroit_rate	0.024				
Michigan	Mich_ex	3 950				
	Mich_ex_child	0				
	Mich_rate	0.0425				
Michigan's earned income tax credit	Mich_EIC_rate	0.06				
credit schedule on city tax	Mich_cr_sch	0				
		0				
		0				
maximum	Mich_cr_max	0				
Pension contributions	pens_rate_er	0.062				
	pens_rate_ee	0.062				
	hosp_rate	0.0145				
Ceiling for employers	pens_ceil	113 700				
Unemployment insurance tax	Unemp_rate	0.06				
	Unemp_dedn_rate	0.054				
	Unemp_max	7 000				
Michigan unemploy insur	Mich_unemp_rate	0.0665				
	Mich_unemp_max	9 500				

2013 tax equations

The equations for the US system in 2012 are mostly calculated on a family basis. There is a special function EIC which is used to calculate the earned income credit. Variable names are defined in the table of parameters above, within the equations table, or are the standard variables "married" and "children". A reference to a variable with the affix "_total" indicates the sum of the relevant variable values for the principal and spouse. And the affixes "_princ" and "_spouse" indicate the value for the principal and spouse, respectively. Equations for a single person are as shown for the principal, with "_spouse" values taken as 0.

	Line in country table and intermediate steps	Variable name	Range	Equation
1.	Earnings	earn		
2.	Allowances:	tax_al	J	IF(Married, Married_al, IF(Children=0, single_al, hh_al)) + +((1+Married)*pers_ex+Children*dep_ex)-(ROUNDUP(Positive(earn_total-IF(Married,ex_thrsh_m,IF(Children>0,ex_thrsh_hh,ex_thrsh_s)))/ ex_dedn_unit,0)*ex_dedn_rate*((1+Married)*pers_ex+Children*dep_ex))
3.	Credits in taxable income	taxbl_cr	J	0
4.	CG taxable income	tax_inc	J	positive(earn-tax_al+taxbl_cr)
5.	CG tax before credits	CG_tax_excl	J	Tax(tax_inc, IF(Married, Fed_sch_m, IF(Children, Fed_sch_h, Fed_sch_s)))
6.	6. Tax credits :	EIC	J	EIC(Children, earn_total, EIC_sch)
		Unemp	J	Unemp_dedn_rate*(MIN(earn,Unemp_max))
		ch_crd_max	J	Children*Positive((chcrd_max-chcrd_rdn*Positive(TRUNC(earn, -3)-IF(Married>0, chcrd_thrsh_m, chcrd_thrsh_oth))/1000))
		ch_crd_tax	J	IF(ch_crd_tax>0, MIN(ch_crd_max, CG_tax_excl), 0)
		ch_crd_ref		IF(ch_crd_tax<ch_crd_max, MIN(ch_crd_max-ch_crd_tax, MAX(chcrd_ref_perct*(earn-chcrd_ref_thresh), 0)), 0)
		tax_cr	J	EIC+Unemp+ch_crd_tax+ch_crd_ref
7.	CG tax	CG_tax	J	CG_tax_excl-tax_cr
8.	State and local taxes	local_tax	J	Detroit_rate* Positive(earn_total-Detroit_ex*(1+Married+Children))+ Mich_rate*Positive(earn_total - Mich_ex*(1+Married+Children) - Mich_ex_child*Children) -MIN(Mich_cr_max, Tax(AJ7, Mich_cr_sch)) - Mich_EIC_rate*EIC
9.	Employees' soc security	SSC	B	pens_rate_ee*MIN(earn, pens_ceil)+hosp_rate*earn+add_hosp_rate*Positive(earn-IF(Married,add_hosp_thresh_m,add_hosp_thresh_oth))
11.	Cash transfers	Cash_tran	J	
13.	Employer's soc security	SSC_empr	B	pens_rate_er*MIN(earn, pens_ceil) +hosp_rate*earn+MIN(earn,Unemp_max)*Unemp_rate +MIN(earn,Mich_unemp_max)*Mich_unemp_rate
	Memorandum item: non-wastable tax credits			
	tax expenditure component	taxexp		(rate_rd_crd+EIC)-transfer
	cash transfer component	transfer		IF(CG_tax<0, -CG_tax, 0)

Key to range of equation B calculated separately for both principal earner and spouse P calculated for principal only (value taken as 0 for spouse calculation) J calculated once only on a joint basis.

Taxing Wages 2014
Changes in structural labour income tax progressivity
over 2000-12 period in OECD member countries

ANNEX

Methodology and limitations

1. Methodology

1. *Introduction*

The personal circumstances of taxpayers vary greatly. This Report therefore adopts a specific methodology to produce comparative statistics covering taxes, benefits and labour costs across OECD member countries. The framework of the methodology is as follows:

- The Report focuses on eight different family types which vary by household composition and level of earnings.
- Each household contains a full-time adult employee working in one of a broad range of industry sectors of each OECD economy. Some of the households also have a spouse working less than full-time.
- The annual income from employment is assumed to be equal to a given fraction of the average gross wage earnings of these workers.
- Additional assumptions are also made regarding other relevant personal circumstances of these wage earners in order to calculate their tax/benefit position.

The guidelines described in the following paragraphs form the basis for the calculations shown in Parts O, I, II and III. Table A.1 sets out the terminology that is used. Where a country has had to depart from the guidelines, this is noted in the text and/or in the country chapters contained in Part III of the Report. The number of taxpayers with the defined characteristics and the wage level of the average workers differ between OECD economies.

2. *Taxpayer characteristics*

The eight household types identified in the Report are set out in Table A.2. Any children in the household are assumed to be aged between six and eleven inclusive.

The family is assumed to have no income source other than employment and cash benefits.

3. *The range of industries covered*

The standard assumption for calculating average wage earnings is based on Sectors B-N of the *International Standard Industrial Classification of All Economic Activities* (ISIC Revision 4, United Nations)[1] (see Table A.3). Many countries (for more detailed country information, see Table 0.6) have now adopted this approach.

Table A.1. **Terminology**

General terms	
Average worker (AW)	An adult full-time worker in the industry sectors covered whose wage earnings represent the average for workers
Single persons	Unmarried men and women
Couple with two children	Married couple with two dependent children between six to eleven years of age inclusive
Labour costs	The sum of Gross wage earnings,employers' social security contributions and payroll taxes
Net take-home pay	Gross wage earnings less the sum of personal income tax and employee social security contributions, plus cash transfers received from general government
Personal average tax rate (tax burden)	The sum of Personal income tax and employee social security contributions expressed as a percentage of gross wage earnings
Tax wedge	The sum of personal income tax,employee and employer social security contributions plus any payroll tax less cash transfers, expressed as a percentage of labour costs.
Elasticity of income after tax	Percentage change in "after-tax" income following an increase in one currency unit of income before tax (defined more precisely as one minus a marginal tax rate divided by one minus a corresponding average tax rate)
Terms used under the income tax	
Tax reliefs	A generic term to cover all the means of giving favourable income tax treatment to potential taxpayers
Tax allowances	Amounts deducted from gross earnings to arrive at taxable income
Tax credits	Amounts which a taxpayer may subtract from his tax liability. They are described as payable if they can exceed tax liability (sometimes the terms "refundable" and "non-wastable" are used)
Standard tax reliefs	Reliefs unrelated to the actual expenses incurred by taxpayers and automatically available to all taxpayers who satisfy the eligibility rules specified in the legislation are counted as standard reliefs. These also include deductions for compulsory social security contributions
Basic relief	Any standard tax relief available irrespective of marital or family status
Marriage allowance	Additional tax relief given to married couples. (In some countries, this is not distinguished from the basic relief which may be doubled on marriage)
Non-standard tax reliefs	Reliefs wholly determined by reference to actual expenses incurred
Average rate of income tax	Amount of income tax payable after accounting for any reliefs calculated on the basis of the tax provisions covered in this Report, divided by gross wage earnings
Schedule rate	The rate which appears in the schedule of the income tax and in the schedule of social security contributions
Terms used under cash transfers	
Cash transfers	Cash payments made by general government (agencies) paid to families usually in respect of dependent children.

Table A.2. **Characteristics of taxpayers**[1]

Marital status	Children	Principal earner	Secondary earner
Single individual	No children	67% of average earnings	
Single individual	No children	100% of average earnings	
Single individual	No children	167% of average earnings	
Single individual	2 children	67% of average earnings	
Married couple	2 children	100% of average earnings	
Married couple	2 children	100% of average earnings	33% of average earnings
Married couple	2 children	100% of average earnings	67% of average earnings
Married couple	No children	100% of average earnings	33% of average earnings

1. The *Taxing Wages* models use 1/3 of average earnings rather than 33% of them, 2/3 of average earnings rather than 67% and 5/3 of average earnings rather than 167%.

This approach broadly corresponds to the previous calculation based on Sectors C-K incl. defined in the *International Standard Industrial Classification of All Economic Activities* (ISIC Revision 3.1, United Nations) which was adopted in the 2005 edition of *Taxing Wages*. The reasons for moving to a broadened average wage definition were set out in the Special Feature of *Taxing Wages* 2003-04.

As stated in Part O, Section 2.4 of this Report, only Turkey has not yet moved to this broadened industry definition. The average wage figures reported for Turkey therefore still refer to the approach used prior to the 2005 edition – manual workers in manufacturing (industry sector D). These differences may affect the comparability of the data.

Table A.3. **International Standard Industrial Classification of All Economic Activities**

	Revision 3.1 (ISIC Rev. 3.1)
A	Agriculture, hunting and forestry
B	Fishing
C	Mining and quarrying
D	Manufacturing
E	Electricity, gas and water supply
F	Construction
G	Wholesale and retail trade; repair of motor vehicles, motorcycles and personal and household goods
H	Hotels and restaurants
I	Transport, storage and communications
J	Financial intermediation
K	Real estate, renting and business activities
L	Public administration and defence; compulsory social security
M	Education
N	Health and social work
O	Other community, social and personal service activities
P	Activities of private households as employers and undifferentiated production activities of private households
Q	Extraterritorial organisations and bodies
	Revision 4 (ISIC Rev. 4)
A	Agriculture, forestry and fishing
B	Mining and quarrying
C	Manufacturing
D	Electricity, gas, steam and air conditioning supply
E	Water supply; sewerage, waste management and remediation activities
F	Construction
G	Wholesale and retail trade; repair of motor vehicles and motorcycles
H	Transportation and storage
I	Accommodation and food service activities
J	Information and communication
K	Financial and insurance activities
L	Real estate activities
M	Professional, scientific and technical activities
N	Administrative and support service activities
O	Public administration and defence; compulsory social security
P	Education
Q	Human health and social work activities
R	Arts, entertainment and recreation
S	Other service activities
T	Activities of households as employers; undifferentiated goods- and services-producing activities of households for own use
U	Activities of extraterritorial organizations and bodies

4. *Defining gross wage earnings*

This section sets out the assumptions underlying the calculation of the average earnings figures for the "average worker". The gross wage earnings data have been established using statistical data and the methodologies for calculating the earnings data in each country are set out in Table A.4. Further information on the calculation of the earnings figure is provided in the country chapters in Part III. The sources of the statistical data for each country are set out in Table A.5.

- The data relate to the average earnings in the industry sectors for the country as a whole.
- The calculations are based on the earnings of a full-time adult worker (including both manual and non-manual). They relate to the average earnings of all workers in the industry sectors covered. No account is taken of variation between males and females or due to age or region.
- The worker is assumed to be full-time employed during the entire year without breaks for sickness or unemployment. However, several countries are unable to separate and exclude part-time workers from the earnings figures (see Table A.4). Most of them report full-time equivalent wages in these cases. In four countries (Chile, Ireland, Slovak Republic and Turkey), the wages of part-time workers can be neither excluded nor converted into full-time equivalents because of the ways in which the earnings samples are constructed. As a result, average wages reported for these countries will be lower than an average of full-time workers (for instance, Secretariat analysis of available Eurostat earnings data for selected European countries has shown that including part-time workers reduces average earnings by around 10%). Also, in most of the OECD countries where sickness payments are made by the employer, either on behalf of the government or on behalf of private sickness schemes, these amounts are included in the wage calculations. It is unlikely that this has a marked impact on the results since employers usually make these payments during a short period and the amounts usually correspond very closely to normal hourly wages.
- Two of the household types include a second earner at 33 per cent of average earnings. Such individuals are more likely to be working part-time rather than full-time (as shown in the Special Feature of the 2005 edition). However, it is also shown that the assumption that all employees are working full-time does not significantly affect the tax rates calculated in *Taxing Wages*, except in the case of Belgium for married couples where the spouse is earning 33 per cent of the average wage level. This is because any special provisions made for part-time workers tend to be either of minor importance or not applicable for the household types currently presented in *Taxing Wages*.
- The earnings calculation includes all cash remuneration paid to workers in the industries covered taking into account average amounts of overtime, cash supplements (e.g. Christmas bonuses, thirteenth month) and vacation payments typically paid to workers in the covered industry sectors. However, not all countries are able to include overtime pay, vacation payments and cash bonuses according to the definition.
- The earnings figures include supervisory and/or management employees, though some countries are not able to do this. In such countries, the reported averages are lower than would otherwise be the case (for instance, OECD Secretariat analysis of available Eurostat earnings data for selected European countries has shown that excluding this type of workers can reduce average earnings by 10% to 18%). In the case of Turkey that has not yet been able to move to the broadened industry definition, the definition includes only manual workers and minor shop-floor supervisory workers in the manufacturing industry.
- Fringe benefits – which include, for example, provision of food, housing or clothing by the employer either free of charge or at below market-price – are, where possible, excluded from the calculation of average earnings. This could affect comparability of tax

Table A.4. **Method used to calculate average earnings**

	Items included and exluded from the earnings base					Types of worker included and excluded in the average wage measure			Basic method of calculation used	Income tax year ends	Period to which the earnings calculation refers
	Sickness[1]	Vacations	Overtime	Recurring cash payments	Fringe benefits	Supervisory workers	Managerial workers	Part-time workers			
Australia	Inc	Inc	Inc	Inc	Exc	Inc	Inc	Exc	Average weekly earnings x 52	30 June	Fiscal year
Austria	Exc	Inc	Inc	Inc	Taxable value Inc	Inc	Inc	Exc	Average annual earnings	31 December	Calendar year
Belgium	Exc	Inc	Inc	Inc	Exc	Inc	Inc	Exc	Monthly earnings in October x 12 (plus recurring bonuses)	31 December	Calendar year
Canada	Exc	Inc	Inc	Inc	Exc	Inc	Inc	Inc[6]	Average weekly hours x average hourly earnings x 52	31 December	Calendar year
Chile	Exc	Inc	Inc	Inc	Exc	Inc	Inc	Inc	Hourly earnings x hours worked	31 December	Calendar year
Czech Republic	Exc	Inc	Inc	Inc	Exc	Inc	Inc	Inc[6]	Average monthly earnings x 12	31 December	Calendar year
Denmark	Exc	Inc	Exc	Inc	Exc	Inc	Inc	Inc[6]	Hourly earnings x hours worked	31 December	Calendar year
Estonia	Inc	Inc	Inc	Inc	Exc	Inc	Inc	Inc	Average earnings	31 December	Calendar year
Finland	Exc	Inc	Inc	Inc	Exc	Inc	Inc[5]	Exc	Hourly wages x usual working time or (monthly earnings x months) + vacation payments+ end of year bonuses	31 December	Calendar year
France	Exc	Inc	Inc	Inc	Exc	Inc	Inc	Exc	Annual earnings	31 December	Calendar year
Germany	Exc	Inc	Inc	Inc	Exc	Inc	Inc	Exc	Annual earnings	31 December	Calendar year
Greece	Exc	Inc	Inc	Inc[2]	Inc	Inc	Inc	Exc	Hourly earnings x hours worked	31 December	Calendar year
Hungary	Exc	Inc	Inc	Inc	Exc	Inc	Inc[5]	Exc	Average monthly earnings x 12	31 December	Calendar year
Iceland	Exc	Inc	Inc	Inc	Exc	Inc	Inc	Exc	Hourly earnings x hours worked x 12	31 December	Calendar year
Ireland	Exc	Inc	Inc	Inc	Exc	Exc	Exc	Inc	Average weekly earnings in each quarter for four quarters/4*52	31 December	Calendar year
Israel	Exc	Inc	Inc	Inc	Exc	Inc	Inc	Exc	Average earnings	31 December	Calendar year
Italy	Exc[3]	Inc	Inc	Inc	Exc[4]	Inc	Inc	Inc[6]	Average monthly earnings x 12	31 December	Calendar year
Japan	Exc	Inc	Inc	Inc	Exc	Inc	Inc	Exc	Monthly earnings in June x 12	31 December	Calendar year
Korea	Exc	Inc	Inc	Inc	Exc	Inc	Inc	Exc	Average monthly earnings x 12	31 December	Calendar year
Luxembourg	Exc	Inc	Inc	Inc	Exc	Inc	Inc	Exc	Aggregate annual earnings divided by annual average number of full-time employees. Any parts of earnings that exceed the upper social contribution limit (7 times the minimum wage) are not recorded.	31 December	Calendar year
Mexico	Exc	Inc	Exc	Inc	Exc	Inc	Inc	Exc	Average monthly earnings x 12	31 December	Calendar year
Netherlands	Exc	Inc	Exc	Inc	Exc	Inc	Inc	Exc	Annual gross earnings	31 December	Calendar year
New Zealand	Exc	Inc	Inc	Inc	Exc	Inc	Inc[5]	Inc[6]	Average weekly earnings in each quarter x 13	31 March	Tax year
Norway	Exc	Exc	Inc	Inc	Exc	Inc	Inc	Inc [6]	Annual wages + estimated overtime	31 December	Calendar year
Poland	Inc	Inc	Inc	Inc	Exc	Inc	Inc	Inc [6]	Average monthly earnings x 12	31 December	Calendar year
Portugal	Exc	Inc	Inc	Inc	Inc	Inc	Inc	Exc	Weighted monthly average x 12	31 December	Calendar year

Table A.4. **Method used to calculate average earnings** *(cont.)*

	Items included and exluded from the earnings base					Types of worker included and excluded in the average wage measure			Basic method of calculation used	Income tax year ends	Period to which the earnings calculation refers
	Sickness[1]	Vacations	Overtime	Recurring cash payments	Fringe benefits	Supervisory workers	Managerial workers	Part-time workers			
Slovak Republic	Exc	Inc	Inc	Inc	Inc	Inc	Inc	Inc	Average monthly earnings x 12	31 December	Calendar year
Slovenia	Inc	Inc	Inc	Inc	Exc	Inc	Inc	Inc	Average monthly earnings x 12	31 December	Calendar year
Spain	Exc	Inc	Inc	Inc	Exc	Inc	Inc	Exc	Weighted monthly average x 12	31 December	Calendar year
Sweden	Exc	Inc	Inc	Inc	Actual value Inc	Inc	Inc	Inc[6]	Average hourly earnings in September x hours worked; and monthly earnings in September x 12	31 December	Calendar year
Switzerland	Exc	Inc	Inc	Inc	Exc	Inc	Inc	Inc[6]	Monthly earnings x 12	31 December	Calendar year
Turkey	Exc	Inc	Inc	Inc	Actual value inc	Exc	Exc	Inc	Average annual earnings	31 December	Calendar year
United Kingdom	Exc	Inc	Inc	Inc	Exc	Inc	Inc	Exc	Average gross annual earnings	5 April	Fiscal year
United States	Exc	Inc	Inc	Inc[2]	Exc	Inc	Inc	Inc[6]	Average weekly earnings x 52	31 December	Calendar year

Note: Exc = Excluded Inc = Included "-" = information not available.

1. Usually includes compensation paid by employer whether paid on behalf of the government or as part of a private sickness scheme.
2. Excludes profit sharing bonuses in Greece and the United States plus end of year bonuses in the United States.
3. Sickness payments are only included to the extent that they are paid by the employer. For manual workers, this is only the case during the first three days of sick leave, while payments for the fourth day onwards are made by INPS.
4. Partly: the (small) taxable part of fringe benefits is included.
5. Except for top management (Finland); except if income from profits exceeds 50% of total income (Hungary); except for proprietors (New Zealand).
6. Part-time wages are converted to full-time equivalents before calculating the average wage measure.

wedges – as the reliance on fringe benefits may vary between countries and over time. However, the lack of comparability is probably limited as fringe benefits rarely account for more than 1-2 per cent of labour costs and are normally more common among high-income employees than in the income ranges covered by *Taxing Wages* (33 to 167 per cent of average earnings). Table A.4 shows that some member countries are not able to exclude fringe benefits from the earnings figures reported and used in *Taxing Wages*. The decision to exclude was been taken because:

- these types of benefits are difficult to evaluate in a consistent way (they may be valued at the actual cost to the employer, their value to the employee or their fair market value);
- in most countries, they are of minimal importance for workers at the average wage level;
- the tax calculations would be significantly more complicated if the tax treatment of fringe benefits were to be incorporated.

- Employers' contributions to private pension, family allowance or health and life insurance schemes are excluded from the calculations, though the amounts involved can be significant. In the United States, for example, these contributions can account for more than 5 per cent of the earnings of employees. The country chapters in Part III indicate of the existence of schemes which may be relevant for an average worker.

Table A.5. **Source of earnings data, 2013**

	Type of sample	Source
Australia	Quarterly survey of firms resulting in a representative sample of wage and salary earners in each industry.	Australian Bureau of Statistics "Average Weekly Earnings, Australia" and "Labour Force, Australia"
Austria	Annual Wage Tax Statistics	"Lohnsteuerstatistik"
Belgium	Data collected or estimated on the basis of an annual establishment survey and social insurance registers of employees	Statistics Division of the Ministry of Economy (Federal Public Service, Economy, SMEs, Self-employed and Energy). Same source as for Eurostat "Annual gross earnings" data.
Canada	Monthly survey of all firms	Statistics Canada, "Survey of Employment Payrolls and Hours"
Chile	Monthly sample of businesse with 10+ employees	National Statistics Institute of Chile (INE)
Czech Republic	Employer survey data	National Statistical Office
Denmark	Danish Employers Confederation survey of earnings	Annual Report Danish Employers Confederation (Dansk Arbejds Giverforening)
Estonia	-	Statistics Estonia/Ministry of Finance
Finland	1) Finnish Employers Federation survey of hourly and monthly earnings; 2) Survey for unorganized employers "Structure of Earnings Statistics" published by the Central Statistical Office	"Wages Statistics" published by the Central Statistical Office
France	Social insurance registers covering all employers.	INSEE, "Déclarations Annuelles des Données Sociales" (DADS)
Germany	Survey carried out by the Federal Statistical Office	National Statistical Office
Greece	Survey carried out by National Statistics Service and Social Security Institutions	National Statistical Service Labour Statistics. Same source as for Eurostat "Annual gross earnings" data.
Hungary	Monthly surveys among enterprises with at least five employees.	Central Statistical Office
Iceland	Monthly survey of earnings in the private sector market	Statistics Iceland
Ireland	Quarterly surveys of industrial employment, earnings and hours worked	Central Statistics Office
Israel	-	Central Bureau of Statistics
Italy	Quarterly indicators of wages in industry and services (OROS)	National Institute of Statistics
Japan	Basic survey on wage structure of all establishments with more than 10 employees	Ministry of Health, Labour and Welfare, Annual Report
Korea	Labour Force Survey at Establishments	Ministry of Employment and Labour

Table A.5. **Source of earnings data, 2013** *(cont.)*

	Type of sample	Source
Luxembourg	Monthly aggregated files of Social security services.	National Statistical Office and Social Security Services.
Mexico	Administrative data from the Mexican Social Security Institute (Instituto Mexicano del Seguro Social [IMSS])	The National Minimum Wage Commission (Comisión Nacional de Salarios Mínimos [CONASAMI])
Netherlands	Survey "Employment and Wages"	Central Bureau of Statistics, Statline
New Zealand	The quarterly employment survey is a sample survey of significant business with an employment count of 1 or more	Statistics New Zealand INFOS
Norway	Sample of enterprises based on published sector statistics for 3rd quarter – except agriculture, forestry and fishing and private households	Statistics Norway Wage
Portugal	April and October survey of earnings carried out by the Ministry of Labour	Ministry of Labour
Poland	Estimates for different sectors	Monthly Statistical Bulletin
Slovak republic	Quarterly and annual statistical data	Slovak Statistical Office
Slovenia	Monthly survey of employees	Statistical Office of the Republic of Slovenia
Spain	Quarterly survey of firms	Instituto Nacional de Estadistica "Encuesta Trimestral de Coste Laboral" (Labour Cost Survey)
Sweden	September survey of Swedish employers	Statistics Sweden
Switzerland	Swiss Statistics Office. Personnes actives occupées selon la branche économique	La vie économique, SECO (Secrétariat d'État à l'économie) table B.8.1, www.bfs.admin.ch/bfs/portal/fr/index/themen/03/04.html
Turkey	Annual Manufacturing Industry Survey	Turkish Statistical Institute
United Kingdom	1% sample of PAYE earnings	Office for National Statistics, Annual Survey of Hours and Earnings (ASHE)
United States	Monthly surveys by Department of Labour on the basis of a questionnaire covering more than 40 million non-agricultural wage and salary-workers	Employment, Hours, and Earnings from the Current Employment Statistics Survey

5. *Calculating average gross wage earnings*

Table A.4 indicates the basic calculation method used in each country while more details are, where relevant, provided in the country chapters in Part III. In principle, countries are recommended to calculate annual earnings by referring to the average of hourly earnings in each week, month or quarter, weighted by the hours worked during each period, and multiplied by the average number of hours worked during the year, assuming that the worker is neither unemployed nor sick and including periods of paid vacation. A similar procedure was recommended to calculate overtime earnings. For countries unable to separate out part-time employees from the data, it is recommended that earnings of part-time employees should if possible be converted into their full-time equivalents.

Statistical data on average gross wage earnings in 2013 are generally not available at present. Estimates of gross wage earnings of average workers in 2013 were therefore derived by the Secretariat on the basis of a uniform approach: all year 2012 earnings levels (or the earnings level in the most recent year for which final average wage earnings country information is available) are multiplied by the country-specific annual percentage change of wages for the whole economy reported in the most recently published edition of the OECD *Economic Outlook*.[2] This transparent procedure is intended to avoid any bias in the results. In some countries, there were varying different approaches;

- The final 2013 average gross wage earnings was used for Australia.
- National estimates were used for the Chile, Estonia, New Zealand and Turkey as the *OECD Economic Outlook* does not provide percentages changes in wages for those countries.

- Average wage earnings were also estimated for prior years for Finland (2012), France (2012), Ireland (2012), the Netherlands (2012) and Switzerland (2007, 2009, 2011, 2012) as no country information on average wage earnings levels was available for these years in these countries.

Sixteen of the OECD member countries have opted to provide national estimates of the level of gross wage earnings of average workers in 2013. These estimates were not used (except for the countries listed above) because of potential inconsistency with the Secretariat estimates derived for other countries. However they are included in Table A.6 to enable comparisons to be made between the estimates obtained by applying the Secretariat formula and those from national sources. In most cases, the two categories are fairly close.

Table A.6. **Estimated gross wage earnings, 2012-13 (in national currency)**

	Average wage 2012	Average wage 2013 (Secret. estimates)	Average wage 2013 (Country estimates)	E094 forecasted Rates for 2013[1]
Australia[2]	73 494	74 978	77 530	2.0
Austria	40 708	41 693	41 824	2.4
Belgium	45 886	46 810		2.0
Canada	46 940	48 078	47 973	2.4
Chile[2]	6 218 613		6 607 476	
Czech Republic	302 993	298 770	310 694	-1.4
Denmark	392 000	395 722	393 910	0.9
Estonia[2]	11 004		11 664	
Finland	41 662	42 493		2.0
France	36 248	36 980		2.0
Germany	44 300	45 170	44 700	2.0
Greece	22 240	20 604	19 558	-7.4
Hungary	2 838 864	2 914 514		2.7
Iceland	5 856 000	6 191 179		5.7
Ireland	32 514	32 381		-0.4
Israel	128 549	131 033		1.9
Italy	29 315	29 704		1.3
Japan	4 893 341	4 901 704		0.2
Korea	38 811 570	39 829 650	39 654 532	2.6
Luxembourg	51 752	52 902		2.2
Mexico	94 875	97 941	98 888	3.2
Netherlands	47 075	48 109		2.2
New Zealand[2]	51 278		53 234	
Norway	504 929	524 177		3.8
Poland	40 205	41 442		3.1
Portugal	17 040	17 335		1.7
Slovak Republic	9 810	10 015	10 004	2.1
Slovenia	17 538	17 611	17 500	0.4
Spain	25 894	26 027	25 802	0.5
Sweden	387 960	391 990	399 211	1.0
Switzerland	87 662	88 161		0.6
Turkey[2, 3]	29 209		31 744	
United Kingdom	34 877	35 548		1.9
United States	47 960	48 463		1.0

1. Increase of compensation per employee in the total economy (*Economic Outlook No. 94*).
2. The country AW estimate is used instead of the OECD Secretariat's AW estimate in the *Taxing Wages* calculations.
3. Turkey wage figures under the old definition of average worker (ISIC D, Rev. 3.)

StatLink http://dx.doi.org/10.1787/888933008114

Table A.7 indicates the exchange rates and purchasing power parities of national currencies for 2013 that are used to calculate comparative earnings figures across countries in the report.

Table A.7. **Purchasing power parities and exchange rates for 2013**

	Monetary unit	Exchange rates[1]	Purchasing power parities
Australia	AUD	1.04	1.47
Austria	EUR	0.75	0.83
Belgium	EUR	0.75	0.83
Canada	CAD	1.03	1.23
Chile	CLP	495.28	347.97
Czech Republic	CZK	19.56	13.30
Denmark	DKK	5.62	7.64
Estonia	EUR	0.75	0.55
Finland	EUR	0.75	0.91
France	EUR	0.75	0.84
Germany	EUR	0.75	0.78
Greece	EUR	0.75	0.65
Hungary	HUF	223.58	127.10
Iceland	ISK	122.17	137.94
Ireland	EUR	0.75	0.81
Israel	ILS	3.61	4.04
Italy	EUR	0.75	0.75
Japan	JPY	97.60	102.61
Korea	KRW	1094.93	846.08
Luxembourg	EUR	0.75	0.92
Mexico	MXN	12.77	7.83
Netherlands	EUR	0.75	0.83
New Zealand	NZD	1.22	1.46
Norway	NOK	5.88	8.80
Poland	PLN	3.16	1.80
Portugal	EUR	0.75	0.60
Slovak Republic	EUR	0.75	0.51
Slovenia	EUR	0.75	0.60
Spain	EUR	0.75	0.68
Sweden	SEK	6.51	8.64
Switzerland	CHF	0.93	1.37
Turkey	TRL	1.90	1.08
United Kingdom	GBP	0.64	0.69
United States	USD	1.00	1.00

1. Average of 12 months daily rates.

StatLink http://dx.doi.org/10.1787/888933008133

6. Coverage of taxes and benefits

The Report is concerned with personal income tax and employee and employer social security contributions payable on wage earnings. In addition, payroll taxes (see Section 10) and in one case church tax (see Section 11) are included in the calculation of the total wedge between labour costs to the employer and the corresponding net take-home pay of the employee.

The calculation of the after-tax income includes family benefits paid by general government as cash transfers (see Section 12). Income tax due on capital income and non-wage labour income, several direct taxes (net wealth tax, corporate income tax) and all indirect taxes are not considered in this Report. However, all central, state and local government income taxes are included in the data.[3]

In this study, compulsory social security contributions paid to general government are treated as tax revenues. Being compulsory payments to general government they clearly resemble taxes. They may, however, differ from taxes in that the receipt of social security benefits depends upon appropriate contributions having been made, although the size of the benefits is not necessarily related to the amount of the contributions. Countries finance compulsory public social security programmes to a varying degree from general tax and non-tax revenue and earmarked contributions, respectively. Better comparability between countries is obtained by treating social security contributions as taxes, but they are listed under a separate heading so that their amounts can be identified in any analysis.

7. Calculation of personal income taxes

The method by which income tax payments are calculated is described in the country tables in Part III. First, the tax allowances applicable to a taxpayer with the characteristics and income level related to gross annual wage earnings of an average worker are determined. Next, the schedule of tax rates is applied and the resulting tax liability is reduced by any relevant tax credits. An important issue arising in the calculation of the personal income tax liability involves determining which tax reliefs should be taken into account. Two broad categories of reliefs may be distinguished:

- *Standard tax reliefs*: reliefs which are unrelated to actual expenditures incurred by the taxpayer and are automatically available to all taxpayers who satisfy the eligibility rules specified in the legislation. Standard tax reliefs are usually fixed amounts or fixed percentages of income and are typically the most important set of reliefs in the determination of the income tax paid by workers. These reliefs are taken into account in the calculations – they include:
  - the *basic relief* which is fixed and is available to all taxpayers or all wage earners, irrespective of their marital or family status;
  - the *standard relief* which is available to taxpayers depending on their *marital status*;
  - the *standard child relief* granted to a family with two children between the ages of six to eleven inclusive;
  - the *standard relief* in respect of *work expenses*, which is usually a fixed amount or fixed percentage of (gross) wage earnings; and,
  - tax reliefs allowed for *social security contributions* and other (sub-central government) *income taxes* are also considered as standard reliefs since they apply to all wage earners and relate to compulsory payments to general government.[4]
- *Non-standard tax reliefs*: These are reliefs which are wholly determined by reference to actual expenses incurred. They are therefore neither fixed amounts nor fixed percentages of income. Examples of non-standard tax reliefs include reliefs for interest on qualifying loans (e.g. for the purchase of a house), private insurance premiums, contributions to private pension schemes, and charitable donations. These are not taken into account in calculating the tax position of employees.

Standard reliefs are separately identified and their impact on average tax rates is calculated in the results tables shown in the Country chapters. The latter include a brief description of the main non-standard reliefs in most cases.

8. State and local income taxes

Personal income taxes levied by sub-central levels of government – state, provincial, cantonal or local – are included in the scope of this study. State income taxes exist in Canada, Switzerland and the United States. Since 1997, Spain has an income tax for the Autonomous Regions. Local income taxes are imposed in Belgium, Denmark, Finland, Iceland, Italy, Japan, Korea, Norway, Sweden, Switzerland and the United States. In Belgium, Canada (other than Quebec), Denmark, Iceland, Italy, Korea, Norway and Spain they are calculated as a percentage of taxable income or of the tax paid to central government. In Finland, Japan, Sweden and Switzerland, local government provides different tax reliefs from central government. In the United States, the sub-central levels of government operate a separate system of income taxation under which they have discretion over both the tax base and tax rates. Except for Canada, Spain and Switzerland, the rate schedule of these sub-central taxes consists of a single rate.

When tax rates and/or the tax base of sub-central government income taxes vary within a country, it is sometimes assumed that the average worker lives in a typical area and the income taxes (and benefits) applicable in this area are presented. This is the procedure followed in Canada, Italy, Switzerland and the United States where the tax base and tax rates vary very widely throughout the country. Belgium, Denmark, Finland, Iceland and Sweden have preferred to select the average rate of sub-central government income taxes for the country as a whole. No problem arises in Norway and Korea where the local rates do not vary in practice. Japan and Spain have used the widely prevalent standard schedule.

9. Social security contributions

Compulsory social security contributions paid by employees and employers to general government or to social security funds under the effective control of government are included in the coverage of this Report. In most countries, contributions are levied on gross earnings and earmarked to provide social security benefits. In Finland, Iceland and the Netherlands, some contributions are levied as a function of taxable income (i.e. gross wage earnings after most/all tax reliefs). Australia and New Zealand do not levy social security contributions.

Contributions to social security schemes outside the general government sector are not included in the calculations. However, information on "non-tax compulsory payments" as well as "compulsory payment indicators" is included in the *OECD Tax Database*, which is accessible at *www.oecd.org/ctp/taxdatabase*.

10. Payroll taxes

The tax base of payroll taxes is either a proportion of the payroll or a fixed amount per employee. In the OECD *Revenue Statistics* payroll taxes are reported under heading 3000. Fifteen OECD countries report revenue from payroll taxes: Australia, Austria, Canada, Denmark, France, Hungary, Iceland, Ireland, Israel, Korea, Mexico, New Zealand, Poland, Slovenia and Sweden.

Payroll taxes are included in total tax wedges reported in this publication, given that they increase the gap between gross labour costs and net take-home pay in the same way as income tax and social security contributions do. The main difference with the latter is that the payment of payroll taxes does not confer an entitlement to social security benefits.

Also, the tax base of payroll taxes may differ from the tax base of employer social security contributions. For example, certain fringe benefits may only be liable to payroll tax. Because this Report presents the standard case, the payroll tax base is – depending on the relevant legislation – gross wage (excluding fringe benefits and other items of compensation that vary per employee), gross wage plus employer social security contributions, or a fixed amount per employee.

Four of the OECD member countries include payroll taxes in the *Taxing Wages* calculations: Australia, Austria, Hungary and Sweden. The other countries reporting payroll tax revenue in *Revenue Statistics* have not included these taxes in the calculations for the present Report for a variety of reasons.

11. Church tax

Some OECD member countries impose a levy known as "church tax", but only Denmark reports such revenues in the OECD *Revenue Statistics*. This is because the Danish State Church is classified as a part of general government. Denmark argues that this inclusion of the church in general government is appropriate because of the high degree of control that the government exercises over the church. Since the Working Party on Tax Policy Analysis and Tax Statistics has agreed that church taxes should be treated consistently in its two main statistical publications, only the Danish church tax is included in the calculations for *Taxing Wages*.

12. Family cash benefits from general government

Tax reliefs and family cash transfers universally paid in respect of dependent children between the ages of six to eleven inclusive who are attending school are included in the scope of the study. If tax reliefs or cash transfers vary within this age range, the most generous provisions are adopted, except that the case of twins is explicitly disregarded. Suppose the child benefit programme of a country is structured as follows:

Age group	Benefits per child
Children 6-8	100 units
Children 9-10	120 units
Children 11-14	150 units

The most favourable outcome arises in the case of 11-year old twins: 300 units. However, as the case of twins is excluded, the best outcome now becomes 270 units (one child 11 years old, one child 9 or 10 years old). This amount would be included in the country table. Often, the amount in benefits is raised as children grow older. The calculations assume that the children have been born on 1 January so the annual amount received in child benefits may be calculated from the benefit schedule that is in place at the start of the year with any revisions to these amounts during the year being taken into account.

Relevant cash payments are those received from general government. In some cases, the cash benefits include amounts that are paid without consideration to the number of children.

13. *Payable tax credits*

Payable (non-wastable) tax credits are tax credits that can exceed tax liability, where the excess, if any, can be paid as a cash transfer to the taxpayer. In principle, these credits can be treated in different ways according to whether they are regarded as tax provisions or cash transfers or a combination of these. A Special Feature in the 2001 edition of *Revenue Statistics* discusses these alternative treatments and the conceptual and practical difficulties that arise in deciding which is the most appropriate approach for the purpose of reporting internationally comparable tax revenue figures.[5]

Based on this review, the Interpretative Guide of the *Revenue Statistics* requires that:

- only the portion of a payable tax credit that is claimed to reduce or eliminate a taxpayer's liability (the "tax expenditure" component)[6] should be deducted in the reporting of tax revenues;
- the part of the tax credit that exceeds a taxpayer's tax liability and is paid to him (the "cash transfer" component) should be treated as an expenditure item and not deducted in the reporting of tax revenues.

However, additional information is provided in *Revenue Statistics* on aggregate tax expenditure components and aggregate transfer components of payable tax credits to show the effect of alternative treatments.[7]

The situation is different in *Taxing Wages* where the full amount of the payable tax credit is taken into account in the income tax calculation.

Strict consistency with the *Revenue Statistics* would require that only the tax expenditure component be offset against derived income tax, with the excess (if any) treated as a cash transfer. However, this approach would diminish rather than strengthen the informational content of the derived results in *Taxing Wages*. In particular, limiting tax credit claims to tax expenditure amounts would yield a zero income tax liability and zero average income tax rate where cash refunds are provided. Where tax credits claims are not constrained in this way, negative income tax liabilities and negative average income tax rates would result where cash transfers are provided. Arguably, these negative amounts more clearly convey the taxpayer's position (which is improved relative to the no-tax situation). Also, not including the cash transfer portion of payable tax credits in the "cash transfers from general government" item of the country tables permits greater transparency of the latter which focuses on "pure" cash transfers only.

However, in order to improve the informational content of country tables as regards payable tax credits, the memorandum item reporting at the bottom of the relevant country tables shows tax expenditure amounts on one line, with a second line showing cash transfer amounts. Where more than one payable tax credit program applies, the figures represent aggregates covering all the programs. Total program costs in each of the household cases considered can be derived by adding the tax expenditure and cash transfer amounts.

14. *The calculation of marginal tax rates*

In most cases, the marginal tax rates are calculated by considering the impact of a small increase in gross earnings on personal income tax, social security contributions and cash benefits. However, in the case of a non-working spouse, the move from a zero to a small positive income is unrepresentative of income changes and therefore of little interest. So, for this case, the marginal rates for the spouse are calculated by considering the impact of an income increase from zero to 33 per cent of the average wage.

2. Limitations

1. *General limitations*

The simple approach of comparing the tax/benefit position of example families avoids many of the conceptual and definitional problems involved in more complex international comparisons of tax burdens and transfer programmes. However, a drawback of this methodology is that the earnings of an average worker will usually occupy a different position in the overall income distribution in different economies, although the earnings relate to workers in similar jobs in various OECD member countries.

Because of the limitations on the taxes and benefits covered in the Report, the data cannot be taken as an indication of the overall impact of the government sector on the welfare of taxpayers and their families. Complete coverage would require studies of the impact of indirect taxes, the treatment of non-wage labour income and other income components under personal income taxes and the effect of other tax allowances and cash benefits. Complete coverage would also require that consideration be given to the effect on welfare of services provided by the state, either free or below cost, and the incidence of corporate and other direct taxes on earnings and prices. Such a broad coverage is not possible in an international comparison of all OECD countries. The differences between the results shown here and those of a full study of the overall impact on employees of government interventions in the economy would vary from one country to another. They would depend on the relative shares of different kinds of taxes in government revenues and on the scope and nature of government social expenditures.

The Report shows only the formal incidence of taxes on employees and employers. The final, economic incidence of taxes may be quite different, because the tax burden may be shifted from employers onto employees and *vice versa* by market adjustments to gross wages.

The income left at the disposal of a taxpayer may represent different standards of living in various countries because the range of goods and services on which the income is spent and their relative prices differ as between countries. In those countries where the general government sector provides a wide range of goods and services (generous basic old age pension, free health services, public housing, university education, etc.), the taxpayer may be left with less cash income but may enjoy the same living standards as a taxpayer receiving a higher cash income but living in a country where there are fewer publicly provided goods and services.

As mentioned in Part O and detailed in the Special Feature of the 2005 edition of *Taxing Wages*, second earners who are earning 33 per cent of the average wage are very likely to be working part-time, although the *Taxing Wages* methodology generally assumes that they are working full-time. However, this only affects the accuracy of the results in *Taxing Wages* for one family type in Belgium (married couple where a second earner is earning 33 per cent of average wages). Therefore, one should be cautious when interpreting the results for this family type for Belgium. In addition, for all countries with hour-based rules, (see the 2005 Special Feature), caution should be used in applying the results in this Report to other household types.

2. Some specific limitations on the income tax calculation

The exclusion of non-wage income and the limited number of tax reliefs covered imply that the average rates of income tax in the tables in this publication will not necessarily reflect the actual rates confronting taxpayers at these levels of earnings. Actual rates may be lower than the calculated rates because the latter do not take into account non-standard expense-related reliefs. On the other hand, actual rates may be higher than calculated rates because the latter do not take into account tax on non-wage income received by employees.

The decision not to calculate separately average rates of income tax taking into account the effect of non-standard tax reliefs was taken because:

- in many cases, expense-related reliefs are substitutes for direct cash subsidies. To take into account these reliefs while ignoring any corresponding direct subsidies would distort comparisons of take-home pay plus cash transfers;
- the special tax treatment of certain expenses may be linked to special treatment of any income associated with these expenses (e.g. the tax treatment of social security contributions and pension income) which is beyond the scope of this study;
- a few countries were unable to estimate the value of these reliefs and even those countries which could do so could not limit their estimates to taxpayers with the characteristics assumed in the above part on methodology; and,
- not all countries could calculate separately the reliefs available to different family-types. Where a split is provided between single individuals and families with children, there are large differences in the value of the reliefs typically received by these two categories of households.

3. Limitations to time-series comparisons

The Calculations of the tax burden on labour income in OECD countries reported in previous editions of *Taxing Wages*, including the 2004 edition, are based on an average earnings measure calculated for manual full-time workers in the manufacturing sector (the "average production worker"). From 1996 onwards there are time-series results covering all 8 family types, whereas there are results from 1979 onwards for two of these family-types: single individuals without children and married one-earner couples with two children with earnings equal to those of an average production worker.

Any analysis of the results has to take into account the fact that the earnings data do not necessarily relate to the same taxpayer throughout the period. The average earnings are calculated for each year. As such, the results do not reflect the changing earnings and tax position of particular individuals over time but rather to the position of workers earning a wage equal to average earnings in the covered industry sectors in each particular year. This, in turn, may mean that the earnings levels referred to may be at different points in the income distribution over the period covered and changes in tax rates may be influenced by these trends.

From the 2005 edition, *Taxing Wages* has reported tax calculations under a broadened average worker definition that includes all full-time employees covering industry Sectors C-K (reference to ISIC Rev. 3.1). The implications of adopting this new definition for time-series comparisons are discussed in the 2005 edition of *Taxing Wages*. As of the 2010 edition of the *Taxing Wages* Report, many countries have started reporting average wage earnings for full-time employees covering industry Sectors B-N of the ISIC Rev. 4 industry classification (which broadly corresponds to Sectors C-K in ISIC Rev. 3.1).

3. A note on the tax equations

Each country chapter contains a section describing in a standard format the equations under-pinning the calculations required to derive the amounts of income tax, social security contributions and cash transfers. These algorithms represent in algebraic form the legal provisions described in the chapter and are consistent with the figures shown in the country and comparative tables. This section describes the conventions used in the definition of the equations and how they could be used by those wishing to implement the equations for their own research.

The earlier sections of the country chapters describe how the tax and other systems work and present the values of the parameters of those systems such as the levels of allowances and credits, and the schedule of tax rates.

In the first part of the equations section is a table showing a brief description of each parameter (such as "Basic tax credit"), the name of the parameter as used in the algebraic equation ("Basic_cred") and the actual value for the relevant year (such as "1098"). Where there is a table of values – for example a schedule of tax rates and the associated thresholds of taxable income – a name is given to the entire table (for example "tax_sch"). These variable names are those used in the equations.

After the table of parameters is the table of equations. The four columns contain information as follows:

- The first two columns give a description and a variable name for the result of the equation on that row of the table. These always include the thirteen main financial value entries in the country tables. Additional rows define any intermediate values which are calculated either to show the detail included in the tables (such as the subdivision of total tax allowances into the different categories) or values which make the calculation clearer.
- The third column shows the range of the calculation in that row. This is necessary to allow for the different way that tax may be calculated for married couples. The options are:
  - B The calculation is carried out separately for both the principal earner and the spouse using their individual levels of earnings. This applies in the case of independent income tax and usually also in respect of social security contributions.
  - P The calculation applies for the principal earner only. An example is where the principal earner can use any of the basic tax allowance of the spouse which cannot be set against the income of the spouse.
  - S The calculation applies for the lower earning spouse only.
  - J The calculation is carried out only once on the basis of joint income. This applies to systems of joint or family taxation and is also usual for the calculation of cash transfers in respect of children.
- The final column contains the equation itself. The equation may refer to the variables in the parameters table and to variables which result from one of the rows of the equations table itself. Use is also made of the two standard variables "Married", which have the value 1 if the family consists of a married couple and 0 in the case of a single individual,

and "Children" which denotes the number of children. Sometimes there is a reference to a variable with the affix "_total" which indicates the sum of the relevant variable values for the principal earner and the spouse. Similarly, the affixes "_princ" and "_spouse" indicate the value for the principal earner and spouse, respectively.

In the equations a number of functions are used. Some of these are used in the same way as in a number of widely available "spreadsheet" computer packages. For example, MAX(X,Y) and MIN(X,Y) find the maximum and minimum of the two values, respectively. IF(condition X,Y) chooses the expression X if the condition is true and the expression Y if it is false. Boolean expressions are also used and are taken to have the value 1 if true and 0 if false. As an example, (Children=2*CB_2 is equivalent to IF(Children=2, CB_2,0).

There are also three special functions commonly used which denote calculations often required in tax and social security systems. These are:

- Tax (taxinc, tax_sch): This calculates the result of applying the schedule of tax rates and thresholds in "tax_sch" to the value of taxable income represented by "taxinc". This function may be used in any part of the equations, not just in the income tax calculation. For some countries it is used for social security contributions or even for allowance levels which may be income dependent.
- Positive (X): This gives the result X when this value is positive and zero otherwise. It is therefore equivalent to MAX(0,X).
- Taper (value, income, threshold, rate): This gives the amount represented by "value" if "income" is less than "threshold". Otherwise, it gives "value" reduced by "rate" multiplied by (income- threshold), unless this produces a negative result in which case zero is returned. This provides the calculation which is sometimes required when a tax credit, for example, is available in full provided that total income is below a threshold but is then withdrawn at a given rate for each currency unit in excess of the threshold until it is withdrawn completely.

In some circumstances, there are country specific special functions. These functions involve programming that is designed to simplify the tax calculations. The programming underlying these functions is based on the description of the particular measure given in the relevant country chapter found in Part III. For example, the Earned Income Credit in the United States is calculated using the function called EIC.

Anyone wishing to make their own implementation of the equations will have to write functions corresponding to these special functions or make appropriate modifications to any equations that use them.

Notes

1. Not all national statistical agencies use ISIC Rev. 3.1 or ISIC Rev. 4 to classify industries. However, the Statistical Classification of Economic Activities in the European Community (NACE), the North American Industry Classification System (NAICS) and the Australian and New Zealand Standard Industrial Classification (ANZSIC) include a classification which is broadly in accordance with industries C-K in ISIC Rev. 3.1 or industries B-N in ISIC Rev. 4.
2. Wage estimates reported in the *OECD Economic Outlook* are consistent with information in the Analytical Data Base (ADB) of the Economics Department (ECO) of the OECD. These estimates are prepared by the ECO country desks. Data in the ADB/EO94 are consistent with the December 2013 issue of the *OECD Economic Outlook*.
3. Information on the fiscal powers of sub-central governments may be found in the publication *Taxing powers of state and local government, OECD Tax Policy Studies* No. 1 (Paris, 1999).

4. In this case, the amount of tax relief is related to actual social security contributions paid by the employee or withheld from his wage – thus in this respect this item deviates from the general definition of standard tax relief under which relief is unrelated to actual expenses incurred.
5. OECD, *Revenue Statistics 1965-2000*, p. 28-31.
6. This characterisation must be viewed as informal, as the determination of tax expenditures requires the identification of a benchmark tax system for each country, or preferably, a common international benchmark. In practice it has not been possible to reach agreement on a common international benchmark for such purposes.
7. See Table D in the latest edition of OECD, *Revenue Statistics*.

ORGANISATION FOR ECONOMIC CO-OPERATION AND DEVELOPMENT

The OECD is a unique forum where governments work together to address the economic, social and environmental challenges of globalisation. The OECD is also at the forefront of efforts to understand and to help governments respond to new developments and concerns, such as corporate governance, the information economy and the challenges of an ageing population. The Organisation provides a setting where governments can compare policy experiences, seek answers to common problems, identify good practice and work to co-ordinate domestic and international policies.

The OECD member countries are: Australia, Austria, Belgium, Canada, Chile, the Czech Republic, Denmark, Estonia, Finland, France, Germany, Greece, Hungary, Iceland, Ireland, Israel, Italy, Japan, Korea, Luxembourg, Mexico, the Netherlands, New Zealand, Norway, Poland, Portugal, the Slovak Republic, Slovenia, Spain, Sweden, Switzerland, Turkey, the United Kingdom and the United States. The European Union takes part in the work of the OECD.

OECD Publishing disseminates widely the results of the Organisation's statistics gathering and research on economic, social and environmental issues, as well as the conventions, guidelines and standards agreed by its members.

OECD PUBLISHING, 2, rue André-Pascal, 75775 PARIS CEDEX 16
(23 2014 02 1 P) ISBN 978-92-64-20916-9 – 2014-2